The Political Economy of International Law

The Political Economy of International Law

A European Perspective

Edited by

Alberta Fabbricotti

Faculty of Law, La Sapienza University of Rome, Italy

EE Edward Elgar
PUBLISHING

Cheltenham, UK • Northampton, MA, USA

Published by
Edward Elgar Publishing Limited
The Lypiatts
15 Lansdown Road
Cheltenham
Glos GL50 2JA
UK

Edward Elgar Publishing, Inc.
William Pratt House
9 Dewey Court
Northampton
Massachusetts 01060
USA

A catalogue record for this book
is available from the British Library

Library of Congress Control Number: 2016931779

This book is available electronically in the **Elgar**online
Law subject collection
DOI 10.4337/9781785364402

MIX
Paper from responsible sources
FSC www.fsc.org FSC® C013056

ISBN 978 1 78536 439 6 (cased)
ISBN 978 1 78536 440 2 (eBook)

Typeset by Columns Design XML Ltd, Reading
Printed and bound in Great Britain by TJ International Ltd, Padstow

Contents

List of Contributors vii
Acknowledgements ix
List of Abbreviations x

Introduction 1
Alberta Fabbricotti

PART I FRAMEWORK ISSUES

1. Political Economy of International Law: Towards a Holistic Model of State Behaviour 9
Anne van Aaken and Joel P Trachtman

PART II POLITICAL ECONOMY AND THE SOURCES OF INTERNATIONAL LAW

2. The Political Economy of Customary International Law 47
Niels Petersen
3. Can Political Economy Help Solve the Riddle of Customary International Law? 62
Alessandra Gianelli
4. The Political Economy of *Jus Cogens* 75
Paul B Stephan
5. The Political Economy of International Treaties 95
Panos Merkouris
6. Political Economy and the Decisions of International Organizations: Choosing Governance Arrangements through Informality 127
Ramses A Wessel and Evisa Kica

PART III POLITICAL ECONOMY AND THE ENFORCEMENT OF INTERNATIONAL LAW

7. Political Economy of International Law: A Convenient Alliance for the Study of Compliance? 159
Barbara Delcourt

8. International Political Economy and the Prisoner's Dilemma: Compliance with International Law 178
Meredith Kolsky Lewis
9. The Political Economy of Judicial Production of International Law 202
Paul B Stephan
10. The Political Economy of the (Non-)Enforcement of International Human Rights Pronouncements by States 230
Andreas von Staden
11. The Political Economy of International Lawmaking by National Courts 258
Eyal Benvenisti
12. Political Economy and the Responsibility of States: The Problem of Many Hands in International Law 278
André Nollkaemper

PART IV POLITICAL ECONOMY AND SUBSTANTIVE FIELDS OF INTERNATIONAL LAW

13. The Political Economy of Regional Trade Agreements 311
Alberta Fabbricotti
14. Political Economy and International Investment Law: The Conclusion of IIAs by Developing Countries during the Twentieth Century 329
Tobias A Lehmann
15. Political Economy and International Water Law: Political Economy Induced Changes to the Uptake of Benefit Sharing in International Water Law 356
Laurence Boisson de Chazournes and Christina Leb
16. Political Economy and the Protection of Human Rights: Political Economy and Compliance with Human Rights Treaties 384
Ulyana Kohut
17. Political Economy and International Migration Law 409
Daniela Vitiello and Marion Panizzon

PART V CONCLUSIONS

18. Political Economy and International Law: Paradoxes and Potential 439
Eyal Benvenisti and Jan Wouters

Index 447

Contributors

Anne van AAKEN, Professor of Law and Economics, Legal Theory, Public International Law and European Law at the University of St. Gallen.

Eyal BENVENISTI, Anny and Paul Yanowicz Professor of Human Rights, Tel Aviv University Faculty of Law and Global Professor at New York University School of Law; from 2016 Whewell Professor of International Law at the University of Cambridge.

Laurence BOISSON de CHAZOURNES, Professor of International Law, University of Geneva; Adviser to international organizations and governments; Director of the Platform for International Water Law, Faculty of Law, University of Geneva.

Barbara DELCOURT, Professor at the Institute for European Studies and at the Faculty of Social and Political Sciences, Université Libre de Bruxelles.

Alberta FABBRICOTTI, Adjunct Professor and Senior Researcher in International Law and EU Law, Faculty of Law, *La Sapienza* University of Rome.

Alessandra GIANELLI, Professor of International Law, Faculty of Law, University of Teramo.

Evisa KICA, Researcher at the Utrecht Centre for Regulation and Enforcement in Europe (RENFORCE), University of Utrecht, and at the Centre for European Studies of the University of Twente.

Ulyana KOHUT, PhD Candidate in International Law, *La Sapienza* University of Rome.

Christina LEB, Senior Water Resources Specialist, Water Global Practice, World Bank; Associate member of the Platform for International Water Law, Faculty of Law, University of Geneva.

Tobias A LEHMANN, PhD Candidate in Law, University of St. Gallen.

Meredith Kolsky LEWIS, Professor of Law and Director, Cross-Border Legal Studies Center, SUNY Buffalo Law School; Associate Professor, Victoria University of Wellington Law School.

Panos MERKOURIS, Assistant Professor of Public International Law at the University of Groningen.

André NOLLKAEMPER, Professor of Public International Law and Director of the Amsterdam Center for International Law at the Faculty of Law of the University of Amsterdam (UvA).

Marion PANIZZON, Senior Research Fellow, University of Bern.

Niels PETERSEN, Professor of Public Law, International Law and EU Law at the University of Münster.

Andreas von STADEN, Assistant Professor of Political Science in the Faculty of Economics and Social Sciences at the University of Hamburg.

Paul B STEPHAN, The John C Jeffries, Jr., Distinguished Professor and Director of Graduate Studies at the University of Virginia School of Law.

Joel P TRACHTMAN, Professor of International Law at The Fletcher School of Law and Diplomacy.

Daniela VITIELLO, Post-Doctoral Research Fellow, University *Roma Tre*.

Ramses A WESSEL, Professor of International and European Law and Governance and Co-Director of the Centre for European Studies at the University of Twente.

Jan WOUTERS, Full Professor of International Law and International Organizations, Jean Monnet Chair *ad personam* EU and Global Governance and Director of the Leuven Centre for Global Governance Studies and Institute for International Law at the University of Leuven (KU Leuven).

Acknowledgements

The contributions in this book are for the most part the proceedings of a conference of the same title held in Rome in May 2014. I would like to express my deep gratitude to *La Sapienza* University of Rome, for its generous financial support of the conference, and to the participants in the conference for their contributions, both formal and informal, which have enriched this publication. I feel profoundly obliged to Anne van Aaken for her valuable suggestions regarding the organization of the conference and the structure of the book resulting from its proceedings. Both the conference and the book would not have seen light without her enthusiastic support. Also, special thanks are deserved by Matilde Dandolo and Michèle Favorite for linguistic assistance. And I am grateful to Ben Booth and Iram Satti at Edward Elgar for their helpfulness and efficiency with the production process of this book.

Abbreviations

ABM	Anti-Ballistic Missile
ACHR	American Convention on Human Rights
Afr Aff	African Affairs
AfrChHPR	African Charter on Human and Peoples' Rights
AfrCmHPR	African Commission of Human and Peoples' Rights
AfrCtHPR	African Court of Human and Peoples' Rights
AJIL	American Journal of International Law
Am Econ Rev	American Economic Review
Am J Pol Sci	American Journal of Political Science
Am L Econ Rev	American Law and Economics Review
Am Pol Sci Rev	American Political Science Review
Am Psychol	American Psychologist
Am Soc Rev	American Sociological Review
Am U Int L Rev	American University International Law Review
American U J Int L Pol	American University Journal of International Law and Policy
AMR	Academy of Management Review
Ann IDI	Annuaire de l'Institut de Droit International/Yearbook of the Institute of International Law
Ann Rep	Annual Report
Ann Rev Econ	Annual Rev of Economics
APHRPE	Draft Articles on Protection of the Human Rights of Persons Who Have Been or Are Being Expelled
ARIO	Draft Articles on the Responsibility of International Organizations
ARSIWA	Articles on Responsibility of States for Internationally Wrongful Acts
ARSP Beiheft	Archiv für Rechts- und Sozialphilosophie Beiheft

ASEAN	Association of South-East Asian Nations
Asian J Int L	Asian Journal of International Law
Asia-Pac J Int L	Asia-Pacific Journal of International Law
ASIL	American Society of International Law
ASIL Proc	American Society of International Law Proceedings
ATS	Alien Tort Statute
AU	African Union
Australian Yb Int L	Australian Yearbook of International Law
AWR Bull	AWR Bulletin: Quarterly on Refugee Problems
BIT(s)	Bilateral Investment Treaty(ies)
Boston U L Rev	Boston University Law Review
British J Pol Sci	British Journal of Political Science
Buffalo HR L Rev	Buffalo Human Rights Law Review
Buffalo J Int L	Buffalo Journal of International Law
BYIL	British Yearbook of International Law
Calif L Rev	California Law Review
Cap Mkts L J	Capital Markets Law Journal
CAS	Court of Arbitration for Sport
Case W Res J Int L	Case Western Reserve Journal of International Law
CAT	Convention against Torture
CATOC	Convention against Transnational Organized Crime
CBD	Convention on Biological Diversity
CED	Committee on Enforced Disappearance
CEDAW	Convention on the Elimination of All Forms of Discrimination against Women
CESCR	Committee on Economic, Social and Cultural Rights
CGD	Center for Global Development
Chi J Int L	Chicago Journal of International Law
Chinese J Int L	Chinese Journal of International Law
CIL	Customary International Law
CITES	Convention on International Trade in Endangered Species of Wild Fauna and Flora

CJEU	Court of Justice of the European Union
CLEER	Centre for the Law of the EU External Relations
CmAT	Committee against Torture
CmEDAW	Committee on the Elimination of all Forms of Discrimination against Women
CMLR	Common Market Law Review
CmRC	Committee on the Rights of the Child
CoE	Council of Europe
Colum L Rev	Columbia Law Review
Comp Lab L Pol J	Comparative Labor Law & Policy Journal
COMPAS	Centre on Migration, Policy and Society
Comunicazioni Studi	Comunicazioni e Studi dell'Istituto di diritto internazionale e straniero dell'Università di Milano
Cornell L Rev	Cornell Law Review
CPS	Comparative Political Studies
CRC	Convention on the Rights of the Child
Crit Rev Int Soc Polit Philos	Critical Review of International Social and Political Philosophy
CRPD	Convention on the Rights of Persons with Disabilities
CRSR	Convention Relating to the Status of Refugees
CRTA	WTO Committee on Regional Trade Agreements
CUP	Cambridge University Press
DC(s)	Developing Country(ies)
DSB	World Trade Organization Dispute Settlement Body
DSP	Dispute Settlement Procedure
Duke L J	Duke Law Journal
EC	European Communities
ECHR	European Convention on Human Rights
Econ Lett	Economics Letters
Econ Pol	Economic Policy
ECOWAS	Economic Community of West African States
ECR	European (EU) Court Reports
ECT	European Energy Charter Treaty

ECtHR	European Court of Human Rights
ED	Economic Dualism (Theory of)
EEC	European Economic Community
EEZ	Exclusive Economic Zone
EJIL	European Journal of International Law
ELJ	European Law Journal
ESIL	European Society of International Law
ESIL Refl	European Society of International Law Reflections
EU	European Union
EUI	European University Institute
Eur J Int Rel	European Journal of International Relations
Eur J Leg Stud	European Journal of Legal Studies
Eur J Migration L	European Journal of Migration and Law
Eur J Pol Econ	European Journal of Political Economy
FDI	Foreign Direct Investment
Finnish Yb Int L	Finnish Yearbook of International Law
For Aff	Foreign Affairs
Fordham Int L J	Fordham International Law Journal
Forum for Social Economics	Forum for Social Economics
FTA(s)	Free Trade Agreement(s)
Game Econ Behav	Games and Economic Behaviour
GATS	General Agreement on Trade in Services
GATT	General Agreement on Tariffs and Trade
GDP	Gross Domestic Product
GEF	Global Environmental Fund
Georgia J Int Comp L	Georgia Journal of International and Comparative Law
German L J	German Law Journal
GHG	Greenhouse Gas
GPG(s)	Global Public Good(s)
GYIL	German Yearbook of International Law
Hague Yb Int L	Hague Yearbook of International Law
Harv Int L J	Harvard International Law Journal

Harv JLPP	Harvard Journal of Law and Public Policy
Harv L Rev	Harvard Law Review
Hastings Int Comp L Rev	Hastings International and Comparative Law Review
Hastings L J	Hastings Law Journal
Houston J Int L	Houston Journal of International Law
HR	Human Rights
HR L Rev	Human Rights Law Review
HR Q	Human Rights Quarterly
HRC	Human Rights Committee
HRLJ	Human Rights Law Journal
IACmHR	Inter-American Commission on Human Rights
IACRDS	Inter-American Convention on Rights and Duties of States
IACtHR	Inter-American Court on Human Rights
ICC	International Criminal Court
ICCPR	International Covenant on Civil and Political Rights
ICESCR	International Covenant on Economic, Social and Cultural Rights
ICJ	International Court of Justice
ICJ Rep	International Court of Justice Reports
ICLQ	International and Comparative Law Quarterly
ICMW	International Convention on the Protection of the Rights of All Migrant Workers and Members of their Families
ICSID	International Centre for Settlement of Investment Disputes
ICTY	International Criminal Tribunal for the Former Yugoslavia
IDI	Institut de Droit International / Institute of International Law
IG	Interest Group
IIA(s)	International Investment Agreement(s)
IL	International Law
ILA	International Law Association

ILC	International Law Commission
ILC Yb	International Law Commission Yearbook
Ill L Rev	Illinois Law Review (also, University of Illinois Law Review)
ILM	International Legal Materials
ILO	International Labour Organization
ILO n 143	ILO Convention Concerning Migration in Abusive Conditions and the Promotion of Equality of Opportunity and Treatment of Migrant Workers
ILO n 49	ILO Convention Concerning Migration for Employment
ILR	International Law Reports
IM	Immigration Market (Theory)
IMI	International Migration Institute
Indian J Int L	Indian Journal of International Law
Indiana J Glob Leg Stud	Indiana Journal of Global Legal Studies
Indiana L J	Indiana Law Journal
Int Aff	International Affairs
Int Comm L Rev	International Community Law Review
Int Econ Rev	International Economic Review
Int J Popul Geogr	International Journal of Population Geography
Int J Innovat Tech Manag	International Journal of Innovation and Technology Management
Int Migr	International Migration
Int Migr Rev	International Migration Review
Int Org	International Organization
Int Org L Rev	International Organizations Law Review
Int Stud Q	International Studies Quarterly
Int Stud Rev	International Studies Review
Int Theo	International Theory
IO(s)	International Organization(s)
IOM	International Organization for Migrations
IPE	International Political Economy
IRLE	International Review of Law and Economics

ISIL	Islamic State of Iraq and the Levant
ISO	International Organization for Standardization
ISSJ	International Social Science Journal
Italian Yb Int L	Italian Yearbook of International Law
ITLOS	International Tribunal for the Law of the Sea
ITLOS Rep	International Tribunal for the Law of the Sea Reports
IWL	International Water Law
IWRM	Integrated Water Resources Management
IZA	Institute for the Study of Labor
J Abnorm Soc Psychol	Journal of Abnormal and Social Psychology
J Cons R	Journal of Consumer Research
J Econ Lit	Journal of Economic Literature
J Emp L Stud	Journal of Empirical Legal Studies
J Ethn Migr Stud	Journal of Ethnic and Migration Studies
J Eur Pub Pol	Journal of European Public Policy
J Int Crim Just	Journal of International Criminal Justice
J Int DS	Journal of International Dispute Settlement
J L Econ	Journal of Law and Economics
J Leg Analysis	Journal of Legal Analysis
J Leg Stud	Journal of Legal Studies
J Peace R	Journal of Peace Research
J Pers Soc Psychol	Journal of Personality and Social Psychology
J Pol Econ	Journal of Political Economy
J Politics	Journal of Politics
J Risk R	Journal of Risk Research
JCR	Journal of Conflict Resolution
JEP	Journal of Economic Perspectives
JIEL	Journal of International Economic Law
JILIR	Journal of International Law and International Relations
JITE	Journal of Institutional and Theoretical Economics
JPP	Journal of Public Policy
JWT	Journal of World Trade

L Contemp Probs	Law and Contemporary Problems
L Prac Int Cts Tribs	The Law and Practice of International Courts and Tribunals
LDCs	Least-Developed Countries
Leiden J Int L	Leiden Journal of International Law
LMS	Labour Market Segmentation (Theory)
LNTS	League of Nations Treaty Series
LOSC	Convention on the Law of the Sea (1982)
LSE	London School of Economics
Max Planck UN Yb	Max Planck Yearbook of United Nations Law
MEA(s)	Multilateral Environmental Agreement(s)
Melb J Int L	Melbourne Journal of International Law
MERCOSUR	Mercado Común del Sur / Southern Common Market
MFN	Most Favoured Nation
Mich J Int L	Michigan Journal of International Law
Mich L Rev	Michigan Law Review
Minn L Rev	Minnesota Law Review
Mod L Rev	Modern Law Review
MT	Migrant Transnationalism (Theory)
NAFTA	North American Free Trade Agreement
NATO	North Atlantic Treaty Organization
Neb L Rev	Nebraska Law Review
NELM	New Economics of Labour Migration
NGOs	Non-governmental Organizations
NILR	Netherlands International Law Review
Nord J Int L	Nordic Journal of International Law
North Carolina J Int L Com Reg	North Carolina Journal of International Law and Commercial Regulation
Notre Dame L Rev	Notre Dame Law Review
NQHR	Netherlands Quarterly of Human Rights
NSA	Non-State Actors
Nw J Int L Bus	Northwestern Journal of International Law & Business

NYIL	Netherlands Yearbook of International Law
NYU JILP	New York University Journal of International Law and Politics
OAS	Organization of American States
OECD	Organization for Economic Cooperation and Development
OHCHR	The Office of the United Nations High Commissioner for Human Rights
OIG(s)	Organised Interest Group(s)
OJ	Official Journal of the European Union
OMVS	Organisation pour la Mise en Valeur du fleuve Sénégal
OSCE	Organization for Security and Co-operation in Europe
OUP	Oxford University Press
Oxford J Leg Stud	Oxford Journal of Legal Studies
ÖZP	Österreichische Zeitschrift für Aussenpolitik
PCIJ	Permanent Court of International Justice
PCIJ Rep	Permanent Court of International Justice Reports
PE	Political Economy
Penn State JLIA	Penn State Journal of Law and International Affairs
Pepp L Rev	Pepperdine Law Review
PIL	Public International Law
PILL	Public International Law Lobby
Pol Gov	Politics and Governance
Pol Sci Q	Political Science Quarterly
Pub Aff Q	Public Affairs Quarterly
PUF	Presse Universitaire Française
Q J Econ	Quarterly Journal of Economics
RDI	Rivista di diritto internazionale
Recueil des Cours	Recueil des Cours de l'Académie de Droit International de La Haye / Collected Courses of the Hague Academy of International Law
Refugee Surv Q	Refugee Survey Quarterly
Rep	Reports

Rev Econ Anal	Review of Economic Analysis
Rev hell dr int	Revue hellénique de droit international
Rev Int Econ	Review of International Economics
Rev IOs	Review of International Organizations
RGDIP	Revue Générale de Droit International Public
RLE	Review of Law and Economics
RTA(s)	Regional Trade Agreement(s)
Scand J Econ	The Scandinavian Journal of Economics
SCC	Stockholm Chamber of Commerce
Sci Eng Ethics	Science and Engineering Ethics
SCM	Subsidies and Countervailing Measures
SDO(s)	Standards Developing Organization(s)
Socio Econ Rev	Socio Economic Review
Southern Calif L Rev	Southern California Law Review
SPS	Sanitary and Phytosanitary (Measures)
SPT	Sub-Committee on the Prevention of Torture
Stanford J Int L	Stanford Journal of International Law
Stanford L Rev	Stanford Law Review
SUNY Press	State University of New York Press
Sup Ct Econ Rev	Supreme Court Economic Review
SWAPO	South West Africa People's Organization
SZIER/RSDIE	Revue suisse de droit international et de droit européen / Schweizerische Zeitschrift für internationales und europäisches Recht
TBT	Technical Barriers to Trade
TEC	Treaty establishing the European Community
TEU	Treaty on European Union
Tex Int L J	Texas International Law Journal
TFEU	Treaty of the Functioning of the European Union
Theo Econ	Theoretical Economics
Theo Inq L	Theoretical Inquiries in Law
TLP	Transnational Legal Process
Touro L Rev	Touro Law Review

TPMH	The Problem of Many Hands
TPP	Trans-Pacific Partnership
TTIP	Transatlantic Trade and Investment Partnership
TWO	Transboundary Waters Opportunity (Analysis)
U Chi L Rev	University of Chicago Law Review
U Ill L Rev	University of Illinois Law Review
U Pa J Int Econ L	University of Pennsylvania Journal of International Economic Law
UDHR	Universal Declaration of Human Rights
UK	United Kingdom
UN	United Nations
UNDP	United Nations Development Programme
UNGA	United Nations General Assembly
UNTS	United Nations Treaty Series
US	United States of America
USSR	Union of Soviet Socialist Republics
USADA	US Anti-Doping Agency
Utah L Rev	Utah Law Review
Vanderbilt J Transnatl L	Vanderbilt Journal of Transnational Law
Vanderbilt L Rev	Vanderbilt Law Review
VCCR	Vienna Convention on Consular Relations
VCLT	Vienna Convention on the Law of Treaties
Virginia L Rev	Virgina Law Review
VJIL	Virginia Journal of International Law
WB	The World Bank
WBAT	World Bank Administrative Tribunal
WHO	World Health Organization
WI	Water International
Wisconsin Int L J	Wisconsin International Law Journal
World Econ	The World Economy
WP	Water Policy
WS	World System (Theory)
WTO	World Trade Organization
Yale J Int L	Yale Journal of International Law

Yale L J	Yale Law Journal
Yale U EGC	Yale University Economic Growth Center
Yb Int Invest L Pol	Yearbook on International Investment Law & Policy

Introduction

Alberta Fabbricotti

As the title clearly suggests, this book ambitiously aims at exploring Public International Law (PIL, or simply IL) through the lens of Political Economy (PE). Although interdisciplinarity seems to have become a must in most areas of academic research and so in the sphere of law, *The Political Economy of International Law – A European Perspective* is the first edited book providing a systematic and coherent review of the interactions between PE and IL. PE considerations have indeed been a late arrival in IL. Such an interdisciplinary approach was only proposed in the 1990s and has gained prominence since 2000, whereas questions of PE have been placed on the scholarly agenda of other legal science branches from time immemorial.

PE is not a unified discipline. This entails that the term 'Political Economy' is used in different ways. In its most common meaning, PE refers to interdisciplinary studies drawing upon economics, law, and political science in explaining how political institutions, the political environment, and the economic system influence each other. Given the overlap between legal and political systems, some of the issues in PE are also raised in Law and Economics – in other words, the application of economic, specifically microeconomic, methods to legal analysis – Constitutional Economics and Political Science. PE is also often associated with rational-choice theories relying on the assumption that an actor, be it an individual, a State or an international organisation, acts intentionally in order to achieve its set of goals.

In this book, PE refers to the study of the 'why' questions (why do we have laws, institutions, courts) using as explanatory variables the 'who' questions (who are the actors – legislators, executives, judges, interest groups within a country, a country itself or international organisations, NGOs, business – that participate in shaping IL) and 'what' motivates them (their preferences) on the one hand and their constraints (power, resources, institutions and laws etc.) on the other hand. A change of the law may lead to a change in the constraints. PE combines a descriptive approach, explaining why we sometimes are unable to achieve the best possible outcome, and a prescriptive approach, suggesting how to move in a way that would be more efficient or democratic.

This book explores how PE can increase our understanding of IL. Whereas international lawyers bring their knowledge of institutions and their experience to the table, PE brings a theoretical framework that helps to capture a problem's underlying structure. The combination of these two elements allows us to find better solutions to problems.

The interdisciplinary perspective offered in this book would have been unthinkable just a few years ago. International lawyers kept on viewing the real world through the (legalistic) Westphalian lens of equal sovereignty of the nation-States. The paradigm that only States' behaviours matter for IL purposes – the so-called 'unitary State perspective' – has however been seriously undermined recently, especially in the context of global governance. The interpenetration of global political and economic life has dramatically changed the context for international lawyers' investigations. It is nowadays almost self-evident that a new way of thinking in IL is needed in order to keep abreast with globalization (that is, with individuals, corporations and nation-States reaching around the world farther, faster and deeper than ever before). PE can lead international lawyers towards a non-unitary State perspective.

The book project came out of a conference that was hosted by *La Sapienza* University in Rome on 16–17 May 2014. Following to a large extent the scheme of the conference programme, the book is divided into five parts and eighteen chapters representing the main categories, subcategories and topics of IL.

In Part I, the seminal introductory chapter by Anne van Aaken and Joel Trachtman shapes the basic concepts and methodological approaches to the investigation which will inspire the following chapters.

In Part II, the authors address the sources of IL. The understanding of Customary International Law (CIL) has always been difficult without social science explanation: the compared chapters of Niels Petersen and Alessandra Gianelli provide pros and cons regarding the use of PE in order to explain custom. Paul Stephan explains the logic of *jus cogens* by drawing on divergent interests of different actors and illuminates his analysis with the decision of the International Court of Justice (ICJ) in *Jurisdictional Immunities of the State*. Panos Merkouris concentrates on treaties: their making and functioning as well as treaty conflicts and interpretation as well as the interests of different actors therein. The chapter of Ramses Wessel and Evisa Kica addresses the decisions by International Organizations (IOs) by pointing to the choice of States (or other actors in the public sphere) to move from formal to informal international decision-making as well as to some consequences of this choice.

Part III highlights the most relevant questions concerning the enforcement of IL. Barbara Delcourt and Meredith Kolsky Lewis ask on the basis of PE why States comply with IL. Delcourt presents a framework for answering this question, embedding a PE analysis in competing theories on that issue. Lewis explores the PE game theory of the prisoner's dilemma in the context of compliance with IL. The role of national and international courts in IL is becoming ever more crucial. Paul Stephan and Eyal Benvenisti explain court behaviour. Benvenisti suggests that domestic courts not only make and enforce IL, but they may actually be responsible for ensuring that international organizations and courts adhere to procedural and substantive norms that protect human rights and ensure accountability of global decisions to diverse stakeholders. They do so to protect their own authority domestically. Stephan offers a PE theory on how international tribunals decide and identifies different PE models of international adjudication. Andreas von Staden picks the (non-) compliance behaviour of States with the international human rights pronouncements and explains it on the basis of a PE analysis. André Nollkaemper presents a PE analysis of shared responsibility in IL.

In Part IV, the book then turns to specific subject matters. Alberta Fabbricotti explains the surge of Regional Trade Agreements (RTAs) on the basis of a PE analysis. Lehmann offers a PE theory, based on the political science selectorate theory on why States conclude international investment treaties. This theory offers an alternative and potentially better theory than the 'competition-for-capital' theory relying on the State as a unit of analysis so far mostly discussed. Laurence Boisson de Chazournes and Christina Leb analyse the PE reasons for (insufficient) benefit sharing in international water law. Ulyana Kohut considers the applicability of the principal theories of compliance with IL specifically to human rights treaty-based obligations. The chapter by Daniela Vitiello and Marion Panizzon reviews key PE theories regarding migration, and considers the suitability, efficiency and democracy of current instruments of global transaction over migration in light of new migratory trends and challenges.

Part V contains the authoritative chapter by Eyal Benvenisti and Jan Wouters, who masterfully conclude the book by highlighting that the relationship between IL and PE turns out to be a story of paradoxes, but also one which carries great potential.

The methodological approach featured in the whole structure of the book has been to take as a point of departure the traditional catalogue of an IL general treatise and to systematically inject insights from PE into each of its sections and chapters. The rationale for this approach assumes that it is up to IL scholars to pioneer the trespassing on the discipline of PE and not vice versa. It is indeed the international lawyers who actually feel the need to open their traditional frontiers to insights from other scientific branches, and particularly from PE. It follows from this perspective that this book takes for granted the reader's basic knowledge of the structure, theories and institutions of PIL.

This method is a distinctive trait which makes the present book completely different from other publications which look at IL in an interdisciplinary context, typically the US literature. The title subheading *A European Perspective* was added in order to emphasize this difference, and not to mean any geographical, cultural background or academic affiliation, which would have been even contradictory given the listing among the contributors of academicians from outside Europe, and particularly from the US.

It would clearly have been impossible to cover all potential PE intersections with each of the IL fundamentals in a single volume. To avoid any misunderstanding it should first be said that this book is not dealing with the PE of IOs, an issue which deserves a specific and autonomous investigation. Moreover, the editor and the authors agreed on discussing, in connection with each IL fundamental, one or more selected issues of particular relevance for the understanding of the PE/IL interplay. For example, concerning the international treaties as a source of IL (by Panos Merkouris), it was deemed that a representative picture of the PE/IL interaction would be offered focusing on areas having a great instructional value: i) non-State determination of the existence of a treaty; ii) evolutive interpretation; iii) normative conflict and iv) termination of treaties.

The main distinctive feature of IL compared to the other branches of the law is probably the extraordinary relevance of custom among its normative sources. Therefore it is not surprising that CIL is the most debated issue in existing PE/IL literature. In light of these considerations, the present book dedicates two chapters to the CIL though from two different perspectives in a dialectic relationship, *The Political Economy of Customary International Law* by Niels Petersen, and *Can Political Economy Help Solve the Riddle of Customary International Law* by Alessandra Gianelli.

Also, it would not have been feasible, in an effort to contain the length of this book within reasonable limits, to review PE game theories systematically. The fact that only the prisoner's dilemma game is investigated in one separated chapter, *International Political Economy and the Prisoner's Dilemma: Compliance with International Law* by Meredith Kolsky Lewis, is simply due to the great popularity gained by this game theory in PE and now also in IL. In other words, this does not imply a doctrinal preference for this strict dominance game over other theories, like coordination games, for example.

To ensure that the many different chapters would merge into a homogeneous and coherent framework, the contributors were asked to address some core themes raised in the basic introductory chapter *Political Economy of International Law: Towards A Holistic Model of State Behaviour* by Anne van Aaken and Joel Trachtman. In particular, they were asked to answer: 1) whether they were adopting a PE or an International Political Economy (IPE) approach; 2) whether they were considering IL as *explanandum* (they had to explain the determinants of its creation) or as *explanans* (they had to explain its consequences and effects); and 3) whether they were going to discuss the determinants of the adherence of the State to IL (why the State enters into a particular treaty, for instance) or of its compliance with IL (why the State obeys given rules). This kind of leitmotiv all along the volume was intended to ensure that the terminology and method in the introductory chapter were maintained in the chapters of the book's main body.

PART I

Framework Issues

1. Political Economy of International Law: Towards a Holistic Model of State Behaviour

Anne van Aaken and Joel P Trachtman

I. INTRODUCTION

International relations have changed considerably since the end of the Cold War. Many new phenomena do not fit into the traditional State-centred Public International Law (PIL) normative frame, such as soft law, Non-State Actors (NSA) and hybrids[1] as well as transnational legal processes.[2] Furthermore, International Law (IL) now deals with many 'behind the border' issues that were not the concern of traditional PIL. How is IL rising to the challenge of capturing these factually new phenomena *de lege lata* and dealing with them in a normative context? When analysing old and new developments and asking why States cooperate and comply with PIL and how they design PIL, 'why' questions need to be asked. Social science provides tools to answer them and, as we submit in this Chapter, additionally we need to look into the 'billiard ball' State in order to answer them, in other words, we need to break up the black box of the State as a unitary actor and instead look at the Legoland – the bits and pieces constituting the 'unitary actor' – we live in.[3]

[1] Kenneth Abbott and Duncan Snidal, 'International Regulation without International Government: Improving IO Performance through Orchestration' (2010) 5 Rev IOs 315 and Kenneth Abbott, Philipp Genschel, Duncan Snidal and Bernhard Zangl (eds), *International Organizations as Orchestrators* (CUP 2015).

[2] Colin Scott, Fabrizio Cafaggi and Linda Senden (eds), *The Challenges of Transnational Private Regulation: Conceptual and Constitutional Debates* (Blackwell 2011); Fabrizio Cafaggi (ed), *The Enforcement of Transnational Regulation. Ensuring Compliance in a Global World* (Edward Elgar 2012).

[3] Anne-Marie Slaughter, 'Remarks, The Big Picture: Beyond Hot Spots & Crises in Our Interconnected World' (2012) 1 Penn State JLIA 286.

Political Economy (PE) has been used in the national realm to understand political outcomes, including laws and jurisprudence applied to all substantive matters. PE identifies the interests of relevant actors as well as the characteristics of the institutions through which they pursue their interests. However, the law in action ultimately sets incentives and channels interests. International Political Economy (IPE), although using a two-level analysis, that is, the interaction between national politics and the behaviour of States on the international plane, has been largely confined to international economic relations as a subject matter. Furthermore, the PIL dimension is predominantly missing in IPE scholarship, although PIL has the potential to reorder values and interests and influence behaviour within the national realm. In order to understand the many other facets of PIL, it is necessary to extend the IPE approach to all subject matter of PIL and to include PIL's behavioural force in the analysis of State behaviour.

As Anne-Marie Slaughter urged some years ago: 'International Relations as a social science approach can make International Lawyers better *lawyers*.'[4] We believe this is the case, without dismissing detailed doctrinal work as a *conditio sine qua non* for a good understanding of the interests and incentives set by PIL: the internal perspective to the law remains most important. This Chapter outlines a general model of PE of PIL. It thereby closes a gap: in PE, the 'international' is missing, in IPE, the non-economic subject matters, as well as the law, are missing, while in PIL, the social science is missing. Combining those approaches allows for a theory of PE of PIL. To paraphrase Kant: 'PE without PIL is empty, PIL without PE is blind.' Let us already stress at this point that we present one basic model only. It is already quite complicated but it can be tweaked further, for example, by integrating other behavioural assumptions or it can be simplified by leaving out one side of the equation. The model is meant to be a starting point and a framework for analysis.

This Chapter first clarifies some methodological misunderstandings commonly arising from a legal perspective in order to clarify the utility of PE in legal analysis (II.). A short overview on the variety of IPE is given to acknowledge the connecting factors between PE and PIL (III.). Second, and as the main focus of this Chapter, we will zoom in on a PE of PIL model for understanding and explaining the formation of and compliance with PIL via internal political processes: the PE of IL is

---

[4] Anne-Marie Slaughter, 'International Law and International Relations: Millenial Lectures' (2000) 285 Recueil des Cours de l'Académie de Droit International (Recueil des Cours) 9, 26.

preliminarily explained as a two-level game (IV.) and the model is described afterwards (V.). The last part concludes (VI.).

II. THE INTEGRATION OF PE INTO PIL: METHODOLOGICAL CLARIFICATIONS FROM A LEGAL PERSPECTIVE

Often, legal scholars focus on law application and wonder why and how social science could complement or help legal analysis. How exactly can social science contribute to PIL scholarship? In order to retain methodological clarity, we will draw on legal theory in order to clarify the role of PE or IPE in law-making or law interpretation.

Traditionally, three categorical statements are possible in law, which in turn means that lawyers may take three different perspectives or roles.[5] The first to introduce this kind of distinction was Hermann Kantorowicz,[6] followed by Max Weber[7] and Hans Albert[8] as well as some of the legal sociologists in the German-speaking countries.[9] Kantorowicz composes an epistemological trilogy[10] consisting of the normative perspective

---

[5] See for an extensive discussion Anne van Aaken, *Rational-Choice in der Rechtswissenschaft. Zum Stellenwert der ökonomischen Theorie im Recht* (Nomos 2003).

[6] Hermann Kantorowicz, *Rechtswissenschaft und Soziologie [Th. Würtemberger ed, C.F. Müller 1962 (first 1911)]*. Of course, classifications are never right or wrong but only more or less useful.

[7] Daniel Bodansky, 'International Law in Black and White' (2006) 34 Georgia J Int Comp L 285, 285 attributes this classification to Max Weber. Weber neither used this categorization in 'Sociology of Law' (1921) nor in 'Objectivity in Social Science and Policy' (1904) though he of course always made a sharp distinction (as Kantorowicz) between normative and empirical knowledge. Weber also knew the paper of Kantorowicz as he commented on the paper 'Rechtswissenschaft und Soziologie' in 1911, see Bibliography of Max-Weber Gesamtausgabe, http://www.mohr.de/en/sociology/text-editions/max-weber-gesamtausgabe/edition.html (accessed 20 Oct 2014).

[8] Hans Albert, 'Erkenntnis und Recht. Die Jurisprudenz im Lichte des Kritizismus', in Hans Albert et al. (eds), *Rechtstheorie als Grundlagenwissenschaft der Rechtswissenschaft*, vol II (Bertelsmann Universitätsverlag 1972) at 80.

[9] For example, Manfred Rehbinder, *Rechtssoziologie* (4th edn, Walter de Gruyter 2000), Hubert Rottleuthner, *Rechtstheorie und Rechtsoziologie* (Alber 1981) at 13.

[10] Kantorowicz (n 6) at 69 ('erkenntnistheoretischer Trialismus').

(*Wertwissenschaft*)[11] (in the social science sense: normative science), the sociological perspective (*Realwissenschaft*; positive science), and the law application or doctrinal perspective (*Normwissenschaft*). He also distinguished between the general level and the specific level within those three columns.[12] The normative and the sociological (or economic) perspective take an external point of view on the law whereas the doctrinal perspective takes an internal point of view.[13]

The normative perspective includes questions of how (international) law *ought* to be. At a general knowledge level this is meant to be legal philosophy: what kind of goals ought PIL pursue? The specific level includes legal policy questions, for example, how to design international institutions (*de lege ferenda*) with a view to achieving the stated goals (for example, peace, human rights, free trade, climate change mitigation), including the effectiveness of the law. The discussion on which goals are to be pursued and how they are to be justified thus belongs to the normative perspective. The question of how best to pursue them, though, necessarily includes social science knowledge; norm idealism without reality check is at best naïve, at worst untruthful. Furthermore, there might be assumptions of what normative goals actors ought to pursue, for example, public welfare; whether politicians pursue them in reality is in turn a question of positive science and enters the assumptions of the PE model, as will be elaborated below.

The second column entails the sociological perspective or positive explanation in the social science sense ('positive analysis' in the social science sense, not to be confused with legal positivism[14]). Here, descriptive, explanatory and predictive questions can be asked. Usually one proceeds by developing a hypothesis which may be (should be) empirically tested. There are thus again two levels: the abstract or theoretical level which can use as underlying theory rational choice (as done by economists and a lot of political scientists), behavioural economics[15] or

---

[11] Bodansky (n 7) at 285 calls this the ethical perspective.

[12] Kantorowicz (n 6) at 92 (generalisierende und individualisierende Erkenntnis).

[13] Seminal: Herbert L A Hart, *The Concept of Law* (3rd edn, OUP 2012).

[14] Lawyers and social scientists use different notions of positivism. Although both deal with 'what is', they are fundamentally different methodological approaches. Whereas legal positivism asks 'what is law', social science positive analysis is descriptive and explanatory with the help of models and empirical analysis. Usually causal relationships are looked for.

[15] See for that approach, Anne van Aaken, 'Behavioral International Law and Economics' (2014) 55 Harv Int L J 421. For a behavioral approach to PE, see Jan

more constructivist approaches. The important point to stress is that different behavioural assumptions may underlie the models of PE of PIL; ideally those should be spelt out explicitly. Differences of approaches in IPE are thus mainly linked to differences in underlying theories and hypotheses. On the level of empirics, quantitative or qualitative methods can be used.

The causes and effects of PIL come to the fore, depending on whether PIL is used as *explanans* (independent variable) or *explanandum* (dependent variable). Social scientific methods can be used both to explain the consequences of PIL, including of whether PIL is effective (law as *explanans*) as well as the determinants of its creation (law as *explanandum*). Whereas much research has focused on the consequences of PIL, the focus of PE and IPE is to explain political and legal outcomes. Although those questions should be distinguished (law is either on the left or right side of the equation: only half of a causal cycle), they are not independent from each other if the whole cycle is to be analysed – depending on the consequences, States are supposed to be more or less inclined to cooperate in international relations, depending on internal interest constellations. This is what the model presented in this Chapter aims to achieve. It has been the merit of IPE to empirically construct the outcome *(explanandum)* by focusing as a first step on the interests of the actors, which are in turn affected by the assumed consequences of norms, for example, trade liberalization norms (*explanans*).[16] Interests of actors in certain policies are thus deduced from the consequences of those policies. Only that kind of knowledge enables IL scholars to understand why and how States cooperate. Here again, one may distinguish the general from the specific level. Whereas on the general level discussions on the merits of different social science theories and their respective hypotheses take place (for example, rationalist vs. constructivist views on how PIL functions), on the specific level, a scholar may work empirically on a specific issue and try to (in)validate a hypothesis.

Schnellenbach and Christian Schubert, 'Behavioral Political Economy: A Survey', CESifo Working Paper No. 4988, available at http://www.cesifo-group.de/portal/page/portal/lang-en/DocBase_Content/WP/WP-CESifo_Working_Papers/wp-cesifo-2014/wp-cesifo-2014-09/cesifo1_wp4988.pdf (2014).

[16] David A Lake, 'International Political Economy', in Barry R Weingast and Donald A Wittman (eds), *The Oxford Handbook of Political Economy* (OUP 2006), 763 ff. Interest or preferences over alternative policies of different groups are derived from the distributional implications of alternative policies.

Last, but not least, there is the third column which is the traditional domain of international lawyers, namely the doctrinal perspective, which Kantorowicz called 'Normwissenschaft' or in legal theory would be called 'Rechtsanwendungswissenschaft' (science of law application). Here, as primary methodology, hermeneutics is used, something social science (including economics) cannot contribute to at first sight. European international lawyers tend to concentrate on this column. Here again, two levels may be distinguished: the level of methods of interpretation on the general level as well as the doctrinal analysis on the specific level.

The systematic starting point for the interpretation of treaties is Arts. 31 and 32 of the Vienna Convention on the Law of Treaties (VCLT).[17] Some interpretative methods not only leave open a window for social science knowledge but even demand it, for example, in teleological interpretation (object and purpose as mentioned in Art. 31 (1) VCLT), in openly consequentialist argumentation, in comparative interpretation, or within the principle of proportionality (for example, necessity under Art. XX (b) GATT or Art. 1 of Protocol No. 1 to the European Convention on Human Rights (ECHR)).[18] All of those interpretive methods are based, structurally, on means-end-rationality. The 'object and purpose' provides a clear example of this. The relationship between the means (the alternative interpretations) and the end (the purpose of the treaty) is a hypothesis on real-world consequences. An evidence-based interpretation would use social science, in order to shed light and convincingly argue for the presumed causal relationship between the end and the means. The same reasoning applies, for example, for proportionality or necessity analysis which request a comparative least intrusive means test.[19] If one does not confine teleological interpretation to legal consequences but includes real world consequences, social science insights are needed, be

---

[17] See instead of many Richard K Gardiner, *Treaty Interpretation* (OUP 2008); Sir Jennings and Arthur Watts (eds), *Oppenheim's International Law*, Vol. I, Parts 2 to 4: Peace (Longman 1992/1905) 1266 ff. Those rules of interpretation are accepted as Customary International Law (CIL). See for supplementary means of interpretation such as *contra preferentem*, *in dubio mitius* or *expressio unius est exclusio alterus* ibid 1277 ff.

[18] Anne van Aaken, 'Defragmentation of International Law through Constitutional Interpretation: A Methodological Proposal' (2009) 16 Indiana J Glob Leg Stud 483.

[19] Extensively, see van Aaken (n 5) and Anne van Aaken, 'Opportunities for and Limits to an Economic Analysis of International Economic Law' (2011) Transnational Corporations Review, available at http://journal.tnc-online.org/ 27.

they hypotheses or, better, empirical insights into causal relationships. Economics is the most advanced discipline in discovering those relationships.[20]

Examples for questions at the doctrinal level are whether the invasion of Iraq in 2003 violated the UN Charter, how to understand the potential victim requirement under the standing norms of regional human rights treaties or whether a country in severe economic crisis could justify its necessity measures under Art. 25 ILC Articles on Responsibility of States for Internationally Wrongful Acts (ARSIWA) or respective essential security escape clauses in Bilateral Investment Treaties (BITs). Here, a PIL scholar takes the perspective of a judge, a legal advisor to government or a lawyer for her client and asks first of all what the law is. Taking this internal perspective on the law has been the traditional task of lawyers. No matter what kind of norms (soft or hard) are relevant for changing States' behaviour, only the sources of IL as stated in Art. 38 (1) International Court of Justice (ICJ) Statute are relevant for this task.[21] On questions of legal validity, legal positivism is probably still the way to go.[22] Nevertheless, interpretation of soft law, since it can be relevant for States' behaviour, is not to be neglected in a social science perspective or if soft law enters 'hard' law, as for example, the incorporation of Codex

---

[20] Edward O Wilson, *Consilience: The Unity of Knowledge* (Alfred A Knopf 1998) at 195: 'This discipline [economics] … deserves the title often given to it, Queen of the social science'.

[21] The debate on the importance of soft law is exploding. Nevertheless, even if one assumes the importance of soft law for changing States' behaviour, as for example, Eibe Riedel, 'Standards and Sources. Farewell to the Exclusivity of the Sources Triad in International Law?' (1991) 2 EJIL 58, there seems to be a wide consensus that the sources of IL should not be extended (though of course there is a wide discussion on the importance of soft law as a means of interpretation of hard law or its role in forming CIL). See instead of many Daniel Thürer, 'Soft Law', in Rudolf Bernhardt (ed), *Encyclopedia of Public International Law*, Vol. 4 (OUP 2000) 452 ff. For a different view including soft law as a source of law, see Andrew T Guzman, 'A Compliance Based Theory of International Law' (2002) 90 Calif L Rev 1823.

[22] This is a small problem for treaties: they are valid through consent even if not effective. Consent would also still be needed on a 'constitutional level', even if there is a delegation of law-making to International Organizations. See for a game theoretical analysis of the trend of eroding the traditional consent model in PIL, Laurence R Helfer, 'Participation, Compliance, and Nonconsensual International Lawmaking' 2008 U Ill L Rev 71. The problem is greater with CIL: here, sociological factors might be necessary in order to determine validity of CIL and a fusion of a doctrinal and a sociological perspective might be necessary.

Alimentarius in the WTO agreements.[23] Differences in approaches to legal science arise forcefully on the question of law application, that is the extent and the way by which the normative and the social science perspective may enter the doctrinal perspective. Here, the difference between European and American IL scholars may be the largest; the latter being generally more open to the normative as well as the positive approach than the former. We firmly believe that a purely internal point of view can gain greatly from including also external perspectives on the law. More than that, we believe that self-contained legal analysis without social science insights tend to be deficient since they do not take into account the underlying social problems to be solved by law. Social science strengthens legal analysis, it does not weaken it.

Those columns or perspectives do not stand unconnected to each other. Positive description, explanation and prognosis can be used to derive normative critique; positive explanation is indispensable to the effective pursuit of certain goals.[24] This shows again how closely interconnected the three columns are in practice. International constitutionalism as a normative approach can benefit from social science insights as to how to pursue those normative goals most effectively. It needs a functional approach, just as does transnational governance.[25] On questions of legal policy and institutional design, there is broad consensus that social science should be taken into account: there is thus a direct input from social science to IL design. Furthermore, when law is taken as *explanandum*, that is, the PE question is asked of why we have a particular PIL rule, a theory is needed to explain why the actors chose what kind of law. This theory will often include law as *explanans*: what consequences the actors expected from the particular legal rule. In PE and IPE, it is assumed that actors follow their interests and theories about the consequences of PIL – that is, actors which expect to benefit (rightly or wrongly) from certain norms are assumed to be in favour of that policy (and lobby for it). This assumption will be taken up below in part IV.

---

23 See the chapter by Ramses A Wessel and Evisa Kica in this Volume.

24 Daniel A Farber, 'Positive Theory as Normative Critique' (1994) 68 Southern Calif L Rev 1565.

25 Anne van Aaken, 'A Functional Approach to International Constitutionalism: The Value Added of a Social Science Contribution' (2012) 127 ARSP Beiheft 155; Joel P Trachtman, *The Future of International Law: Global Government* (CUP 2013).

III. VARIETIES OF INTERNATIONAL POLITICAL ECONOMY

The holistic study of law, politics and economics has its roots in moral philosophy (Adam Smith, JS Mill, Karl Marx) when politics, law and economics were not yet separated and law was not yet reduced to irrelevance as in (most) economic models of law starting in the 1880s with the marginal revolution. Thus, PE and IPE have ancient roots. Since we zoom in on PE of PIL in the next part, explaining how the national and international realm interconnect, we will deal with IPE first.

Economics is not only a subject matter but also a specific methodological approach – the rational choice approach which is also used by political scientists.[26] A prominent misunderstanding arises from the fact that economics is often viewed as dealing only with the subject matter of the economy or business, that is only economic variables are looked at and everything else is irrelevant to the analysis. Some parts of economic science indeed confine themselves to purely economic variables, for example, classical macroeconomics. Traditionally, also, IPE has been confined to economic matters,[27] namely international economic relations. Then it is also more permissible to confine the analysis to purely economic goals, such as efficiency, economic growth or distributional questions. But increasingly, economics as a social science methodology analyses other subject matters, including IL with all its substantive areas that justify and even call for a broader definition of goals – public welfare (welfarism) which in turn then has to be refined for each subject matter and can include goals such as environmental protection, health or other human rights. Taking economics as a methodology, legal scholars have used economic approaches, including game theory and contract theory, to explain States' behaviour in international relations but have largely concentrated on the State as a 'billiard ball', thus leaving out the two-level PE analysis.[28] Furthermore, the economic approach has been extended ever more towards behavioural economics, abandoning the

---

26 Jeffrey L Dunoff and Mark A Pollack (eds), *Interdisciplinary Perspectives on International Law and International Relations. The State of the Art* (CUP 2013).

27 See Lake (n 16) at 758.

28 Jeffrey L Dunoff and Joel P Trachtman, 'Economic Analysis of International Law' (1999) 24 Yale J Int L 1; Jack L Goldsmith and Eric A Posner, *The Limits of International Law* (OUP 2005); Andrew T Guzman, *How International Law Works: A Rational Choice Theory* (OUP 2008); Joel P Trachtman, *The Economic Structure of International Law* (Harvard University Press 2008).

assumption of full rationality, and using psychological insights.[29] PE is the application of economic methodology to the field of politics, traditionally in the national realm only, without connection to the international plane. PE is therefore not confined to economic matters but can be and is extended to virtually all issues by drawing on the economic (social scientific) approach.[30] PE studies political processes to explain outcomes, including law (law as *explanandum*); this research is conducted by positive political theory, Public Choice or (New) Institutional Economics. It is the second column in the categorization of Kantorowicz and it is needed for the explanation of State behaviour in law creation and compliance.

Whereas PE is rather defined by its economic methodology, being focused on national politics, IPE has long been defined by its substantive subject matter, namely international economic relations, when rediscovered as a field of research.[31] IPE always recognized that decisions concerning international economy rested on domestic policies but still was mostly confined to the substantive field of economics (whereas the rest of PE is mainly unified by research questions and methodology but confined to explaining national policies and institutions). In spite of this, there are many understandings of IPE: it is 'a notoriously diverse field of study'[32] and is becoming ever more diverse.

Cohen orders the diversity of IPE approaches by dimensions of substance or style.[33] *First*, is the question of which units are the basic unit of analysis (ontology): States, firms, Non-governmental Organizations (NGOs), courts, individuals or the system as a whole? Although all theories are at their core individualist, for pragmatic purposes, researchers often bundle together individuals that can reasonably be assumed to share their interests into groups, for example, firms, NGOs,

---

29 van Aaken (n 15) with further references.

30 See for the subjects of study of PE, Barry R Weingast and Donald A Wittman (eds), *The Oxford Handbook of Political Economy* (OUP 2006) with contributions ranging from voter behaviour and pressure groups to legislative bodies, constitutional theory, property rights protection democracy and capitalism.

31 See the seminal article of Susan Strange, 'International Economics and International Relations: A Case of Mutual Neglect'(1970) 46 Int Aff 304.

32 Anthony Payne, 'The Study of Governance in a Global Political Economy', in Nicola Phillips (ed), *Globalizing International Political Economy* (Palgrave Macmillan 2005) 69.

33 Benjamin J Cohen, *International Political Economy* (Edward Elgar 2014) 8.

unions.[34] *Second*, the agenda: what are the most important issues to be addressed? Is it material welfare and its distribution, or is it the interest in governance and decision-making? Are those questions confined to regions, continents or rather global? *Third*, very importantly, is the question: is the research normatively driven, seeking to achieve certain values, or is the research 'positive', focused on explanation, intended to enhance our understanding of the world? *Fourth*, how open to other disciplines is the conducted research? Is rational choice the only way to go or are other disciplines, such as psychology, anthropology, and history, easily incorporated? And *last, but not least*, epistemology: what methodologies are used? Analytical theories, empirical work, the latter only quantitative or also qualitative? The illumination of the different dimensions is useful in order to understand the permissible variety of research conducted under the heading of 'IPE' included in this book.

Cohen regrets that mostly IPE has been identified with English speaking research, neglecting the diversity existing worldwide.[35] Those other perspectives take different approaches to the above-mentioned dimensions. Traditionally, there has been an American and a British School of IPE (although there are others as well). All schools are concerned with the interaction of the State (viewed as the relevant actor) and economics as well as international economic relations. As Helen Milner has put it: 'The central questions all relate to the interaction of politics and economics among States'.[36] Nevertheless, they differ considerably in their assumptions and normative thrust. Whereas one theory, dependency theory, dealt with the question of the economy and prospects of development in poor countries in the 1970s,[37] hegemonic stability theory asked whether a single hegemonic State was necessary and sufficient for international economic cooperation to arise.[38] Often, IPE has been equated with Open Economy Politics (OEP), although this is just one branch of IPE and close to the American school, using the

---

[34] Lake (n 16) 763.

[35] Cohen (n 33) 4 ff. He deals in this book with the American and the British School (including their fringes) as well as the continental European, the Latin American and the Chinese approach.

[36] Helen Milner, 'Reflections on the Field of International Political Economy', in Michael Brecher and Frank P Harvey (eds), *Conflict, Security, Foreign Policy, and International Political Economy: Past, Paths and Future Directions in International Studies* (University of Michigan Press 2002) 214.

[37] Cohen (n 33) 96 ff.

[38] For more details, see Lake (n 16) 761 ff.

rationalist approach, focusing on the interaction of domestic and international frontiers, still involved with the subject matter of economics.[39] It is concerned with defining or deriving the interest of the different national constituencies, the institutions aggregating societal conflicts and the conditions of bargaining of opposing domestic groups. With those national interests aggregated through institutions towards a 'national policy', OEP can then turn to the international bargaining necessary because of externalities. Usually this direction of causal inference is taken. Less focus has been placed on the influence of IL and institutions on domestic policies. This influence will be taken into consideration in the model developed below.

Whereas the American School of IPE used the rational choice approach and was more free-trade leaning, the British School used also a constructivist approach and exhibits more critical thinking, including distributional issues. Thus, while IPE uses a two-level analysis in order to explain international relations, it is mainly confined to economic international relations, by tradition mostly trade relations.[40] Furthermore, while it views PIL sometimes as an outcome of international bargaining, it neglects the influence of PIL on domestic outcomes.

In the following, a model is developed which integrates PIL more holistically in a PE model: PIL is viewed as *explanans* as well as *explanandum*, closing the causal cycle. The central unit of analysis is thus domestic interests.

In order to qualify as an IPE model, it must incorporate a theory of political decision-making. The model developed focuses on the balance of interests and power in the domestic setting, examining how the domestic PE determines the ability of States to form and comply with IL in the international context. It is not confined to international economic relations but is applicable to all subject matters. It incorporates PIL as an *explanandum* by assuming that IL is formed only when national politics produces a demand for international cooperation. So it is domestic preferences of the demanding country that cause the initial unilateral

---

[39] Seminal, Peter Katzenstein, 'International Relations and Domestic Structures: Foreign Economic Policies of Advanced Industrial States' (1976) 30 Int Org 1. See for an example of topics connected to economics, but analysing different actors, Anthony Payne and Nicola Phillips (eds), *Handbook of the International Political Economy of Governance* (Edward Elgar 2014).

[40] See the chapters of Lehmann and Fabbricotti in this Volume.

demand for international cooperation, and domestic preferences of partner countries that determine whether there is sufficient reciprocity – specific or diffuse – to make acceptance of an international legal rule attractive.

But in order to have a complete theory of why States demand and create IL, we must also develop a theory of how IL has effects in the real world of domestic politics. Here again, we focus on the interests of States, and assume that, in addition to the constellation of national interests that result in demand for the international legal rule, and may continue to support the reciprocal rule initially agreed, there are also national interests – including the government itself or national courts – that are interested in promoting the international legal system and its reliability, either for selfish or altruistic reasons. Lawyers have for a long time looked at those interactions – national to international and back – but without using social science. In the view of the present authors this neglect is to be remedied.

In a sense, the PE model of PIL developed in the next paragraph is simply an extension of the national PE model of public policy. The extension is into the international setting, where an expanded range of tradeoffs and exchanges is possible. Exchange of public policy commitments across borders, as in the market for goods and services, takes place when exchange can increase the welfare of the participants in the exchange. PIL is one instrument of international cooperation – one instrument of international exchange of policy commitments.

IV. POLITICAL ECONOMY OF INTERNATIONAL LAW AS A TWO-LEVEL GAME

In this Section, we explore the application to PIL of Kantorowicz's second pillar: the sociological perspective (Realwissenschaft; positive science). As we stated in Section II, we are concerned in the second pillar with the causes and effects of IL – why States make IL, and why they comply with IL.

A PE approach to IL must be based on welfarism, which suggests theories that assume that individuals make IL through States in order to better their lot. This is a liberal, methodologically individualist, and preference-based approach. Having said that, there is room for ideational or constructivist reasons for IL. This is because legal change is always mediated through perception and ideas. Legal change is also mediated through political mechanisms, which achieve welfare with varying degrees of fidelity.

An important alternative perspective focuses not on public welfare, but on political welfare – the welfare of government officials, including their efforts to secure political support. This 'public choice' approach has important descriptive power, but it must either incorporate a measure of public welfare, or concede incompleteness. It can incorporate a measure of public welfare by recognizing that to some extent political support will be based on the ability of politicians to deliver enhanced welfare to their citizens.

Reconciling public welfare, public choice, and constructivism, it might be said that public welfare is mediated through ideas, and that our ideas about public policy are largely mediated – are given effect – through national political systems.

As noted above, a model that included in the determinants of national policy only public welfare would be deficient, as would a model that included in the determinants of national policy only political welfare. Rather, national policy will be determined by a combination of the welfare of political actors and their constituents. Public choice models that include public welfare as a determinant of political welfare are sufficient to do so. So are public welfare models that recognize the mediating effect of politics. Whatever model is chosen, there will be circumstances in which a greater aggregate of public and political welfare may be achieved by international cooperation. To the extent that public welfare is a vector in national decision-making, national governments will tend to seek international cooperation that enhances public welfare.

Any understanding of international cooperation through law must be infused with respect for the practical, State-based, political process by which formal cooperation occurs, and it must include a mechanism by which States would determine to create organizational structures which facilitate cooperation. It must develop a perspective on the interaction between multiple domestic political processes, and it must develop a theory of the creation of international organizations.

Mitrany observed as follows:

> Our social activities are cut off arbitrarily at the limit of the State and, if at all, are allowed to be linked to the same activities across the border only by means of uncertain and cramping political ligatures. What is here proposed is simply that these political amputations should cease. Whenever useful or necessary the several activities would be released to function as one unit throughout the length of their natural course.[41]

---

[41] David Mitrany, *A Working Peace System* (Chicago Quadrangle Press 1966) 82.

Yet Mitrany did not develop the full implications of the extension of politics across borders. IL is the formal mechanism by which such extension occurs in the modern world, and international legal rules and institutions make up the formal link between separate domestic political systems.

International relations and IL form a mechanism by which the domestic politics of different States may be linked, modifying the otherwise applicable political equilibrium in different States. The interaction of States matters for domestic politics, and in fact is simply an extension of domestic politics. But it is an extension that constitutes functional cross-national political equilibria, and in effect, communities. These communities often require law, and increasingly require international organizations.

IV.1. The Methodological Individualism from Unilateralism to Multilateralism

The liberal theory of international relations, developed by Andrew Moravcsik, calls attention to the domestic sources of international relations preferences.[42] Thus, 'the demands of individuals and societal groups are treated as analytically prior to politics.'[43] Liberal theory focuses on preferences of States, resulting from the aggregation of individual preferences by the State's political mechanisms. Governments then act purposively in world politics on the basis of these preferences. Thus, preferences are the cause of State behaviour within a world system that provides constraints based on other States' preferences.

States are dynamic systems, with individuals and groups of individuals vying with one another for influence. To the extent that these systems are assumed to be closed, it may be appropriate to expect a fairly stable equilibrium among these individuals and groups. Coalition politics may be relatively stable, with change occurring based on demographic, technological, ideational, or other factors that disrupt the equilibrium. The market of international relations, in which States seek modifications of the behaviour of other States, provides an additional, dynamic source of stimuli that may disrupt otherwise extant national political equilibria.

---

[42] See Andrew Moravcsik, 'Taking Preferences Seriously: A Liberal Theory of International Politics' (1997) 51 Int Org 513, 516–21 (giving an overview of the assumptions underlying the liberal theory and explaining how domestic politics exerts an influence in world politics).

[43] Ibid at 517.

As the market of international relations becomes deeper and more efficient, it will increasingly be a part of a normal national equilibrium.

Thus, while as Putnam explains, 'it is fruitless to debate whether domestic politics really determine international relations, or the reverse',[44] the relationship between domestic politics and international relations has a particular directional structure. Liberal theory envisions States entering the 'market' of international relations to satisfy preferences.[45] The State is a dynamic aggregator of individual, group, and coalition preferences.

IV.2. The Domestic Causes of International Law

A number of factors within the domestic politico-legal sphere may cause States to make (adhere to), and to comply with, IL. It is unlikely that any mono-causal explanation would be broadly successful, and this field would benefit from empirical evaluation of the relative causal power of different factors in different contexts. The literature has focused on the following categories of causal factors: (i) domestic structure,[46] (ii) ideas and managerial factors,[47] (iii) domestic litigation and interest groups, and (iv) domestic interests and partisan politics. We focus here on domestic interests and partisan politics, or preferences, simply because we speculate that a preference-based explanation of entry into and compliance with law will generally provide the greatest explanatory power. Our speculation is supported by a broad consensus in social science that preferences have great (although definitely not exclusive) causal power. However, this is not based on empirical validation in particular cases, and we would expect other causal factors to be important in specific circumstances.

---

[44] See Robert D Putnam, 'Diplomacy and Domestic Politics: The Logic of Two-Level Games' (1988) 42 Int Org 427. On Putnam's Two-Level Game Theory see the chapter by Benvenisti in this Volume.

[45] See, for example, Dunoff and Trachtman (n 28) analogizing the 'market of international relations' to the market of goods, except that states trade in units of power.

[46] Helen Milner and Peter Rosendorff, 'Democratic Politics and International Trade Negotiations' (1997) 41 JCR 117–46.

[47] See, for example, Harold Hongju Koh, 'Internalization Through Socialization' (2005) 54 Duke L J 975; Harold Hongju Koh, 'Why Do Nations Obey International Law?' (1997) 106 Yale L J 2599; Abram Chayes and Antonia Handler Chayes, 'On Compliance' (1993) 47 Int Org 175; Abram Chayes and Antonia Handler Chayes, *The New Sovereignty: Compliance with International Regulatory Agreements* (Harvard University Press 1995).

In his seminal 1978 article, 'The Second Image Reversed: The International Sources of Domestic Politics',[48] Peter Gourevitch develops the implications of the fact that the international system can affect the structure of domestic politics. This is the second image (an image of the impact of domestic politics on international relations) reversed.[49] In his leading article, 'Diplomacy and Domestic Politics: The Logic of Two-Level Games',[50] Putnam focuses attention on the role of international pressure – foreign demands – in inducing domestic political change.

Putnam's two-level game theory suggests that the role of the national government in international relations is to mediate between two separate 'games', the international game and the domestic game: 'The unusual complexity of this two-level game is that moves that are rational for a player at one board (such as raising energy prices, conceding territory, or limiting auto imports) may be impolitic for that same player at the other board.'[51]

While this provides important insights, especially as to the position of government officials caught in between, another perspective might suggest that there is no real conflict between these games. Rather, opportunities in the international game shape the strategy for maximizing an aggregate basket of preferences in the domestic game. The State is always maximizing its preferences under constraint. It is as erroneous to say that there is an inconsistency between the international and the domestic as it is to say that a corporation, entering the market, is in conflict with the market. It seeks the benefits of the market, in terms of the ability to purchase and to sell.[52]

Putnam is right in his core insight that if we examine the domestic game, we may find that there is an opportunity for a domestic equilibrium which would not exist except for the existence of the international game (what Putnam refers to as a 'synergistic linkage').[53] This is not the

---

48 Peter Gourevitch, 'The Second Image Reversed: The International Sources of Domestic Politics' (1978) 32 Int Org 881.

49 Kenneth Waltz developed the idea of three images. The first image examines the role of individuals in international relations. The second focuses on the effects of domestic politics on international relations, while the third focuses on the effects of the international system on international relations. Consider Kenneth Waltz, *Man, The State, and War: A Theoretical Analysis* (Columbia University Press 1959).

50 See Putnam (n 44).

51 Ibid at 434.

52 For a broader argument along these lines, consider Trachtman (above, n 25).

53 Putnam (n 44) at 447–48.

exception, however, but the rule in international cooperation and IL. As Jongryn Mo points out, domestic bargaining is endogenous to international cooperation – it is affected by opportunities for international cooperation.[54] Domestic bargaining is constrained by the range of international opportunities, wherever the international opportunities allow a superior outcome compared to a purely domestic equilibrium. We must assume that international cooperation will only be efficient, and will only ensue, where it allows a superior aggregate outcome, either from a political welfare or from a public welfare standpoint.

It is important to focus on the role of realignments on the domestic board: on the fact that entry into, and compliance with, IL is *always* motivated by either the prospect of change in domestic coalitions that the new IL causes, or by the prospect of avoiding unattractive change from an existing beneficial coalition. It focuses on the implications of these realignments for compliance. If there were no modification of domestic coalitions, there would be no purpose for IL – once it is accepted that compliance is always a domestic political decision, IL will only be effective if it modifies domestic politics.

Mo develops a formal bargaining model of the interplay between domestic and international bargaining. He examines the context in which the negotiator has preferences different from those of her domestic constituents: the case of conflicting domestic interests. The model presented is also an example of a nested game. We can think of international bargaining as consisting of domestic and international games that are played simultaneously. In the domestic game, the incentives of groups trying to form a domestic coalition are structured by the international game. Because groups need to make a proposal attractive to the foreign country, their incentives in choosing domestic coalition partners thus do not depend exclusively on domestic considerations.[55]

V. A MODEL OF ADHERENCE TO, AND COMPLIANCE WITH, INTERNATIONAL LAW

In this Section, we begin to develop this Chapter's model, based, in part, on the Gene Grossman–Elhanan Helpman political support model

---

[54] Jongryn Mo, 'The Logic of Two-Level Games with Endogenous Domestic Coalitions' (1994) 38 JCR 402.

[55] Ibid at 406.

designed for use in connection with international trade negotiations.[56] In that model, incumbent governments are assumed to seek to maximize a political support function. This political support function is assumed to have two components. *First*, organized interest groups are assumed to make political contributions that can assist in re-election, providing an incentive for governments to implement policies that enhance organized interest group welfare. *Second*, voters are assumed to respond in their voting behaviour to their own welfare, and so one can expect some incentive to implement policies that enhance voter welfare.[57] The government then sets its policy to aggregate a weighted sum of total contributions and aggregate social welfare. Politicians thus seek to please the 'winning' lobbies and the electorate as a whole.

We adapt the Grossman–Helpman model of the lobbying process as follows: Each lobby, representing a particular policy decision in connection with IL (whether for or against the adherence or compliance decision), confronts the government with a contribution schedule. The contribution schedule arrays contributions against policy decisions. The government then sets a policy and collects from each lobby the appropriate contribution. 'An equilibrium is a set of contribution schedules such that each lobby's schedule maximizes the aggregate utility of the lobby's members, taking as given the schedules of the other lobby groups.'[58] This model has the structure of a common agency problem: a situation where several principals seek to influence the behaviour of a single agent. 'The government here serves as an agent for the various (and conflicting) special interest groups, while bearing a cost for implementing an inefficient policy that stems from its accountability to the general electorate.'[59]

The Grossman–Helpman model is designed to explain the effectiveness of lobbying in regard to trade policy, and specifically, tariffs and subsidies.[60] Individual preferences over protectionism are assumed to

---

[56] See Gene M Grossman and Elhanan Helpman, 'Trade Wars and Trade Talks' (1995) 103 J Pol Econ 675, 678.

[57] It may also be that politicians are civic-minded, resulting in precisely the same motivation, assuming that the voter's utility is actually congruent with the politician's civic vision.

[58] Gene M Grossman and Elhanan Helpman, 'Protection for Sale' (1994) 84 Am Econ Rev 833, 836.

[59] Ibid.

[60] Ibid at 834 ('This paper seeks to explain the equilibrium structure of trade protection. We are interested in understanding which special interest groups will be especially successful in capturing private benefits from the political process.').

arise from their sector-specific endowments. Following Mancur Olson, there are some owners of factors of production who are able to organize, and some who are unable to do so.[61] The unorganized owners of factors of production do not make contributions, and so lack this type of influence over policy. We assume that each lobby structures its contribution schedule to maximize the total welfare of its members. Like Grossman and Helpman, we are first 'interested in the political equilibrium of a two-stage noncooperative game, in which the lobbies simultaneously choose their political contribution schedules in the first stage and the government sets policy in the second.'[62]

The Grossman–Helpman model relates a lobby's equilibrium success in obtaining trade protection to: (i) the State of its political organization, (ii) the ratio of domestic output in the relevant industry to net trade, (iii) the elasticity of import demand, (iv) the relative importance to the government of campaign contributions versus voter welfare, and (v) the fraction of voters that belong to the lobby group. Items (ii) and (iii) are specific to the trade context, but one would expect to find other measures of lobby welfare in other international legal contexts.

In their 1995 work, 'The Politics of Free Trade Agreements',[63] Grossman and Helpman extend their 1994 model to examine the conditions under which two States might agree to a free trade agreement. This model uses assumptions about the welfare effects of trade liberalization and addresses adherence rather than compliance. Therefore, this extended model is not directly adaptable to a general IL model of compliance. However, it provides a good basis for a broader model of entry into IL (adherence), and can be extended to analyse compliance.

Grossman and Helpman assume that the status quo prior to an international agreement is itself a domestic political equilibrium in each State.[64] This assumption seems appropriate. Thus, the opportunity for an international agreement can be understood as an exogenous shock to the existing domestic equilibrium. The opportunity for an international agreement changes the relative prices. In the trade context, the possibility for foreign compliance with a commitment to liberalize makes the price

---

[61] See Mancur Olson Jr, *The Logic of Collective Action: Public Goods and the Theory of Groups* (Harvard 1965) at 53–65 (providing a model predicting under what conditions organized political groups are likely to emerge).

[62] Grossman and Helpman (n 58) at 838.

[63] Gene M Grossman and Elhanan Helpman, 'The Politics of Free-Trade Agreements' (1995) 85 Am Econ Rev 667.

[64] Ibid at 668–70.

of domestic protectionism higher by engaging the concerns of domestic producers for export.

Grossman and Helpman, in the context of the establishment of a free trade agreement, find that in order for an agreement to be entered into, there must be a sufficient number of exporters in each country prepared to lobby for the agreement, on the basis of the welfare gains these lobbies would achieve by virtue of the performance by the other State of its market liberalization obligations under the agreement.[65] They use the concept of a politically Pareto efficient agreement, meaning an agreement with the property that no party could gain politically except at the expense of the other.[66] The specific equilibrium selected would depend, under perfect information, on the relative positions of the two States, including their discount factors or degree of patience, and each State's relative aggregate welfare under the status quo.

In the trade context where Grossman and Helpman develop their model, it is possible to assume that specific industry groups, or lobbies, have specific types of interests in trade policy. In the broader IL context, lobby interests will be more diverse, and preferences cannot be assumed to be confined to narrow wealth gains. However, there may be industry groups, ethnic groups, or other groups that have narrower interests.

While in the Grossman–Helpman model, lobbies make their contributions contingent on trade policy, we may generalize to assume that lobbies make their contributions contingent on international legal policy. For example, within domestic societies there will be a lobby group that is interested in increased human rights in other States. While this interest may be explained in terms of preferences, the types of preferences involved will depend on the particular legal rule involved, and this type of interest cannot be compared directly with other types of interests that may be measured in monetary terms. Nor are we able to make any assumptions about the utility function of any particular group. Rather, the only assumption that seems defensible is that each IL rule will harm some groups and help some other groups. However, there is one type of lobby that generally appears to be in favour of international legal

---

[65] Grossman and Helpman (n 58) at 847–49 (describing under what conditions that the interests of various lobbying groups may align to make trade agreements across coalitions and countries possible).

[66] See Gene M Grossman and Elhanan Helpman, *Interest Groups and Trade Policy* (Princeton University Press 2002) 27 (describing the concept of a Pareto efficient agreement).

adherence and compliance.[67] That type of lobby is exemplified by organizations of international lawyers such as, in the US, the members of the American Society of International Law (ASIL). We will discuss this type of lobby in greater detail below.

Turning now to the issue of compliance, it is important to recognize that, in this PE model, 'compliance can be rational even if the country as a whole pays for it more than benefits from it', because political power is not necessarily congruent with public welfare.[68] And the converse is true: compliance may be irrational, in the sense that it is not supported by sufficient political force, even if the country as a whole benefits from it more than it pays. However, if public welfare is included in the government's utility function, as in the Grossman–Helpman model, through the mechanism of voting, then international legal rules that increase public welfare are more likely to meet with both adherence and compliance.

The question regarding compliance is: conditional upon entry into an international legal rule at an initial time (t_1), what are the circumstances under which a particular country will comply with that legal rule at a later time (t_2)? We also assume that domestic politics change, in an 'obsolescing bargains'[69] sense.[70] Thus, the coalition that supports adherence at t_1 may not have the same structure or magnitude, and may not even support compliance, at t_2.

We assume an international legal rule with some 'depth' in the sense described in the 'legalization' literature:[71] the rule requires behaviour that would not occur without the added inducement that arises from operation of the rule. In our context, the domestic political process by itself and without any effect of IL would not decide to conform national behaviour to the rule. This is a slightly different issue from the question, addressed for example by Grossman and Helpman, of whether the domestic political process would decide to adhere to an international agreement. It

---

[67] Of course, there will be exceptions. For example, some rules of IL may be found to be objectionable by some portion of the membership of the ASIL.

[68] Xinyuan Dai, *International Institutions and National Policies* (CUP 2007) 6.

[69] See Raymond Vernon, *Sovereignty at Bay* (Basic Books 1971) 46–53.

[70] See Giovanni Maggi and Andrés Rodríguez-Clare, 'The Value of Trade Agreements in the Presence of Political Pressures' (1998) 106 J Pol Econ 574–601 (examining the utility of trade agreements to assist governments in opposing changing political pressure).

[71] Consider Judith Goldstein, Miles Kahler, Robert Keohane and Anne-Marie Slaughter (eds), *Legalization and World Politics* (MIT Press 2001).

is possible that *adherence* to an international agreement would be supported purely by domestic political forces, while *compliance* with the same agreement would require the additional effect of IL. Indeed, domestic *adherence* under 'depth' for the adhering State would presumably be conditioned on an expectation of foreign *compliance*, depending on the magnitude of other, non-reciprocal, incentives for compliance.

It is here further assumed that in order for any State to decide to comply with an international legal rule, there must be a coalition of domestic lobbies that is strong enough to determine national behaviour. This assumption can survive the diversity of national politics: it is not necessary to have an interest-group-based politics such as that of the US for this type of model to apply. Even autocracies involve sensitivity to political support, although the relative importance of political support compared to government policy may differ markedly. Furthermore, decision-making may, in some circumstances, take place in arenas that are insulated from interest group politics, and even from executive policy. This is the case with international legal rules that have direct effect, in which the decision is delegated exclusively to courts. We focus on lobbies more broadly, recognizing that other mechanisms, such as courts, may play the critical role in compliance.[72]

V.1. Reciprocity

A number of scholars have examined reciprocity, or retaliation, as a means of inducing compliance with IL.[73] This theoretical approach is elegant and compelling: States comply with IL in order to induce other States to comply, or in order to induce other States to continue to refrain from retaliation. In Keohane's 'specific reciprocity' (as opposed to diffuse reciprocity) sense, there is little difference between reciprocity and retaliation.[74]

---

[72] See Anne van Aaken, 'Effectuating Public International Law Through Market Mechanisms' (2009) 165 JITE 33.

[73] See, for example, Robert O Keohane, *After Hegemony* (Princeton University Press 2005) 104–05, 128–31; Guzman (n 28) 33–48, 211–12 (listing reputation, reciprocity, and retaliation as costs that deter States from noncompliance).

[74] Robert O Keohane, 'Reciprocity in International Relations' (1986) 40 Int Org 1, 4.

Most work in this area has arisen from a growing rationalist debate regarding compliance with Customary International Law (CIL).[75] Norman and Trachtman,[76] for example, developed a repeated multilateral prisoner's dilemma model of formation of, and compliance with, CIL. This model is based on the potential for retaliatory defection. It focuses on the parameters of the multilateral prisoner's dilemma in the CIL context. These parameters include: (i) the relative value of cooperation versus defection, (ii) the number of States effectively involved, (iii) the extent to which increasing the number of States involved increases the value of cooperation or the detriments of defection, including whether the particular issue has characteristics of a common problem, a public good, or a network good, (iv) the information available to the States involved regarding compliance and defection, (v) the relative patience of States in valuing the benefits of long-term cooperation compared to short-term defection, (vi) the expected duration of interaction, (vii) the frequency of interaction, and (viii) the existence of other bilateral or multilateral relationships among the States involved.[77]

Norman and Trachtman highlighted some of the characteristics of different States' domestic politics that might affect their level of patience and their resulting propensity to accept and comply with rules of CIL. (In custom, the adherence phase and compliance phase may be less distinct than in treaty.) However, they did not analyse the *decision-making* process within States or the lobbying game within States. Other rationalist approaches focusing on reciprocity or retaliation are characterized by the same limitation.

However, it is clear that a State's decision to adhere to and comply with IL is dependent on domestic politics. We must recognize that States have a variety of interests, represented by different interest groups. Certain domestic lobbies are motivated by the possibility of direct foreign reciprocity and other domestic lobbies are motivated by respect for IL. As discussed in more detail below, it is possible that respect for IL may also be understood as a special kind of diffuse reciprocity.

---

75 Consider Goldsmith and Posner (n 28); Guzman (n 21) 1823; Edward T Swaine, 'Rational Custom' (2002) 52 Duke L J 559; Pierre-Hugues Verdier, 'Cooperative States: International Relations, State Responsibility and the Problem of Custom' (2002) 42 VJIL 839. The Goldsmith and Posner book has spawned a rich responsive literature. See, for example, George Norman and Joel P Trachtman, 'The Customary International Law Game' (2005) 99 AJIL 541, 541.

76 Norman and Trachtman, ibid.

77 Ibid at 542.

A good example of the type of specific reciprocity and engagement of domestic interests that benefit from reciprocity comes from the trade context. As discussed by Grossman and Helpman,[78] exporters are a domestic constituency interested in foreign liberalization. Therefore, exporters are concerned with domestic compliance with liberalization commitments in order to ensure against reciprocal punishment in the form of protectionism abroad.

It is important to note that reciprocity may be complex: it is not necessarily tit-for-tat where each State promises the same performance.[79] Indeed, the possibility for complex barter or package deals increases the set of possible transactions. For example, while State A may be concerned with human rights in State B, for any number of reasons, State B may be unconcerned with human rights in State A. But State B may be concerned with trade liberalization in State A, perhaps because State A already has sufficient autonomous reasons for providing a satisfactory level of human rights. In fact, IL increases the opportunities for complex barter by allowing diverse performances to be linked and supported by broad fidelity to IL.

Uncertainty as to which commitments the counterparty will suspend in response to a violation would limit the likelihood that the domestic lobby concerned with those commitments will lobby for compliance. There may be a collective action problem among possible lobbies. One way to reduce the effects of this collective action problem would be to designate in advance, and specifically, the type of retaliatory action that the counterparty will take.[80]

V.2. The Role of Government and the Public International Law Lobby

It is useful to examine two sources of influence that might provide a more general influence on adherence to and compliance with IL. Each State will have a government interested in maximizing political support or welfare more generally. The availability of IL as a general tool is important to each government, because each government will value the ability to deliver greater welfare to its citizens where IL serves to do so.

---

[78] Grossman and Helpman (n 56) at 687.

[79] See Putnam (n 44) 446–47.

[80] This would be one benefit of the type of 'contingent liberalization commitments' suggested by Robert Lawrence as a structure for remedies in the trade context. Robert Z Lawrence, *Crimes and Punishments? Retaliation under the WTO* (Peterson Institute for International Economics 2003) 79–89.

For this reason, each government will have at least some interest in supporting the international legal system. Each State may also have a private group interested in supporting the international legal system in general. This might be called the 'Public International Law Lobby' or 'PILL.' One might expect the PILL to be composed largely of international lawyers.

The government and the PILL can be included in a model of the domestic politics of IL in the same way that other lobbies are included. The PILL may be motivated by altruism, including a general idea that IL provides broad benefits. It may be motivated in addition or instead by an expectation that more IL will bring more power and income to international lawyers. This could not only cause the PILL to argue for more IL, but also cause it to argue for more compliance, as more compliance would be expected to evidence the importance of IL. Evidence for the importance of IL, in turn, would add to the prestige and income of international lawyers. Furthermore, more compliance with IL might result in more IL, further benefiting the PILL. It is in connection with the PILL, and with the government as a 'lobby' itself as described below, that the constructivist model may have the greatest power: ideas and engagement may support compliance through the PILL and the government.

The PILL would thus be expected to support compliance with IL under most circumstances. The word 'most' rather than 'all' is used here because there is an occasional debate regarding whether 'legitimacy' may trump legality, especially in connection with humanitarian intervention.[81] Putting those exceptional circumstances aside, the PILL effect might be considered as fairly constant across IL rules.

Furthermore, while the PILL might advocate *adherence* to international legal rules in many cases, it would not advocate adherence in all cases. For example, it would not necessarily take a position with respect to a particular State's entry into further preferential trade agreements, into stronger intellectual property protection treaties, or into further BITs. On the other hand, the PILL might more broadly advocate adherence to more IL restraining the use of force or promoting human rights. However, one would expect the PILL to be more likely to advocate *compliance* with IL in all but the exceptional circumstances mentioned above.

In addition to the public choice explanation of the PILL influence described above, the PILL, and government officials, may have an

[81] Consider Simon Chesterman, 'Legality versus Legitimacy: Humanitarian Intervention, the Security Council, and the Rule of Law' (2002) 33 Security Dialog 293.

altruistic or civic-minded position, related to the fact that compliance with IL in general may be broadly beneficial due to network effects among international legal rules. While adherence to IL might have some network effects also, these would appear to be weaker. Importantly, this public welfare position may be held both by the PILL and by government officials. The PILL may seek to educate government officials as to the public welfare effects of compliance with IL. The altruistic position might be based on facts or based on beliefs.

It is important to note that there may also be an anti-IL lobby.[82] To the extent that such a lobby exists, its effects can be netted against the PILL, and to the extent that the anti-IL lobby is stronger than the PILL, then the PILL variable would simply be negative.

V.3. Towards a Model

The following discussion is intended to outline a model of how domestic coalitions would be affected by, and would affect, adherence to and compliance with IL.

Assume two States, H and F. Assume H and F each has exactly four lobbies, and that the respective governments of H and F represent a fifth 'interest group', each with the policy goal profiles set forth below. Assume perfect knowledge by each player of the policy preferences and magnitudes of each lobby. Magnitude is a measure of the political valence of each lobby, although as noted above it could include knowledge endowment as to compliance. The model would involve four stages. In the first stage, the lobbies in each country set contribution schedules to influence their government. In the second stage, the governments negotiate an agreement. In the third stage, lobbies (perhaps including new or different ones, and perhaps with different magnitudes) lobby about compliance. In the last stage, governments simultaneously choose whether or not to comply. In the following discussion, we focus on two stages: t_1 when the governments negotiate an agreement, and t_2 when the governments choose whether or not to comply. But it is important to note that lobbies at the first and second stages would be expected to anticipate the situation at the third and fourth stages, and respond accordingly.

---

[82] Consider Peter Spiro, 'The New Sovereigntists' (Nov/Dec 2000) 79 For Aff 6.

H lobbies:

J: policy goal is x (for example, *either* consumers seeking free trade in bananas imported to H,[83] *or* environmentalists seeking carbon reduction).
K: policy goal is not x (for example, *either* import competing producers seeking protection in bananas in H, *or* oil companies seeking to avoid carbon reduction).
L: policy goal is y (for example, *either* orange producer seeking free trade in oranges exported to F, *or* separate group of environmentalists seeking protection of the rain forest in F).
P_h: policy goal is adherence to IL at t_1 (P_{h1}) and compliance with IL at t_2 (P_{h2}). Assume that $P_{h2} > P_{h1}$ (IL lobbies are harmed more by non-compliance than by non-adherence).
G_h: government of H (excluding the effects already reflected by J, K, L and P_h), as a separate 'interest group' that seeks to maximize its voting support by maximizing general public welfare in connection, *inter alia,* with adherence and compliance and concern for reciprocity and retaliation in connection with non-adherence at t_1 (G_{h1}) and non-compliance at t_2 (G_{h2}). Assume that $G_{h2} > G_{h1}$ (there is greater concern for retaliation against non-compliance than against non-adherence).

If domestic equilibrium at t_1 were x (the preferred policy of J), that is $J > K$, then no IL would be needed to induce x. However, assume that at t_1, $K > J$. (We are assuming IL with 'depth.') Therefore, the domestic equilibrium at t_1 is not x: H would not enter into an international agreement. However, assume that $J + L + P_{h1} + G_{h1} > K$. Therefore, IL that engages the lobbying power of L could cause a shift from not x to x at the adherence stage (t_1), inducing adherence to a rule of IL. Once that rule of IL is established, there is a shift from P_{h1} to P_{h2}, and from G_{h1} to G_{h2}. According to our assumptions, these shifts would be expected to

83 These policies in parentheses are merely provided as examples. Any policy where reciprocity is valuable and the magnitudes are appropriate could be substituted. For example, y could be protection of the ozone layer, while x is avoidance of terrorist attacks. The point is that within each domestic system, there is (i) a lobby on each side of the contention regarding the domestic measure, (ii) a lobby that cares about foreign measures, (iii) a PILL that cares about the growth of and compliance with IL, and (iv) the government which, aside from its interest in lobbies' support, is also interested in public welfare as a way to increase voting support.

increase the tendency to comply. In order to determine actual compliance, we would need to examine whether at any given time $J + L + P_{h2} + G_{h2} > K$.

It is important to note that in this model, IL only affects State behaviour pursuant to the above assumptions regarding relative magnitudes of lobbies. This model does not utilize 'compliance pull' or other effect of IL, separate from the force of the national lobbies that care about compliance with IL. But in assuming that $P_{h1} < P_{h2}$, and $G_{h1} < G_{h2}$, we are assuming a tendency to comply, conditional on adherence. The magnitudes of these differences tell us something about the level of vulnerability of continued compliance to changes in other factors.

Also, recall that the issue specific lobbies are not the only determinants of public policy. Under the assumptions of the Grossman–Helpman model, broader public welfare enters the equation through G by virtue of voting.[84] Therefore, an international legal rule that increases public welfare is more likely to achieve both adherence and compliance.

As outlined above, H's decision to adhere and comply is partially dependent on the decision of F to reciprocate, inducing L to lobby for adherence and compliance. The situation in F is a mirror image of H, with adherence and compliance by both increasing their joint welfare, according to the assumptions of this model. The F lobbies are described below.

F lobbies:

M: policy goal is y (for example, *either* consumers seeking free trade in oranges imported to F, *or* protection of rain forest).
N: policy goal is not y (for example, *either* import competing producers seeking protection in oranges in F, *or* seeking to develop the rain forest).
Q: policy goal is x (for example, *either* banana producer seeking free trade in bananas exported to H, *or* oil companies seeking to avoid carbon reduction).
P_f: policy goal is adherence to IL at t_1 (P_{f1}) and compliance with IL at t_2 (P_{f2}). Assume that $P_{f2} > P_{f1}$ (IL lobbies are harmed more by non-compliance than by non-adherence).
G_f: government of F (excluding the effects already reflected by M, N, Q, and P_f), as a separate 'lobby' that seeks to maximize its voting support by maximizing general public welfare in connection, *inter alia,* with adherence, compliance, and concern for reciprocity and retaliation

84 Grossman and Helpman (n 58) at 847–49.

in connection with non-adherence at t_1 (G_{f1}) and non-compliance at t_2 (G_{f2}). Assume that $G_{f2} > G_{f1}$ (there is greater concern for retaliation against non-compliance than against non-adherence).

Assume that at t_1, $N > M + P_{f1} + G_{f1}$, therefore domestic equilibrium is not y. However, assume that, $M + Q + P_{f1} + G_1 > N$. The situation of F then parallels that of H.

Therefore, and this points to the critical function of international cooperation, if H and F are considered separately, they have separate equilibria of not x and not y. But at t_1, if H and F are considered together – their ability to interact is an exogenous shock to each of their separate equilibria – they are able to reach an international exchange of policy. This international exchange of policy is politically Pareto superior, as it results in greater support for each government.[85] We have assumed that L and Q (the parties in each of H and F concerned about the measures taken by the other State), when their respective influence is added to J and M, respectively, is able to overcome K and N, respectively. So, at t_1, under interaction, a new equilibrium arises, of x and y, inducing adherence to an international agreement.

However, at t_2, the compliance phase, this structure may take on the characteristics of a prisoner's dilemma game. That is, if H can defect and move to not x, while F plays y, it might be that H can garner the most political support.[86] However, assuming all positions remain the same as at t_1, if H defects, then F can defect in response, resulting in a non-cooperative equilibrium. But, assuming that $P_2 > P_1$, and $G_2 > G_1$, the differences in these factors may be sufficient in magnitude, especially when aggregated over time or over multiple cooperation contexts, to exceed the value of defection, avoiding the prisoner's dilemma.[87] In fact concern regarding the integrity of the IL system to enable it to continue to produce political welfare-increasing agreements may be included in P_2 and G_2.

Note that at t_1, the forces in H and F supporting not x and not y, respectively, will be expected to oppose the creation of the international

---

85 It is not necessarily superior from a public welfare standpoint.

86 Putnam suggests that policymakers generally have an incentive to cheat. Putnam (n 44) 438 (citing Matthew E Canzoneri and Jo Anna Gray, 'Two Essays on Monetary Policy in an Interdependent World' (Feb 1983), International Finance Discussion Paper, 219 (Board of Governors of the Federal Reserve System)).

87 For a full discussion of the prisoner's dilemma dynamic see the chapter by Meredith Kolsky Lewis in this Volume.

linkage that changes the equilibrium to their detriment. In addition, these forces will be expected to oppose the creation of international legal rules that will result in the shift from P_1 to P_2 and from G_1 to G_2, which these forces anticipate will entrench their disfavoured policy. However, the fact that they anticipate these effects does not mean that they have the lobbying power to avoid these effects. Nevertheless, they may seek to engage sovereigntist or other generally opposing forces in order to supplement their policy position.

Further development and use of this model will depend on policymakers' ability to identify proxies for power and interest of lobbies. In international economic law areas, wealth and amount at stake may serve as a proxy. In other areas, such as human rights or international environmental law, size of membership in relevant groups, such as ethnic groups, and survey data regarding the magnitude of individual concern, may be helpful. However, as a guide to negotiators and policymakers, this approach may be useful without further formalization. If it is helpful to know about compliance, there is no more complete or precise approach. The test of a model is not whether it answers every question perfectly, but whether it answers questions that need to be answered in a useful way and better than the other tools available.

What systematic features does this model exhibit? First, because we assume that $P_2 > P_1$, and $G_2 > G_1$, this model exhibits a systematic bias towards compliance, conditional on adherence. However, while this is a systematic bias, it cannot be expected to overcome changes in other parameters in all cases. Moreover, the magnitude of this systematic bias depends on the individual magnitude of P_2 and G_2 in each State. This focus on P_2 and G_2 may either supplement or supplant the 'liberal States' theory, depending on the cause of P_2 and G_2. These differentials between P_2 and G_2 may also be understood within a reputation or reciprocity model, as determinants of the importance to the particular State of its 'reputation' or of diffuse reciprocity in determining whether to comply. In a prisoner's dilemma model, these differentials can be seen as a measure of the extent to which the shadow of the future, including compliance in connection with other rules, affects the behaviour of the subject State.

Second, this model accepts that domestic lobbies may vary in intensity from t_1 to t_2. This variation may be for exogenous reasons, or it may systematically be that lobbies that achieve their preferences at t_1 become wealthier or otherwise stronger at t_2 as a result. If this is the case, we would again see a systematic bias towards compliance, conditional on adherence.

How can policy preferences change in ways that might give rise to non-compliance? In other words, in what ways are international cooperation arrangements not self-enforcing?

First, the timing of performance by one State may differ from the timing of performance by another, and this may give rise to asset specificity after t_1 adherence. In this context, by 'asset specificity', we mean that the investment in compliance by one party would be less valuable to that party if the other party does not carry out its side of the bargain. This is no different from any other asset specificity in contracting. But under asset specificity, a greater role for a PILL, or for governmental preferences for compliance, may be required to induce compliance with IL, as the H lobbies that benefit from the asset specific investment by F would have little reason to lobby in support of compliance after performance by F. Obviously, to the extent that performance is expected to take place symmetrically at multiple moments over an extended period of time, this type of asset specificity may be reduced. If the period of time is finite, it is still possible for cooperation to unravel in anticipation of the last period.

Second, either State may have acted strategically or opportunistically at the adherence stage, developing a coalition to adhere in order to reap benefits that may arise from adherence, with no intent or political power to actually comply. This is a sub-case of the first type of change, as it assumes that the non-defecting State gives some performance after t_1 adherence, while the defecting State fails to comply at t_2.

Third, the political magnitude of various lobbies may change over time. A prediction made at t_1 regarding the lobbying valence of various lobbies may have a high probability of being accurate at t_1, but would be expected to become less likely to be accurate over time. Consider, for example, circumstances of sudden great political change, such as a revolution.

Fourth, this model suggests that uncertainty regarding domestic coalitions to support compliance would increase over time. It thus might suggest that governments may assess the value of reciprocal commitments over a delimited period of time, rather than over an indefinite period of time. This would reduce the magnitude of the shadow of the future in inducing compliance at any stage.

Fifth, we can show that international retaliation, reputation, and reciprocity cannot ensure compliance. Compliance will always depend on the constellation of domestic political forces in the relevant State.

Sixth, we may be able to suggest reasons for bilateralism versus multilateralism, *mutatis mutandis*: bilateralism might allow for the construction of more nuanced political coalitions to induce compliance, individualized to the particular international legal transaction.

Seventh, we might be able to explain the use by domestic governments of international legal commitments at t_1 to lock in a policy that is supported by a domestic equilibrium at t_1, where there is a preference over future policy. Government at t_1 may do so by increasing the effect of P and G through adherence, and inducing support from a separate domestic lobby through reciprocity.

Eighth, we may be able to assist in determining whether entry into a particular international legal commitment is done insincerely, without intent to comply. Counterparties would wish to evaluate whether there is sufficient domestic support for compliance with the commitments on which they rely.

VI. OUTLOOK: THE POTENTIAL AND THE LIMITS OF PE OR PIL

This Chapter theorizes that IL is made by strategic States willing to reduce their autonomy along certain dimensions in order to increase the satisfaction of their preferences along other dimensions, where after the commensuration of these two dimensions, each State's government counts itself better off. The mechanism of the State's decision-making regarding this trade-off and commensuration is domestic politics. In this theory, when domestic coalition A stands to achieve a benefit greater than the loss that is expected by domestic coalition B, coalition A is able to enter the political arena and overcome coalition B, all other things being equal. Where an international transaction – one type of which is IL – could result in a political surplus, that surplus may induce a coalition to act to achieve it.

The Chapter has developed a rationalist theory of adherence to and compliance with IL that takes account of the internal decision-making processes of States. It has always been true that the domestic public policy process has formed coalitions in order to make public policy, and that there have always been dissenters. The international relations context can be understood as an expansion of the possibilities for trade-offs and agreement – for formation of coalitions. The set of possible coalitions that may be formed is effectively increased by the ability to engage in international legal agreements.

Formation and compliance with IL is dependent on the identification and negotiation of efficient transnational political linkages. In an important sense, the scope of domestic politics is extended by the capability of entering into international agreements. While we do not have a continuous transnational political system, IL forms a transmission belt that can link domestic lobbies transnationally. Indeed, by virtue of the expansion of the scope of the possibilities for Pareto improving political transactions, the international extension of the scope of domestic politics, where it occurs, would generally be expected to increase *domestic* welfare. Of course, the move from domestic *political* welfare to actual welfare depends on the extent to which domestic politics reflects actual welfare. In any event, a government that wishes to deliver the most to its people, or at least to get the most political support, will be required to enter the IL market for some transactions.

The rationalist theory of adherence and compliance developed here provides a novel way of analysing the possibilities for compliance with IL. It suggests a number of empirical research strategies that may be followed in order to evaluate and possibly revise or extend the theory developed here. Perhaps more importantly, it provides a useful template by which States may evaluate the possibility that their counterparties will comply with their international legal obligations. As States approach important international public policy issues such as global warming, terrorism, and international financial crises, this evaluative tool will allow them to be realistic regarding the utility of proposed international legal rules. Although the model might be difficult to test in various settings, it gives a template to the researcher with all important variables which should be included. In this sense, it provides a frame and a guideline within which PE of IL can be applied to different research questions.

There are limits to the model presented in two respects. It is at the same time over- and under-complex. We are aware that partial models have great merits and it surpasses the capacity of any article dealing with a PE question of IL to deal with the holistic model, that is, both sides of the equation. Thus, concentrating only on one side is surely justified; however, it is important to keep the whole picture in mind. The model helps to do that by creating a thinking frame, a template. At the same time, the model is under-complex since it is impossible for epistemological reasons to capture reality one-to-one. Every social science insight necessarily has to abstract and concentrate on the most important explanatory variables. This is sometimes quite unsatisfactory from a lawyer's perspective, being used to delving into the intricacies of single cases.

A model of PE of PIL helps to add social science insights and answer the 'why' questions urgently posed to international lawyers in a changing world. We need to zoom in and understand the micro-foundations of behaviour in connection with PIL. This template model is a first attempt to bring different questions together and build a frame within which international lawyers can answer questions on the current, not yet normatively captured developments of international relations.

PART II

Political Economy and the Sources of International Law

2. The Political Economy of Customary International Law

Niels Petersen

I. INTRODUCTION

When legal research discovered International Law (IL) as a field for political and economic analysis in the late 1990s, Customary International Law (CIL) was one of the first issues they turned to.[1] One of the fascinations of CIL stems from the fact that it perfectly fits the image of spontaneous and decentralized rule-making that is a prominent subject of social science research,[2] but largely absent in nation-State legal systems. This contribution aims to give an overview of the different approaches discussed in the literature and to highlight the virtues and the limits of social science analysis of CIL. The political and economic analysis of CIL primarily has two foci. This Chapter will first discuss the formation of CIL and examine under which conditions customary norms evolve. In Anne van Aaken and Joel Trachtman's terminology, law is considered as

[1] See Jack L Goldsmith and Eric A Posner, 'A Theory of Customary International Law' (1999) 66 U Chi L Rev 1113; Mark A Chinen, 'Game Theory and Customary International Law: A Response to Professors Goldsmith and Posner' (2001) 23 Mich J Int L 143; Edward T Swaine, 'Rational Custom' (2002) 52 Duke L J 559; Andrew T Guzman, 'Saving Customary International Law' (2005) 27 Mich J Int L 115; George Norman and Joel P Trachtman, 'The Customary International Law Game' (2005) 99 AJIL 541.

[2] See, for example, Toshio Yamagishi, 'The Provision of a Sanctioning System as a Public Good' (1986) 51 J Pers Soc Psychol 110; Elinor Ostrom, *Governing the Commons: The Evolution of Institutions for Collective Action* (CUP 1990); Ernst Fehr and Simon Gächter, 'Cooperation and Punishment in Public Goods Experiments' (2000) 90 Am Econ Rev 980.

explanandum.[3] In the second part, research on the effectiveness of CIL will be addressed, where law is considered as *explanans*.

II. THE FORMATION OF CUSTOMARY INTERNATIONAL LAW

According to Art. 38 (1) lit. b of the International Court of Justice (ICJ) Statute, CIL consists of two elements: a general practice and an *opinio iuris* that the practice is required by law. On the basis of this definition, traditional social science approaches analyse the conditions under which patterns of State practice emerge. They use simple game-theoretical models to describe the incentive structure of State actors and to predict the formation of customary rules. The first part of this section will show that we should be wary of drawing premature conclusions about the state of international relations from such models. Rather, experimental research shows that people do not always behave according to the game-theoretical predictions.

The second part of this section will deal with the political economy of judging. Approaches trying to predict the emergence of patterns of State practice seem to assume that CIL is all about counting and systematizing the practice and *opinio juris* of State actors. However, when international courts identify customary rules, they do not confine themselves to the analysis of State practice. Instead, we often observe a great deal of judicial pragmatism in identifying CIL. The second part will look at the incentives of international judges when identifying CIL.

II.1. Customary Law and Patterns of State Practice

Traditionally, the political and economic analysis of CIL focuses on predicting State patterns leading to the formation of a customary rule.[4] The most polarizing account in this respect stems from Jack Goldsmith and Eric Posner.[5] Goldsmith and Posner identify different patterns of

---

[3] On the distinction between law as *explanans* and law as *explanandum*, see Anne van Aaken and Joel P Trachtman, 'Political Economy of International Law: Towards a Holistic Model of State Behaviour', above in this Volume.

[4] The argument in this section is, in part, based on Niels Petersen, 'Rational Choice or Deliberation? – Customary International Law between Coordination and Constitutionalization' (2009) 165 JITE 71, 72–75.

[5] Goldsmith and Posner (n 1). See also Jack L Goldsmith and Eric A Posner, *The Limits of International Law* (OUP 2005) 19–78.

State conduct with the help of simple game-theoretical models. They argue that multilateral customary norms only emerge in cases where States have coinciding interests, in other words, when they would perform the observed conduct even without a legal obligation.[6] Furthermore, they acknowledge that patterns may also emerge in bilateral coordination or cooperation games.[7]

However, they claim that coordination or cooperation was impossible if more than two States were involved, because of the high costs of decentralized coordination.[8] On the one hand, reciprocity is the driving force for cooperation in bilateral situations. However, according to Goldsmith and Posner, reciprocity is much less effective in a multilateral setting: If one State overexploits a common pool resource, the reciprocal overuse by all other States is no effective response to protect this resource.[9] Furthermore, the costs of monitoring increase with the number of States, which could lead to more undetected free-riding.[10]

The claims of Goldsmith and Posner were challenged in several contributions. Edward Swaine pointed out that cooperation might not only be possible in cases of coinciding interests, but also in situations with multiple equilibria.[11] In some cases, States may have incentives to cooperate even if there is uncertainty about the equilibrium on which they should coordinate. It is important to note that, in practice, CIL is not a one-shot game in which all States move at the same time without knowing what the other States do. Instead, States may observe the existing practice and decide whether to follow suit. In cooperation games with multiple equilibria, CIL may have an expressive function.[12] States will follow the practice of certain first-mover States because they have an incentive to cooperate even if they would have preferred to coordinate on a different equilibrium.

Furthermore, George Norman and Joel Trachtman refuted the argument by Goldsmith and Posner that cooperation was impossible in multilateral

---

[6] Goldsmith and Posner (n 1).

[7] Goldsmith and Posner (n 1) 1125–27.

[8] Goldsmith and Posner (n 1) 1129–30.

[9] Goldsmith and Posner (n 1) 1129–30.

[10] Goldsmith and Posner (n 1) 1130.

[11] Swaine (n 1).

[12] On the expressive function of law, see Iris Bohnet and Robert D Cooter, 'Expressive Law: Framing or Equilibrium Selection' (2003) UC Berkeley School of Law Public Law and Legal Theory Research Paper No. 138; Richard H McAdams and Janice Nadler, 'Testing the Focal Point Theory of Legal Compliance: The Effect on Third Party Expression in an Experimental Hawk/Dove Game' (2005) 2 J Emp L Stud 87.

prisoners' dilemma situations.[13] They point out that reciprocity must not be impossible in multilateral settings.[14] This is particularly the case if multilateral obligations can be divided into multiple bilateral obligations. But even in situations involving the protection of a public good or a common pool resource, cooperation is – even if less likely – not impossible. Norman and Trachtman highlight reputation effects and possibilities of punishing defecting States by suspending cooperation in other fields.[15]

Moreover, Goldsmith and Posner assume that all States are potential free-riders that seek to maximize their short-term goals. However, experimental research shows that the majority of individuals are usually conditional cooperators when playing public-good games.[16] Linear public-good games are one example of the multilateral prisoners' dilemma discussed by Goldsmith and Posner. Conditional cooperators are, in principle, willing to contribute to the public good. However, they only contribute as long as the other participants contribute as well. They are thus inclined to advance the common cause, but do not want to be exploited. For them, cooperation depends on the beliefs about the other participants' readiness to cooperate.[17] Such beliefs are usually formed by observing the conduct of the latter.[18] If we assume that State actors behave like individuals in the lab, most States are not to be classified as free-riders, but rather as conditional cooperators. Therefore, if they observe cooperative conduct by other States, they may be inclined to

---

13 Norman and Trachtman (n 1).

14 Norman and Trachtman (n 1) 556–59.

15 Norman and Trachtman (n 1) 567.

16 Claudia Keser and Frans van Winden, 'Conditional Cooperation and Voluntary Contributions to Public Goods' (2000) 102 Scand J Econ 23; Urs Fischbacher, Simon Gächter and Ernst Fehr, 'Are People Conditionally Cooperative? Evidence from a Public Goods Experiment' (2001) 71 Econ Lett 397; Urs Fischbacher and Simon Gächter, 'Social Preferences, Beliefs, and the Dynamics of Free-Riding in Public Goods Experiments' (2010) 100 Am Econ Rev 541.

17 Martin Dufwenberg and Georg Kirchsteiger, 'A Theory of Sequential Reciprocity' (2004) 47 Game Econ Behav 268; Armin Falk and Urs Fischbacher, 'A Theory of Reciprocity' (2006) 54 Game Econ Behav 293.

18 Fischbacher and Gächter (n 16) 548–49. See also Keser and Winden (n 16) 32; Christoph Engel, 'The Emergence of a New Rule of Customary Law: An Experimental Contribution' (2011) 7 RLE 767, 780–81; Christoph Engel et al., 'First impressions are more important than early intervention: Qualifying broken windows theory in the lab' (2014) 37 IRLE 126, 129–30 (showing that the first round in public-good games usually sets the stage for subsequent cooperation).

cooperate as well, which may facilitate cooperation in multilateral prisoners' dilemma situations.[19]

II.2. The Public Economy of Judicial Identification of Customary Law

In its jurisprudence since the Second World War, the ICJ has not always based the identification of a rule of CIL on a detailed analysis of State practice.[20] The most famous example is probably the Court's judgment in the Nicaragua case,[21] where the ICJ stated the existence of customary prohibition of the use of force without bothering to discuss the State practice on the matter in detail.[22] This led Sir Robert Jennings to argue famously that 'most of what we perversely persist in calling CIL is not only not customary law: it does not even faintly resemble a customary law.'[23]

What determines the strategies of the ICJ when identifying rules of CIL? When we consider the factors that might influence judicial decision-making, two are of particular importance. On the one hand, the uncertainty underlying the identification of customary norms gives judges a large degree of freedom in identifying and interpreting CIL. On the other hand, international courts cannot implement their own judgments. Therefore, they are dependent on the acceptance of their decisions by the parties and by the international community. While the former consideration could lead to international courts making a rather progressive use of CIL, the latter suggests a conservative approach.

---

19 Niels Petersen, 'Customary International Law and Public Goods', in Curtis A Bradley (ed), *Custom's Future: International Law in a Changing World* (CUP 2015).

20 See Michael Wood, *First report on formation and evidence of customary international law*, UN Doc. A/CN.4/663 (17 May 2003) para. 62 (distinguishing two approaches of the ICJ with regard to CIL – one with and one without detailed analysis of state practice).

21 *Military and Paramilitary Activities in and against Nicaragua (Nicaragua v. U.S.)*, [1986] ICJ 14.

22 See Bruno Simma and Philip Alston, 'The Sources of Human Rights Law: Custom, Jus Cogens, and General Principles' (1992) 12 Australian Yb Int L 82, 96–97.

23 Robert Y Jennings, 'The Identification of International Law' in Bin Cheng (ed), *International Law. Teaching and Practice* (Stevens and Sons 1982) 3, 5.

There is a lot of uncertainty with regard to the factors for identifying CIL.[24] IL scholars debate about how much practice is necessary to establish a customary norm,[25] whether the practice of different States should be weighted differently[26] and whether it may even be dispensable in some instances.[27] There is no agreement either on the indicators for

---

24 Holger Hestermeyer, 'Access to Medication as a Human Right' (2004) 8 Max Planck UN Yb 101, 158; Niels Petersen, 'Customary Law without Custom? – Rules, Principles, and the Role of State Practice in International Norm Creation' (2008) 23 Am U Int L Rev 275, 276–77; László Blutman, 'Conceptual Confusions and Methodological Deficiencies: Some Ways that Theories on Customary International Law Fail' (2014) 25 EJIL 529; Curtis A Bradley, 'A State Preferences Account of Customary International Law Formation', in Curtis A Bradley (ed), *Custom's Future: International Law in a Changing World* (CUP 2015). See also Martti Koskenniemi, 'The Pull of the Mainstream' (1990) 88 Mich L Rev 1946, 1947 (referring to CIL as a 'theoretical minefield').

25 See Jonathan I Charney, 'The Persistent Objector Rule and the Development of Customary International Law' (1985) 56 BYIL 1, 19; Brian D Lepard, *Customary International Law. A New Theory with Practical Applications* (CUP 2010) 152–53; Olufemi Elias, 'Persistent Objector', in Rüdiger Wolfrum (ed), *Max Planck Encyclopedia of Public International Law* (OUP 2012).

26 See Richard R Baxter, 'Treaties and Custom' (1970) 129 Recueil des Cours 25, 66; Karol Wolfke, *Custom in Present International Law* (Martinus Nijhoff Publishers 1993) 78; Anthony Clark Arend, *Legal Rules and International Society* (OUP 1999) 92–93. See also Anthony D'Amato, *The Concept of Custom in International Law* (Cornell University Press 1971) 96–97 (attributing different weight according to the degree of the State's 'sophistication' in IL).

27 See Bin Cheng, 'United Nations Resolutions on Outer Space: "Instant" International Customary Law?' (1965) 5 Indian J Int L 23; Louis B Sohn, 'The Human Rights Law of the Charter' (1977) 12 Tex Int L J 129, 133; Bin Cheng, 'On the Nature and Sources of International Law', in Bin Cheng (ed), *International Law. Teaching and Practice* (Stevens and Sons 1982) 203, 222–29; Frederic L Kirgis, 'Custom on a Sliding Scale' (1987) 81 AJIL 146; John Tasioulas, 'In Defence of Relative Normativity: Communitarian Values and the Nicaragua Case' (1996) 16 Oxford J Leg Stud 85; Fernando R Tesón, 'Two Mistakes about Democracy' (1998) 92 ASIL Proc 126, 127; Anthea Elizabeth Roberts, 'Traditional and Modern Approaches to Customary International Law: A Reconciliation' (2001) 95 AJIL 757; Guzman (n 1) 122; Lepard (n 25) 98. See also William Schabas, 'Customary Law or "Judge-Made" Law: Judicial Creativity at the UN Criminal Tribunals', in José Doria, Hans-Peter Gasser and M Cherif Bassiouni (eds), *The Legal Regime of the International Criminal Court. Essays in Honour of Professor Igor Blishchenko* (Martinus Nijhoff 2009) 77; Roozbeh B Baker, 'Customary International Law in the 21st Century: Old Challenges and New Debates' (2010) 21 EJIL 173; Rudolf Geiger, 'Customary International Law in the Jurisprudence of the International Court of Justice: A Critical Appraisal', in Ulrich Fastenrath, Rudolf Geiger, Daniel-Erasmus Khan,

opinio iuris and how to evaluate incoherent expressions of *opinio iuris*.[28] Finally, there is debate whether States may opt out of customary obligations through persistent objection.[29] This uncertainty often leads to an expansive identification of customary norms in international legal scholarship. This is particularly true for the field of international human rights. Many fundamental human rights are thought to form part of CIL, even though they are still frequently violated.[30] This confusion in the methodology for identifying customary norms is probably best summarized by Martti Koskenniemi in a review article of Theodore Meron's book on human rights in CIL:

> The feeling is, in other words, that Professor Meron has quite strong opinions about which norms should be included among those that are binding even beyond specific treaties, and that he uses whichever arguments are available to support them.[31]

This observation not only applies to Meron's book, but to a large part of the scholarship dealing with human rights and CIL. In other words, the uncertainty surrounding the identification of CIL gives legal practitioners a large amount of discretion and thus favours a progressive jurisprudence.

However, the mere fact that judges have a large measure of discretion does not automatically mean that they use this discretion for the progressive development of IL. Instead, they face structural constraints.

Andreas Paulus, Sabine von Schorlemer and Christoph Vedder (eds), *From Bilateralism to Community Interest: Essays in Honour of Bruno Simma* (OUP 2011) 673 (observing that international courts and tribunals increasingly refrain from detailed analyses of the State practice and instead recur to interpretative methods of identifying CIL).

28 See Simma and Alston (n 22); Petersen (n 24).

29 Ian Brownlie, *Principles of Public International Law* (OUP 1966) 8; Ted L Stein, 'The Approach of the Different Drummer: The Principle of the Persistent Objector in International Law' (1985) 26 Harv Int L J 457; Pierre-Marie Dupuy, 'À propos de l'opposabilité de la coutume générale: enquête brève sur l' "objecteur persistant "' in *Le droit international au service de la paix, de la justice et du développement. Mélanges Michel Virally* (Editions A Pedone 1991) 257; Prosper Weil, 'Le droit international en quête de son identité' (1992) 237 Recueil des Cours 9; Wolfke (n 26) 66–67; Elias (n 25). See also the critique of the doctrine voiced by Charney (n 25); Christian Tomuschat, 'Obligations Arising for States without or against their Will' (1993) 241 Recueil des Cours 195, 284–90; Patrick Dumberry, 'Incoherent and Ineffective: The Concept of Persistent Objector Revisited' (2010) 59 ICLQ 779.

30 Simma and Alston (n 22) 84–85.

31 Koskenniemi (n 24) 1952.

International courts do not have any means to implement their judgments. Consequently, they are dependent on the acceptance of their decisions. This acceptance has two levels. First, the judgment has to be accepted by the parties to the case. However, losing parties will not be very inclined to follow a decision that has not been in their favour.[32] Therefore, courts have a tendency to make compromises and to try to give all parties a share of the cake. Second, international courts and tribunals depend on their legitimacy within the international community. The higher the general acceptance of a court, the more likely it is that the reputation of a country will be damaged if it does not comply with a particular judgment. Furthermore, a State will also be more likely to accept an unfavourable judgment of a court if it generally holds the court in high esteem. In order to increase their legitimacy, courts try to give the impression that they are neutral arbiters without a political agenda. This suggests that courts would rather adopt a conservative approach with regard to CIL.

In order to examine which of these two factors prevails in the jurisprudence of the Court, we would need a detailed empirical assessment of the Court's case law. Such an assessment would be beyond the scope of this contribution.[33] However, I would like to make some preliminary observations. The approach of the ICJ is probably neither always progressive, nor always conservative. Rather, we will observe some judgments in which the Court relies on a detailed analysis of State practice,[34] while it refrains from such an analysis in other cases.[35] The

---

[32] For a recent example, see Judgment 238/2014, Italian Constitutional Court, 22 October 2014, unofficial translation by Alessio Gracis, available at http://italyspractice.info/judgment-238-2014 (declaring that the execution of a judgment of the ICJ granting Germany immunity before Italian courts for war crimes committed during the Second World War would violate the Italian constitution).

[33] For an empirical analysis of the identification strategies of the ICJ regarding CIL, see Mitu Gulati, 'Customary International Law: How do Courts Do It?', in Curtis A Bradley (ed), *Custom's Future: International Law in a Changing World* (CUP 2015). See also Niels Petersen, 'The Political Economy of the International Court of Justice: Judicial Strategies to Identify Customary International Law', Conference Paper, ESIL Annual Conference 2015.

[34] See, for example, *North Sea Continental Shelf (Germany v. Denmark/Netherlands)*, [1969] ICJ 3, at ¶¶ 75–81 (20 Feb); *Jurisdictional Immunities of the State (Germany v. Italy)*, [2012] ICJ 99 (3 Feb).

[35] See, for example, *Legality of the Threat or Use of Nuclear Weapons*, [1996] ICJ 226, at ¶ 79 (8 July); *Application of the Convention on the Prevention and Punishment of the Crime of Genocide (Bosnia v. Serbia)*, [2007] ICJ 43, at ¶¶ 160, 385, 388, 398, 420 (26 Feb); *Navigational and Related Rights (Costa*

difference in approaches can probably be explained by the strength of the moral appeal of the norm in question. If a norm has a high moral appeal, the legitimacy of the Court's finding is grounded on this moral appeal. The Court might fear to undermine its own legitimacy if it refused to give such fundamental principles as the prohibition of the use of force or the prohibition of torture the status of a customary norm. By contrast, if a norm is lacking such an extraordinary moral appeal, the Court still feels compelled to base its identification of custom on State practice and/or *opinio iuris*. This is probably only a rough distinction that would need further refinement. However, such refinement should be dedicated to a more detailed empirical analysis of the matter.

III. COMPLIANCE WITH CUSTOMARY INTERNATIONAL LAW

The question of compliance with norms of CIL differs considerably from the question of norm formation. In the latter case, law is not a decisive factor of the analysis. However, when we look at compliance, the crucial question is whether the existence of customary norms changes the incentive patterns.[36] Does the fact that states are legally obliged to perform a specific type of conduct impose additional costs on them if they do not comply? But States may not only comply with legal norms because they fear sanctions in case of non-compliance. Rather, compliance may also be due to acculturation. Therefore, the second part of this section analyses constructivist accounts of compliance with CIL.

III.1. Rational Choice Approaches

According to rational choice approaches, States comply with IL if they fear additional costs in case of non-compliance.[37] Compliance is a central issue in discussions on IL as a regulatory tool because of the lack of a

---

Rica v. Nicaragua), [2009] ICJ 213, at ¶ 47 (13 July); *Pulp Mills on the River Uruguay (Argentina v. Uruguay)*, [2010] ICJ 14, at ¶¶ 64–65, 121, 145 (20 Apr.); *Questions relating to the Obligation to Prosecute or Extradite (Belgium v. Senegal)*, [2012] ICJ 422, at ¶¶ 99, 113 (20 July).

[36] Anne van Aaken, 'To Do Away with International Law? Some Limits to "The Limits of International Law"' (2006) 17 EJIL 289.

[37] The argumentation in this section is, to a significant extent, based on Niels Petersen, 'How Rational is International Law?' (2009) 20 EJIL 1247, 1249–50.

centralized sanctioning mechanism. However, the lack of central sanctions does not mean that there are no means to punish deviant conduct. Andrew Guzman has identified three factors that may induce compliance: reciprocity, retaliation and reputation.[38]

The reciprocal structure of many legal obligations gives States incentives to comply because they expect other States to comply as well. There are two different forms of reciprocity – specific and diffuse reciprocity.[39] In cases of specific reciprocity, legal obligations can usually be broken down into bilateral relations. If a State does not comply with a legal obligation, other States may hurt the non-complying State directly by deviating as well and thus denying the non-compliant State the benefits of cooperation.[40] In contrast, if obligations are diffusely reciprocal, deviation is no viable punishment option.[41] In some cases, reciprocal conduct does not affect the violating State at all. If a State violates human rights obligations, it will not be affected if other States equally refuse to comply with their human rights obligations. In other instances, reciprocal denial of fulfilling legal obligations may have the unintended effect of cooperation breaking down entirely. If States, for example, have a legal obligation to contribute to a global public good, reciprocal non-compliance would not only hurt the State violating its legal obligations, but all other States as well.

Concerning CIL, however, reciprocity may be an issue in a different sense. Non-compliance of certain States might also set a precedent and lead to the disintegration of a customary norm.[42] If States are conditional cooperators,[43] they may cease to follow customary obligations if other States refuse to comply. There are two things to note. First, non-compliance of one State will usually not lead to the immediate disintegration of a customary norm. Instead, there will be a tipping point, at which we observe deviant conduct of a significant number of States, after

---

[38] Andrew T Guzman, *How International Law Works: A Rational Choice Theory* (OUP 2008).

[39] Robert Owen Keohane, 'Reciprocity in International Relations', in Robert Owen Keohane (ed), *International Institutions and State Power* (Westview Press 1989) 132.

[40] But see also Pierre-Hugues Verdier and Erik Voeten, 'Precedent, Custom and Change in Customary International Law: An Explanatory Theory' (2014) 108 AJIL 389 (arguing that States usually apply customary rules to 'all foreign States on a non-reciprocal and non-discriminatory basis', so that reciprocity is no effective means of punishing non-compliant States).

[41] Guzman (n 38) 65.

[42] Verdier and Voeten (n 40).

[43] See above, I.1.

which most States will not consider it to be favourable to continue to comply with a customary norm.[44] Moreover, some States will be more important than others because their conduct has a greater effect than the conduct of an average State. In norms concerning trade relations, the conduct of the main importing and exporting nations will probably have a significantly greater impact on the conduct of other States. The international community will probably react differently to deviant conduct of Samoa than to deviant conduct of the United States.

The second factor that should induce compliance is retaliation. States may punish deviant States and thus impose costs for non-compliance. However, punishment itself is costly. For this reason, a decentralized punishment mechanism is a second-order public good.[45] Consequently, States have incentives to free-ride and to hope that other States will punish the deviator.[46] Yet, experimental evidence shows that individuals do punish anti-social behaviour under certain circumstances.[47] The occurrence of punishment in public-good experiments is explained by the existence of fairness preferences, which lead certain participants to exert punishment even if it is individually rational to refrain from punishing.[48] It is unclear whether these observations also apply to the diplomatic relationships between different States. Moreover, incentives to free-ride will probably increase with an increasing group size. Consequently, decentralized retaliation is also a less than perfect mechanism to induce compliance.

The central factor inducing compliance is reputation.[49] States incur costs for non-compliance if their reputation for making credible commitments decreases. Other States may not want to enter into legal relationships with States known to have a poor compliance record or to extract higher returns for their cooperation.[50] For this reason, States comply with a legal norm if the gains from the prevention of a reputational loss are higher than the short-term benefits of a law violation. However, reputation probably works better with regard to compliance with treaty law than with regard to CIL. This is all the more valid as some authors argue that

---

44 Verdier and Voeten (n 40).

45 Yamagishi (n 2) 111.

46 Guzman (n 38) 66.

47 See Fehr and Gächter (n 2).

48 Fehr and Gächter (n 2).

49 Seminally, Robert Owen Keohane, *After Hegemony. Cooperation and Discord in the World Political Economy* (Princeton University Press 1984) 105–06.

50 Guzman (n 38) 34.

reputation is compartmentalized.[51] If a State is considered reliable with regard to trade or investment agreements, its reputation for future economic cooperation may not suffer much from human rights violations. In the same vein, a State that does not comply with CIL may not find it difficult to conclude further treaties if it has a reputation for honouring international agreements. However, there is some hope. Reputation is probably not completely compartmentalized. Instead, there may be some spillover effects. If non-compliance with fundamental norms of CIL translates into a general reputational loss that is an obstacle to future cooperation, reputational effects may be a mechanism to enhance compliance with CIL.

Rational choice theory paints a rather bleak picture of the ability of CIL to induce compliance. The three factors that enhance compliance of States with IL and that are discussed in the rational-choice literature – reciprocity, retaliation and reputation – have a limited effectiveness in the context of CIL. Reciprocity does not induce compliance if the legal obligations are diffusely reciprocal. Retaliation is itself a second-order public good, so that States may often be reluctant to punish deviant States; finally, reputation is probably a more important factor when it comes to treaty law than in the context of customary obligations. However, this does not mean that CIL is inherently instable. If customary norms represent behavioural equilibria, then States usually have little incentive to defect in the first place. Furthermore, the next section will analyse whether the normativity of CIL has – as constructivists argue – a positive effect on compliance even in the absence of effective sanctioning mechanisms.

III.2. Constructivism and the Shaping of Preferences Through Norms

Constructivists argue that legal norms make a difference in State conduct regardless of the strength of potential sanctions.[52] Rational choice

---

[51] Guzman (n 38) 100–06.

[52] See, for example, Margaret E Keck and Kathryn Sikkink, *Activists beyond Borders. Advocacy Networks in International Politics* (Cornell University Press 1998); Alexander Wendt, *Social Theory of International Politics* (CUP 1999); Thomas Risse, 'Konstruktivismus, Rationalismus und Theorien Internationaler Beziehungen – Warum empirisch nichts so heiß gegessen wird, wie es theoretisch gekocht wurde', in Gunther Hellmann, Klaus Dieter Wolf and Michael Zürn (eds), *Die neuen Internationalen Beziehungen* (Nomos 2003) 99; Ryan Goodman and Derek Jinks, 'How to Influence States: Socialization and International Human Rights Law' (2004) 54 Duke L J 621; Ryan Goodman and Derek Jinks,

theorists assume that actors have constant, transitive and exogenous preferences. However, they do not deal with the question how preferences are formed.[53] In contrast, constructivists are precisely preoccupied with the process of preference formation. They argue that preferences depend on the ideals which a person tries to live up to, and that these ideals are shaped by history, culture, religion, language and the social environment.[54] According to such a conception, human behaviour cannot only be influenced by imposing costs on specific conduct, but also by shaping the actors' preferences.[55]

Social psychology research suggests that individual preferences are indeed very much formed by people's social environment.[56] Furthermore, there is empirical evidence that the mere existence of norms has a positive effect on contributions to public goods.[57] It is certainly not self-evident that these findings from research with individuals also apply to the conduct of States. However, there is some evidence that suggests that norms also shape the conduct of actors in international relations. Derek Jinks and Ryan Goodman have argued that State behaviour is, to a significant extent, influenced through acculturation.[58] They claim that actors

> routinely internalize, via acculturative processes, the cognitive frames and behavioural expectations of socially relevant others. Accordingly, state actors often embrace common beliefs and practices because they reflect taken-for-granted scripts of how 'liberal' or 'modern' states behave.[59]

In particular, if actors do not have fixed preferences, their conduct is often influenced by the expectations of others as expressed by legal norms. For example, after political transitions, States often incorporate

---

'Incomplete Internalization and Compliance with Human Rights Law' (2008) 19 EJIL 725; Ryan Goodman and Derek Jinks, *Socializing States: Promoting Human Rights through International Law* (OUP 2013).

[53] The argument in this section is, in part, based on Petersen (n 37) 1258–60; Petersen (n 4) 81–82.

[54] Jennifer L Hochschild, 'How Ideas Affect Actions', in Robert E Goodin and Charles Tilly (eds), *The Oxford Handbook of Contextual Political Analysis* (OUP 2006) 284, 290.

[55] Petersen (n 37) 1259.

[56] Paul Slovic, 'The Construction of Preference' (1995) 50 Am Psychol 364.

[57] Christoph Engel and Michael Kurschilgen, 'The Coevolution of Behavior and Normative Expectations: An Experiment' (2013) 15 Am L Econ Rev 578, 585–88.

[58] Goodman and Jinks, 'Incomplete Internalization' (n 52).

[59] Goodman and Jinks, 'Incomplete Internalization' (n 52) 728.

international human rights norms in their newly emerging constitutions in order to signal that they are 'good' members of the international community.[60]

Moreover, Thomas Risse and some colleagues have argued, in several contributions, that law can influence actors in the field of human rights law even though sanctions have only a very limited effectiveness in this area.[61] They show in several case studies how human rights obligations gradually affect the conduct of governments and force them to compliance. The basic idea is that governments enter into a discourse with actors in transnational advocacy networks, and are then caught in a deliberative trap. Risse distinguishes five different stages: repression, denial, tactical concessions, prescriptive status and rule-consistent behaviour.[62]

In the first stage of the model, international human rights NGOs and other transnational activists accuse specific governments of human rights violations. Initially, the accused government will usually refute these accusations. Either it will doubt the validity of the international human rights norm or deny the factual allegations underlying the accusation. If international pressure persists, the government will often agree to make cosmetic changes in order to pacify the criticism. These changes may open up opportunities for national human rights advocates to oppose the government. Facing pressure from two sides, the government may feel compelled to initiate a controlled liberalization. Others miscalculate and are overthrown by the domestic opposition. Human rights norms do not necessarily lead to such an argumentative spiral. However, they may do so, thus gradually increasing compliance with human rights obligations. Thomas Risse and his colleagues cite several examples where human rights norms have led to a gradual increase of the human rights situation.[63]

---

[60] Tom Ginsburg, Svitlana Chernykh and Zachary Elkins, 'Commitment and Diffusion: How and Why National Constitutions Incorporate International Law' (2008) 2008 U Ill L Rev 201.

[61] Thomas Risse, 'International Norms and Domestic Change: Arguing and Communicative Behavior in the Human Rights Area' (1999) 27 Politics and Society 529; Thomas Risse, '"Let's Argue!": Communicative Action in World Politics' (2000) 54 Int Org 1; Thomas Risse, Anja Jetschke and Hans Peter Schmitz, *Die Macht der Menschenrechte* (Nomos 2002); Cornelia Ulbert and Thomas Risse, 'Deliberately Changing the Discourse: What Does Make Arguing Effective?' (2005) 40 Acta Politica 351.

[62] Risse, 'International Norms' (n 61) 538.

[63] Risse, Jetschke and Schmitz (n 61).

These considerations show the limits of pure rational choice approaches to IL. Rational choice models explain a wide range of phenomena that we observe in international relations. However, they do not provide a holistic account of 'how international law works'.[64] Instead, the mere normativity of CIL may sometimes already induce compliance as the preferences of international actors are often shaped by the norms of IL.

IV. CONCLUSION

This contribution intended to give an overview of rational choice approaches to CIL. Rational choice scholarship concerning custom usually has two foci. On the one hand, it deals with the formation of customary norms. I have approached this issue from two angles. The rational choice literature usually concentrates on the identification of patterns of State practice. We have seen that CIL may emerge under different incentive structures, not only when the interests of the States coincide. But CIL may also be judge-made law. I have argued that judges sometimes have incentives to 'declare' CIL even if the norm is not supported by a sufficient amount of State practice. This is particularly the case when norms have a high moral appeal.

On the other hand, we have also taken a look at compliance with CIL once a customary norm has emerged. According to rational choice theory, the effectiveness of CIL is limited. The three factors upon which rational choice theorists usually rely to explain the effectiveness of IL have a limited scope in the realm of custom. Reciprocity only works in specifically reciprocal relationships; decentralized punishment is a second-order public good and may thus suffer from free-riding; finally, reputation is more effective as a compliance mechanism in some fields of IL than in others. The final section leaves the world of rational choice and analyses alternative explanations for the effectiveness of CIL. Norms may not only impose additional costs on State conduct, but they may also shape the preferences of actors on the international plane. It may thus be that rational choice accounts underestimate the effectiveness of CIL.

---

64 Petersen (n 37) 1260.

3. Can Political Economy Help Solve the Riddle of Customary International Law?

Alessandra Gianelli

I. INTRODUCTION

Customary International Law (CIL) has been the subject of scholarly reflections for a long time. While its binding force appears still in doubt for some International Relations/Political Economy scholars,[1] the majority of international lawyers have, since the sixteenth century, assumed that custom is a source of law among States, a concept clearly expressed in the 1920 Statute of the Permanent Court of International Justice (PCIJ).[2] Notwithstanding the relative paucity of customary rules, custom's role is today considered ever more crucial given the variety and number of treaty regimes, a situation often described as fragmentation. Because of its general scope and because some fundamental rules, like *pacta sunt servanda* or the law of State responsibility for wrongful acts, are first and foremost customary, custom fulfills the role of the background set of rules upon which all conventional norms more or less rely. The systemic function of CIL is also apparent regarding interpretation of treaty rules, a function enhanced by Article 31, para. 3 c) of the 1969 Vienna Convention on the Law of Treaties (VCLT).[3] All this notwithstanding, a

[1] Jack L Goldsmith and Eric A Posner, *The Limits of International Law* (OUP 2005) 23 ff., are a prominent example.

[2] Scholars were more interested in debating the nature of CIL, particularly whether a type of natural law or a tacit agreement, rather than its being a body of binding law. Among the authors who have denied, in different degrees, the existence of a law among nations one may recall Hobbes, Spinoza or Austin.

[3] International Law Commission (ILC), *Conclusions of the work of the Study Group on the Fragmentation of International Law: Difficulties arising from the Diversification and Expansion of International Law*, 2006, paras 5 ff., 17 ff.; *Fragmentation of International Law: Difficulties arising from the Diversification*

precise and commonly shared notion of custom may still be a work in progress in International Law (IL).[4]

Generally speaking, Political Economy (PE) scholars and international lawyers ask themselves different questions. Concerning CIL, the former are interested in investigating why there are such rules; who are the actors behind its emergence or change; what are the reasons behind those actors; what are the implications of a certain rule? International lawyers typically question what the law says; what conduct is required for its implementation; what are the consequences of its violation?

A central point of discussion in PE appears to be whether IL in general, and CIL more specifically, affects States' behavior. The question receives different answers from different scholars. That States may decide to violate the law to pursue some political goals, and may discount the consequences of such a breach, or that, on the contrary, they may follow the law mainly because it is in their self-interest, follows from States being political entities, which pursue a certain agenda. To suppose that they obey IL just because it is law, is unrealistic. It is also unrealistic to think that international lawyers are unaware of that.[5]

Conversely, IL may have answers to the question of why States follow CIL, which might be of some relevance also for PE. The endogenous nature of CIL makes it easier for self-interest and law to identify and therefore for States to comply with law. Also, the reciprocity character of the great majority of customary rules is a strong incentive for a State to comply even when it holds a duty under the specific relationship, because it is likely that that same State will hold a right at some other time or with some other State.[6] The compliance with IL may also be systematically assured through mechanisms of incorporation into municipal law,

and Expansion of International Law, Report of the Study Group of the International Law Commission, Finalized by Martti Koskenniemi, A/CN.4/L.682, 13 April 2006, paras 410 ff. For the assertion that CIL 'is a good thing', see Andrew T Guzman and Jerome Hsiang, 'Some Ways that Theories on Customary International Law Fail: A Reply to Làszló Blutman' (2014) 25 EJIL 553, at 557. For a different view, see Joel P Trachtman, 'The Obsolescence of Customary International Law' (2014), available at http://ssrn.com/abstract=2512757.

[4] The ILC is currently studying the identification of CIL, which was put on its agenda in 2012.

[5] Oscar Schachter, *International Law in Theory and Practice* (1982), 178 *Hague Academy of International Law* 21 ff.

[6] Barbara Delcourt, 'Political Economy of International Law: A Convenient Alliance for the Study of Compliance?', in this Volume, gives a thoughtful and critical portrait of how IR theorists approach compliance of IL.

sometimes at the constitutional level.[7] Above all, the possibility of non-compliance does not appear to be a characteristic feature of CIL, or treaties. Indeed, non-compliance is a possibility with all forms of law.

More interesting in an IL perspective is the question, also addressed by PE scholars, about why States infringe the law. If it were possible to find a guidance tool among the apparently most different causes of the choice of States not to obey the law, this might greatly help in understanding how to anticipate and navigate such behavior, possibly through a change in the law.

The present Chapter purports to discuss some basic issues facing any IL scholar dealing with custom, in a PE perspective. The limits of the contribution suggest evaluating how PE can help address and solve those issues, rather than addressing and comparing theoretical underpinnings in the two areas. Referring to the different approaches maintained in this Volume,[8] the perspective is to take customary IL both as an *explanandum* and as an *explanans*, as the role of the interpreter of an unwritten rule extends in both directions. The assumption is that PE works through models, which may relay information about rules and States' conduct not otherwise available to IL. Some PE scholars deny that game-theoretic models may predict behavior. Rather, their aim would only be to generate and test hypotheses about States' conduct.[9] Other scholars, though, claim more openly a prognostic goal of the models.[10] I will take account of various views and consider: creation and change of CIL; interpretation and implementation; the notion of State. I will conclude that a deeper understanding of PE may be helpful for international lawyers, as a tool to try to rationalize the many factors underlying CIL and its implementation.

II. CREATION AND CHANGE OF CUSTOMARY INTERNATIONAL LAW

The very first task of any IL scholar is to distinguish law from what is not law. States remind us that this is not just an academic pursuit by

---

[7] Schachter (n 5) gives a synthetic but thorough and still valid picture of the different reasons that lie behind observance of IL.

[8] Anne van Aaken and Joel P Trachtman, 'Political Economy of International Law: Towards a Holistic Model of State Behaviour', in this Volume.

[9] Joel P Trachtman, *The Economic Structure of International Law* (Harvard University Press 2008) at 74.

[10] Goldsmith and Posner (n 1).

paying careful attention to the choice of words when making official statements in a variety of circumstances or by stressing that a certain conduct should not be taken as a precedent for the coming into existence of a certain obligation.

The notion of source of law/rules of recognition allows us to identify under which conditions we have a rule/norm.[11] It is usually clear when a treaty comes into existence, although there may be exceptions. Custom is always much more difficult to ascertain. Practice of States plus *opinio juris* is a code expression, borrowed from municipal law, which States, courts, scholars have long come to use to refer to the process through which a branch of IL is created.[12]

Can PE help answer the question of *how* CIL is created? Among the various descriptions of PE scholars, one of the more interesting is the definition of custom as a 'feat of levitation' built 'on a fabric of rational acts, woven through a multiplicity of relations over time'.[13] The expression stresses both the absence of a formal and immediately perceptible process of making of the rules, as well as CIL's intimate connection with the social context to which it refers.[14] PE illustrates and analyzes in detail the logical/rational reasons behind States' behaviors, in the absence of binding treaties. That is, PE abundantly discusses why States create CIL, and does so through rational models. The model to assess the various behaviors is, typically, the prisoner's dilemma, with some relevant differences among authors.[15] Some consider that only the bilateral prisoner's dilemma is relevant,[16] while others consider more appropriate a multilateral prisoner's dilemma.[17] Custom has, by its very nature, a general scope, which does not mean, however, that it is always applied

---

[11] For a convincing reaffirmation of the relevance of a formalist approach to sources see Jean D'Aspremont, *Formalism and the Sources of International Law: A Theory of the Ascertainment of Legal Rules* (Oxford University Press 2011). A different view is maintained by Làszló Blutman, 'Conceptual Confusion and Methodological Deficiencies: Some Ways that Theories on Customary International Law Fail' 25 EJIL 529.

[12] The Special Rapporteur of the ILC on the topic identification of customary international law, Michael Wood, has stressed how the dualistic concept of international custom is widely accepted also by States. See *Second report on identification of customary international law*, A/CN.4/672, 22 May 2014, 7 ff.

[13] Trachtman (n 9) 72, 116.

[14] See van Aaken and Trachtman (n 8).

[15] Meredith Kolsky Lewis, 'International Political Economy and the Prisoner's Dilemma: Compliance with International Law', in this Volume.

[16] Goldsmith and Posner (n 1).

[17] Trachtman (n 9) 77 ff.

multilaterally. Its general scope means that custom may be applied in nth specific situations, but that very often those situations will concern only two States. The relevant practice regarding custom often refers to the behavior of pairs of States, where third States may comment on this behavior. The game appears at the same time bilateral and multilateral, because if the practice is limited to one or a few pairs of States, we cannot discern a general pattern.

The parameters of the game also play a central role, and also vary from author to author. Some[18] may consider: value of cooperation vs. defection; number of States involved; type of interest to be protected, whether individual or concerning global commons; information available; 'patience' of States; duration and frequency of interaction; presence of other relationships with the State/s involved; or reputation.[19]

Indeed, the relevance and type of parameters involved may lead us to question whether this is still a prisoner's dilemma framework, or whether there are other parameters one should take into account in any specific case. In such circumstance, one must wonder whether any possible model could be built. This appears to be a concern shared by social norms literature.[20] In particular, some commentators say[21] that what distinguishes the traditional prisoner's dilemma from the current state of CIL is the fact that States can communicate; that they know how compliant each State is. One would add that usually the game of promoting new rules is played not between single States, but among groups of States; that there is not necessarily a conflict of interests among States; that the assumption of CIL as a non-cooperative game may be questioned; that States always have the option to conclude treaties.[22]

Another issue with the prisoner's dilemma is the choice of strategy. Some authors decline to consider strategies like tit-for-tat for reasons which are not always clear.[23] In the creation of a CIL rule, reciprocity has a crucial role, and not to consider it appears to greatly undermine a

---

[18] Trachtman (n 9) 77 ff.

[19] Andrew T Guzman, *How International Law Works* (OUP 2008), Chapter 3.

[20] Trachtman (n 9) 79. See also Niels Petersen, 'The Political Economy of Customary International Law', in this Volume.

[21] Trachtman (n 9) 84.

[22] Meredith Kolsky Lewis (n 15) takes some examples of customary rules cast in the prisoner's dilemma framework to conclude that in these cases the law solves the dilemma. She also underlines, more generally, the 'limitations of the model as applied to real-world situations'. Along the same line see also Niels Petersen, in this Volume.

[23] Trachtman (n 9) 85.

realistic vision of the process. Most of the conducts/positions/declarations significant to the emergence of CIL concern possible rules to be applied in specific circumstances to the same States both as right-holders and as duty-bearers.

PE interaction with traditional international lawyering appears necessary to give a satisfactory answer about how CIL can be distinguished from non-legally significant conduct. Some scholars deny the existence of CIL as a body of rules for reasons which, however, are either very much in line with the traditional notion of custom, like the lack of a consistent State practice, or not accurate, like a supposed necessary desire to obey the law. Rather, the subjective element of custom consists in what the same scholars recognize with some puzzlement: that States declare their adherence to a certain rule, and try to justify a discordant behavior always in accordance with IL.[24] This is precisely the *Nicaragua* canon.[25]

The Goldsmith–Posner argument is that it is indeed political/economical interests, not obedience to the law, which gives rise to States' conduct. No international lawyer would deny this. The real test is whether States feel free to act in a certain way and therefore admit no (legal) restraints, or rather feel they have to justify their conduct according to IL. An international lawyer would answer that the economic/political/strategic reasons for a State to adopt a certain conduct concern the 'substantial source' of the law, that is, the reasons for law. Gaetano Morelli started his Course of International Law[26] by precisely pointing out that States have various interests, which may be conflicting or mutual, and that one way to solve or regulate them is by way of fact, when one State prevails over the other, or one ceases from pursuing its interest; while another way is through law, that is, by establishing rules of conduct.

Another test, which is sometimes invoked for discerning CIL from mere social conduct, is third party sanctioning, following a conduct in conflict with an alleged customary international rule.[27] This approach, however, misunderstands the very nature of IL. As the law of an anarchic

---

[24] Goldsmith and Posner (n 1) 54, 167 ff.

[25] *Case Concerning Military and Paramilitary Activities in and against Nicaragua (Nicaragua v. United States of America)* (Merits) [1986] ICJ Rep 14, at 98. See Michael Wood, *Second report on identification of customary international law* (n 12) paras 60 ff.

[26] Gaetano Morelli, *Nozioni di diritto internazionale* (7th edn, CEDAM 1967) 1 ff.

[27] Only to some extent, Trachtman (n 9) 117.

society, 'sanctioning' not only is in principle left up to the injured party, but this party may or may not do so at its discretion.[28] The International Law Commission (ILC) 2001 Articles on State responsibility are very clear on this point. With regard to breaches of customary obligations, only in case of *erga omnes* obligations *may* other parties (among the *omnes*) take initiatives and only in case of breaches of peremptory norms[29] must third parties take some actions, which, in any case, do not have a punitive character. Looking for consistent punishing or penance would deny the qualification of law to a large part of IL, whether customary or treaty. This is indeed just an aspect of the never-ending debate about the nature of IL, and greater detail on this point is beyond the scope of this Chapter.

In sum, investigating the way States' interests may combine or conflict is certainly interesting and helps understanding how a need for the law may arise. However, PE by itself does not seem to answer the question of how we move from comprehending States' needs/interests/behaviors to having legal rules rather than mere social conducts.[30] Those PE scholars who deal with the issue[31] rely on the traditional elements of *opinio iuris* and State practice, or only *opinio iuris*,[32] sometimes dwelling on the classical problem of how to interpret the subjective element in the first States to lead the way – their intention to promote a new rule of law.

Interestingly, by defining States' conduct as rational, PE helps support the theory of custom as the product of deliberate choices, rather than a spontaneous phenomenon, as some Italian scholars have maintained in the past.[33] As for the opinion that some principles would not require State

---

[28] For the observation that 'decentralized retaliation is also a less than perfect mechanism to induce compliance', see Petersen (n 20) para. II 1.

[29] Eric A Posner, 'Erga Omnes Norms, 'Institutionalization and Constitutionalism in International Law' (2009) 175 JITE 5, appears to believe that an *erga omnes* norm exists when States other than the injured retaliate against a violator.

[30] Jeffrey L Dunoff and Mark A Pollack, 'Reversing Field: What Can International Law Teach International Relations?' 3 ESIL Refl 3, available at www.esil-sedi.eu.

[31] Trachtman (n 9) 111.

[32] Guzman (n 19) 190 ff.

[33] Mario Giuliano, 'Considerazioni sulla costruzione dell'ordinamento internazionale' (1946) 2 Comunicazioni Studi 175; Roberto Ago, *Scienza giuridica e diritto internazionale* (Giuffrè 1950); Giuseppe Barile, 'La rilevanza e l'integrazione de diritto internazionale non scritto e la libertà di apprezzamento del giudice' 5 Comunicazioni Studi 150. A very similar conclusion is recently reached by Blutman (n 11) at 551. For a critical review of that doctrinal debate, see Gaetano Arangio-Ruiz, 'Customary Law: A Few More Thoughts About the

practice,[34] one notes that the ICJ case-law appears to be to the contrary,[35] as well as the ILC current work,[36] although the opinion is shared by some IL scholars as well.[37]

A question that PE may well help answer is *when* is it likely that law is created through custom. PE tries to identify the set of circumstances (parameters) under which CIL is likely to develop, and studies the conditions which should occur for CIL to emerge. Again, these conditions may vary according to different scholars. For example, Trachtman[38] believes that CIL is likely to emerge when returns from cooperation are high and returns from unilateral defection are low; when States are patient; when interaction among participating States is high. These are all conditions which the IL interpreter may well take into account in reading State practice and considering whether a customary rule is about to come into existence.

Also interesting are the various cases analyzed for multilateral customary rules to arise. The analysis closely connects with the concept of *erga omnes* obligations, and helps to clarify it; it may lead to reconsideration of whether the expression employed in Articles 60, para. 2 c) of the VCLT and 42 b) ii) of the ILC's 2001 Articles on State Responsibility exhausts the notion of those obligations ('an obligation which is owed to a group of States or the international community as a whole and the breach of the obligation is of such a character as radically to change the position of all the other States to which the obligation is owed with respect to the further performance of the obligation'). More generally, the PE approach may help better define normatively multilateral customary regimes, which are only roughly drawn. This is a consideration various PE scholars seem to agree upon.[39]

One reason why this operation may be more fruitful concerning multilateral general rules could be that in this case the identification of a

---

Theory of "Spontaneous" International Custom' in *Droit du Pouvoir, Pouvoir du Droit: Mélanges offerts à Jean Salmon* (Bruylant 2007) 93.

[34] Niels Petersen, 'Customary Law Without Custom? Rules, Principles and the Role of State Practice in International Norm Creation' (2008) 23 Am U Int L Rev 275.

[35] For example, *Jurisdictional Immunities of the State (Germany v. Italy: Greece intervening)* (Merits) [2012] ICJ Rep 99, at 122.

[36] Michael Wood (n 12) at 11/68–12/68.

[37] For example, Enzo Cannizzaro, *Diritto internazionale* (2nd edn, Giappichelli 2014) at 116.

[38] Trachtman (n 9) 104.

[39] Trachtman (n 9) 108, 116; Posner (n 29) 9 ff.; Petersen, 'The Political Economy of Customary International Law', in this Volume.

common interest/public good to safeguard reduces the number of variables that affect other models and simplify the solutions. Another reason may lie with the relatively recent emergence of *erga omnes* obligations, which leaves room for further speculation on the applicable regime.

From a PE perspective, the considerations which apply to the likelihood of a new CIL arising are the same as in the case of a change of an existing CIL rule. The analysis and different scenarios provided by the models help us to better understand when such a change may come about. Like traditional IL, PE scholars who deal with this question stress the relevance of the *opinio iuris* of States when adopting conduct not in line with the existing rule.[40]

The most interesting contribution of PE is perhaps its ambition to indicate the best rule, in terms of the efficient rule or the efficient equilibrium States may want to pursue. If a PE approach were widely shared among the different stakeholders in CIL, this would allow for a rationalization of the solutions achieved through CIL. However, here too the way different States appreciate their interests, at different moments, may be a challenging obstacle.

The kind of input PE offers may be particularly relevant regarding codification of CIL. In all of the different areas where the ILC has produced its codification work, there is a measure of progressive development, in line with Article 13 of the UN Charter. ILC work is regularly submitted to States at the General Assembly's Sixth Committee for evaluation and comment. If a line of reasoning were clearly developed by the ILC pointing out why a certain solution should be considered better than others, States would be forced to comment on it and might be persuaded to accept it and adapt to it. In order to take the ILC and States along this path, maybe a simplification of the game-theoretical models might be useful. One should also consider that there are private institutions which pursue a quasi-codification effort, like the Institut de Droit International (IDI), and that it could be helpful conveying to them the same message.

III. INTERPRETATION AND IMPLEMENTATION OF CUSTOMARY RULES

PE may help in the interpretation of CIL. As unwritten rules are by necessity generic, interpretation is more crucial than for treaties, and the

---

40 Trachtman (n 9) 114–115.

role of the interpreter much wider and creative, arriving at consideration of whether a rule even exists or not, or if it is undergoing change. Interpretation of custom is therefore a process interconnected with its creation and change. Besides, there is not an established set of rules concerning interpretation of custom, as there is with regard to treaties.[41] If we add that, apart from international scholars or lawyers, the players who apply and therefore interpret IL are various, both at the municipal and international level,[42] it is clear how critical the reading of custom is.[43] Among the different readers/interpreters, courts command special attention.[44]

PE can provide useful tools to organize in a rational framework interests, reasons and outcomes behind possible, divergent readings. In other words, it can try to lead to more rational choices. 'Rational', though, again, depends very much upon the interpreter's definition. If a government may find it rational to follow an interpretation given by the International Court of Justice, because by doing so the State complies with IL and does not commit a wrongful act, a constitutional court may decide that the responsibility of the State is the price to pay to promote a change of that rule, consistent with the municipal set of fundamental rights. In other words, different interpreters may have different priorities, and may discount negative effects at different rates even within the same State.[45] The above remarks with regard to creation and change of custom apply to its interpretation as well. PE's tools help the process of interpretation, but may not anticipate the result of that process.

A coterminous problem is the predictability and assessment of a breach. From the IL standpoint, PE models might provide value by offering a rational scheme to describe what determines States' compliance and, conversely, States' breaches of CIL. Relevant to these aspects are also those studies that consider why States comply with CIL.[46] A problem of the models may however be the blind spot of States'

[41] An effort to provide a comprehensive and critical study of interpretation of the whole of IL is now carried out in Andrea Bianchi, Daniel Peat and Matthew Windsor (eds), *Interpretation in International Law* (OUP 2015).

[42] Anne van Aaken and Joel P Trachtman (n 8).

[43] This is certainly not an original statement: see, among many, Robert Y Jennings, 'What is International Law and How Do We Tell it When We See It?' (1981) 37 *Schweitzerisches Jahrbuch für Internationales Recht* 59, 65 ff.

[44] Petersen (n 20).

[45] The rational approach is being revisited also concerning IR/IL: see Anne van Aaken, 'Behavioral International Law and Economics' (2014) 55 Harv Int L J 421.

[46] Like Guzman (n 19).

preferences and priorities, which are difficult to anticipate or rationalize and which are crucial in the decision to breach CIL. More particularly, it is the assumption of the rationality of the various actors involved in the decision which may be questioned.[47]

Furthermore, tools like the theory of efficient breach are already considered by PE specialists of little relevance for non-compliance of treaty obligations.[48] The reasons given to limit its relevance for non-performance of treaties may be even stronger for breaches of CIL.

IV. THE NOTION OF STATE IN POLITICAL ECONOMY AND ITS CONSEQUENCES ON CUSTOM

PE is very much aware of the complexity of the decision-making process, both regarding promotion and implementation of CIL, inside as well as outside States.[49] Should this understanding promote a new and different notion of State as a subject of IL?

The current, still prevailing black-box notion of States in IL is nowadays negatively assessed with regard to some of its implications, like the supposed irrelevance of human rights protection or internal self-determination. That notion, however, serves in principle the function of having only one, clearly defined accountable entity. It has been a widely accepted rule for over a century and works well in matters of responsibility. Attribution of a certain conduct to a State has indeed been extensively studied in conjunction with the ILC's work on State responsibility for wrongful acts (ARSIWA). The black-box notion would seem to differ from the billiard-ball definition of States supported by part of the international relations theory, in that it does not deny that conduct of States concerning IL is the result of various factors including municipal political coalitions, the kind of government in power, powerful lobbies or the way municipal law opens up to IL,[50] as well as the relationships with other States. On the contrary, it is precisely because the dynamics, actors or decisions-making processes vary substantially from one State to

---

[47] Andreas L Paulus, 'Potential and Limits of the Economic Analysis of International Law: A View from Public International Law' (2009) 175 JITE 170.

[48] Jeffrey L Dunoff and Joel P Trachtman, 'Economic Analysis of International Law' (1999) 24 Yale J Int L 32.

[49] Jeffrey L Dunoff and Joel P Trachtman (eds), *Ruling the World? Constitutionalism, International Law and Global Government* (CUP 2009).

[50] van Aaken and Trachtman (n 8).

another, that IL chooses not to take into account what happens inside the State. The concept of separation between the municipal and international systems, usually defined as dualism, helps in understanding such a basic approach.

This does not mean that international lawyers are unaware of how a certain conduct or change of conduct may be generated from a certain State. Typically, it is international lawyers who draft provisions in constitutions or provide arguments for courts about the incorporation of customary – and conventional – IL in municipal systems, as well as about its existence and interpretation. Incorporation actually takes place with many different nuances. Conversely, those interested in a change of attitude of a State towards customary IL will have to understand which entities may be able to implement a certain conduct by the State, relevant at the international level. This is more complex for customary than for treaty rules. The latter require executive input and sometimes a parliament authorization; the process of creation of treaty rules, from a municipal perspective is close to the process established for enacting national laws or decrees. The various stakeholders may have little difficulty in understanding whom to approach and how, in order to reach a certain result concerning conventions to be stipulated or terminated. The process of creation of CIL may be much more 'mysterious' to them. Decision-making within the State must therefore be accompanied by the ability to understand how to contribute to the creation, development and change of custom in IL. On the other hand, international lawyers are not blind: they cannot possibly ignore why States change or maintain a certain behavior, when peering through the different documents, correspondence, declarations, position papers and so on, described as States' practice.[51]

The PE approach of investigating and possibly relying on models of the municipal dynamics that lead to a certain State conduct, relevant also for the purposes of CIL, seems actually close to the scholarly perspective, which denies that IL provides rules of attribution of a certain conduct to a certain State. According to this opinion, the way a State comes to assume and express a certain position is only a matter of fact, and, as such, the outcome of historical, economic, political factors. For this opinion, there can never be a proper agency question under IL.[52]

---

[51] Schachter (n 5), particularly at 24.

[52] Gaetano Arangio-Ruiz, 'The Normative Role of The General Assembly of The United Nations and The Declaration of Principles of Friendly Relations' (1972) 137 Recueil des Cours 419, 646–63.

V. CONCLUSIONS

A great contribution by PE to the theory and understanding of CIL is its rationalization of State practice. Having a clearer idea about the different scenarios and rationalizing about the outcomes of possible choices helps States, other international actors, judges, scholars and NGOs to better evaluate the kind of rule they want to support.

However, theoretical discrepancies among PE specialists may translate into international lawyers' disorientation and skepticism about the aptitude of models to reflect reality. The often-mentioned problem of the blind spot of States' preferences/interests remains a question, which may only be addressed on a case-by-case basis. The real challenge of PE, from an IL perspective and concerning in particular custom, is to develop empirical methods to measure factors like patience, horizon, payoffs, as well as externalities.

In the end, it appears unrealistic to imagine that PE can provide actual forecasts of States' future behavior. It is probably more fruitful, for an international lawyer, to look at PE as a (rational) method of evaluation of the different factors, reasons, actors, outcomes (the why, who, what PE questions) relevant when assessing the creation, development and change of general IL. On a methodological level, because PE uses mathematical/economical models to rationalize different settings, but at the same time openly calls for more empirical data to evaluate those models, a closer interaction between the two disciplines may bear interesting results for both parties. Those data should indeed result from an analysis of practice of States, a well-known area of study for traditional IL scholars. PE can help solve the riddle of customary IL, as long as PE scholars are willing to hear international lawyers' side of the story.

4. The Political Economy of *Jus Cogens*

Paul B Stephan

I. INTRODUCTION

No concept has greater salience than *jus cogens* in contemporary debates about International Law (IL). It proposes that humanity, unmediated by States or other entities, insists on the recognition of fundamental human rights that all subjects of IL must respect. *Jus cogens* displaces the regular processes of international lawmaking. Its norms occupy the highest level of law's hierarchy and invoke the deepest moral commitments.[1]

So stated, the *jus cogens* concept would seem to defy the kinds of analysis that Political Economy (PE) might offer. Its premise is the existence of transcendent moral commitments that exclude normal politics. It implicates constitutional politics, not PE. Economic analysis, with its emphasis on rational self-interest and welfare maximization, would seem to have little to say about such values.

This view of *jus cogens*, however, is too narrow. The core of the concept is not a set of particular claims about human rights. Rather, it is three related assertions: that a body of peremptory norms exists, that these norms operate on a higher plane than normal IL, and that they derive their legitimacy and binding nature from something other than State consent. *Jus cogens* is fundamentally about a lawmaking process, not about the content of the law made.

---

[1] Alexander Orakhelashvili, *Peremptory Norms in International Law* (OUP 2006); Case T-315/01, *Kadi v. Council*, [2005] ECR II-3649, revised, Joined Cases C-402/05 and C-415/05, *Kadi v. Council*, [2008] ECR I-6351; *Nada v. State Secretariat for Economic Affairs and Federal Department of Economic Affairs, Bundesgericht* [BGer] [Federal Supreme Court], ¶ 7, Nov. 14, 2007, 133 *Entscheidungen des Schweizerischen Bundesgerichts* [BGE] II 450 (Switz.).

So understood, *jus cogens* readily lends itself to a political-economy analysis. Choices about processes to reach significant outcomes necessarily entail consideration of who will gain, and who will lose, as a result of these choices. The choices are political, and economics can help us think in an orderly manner about what gain and loss means.

I develop this argument in three steps. First, I discuss the history of the *jus cogens* concept in IL. This history demonstrates that the present manifestation of the concept – one that makes human rights central to the enterprise – is only the most recent version. It confirms the appropriateness of looking at the procedural dimension of the concept, rather than any substantive outcome. Second, I describe the basic elements of political-economy analysis as it applies to IL. This discussion concentrates on a particularly significant subset of political economy, namely the theory of public choice. I then show how this theory can inform an analysis of *jus cogens*. In particular, I demonstrate how political economy helps us understand the implications of the majority and dissenting opinions of the International Court of Justice (ICJ) in *Jurisdictional Immunities of the State*, that body's most recent and significant consideration of the *jus cogens* concept.

This exercise establishes two things. First, it demonstrates the resiliency and flexibility of political economy as a method of attacking fundamental IL problems. Second, it invites us to reconsider core assumptions about how IL works, and thus opens up space for critical thinking about the field.

As van Aaken and Trachtman propose in the model found at the beginning of this Volume, this Chapter links the domestic politics of preference formation at the national level to the construction of a particular rule of IL (IL as *explanandum*). It considers why particular groups would prefer widespread international recognition of a *jus cogens* idea, and others would not. The Chapter also considers the functional consequences of *jus cogens* within the international system (IL as *explanans*), in part to tie the preferences of its proponents to the outcomes that it generates. Acceptance of the rule redistributes power both among non-State actors and among States. Discovering these results validates the use of the political economy of IL both as a means of explaining the stakes in debates over particular IL constructs, and as a tool for framing a normative assessment of the potential outcomes of these debates.

The concept of *jus cogens* in IL has enjoyed multiple lives.[2] The term itself has its origins in continental analysis of private law. A 'peremptory rule' overrides private preferences in favor of a public policy. The concept thus implied a hierarchical relationship, with otherwise legitimate public law always taking precedence over private law.[3]

Alfred von Verdross, a leading Austrian academic and diplomat, first borrowed the concept for use in IL, at least among writers in English. He argued that IL contained higher principles that themselves constituted the international system and thus operated independently of the will of States. Writing shortly before the *Anschluss* and anticipating what was to come, he invoked *jus cogens* as a basis for invalidating treaties that destroyed the capacity of a State to function as a sovereign and to fulfill its essential tasks within the international community. He provided as examples maintenance of internal law and order, defense against external attacks, care for the welfare of its subjects, and protection of subjects abroad.[4] All these disabilities were those that the German Reich soon would impose on victims of its aggression.[5]

After the War, von Verdross acquired surprising bedfellows. The Soviet Union found itself in the unanticipated position of a superpower with extensive international relations, but not the leader of a globally socialist world.[6] It required a new conception of IL to reflect its international position. Soviet theorists arrived at the concept of peaceful coexistence, a second-order theory of international lawmaking that shared structural elements with von Verdross's concept. In essence, the theory of peaceful

---

[2] In this Section of this Chapter, I draw heavily on Paul B Stephan, 'The Political Economy of Jus Cogens' (2011) 44 Vanderbilt J Transnatl L 1073, 1081–96.

[3] On the private law origins of *jus cogens*, see Levan Alexidze, 'Legal Nature of Jus Cogens in Contemporary International Law' (1981) 172 Recueil des Cours 219, 233–42.

[4] Alfred von Verdross, 'Forbidden Treaties in International Law' (1937) 31 AJIL 571 at 574.

[5] Von Verdross initially had agreed in 1932 to take up a prestigious academic post in Munich, but he withdrew his acceptance after Hitler came to power and remained in Austria. After the Anschluss the Nazi government constrained his work but allowed him to continue to do international law. 'Biographical Note with Bibliography' (1995) 6 EJIL 103 (appended to Festschrift commemorating von Verdross).

[6] See Paul B Stephan, 'The Impact of the Cold War on Soviet and US Law: Reconsidering the Legacy', in Tatiana Borisova and William B Simons (eds), *The Legal Dimension in Cold War Interactions: Some Notes from the Field* (Martinus Nijhoff 2012) 141, 143–45.

coexistence posited that the prevention of a cataclysmic confrontation between the two social and economic regimes that the Soviets called socialism and capitalism had become the fundamental and overriding imperative of IL. Although the Soviets had supreme confidence in the ultimate triumph of their system, they recognized that the invention of nuclear weapons had raised the possibility of a conflagration that would interrupt history and end civilization of any sort. To hold off such an appalling outcome, IL had to exclude any outcome that would increase the risk of confrontation.

The Soviet argument did much more than define the rules for formation of Customary International Law (CIL). Rather it embraced as a fundamental norm the principle that no IL, including any treaty commitment, could come into being without the consent of the two regimes. In effect, the theory gave the Soviet Union a veto over all IL, conventional as well as customary. To take a concrete instance, the argument provided a basis for arguing that the NATO Treaty, because it facilitated intercamp armed confrontation, exceeded the capacity of States to make international obligations and hence was profoundly illegitimate.[7]

The approaches of von Verdross and the Soviet Union to *jus cogens* invite comparison and contrast. Both posited the existence of higher order norms that limited the capacity of States to make IL. Both focused on the limiting role of these norms, rather than suggesting that they could form an independent source for an international legal obligation. Both agreed that the norms derived from fundamental principles underlying the international system functioned primarily as a limit on treatymaking. Just as *jus cogens* in private law constrains freedom of contract, *jus cogens* in both the Verdross and Soviet understanding constrains the power of States to make treaty law.

But the premises of the Verdross and Soviet higher order norms differed considerably. Von Verdross regarded these norms as limiting the power of States to surrender their capacity to function as States. State sovereignty formed the heart of his theory, even though it meant, paradoxically, that in one crucial respect it limited sovereignty (specifically, the right to bargain away the attributes of sovereignty).

The focus of the Soviet theory, in contrast, was on the international order. The international order would not tolerate exercises of State

[7] See Nikita S Khrushchev, 'On Peaceful Coexistence' (Oct. 1959) 38 For Aff 1, 3–4; Grigorij I Tunkin (ed), *Problemy Mezhdunarodnogo Prava [Problems of International Law]* (1961); Leon Lipson, 'Peaceful Coexistence' (1964) 29 Law and Contemporary Problems 871, 872.

authority that threatened the survival of that order. This in turn presupposed the consent of the socialist and capitalist camps (but in any event, that of the Soviet Union) as a condition for the formation of any international norm or treaty.

These streams of IL theory came together in the UN International Law Commission (ILC) and what may be its most important achievement, the Vienna Convention on the Law of Treaties (VCLT). GI Tunkin, the Soviet scholar most closely associated with the theory of peaceful coexistence, served on this body during the promulgation of the treaty, as did von Verdross. Both pushed for explicit recognition of the limits of treatymaking authority based on a hierarchy of norms. Many in the West, particularly the United States (US), the United Kingdom (UK) and France, pushed back against this idea, arguing that the international community had not realized a set of norms that could be said to operate independently of the will of States.[8] The Soviet view largely prevailed, as embodied in Article 53 of the VCLT.[9] The text as adopted nodded in the direction of the objectors by limiting the concept to *jus cogens* norms recognized by 'the international community of States as a whole'. But the absence of rules to determine what counts as recognition and to define the 'whole' of the international community meant that the proponents had gained most of what they desired.[10]

The next stage in the life of the *jus cogens* concept came with the human rights revolution of the 1970s. Although the movement claims a lineage that passes through Nuremberg and back to natural law traditions, its role as a systematic legal program within IL effectively began with the inclusion of human rights topics in the Helsinki Declaration of August 1975.[11] The entire Declaration was framed as a statement of political principles, rather than binding legal commitments. But a wide range of

---

8 See Stephan (n 2) at 1085–88.

9 VCLT art. 53, May 23, 1969, 1155 UNTS 331.

10 Article 53 was one of the provisions that made it impossible for the US and France to join the Convention. For academic criticism of Article 53 as well as the *jus cogens* concept generally, see Georg Schwarzenberger, *International Law and Order* (Stevens and Sons 1971) 27–56; Jerzy Sztucki, *Jus Cogens and the Vienna Convention on the Law of Treaties: A Critical Appraisal* (Springer-Verlag 1974). Hans Kelsen, like Schwarzenberger a prominent international legal scholar whom the Nazis forced to emigrate, kept his distance from the concept but did not attack it head on. Hans Kelsen, 'Limitations on the Functions of the United Nations' (1946) 55 Yale L J 997, 1007.

11 The Final Act of the Conference on Security and Cooperation in Europe, Part VII, August 1, 1975, 14 ILM 1292; Samuel Moyn, *The Last Utopia: Human Rights in History* (Harvard University Press 2010).

political movements – particularly anti-Soviet nationalists in Central and Eastern Europe, opponents of authoritarian regimes in Latin America and Southern Europe and foes of apartheid – sought to translate the principles into law. *Jus cogens* offered itself as a useful mechanism, dispensing as it does with impediments such as State consent or evidence of State practice. Once these political movements prevailed, the triumph of human rights as a bedrock concept of the international system seemed inevitable.

In the US, the transition from the Carter to the Reagan Administration added salience to this move. The Carter Administration was the first postwar US government to move human rights to the foreground in foreign policy, while at least some of Reagan's foreign policy intellectuals embraced authoritarian regimes for anticommunist purposes. US international lawyers sought to entrench human rights in the legal system, where courts could protect them from the vagaries of the political branches.[12] As a result, by the 1980s US courts and lawyers, although not necessarily the US government, had fully embraced a version of *jus cogens* that mandated respect for human rights. Many other publicists around the world also signed up for this new conception of *jus cogens*.[13]

This latest version of the *jus cogens* concept marked a break from past iterations in at least two respects. Like its predecessors, it presumed a set of higher order norms that exist independent of State consent and thus arise outside the normal international lawmaking process. But the differences are profound. First and most obviously, the new *jus cogens* substantive norms derive not from claims about sovereignty or the international order, but from the perceived needs of humanity. Moreover, the rights claimed extend against all subjects of IL, including, most importantly, the claimant's own sovereign.

---

[12] The most concrete aspect of this entrenchment was the US government's amicus brief in *Filártiga v. Peña-Irala*, 630 F.2d 876 (2d Cir. 1980), a case that opened up the federal courts to human rights litigation. See PB Stephan, 'Courts, the Constitution, and Customary International Law – The Intellectual Origins of the Restatement (Third) of the Foreign Relations Law of the United States' (2003) 44 VJIL 33.

[13] Christopher A Ford, 'Adjudicating Jus Cogens' (1994) 13 Wisconsin Int L J 145; GD Haimbaugh, Jr., 'Jus Cogens: Root and Branch (An Inventory)' (1987) 3 Touro L Rev 204, 207–11; Stefan Kadelbach, 'Jus Cogens, Obligations Erga Omnes and Other Rules – The Identification of Fundamental Norms', in C Tomuschat and J-M Thouvenin (eds), *The Fundamental Rules of the International Legal Order: Jus Cogens and Obligations Erga Omnes* (Martinus Nijhoff 2006) 21; Karen Parker and Lyn B Neylon, 'Jus Cogens: Compelling the Law of Human Rights' (1989) 12 Hastings Int Comp L Rev 411.

Second, under this version *jus cogens* norms function not only as a limit on the making of IL, but on all exercises of State authority. The shift is subtle, but significant. The concept evolved from a constraint on the ability of States to bind each other through IL to an international-law-based limit on the State's ability to dispose of matters within its own territory and regarding its own subjects. In Hohfeldian terms, earlier versions of *jus cogens* created privileges in favor of a State, and non-rights on the part of the international order. In other words, the von Verdross–Tunkin conception gives States the privilege of transgressing an obligation that violates *jus cogens*. Correspondingly, the international order has no right to require the State to adhere to an obligation that *jus cogens* treats as invalid.

The human rights conception of *jus cogens*, in contrast, creates a right on behalf of humanity and the international community as a whole and a corresponding duty on the part of States. States must comply with this duty, and rights holders may hold them accountable. The new conception thus combined a different set of substantive norms with a more comprehensive enforcement mechanism, all while asserting continuity with a past concept.[14]

This brief history demonstrates several things. First, the modern idea that IL, although fully secular and thus divorced from religious mandates, still might rest on higher level norms that limit the discretion of States, has proven useful in several quite different historical and geopolitical periods. Second, the content of these higher level norms has changed dramatically, in part because the concept is not self-defining. Each period finds its own imperatives, which show no continuity with past ones. Third, the concept has functioned as something of a wild card, enabling an actor dissatisfied with the status quo to ascribe legal status to norms that under conventional criteria seem to be only aspirations. Fourth, the concept can function either as a limit on international lawmaking (as illustrated by von Verdross and the Soviet theory of peaceful coexistence) or as an extension (as the contemporary human rights movement insists).

The broader point is that the concept of *jus cogens* is neither fixed nor inevitable. The current conception of *jus cogens*, in other words, is an episode, not a conclusion. Asserting the existence of the concept *vel non*, as well as choosing which variant of the concept to embrace, rests on a calculus in which interest plays a part.

---

[14] Wesley N Hohfeld, 'Some Fundamental Legal Conceptions as Applied in Judicial Reasoning' (2013) 23 Yale L J 16, 32–44; Stephan, (n 2) at 1077 n 10.

Having established the historical contingency of the *jus cogens* concept, I now consider how the concept might be adapted to new challenges. Political economy enters the story as a form of positive analysis that relates various political and economic configurations to particular uses of the concept. In the US, it plays an important role in many legal fields, although it has come to IL relatively recently.

II. POLITICAL ECONOMY

The field of political economy involves the use of economic principles to analyze the making of political choices.[15] It does not exclude normative goals, such as moral justification, which may shape preferences for which actors seek optimal satisfaction. It does not, however, itself provide normative goals and generally is agnostic as to moral justification. Accordingly, some critics see the field as wicked.[16]

A scholar who uses the insights of political economy to explore the generation and application of IL might justify this method as necessary but not sufficient for prescribing law. One cannot translate moral claims into social action, the argument goes, without considering the mechanisms that constrain social action. To the extent one believes that morally attractive arguments in and of themselves induce desirable social behavior, political economy is irrelevant. One cannot take political economy seriously unless one is willing to concede that something more than moral conviction matters in making social choices.

Political economy involves identifying the interests of relevant actors as well as the characteristics of the institutions through which they pursue their interests. In the case of IL, the actors include the governments of States, legislators that hold these governments accountable, domestic judges, international officials and judges, jurists seeking to shape IL, and various private organizations generating information and publicity about international legal arguments (what I will call activists).[17]

Political economy assumes that actors seek to maximize whatever it is that they want. It posits that actors, besides pursuing preferences based

---

[15] See the chapter of Joel Trachtman and Anne van Aaken, above in this Volume, at 9.

[16] For example, Jeffrey Rosen, 'Overcoming Posner' (1995) 105 Yale L J 581.

[17] See Paul B Stephan, 'International Law as a Source of Law', in Francesco Parisi (ed), *Production of Legal Rules – Encyclopedia of Law and Economics* (2nd edn, Edward Elgar 2011) 255.

on moral conviction, seek to maximize interests such as prestige, influence and material resources (on either a personal or affiliation-group basis). These forces drive social behavior, including political contestation. To put it simply, even morally convinced actors wish to maximize their influence, if only to fulfill their convictions. And political economy rests on the assumption that persuasion through rational appeal is not the only way to maximize influence.

Within the general subject of political economy, the theory of public choice has a prominent place. These ideas, associated particularly with the Nobel Prize winning work of the economist James Buchanan, look at how the design of decisionmaking institutions affects the kinds of choices made. It concentrates on the structure and incentives of coalitions that influence democratic decisionmaking. It observes that asymmetries in access to information as well as the ability to capture private benefits from public law (commonly called rents, in analogy to the returns from property rights) enable compact, homogenous groups to have outsized influence in the lawmaking process. More generally, the theory explores the incentives facing public actors as well as those who seek public action.[18]

One can trace back the application of public choice theory to IL over many years.[19] In the last two decades, however, Eyal Benvenisti and I have independently drawn the attention of international lawyers to the subject. We argue that the public choice literature provides a useful toolbox for international lawyers to attack problems of collective action and the distribution of rights and duties.[20]

---

[18] On public choice theory as a branch of political economy, see James M Buchanan and Gordon Tullock, *The Calculus of Consent: Logical Foundations of Constitutional Democracy* (University of Michigan Press 1962); Dennis C Mueller, *Public Choice III* (CUP 2003); Mancur Olson, *The Logic of Collective Action: Public Goods and the Theory of Groups* (Harvard University Press 1965). On the closely related field of institutional economics, Nobel Prize winning work includes Douglass C North, *Institutions, Institutional Change and Economic Performance* (CUP 1990); Elinor Ostrom, *Governing the Commons: The Evolution of Institutions for Collective Action* (CUP 1990); Herbert A Simon, *Administrative Behavior* (2nd edn, MacMillan 1961); Oliver E Williamson, *The Economic Institutions of Capitalism* (Chenggeng Books 1985); Ronald H Coase, 'The Nature of the Firm' (1937) 4 Economica 386.

[19] For example, Vilfredo Pareto, *Manual of Political Economy* 324 (AS Schwier & AN Page eds, AS Schwier trans, 1971) (1927).

[20] Eyal Benvenisti, 'Exit and Voice in the Age of Globalization' (1999) 98 Michigan L Rev 167; Paul B Stephan, 'Accountability and International Lawmaking: Rules, Rents and Legitimacy' (1996–97) 17 Nw J Int L Bus 681; Paul B

What does public choice theory have to say about *jus cogens*? In the previous part of this Chapter, I demonstrated that the principal feature of *jus cogens* arguments in IL is the premise that a higher order set of rules either limit or expand the set of international obligations that otherwise rest on State consent. To refer back to the civil law origins of the term, *jus cogens* sets boundaries on the freedom of contract that States possess and exercise in the construction of IL, just as public law limits private law. Definition of those boundaries in turn permits arguments that do not rest on traditional sources of authority in IL, such as treaty texts or State practice. *Jus cogens* both enlarges the set of arguments that one might make concerning the content of IL and frees the person making the argument from having to defer to traditional sources of authority.

By hypothesis, this enlargement in the range of arguments and outcomes should most serve the interests of those actors who do not directly participate in the conventional processes of IL formation. State practice varies, of course, but in general foreign offices (in the US, the Department of State) have the most direct responsibility for engagement in the conventional processes. Other specialists in national bureaucracies, such as career military lawyers, also might have an interest in the lawmaking status quo. These are the actors, then, that public choice theory predicts will show the greatest resistance to *jus cogens*, because they have the most to lose.

Extending this hypothesis, one can make further predictions about the popularity of *jus cogens* arguments among various interest groups. Litigation provides an interesting case. Judges play various roles in societies, and scholars debate the shape of the judicial welfare function, that is, the interests that judges seek to maximize. In earlier work I have suggested that, absent other constraints such as screening by appointing authorities, patronage or risk of removal, judicial welfare functions might correspond roughly to those of the lawyers who appear before judges.[21] This correspondence rests on several factors: In many systems, especially those based on the Anglo-American model, judges are drawn from the ranks of litigators; litigators have some control over the distribution of litigated claims, leading judges to reach outcomes that reflect the median preference of these litigators; and resisting outcomes generally preferred by litigators will cost judges greater effort.

Stephan, 'Barbarians Inside the Gate: Public Choice Theory and International Economic Law' (1995) 10 American U J Int L Pol 745.

[21] Paul B Stephan, 'The Political Economy of Extraterritoriality' (2013) 1 Pol Gov 92.

Litigators, one may presume, are likely to have at least a mild preference for *jus cogens* arguments. Moderate increases in legal instability raise the value of their services by increasing demand for them. *Jus cogens* also opens up the range of permissible legal arguments, rewarding creativity and ingenuity. If judges in turn are drawn at least in part to satisfying litigator preferences, a conjecture that impartial and independent judges should be more open to *jus cogens* arguments than officials working in the government and legislature would be plausible.

Jurists and activists also should prefer *jus cogens* arguments, perhaps even more strongly than litigators and judges. Persons in these groups are less likely to have a direct role in the traditional means of international lawmaking. To maximize their influence and prestige, they need to challenge the State monopoly over this process. *Jus cogens* provides the perfect mechanism for achieving this.

Finally, these arguments also indicate the likelihood of dynamic interactions among governmental and legislative actors, judges and litigators, and jurists and activists. To protect their asserted monopoly over international lawmaking, government and legislative actors might push back against those victories for the *jus cogens* concept that materialize in the courts or elsewhere. Such resistance would not affect the international consequences of these victories, because the concept precludes State nullification of its norms. But domestic political actors might adjust the domestic legal landscape. They also might try to weed out judges who showed excessive receptivity to *jus cogens.* Some of this screening might take place during the appointment process in those jurisdictions where political actors have a say in judicial selection. Political actors also might veto the reappointment of judges who rely too much on the concept, in those contexts where political approval of reappointment exists.

Also by hypothesis, not only would the competences of particular actors affect their attitude toward *jus cogens*, but, *ceteris paribus*, those States that have the greatest investment in the legal status quo would be most likely to resist a destabilizing, open ended theory that makes it possible to dispense with prior international norms. Symmetrically, State actors with the least stake in the legal status quo would be most receptive to *jus cogens*. These actors would prefer both to reshape IL to their own purposes and to avoid veto points such as the consent of other States.

Accordingly, a State that has experienced a rapid and profound change in its geopolitical position might most welcome the construction of new international norms without the cost of obtaining agreement with other actors. The Soviet concept of peaceful coexistence, for instance, gave a newly powerful and internationally engaged State a theoretical basis for editing the existing set of international norms so as to exclude those it found inconvenient. *Jus cogens* solved a dilemma for the newly hegemonic Soviet Union: it reconciled the use of IL as authority with the need to jettison much of the legal status quo.

In summary, the theory of public choice offers several hypotheses about the scope and impact of the *jus cogens* concept. These hypotheses, one must stress, focus on the concept as a mechanism, rather than on any particular set of substantive norms (such as human rights) that might be ascribed to *jus cogens.* They presume, in other words, that actors might embrace or reject the concept independently of what norms currently are seen as *jus cogens*, because of the concept's capacity for advancing different norms in the future.

III. THE POLITICAL ECONOMY OF *JURISDICTIONAL IMMUNITIES OF THE STATE*

Having derived hypotheses from public choice theory, and political economy more generally, about the expected receptivity of various actors and regimes to *jus cogens* arguments, one then must devise a strategy for testing them. Ideally, one might develop a large database of incidents where *jus cogens* could arise to determine which actors embrace, and which reject, the concept. This approach would meet the highest standards of social science.

Such a quantitative analysis presents significant challenges, however. There simply are not enough instances of international lawmaking to generate a sizable data set susceptible to robust testing. Even more fundamentally, definition of negative findings – instances where an actor might have embraced a *jus cogens* argument but did not – presents great challenges.

Solutions to these problems doubtlessly exist, but this Chapter will not offer any. Instead, it will discuss an especially salient instance of contestation over *jus cogens*, the ICJ's decision in *Jurisdictional Immunities of the State*.[22] It explores which actors invoked the concept, which resisted it, and how these actions conform to the hypotheses developed in

[22] *Jurisdictional Immunities of the State* (*Germany v. Italy*), Judgment (Feb. 3, 2012), available at http://www.icj-cij.org/docket/files/143/16883.pdf [hereinafter ICJ Judgment]. For my earlier discussion of the decision, see Paul B Stephan, 'Sovereign Immunity and the International Court of Justice: The State System Triumphant', in John N Moore (ed), *Foreign Affairs Litigation in the United States* (Brill/Nijhoff 2013) 67.

the previous part of this Chapter. This case study lacks the empirical rigor of quantitative analysis, but it does illuminate the hypotheses derived from political economy. It establishes their relevance, if not necessarily their conclusiveness.

The dispute in *Jurisdictional Immunities of the State* involved private lawsuits brought in Greek and Italian domestic courts against the Federal Republic of Germany. The plaintiffs alleged that they suffered grave human rights injuries at the hands of the German Reich during World War II. Successive German governments and legislatures had adopted various compensation schemes for many victimized by the Reich's atrocities, but none extended to the particular Greek or Italian plaintiffs. These victims brought civil suits for compensation, first in Greece and later in Italy.

Greek and Italian courts apply the CIL of State immunity, because these countries are not parties to treaties that supplant this law and their legislatures have not enacted domestic statutes regulating this subject. The Greek *Areios Pagos* held that CIL recognized an exception to the general rule of State immunity from domestic judicial process in the case of claims based on allegations of grave human rights abuses.[23] The Italian *Corte Suprema di Cassazione* reached a similar conclusion a few years later.[24] After German courts refused to enforce the Greek judgment, the plaintiffs sought to collect in Italy.[25] Germany then invoked a treaty which required Italy to resolve such disputes of this sort in the ICJ. The

---

[23] *Prefecture of Voiotia v. Germany*, Areios Pagos [A.P] [Supreme Court] 11/2000 p. 2 (Greece), summarized in M Gavouneli and I Bantekas, 'Sovereign Immunity – Tort Exception – Jus Cogens Violations – World War II Reparations – International Humanitarian Law' (2001) 95 AJIL 198. Two years later a higher Greek tribunal denounced this decision. *Germany v. Margellos*, Anotato Eidiko Dikastirio [A.E.D] [Special Supreme Court] 6/2002 (Greece), translated in 129 ILR 525 (2002), summarized in Maria Panezi, 'Sovereign Immunity and Violation of Jus Cogens Norms' (2003) 56 Rev hell dr int 199.

[24] *Ferrini v. Federal Republic of Germany*, cass., sez. un., 11 marzo 2004, n. 5044, Giustizia Civile 2004 II, 1191, reprinted in (2004) 87 RDI 539, summarized in Andrea Bianchi, 'Ferrini v. Federal Republic of Germany' (2005) 99 AJIL 242.

[25] *Bundesgerichtshof* [BGH] [Federal Court of Justice] 2003 *Entscheidungen des Bundesgerichtshofes in Zivilsachen* [BGHZ] 155 (Ger.), summarized in Sabine Pittrof, 'Compensation Claims for Human Rights Breaches Committed by German Armed Forces Abroad During the Second World War: Federal Court of Justice Hands Down Decision in the Distomo Case' (2004) 5 German L J 15.

ICJ confirmed its jurisdiction in the main case but rejected an Italian counter-claim for compensation, ruling that it lacked jurisdiction over the latter.[26]

On the merits, a large majority sided with Germany and ruled that the lawsuits fit within no recognized exception to the CIL of State immunity.[27] It framed the inquiry as whether State practice had emerged that could provide a basis for an exception, and found none. No States other than Italy and Germany in the cases before the Court, and no international tribunal, had recognized any exception to sovereign immunity for grave human rights abuses. The Court was unwilling to create such an exception on its own.

As a technical matter, the majority understood the concept of State practice rather broadly. It did not simply add up national court cases that had addressed the existence of a CIL exception to immunity. Many courts have rejected the idea of a *jus cogens* exception of immunity, but most of these based their conclusion on interpretation of a national statute or, in the case of the European Court of Human Rights (ECtHR), the text of the European Convention on Human Rights (ECHR).[28] The ICJ treated these cases as significant because it regarded a State's decision to decline the exercise of jurisdiction, whatever the legal theory on which it relied, as significant. State practice, the ICJ assumed, means acts by accountable State actors, whether legislatures in enacting immunity laws or courts in applying them.

In striking contrast to all the other opinions in the case, including the other dissents, Judge Cançado Trindade rejected the proposition that a question of fundamental moral importance, such as the abolition of

---

[26] *Jurisdictional Immunities of the State* (*Germany v. Italy*), [2010] ICJ 310.

[27] Besides the opinion for the Court (above n 22), three other judges wrote separate opinions expanding on the meaning of the decision. Separate opinion of Judge Koroma, http://www.icj-cij.org/docket/files/143/16885.pdf; Separate opinion of Judge Keith, http://www.icj-cij.org/docket/files/143/16887.pdf; Separate opinion of Judge Bennouna, http://www.icj-cij.org/docket/files/143/16889.pdf. Three judges dissented, two on the grounds that State practice had recognized exceptions to immunity limited to the specific circumstances of the case, Dissenting opinion of Judge ad hoc Gaja, http://www.icj-cij.org/docket/files/143/16895.pdf, and dissenting opinion of Judge Yusuf, http://www.icj-cij.org/docket/files/143/16893.pdf, and one on the ground that State practice was irrelevant in questions involving the rights of humanity, Dissenting opinion of Judge Cançado Trindade, http://www.icj-cij.org/docket/files/143/16891.pdf.

[28] The cases relied upon by the ICJ include those from Canada, France, Slovenia, New Zealand, Poland and the UK, as well as the ECtHR. *Jurisdictional Immunities of the State* (*Germany v. Italy*), (above n 22) ¶¶ 85–90.

impunity for grave human rights violations, could rest on State practice. He instead combined references to the aspirations of prominent jurists with arguments from moral principles. Overall, the opinion is much more deductive than inductive. Its stance is fearless. Past precedents, including the Court's, present no impediments. He hoped to open up the Court to the pleas of moral reasoning and the interests of all humans, unmediated by States or even the Court's past jurisprudence.

Finally, the *Corte costituzionale della Repubblica Italiana* provided an epilogue to the dispute. Once the Italian parliament adopted a law implementing the Court's decision, the plaintiffs asserted that barring their suit would violate their right under the Italian constitution to judicial protection of their fundamental rights. The Italian constitutional tribunal agreed. Because IL as authoritatively determined by the ICJ transgressed a constitutional right, it could not serve to justify the law implementing the decision. Instead Italy would defy the Court, privileging constitutional order over IL.[29] Accordingly, *jus cogens* dropped out of the story.

In this episode, who made claims based on *jus cogens* and who resisted? In no jurisdiction had a legislature responded to the appeal of the *jus cogens* argument by carving out an exception to immunity from judicial process. Nor did any government support the argument in domestic courts, although Italy and Greece did defend the outcomes of domestic litigation once called to do so before the ICJ. Rather, the lawyers representing the Greek and Italian plaintiffs advocated the *jus cogens* claim, and the courts, indifferent to the enactments or views of the respective governments, agreed.

What should one make of actions of the ICJ itself? PE would begin with the observation that, whatever its honor and accomplishments, the ICJ functions under greater political constraints than does a typical national court. By custom, the power to appoint jurists to the Court rotates among certain States. The UN General Assembly (UNGA) ratifies these choices, but rarely if ever does this body upset these nominations. Thus individual States screen candidates and are likely to exclude individuals whose professional accomplishments might indicate a risk of voting to undermine important national interests. Moreover, the possibility of reappointment exists, which means judges once appointed must

---

[29] 'Accordingly, the incorporation, and thus the application, of the international norm would inevitably be precluded, insofar as it conflicts with inviolable principles and rights.' Italian Constitutional Court, Judgment n. 238 of October 22, 2014, at ¶ 3.4. Unofficial English translation by Alessio Gracis, available at http://italyspractice.info/judgment-238-2014.

take into account the reaction of the nominating State to particular votes. None of these mechanisms achieves anything like domination and control, but they do make it less likely that the persons who serve on the Court will embrace outlier positions that significantly undermine the interests of selecting States.[30]

Nor is the power to nominate distributed randomly. The five permanent members of the UN Security Council – China, France, the Union of Soviet Socialist Republics, then Russia, the UK and the US – have had a disproportionate number of their nationals on the Court.[31] Not only do these States share a veto power in the Council, but they all are relatively large, have extensive international engagements, and are the only States with a legal right to possess nuclear weapons. One might predict that they would have a moderate to strong preference for the international legal status quo, that they would want to manage human rights issues through governments rather than by independent adjudication (especially in other countries' courts), and that they generally would worry about an international court that marginalized the importance of State involvement in the making of IL.[32] Perhaps not surprisingly, then, all five of the P5 judges, as well as most of the others, rejected a strong reading of the *jus cogens* principle.

The prominent exception, of course, is Judge Cançado Trindade. His position in *Jurisdictional Immunities of the State*, however, is consistent with his earlier career as an academic, human rights advocate and a judge on the Inter-American Court of Human Rights (IACtHR). The Brazilian government that nominated him to the Court was somewhat to the left of its immediate predecessors and populated by politicians who had begun their career opposing a military junta that had committed many human rights abuses. The strongest advocate of *jus cogens* on the Court thus was a person who made his way in advocacy and international service, rather than working mostly within a State's foreign relations structure, and who was nominated by a government that had a relatively low investment in

---

[30] For empirical evidence providing some support for the proposition that the votes of ICJ judges tend to align with national interests, see Eric A Posner and Miguel FP de Figueiredo, 'Is the International Court of Justice Biased?' (2005) 34 J Leg Stud 599.

[31] In the 68-year history of the Court, a French, Soviet or Russian, UK and US judge has served all or nearly all of time. A Chinese judge has served for 39 years, with a gap from the Cultural Revolution to 1985, when the competing claims of Taiwan and the People's Republic were clarified.

[32] For example, China, Russia and the US have declined to accept the jurisdiction of the International Criminal Court.

the international legal status quo and that relied on human rights advocacy to strengthen its domestic legitimacy.

Finally, the scholarly community generally has greeted *Jurisdictional Immunities of the State* critically. More moderate authors have tried to find some daylight in the decision for enforcement of human rights, while the stronger critics have deplored the decision as conservative and short-sighted. Interestingly, proponents of *jus cogens* largely have taken the connection to human rights for granted and have not explored the broader implications of procedural mechanism that is the foundation of the concept.[33]

All of these outcomes are broadly consistent with what this Chapter's political-economy analysis would predict. In *Jurisdictional Immunities of the State*, persons and institutions interested in freeing themselves from the traces of the past pressed *jus cogens* arguments. Affected States as well as institutions over which national governments have substantial influence resisted.

This one case, I must repeat, does not prove that a political-economy analysis unlocks all mysteries in the development of international legal doctrine. It does not even prove that the interests of the principal actors in the drama caused their actions. What the case does is establish the conditional plausibility of the analysis and lend great shade and color to the theory. It illustrates a great deal, even if it proves nothing.

IV. CONCLUSION: THE FUTURE OF *JUS COGENS*

The evolution of IL from a set of norms made exclusively by sovereigns to an open legal system with multiple points of entry and a wide range of acceptable claims reflects profound underlying changes in the world

---

[33] Excluding work by Italian scholars who criticized technical aspects of the opinion, the negative scholarly chorus includes Christopher A Whytock, 'Foreign State Immunity and the Right to Court Access' (2013) 93 Boston U L Rev 2033; Winston P Nagan and Joshua L Root, 'The Emerging Restrictions on Sovereign Immunity: Peremptory Norms of International Law, the U.N. Charter, and the Application of Modern Communications Theory' (2013) 38 North Carolina J Int L Com Reg 375; Suzanne Katzenstein, 'International Adjudication and Custom Breaking by Domestic Courts' (2012) 62 Duke L J 671; Paul C Bornkamm, 'State Immunity Against Claims Arising from War Crimes: The Judgment of the International Court of Justice in Jurisdictional Immunities of the State' (2012) 13 German L J 733; Markus Krajewski and Christopher Singer, 'Should Judges be Front-Runners? The ICJ, State Immunity and the Protection of Fundamental Human Rights' (2012) 16 Max Planck UN Yb 1.

economy, global culture, and the alignment of geopolitical forces.[34] *Jus cogens* constitutes only one mechanism by which IL has diminished the juridical monopoly of sovereigns. For all the reasons that explain the growth of privatization in IL, one should expect the *jus cogens* concept to persist.

Seen in this perspective, the outcome of *Jurisdictional Immunities of the State* is an episode, not a definitive moment. The failure of the concept to make much headway in the ICJ does not preclude others from embracing these arguments. National courts and international tribunals that face fewer national checks still might use *jus cogens* to override legal rules that they dislike.[35]

How might *jus cogens* evolve? If the human rights community has its way, it ultimately will overcome procedural as well as substantive obstacles to the vindication of fundamental human rights. Debates in the future might focus on what constitutes a fundamental human right and what qualifies as an obstacle, but the basic thrust of the concept will become conventional wisdom.

PE asks what kind of alignment of political, economic and technological forces will compel such an outcome. Moral education alone might demand a full victory for the human rights movement, but an economic analysis of political decisionmaking cannot stop there. Here I must admit to a failure of imagination. I do not see how to sustain a devolution of power to judges, jurists, academics and activists, whatever the short-term appeal of such a move. Blunders will beget cynicism, some will be revealed as wielding this authority for personal gain, and a backlash will emerge. This unhappy future is not inevitable, but neither is it unlikely.

Another possibility is that a new international actor might take advantage of a significant change in the correlation of forces to propose new work for *jus cogens*. At the moment China seems the most likely candidate for occupying this position, based on its remarkable economic growth and increasing willingness to project its economic and military

---

34 See Paul B Stephan, 'Privatizing International Law' (2011) 97 Virginia L Rev 1573; Nico Krisch, 'The Decay of Consent: International Law in an Age of Global Public Goods' (2014) 108 AJIL 1.

35 Presumably the ECtHR, for example, might embrace the principle, as State influence over the selection of judges is less than with respect to the ICJ. After *Jurisdictional Immunities of the State*, however, the European Court affirmed an earlier ruling, based on the ECHR rather than CIL, that States need not create a torture exception to sovereign immunity in civil suits. Case of *Jones et al. v. United Kingdom*, Applications Nos. 34356/06 and 40528/06, Jan. 14, 2014.

power externally. How might a less risk-averse and conservative Chinese leadership than we see at present recruit *jus cogens* to advance its interests?

It is not too wild to imagine China embracing something not too removed from von Verdross's conception of *jus cogens* as a sovereignty-protecting structure. This concept would limit State discretion to bargain away inherent practical powers long associated with exclusive State authority, such as ownership and control of subsurface resources. This concept might nod in the direction of the 'matters which are essentially within the domestic jurisdiction of any State' that the UN Charter excludes from international regulation.[36] References to the 'New International Economic Order' of the 1970s also would pop up.[37]

Such a repurposing of *jus cogens* might serve as a useful mechanism to reconfigure the IL of trade and investment protection, and particularly to shift power from large private actors to States. China might object in particular to the liberal idea of private power as a check on State power, a concept that runs through contemporary trade and investment law. *Jus cogens* might serve to correct what it might see as an imbalance in current IL.

This speculation is, of course, only a thought experiment. How the world system might evolve, how these changes would create new interests and imperatives, and how these imperatives might find themselves expressed through *jus cogens* is unknowable. Still, the enterprise has a point.

The modern conception of *jus cogens* is seen by its proponents as providing a foundation for the international legal system, a centripetal force that can check pernicious fragmentation and lost legitimacy.[38] But, as PE teaches us, it is the structure rather than the content of *jus cogens* that over time does the heavy lifting. Procedurally, *jus cogens* can make it

---

36 UN Charter art. 2(7).

37 See, for example, Burns H Weston, 'New International Economic Order and the Deprivation of Foreign Proprietary Wealth: Some Reflections upon the Contemporary International Law Debate', in Richard B Lillich (ed), *International Law of State Responsibility for Injuries to Aliens* (University Press of Virginia 1983) 89.

38 For example, Tomer Broude, 'Fragmentation(s) of International Law: Normative Integration as Authority Allocation', in Tomer Broude and Yuval Shany (eds), *Sovereignty, Supremacy, Subsidiarity: The Shifting Allocation of Authority in International Law* 99 (Hart 2008) (criticizing argument).

harder, not easier, to make IL, and thus can undermine rather than bolster the international legal order. When we think about *jus cogens*, we must be careful about what we wish for.

5. The Political Economy of International Treaties

Panos Merkouris

I. INTRODUCTION

In 1996 the WTO Appellate Body made the following oft-cited quote: 'WTO agreements are not to be read in clinical isolation from public international law'.[1] What this meant was that WTO law, and any other specialised field of International Law (IL) for that matter, could not be considered as an isolated island.[2] All areas of IL are inter-connected and in a constant state of amphidromous[3] influence. In the spirit of the Volume, the above quote could be paraphrased thus: 'Public International Law is not to be read in clinical isolation from other sciences'.

Political Economy (PE) has much to offer in the understanding and study of Public International Law (PIL). Every contribution to this Volume attempts to make up for the shortcomings and fill the *lacunae* in existing analysis of PIL under the PE or International Political Economy (IPE) lens. Van Aaken and Trachtman very poignantly observe that despite the undeniable merits of the existing PE and IPE approaches to PIL those approaches are far from flawless.[4] PE has been used at the national level to understand the interaction of a multitude of different 'interest groups' and their influence on the form, substance and application of the law, but it 'often lacks sufficient focus on intricate norms'.[5] IPE, although using a 'two-level analysis', focuses mostly on economic

---

1 *US – Standards for Reformulated and Conventional Gasoline* – Report of the Appellate Body (20 May 1996) WT/DS2/AB/R, Sec III.B.

2 Joost Pauwelyn, 'Bridging Fragmentation and Unity: International Law as a Universe of Inter-connected Islands' (2004) 25 Mich J Int L 903.

3 Or omni-dromous to be more precise.

4 Anne van Aaken and Joel P Trachtman, 'Political Economy of International Law: Towards a Holistic Model of State Behaviour', above in this Volume.

5 Ibid.

relations, disregarding the wide gamut of other areas in which international regulation occurs. PIL academic discourse, finally, sometimes falls prey to solipsistic tendencies; PIL is analysed only through the lens of law, as an isolated island. In this manner, though, the lessons that could be learned and the information gained by taking stock of the experience and achievements of other sciences and/or approaches remain regrettably underused.

Therefore, the *telos* of this Volume could be considered as a 'call to arms' for a more systematic and systemic PE and IPE study of PIL: to demonstrate that our understanding of PIL can only be augmented by PE tools and that the combination of PE, IPE and PIL is considerably superior to the sum of each of its individual elements. In this *milieu*, the present Chapter will tackle the task of demonstrating the need for a PE and IPE study of international treaty law and of treaties. This will not be attempted in a complete vacuum. We have come a long way from the original studies of international relations (IR) on PIL, where the focus was 'on understanding and avoiding interstate conflict, with this concern stemming from a Hobbesian interpretation of international affairs in which States interact in a perilous state of nature where meaningful cooperation is precluded by insecurity, mutual fear and distrust', to nowadays more nuanced discussions on cooperation and compliance in decentralised or more centralized regimes/instruments.[6] Similarly, in PE and IPE there has been a significant shift from the analysis of the actions of a State on the international plane being viewed only as a unitary actor (as a 'black box'[7] or as a 'billiard ball'[8]) to more complex alternatives offered by the 'two-level game' analysis,[9] where 'moves that are rational

[6] Dunca Snidal and Michael Sampson, 'Interstate Cooperation Theory and International Institutions' (25 November 2014) in *Oxford Bibliographies Online* <http://www.oxfordbibliographies.com/view/document/obo-9780199743292/obo-9780199743292-0093.xml> accessed 15 December 2014.

[7] Anne van Aaken, 'Rational Choice Theory' (23 March 2012) in *Oxford Bibliographies Online* <http://www.oxfordbibliographies.com/view/document/obo-9780199796953/obo-9780199796953-0051.xml?rskey=IGLEI7&result=2&q=rational+choice+theory#firstMatch> accessed 15 December 2014.

[8] Jack L Goldsmith and Eric A Posner, *The Limits of International Law* (OUP 2008); Joel P Trachtman, *The Economic Structure of International Law* (Harvard University Press 2008).

[9] Robert D Putnam, 'Diplomacy and Domestic Politics: the Logic of Two-Level Games' (1988) 42 Int Org 427, 433–434; Helen Milner, *Interests, Institutions and Information: Domestic Politics and International Relations* (Princeton University Press 1997); Jongryn Mo, 'The Logic of Two-Level Games with Endogenous Domestic Coalitions' (1994) 38 JCR 402.

for a player at one board [either the domestic or the international one] may be impolitic of that same player on the other board'.[10]

The aforementioned are great strides in adopting a PE/IPE perspective in the study of IL. However, with respect to treaties which are the focus of the present Chapter, there is still a long way to go. The reason is that the existing literature tends to apply PE/IPE approaches in the study of treaties around two main attractors: i) the emergence of a treaty (negotiation, signing and ratification)[11] and ii) compliance or non-compliance with the obligations undertaken through that treaty.[12] This approach is extremely fragmented. Treaties are not still images frozen in time. They are 'living instruments' that are born, evolve and sometimes die. Using this information as a guide, the present Chapter will highlight the existence of a veritable cornucopia of uncharted areas in a treaty's 'life-cycle' where a strictly legal approach is not sufficient and where PE/IPE can yield valuable insight as to how PIL is formed and functions.

For this reason, law of treaties will be examined mainly through the lens of IPE, avoiding, however, the pitfall of being focused only on economic relations but using examples from all PIL areas. PIL will also be examined as *explanandum* (dependent variable),[13] while methodologically the analysis for the most part, will be conducted under the

---

[10] Putnam (n 9) 434.

[11] Jeffrey L Dunoff and Joel P Trachtman, 'Economic Analysis of International Law' (1999) 24 Yale J Int L 1; Gene M Grossman and Elhanan Helpman, 'The Politics of Free-Trade Agreements' (1995) 85 Am Econ Rev 667; Gene M Grossman and Elhanan Helpman, 'Trade Wars and Trade Talks' (1995) 103 J Pol Econ 675; Rachel Brewster, 'The Domestic Origins of International Agreements' (2003–2004) 44 VJIL 501; Mo (n 9); Putnam (n 9).

[12] Robert O Keohane and Joseph S Nye, *Power and Interdependence: World Politics in Transition* (Little, Brown 1977); Harold H Koh, 'Why do Nations Obey International Law?' (1996–1997) 106 Yale L J 2599; Edith Brown Weiss and Harold K Jacobson (eds), *Engaging Countries: Strengthening Compliance with International Environmental Accords* (MIT Press 1998); Abram Chayes and Antonia Handler Chayes, *The New Sovereignty: Compliance with International Regulatory Agreements* (Harvard University Press 1998); Andrew T Guzman, 'A Compliance-Based Theory of International Law' (2002) 90 Calif L Rev 1823; Markus Burgstaller, *Theories of Compliance with International Law* (Martinus Nijhoff 2005); Laurence R Helfer, 'Nonconsensual International Lawmaking' (2008) 1 U Ill L Rev 71; Anne van Aaken, 'Effectuating Public International Law through Market Mechanisms ?' (2009) 165 JITE 483.

[13] Although in Section III in this Chapter, PIL will be briefly examined as *explanans* (independent variable) as well.

second column of Kantorowicz's epistemological trilogy,[14] that is, *Realwissenschaft* (sociological perspective). However, for 'Evolutive Interpretation' the third column, that is, *Normwissenschaft* (doctrinal perspective), will also be used, given the nature of that analytical part, which renders *Normwissenschaft* the more apposite analytical lens.

Finally, the aim of this Chapter is not to provide a complete list of all IPE approaches and tools to explain law of treaties *in toto*. The open-ended nature of this field of law would transmute any such exhaustive attempt into an exercise in futility. The aim is to highlight the fact that there is a multitude of areas of the law of treaties which have not yet been the subject of IPE analysis and to pinpoint those where IPE considerations, approaches and tools may or are needed to come into play in order to understand the outcome. Consequently, the content of this Chapter has been structured following a 'from cradle to grave' approach and the following areas have been selected for their instructional value: i) non-State determination of the existence of a treaty; ii) evolutive interpretation; iii) normative conflict; and iv) termination of treaties.

II. NON-STATE DETERMINATION OF THE EXISTENCE OF A TREATY

As mentioned above, the existing literature on PE in the field of law of treaties concerns itself mainly with how and why States decide to sign and ratify a treaty. Article 2(1) of the Vienna Convention on the Law of Treaties (VCLT) provides the deceptively simple definition of a treaty: '[A treaty is] an international agreement concluded between States in written form and governed by IL, whether embodied in a single instrument or in two or more related instruments and whatever its particular designation'. However, as Jessup very poignantly underlined as early as 1962 '[t]he notion that there is a clear and ordinary meaning of the word "treaty" is a mirage'.[15]

---

[14] Hermann Kantorowicz, *Rechtwissenschaft und Soziologie* (CF Müller 1962) 11; see also Daniel Bodansky, 'International Law in Black and White' (2006) 34 Georgia J Int Comp L 285; van Aaken and Trachtman (n 4).

[15] *South West Africa (Ethiopia v South Africa; Liberia v South Africa)* (Preliminary Objections, Separate Opinion of Judge Jessup) [1962] ICJ Rep 319, 402. See also, Godefridus JH van Hoof, *Rethinking the Sources of International Law* (Kluwer Law and Taxation Publishers 1983) 117.

The definition of Article 2 VCLT makes it clear that the nomenclature of the instruments in question is of no consequence,[16] and as the ICJ has stated in an unequivocal manner '[t]erminology is not a determinant factor as to the character of an international agreement or undertaking'.[17] This, however, raises the very interesting possibility of a treaty existing despite one of its parties objecting to its very existence. Existing literature focuses on the State, either as a 'billiard ball' or on the negotiations surrounding a treaty being a reflection of a 'two-level game' where the State's choices will be the outcome of forces and pressure from its interaction with other States, on the one hand, and of domestic interactions amongst the various 'interest groups', on the other. The merit of these analyses is undeniable and proves the importance of PE/IPE in the study of treaties. However, they all share as a starting point the assumption that the existence of a treaty will always be self-evident. Nonetheless, this is a gross oversimplification. There have been a number of cases where the question of the existence or not of a treaty was at the heart of an international dispute, and the 'actors' that determined the treaty's existence were not the States but international judicial bodies. Consequently, this is a so far neglected 'point of entry' through which IPE may offer valuable insights as to the creation of treaties as an *explanandum*. This would mean that with respect to this area of the law of treaties the focus should not only be the State[18] but also the international judiciary.

On this point, let us examine the cases where the existence of a treaty was disputed between States. In *Aegean Sea Continental Shelf* the ICJ examined a Joint Communiqué of the Greek and Turkish Prime Ministers and determined that, bearing in mind the terms employed and the circumstances of its conclusion, it could not be considered a treaty.[19] In *Qatar/Bahrain*, Joint letters and Minutes of meetings between the two States were considered by the Court to satisfy the requirements of IL in order for them to be considered as treaties.[20] However, in a different case,

---

[16] ILC, 'Reports of the International Law Commission on the Second Part of its Seventeenth Session and on its Eighteenth Session' (3–28 January 1966) UN Doc A/6309/Rev.l, [1966] II ILC Yb 169, 188 (Commentary to Draft Article 2).

[17] *South West Africa* (Preliminary Objections) (n 15) 331.

[18] Or any other subject of IL with treaty-making capacity (IOs, for instance).

[19] *Aegean Sea Continental Shelf (Greece v Turkey)* (Jurisdiction) [1978] ICJ Rep 4 para 96.

[20] *Maritime Delimitation and Territorial Questions between Qatar and Bahrain* (*Qatar v Bahrain*) (Jurisdiction and Admissibility) [1994] ICJ Rep 112 paras 23–30.

again on maritime delimitation, the International Tribunal for the Law of the Sea (ITLOS) found that a similar set of Minutes between Bangladesh and Myanmar did not constitute a treaty.[21] Finally, in *Cameroon v Nigeria* the ICJ not only held that the Maroua Declaration was an international agreement but also that Nigeria could not invoke the exception of Article 46 VCLT.[22] Nigeria had argued that according to its constitution the Nigerian Head of State did not have the capacity to bind Nigeria, without the express approval of the Nigerian Supreme Military Council.[23] However, the ICJ held that the violation was not manifest for the purposes of Article 46 VCLT, and consequently the Maroua Declaration was a valid and binding international agreement.[24]

As can be seen from the aforementioned jurisprudence, disputes where the determination of whether a particular document is a treaty or not, although not very common, have not been a 'one-off' occurrence. Understanding the underlying rationale both legal and non-legal is of critical importance for scientifically and objectively predicting future outcomes especially considering that all of these cases dealt, one way or another, with delimitation.

Understanding the factors that affect judges in the execution of their functions has been the subject of several critical studies employing a wide array of theories from a plethora of sciences (legal, social sciences, economics, psychology to name but a few). But which one is correct? Regarding rational choice-based theories

> [t]he answer depends on who you ask and when. *Legal model* researchers would reply that justice's considerations are rooted in law, and that the law is essentially comprised of its plain meaning, the lawmaker's intent, and

---

[21] *Dispute Concerning the Land and Maritime Boundary between Bangladesh and Myanmar in the Bay of Bengal* (*Bangladesh/Myanmar*) (14 March 2012, Judgment) ITLOS Rep 2012 paras 92–94.

[22] *Case Concerning the Land and Maritime Boundary between Cameroon and Nigeria* (*Cameroon v Nigeria; Equatorial Guinea, Intervening*) (Merits) [2002] ICJ Rep 303 paras 263–265.

[23] Ibid at para 258.

[24] There are two additional cases: i) *Legal Status of Eastern Greenland* (*Denmark v Norway*) PCIJ Rep Series A/B No 53; and ii) *Nuclear Tests* (*New Zealand and Australia v France*) (Judgment) [1974] ICJ Rep 457. In these cases the parties disputed the existence or not of binding international obligations. However, unlike in the previously mentioned cases, the source of obligations was not a written treaty, but a unilateral statement (or an oral treaty as some authors argue for *Legal Status of Eastern Greenland*). Consequently they are not relevant to the present analysis.

> precedent. *Attitudinal model* researchers would answers that the law camouflages the true main consideration: the judge's attitude vis-à-vis the facts of the case. A *rational choice* model would agree with the attitudinalists, yet add strategic considerations related to the odds of the judge's opinions being accepted and ultimately realized. A *neo-institutionalist* would also claim that judges' own attitudes are a main consideration. Such a researcher would also agree that the strategic considerations, which often stem from various institutional arrangements and norms, influence judges' decisions. Yet in the eyes of the neo-institutional, variables also have their own influence on court decision making. A main institutional variable is 'the law' which is defined as a dynamic mindset instead of a formal definition as per the legal model.[25]

Posner, starting from economics and trying to compensate for the fact that judges are 'generally insulated from market incentives' and that the cases they decide do not affect their own well-being,[26] draws analogies with managers of non-profit organizations, voters and theatre-goers.[27] Behavioural economics,[28] combining economics and cognitive sciences examines the judicial function by focusing on 'the three primary contrasts between the economic and the behavioural perspectives [i.e.] deviations from the assumption of cognitive rationality [heuristics and biases], departures from the assumption of motivational rationality … , and divergences from consequentialist morality'.[29]

The truth, as in most situations, lies somewhere in the middle. None of these theories can or attempts to describe holistically the role of the judges and the factors that affect their decision-making. They are similar to the blind men in Buddha's parable. All these theories provide a useful

---

25 Doron Teichman and Eyal Zamir, 'Judicial Decision-Making: A Behavioral Perspective', in Eyal Zarim and Doron Teichman (eds), *The Oxford Handbook of Behavioral Economics and the Law* (OUP 2014) 665 citing Keren Weinshall-Margel, 'Attitudinal and Neo-Institutional Models of Supreme Court Decision-Making: An Empirical and Comparative Perspective from Israel' (2011) 8 J Emp L Stud 556, 569.

26 Hence the standard starting point of economic analysis, in other words, that the individual is a rational being aiming at maximizing its own utility, is inapplicable.

27 Richard A Posner, 'What Do Judges and Justices Maximize? (The Same Thing Everybody Else Does)' (1993) 3 Sup Ct Econ Rev 1.

28 Generally on behavioural economics and the need to use this tool in PE/IPE: Eyal Zarim and Doron Teichman (eds), *The Oxford Handbook of Behavioral Economics and the Law* (OUP 2014); Anne van Aaken, 'Behavioral International Law and Economics' (2014) 55 Harv Int L J 421; Deborah Kay Elms, 'New Directions for IPE: Drawing from Behavioral Economics' (2008) 10 Int Stud Rev 239.

29 Teichman and Zamir (n 25) 667.

but partial insight, a small pebble in the understanding of the wide structure that is the judicial function. This demonstrates the need to transpose these theories and tools to the international plane in order to study the function of international judges from the perspective of a variety of different sciences.

Regarding the object of our analysis in the present Section, that is, the non-State determination of the existence of treaties, the abovementioned tools can prove extremely useful. A hermetically strict *legal model* is not sufficient to describe the outcome in the above cases. It is true that Article 2 VCLT allows for flexibility by not focusing on the nomenclature of the relevant instruments and that it is the intention of the parties that is the critical element. However, on the one hand, the determination of a fictional presumed common intent where none has been articulated *expressis verbis* is notoriously susceptible to being found in snippets taken from the preparatory work as a *tabula in nauflagrio*,[30] while, on the other hand, similar documents in similar circumstances were given diametrically opposite legal characterisations (Minutes were found to be binding in *Qatar/Bahrain*, and non-binding in *Bangladesh/Myanmar*). The feeling is that the strictly *legal model* cannot account for these discrepancies, and that additional factors might be at play here. It is at this point where PE/IPE tools, theories and approaches can shed a revealing light.

Take, for instance, the nature of cases where non-State determination of the nature of international documents has arisen. All of them involve delimitation. Such a lack of subject-matter diversity cannot be a mere statistical aberration. *Attitudinal*, *rational choice* and *neo-institutionalist* approaches alike would agree that there must be an additional factor/s underlying such jurisprudential subject-matter consistency. Such factor/s may be revealed by considering the judicial welfare function, i.e the interests that the judges seek to maximize.[31] It is true that such function is qualitatively and quantitatively different from that of national judges. The lack of a common legislative body and of a normative hierarchy makes it impossible for all international judges to share the same interests they seek to maximize.[32] However, that is not to say that certain

---

[30] Comments by Sir Erick Beckett in: Institut de Droit International (IDI), 'De l'interprétation des traités' [1950] I Ann IDI 438–440.

[31] Paul B Stephan, 'The Political Economy of Extraterritoriality' (2013) 1 Pol Gov 92; Paul B Stephan, 'The Political Economy of *Jus Cogens*', above in this Volume.

[32] As will also be shown in the following Section on 'Evolutive Interpretation'.

of the interests may be common irrespective of the competence of the particular court. One such interest would be ensuring or increasing the stability of international relations and the international community as a whole. Boundary treaties are the most common form of such an increase as can be seen for instance from the fact that in cases of State succession, one of the few treaties not affected by the emergence of new States are border treaties.[33] Consequently, it is only *rational* that international judges would resort to the non-State determination of the existence of a treaty as an exceptional measure (which explains the small number of cases) in order to maximize the ubiquitous interest of international stability (which explains why we can identify the same pattern in different courts).

If that were the only consideration, though, then how can one account for the fact that not in all the cases where the issue arose have the international courts not acknowledged the existence of a treaty. At this point, rational choice, behavioral economics and considerations of the international judicial welfare function may come to our aid. Whereas rational choice theory suggests that 'the relative ranking of two options is context-independent',[34] studies have demonstrated that decisions may often be context-dependent, even despite the fact that the additional choices offered objectively should be immaterial as to the evaluation of the existing two choices.[35] The two main mechanisms of context-dependence are the compromise effect and the contrast effect.[36] In *Bangladesh/Myanmar*, for instance, one of the elements that ITLOS took into account was that during the discussions there was reference to entering into a separate agreement on delimitation of the maritime

---

[33] Vienna Convention on Succession of States in Respect of Treaties (adopted 23 August 1978, entered into force 6 November 1996) 1946 UNTS 3, Art 11.

[34] Teichman and Zamir (n 25) 670.

[35] Indicatively: Joel Huber, John W Payne and Christopher Puto, 'Adding Asymmetrically Dominated Alternatives: Violations of Regularity and the Similarity Hypothesis' (1982) 9 J Cons R 90; Itamar Simonson, 'Choice Based on Reasons: The Case for the Attraction and Compromise Effects' (1989) 16 J Cons R 158; Mark Kelman, Yuval Rottenstreich and Amos Tversky, 'Context-Dependence in Legal Decision Making' (1996) 25 J Leg Stud 287; Itamar Simonson and Amos Tversky, 'Choice in Context: Tradeoff Contrast and Extremeness Aversion' (1992) 29 Journal of Marketing Research 281; Geoffroy de Clippel and Kfir Eliaz, 'Reason-based Choice: A Bargaining Rationale for the Attraction and Compromise Effects' (2012) 7 Theo Econ 125.

[36] Teichman and Zamir (n 25) 671.

zones.[37] However, the non-existence of such an agreement should have been irrelevant as to the determination of whether the Minutes were a treaty. Especially considering that if ITLOS found that the Minutes were a treaty, such delimitation would occur through ITLOS, hence the effect on the value of the two choices on offer (Minutes as treaty or non-treaty) should have been zero. In *Cameroon v Nigeria*, on the other hand, the ICJ was reluctant to question the validity of the Joint letters and the Maroua Declaration, because a non-treaty finding would then bring into question the treaty status of the Yaounde Declaration as well.

Finally, the international judicial welfare function can also come into play. As mentioned, one of the interests that international judges seek to maximize is the stability of international relations. However, this is not left completely unchecked. A counter-balancing interest is the consent-based construction of the international system. A judicial determination on the existence of a treaty may raise questions as to whether the consent of the parties was a merely a legal construct rather than actually given. For this reason, international courts may prefer to reject the non-State determination on the existence of a treaty, especially when there are other agreements or mechanisms in place that ensure that States will agree or attempt to agree on their own on a treaty (*Bangladesh/Myanmar*). When no such mechanism exists, then the international judiciary might be more partial to determining itself the boundaries as otherwise it is highly unlikely that the States will reach an agreement (*Qatar/Bahrain*).

The present analysis has just scratched the surface of the possible contributions of examining the relevant jurisprudence in this area of the law of treaties from an IPE perspective. It was merely meant to demonstrate that these cases may make more sense and may lead to better predictions by utilizing the wide arsenal of tools that have been developed by a number of sciences and that can easily be transposed to the field of the law of treaties.

III. EVOLUTIVE INTERPRETATION

We will now move along the temporal axis of the life-cycle of a treaty and try to identify other 'points of PE/IPE entry'. One such point is treaty interpretation. As Lord McNair mused, 'there is no part of the law of treaties which the text-writer approaches with more trepidation than the

---

[37] *Bangladesh/Myanmar* (n 21) para 93.

question of interpretation'.[38] PE and IPE have much to offer in clarifying the mercurial interpretative process, irrespective of whether one examines interpretation holistically or from the lens of the schools of interpretation, in other words, i) textual/grammatical,[39] ii) intentions/drafters' approach,[40] iii) teleological.[41] For the purposes of the present Chapter evolutive interpretation was selected as the most illustrative example of an interpretative method that by its nature cries for a PE/IPE based analysis.

III.1. What is Evolutive Interpretation?

Sir Gerald Fitzmaurice identified amongst the various principles of interpretation, one that he called the 'principle of contemporaneity', by virtue of which '[t]he terms of a treaty must be interpreted according to the meaning which they possessed, or which would have been attributed to them, and in the light of current linguistic usage, *at the time when the treaty was originally concluded*'.[42] There is an exception to this principle. '[W]here it can be established that it was the intention of the parties that the meaning or scope of a term or expression used in the treaty should follow the development of the law, *the treaty must be interpreted so as to give effect to that intention*'.[43] Various terms have been used to describe this exception to the principle of contemporaneity, 'evolutionary',[44]

---

38 Arnold D McNair, *The Law of Treaties* (Clarendon Press 1961) 364.

39 Since this approach focuses on the text, a PE/IPE analysis might be closely connected to the analysis as to the creation of the treaty.

40 Within this approach, PE/IPE may found close ties not only with the relevant PE/IPE analysis as to the creation of treaties but also as to compliance with its obligations.

41 As van Aaken and Trachtman argue, 'some interpretative methods not only leave open a window for social science knowledge but even demand it, for example, in teleological interpretation … , in openly consequentialist argumentation, in comparative interpretation, or within the principle of proportionality': van Aaken and Trachtman (n 4). On a PE analysis of the principle of proportionality see Anne van Aaken, 'Defragmentation of International Law through Constitutional Interpretation: A Methodological Proposal' (2009) 16 Indiana J Glob Leg Stud 483.

42 Gerald Fitzmaurice, 'The Law and Procedure of the International Court of Justice 1951–54: Treaty Interpretation and Other Points' (1957) 33 BYIL 203, 212 (emphasis added).

43 Hugh Thirlway, 'The Law and Procedure of the International Court of Justice 1960–1989: Supplement 2006: Part Three' (2006) 77 BYIL 1, 57 (emphasis added).

44 *Gabčíkovo-Nagymaros Project (Hungary/Slovakia)* (Separate Opinion of Judge Bedjaoui) [1997] ICJ Rep 7 para 5; *Mayagna (Sumo) Awas Tingni*

'evolutive'[45] and 'dynamic' interpretation.[46] All stem from the idea that certain treaties can be considered as 'living instruments'[47] that need to adapt and evolve in order to remain relevant. For reasons of simplicity the term that will be used from this point onwards will be evolutive interpretation as more closely linked than 'dynamic interpretation' to the idea of 'survival of the fittest',[48] where fittest is not always necessarily the strongest but also the most adaptable.[49] This fits squarely within the concept of treaties adapting through evolutionary interpretation in order to survive and avoid devolving to a state of *desuetudo.*

III.2. The Legal Basis of Evolutive Interpretation

The principle of contemporaneity juxtaposed with evolutive interpretation is a small-scale reflection of the greater ebb and flow between stability and change that is characteristic of the international system as a whole. Although 'evolutive interpretation' is not mentioned *expressis verbis* in Articles 31–33 VCLT, which reflect the customary rules on interpretation,[50] nonetheless it can easily be deduced from the provisions (for

---

Community v Nicaragua (Judgment on Merits, Reparations and Costs) Inter-American Court of Human Rights Series C No 79 (31 August 2001) para 148; Eirik Bjorge, *The Evolutionary Interpretation of Treaties* (OUP 2014).

[45] *Daimler Financial Services AG v Argentina* (Award, 22 August 2012) ICSID Case No ARB/05/1 para 267; *Mondev International Limited v USA* (Award, 11 October 2002) ICSID Case No ARB(AF)/99/2 para 123.

[46] Malgosia Fitzmaurice, 'Dynamic (Evolutive) Interpretation of Treaties – Part I' (2008) 21 Hague Yb Int L 101; Malgosia Fitzmaurice, 'Dynamic (Evolutive) Interpretation of Treaties – Part II' (2009) 22 Hague Yb Int L 1.

[47] *Tyrer v UK* (25 April 1978) App No 5856/72 para 31; *Loizidou v Turkey* (Preliminary Objections) [GC] (23 March 1995) App No 15318/89 para 71; *Vo v France* [GC] (8 July 2004) App No 53924/00 para 82; *Yakye Axa Indigenous Community v Paraguay* (Judgment on Merits, Reparations and Costs) Inter-American Court of Human Rights Series C No 125 (17 June 2005) para 125; *Case of the Mapiripán Massacre v Colombia* (Judgment on Merits, Reparations and Costs) Inter-American Court of Human Rights Series C No 122 (15 September 2005) para 106.

[48] A phrase that was coined by Herbert Spencer, *The Principles of Biology* (Williams and Norgate 1864), vol I, 444.

[49] 'Evolutionary interpretation' was not selected, as the term 'evolutive interpretation' has been more widely used in writings and international jurisprudence.

[50] Indicatively: *Arbitral Award of 31 July 1989* (*Guinea-Bissau v Senegal*) [1991] ICJ Rep 53 para 48; *Oil Platforms* (*Islamic Republic of Iran v USA*) (Preliminary Objections) [1996] ICJ Rep 803 para 23.

example, Article 31(1), 31(3)(c) VCLT) and from the three main approaches to treaty interpretation.[51] So much so, in fact, that each of these has been used as a separate basis through which the validity of evolutive interpretation has been argued to be established: i) the intention of the parties is the easiest one to accept, the one most widely supported[52] and in conformity with the consent-based structure of the international legal system; ii) another argument put forward is that certain treaties are by their 'nature' (their object and purpose) evolutive. This argument is particularly relevant to human rights treaties (and to a lesser degree environmental treaties),[53] on the one hand, and constitutive treaties of International Organizations (IOs),[54] on the other hand. Interestingly, in recent years a reverse presumption has been gaining traction

---

[51] In more detail on the topic see: Panos Merkouris, '(Inter)temporal Considerations in the Interpretative Process of the VCLT: Do Treaties Endure, Perdure, or Exdure?' (2014) 45 NYIL 121–156.

[52] *Legal Consequences for States of the Continued Presence of South Africa in Namibia (South West Africa) notwithstanding Security Council Resolution 276* (Advisory Opinion, Dissenting Opinion of Judge Fitzmaurice) [1971] ICJ Rep 16 para 85; Rosalyn Higgins, 'Some Observations on the Inter-temporal Rule in International Law', in Jerzy Makarczyk (ed), *Theory of International Law at the Threshold of the 21st Century* (Kluwer Law International 1996) 173, 180–181; Mustafa K Yasseen, 'L'interprétation des traités d'après la Convention de Vienne sur le Droit des Traités' (1976) 151 Recueil des Cours 1, 66–67; Ian Sinclair, *The Vienna Convention on the Law of Treaties* (2nd edn, Manchester University Press 1984) 140.

[53] *Loizidou v Turkey* (n 47) para 75; *'Other Treaties' Subject to the Advisory Jurisdiction of the Court*, Advisory Opinion OC-1/82, Inter-American Court of Human Rights Series A No 1 (24 September 1982); *The Effect of Reservations on the Entry Into Force of the American Convention on Human Rights*, Advisory Opinion OC-2/82, Inter-American Court of Human Rights Series A No 2 (24 September 1982); *Restrictions to the Death Penalty*, Advisory Opinion OC-3/83, Inter-American Court of Human Rights Series A No 3 (8 September 1983).

[54] *Rights of Nationals of the United States of America in Morocco (France v USA)* [1952] ICJ Rep 176, 211; Henry G Schermers and Niels M Blokker, *International Institutional Law: Unity with Diversity* (5th rev edn, Martinus Nijhoff 2011) paras 1155–1156 and 1347; Philippe Sands and Pierre Klein, *Bowett's Law of International Institutions* (6th edn, Sweet and Maxwell 2009) 454; Tetsuo Sato, *Evolving Constitutions of International Organizations: A Critical Analysis of the Interpretative Framework of the Constituent Instruments of International Organizations* (Kluwer Law International 1996) 150–160. However, see Brölmann, who rightly points out that teleological and evolutive interpretation are sometimes conflated, and that to these instruments teleological interpretation is more apposite; Catherine Brölmann, 'Specialized Rules of

concerning bilateral investment treaties (BITs), in other words, that by their nature they are static, 'non-evolutive' and that the terms therein must be understood as they stood at the time of the conclusion of the treaty;[55] iii) finally, another argument, linked to the grammatical/textual school of interpretation, that has been raised is that certain terms are by their nature evolutive. These terms are known as 'generic terms'.[56]

Irrespective of whether these bases for evolutive interpretation are valid or whether they are all different manifestations of the will (intention) of the parties and in particular their 'time-will',[57] they all remain a basis of analysis of evolutive interpretation within a strictly legal model and IPE/PE analysis does not seem to be applicable.

III.3. IPE/PE Relevance within the Process of Evolutive Interpretation

This 'magic picture' dissolves when we ask the right questions. What form can evolutive interpretation take? Evolutive interpretation can reflect: i) evolution of fact ('*ouverture du texte*') and ii) evolution of law ('*renvoi mobile*').[58]

When we are dealing with situations of evolution of fact, the rule that is being interpreted changes alongside the factual situation contemplated, for example, the evolution of medical knowledge and scientific advancements,[59] societal and cultural changes,[60] moral developments,[61]

Treaty Interpretation: International Organizations', in Duncan B Hollis (ed), *The Oxford Guide to Treaties* (OUP 2012) 512–514.

[55] *ICS Inspection and Control Services Limited v Argentina*, (PCA) (Award on Jurisdiction, 10 February 2012), para 289; *RosInvest Co. UK Ltd. v the Russian Federation* (Award on Jurisdiction, 5 October 2007), SCC Case No V 079/2005 paras 39–40 and 121.

[56] *Aegean Sea Continental Shelf* (n 19) paras 74–77; *Gabčíkovo-Nagymaros Project* (n 44) para 112; *Dispute Regarding Navigational and Related Rights (Costa Rica v Nicaragua)* [2009] ICJ Rep 213 paras 65–67.

[57] Merkouris (n 51) 139–144.

[58] Théodore Georgopoulos, 'Le droit intertemporel et les dispositions conventionelles évolutives – quelle thérapie contre la vieillesse des traités?' (2004) 108 RGDIP 123, 132–134.

[59] *Gabčíkovo-Nagymaros Project* (n 44) paras 104–107; *Vo v France* (n 47), Dissenting Opinion of Judge Ress, para 5.

[60] *Öztürk v Germany* (21 February 1984) App No 8544/79, Dissenting Opinion of Judge Bernhardt.

[61] *Cossey v UK* (27 September 1990) App No 10843/84, Joint Dissenting Opinion of Judges Palm, Foighel and Pekkanen, para 5.

developments in public opinion,[62] current living conditions,[63] and the socio-economic situation of a State.[64] From this indicative list it is evident that PE/IPE analysis may easily and should enter into the interpretative realm.

In the case of evolution of law ('*renvoi mobile*') the norm interpreted reflects the evolution of the law to which it is connected. As the law changes so does the content of that norm. The form or the source of the law is irrelevant. Customary International Law (CIL),[65] international treaties,[66] and domestic law[67] have all been considered alike for purposes of 'evolution of law'. At this point PE/IPE analysis might be somewhat indirect, as it will first examine the changing law and then the rule being interpreted. Nonetheless its usefulness is of equal value as that of the more direct analysis in the case of 'evolution of fact'.

Moreover, the relevance of PE/IPE for evolutive interpretation can be seen with respect to two different 'actors': the international judiciary and the various 'interest groups'. As far as the international judiciary is concerned, the analysis and conclusions of the previous Section apply here as well. An IPE study of the role and function of the judges is necessary, utilizing rational choice theory, economics, behavioural economics, cognitive and social science tools. For reasons of brevity, suffice it here to say that, with respect to evolutive interpretation, the judges of international human rights courts have an additional and more narrowly defined interest compared to their 'general international law' counterparts, that they may seek to maximize within their judicial welfare function: the protection of human rights. Not only is their interest more specific, but it is also connected with concepts of morality and maybe

---

62 *Öztürk v Germany* (n 60), Dissenting Opinion of Judge Bernhardt.

63 *Yakye Axa Indigenous Community v Paraguay* (n 47) para 125; *Tyrer v UK* (n 47) para 31; *Gómez Paquiyauri et al. (on behalf of Gómez Paquiyauri and Gómez Paquiyauri) v Peru* (Judgment on Merits, Reparations and Costs) Inter-American Court of Human Rights Series C No 110 (8 July 2004) para 165; *Case of the 'Street Children' (Villagrán Morales et al.) v Guatemala* (Merits) Inter-American Court of Human Rights Series C No 63 (19 November 1999) para 193.

64 *Yakye Axa Indigenous Community v Paraguay* (n 47), Partly Concurring and Partly Dissenting Opinion of Judge Ramon Fogel para 33.

65 *Mondev International Limited v USA* (n 45) paras 116–125.

66 *Yakye Axa Indigenous Community v Paraguay* (n 47) paras 124–131; *Case of the 'Street Children' v Guatemala* (n 63) paras 193–194.

67 *Öcalan v Turkey* (12 May 2005) App No 46221/99 paras 162–164; *Marckx v Belgium* (13 June 1979) App No 6833/74; *Dudgeon v UK* (22 October 1981) App No 7525/76 para 60.

with the judges' own personal views,[68] facts which may be useful in explaining why human rights courts have been more prone to evolutive interpretation than other international courts and tribunals.

However, the international judiciary is not the only relevant 'actor' for a PE/IPE analysis of evolutive interpretation. The actions of 'interest groups' can influence IL both indirectly and directly. Their influence is indirect at the domestic level when their actions/pressure leads either to the adoption of laws by the legislature or to the emergence of a factual situation (for example, societal and cultural changes, moral developments, developments in public opinion). Irrespective of which form their indirect influence takes, it will be taken into account by the international judiciary for interpretative purposes. In this context, the analysis of the actions and effects of these 'interest groups' would move along the same lines as classical PE analysis on 'interest groups'. This is corroborated by the fact that the European Court of Human Rights (ECtHR) always counterbalances the private 'interest groups' with the interests of the State (this power struggle between private and State 'interest groups' is central to PE analysis on the formation of law) when contemplating on whether to consider the evolution of fact or law as relevant and sufficient for interpretative purposes. It does so by using concepts such as the 'margin of appreciation'[69] and the existence of a 'European consensus' or a 'European common standard'.[70] In sum, the above could be considered as a 'second order' influence of 'interest groups', as they affect the content of the international norm indirectly through contributing to the evolution of fact and/or law.

Domestic 'interest groups', however, can influence IL directly as well. The ECtHR allows individual applications. Consequently, 'interest groups' that have a vested interest in a particular right being interpreted evolutively[71] can appear before an international court and make their case

---

[68] Compare that to the issues of territorial and maritime delimitation of the previous Section. It is easier to see a judge having personal and strong views on issues of human rights rather than on delimitation.

[69] *Schalk and Kopf v Austria* (24 June 2010) App No 30141/04; *RR v Poland* (26 May 2011) App No 27617/04 paras 186–187.

[70] *Vo v France* (n 47) [82]; *Scoppola v Italy* (17 September 2009) App No 10249/03 para 104.

[71] Consider the evolutive interpretation of Article 8 of the European Convention on Human Rights (ECHR) which has been used to protect, for instance, the rights of same-sex couples and even offer a rudimentary protection of the environment.

directly on the international plane[72] either as an applicant or as an expert asked for a technical advice or through submission of *amicus curiae* briefs. This possibility opens up the option of exploring through PE/IPE the manner in which such 'interest groups' may influence IL not in the classical PE sense but *directly* by virtue of being international 'actors'.

A final point that needs to be raised is the reversal of the 'two-level game' analysis that may occur as a result of evolutive interpretation and a judgment of the ECtHR. If the ECtHR adopts an evolutive interpretation and finds the State in violation of a right enshrined in the ECHR, then the State will have to take measures to address that violation. Such measures could include withdrawal and amendment of domestic laws.[73] In such a situation: i) IL affects domestic politics, which is a reverse image of the classical 'two-level game' PE analysis;[74] ii) domestic 'interest groups' affect domestic law in a non-classical way, in other words, exercising pressure from the international plane and not only the domestic one; and iii) IL (and its evolutive interpretation) becomes the *explanans* of the amended domestic law, the latter, in turn, becoming the *explanandum.*

IV. NORMATIVE CONFLICT: THE AB/AC CONFLICT

IV.1. Normative Conflict is Endemic in International Law

Kelsen, in *Reine Rechtslehre*,[75] described all legal systems as a pyramid of norms 'with a transcendental *Grundnorm* at the apex of the pyramid ... [where] it [would] always be possible to determine the relationship between two or more norms'.[76] Based on this assumption, he argued that a perfect legal system did not allow for normative conflict because any such a situation would presuppose a flaw in the *Grundnorm*, a conclusion that would be an *absurdum*. Consequently, he concluded that a perfect legal system was conflict-free.[77]

---

[72] After having exhausted domestic remedies.

[73] Putnam calls this reversal a 'synergistic linkage': Putnam (n 9) 447–448.

[74] Peter Gourevitch, 'The Second Image Reversed: International Sources of Domestic Politics' (1978) 32 Int Org 881.

[75] Hans Kelsen, *Pure Theory of Law* (University of California Press 1970).

[76] Anja Lindroos, 'Addressing Norm Conflicts in a Fragmented Legal System: The Doctrine of *Lex Specialis*' (2005) 74 Nord J Int L 27.

[77] Kelsen reversed this position in the second edition of *Reine Rechtslehre* as he concluded that conflict of norms is a conflict of will, *not a logical contradiction.* Hans Kelsen, 'Derogation', in Ralph Newmann (ed), *Essays in Jurisprudence in Honour of Roscoe Pound* (Bobbs-Merrill 1962) 339–361.

IL is far from a perfect system, and irrespective of whether Kelsen's theoretical structure holds water, it is generally accepted that conflict is 'endemic' to IL, due to its 'spontaneous, decentralized and unhierarchical nature of international law-making'.[78] Various definitions of conflict have been proposed, varying from strict[79] to more open-ended.[80] The most cited one is that offered by Jenks: '[a] conflict in the strict sense of direct incompatibility arises only where a party to the two treaties cannot simultaneously comply with its *obligations* under both treaties'.[81]

The manner in which IL and its actors have attempted to address normative conflict is firstly, through a presumption against conflict,[82] and secondly, by harmonization through interpretation.[83] Despite their usefulness, these tools 'cannot eliminate the problem of conflict'.[84] For genuine conflicts a wide arsenal is available to the international judge: *lex superior derogat inferiori*, conflict clauses, *lex specialis derogat generali*

---

78 ILC Study Group, 'Report on Fragmentation of International Law' (13 April 2006) UN Doc A/CN.4/L.682 para 486 (ILC Study Group); Nele Matz-Lück, 'Treaties, Conflicts between' MPEPIL 1485 (December 2010) para 2.

79 Joel Trachtman and Gabrielle Marceau, 'TBT SPS, and GATT: A Map of WTO Law and Domestic Regulation', in Federico Ortino and Ernst-Ulrich Petersmann (eds), *The WTO Dispute Settlement System 1995–2003* (Kluwer Law International 2004) 330–331; Gabrielle Marceau, 'Conflict of Norms and Conflict of Jurisdictions: The Relationship between the WTO Agreement and MEAs and Other Treaties' (2001) 35 JWT 1081, 1087; Rüdiger Wolfrum and Nele Matz, *Conflicts in International Environmental Law* (Springer 2003) 4–11.

80 Joost Pauwelyn, *Conflict of Norms in Public International Law: How WTO Law Relates to Other Rules of International Law* (CUP 2003); Wladyslaw Czapliński and Gennady Danilenko, 'Conflict of Norms in International Law' (1990) 21 NYIL 3, 12–13; Seyed Ali Sadat-Akhavi, *Methods of Resolving Conflicts between Treaties* (Martinus Nijhoff 2003) 5–6.

81 Wilfred Jenks, 'Conflict of Law-Making Treaties' (1953) 30 BYIL 401, 426.

82 Hersch Lauterpacht, 'Second Report on the Law of Treaties' (8 July 1954) UN Doc A/CN.4/87, [1954] II ILC Yb 123, 137–138; Jenks (n 81) 427–429; Michael Akehurst, 'The Hierarchy of the Sources of International Law' (1977) 47 BYIL 273, 275; Hans Aufricht, 'Supersession of Treaties in International Law' (1952) 37 Cornell L Rev 655, 657.

83 Pauwelyn (n 80) 240–244; Czapliński and Danilenko (n 80) 13; Charles Rousseau, 'De la compatibilité des normes juridiques contradictoires dans l'ordre international' (1932) 39 RGDIP 133; Georg Schwarzenberger, *International Law: International Law as Applied by International Courts and Tribunals* (3rd edn, Stevens 1957) vol I, 474.

84 Jenks (n 81) 429.

and *lex posterior derogat priori*.[85] Leaving aside that the exact normative value of these conflict resolution techniques is still debated[86] and that they all have inherent limits, one major problem is that they require identity of the disputing parties in the conflicting treaties. But what happens if only one of the disputing parties is party to the conflicting treaties?

IV.2. The Infamous AB/AC Conflict

This brings us to the notorious AB/AC conflict. In this scenario, State A has ratified treaty X with State B, and later it has ratified treaty Y with State C. However, the obligations owed to State B and C conflict with each other. Adhering to one set of obligations would *eo ipso* mean a violation of the other set.

The AB/AC conflict is a troubling concept and authors have tried to offer workable solutions. One suggested by some of the titans in the field of IL was that the *lex prior* should prevail, and that the later one should be invalid.[87] The reason was two-fold. First, that the rule *lex prior derogat posteriori* is not a mere inversion of *lex posterior derogat priori*. Whereas the latter requires identity of parties, the former does not.[88] Second, the superiority of the earlier treaty and the resulting nullity of the

---

[85] For a critical overview of these conflict resolution techniques: ILC Study Group (n 78).

[86] In other words, whether they are customary rules, principles, interpretative criteria or tools. For a discussion see: ILC Study Group (n 78); Schwarzenberger (n 83) 472–473; Pauwelyn (n 80) 388; Neil McCormick, *Legal Reasoning and Legal Theory* (Clarendon Press 1978) 100–128; Malgosia Fitzmaurice and Olufemi Elias, *Contemporary Issues in the Law of Treaties* (Eleven International Publishing 2005) 322; Nancy Kontou, *The Termination of Treaties in Light of New Customary International Law* (Clarendon Press 1994) 142.

[87] Emmerich de Vattel, *The Law of Nations or Principles on the Law of Nature Applied to the Conduct and Affairs of Nations and Sovereigns* (GGJ and J Robinson 1793) Book II, Ch XVII [315]; Hersch Lauterpacht, 'Contracts to Break a Contract', in Elihu Lauterpacht (ed), *International Law: The Collected Papers of Hersch Lauterpacht* (CUP 1978) 374; Hersch Lauterpacht, 'The Covenant as the "Higher Law"' (1936) 17 BYIL 54, 63–64.

[88] Wolfram Karl, 'Conflicts between Treaties' in *Encyclopedia of Public International Law* (North-Holland 1984) vol II, 469. Cases where the *lex prior* rule has been applied: *Customs Regime between Germany and Austria* (Advisory Opinion) PCIJ Rep Series A/B No 41; *Oscar Chinn (UK v Belgium)* (Separate Opinions of Judge Eysinga and of Judge Schücking) PCIJ Rep Series A/B No 63.

posterior one 'followed cogently' from the principle of good faith and requirements of international public policy,[89] and secured the unity of law.[90]

However, when the issue arose during the International Law Commission (ILC) discussions of the VCLT, most members considered it too dogmatic and unrepresentative of existing practice.[91] AB/AC conflict did not lend itself to a strict conflict resolution rule, and States had to decide *ad hoc* which obligations to comply with and which to violate. As Fitzmaurice very succinctly put it, this 'does not mean that international law confers a "right of election", but only that … it may not be possible to prevent a *power* of election from being exercised'.[92] Consequently, this 'power of election' was considered to be the *optimal solution*,[93] and mirrored indirectly through Article 30(4)(b) VCLT and also through the silence of Article 30 on the issue of AB/AC conflict.

IV.3. EU/Russia and the South Stream Project: A Contemporary Case of AB/AC Conflict

The use of the term 'power' of election *in lieu* of the term 'right' clearly demonstrates that in AB/AC conflicts it is the States that decide which rules to uphold and which to violate. So despite the fact that we already have an existing treaty, at this point we are in a *sui generis* situation where States face similar concerns and influences as during the treaty negotiations; and as PE has and continues to offer valuable insight as to how, why and when States decide to become party to a treaty, in the same manner here PE could be quintessential in comprehending why and how

---

[89] Hersch Lauterpacht, 'First Report on the Law of Treaties' (24 March 1953) UN Doc A/CN.4/63, [1953] II ILC Yb 90, 157.

[90] Lauterpacht, 'Second Report' (n 82) 136 para 7.

[91] Gerald Fitzmaurice, 'Third Report on the Law of Treaties' (18 March 1958) UN Doc A/CN.4/115, [1958] II ILC Yb 20, 41 ff.; Humphrey Waldock, 'Second Report on the Law of Treaties' (20 March–5 June 1963) UN Doc A/CN.4/156 and Add. 1–3, [1963] II ILC Yb 36, 56 ff.; ILC, 'Summary Record of the 857th Meeting' (24 May 1966) UN Doc A/CN.4/SR.857 paras 49, 88–91; ILC, 'Summary Record of the 858th Meeting' (25 May 1966) UN Doc A/CN.4/SR.858 para 10.

[92] Fitzmaurice, 'Third Report' (n 91) 42 para 85; Zuleeg calls this *power of election* the 'principle of political freedom': Manfred Zuleeg, 'Vertragskonkurrenz im Völkerrecht. Teil I: Verträge zwischen Souveränen Staaten' (1977) 20 GYIL 246, 267–268.

[93] ILC, '857th Meeting' (n 91) para 49, 88–89; ILC, '858th Meeting' (n 91) para 10.

States select to violate a particular set of obligations (treaty X) and not the other (treaty Y). Therefore, AB/AC conflicts constitute another 'point of entry' of PE into PIL and an area where the veil, if it exists at all, between PE and IL demonstrates a great degree of permeability.

But in this day and age, should the AB/AC conflict not be anything more than a thing of the past, an archaic concept of little, if any, consequence? This could not be further from the truth. The proliferation of information, treaties and areas of IL-regulation are the exact reason why AB/AC conflict will arise with increasing frequency. Take for example the EU/Russian South Stream dispute. The South Stream is a proposed gas pipeline that is planned to transport Russian natural gas through several EU countries. A number of bilateral treaties were signed between Russia and six EU member States.[94] Construction started in December 2012. However, on 4 December 2013, the European Commission threw a monkey wrench into these projects and agreements. Klaus-Dieter Borchardt, director for energy markets at the Commission, stated that these bilateral agreements breached EU law[95] and had to be either denounced and renegotiated or extensively amended.[96] Russia, in turn, claimed that these agreements were governed by IL and valid. Consequently, it was the EU that had to renegotiate its Third Energy Package to conform to the bilateral agreements and not the opposite. The Commission responded by claiming if a renegotiation did not happen it had the competence to ensure that EU law is respected within the EU, implying that if the agreements were not changed, it would lodge infringement proceedings against its member States.[97]

On 12 December 2013, Energy Commissioner Günther Oettinger stated that the States concerned gave the Commission the mandate to negotiate on their behalf the required changes.[98] These negotiations proved fruitless. In mid-2014, however, EU member States started making moves aimed at the continuance of the South Stream Project.

---

[94] Bulgaria, Hungary, Greece, Croatia, Slovenia and Austria. Additionally, Russia has signed a bilateral agreement with Serbia, which, although not an EU-member, is a party to the Energy Community.

[95] 'South Stream Bilateral Deals Breach EU Law, Commission Says' (*Euractiv*, 4 December 2013) <http://www.euractiv.com/energy/commission-south-stream-agreemen-news-532120> accessed 15 December 2014.

[96] Ibid.

[97] Ibid.

[98] 'Oettinger Takes the Lead in Legal Spat with Russia over South Stream' (*Euractiv*, 12 December 2013) <http://www.euractiv.com/video/oettinger-takes-lead-legal-spat-russia-over-south-stream-307362> accessed 15 December 2014.

Austria signed an agreement with Gazprom, while stating that the agreement and its implementation would not violate EU law.[99] Bulgaria in order to continue with the construction of the pipeline amended its own domestic legislation. According to these amendments, the pipeline was not a pipeline but an 'interconnector', hence it fell outside the scope of relevant EU law, and alternatively even if it were a pipeline it was not a 'land pipeline' because part of it would be going through the Black Sea, once again falling outside the scope *ratione materiae* of EU law.[100] Responding to this, the EU launched infringement procedures against Bulgaria,[101] although later on it withdrew those pending negotiations.

It is apparent that the South Stream Project is a veritable *smorgasbord* of issues where PE and IPE may shed illuminating light. With respect to the States involved, this is a situation where they have the 'power of (s)election'. The influence of domestic 'interest groups' will be even more pronounced because external compliance-inducing factors do not apply in favour of one set of obligations, as both sets are binding and based on international treaties. Consequently, each State may adopt a different solution based on the particular domestic equilibrium. This may explain the somewhat different approaches of Austria and Bulgaria. Despite their differences, though, both these solutions share a common denominator, that of rejection of the existence of the conflict. This is a *rational choice* – based solution as the non-existence of a normative conflict would maximize the sum of the potential gains of the States, as they would be able to benefit from both sets of obligations.

Obviously, however, acting as if a conflict does not exist does not mean that the conflict did not arise. Both States have undertaken the risk that the EU, presently or in the future, does not agree with them, as was already shown by the lodging of infringement proceedings against Bulgaria. Such a potential defection from EU obligations can be explained through the economics-based approach to contracts and law,

---

[99] 'Austria Seals South Stream deal with Gazprom' (*Euractiv*, 25 June 2014) <http://www.euractiv.com/sections/energy/austria-seals-south-stream-deal-gazprom-303046> accessed 15 December 2014.

[100] 'Bulgaria, Commission, Lost in Translation over South Stream' (*Euractiv*, 25 April 2014) <http://www.euractiv.com/sections/energy/bulgaria-commission-lost-translation-over-south-stream-301751> accessed 15 December 2014.

[101] 'Two Energy Law Infringement Procedures Threaten Bulgaria' (*Euractiv*, 4 April 2014) <http://www.euractiv.com/sections/energy/two-energy-law-infringement-procedures-threaten-bulgaria-301365> accessed 15 December 2014.

and in particular the 'price theory' and the 'efficient breach hypothesis'.[102] Furthermore, Trachtman's parameters of the multilateral prisoner's dilemma in the context of CIL may be equally useful here and applicable *mutatis mutandis*.[103]

Nonetheless, this is only one side of the coin, as the situation includes an IO with international legal personality, the EU. For this reason, any PE/IPE analysis needs to take into account theories of interstate cooperation and of IOs. Originally, the literature on interstate cooperation focused on 'international regimes',[104] which downplayed the importance of formal institutions. Nowadays, however, the analysis has shifted to 'international institutions' defined as 'humanly devised constraints that structure political, economic and social interaction',[105] as 'the result of power but also as playing a role in constraining and shaping power'.[106] There is extensive literature explaining the reasons for the creation of IOs[107] (an interesting theory here is the theory of the firm, based on the Coase Theorem),[108] their design[109] and the problems of cooperation and enforcement.[110]

---

[102] Dunoff and Trachtman (n 11) 31–32.

[103] George Norman and Joel P Trachtman, 'The Customary International Law Game' (2005) 99 AJIL 541, 542. Indicatively, some of the relevant parameters are: i. the relative value of cooperation versus defection; ii. the number of States effectively involved; iii. the information available to States regarding compliance and defection; iv. the relative patience of States in valuing the benefits of long-term cooperation compared to short-term defection; and v. whether there are other bilateral/multilateral relationships between the involved States.

[104] Stephen D Krasner (ed), *International Regimes* (Cornell University Press 1983).

[105] Douglas North, 'Institutions' (1991) 5 JEP 97.

[106] Snidal and Sampson (n 6).

[107] Kenneth W Abbott and Duncan Snidal, 'Why States Act Through Formal International Organizations' (1998) 42 JCR 3.

[108] Joel P Trachtman, 'The Theory of the Firm and the Theory of the International Economic Organization: Toward Comparative Institutional Analysis' (1997) 17 Nw J Int L Bus 470, 543–554; Dunoff and Trachtman (n 11) 36–38.

[109] Focusing on their rational design: Barbara Koremenos, Charles Lipson and Duncan Snidal (eds), The Rational Design of International Institutions (CUP 2001); Abbott and Snidal (n 107). Focusing specifically on the 'principle-agent model': Beth A Simmons and Lisa L Martin, 'International Organizations and Institutions', in Walter Carlsnaes, Thomas Risse and Beth A Simmons (eds), *Handbook of International Relations* (SAGE 2002) 192; Snidal and Sampson (n 6).

[110] Abram Chayes and Antonia H Chayes, 'On Compliance' (1993) 47 Int Org 175; Jeffrey T Checkel, 'Why Comply? Social Learning and European

However, a majority of the writings tends to focus on forms of interstate cooperation, that are decentralized in nature and using 'soft' forms of compliance, which are not applicable to the EU.[111] Furthermore, what is not examined is how the compliance with the obligations of an IO may affect the compliance with other international obligations or the capacity of the States to enter into international relations.

With respect to the present case, and based on the existing PE/IPE tools on IOs, the actions of the EU can be explained as an attempt to achieve the following three goals:

i. increase the cost of non-compliance (infringement proceedings against Bulgaria), and thus reverse the outcome to which Bulgaria and Austria arrived at by applying the 'price theory' and the 'efficient breach hypothesis';
ii. maximize its own utility (rational choice theory) by reinforcing the autonomy of its legal order[112] and negotiating on behalf of its member States; and
iii. reinforce the 'folk theorem', in other words, that 'any outcome that makes a side better off can (in principle) be achieved provided that that the cooperating parties care enough about maintaining their future cooperative relations so as not to be tempted by short-run actions that would undermine cooperation'.[113]

This is, of course, only the tip of the iceberg. The South Stream Project reveals that modern international treaty practice is a wild landscape with a plethora of actors connected in a multitude of manners and at various levels of integration. As PE requires that a State not be examined only as a 'billiard ball', but also through a 'two-level game' analysis, similarly in the situation described above where we also have an IO attempting integration at a European level, we should not examine the IO as merely a 'billiard ball' but also internally. Due to the number of actors involved and the levels of internality ('interest groups', States etc.), perhaps the

---

Identity Change' (2001) 55 Int Org 553; Anne Marie Burley and Walter Mattli, 'Europe Before the Court: A Political Theory of Legal Integration' (1993) 47 Int Org 41.

[111] Ramses A Wessel and Evisa Kica, 'Political Economy and the Decisions of International Organizations: Choosing Governance Arrangements through Informality', below in this Volume.

[112] As established in *Costa*; *Case 6/64, Flaminio Costa v ENEL* [1964] ECR 585.

[113] Snidal and Sampson (n 6).

'billiard ball' image could be supplemented with that of a Russian doll (a *matryoshka* doll). When you open a *matryoshka* doll you find another one inside and so on and so forth, so in the case of IOs, and the EU in particular, this could reflect the 'pluri-level game' analysis. The dolls can be set apart and interact with each other ('billiard ball' image), while also be put one inside the other ('pluri-level game' analysis). In conclusion, normative conflict, especially when IOs are also involved, is an area of PIL where PE/IPE analysis can shed much needed light.

V. TERMINATION OF TREATIES

A final 'point of entry' of PE considerations is that of termination of treaties. It goes without saying that when a treaty is terminated or when a State withdraws from a treaty this will be a result of the negotiating parties' intent. This intent will usually be reflected in the treaty text, with the adoption of relevant clauses regulating withdrawal and/or termination of a treaty.[114] In this context, the PE analysis of this topic would be similar to that relating to the negotiation of treaties. Concepts such as 'two-level game', 'relative vs absolute gains', 'interest groups', 'the Pareto efficiency', to name but a few, will all come into play in clarifying why States opted for a particular method of withdrawal/termination, as well as why and when they opt for utilizing it. However, once again things are not as clear-cut as they seem.

In PE analysis on IL we often, and rightly so, encounter criticism of the 'billiard ball' model (stemming from the realist theory). Just as we criticize the billiard ball model for failing to take into account the internal dynamics of a State, the consideration of the State as a solo actor on the international plane, acting and reacting only in and to its relations with other States, does not reflect the complexity of the modern international legal system, with an ever-increasing number of subjects, 'actors', 'participants' and 'users'.[115]

---

[114] The VCLT has an entire Section devoted on this topic (Section V).

[115] On the need to expand the theory of subjects of IL, see: Rosalyn Higgins, *Problems and Process: International law and How we Use it* (Clarendon Press 1994) 39–55; Rosalyn Higgins, *Themes and Theories: Selected Essays, Speeches, and Writings in International Law* (OUP 2009) 79–90; Emmanuel Roucounas, 'The Users of International Law', in MH Arsanjani et al. (eds), *Looking to the Future: Essays on International Law in Honor of W. Michael Reisman* (Martinus Nijhoff 2011) 217.

Within the context of this Chapter, we will try to demonstrate that the choice of termination/withdrawal from a treaty may, in certain circumstances, be *de facto* and *de jure* in the hands of another subject of IL. Let us take for instance Article 351 (ex Article 307 TEC) of the Treaty of the Functioning of the European Union (TFEU):

> The rights and obligations arising from agreements concluded before 1 January 1958 or, for acceding States, before the date of their accession, between one or more Member States on the one hand, and one or more third countries on the other, shall not be affected by the provisions of the Treaties.
>
> To the extent that such agreements are not compatible with the Treaties, the Member State or States concerned shall take all appropriate steps to eliminate the incompatibilities established …

Article 351 TFEU, although logical and seemingly clear in its content, has been the subject of much controversy. Views range from the extremely positive, with Petersmann describing it as an example of the immense *Völkerrechtsfreundlichkeit* (friendliness towards IL) of the EU,[116] to the more grim critique by Klabbers that the positive assessment of Article 351 TFEU 'owes more to mythology than to analysis',[117] and that the case-law of the courts of the EU has narrowed Article 351's scope, 'to such an extent that Article 351 has been stripped of much of its content'.[118]

At first glance, the scope of Article 351 TFEU seems pretty straightforward. In order for it to apply, the following conditions need to be cumulatively satisfied:

i. a treaty must have been entered into prior to 1 January 1958 or prior to the date of accession to the EU of the affected State;
ii. the treaty must be between an EU member State and a non EU member State. Article 351 TFEU does not apply between EU member States; and
iii. the treaty must create rights and obligations.

---

[116] E-U Petersmann, 'Artikel 234', in H von der Groeben et al. (eds), *Kommentar sum EWG-Vertrag* (Nomos 1991) 5725–5753.

[117] Jan Klabbers, 'The Validity of EU Norms Conflicting with International Obligations', in Enzo Cannizzaro et al. (eds), *International Law as Law of the European Union* (Martinus Nijhoff 2011) 120.

[118] Jan Klabbers, *International Law* (CUP 2013) 56.

The development of the jurisprudence of Article 351 TFEU is quite revealing. The *Burgoa* and *Levy* cases were the first ones where the Court held that Article 351 applied to all treaties irrespective of their subject-matter as long as they are capable of affecting the application of the EC treaty.[119]

However, it is from this point onwards that the jurisprudence of the Court of Justice of the European Union (CJEU) started interpreting Article 351's scope of application more and more restrictively. The evolution of the jurisprudence seems to have occurred in various stages. At the first stage, the term 'rights and obligations' of Article 351(1) was found by the CJEU to be tantamount to 'rights of third States and obligations of EU member States'.[120] Consequently, Article 351 cannot be invoked by an EU member State, if it wants to exercise a *right* under another treaty. In such a case it *must refrain from exercising that right.*

Although not easily deducible from the text itself, such an interpretation still seems to be within reason. In recent cases, however, the CJEU seems to have imposed a limit as to the 'obligations' that can be invoked. In the infamous *Kadi* case the CJEU concluded that such an invocation is permitted as long as it does not conflict with 'the constitutional principles of the EC Treaty', 'a constitutional guarantee forming part of the very foundations of the Community', 'a foundation of the Union' or 'the principles that form part of the very foundations of the Community legal order'.[121]

In another set of cases the CJEU reduced the term 'appropriate steps' of Article 351(2) TFEU to rubble. These cases dealt with a number of BITs signed between EU member States and third States. The CJEU held that despite the fact that there existed other alternatives to resolving the incompatibilities between the treaties and EU law, the States had to denounce or withdraw from the external treaty, because that was the optimal solution as it was the most expedient and fireproof way to ensure avoidance of present and future incompatibilities.[122] In essence, the

---

119 Case 812/79, *Attorney General v Burgoa* [1980] ECR 2787 para 6; Case C-158/91, *Levy* [1993] ECR I-4287 para 11.

120 Case 10/61, *Commission v Italy* [1962] ECR 1, 8-10; Case C-158/91, *Levy* (n 119) para 12.

121 Joined Cases C-402/05 P and C-415/05 P, *Yassin Abdullah Kadi and Al Barakaat International Foundation v Council of the European Union and Commission of the European Communities* [2008] ECR I-6351 paras 285, 290, 303 and 304 respectively.

122 C-170/98, *Commission v Belgium* [1999] ECR I-5493 paras 41–43; Case C-62/98, *Commission v Portugal* [2000] ECR 1-5171 paras 34–52; Case C-84/

CJEU transformed the text of Article 351(2) from '[EU member States] shall take all appropriate steps to eliminate the incompatibilities' to '[EU member States] shall denounce/withdraw from the incompatible treaty, as soon as this is possible'. In this manner the CJEU has made paragraph 2 of Article 351 TFEU the *lex superior*. It is irrelevant to decide whether denunciation is actually appropriate or not: as long as States have the option of denouncing an incompatible treaty, they should do so.[123] Ultimately, the jurisprudence seems to have created a presumption that the most appropriate step will be denunciation, an interpretation which seems to go against the grain of an ordinary reading of Article 351 TFEU.

Further restrictions to the scope of Article 351 TFEU occurred in the *Open Skies* cases. These concerned the validity of certain international air transfer agreements between the US and eight EU member States.[124] The original agreements had been concluded during the 1940s, consequently they fell within the scope of Article 351 TFEU *ratione temporis*. However, in the 1990s the US started renegotiating some of the articles of these agreements, with a view to amending them. The EU requested that the relevant EU member States refrain from adopting any amendments in the interest of the common (EU) good and in order to reinforce the EU's negotiating capital. However, the aforementioned eight EU member States did not heed the EU's request and adopted these amendments.[125] The EU brought infringement proceedings against them. Surprisingly, the CJEU held that Article 351 TFEU was not applicable, the reasoning being that although the original treaties had been ratified in the 1940s, these amendments should not be considered as a mere change to the original treaties, but as *new treaties*. Based on that, and since the amendments/new treaties occurred in the 1990s, they fell outside the *ratione temporis* scope of Article 351 TFEU. Once again, the CJEU expanded the notion of a term of Article 351 TFEU, 'treaty', to include

98, *Commission v Portugal* [2000] ECR 1-5215 paras 49–61; C-203/03, *Commission v Austria* [2005] ECR I-935 paras 61–64.

[123] For instance, in the aforementioned cases, only Austria was found not to be in violation of its obligations under EU law, because it was unable at the time to denounce the relevant ILO Convention: C-203/03, *Commission v Austria* [2005] ECR I-935 paras 61–64.

[124] Austria, Belgium, Germany, Denmark, the UK, Luxembourg, Sweden and Finland.

[125] This decision of the member States to go against the forceful suggestion of the EU may be in and of itself also an area of extreme interest to study from a PE/IPE perspective.

'amendments' and in this manner reduced even further the scope of Article 351 TFEU.

In a final group of cases, the CJEU found yet another innovative way to reduce the scope of Article 351 TFEU. These cases concerned BITs concluded between EU member States and third States that ensured the free transfer of funds relating to investments. The CJEU opined that although these BITs were not *per se* and at present incompatible with EU law, nonetheless they did not provide for an exemption clause that would allow the EU to impose in the future restrictions in the free transfer of funds in the exercise of its powers.[126] What is interesting is that the CJEU expanded the notion of 'incompatibility' of Article 351 TFEU to include not only existing and present incompatibilities, but also *possible future ones* in areas where the EU may not even have exercised its powers yet.[127]

One would be hard pressed to find anybody who on a first reading of Article 351 TFEU would consider as 'ordinary meaning' all the restrictive interpretations that the CJEU has read into that Article. Each interpretation taken separately could perhaps be ultimately agreed with (although even this is highly debatable) but definitely all of them taken in aggregate seem to have stretched the meaning of the text to its breaking point. The text seems to have been buried under a multitude of teleological and '*faux*-grammatical' interpretations. If the Article may have started as an example of EU's *Völkerrechtsfreundlichkeit*, that is no longer the case. In fact the Commission has even argued before the CJEU the exact opposite: 'The Commission argues that [Article 351 TFEU] does not establish that PIL obligations prevail over Community law, but rather the reverse'.[128] The jurisprudence of the CJEU seems to have vindicated Klabbers when he claimed that Article 351 TFEU 'has been stripped of much of its content'.

However, if the very restrictive interpretation of Article 351 TFEU may not be easily explained by strictly legal models of treaty interpretation, then this might be an indication that this is an area where PE/IPE analysis can offer some much needed insight. In previous Sections we analysed the importance of a PE/IPE analysis of the role of international

---

[126] Such restrictions could be for instance the freezing of assets of individuals suspected of having ties with or funding terrorist cells, similar to *Kadi*.

[127] Case C-249/06, *Commission v Sweden* [2009] ECR I-1335 paras 20, 38 and 41–45; Case C-205/06, *Commission v Austria* [2009] ECR I-1301 paras 21 and 37–45; Case C-118/07, *Commission v Sweden* [2009] ECR I-10889 paras 31, 35 and 49.

[128] Case T-2/99, *T Port GmbH v Council* [2001] ECR II-2093 para 69.

judges (in this case the interest they would be attempting to maximize would be the autonomy of EU's legal order), of the restrictions imposed by IOs to the treaty-making, treaty-amending and treaty-terminating capacity of States (here the States are forced to terminate treaties, despite the fact that they do not wish to, and any decision to breach their EU obligations would not be supported by the 'price theory' and the 'efficient breach hypothesis'). These considerations equally apply here and there is no need for repetition. However, one additional point that needs to be raised is what the catalyst was for this change of behaviour of the EU. Van Aaken points out that according to classical rational choice assumptions '[a] change in behaviour is attributed to a change in restraints ... not a change in preferences'.[129] If we examine carefully the CJEU jurisprudence on Article 351, what becomes evident is that the scope of Article 351 TFEU is inversely proportional to the level of EU integration. The greater the degree of integration, the more reduced the scope of Article 351 TFEU. With every new/amended EC/EU treaty the Pareto frontier shifted. This allowed the organs of the EU to adopt an increasingly more restrictive interpretation of Article 351 TFEU. This has on several occasions led EU member States to face an impossible situation of having to choose between violating their EU obligations and terminating their treaty with a third State. The choice has been skewed in favour of the latter, since through the greater vertical integration of the EU and the extremely restrictive interpretation of Article 351 TFEU, complying with EU obligations has been rendered Pareto-efficient, or Pareto-superior compared to maintaining conflicting obligations under treaties with third States. Such treaties have now become almost automatically Pareto-inefficient.

All the above demonstrate that termination of treaties is another 'point of entry' of PE/IPE considerations in the law of treaties. The EU jurisprudence analysed illustrates that the question of when a treaty is to be terminated, is no longer a decision *taken only by the State*, but in some instances may be *taken for the State* by other international actors. In such a complex field where the result is the death of international obligations, PE/IPE analysis is essential in order to better understand the contours of the forces that may lead to treaty termination.

---

[129] van Aaken (n 7).

VI. CONCLUSION

The present Chapter's aim was to demonstrate that the law of treaties can be viewed from an additional PE/IPE perspective. The existing approaches of explaining States and their actions as a 'billiard ball', or as a result of a 'two-level game' analysis are extremely useful, and were the building blocks of our analysis in several Sections. However, despite their undisputed usefulness, these approaches are far from exhaustive. Important insight can also be offered by examining other 'actors' on the international plane as well as different versions of interstate cooperation. The approaches that take these elements into account I have described as '*matryoshka* doll' and 'pluri-level game' analysis (in the Section 'Normative Conflict: The AB/AC Conflict'). The inclusion of all these approaches ('billiard ball', '*matryoshka* doll', 'two-level game' and 'pluri-level game' analysis) to the study of the law of treaties will allow current research in the field to grow and offer a more cohesive and accurate description and explanation of:

- *who* influences the acts of States and international organizations;
- *how* this influence is exercised;
- *what* the end result is; and
- *why* it has the form it ends up having.

This holistic approach to the study of the law of treaties has as an added benefit that this area of IL is dissected using both a bottom-up approach (that is, how domestic actors/interest groups affect events/laws at the international level) and a top-down one (how international actors/interest groups influence events/laws at the domestic level). This goes to demonstrate even further that the relationship between State and international community cannot be seen as a one-way relationship, where the State (and its interest groups) affect the international community, but rather as an amphidromous one where the international actors and interest groups can equally influence events and processes within a State.

The *telos* of the present Chapter was to identify areas of the law of treaties, not yet analysed in this light, which function as 'points of entry' for a PE/IPE analysis. Following a 'cradle to grave approach' of the life-cycle of treaties, four key areas were identified as such possible 'points of entry':

i. non-State determination of the existence of a treaty;
ii. evolutive interpretation;
iii. normative conflict (with special focus on the AB/AC conflict);
iv. termination of treaties.

In all of them, PE/IPE tools were indispensable in the comprehension and description of the phenomena observed. Apart from the ones already mentioned above, and to name but a few more of the tools that were resorted to during the present analysis: rational choice-based theories, behavioural economics, international judicial welfare function, cognitive and social science tools, multilateral prisoner's dilemma, theories of interstate cooperation and of IOs, theory of the firm, 'folk theorem', 'price theory', 'efficient breach hypothesis', and 'Pareto-efficiency'. This list is far from a *numerous clausus*. With it we have barely scratched the surface. The usefulness, however, of this enumeration of tools is to demonstrate beyond a shadow of a doubt that a hermetic approach to the study of the law of treaties without drawing inspiration from other sciences is an approach similar to Buddha's parable of blind men and the elephant. As those blind men described the elephant depending on the part of its body they were touching (leading them to describe the elephant in such diverse terms as similar to a 'pot', a 'plow', a 'pillar', or a 'brush'), similarly examining the law of treaties only from the perspective of the law *strict sensu* offers an incomplete, fragmented and in the end erroneous description of this complex area. Such an approach fails to recognize that IL and the law of treaties *is not a singularity but a multiplicity*. Consequently, and the realization of this conclusion was one of the main aims of the present Chapter, a more systematic examination of the law of treaties is needed, in which the utilization of PE/IPE tools and concepts is essential for the fuller understanding of the forces and mechanics at work in this area of law.

6. Political Economy and the Decisions of International Organizations: Choosing Governance Arrangements through Informality

Ramses A Wessel and Evisa Kica

I. INTRODUCTION

Traditionally, legal scholarship on International Organizations (IOs) is largely doctrinal. As a branch of Public International Law (PIL), the law of IOs (or international institutional law) focuses on *traditional actors* (States), *processes* (international (institutionalized) governmental negotiations) and *instruments* (treaties, decisions of formal IOs). Yet, questions on *why* (or *how*) States act through IOs – reflecting a Political Economy (PE) approach[1] – have been raised by many ever since the large scale emergence of IOs since 1945. Indeed, these are not traditional legal questions, and they have mainly been approached from the perspectives (and on the basis of theoretical insights) of other, or meta-legal, academic disciplines. Thus, Trachtman, for instance, articulated economic reasons for the international structure[2] and Abbott and Snidal[3] pointed to the importance of *centralization* and *independence* and argued that these 'two characteristics distinguish IOs from other international institutions: centralization (a concrete and stable organizational structure and an

[1] See Anne van Aaken and Joel P Trachtman, 'Political Economy of International Law: Towards a Holistic Model of State Behaviour', above in this Volume.

[2] Joel P Trachtman, *The Economic Structure of International Law* (Harvard University Press 2008). More recently, Trachtman analysed a more general set of reasons why States might move to cooperation: Joel P Trachtman, *The Future of International Law: Global Government* (CUP 2013) Chapter 2.

[3] Kenneth W Abbott and Duncan Snidal, 'Why States Act through Formal International Organizations' (1998) JCR 3–32 at 9.

administrative apparatus managing collective activities) and independence (the authority to act with a degree of autonomy, and often with neutrality, in defined spheres).' The focus of Abbott and Snidal was on formal intergovernmental organizations and could be seen as a reaction to the vast literature on international regimes, initiated by authors such as Krasner and Keohane.[4]

At the same time, in studies on the appropriate choice for international/transnational governance arrangements political studies and IR-theory have never excluded informal bodies and networks. In fact, according to Simons and Martin, the turn in the latter disciplines from the study of formal institutions to regimes 'was instigated by the observation that much of what was interesting about world politics – especially during the Cold War period – seemed to take place among intensely independent actors but beyond the purview of formal inter-State organizations'.[5] It is this insight that only slowly starts to affect international legal doctrinal analysis.

Realizing that there is a whole world of international cooperation beyond the boundaries that were defined for PIL, international lawyers started to show an increased[6] interest in attempting to describe and even explain normative processes that traditionally sit uneasy with International Law (IL). To name just a few (key) examples: Slaughter drew our attention to 'transgovernmental regulatory networks';[7] Kingsbury and others pointed to an emerging 'global administrative law';[8] Alvarez noted that more and more technocratic international bodies 'appear to be engaging in legislative or regulatory activity in ways and for reasons that might be more readily explained by students of bureaucracy than by scholars of the traditional forms for making customary law or engaging

---

[4] Stephen D Krasner, *International Regimes* (Cornell University Press 1983); Robert O Keohane, *After Hegemony: Cooperation and Discord in the World Political Economy* (Princeton University Press 1984).

[5] Beth A Simons and Lisa L Martin, 'International Organizations and Institutions', in Walter Carlsnaes, Thomas Risse and Beth A Simmons (eds), *Handbook of International Relations* (Sage 2001) 192–211 at 192.

[6] Or perhaps a *renewed* interest, considering the fact that ancient legal approaches clearly included non-State actors and informality – think of the *lex mercatoria*, which functioned as the international law of commerce throughout medieval Europe.

[7] Anne-Marie Slaughter, *A New World Order* (Princeton University Press 2004) Chapter 6.

[8] Benedict Kingsbury, Nico Krisch and Richard B Stewart, 'The Emergence of Global Administrative Law' (2005) 68 L Contemp Probs 15–61.

in treaty-making';[9] von Bogdandy and others argued that international public authority may have different sources;[10] Pauwelyn, Wessel and Wouters introduced us to 'informal international law-making';[11] the project on 'Private Transnational Regulatory Regimes' draws attention to transnational private actors;[12] and all of this returns in the project on 'The Architecture of Postnational Rulemaking'.[13] The study of international institutional law (the law of IOs) is moving from a very descriptive (and admittedly, occasionally not too exciting) analysis of the set-up of the various existing IOs, their organs and decision-making procedures, to a more conceptual analysis of the changing role of international institutions in global governance.[14] Lawyers increasingly seem to be able to set aside their traditional hesitations by accepting a reality of many different forms, actors and processes in the formation of international norms. Obviously, to political scientists and international relations theorists, the existence of 'transnational' normative processes does not come as a surprise and, in a way, always formed part of their 'reality of global governance'.[15]

---

[9] José E Alvarez, *International Organizations as Law-Makers* (OUP 2005) at 217.

[10] Armin von Bogdandy, Rüdiger Wolfrum, Jochen von Bernstorff, Philipp Dann and Matthias Goldmann (eds), *The Exercise of Public Authority by International Institutions: Advancing International Institutional Law* (Springer 2010).

[11] Joost HB Pauwelyn, Ramses A Wessel and Jan Wouters (eds), *Informal International Lawmaking* (OUP 2012); and Ayelet Berman, Sanderijn Duquet, Joost HB Pauwelyn, Ramses A Wessel and Jan Wouters (eds), *Informal International Lawmaking: Case Studies* (Torkel Opsahl Academic E Publisher 2012), available at http://www.fichl.org/fileadmin/fichl/documents/LOTFS/LOTFS_3_Web.pdf.

[12] See 'Private Transnational Regulatory Regimes', available at http://privateregulation.eu and Fabrizio Cafaggi (ed), *Enforcement of Transnational Private Regulation* (Edward Elgar 2012).

[13] See 'The Architecture of Postnational Rulemaking: Views from International Public Law, European Public Law and European Private Law', available at www.uva.nl/architecture.

[14] A recent example is Roberto Virzo and Ivan Ingravallo (eds), *Evolutions in the Law of International Organizations* (Brill Nijhoff 2015).

[15] Jonathan GS Koppell, *World Rule: Accountability, Legitimacy, and the Design of Global Governance* (University of Chicago Press 2010) Chapter 1. Koppell sketched – both empirically and conceptually – the 'organization of global rulemaking'. Even in the absence of a centralized global State, the population of Global Governance Organizations (GGOs) is not a completely atomized collection of entities: 'They interact, formally and informally on a

This turn in the study of international institutional law reflects empirical developments and may be based on the idea that 'Formal international law is stagnating in terms both of quantity and quality' and that over the years actors have more frequently opted for informal governance arrangements.[16] These arrangements come in many different varieties.[17] While regulation may be left to private actors entirely,[18] many arrangements still foresee some kind of role for governments. And, in fact, many arrangements are simply less formal forms of institutionalized cooperation between States; for instance through what it sometimes referred to as 'soft international organizations'.[19] A PE question would be *why* international actors would opt for more informal settings and output and what the consequences of this choice are in terms of elements that are traditionally perceived as being weak in traditional law, such as legitimacy and compliance. This question relates to the choice for a certain governance arrangement. As this is not a legal question *per se*, we will use insights offered by other disciplines to shed some more light on this choice. In political studies, for instance, questions on 'why institutions exist, how they function and what effects they have on world politics have become increasingly refined and the methods employed in empirical work more sophisticated.'[20] While it remains generally true that in IL 'theoretical reflection in the field of international organizations has been limited',[21] not only the recognition of the increased role of IOs, but in particular the acknowledgment of normative functions of *other* international bodies, often composed of non-governmental actors such as scientific experts, have called for new legal theoretical approaches. This Chapter will make an attempt to contribute to that debate by pointing to the choice of States (or other actors in the public sphere) to move from

---

regular basis. In recent years, their programs are more tied together, creating linkages that begin to weave a web of transnational rules and regulations'.

[16] Joost HB Pauwelyn, Ramses A Wessel and Jan Wouters, 'When Structures Become Shackles: Stagnation and Dynamics in International Lawmaking' (2014) 25 EJIL 733–763.

[17] See Felicity Vabulas and Duncan Snidal, 'Organizations without Delegation: Informal International Organizations (IIGO) and the Spectrum of Intergovernmental Arrangements' (2013) Rev IOs 193–220.

[18] See n 13.

[19] Angela Di Stasi, 'About Soft International Organizations: An Open Question', in Virzo and Ingravallo (n 14) 44–69.

[20] Simons and Martin (n 5). This publication offers a good overview of the different approaches in IR theory towards international institutions.

[21] Henry G Schermers and Niels M Blokker, *International Institutional Law: Unity within Diversity* (Martinus Nijhoff 2011) at 9.

formal to informal international decision-making as well as to some consequences of this choice. Section II will further explain what we mean by the 'turn to informality' and address some possible explanations for this turn, by assessing reasons for actors to choose certain governance arrangements. Using a social science approach, these theoretical assumptions will then be assessed in the framework of a case study on the International Organization for Standardization (ISO) when dealing with the regulatory governance of nanotechnologies (Section III). Section IV will draw some conclusions.

II. EXPLAINING THE TURN TO INFORMALITY

As also indicated in the introduction to this Chapter, the evidence of a slowdown in formal international law-making has been extensively noted in academic literature.[22] Reasons for this may be both negatively and positively inspired.

II.1. Negative Reasons to Opt for Informal Law

The debate on choosing the most appropriate governance arrangement largely concentrated on the pros and cons of the use of soft law. As indicated by, for instance, Guzman and Meyer, soft law would work well for mere *coordination*, but will be less easy to use to establish *cooperation*.[23] However, the legal scholarly debates have clearly moved beyond the soft law debate and it would be too easy to equate informal with soft and formal with hard rules. The shift from formal to informal international law-making can partly be explained by saturation with the existing treaties and changed policy preferences of States. This goes well beyond the phenomenon of soft law[24] as it addresses not only informal output but also new and informal actors and processes. Moreover, even in

---

[22] See, also for further referencing, Pauwelyn, Wessel and Wouters (n 16); Pauwelyn, Wessel and Wouters (n 11). Credits are due to the co-authors of those publications.

[23] See for instance Andrew T Guzman and Timothy Meyer, 'International Soft Law' (2010) 2 J Leg Analysis 171.

[24] See Jules Basdevant, 'La conclusion et la rédaction des traités et des instruments diplomatiques autres que les traités' (1926) 15 Recueil des Cours 539; Bruno Simma, 'Völkerrecht in der Krise' (1980) 20 ÖZP 280; Anthony Aust, 'The Theory and Practice of Informal International Instruments' (1986) 35 ICLQ 787; Charles Lipson, 'Why Are Some International Agreements Informal?' (1991) 45 Int Org 495–538.

terms of output, there is nothing 'soft', in other words, vague, aspirational or deeply contested about most of the norms and standards developed in recent years. If anything, the process of their development is highly regulated and strict. What characterizes these norms is not so much that they are non-binding under IL (the hallmark of 'soft law') but rather that they are outside traditional IL altogether.[25]

The approach comes close to the different types of 'legalization' used in political science literature. Thus, Abbott et al. define 'legalization' on the basis of three dimensions:

1. *obligation* (States and other actors are bound by a rule or commitment or by a set of rules or commitments);
2. *precision* (rules unambiguously define the conduct they require, authorize or prescribe); and
3. *delegation* (third parties have been granted authority to implement, interpret, and apply the rules).[26]

They argue that

> [e]ach of the dimensions is a matter of degree and graduation, not a rigid dichotomy, and each can vary independently. Consequently, the concept of legalization encompasses a multidimensional continuum, ranging from the 'ideal type' of legalization, where all three properties are maximized; to 'hard' legalization, where all three (or at least obligation and delegation) are high; through multiple forms of partial or 'soft' legalization involving different combinations of attributes; and finally to the complete absence of legalization, another ideal type.[27]

While this variety is also recognized in international legal scholarship, the question is whether informal settings or output do allow actors to escape legal commitments. Obviously, this in turn raises questions about the legal nature of the informal output. Could these decisions be a source of IL? Elsewhere, one of the present authors has tentatively argued that consensus within an international professional community on the best available knowledge and expertise can offer a foundation for legal powers

---

25 As argued earlier by Pauwelyn, Wessel and Wouters (n 11).

26 Kenneth W Abbott, Robert O Keohane, Andrew Moravcsik, Anne-Marie Slaughter and Duncan Snidal, 'The Concept of Legalization', in Judith L Goldstein, Miles Kahler, Robert O Keohane and Anne-Marie Slaughter (eds), *Legalization and World Politics* (MIT Press, 2001) 17–35 at 17.

27 Ibid at 17–18.

to issue exhortations enjoying validity under IL.[28] It is well accepted that not all law or legal norms impose or proscribe specific behaviour or legally binding rights and obligations. Normativity must not be confused with imperativity.[29] Indeed, the debate between those who argue in favour of a bright line between law and non-law,[30] and those arguing for the existence of a grey zone[31] is well known. In practice the divide may not always be clearly visible: 'for the bright line school something may be law; for the grey zone school it may not be law (or fall in the grey zone between law and non-law), but still have legal effects, with little practical difference between the two approaches'.[32] Yet, large parts of the debate have been devoted to the establishment of one or more criteria to decide what makes an instrument law (be it sanctions, formalities, intent, effect, substance, or belief). Thus, depending on how one distinguishes between law and non-law, informal output may or may not be part of IL. If formalities or intent matter, a lot of the informal output would not be law. If, in contrast, effect or substantive factors decide, a lot would be law.[33]

We may indeed have to focus more on the actual effects and the acceptance of the norms as playing a role in legal orders, but we feel that acceptance cannot be decoupled from the origin of the norms both in terms of the authority (or authorities) they emanate from and their procedural pedigree. Many of the case studies in the informal international law-making project indicate that the acceptance of the norms – and perhaps

---

[28] Dick WP Ruiter and Ramses A Wessel, 'The Legal Nature of Informal International Law: A Legal Theoretical Exercise', in Pauwelyn, Wessel and Wouters (n 11) 162–184.

[29] André Lalande, *Vocabulaire technique et critique de la philosophie* (Presses Universitaires de France 1993), *sub verbo* 'Normatif'.

[30] For example, Prosper Weil, 'Towards Relative Normativity in International Law?' (1983) 77 AJIL 413–442 at 417–418; Jan Klabbers, 'The Redundancy of Soft Law' (1996) 65 Nord J Int L 167–182 at 181; and Jan Klabbers 'The Undesirability of Soft Law' (1998) 67 Nord J Int L 381–391.

[31] For example, Richard R Baxter, 'International Law in *Her Infinite Variety*'(1980) 29 ICLQ 549–566; and Oscar Schachter, 'The Twilight Existence of Nonbinding International Agreements' (1997) 71 AJIL 296–304.

[32] Joost HB Pauwelyn, 'Informal International Lawmaking: Framing the Concept and Research Questions', in Pauwelyn, Wessel and Wouters (n 11) 13–34.

[33] See on this debate Jan Klabbers, 'Law-making and Constitutionalism', in Jan Klabbers, Anne Peters and Geir Ulf (eds), *The Constitutionalization of International Law* (OUP 2009) 81–125; as well as Pauwelyn, Wessel and Wouters (n 11).

their legitimacy – is based on the fact that they are created by people who know what they are talking about and in such a way that takes account of many (if not always all) affected stakeholders. 'Expertise-based legitimacy' or 'executive authority' are not new phenomena but may form a key to a more inclusive understanding of international norms. Again, this is not groundbreaking. As argued by Paul Craig, in national polities also, law-making is legitimated in three ways:

1. through legislative oversight/imprimatur from the top;
2. through participation from the bottom by input from those affected by the rules; or
3. through executive authority combined with technocratic expertise.[34]

While the second way (that is, participation) is relevant for informal international law-making as well, the fact that only a limited number of stakeholders may be involved renders the third possibility (that is, executive authority) equally relevant. However, 'executive authority' is usually used to describe (or promote) the role of 'the executive' in situations of secondary rule-making in (domestic) constitutional systems.[35]

In the case of informal international law-making, however, it is not about authority to make secondary norms on the basis of primary legislation, it is in fact about primary norms. This may make it difficult to apply the 'executive authority' argument in our case.

In addition, the technocratic (rather than the bureaucratic) version of executive authority seems to suffer from a changing societal attitude towards technocratic expertise.[36] This, obviously, may have consequences for the extent to which the norm-setters can actually be seen as

[34] Paul Craig, 'Postnational Rulemaking: Conceptions of Legitimacy' Unpublished paper presented at the conference *Postnational Rulemaking between Authority and Autonomy*, University of Amsterdam, 20–21 September 2012.

[35] See Paul Craig and Adam Tomkins (eds), *The Executive and Public Law: Power and Accountability in Comparative Perspective* (OUP 2005); and, with regard to the EU, Deirdre M Curtin, *Executive Power of the European Union: Law, Practices and the Living Constitution* (OUP 2009).

[36] Craig and Tomkins (n 35) at 25: 'There is less trust in technocracy than there was a generation ago. The idea that we should trust in those who know best, and that those with technical expertise should be regarded as primus inter pares in this respect, is now viewed with greater scepticism. The related idea that science provides 'objective' answers to certain problems that have to be dealt with in the political arena, has likewise come under strain. It has been recognized that the "answer" may be contentious in scientific terms, and that any one version of the scientific solution may embody value judgments of a social, moral

representing the final addressees of the norms,[37] and whether 'expertise' can form an additional source for legal norms.[38]

II.2. Positive Reasons to Opt for Informal Law

Much has been written in general on the question of why States cooperate and are willing to create and expand international institutions. The most common approach to this question seems to be the functionalist approach.[39] Functionalists' starting points are also used to explain the choice for formal or informal settings as they theorize about 'the respective advantages and disadvantages of formal and informal approaches in responding to problems of collective action, incomplete contracting, and uncertainty, and making predictions about the conditions under which States might choose formal or informal approaches to lawmaking'.[40] Indeed, these types of arguments have generally formed the basis for the debate on soft law in international relations. Thus, Abbott and Snidal have argued that

> international actors choose softer forms of legalized governance when those forms offer superior institutional solutions. [...] By using hard law to order their relations, international actors reduce transaction costs, strengthen the credibility of their commitments, expand their available political strategies, and resolve problems of incomplete contracting. Doing so, however, also entails significant costs: hard law restricts actors' behaviour and even their sovereignty.[41]

---

or political nature, even if such factors are not immediately apparent on the face of the decision.'

37 William Wallace and Julie Smith, 'Democracy or Technocracy? European Integration and the Problem of Popular Consent', in Jack ES Hayward (ed), *The Crisis of Representation in Europe* (Frank Cass 1995) 137–157 at 140.

38 See for recent contributions in various policy fields: Alberto Alemanno, 'Science and EU Risk Regulation: The Role of Experts in Decision-Making and Judicial Review', in Ellen Vos, *European Risk Governance: Its Science, its Inclusiveness and its Effectiveness* (Connex Report Series 2008); Monika Ambrus, Karin Arts, Helena Raulus and Ellen Hey (eds), *Irrelevant, Advisors or Decision-Makers? The Role of 'Experts' in International Decision-Making* (CUP 2013).

39 Cf. recently also Trachtman, *The Future of International Law* (n 2) at 13–18, who at the same time links functionalism to new institutional economics.

40 Mark A Pollack and Gregory C Shaffer, 'The Interaction of Formal and Informal Lawmaking', in Pauwelyn, Wessel and Wouters (n 11) 241–270 at 244.

41 Kenneth W Abbott and Duncan Snidal, 'Hard and Soft Law in International Governance', in Goldstein et al. (n 26) 37–72 at 37–38.

The hard- or softness of the legalization is then measured against the extent of obligation, precision and delegation.

Similar arguments were made by Di Stasi, who argued that

> countries choose soft IOs when they value rapid decision-making and confidentiality, when they prefer to have a broad range of issues on which the body's activity can be centred according to subjective and/or objective changing circumstances, when they want to start an activity of soft cooperation representing the first step in the creation of a formal international organization, *etc*.'[42]

At the same time, Pollack and Shaffer have made a case for a 'distributive approach', to 'help explain why and under what conditions formal and informal procedures can interact as antagonist as well as complements'.[43] They point to the fact that

> [i]n a setting of distributive conflict, IN-LAW [informal law-making] procedures can provide alternative fora within which coalitions of States – and of non-State actors frozen out of participation in formal treaty-making – can advocate for their preferred international norms or counter-norms that would otherwise be out of reach'.[44]

As stated above, formalities have to do with *output*, *process* or the *actors involved*. At the same time, escaping these same formalities is also what is said to make informal law more desirable and effective. Lipson, for example, explains that 'informality is best understood as a device for minimizing the impediments to cooperation, at both the domestic and international levels'.[45] Indeed, in today's increasingly complex and fast-paced world, informality may not only be the less costly option – with new technologies cutting down communication costs, the participation of diverse stakeholders through novel processes has become less costly – it may also be the more effective option, in that a treaty or formal international organization can be too rigid and States may not be able to do it alone (due to limited resources, knowledge or implementation capacity).[46]

---

[42] Angela Di Stasi, 'About Soft International Organizations: An Open Question' (n 19).

[43] Pollack and Shaffer (n 40) at 244.

[44] Ibid at 269.

[45] Lipson (n 24) at 500.

[46] Similar arguments are observed also by Sigrid Quack, 'Law, Expertise and Legitimacy in Transnational Economic Governance: An Introduction' (2010) 8 Socio Econ Rev 5–7; Evisa Kica, and Diana M Bowman, 'Regulation by

Yet, in making the choice for formal or informal settings or output, actors are aware of the fact that in practice this distinction may be less relevant and classic 'legalization' criteria may be less helpful. Informal rules can be committing, quite precise and the authority to implement, interpret, and apply the rules may be delegated to certain third parties. In one of his contributions to the 'Informal International Lawmaking' project, Pauwelyn pointed to one of the ironies inherent in the choice for formal (or hard) IL. He raised the following question: 'if making an instrument legally binding under international law may not make much of a difference anyhow, why should negotiators be so afraid of making something legally binding? Rather than a move away from law we should then perhaps see a move back to international law'.[47] This underlines that the question of why international actors opt for either formal or informal cooperation is much more complex and political science and institutional economics have only been able to provide part of the answer. The turn to informality seems to be much more related to the involvement of non-State actors in norm-setting and the realization by State actors that it is simply impossible (and indeed perhaps not at all necessary) to mould all their agreements into traditional formal legal instruments. International cooperation has moved from agreements on general larger issues, to detailed, often quite technical, issues. At the same time, classic explanations referring to the need for legal certainty and stability to reduce (transaction) costs seem to be confronted with a need for flexibility, to be able to take new and fast (technological) developments into account and prevent IL from being outdated the moment a consensus on a treaty provision has been reached.

In the following Sections we discuss the turn to informality more specifically in relation to newly emerging technologies. The high level of scientific uncertainties and lack of sufficient knowledge have been considered by many as key factors for pushing State actors to rely on IOs, and their activities in regulating these complex issues.[48] In the

---

Means of Standardization: Key Legitimacy Issues of Health and Safety Nanotechnology Standards' (2011) 53 Jurimetrics 11–56.

[47] Joost HB Pauwelyn, 'Is it International Law or Not, and Does it Even Matter?', in Pauwelyn, Wessel and Wouters (n 11) at 151.

[48] See, for example: Christopher J Bosso, 'Policy Consequences of the *Next Industrial Revolution*', in Christopher J Bosso (eds), *Governing Uncertainty: Environmental Regulation in the Age of Nanotechnology* (RFF Press 2010); Karin Bäckstrand, 'Science, Uncertainty and Participation in Global Environmental Governance' (2004) 13 Environmental Politics 650–656; Fabrizio Cantelli, Naonori Kodate and Kristian Krieger, 'Towards Democratic Governance of

following we focus on the field of nanotechnologies,[49] an emerging technology which is expected to provide the next 'industrial revolution' but at the same time, the regulation of which has generated many debates amongst State and non-State actors. By analysing the role of international standards in the field of nanotechnologies, we aim to reflect much more on the extent to which State actors accept the rules set by IOs, such as the ISO. In earlier work the present authors[50] discussed six attributes according to which the potential of the particular transnational/ international arrangements to contribute to the regulatory governance of nanotechnologies can be explained. These attributes include:

1. the *actors involved* in governance arrangements;
2. the *functions* related to such arrangements or organizations;
3. their *degree of institutionalization*;
4. the *regulatory stages* in which they contribute; as well as
5. the *normative scope*; and
6. the *substantive depth* of transnational/international outcomes.

However, what this research does not explain is how these organizations are accepted in practice. In other words, what are the perceptions of actors in relation to this informality turn to IOs. The following Section aims to contribute to answering that question.

Uncertainty? Contesting Notions of Participation, Control And Accountability' (2011) 14 J Risk R 919–932; Geoffrey Hunt and Michael Riediker, 'Building Expert Consensus on Problems of Uncertainty and Complexity Nanomaterial Safety' (2011) 7 Nanotechnology Perceptions 82–98; Robert Falkner and Nico Jaspers, 'Regulating Nanotechnologies: Risk, Uncertainty and the Global Governance Gap' (2012) 12 Global Environmental Politics 30–55.

[49] The term 'nanotechnologies' refers to technologies that are executed on a scale of nanometers (nm). These technologies concern the application and use of materials, structures, devices and systems, which have new properties and functions due to their small size that ranges between 1 to 100 nm, as well as their ability to manipulate materials at this scale.

[50] Evisa Kica and Ramses A Wessel, 'Transnational Arrangements in the Governance of Emerging Technologies: The Case of Nanotechnology', in Elen Stokes, Diana Bowman and Arie Rip (eds), *Embedding and Governing New Technologies: A Regulatory, Ethical & Societal Perspective* (Pan Stanford Publishing 2016) (forthcoming).

III. CASE STUDY: INFORMALITY AND ITS CONSEQUENCES IN THE FIELD OF NANOTECHNOLOGY

As indicated above, a turn to informality may be discovered in many different policy fields. Yet, informal regulation has become particularly popular in areas where technical expertise is crucial and supersedes national political interests and preferences. While one might assume that scientific expertise would enhance the legitimacy and acceptance of the norms,[51] the question is whether that is actually the case. The scope of this Chapter does not allow us to extensively study this topic. Instead we chose to focus on a topical issue area and an international (informal) organization which is well known, more as an illustration than as a case on the basis of which generalized conclusion can be drawn. At the same time, by using a social science approach, this case study allows us to help understand a legal development that cannot be explained on the basis of legal doctrinal analysis itself.

III.1. ISO Technical Committee on Nanotechnology (ISO/TC229)

ISO commenced its work in 1947. It develops international standards with a view to 'facilitating trade, spreading knowledge, disseminating innovative advances in technology, as well as sharing good management and conformity assessment practices'.[52] As of the beginning of 2014, ISO has developed over 19,000 standards.[53] These standards are expected to provide benefits for almost all sectors, such as 'agriculture, engineering, construction, manufacturing, transport, medical devices, information and

---

[51] See for example: Martin Carrier, 'Scientific Knowledge and Scientific Expertise: Epistemic and Social Conditions of Their Trustworthiness' (2011) Analyse & Kritik 195–212; Quack (n 46) at 5–7; Anne Peters, Lucy Koechlin and Gretta F Zinkernagel, 'Non-State Actors as Standard Setters: Framing The Issue in an Interdisciplinary Fashion', in Anne Peters et al. (eds), *Nonstate Actors as Standard Setters* (CUP 2009); Brian Hilligoss and Soo Y Rieh, 'Developing a Unifying Framework of Credibility Assessment: Construct, Heuristics, and Interaction in Context' (2008) Information Processing and Management 1467–1484; Silvio Funtowicz and Roger Strand, 'Change and Commitment: Beyond Risk And Responsibility' (2011) 14 J Risk R 995–1003.

[52] ISO, 'ISO Strategic Plan: 2011-205, Solutions to Global Challenges' (2011), available at http://www.iso.org/iso/iso_strategic_plan_2011-2015.pdf.

[53] See: *ISO Standards in Action*, available at http://www.iso.org/iso/home/news_index/iso-in-action.htm.

communication technologies, the environment, conformity assessment and services'.[54]

ISO moved into the arena of nanotechnologies relatively recently. The official functioning of TC 229 however started in November 2005, with the first plenary meeting in London. Functionality and the need to develop an institutional structure for TC 229 and Working Groups (WGs), as well as a strategic policy statement and the business plan, drove much of the first meetings. TC 229 consists of four WGs working on:

1. *Terminology and Nomenclature* – WG1 – develops uniform terminology and nomenclature for nanotechnologies to facilitate communication and promote common understanding;
2. *Measurement and Characterization* – WG2 – develops measurement and characterization standards for use by industry in nanotechnology-based products;
3. *Health, Safety and Environment* – WG3 – develops science-based standards that aim to promote occupational safety, consumer protection and environmental protection;[55] and
4. *Material Specifications* – WG4 – develops standards that specify relevant characteristics of engineered nanoscale materials for use in specific applications.

WGs conduct the main work at TC 229 (ISO/IEC 2012). Experts, who are individually appointed by a participating ISO member body, a *liaison* organization or both, carry out the main tasks within the WGs. The inclusion of various WGs with different aims and objectives emphasizes that TC 229 has shifted the focus from working only on technical issues related to defining the size and concept of nanomaterials, to addressing broader aspects of the technology, such as risk management, health, environment and safety issues.[56] Furthermore, in 2011 TC 229 took a leading role in developing a guidance document related to the labelling of nanomaterials, which complements the current regulatory initiatives on

---

54 ISO (n 52) at 2.

55 ISO, 'ISO TC/229 Business Plan 8' (2012), available at http://isotc.iso.org/livelink/livelink/fetch/2000/2122/687806/customview.html?func=ll&objId=687806&*objAction*=browse&sort=name.

56 Evisa Kica and Diana Bowman, 'Transnational Governance Arrangements: Legitimate Alternatives to Regulating Nanotechnologies?' (2013) 7 NanoEthics 69–82.

the labelling of food and cosmetic products containing manufactured nano-objects.

Following this evolution in the development of nanotechnology standards, in 2009 the former chair of TC 229 stated that ISO standards now serve three key objectives:

1. supporting commercialization and market development;
2. providing a basis for procurement through technical, quality and environmental management; and
3. supporting appropriate regulation and voluntary governance structures.[57]

In this way, TC 229 and its standards seem to have multiple functions. Furthermore, the Committee provides a forum for debate for various stakeholders. Its plenary meetings organized every tenth month of the year, as well as WG meetings provide opportunities for experts to meet with other delegates, exchange information on standardization issues and set uniform standards. As of March 2015, TC 229 has had 17 plenary meetings, followed by many other conferences and expert meetings. ISO applies the principle of national delegation and its administrative work takes place through a Secretariat located in one of the National Standardization Bodies (NSBs).[58] Delegates participate in ISO/TC meetings in negotiations and consultations. There are 34 participatory ('P') and 14 observatory ('O') members involved in the work of TC 229.

ISO has established procedures for including industrial actors as well as other actors in the standardization process.[59] Within ISO the participating actors are divided into: industry and trade associations; consumer associations; governments and regulators; as well as societal and other interests. TC 229 has a number of collaborations and relationships with other organizations and standardization bodies as well.[60] These stakeholders are known as *liaison* members, and include, amongst others,

---

[57] Peter Hatto, 'Innovative Approaches to Nanotechnology Environmental Governance: Standardization – In Support of 'Nanogovernance' (2008) Presentation at The George Washington University Law School Nanogovernance, available at http://www.nanogovernance.com/images/Hatto.pdf.

[58] ISO/IEC, 'Directives Part 1: Procedures for the Technical Work 1' (2012), available at http://www.jisc.go.jp/international/pdf/isoiec_directives_part1_2012.pdf.

[59] Ellen-Marie Forsberg, 'The Role of ISO in the Governance of Nanotechnology' (2010) Work Research Institute of Norway 1–76.

[60] David S Ensor, 'Update on ISO Nanotechnology Standards Activities' (2007) Clean Rooms 12, 12–13.

groups concerned with the rights of consumers, workers and the environment.[61] TC 229 has also established two Task Groups (TGs) working on Sustainability (TGS) and on Consumer and Societal Dimensions (TGCSDN).[62] These TGs advise TC 229 on the priorities for standards development in the area of consumer and societal dimensions, and the mechanisms that the Committee may develop to receive input from consumer, societal or other relevant organizations.[63]

After analyzing the functioning of the TC 229, we looked at the perceptions of State actors to understand the extent to which transnational rules set by ISO are accepted and followed in practice. In particular we conducted 14 surveys with actors coming from governmental and regulatory agencies (n=14). The questions, as we shall see in the next Section, focused on the procedural pedigree of the TC 229, expertise, as well as the outcomes of this Committee.

III.2. The Perceptions of State Actors on Informal Transnational Rules Set By International Organizations

As this Chapter mainly aims at shedding more light on the shift from formal to informal governance arrangements, our focus is on the 'public' participants in these arrangements. In particular, we conducted 14 interviews with actors coming from regulatory and governmental agencies. We set up a survey questionnaire consisting of 65 questions that focused on:

A. The decision-making process: we asked respondents in the survey to indicate their level of involvement in the process as well as the extent to which they felt included in the process and were able to communicate with other members in the committee. Questions on the process related also to the ability of these actors to access the documents and decisions of the Committee. More specifically, as emphasized in Table 6.1, questions related to whether:

1. the international organization provided appropriate opportunities and resources for these actors to participate actively in developing transnational rules. In particular we looked at:

---

[61] Such as for example the European Consumer Voice in Standardization (ANEC); the European Environmental Citizens Organization for Standardization (ECOS); the European Trade Union Institute (ETUI).

[62] ISO (n 52) at 8.

[63] Ibid.

   (a) *inclusiveness* – which refers to the scope of stakeholder participation, in particular, to the possibility for as many stakeholders as possible to get involved in a governance arrangement;
   (b) *representation* – which refers to the quality of participation. It denotes the commitment of the transnational governing authority to ensure that the active participation of a wide range of stakeholders is guaranteed in practice, regardless of their differences;[64] and
   (c) *resources* – which refers to the allocation of resources provided to participants to support their inclusion in relevant arrangements of technology regulation;[65]
2. the international organization provided appropriate opportunities for these actors to contribute to the decision-making process, communicate and discuss the reasons on which decisions are based, and develop solutions through cooperation and joint agreements. In particular we looked at:
   (a) *participatory decision-making* – which refers to the extent to which participants have the appropriate opportunities to present and amend proposals during the setting of transnational rules;[66]
   (b) *comprehensive agreements* – which refers to the extent to which a governance arrangement provides for the sincere consideration of the arguments of the participants; and
   (c) *communicative agreements* – which refers to the quality of interaction amongst participants to achieve acceptable regulatory outcomes;[67]

---

[64] See Klaus Dingwerth, *The New Transnationalism: Transnational Governance and Democratic Legitimacy* (Palgrave Macmillan 2007) at 41; Ingo Take, 'Regulating the Internet Infrastructure: A Comparative Appraisal of the Legitimacy of ICANN, ITU and WSIS' (2012) 6 Regulation and Governance 499–523.

[65] Timothy Cadman, *Quality and Legitimacy of Global Governance* (Palgrave Macmillan 2012); Ellen-Marie Forsberg, 'Standardization in the Field of Nanotechnology: Some Issues of Legitimacy' (2012) 18 Science and Engineering Ethics 719–739.

[66] Victor Bekkers and Arthur Edwards, 'Legitimacy and Democracy: A Conceptual Framework for Assessing Governance Practices', in Victor Bekkers et al. (eds), *Governance and the Democratic Deficit* (Ashgate Publishing 2007) at 35–61; Dingwerth (n 64).

[67] Marianne Beisheim and Klaus Dingwerth, 'Procedural Legitimacy and Private Transnational Governance: Are the Good Ones Doing Better?' (2008) SFB-Governance Working Paper Series 9, Berlin; Cadman (n 65).

3. the international organization provides appropriate mechanisms of transparency and accountability and ensures that actors have a realistic chance of being heard. In particular we looked at:
   (a) *transparency* – which refers to the readiness of the rule-maker to share information and open up the process to affected stakeholders;[68] and
   (b) *accountability* – which refers to the internal institutionalized procedures that compel the agent to inform and justify their actions, and be held to account by individuals or groups with whom the agent is institutionally linked.[69]

B. Expertise: we asked respondents in the survey about their perceptions of whether they consider ISO to ensure that transnational rules derive from highly-qualified experts, and are based on accurate and reliable scientific information, as well as robust evidence. More specifically we looked at four elements:

(a) *competent expertise* – which refers to the familiarity, the skills and the experience of the rule-makers/participants with the technicalities of the relevant domain;[70]
(b) *robustness* – which refers to the extent to which the decisions of the participants are based on scientifically robust evidence that remains largely constant even in cases when the factual conditions change or are unknown;[71]
(c) *scientific validity* – which refers to the ability of participants to provide for reliable and verified results, which are scientifically relevant to the issue at stake;[72] and

---

[68] Dingwerth (n 64).

[69] Mark Bovens, 'Analysing and Assessing Accountability: A Conceptual Framework' (2007) 13 ELJ 447–468; Robert O Keohane, 'Global Governance and Democratic Accountability', in David Held and Mathias Koenig-Archibugi (eds), *Taming Globalization: Frontiers of Governance* (Polity Press 2003) at 130–160.

[70] Hilligoss and Rieh (n 51) at 1467–1484; Funtowicz and Strand (n 51) at 995–1003.

[71] Carrier (n 51) at 195–212.

[72] Eva Lövbrand, Roger Pielke and Silke Beck, 'A Democracy Paradox in Studies of Science and Technology' (2011) 36 Science, Technology and Human Values 474–496.

(d) *objective judgements* – which refers to the independency of participants from politics or other individual interests.[73]

C. Benefits of the rules: our main focus here was to see the perceptions of State actors on whether they found ISO to provide outcomes that solve collective problems, are understandable, beneficial and followed by in practice. Therefore we looked at four elements, such as: *problem-solving capacity, rule clarity, rule benefits* and *compliance:*

(a) *problem-solving capacity* – which refers to the capacity of transnational rules to solve the problems they were created (or are expected) to address;[74]
(b) *rule benefits* – is closely related to problem solving because it also refers to the potential of the transnational rules. However, this attribute is more narrow in content, since it aims to demonstrate the extent to which transnational rules correspond to the individual interests of stakeholders;[75]
(c) *rule clarity* – indicates the extent to which transnational rules are clearly drafted and understandable;[76] and
(d) *compliance* – relates to the willingness of the ruled to act in accordance with transnational rules.[77]

The perceptions of State actors in relation to the decision-making process, expertise and rule benefits were evaluated using a Likert scale ranked from 1 (very low) to 5 (very high). The cumulative values given by respondents on each of the attributes indicated in Table 6.1 emphasize

---

[73] Yannis Papadopoulos, 'Problems of Democratic Accountability in Network and Multilevel Governance' (2007) 13 ELJ 476–486.

[74] Fritz W Scharpf, *Governing in Europe: Effective and Democratic* (OUP 1999); Fritz W Scharpf, 'Problem-Solving Effectiveness and Democratic Accountability in the EU' (2006) Political Science Series 107; Neil Gunningham, 'Enforcement and Compliance Strategies', in Robert Baldwin, Martin Cave and Martin Lodge (eds), *The Oxford Handbook of Regulation* (OUP 2010) at 120–146.

[75] Renate Mayntz, 'Legitimacy and Compliance in Transnational Governance' (2010) MPIfG Working Paper 10/5, Max Planck Institute for the Study of Societies, Cologne.

[76] Martha Finnemore and Stephen J Toope, 'Alternatives to "legalization": Richer Views of Law and Politics', (2001) 55 Int Org 3, 743–758.

[77] Ibid at 743; Helen Keller, 'Corporate Codes of Conduct and their Implementation: The Question of Legitimacy' (2006), available at http://www.yale.edu/macmillan/Heken_Keller_Paper.pdf; Mayntz (n 75).

the extent to which actors coming from governmental and regulatory agencies perceive the decision-making processes, expertise and rule benefits as leading factors of informal international law-making.

By looking at Table 6.1 we can observe that State actors seem relatively satisfied (mean = 3.7) with their level of participation and representation on nanotechnology standardization activities. In the survey, however, respondents identified several barriers, which as they argue, impacted their participation in nanotechnology standardization activities. Respondents considered the travelling expenses, lack of human resources/personnel and lack of time, to be amongst the main barriers to their participation in nanotechnology standardization activities. However, the provision of resources appears to be a major barrier for these respondents. The fact that some NSBs finance themselves through membership fees has caused many concerns amongst actors coming from these groups, who fear that these practices may lead to a participation gap of under-resourced groups. At the international level, ISO and its TCs, including TC 229, are reliant on harnessing technical expertise and building consensus between the different sectors and jurisdictions that make up its constituency. However, for the most part, TC 229 is open to members who pay their own membership fees. This 'pay-to-play' requirement has led to the under-representation of actors coming from the not-for-profit arena. ISO has taken several initiatives to assist the participation of developing countries in the standardization process, including for example the establishment of the Committee on Developing Country Matters (DEVCO) and Committee on Consumer Policy (COPOLCO).[78] The data from the survey suggest that non-industrial actors coming from less developed countries seem relatively satisfied with these initiatives, but recommend that more needs to be done on the way these actors are involved in the process.

Regarding the contribution that State actors have made to the setting of international standards, the formal procedures of the ISO emphasize that there are several stages in the development of standards, which provide an opportunity for various stakeholders to influence the technical specifications and the final draft of a standard.[79] The process of developing standards indicates that inclusion in the decision-making is important for various actors to communicate their interests and shape the development of international standards. At this point, it is important to note, that

---

[78] ISO (n 52).

[79] For a detailed description of the stages of the development of the ISO standards see: Kica and Bowman (n 46) at 11–56.

whereas 'P' members have a more active role in the process by commenting on the proposals from the initial to the final stages, the 'O' members and liaison organizations are allowed to nominate experts to work on projects, but have no right to vote. However, the survey data suggest that respondents from governmental and regulatory agencies were generally active participants in TC 229 and perceive the process to be relatively deliberative (mean = 3.8).

Decisions on draft standardization proposals, including the technical content of TC 229 standards, are taken through consensus, whereas approvals on final standardization proposals depend on member ballots. In ISO each country has one vote. However, the process of achieving consensus on the purpose and the technical content of the standard involves a mixture of bargaining and arguing amongst participants until resolution of all significant technical disagreements is achieved.[80] As such, the contribution of the experts and the extent to which their perspectives are taken into account impacts highly on the content of the final draft of the standard. Formally, the best opportunities for the experts to meet with other delegates and make rapid progress in developing a particular document are the 'plenary week' meetings of the TC 229.[81] These meetings are face-to-face and are held every tenth month of the year in various countries of the world. The meetings aim to bring experts together to discuss relevant standardization issues that have come up in previous teleconference discussions, to meet with colleagues from different projects, or to discuss future work.

Therefore, as Delemarle and Holst indicate, these meetings provide invaluable opportunities for participants to network, discuss and lobby.[82] The discussions take place during the working group meetings, in which experts interested in particular areas participate to contribute to the debate. When decisions are not made the discussions continue through teleconferencing. The mean scores provided in Table 6.1 for comprehensive and communicative agreements (that is, mean 3.8) emphasize that State actors are relatively satisfied with the opportunities they have had to

---

[80] ISO (n 52).

[81] Peter Hatto, 'Standards and Standardization: A Practical Guide for Researchers' (2010) 4–5, European Commission Directorate-General for Research & Innovation, available at http://ec.europa.eu/research/industrial_technologies/pdf/practical-standardisation-guide-for-researchers_en.pdf.

[82] Aurélie Delemarle and Harald Th Holst, 'The Role of Standardization in the Shaping of a Vision for Nanotechnology' (2012) 10 Int J Innovat Tech Manag 20.

influence the content of the standards and communicate with other members in the committee.

The organizational structure of the TC 229 allows for a high degree of expertise through the national mirror committees, working groups, task groups as well as liaison organizations. In their analysis of TC 229 plenary meetings, Kica and Bowman observe that a wide range of experts are involved to develop international standards.[83] The majority of experts in the process are chemists, physicists and engineers by background, with toxicologists, occupational health practitioners, industrial hygienists, pharmacologists, academics and other socio-environmental actors having a lower representation. The role of knowledgeable experts is considered important for the development of new work item proposals or the approval of other standardization proposals.[84] However, in her study of nanotechnology standardization, Ellen-Marie Forsberg indicates that experts at national level have the tendency to vote positively on certain decisions rather than abstain or be against them, even in cases when the standardization committee lacks the expertise to assess the proposals.[85] These issues appear to have been acknowledged by the TC 229 with the former Chairman advising NSBs to introduce additional – unwritten – questions to the ballot form, which would ask delegates to indicate if they have the appropriate expertise to comment on the documents.[86]

Expertise and expert knowledge in TC 229 are highly evaluated by State actors. As emphasized in Table 6.1 competent expertise has the highest mean score (mean = 3.9) compared to other attributes related to expertise, which emphasizes that respondents are highly satisfied with the knowledge of experts that contribute to the setting of TC 229 standards. In the literature on IOs, scholars often use expert knowledge as a key element for legitimating the activities of these organizations as well as their standards.[87] This is because standardization committees are considered to provide forums that consist of actors having considerable

---

[83] Kica and Bowman (n 56) at 69.

[84] Hatto (n 81) at 4–5.

[85] Forsberg (n 59) at 70.

[86] Peter Hatto and Stuart MacLachlan, 'Standardizing Nanotechnologies' (December 2010) Materials World Magazine.

[87] Olivier Borraz, 'Governing Standards: The Rise of Standardization Process in France and in the EU' (2007) 20 Governance: An International Journal of Policy, Administration, and Institutions 57–84; Bengt Jacobsson, 'Standardization and Expert Knowledge', in Nils Brunsson and Bengt Jacobsson (eds), *A World of Standards* (OUP 2002) at 40–49.

knowledge in the field concerned.[88] The results of the survey emphasize that experts participating in the WGs of TC 229 are considered highly knowledgeable and experienced by their peers on issues related to nanotechnologies. The development of nanotechnology standards, as the respondents generally argue, relies on expert knowledge, founded mainly in private companies, research institutes, governmental and regulatory agencies. However, in the WGs we observed a domination of the views of the respondents coming from industry, research institutes and governmental agencies, who have a background in chemistry, materials science and physics.

The domination of some actors in the process raises many questions about the extent to which experts are independent in their decisions and judgements at TC 229. We have come to learn from various scholars that the main reason why private organizations, and in particular SDOs, are trusted to contribute to setting various rules, is because they are considered to provide the best solutions, that derive from highly qualified and independent experts.[89] However, in TC 229 the independency of experts is perceived to be low (mean = 3.3). As argued by some respondents (that is, five respondents), some WG members have a tendency to support proposals based on their country or employers' priorities, rather than on the technical merits of such proposals.

Besides objectivity, a number of respondents appear concerned with the scientific basis of the nanotechnology standards. In its business plan, TC 229 commits itself to developing high quality standards that promote the best available knowledge and practices in the production, use and disposal of nanomaterials, nanotechnology products and nanotechnology enabled systems. The need for standards to be based on scientifically valid and robust results has been acknowledged in various documents and reports.[90] However, the lack of diverse experts, as well as the lack of sufficient scientific knowledge and certainty on relevant nanotechnology

---

[88] Michelle Egan, *Constructing a European Market* (OUP 2001).

[89] Kai Jakobs, 'How People and Stakeholders Shape Standards – the Case of IEEE 802.11', in *Proceedings of WEBIST, Institute for Systems and Technologies of Information, Control and Communication* (2010); Kristina T Hallström and Magnus Boström, *Transnational Multi-Stakeholder Organization: Organizing Fragile Non-State Authority* (Edward Elgar 2010).

[90] See, for example, ISO/IEC (n 58); Markus Widmer, Christoph Meili, Elvio Mantovani and Andrea Porcari, 'The Framing Nano Governance Platform: A New Integrated Approach to The Responsible Development of Nanotechnologies' (2010) http://www.innovationsgesellschaft.ch/media/archive2/publikationen/FramingNano_Complete_Final_Report.pdf.

issues, seem to be the main challenges which, as the respondents argue, call into question the validity and robustness of the results guiding the development of nanotechnology standards.

Several questions guided our survey on the problem-solving capacity of the standardization outcomes set by TC 229. The business plan of TC 229 indicates that the key objectives of this Committee are to develop (amongst others) standards that:

1. reduce scientific uncertainties and contribute to the smooth transition of the products to the marketplace;
2. support the introduction and use of nanotechnologies to new applications and markets and facilitate global trade; and
3. support regulation, develop risk assessment tools and occupational health protocols in the area of nanotechnologies.[91]

To understand the perceptions of stakeholders on the problem-solving capacity of standardization outcomes, respondents were asked to indicate the extent to which they perceive TC 229 standards to fulfil the global aims that are emphasized in the business plan (in other words, to reduce scientific uncertainties, enable risk and regulatory analysis, facilitate global trade). The perceptions of the respondents emphasize that there is a considerable difference between the stated goals of TC 229, as well as the perceived benefits and problem-solving capacity of TC 229 standards. The results of the survey emphasize that respondents are relatively satisfied with the effectiveness of the TC 229 standards to solve the issues indicated in the business plan. This is verified by the mean 3.6, which on a scale of 1 (very low) to 5 (very high) corresponds to 'medium' level of effectiveness (see Table 6.1). However, when asked about the benefits that TC 229 standards provide to the organizations with which State actors surveyed in this study were associated, respondents perceived these deliverables to be relatively beneficial (mean = 3.4). An explanation for this could be also the fact that compliance with TC 229 standards remains low amongst State actors (mean = 2.0). The clarity of the rules is also perceived to be lower than other attributes related to the benefits of TC 229 standards. As such the overall mean score (mean = 3.0) is much lower than the scores given for the decision-making process and expertise. This is interesting given that State actors, such as those associated with governmental and regulatory agencies, have been active in influencing the setting of these deliverables. The survey

[91] ISO (n 52) at 8.

responses seem to suggest that higher inclusiveness and participation in the decision-making process did not lead governmental and regulatory agencies to perceive TC 229 outcomes as more beneficial and effective in solving various issues at global level nor as resulting in higher compliance with these transnational rules. In fact, these actors appear to be generally more concerned with the benefits and problem-solving capacity of TC 229 standards. The weaknesses of the standards with regard to these points seem to be attributed partially to the fact that the majority of standards developed at TC 229 are not followed in practice, but also to the nature of the deliverables produced by TC 229 and the experience of the respondents with TC 229 deliverables. Only two respondents comply with TC 229 standards. This may be, in part, due to the brief life span of these deliverables (in other words, the majority of TC 229 deliverables are set after 2009) as well as uncertainties characterizing the field of nanotechnologies.[92] Furthermore, given that the majority of deliverables produced by TC 229 are process standards, compliance seems to be costly for most of the respondents.

Most of the TC 229 deliverables are process (horizontal) standards. As of March 2015, there were over 40 deliverables published under the direct responsibility of TC 229. As articulated in the TC 229 business plan, the Committee has given priority to developing horizontal standards

---

[92] Scientific reviews, such as those carried out by the *United Kingdom's Royal Society and Royal Academy of Engineering* in 2004, the *United Kingdom's Royal Commission on Environmental Protection* in 2008 and the *Center for International Environmental Law* in 2012, emphasize that there are scientific and knowledge gaps on the hazardous components, the specific properties of the components, the behaviour of nanomaterials in the environment and/or living organisms, as well as the duration of the anticipated levels of exposure. Significant uncertainties similarly exist in relation to how human exposure to nanomaterials may occur in different environments (for example, exposure from inhalation, oral or dermal penetration), as well as how it can be controlled and measured. There are many uncertainties as to how a nanomaterial comes into contact with humans and/or environmental organisms, and whether it penetrates areas of high concern (such as for example brain cells). See, for example, Carrier (n 51) at 195–212; Quack (n 46) at 5–7; Peters, Koechlin and Zinkernagel (n 51); Royal Communication on Environmental Pollution (RCEP), 'Pollution, Twenty-Seventh Report: Novel Materials in the Environment: The Case of Nanotechnology' (2008) 32, available at http://www.official-documents.gov.uk/document/ cm74/7468/7468.pdf; David Azoulay, 'Just out of REACH. The Center for International Environmental Law, Geneva' (2012), available at http://www.ciel.org/Publications/Nano_Reach_Study_Feb2012.pdf.

that 'provide foundational support across all sectors that use nanotechnologies or nanomaterials'.[93] These standards, as compared to the product standards, are not focused on the product, but instead focus on the method of production or processing, and may impose a set of techniques that can be used to minimize for instance the occurrence of hazardous activities that may lead to several problems and accidents.[94] For instance, the process standards may require an entire industry or a class of operation to achieve optimal levels of pollution control by installing the best available pollution control technology or to utilize a set of procedures along the supply chain to avoid the occurrence of food safety problems.[95] The majority of TC 229 standards also aim to provide resources that relevant actors can use for their own standards in terms of products and applications. For instance, WG4 of TC 229 has focused on setting standards that are not focused on characterizing manufactured nanomaterials (for example, carbon nanotubes) for use in a particular application, but standards that help relevant actors to know the diameters, length and quality of the carbon nanotube through the use of various techniques.

In a similar way, WG1 of TC 229 has set standards that, so far, provide generic definitions for nanotechnology, nanoscience, nanomaterial, engineered nanomaterial and manufactured nanomaterials, to help relevant actors to make use of those definitions in terms of their standards for their own products. The same applies to the deliverables of WG3 of TC 229, which has also provided risk assessment frameworks and generic methods for use by industry in handling nanomaterials in occupational settings.[96] In this way, whereas process standards may help companies and/or other non-industrial actors across borders to be more certain that products result from qualitative and consistent manufacturing processes, these standards come with many challenges as well. Process standards often require that manufacturers and/or suppliers make changes in

---

[93] ISO (n 52) at 8.

[94] Ronald D Knutson and Tim Josling, 'New Generation of Standards', presented at the NAAMIC Conference, Austin, TX, USA (May 2008).

[95] Dinah Shelton and Alexandre Ch Kiss, 'Common Legal Mechanisms of Environmental Protection', in Dinah Shelton and Alexandre Ch Kiss (eds), *Judicial Handbook on Environmental Law* (UNEP 2005) at 33–35.

[96] See also Steffi Friedrichs, Barry Park and James Johnstone, 'Current Developments in Standards and Regulation for Nanotechnologies', Joint NanoKTN/NIA meeting report, 19 March 2013, London, available at http://www.nanotechia.org/sites/default/files/files/20130319_NIA_MeetingNote_Standards_FINAL_Cover_ANNEX.pdf.

Table 6.1 The perceptions of State actors on ISO/TC 229 standardization process and outcomes

		V. High	High	Medium	Low	V. Low	
	Attributes	***Number of Respondents***					***Mean***
Decision-making process	Inclusiveness	4	7	3	0	0	4.2
	Representation	3	7	2	1	0	4.0
	Resources	1	4	2	5	2	2.8
	Overall Score						**3.7**
	Participatory Decision-making	1	8	3	0	0	3.6
	Comprehensive Agreements	2	8	3	0	0	4.0
	Communicative Agreements	3	5	4	1	0	3.8
	Overall Score						**3.8**
	Transparency	3	6	3	0	1	3.8
	Accountability	1	5	6	1	0	3.5
	Overall Score						**3.6**
Expertise	Competent Expertise	1	9	3	0	0	3.9
	Robustness	1	6	6	0	0	3.6
	Scientific Validity	1	6	6	0	0	3.6
	Objective Judgements	1	2	8	2	0	3.3
	Overall Score						**3.6**
Benefits of the rules	Problem-Solving Capacity	4	23	6	3	2	3.6
	Rule Benefits	0	9	4	0	0	3.4
	Rule Clarity	0	5	5	1	0	3.3
	Compliance	0	0	0	0	2	2.0
	Overall Score						**3.0**

production techniques or even implement new techniques to meet the specifications of particular standards. These can bring additional costs to different actors, which may lack the financial means to afford the changes in the manufacturing processes as well as the expertise to implement new techniques.[97] In fact, looking back to the perceptions of respondents that we discussed earlier, we can observe that financial costs and expertise were amongst the main barriers they faced in complying with TC 229 standards. Compliance is an important issue here. In particular, if standards are not used or complied with in practice it may be difficult to know to what extent they can contribute to facilitating global trade, reducing scientific uncertainties or enabling risk and regulatory analysis.

IV. CONCLUSION

PE often raises 'why' and 'how' questions. Yet, these questions are traditionally left out of doctrinal legal analysis. Our overall objective in the present Chapter was to introduce a PE approach to a specific branch of IL, in other words, international institutional law, or the law of IOs, with the specific aim of explaining a turn to informality by (State) actors in choosing international or transnational governance arrangements. We pointed to potential explanations for an increase in informal international law-making at the cost of traditional treaties concluded between States. At the same time we chose one particular area to shed more light on our legal theoretical assumptions by making use of a limited empirical study.

This empirical study was not chosen randomly. Key reasons for a turn to informality seem to relate to the increasing technical nature of international/transnational cooperation and the need to include experts. Formal IOs, consisting of State representatives only, would no longer be able to do the job.[98] Apart from this pragmatic view, a more normative assumption also underlies the choice for informality. Studies pointed to the fact that informal international/transnational cooperation could increase the legitimacy of the norms, given the fact that from the outset stakeholders are at the table and that traditional alternatives are often less legitimate.[99] In fact, it has been argued that, given the legitimacy

---

[97] Shuib Basri and Rory V O'Connor, 'Understanding the Perception of Very Small Software Companies towards the Adoption of Process Standards' (2010) Communications in Computer and Information Science 99, 153–164.

[98] See for a further development of this argument Kenneth W Abbott, Philip Genschel, Duncan Snidal and Bernhard Zangl (eds), *International Organizations as Orchestrators* (CUP 2015).

[99] See Ravi A Pereira, 'Why Would International Administrative Activity be Less Legitimate? – A Study of the Codex Alimentarius Commission', in von Bogdandy et al. (n 10) 541–571. See also Luis M Poiares Maduro, 'Europe and

problems of traditional international law-making, 'informal international law-making' may have to prevail because it replaces a 'thin State consent' with a 'thick stakeholder consensus'.[100]

In our case study on the regulation of nanotechnologies, we tested a few of these assumptions and basically found that a more nuanced picture may be needed. At least in this particular case (which may nevertheless represent similar arrangements concerning the governance of emerging technologies) our study revealed that informality does not necessarily lead to that higher inclusiveness and participation in the decision-making process, nor does it lead to more beneficial and effective outcomes. In addition, the survey responses in the case study emphasize that higher inclusiveness and participation in the decision-making process does not necessarily lead respondents to perceive transnational rules as more beneficial and effective in solving various issues at global level. In fact, respondents from governmental agencies seem to be more concerned with the benefits and problem-solving capacity of nanotechnology standards. The weaknesses of these standards with regard to these points seem to be attributed partially to the fact that the majority of these deliverables are not followed in practice (which creates difficulties in determining the extent to which nanotechnology standards are beneficial and contribute to solving various issues at global level), but also to the nature of the deliverables produced by the Committee and the experience of respondents with these deliverables.

However, at the practical level, the responses of those surveyed (even though limited in numbers) seem to suggest that for a transnational governance arrangement to be accepted by relevant actors, both its *processes* and *outcomes* are crucial. It is clear from this research that the participation gap, as well as the challenges to accessing, controlling and

---

the Constitution – What if this is as Good as it gets?', in Joseph HH Weiler and Marlene Wind (eds), *European Constitutionalism beyond the State* (CUP 2003); and Neil K Komesar, *Imperfect Alternatives, Choosing Institutions in Law, Economics and Public Policy* (University of Chicago Press 1994). At the same time, the side-effects of having experts rather than democratically elected politicians in the driver's seat have also been acknowledged. See for instance Gerd Junne, 'International Organizations in a Period of Globalization: New (Problems of) Legitimacy', in Jean-Marc Coicaud and Veijo Heiskanen, *The Legitimacy of International Organizations* (United Nations University 2001) 189–220 at 219: 'It is the rise of such alternative structures as a result of the globalization process that might prove to be a bigger challenge to the legitimacy of IOs that the direct impact of globalization on the demand for IO activity and on the effectiveness of their actions.' Cf. also Ambrus et al. (n 38).

[100] Pauwelyn, Wessel and Wouters (n 16).

influencing the decision-making process, and benefiting from standardization deliverables, are likely to have important implications for the perceptions of stakeholders, in this case on the role of TC 229 in the regulatory governance of nanotechnologies.

This Chapter could also be seen as a plea for new approaches linking theoretical analysis and empirical studies in international institutional law. International legal scholarship is challenged by the fact that its 'doctrines' are no longer able to explain and deal with changes in global governance. The turn to informality in the real world can only lead to an acceptance in international legal scholarship when empirical findings and insights from social sciences are taken on board.

PART III

Political Economy and the Enforcement of International Law

7. Political Economy of International Law: A Convenient Alliance for the Study of Compliance?

Barbara Delcourt

I. INTRODUCTION

Political Economy of International Law (PEIL) as a theoretical framework aimed at answering the 'why' questions (why do we have law, courts ...), the 'who' questions (who are the actors who participate in shaping the law), and 'what' motivates them (what preferences and constraints, such as power and resources, affect their decisions ...)[1] is a promising venue for scholars and professionals who are particularly interested in understanding the interactions between legal rules, the social and economic environment and agencies in the international setting. One of the most popular but also controversial debates in this field is the issue of compliance. Broadly speaking, compliance is defined as the correspondence between a rule and a behaviour.[2] It has to be distinguished from implementation and effectiveness insofar as

> [u]nlike those two concepts, compliance focuses neither on the effort to administer authoritatively public policy directives and the changes they undergo during this administrative process (implementation) nor the efficacy of a given regulation to solve political problem that preceded its formulation (effectiveness).[3]

---

[1] Anne van Aaken and Joel P Trachtman, 'Political Economy of International Law: Towards a Holistic Model of State Behaviour', above in this Volume.

[2] Kal Raustiala and Anne-Marie Slaughter, 'International Law, International Relations, and Compliance', in Walter Carlsnaes, Beth Simmons and Thomas Risse-Kappen (eds), *Handbook of International Relations* (Sage 2002) 539.

[3] Jürgen Neyer and Dieter Wolf, 'The Analysis of Compliance with International Rules: Definitions, Variables, and Methodology', in Michael Zürn and

In order to investigate this relationship between rule and behaviour, not only the rule itself has to be questioned but also the context in which it operates, and the motives of the actors to comply or not, etc. Unsurprisingly, then, the concept of compliance could be conceived either as a bridge between Public International Law (PIL) and International Relations (IR) and as an asset for the development of PEIL.

On the one hand, the concept of compliance is likely to enter into play, thereby narrowing the gap between PIL and IR and, more generally, coordinating the divergent outcomes arising from the different disciplines of the law, which are mainly theoretical, and the social sciences, which provide toolboxes, methods and more empirical findings. In this respect, Dirk Pulkowski noted that the legal method is poorly equipped to address causal questions like 'why States obey law'.[4] Against this backdrop, the use of this concept could be seen as having fostered the interparadigmatic debate, allowing the emergence of a more comprehensive view on the nature of interactions between law, politics and economics.

The literature on the issue of compliance generally addresses questions like: Are international legal rules autonomous variables in international life? How can we understand the engineering process through which rules are transformed into patterns of behaviour? How efficient is PIL in achieving certain goals (peace, cooperation, liberalization …)? Thus, at first glance, trying to answer these questions fits in quite well with the main objective of any interdisciplinary research agenda.[5]

But at the very same time, one would agree with Benedict Kingsbury's assumption that

> the concept of 'compliance' with law does not have, and cannot have, any meaning except as a function of prior theories of the nature and operation of the law to which it pertains. 'Compliance' thus is not a free-standing concept,

---

Christian Joerges (eds), *Law and Governance in Postnational Europe: Compliance beyond the Nation-State* (CUP 2005) 41–42.

[4] Dirk Pulkowski, 'Review essays: Testing Compliance Theories: Towards US Obedience of International Law in the *Avena Case*' (2006) 19 Leiden J Int L 513; Jana von Stein, 'The Engines of Compliance', in Jeffrey L Dunoff and Mark A Pollack (eds), *Interdisciplinary Perspectives on International Law and International Relations. The State of the Art* (CUP 2013) 477.

[5] For a comprehensive review of the historical roots of the 'dual agenda' (IL/IR), see Jeffrey L Dunoff and Mark A Pollack, 'International Law and International Relations: Introducing an Interdisciplinary Approach', in Dunoff and Pollack (eds) (n 4) 3–32.

> but derives meaning and utility from theories, so that different theories lead to significant different notions of what is meant by 'compliance'.[6]

To that extent, the concept of 'compliance' can turn into a trigger bursting disciplinary, paradigmatic and political disputes. Indeed, criticism against and debates over the theories of compliance (within each discipline and between them) cast a doubt on the ability of the concept to be a promising venue for further interdisciplinary research or, at least, signal the limits of the interparadigmatic and interdisciplinary dialogue. The literature dealing with this topic shows a great variety of approaches and explanations (II), something that is worth remembering in order to fully understand the backdrop against which to build the PEIL and to test its relevance (III).

II. TAKING STOCK OF THE DIVERSITY

Analyses about compliance to which we are nearly accustomed mainly deal with compliance by World Trade Organization (WTO) members, with adverse WTO dispute settlement rulings;[7] there are also attempts to predict compliance or to establish a correlation between compliance and cooperation.[8] Besides, normative works focus on the issue of incentives and the means to overcome non-compliant behaviour, resorting to enforcement mechanisms for instance.[9] All these studies imply collecting a lot of data[10] and require more empirical research to understand why States obey the law, whereas what we really need in order to interpret compliant behaviours is a framework explaining State behaviour by answering questions such as: Is the source of non-compliant behaviour

---

[6] Benedict Kingsbury, 'The Concept of Compliance as a Function of Competing Conceptions of International Law' (1998) 19 Mich J Int L at 346.

[7] John Magnus, 'Compliance to WTO Dispute Settlement Decisions: Is There A Crisis?', in Rufus Yerza and Bruce Wilson (eds), *Key Issues in WTO Dispute Settlement: The First Ten Years* (WTO Publications 2005) 242–250.

[8] George W Downs, David M Rocke and Peter N Barsoom, 'Is the Good News about Compliance Good News about Cooperation?' (1996) 50 Int Org 379–406.

[9] Clifford J Carrubba, 'Courts and Compliance in International Regulatory Regimes' (2005) 67 J Politics 669–689.

[10] James Morrow, 'When Do States Follow the Laws of War' (2007) 101 Am Pol Sci Rev 559–572.

voluntary or non-voluntary?[11] Is the lack of capacity the main cause of a wrong behaviour? What is the logic behind the behaviour: threat of sanctions, coercion, acculturation or persuasion?[12]

These questions clearly require scientific explanations that are hardly traceable. Some of them are obtained by resorting to quantitative analysis, statistics and regression techniques for pooled data, that are used to test hypotheses such as 'the smaller the number of the States that comply with an international rule, the more probable it is that even States, which were initially inclined to comply with the rule, infringe on it'.[13] For sure, not all hypotheses can be tested by using quantitative methods, because of the lack of data or the absence of valid indicators, as in the case of measuring misfits for example, which points to the fact that only inconvenient norms give rise to compliance problems because they generate significant pressure for adaptation.[14] Game theory,[15] rational choice, behavioural methods,[16] and other qualitative methods like tracing

---

[11] Kal Raustialia and David G Victor, 'Conclusions', in David G Victor, Kal Raustalia and Eugene B Skolnikoff (eds), *The Implementation and Effectiveness of International Environmental Commitments: Theory and Practice* (MIT Press 2007) 659–708.

[12] Jana von Stein (n 4) 488–489.

[13] See the research project by Tanja A Börzel, Tobias Hofmann and Carina Sprungk, 'Why Do States Not Obey the Law? Non-Compliance in the European Union' (2004) <http://userpage.fu-berlin.de/~europe/forschung/docs/boerzel_hofmann_sprungk_2004.pdf> accessed 6 December 2014; Tanja A Börzel, Tobias Hofmann and Diana Panke, 'Caving In or Sitting it Out? Longitudinal Patterns of Non-compliance in the European Union' (2012) 19 J Eur Pub Pol 454–471; Alexander Warkotsch, 'Realpolitik and International Reaction to Non-Compliance with Liberal Democratic Norms: Comparing EU and US Response Patterns' (2010) 45 Cooperation and Conflict 80–106; Judith G Kelley, 'Who Keeps International Commitments and Why? The International Criminal Court and Bilateral Non-Surrender Agreements' (2007) 101 Am Pol Sci Rev 573–589.

[14] Tanja A Börzel and Thomas Risse, 'Conceptualizing the Domestic Impact of Europe', in Kevin Feartherstone and Claudio M Radaelli (eds), *The Politics of Europeanization* (OUP 2003) 57–80.

[15] Examples of the added value of the game theories are provided by Jeffrey L Dunoff and Joel P Trachtman, 'Economic Analysis of Law' (1999) 24 Yale J Int L at 35–36 and 43–44.

[16] According to Anne van Aaken, rational choice has been the favoured paradigm but behavioural law and economics (political psychology) could be even more relevant for understanding PIL even if it raises serious methodological difficulties especially when the behaviour of a State and not of an individual is to be explained. See Anne van Aaken, 'Behavioral International Law and Economics' (2013) 2 ESIL Refl 1–2.

causal mechanisms for explaining processes of persuasion, learning, and legal internalization, have also been utilized in compliance studies.[17]

This growing literature on IR or European Studies on compliance issues cannot however be considered the only source of theories and formulae within the interdisciplinary debate. There are indeed many examples of previous works, more anchored in the PIL, which have given birth to well-known schools of thought in this field.[18] To mention a few:

a. The managerial model relies on a cooperative problem-solving approach.[19] Three factors are identified for explaining compliance. First, treaties are based on the free consent of States and thus embody their national interests; it is therefore quite normal that States abide by their international obligations. Second, compliance avoids the need to recalculate the costs and benefits of a particular decision. Third, it generates an efficiency-based rationale for further compliance. Hence, States obey the law because they are persuaded to stick to a dynamic created by a regime to which they belong. Enforcement plays little or no role. The main goal is to design more effective strategies for overcoming compliance problems in regulatory regimes.
b. The legitimacy model is illustrated in Thomas Franck's book.[20] He posits that the key element for compliance lies in the rules themselves and depends heavily on their fairness and, more broadly, on their inherent qualities. In this case, legitimacy and distributive justice outweigh other factors like selfish interests or managerial concerns. Compliance is triggered by a process of reflexive interaction, which leads to a general perception of law being fair

---

[17] Jeffrey T Checkel, 'Why Comply? Social Learning and European Identity Change' (2001) 55 Int Org 553–588.

[18] See Barbara Delcourt, 'Compliance (theories of)', in Rüdiger Wolfrum (ed), *Encyclopedia of Public International Law*, vol. II (OUP 2012) at 557; Michael Scharf and Paul R Williams, 'The Compliance Debate', in Michael Scharf and Paul R Williams (eds), *Shaping Foreign Policy in Times of Crisis* (CUP 2010) 1–13; von Stein (n 4).

[19] Abram Chayes and Antonia Handler Chayes, 'On Compliance' (1993) 47 Int Org 175–205; Abram Chayes and Antonia Handler Chayes, *The New Sovereignty: Compliance with International Regulatory Agreements* (Harvard University Press 1995).

[20] Thomas M Franck, *Fairness in International Law and Institutions* (Clarendon 1995); Thomas M Franck, 'Legitimacy in the International System' (1988) 82 AJIL 705–759.

because it allocates resources in an equitable fashion and it emanates from a 'right process' where actors have equal access to law-making.

c. The compliance-based theory can also be grounded in a model of rational and self-interested actors. Against this background, PIL could affect their behaviour insofar as they fear sanctions and are conscious of their reputation. Andrew Guzman, for instance, explains that failure to comply hurts a State's reputation because it appears to be prepared to breach others' obligations.[21] Coupled with the threat of direct sanctions, the 'reputational effect' – even if it is not always sufficient – provides a powerful incentive for compliance.[22]

d. The transnational model has been proposed by Harold Hongju Koh. It finds that compliance is more a matter of the internalization of international legal rules by the domestic legal systems than a matter of 'fairness' or 'managerial setup'.[23] His analysis aims at demonstrating that traditional answers focused on values, interests, or identity fail to describe the mechanisms that allow international rules to penetrate into a domestic system and the process by which repeated compliance becomes habitual obedience. In a way, internalization of norms[24] proves to be the condition for rule obedience. As a rationalist, he would have underestimated the transformative influence of law on social activities and institutions within the domestic sphere, which affects traditional ways of conducting politics. In this regard, the adoption of a constructivist perspective

---

[21] Reciprocity and Retaliation also play an important role in explaining compliance, Andrew T. Guzman, 'Reputation and International Law' (2006) 34 Georgia J Int Comp L 379–391; Andrew T Guzman, 'A Compliance-based Theory of International Law' (2002) 90 Calif L Rev 1823–1887. His thesis is criticized in Lisa L Martin, 'Against Compliance', in Dunoff and Pollack (n 4) 602.

[22] This issue is discussed in von Stein (n 4) 481–482 and more extensively in the same book by Rachel Brewster, 'Reputation in International Relations and International Law Theory' 525–543; George W Downs and Michael A Jones, 'Reputation, Compliance, and International Law' (2002) 31 J Leg Stud 95–114.

[23] Harold H Koh, 'Why Do Nations Obey International Law?' (1997) 106 Yale L J 2599–2659.

[24] Asher Alkoby, 'Theories of Compliance with International Law and the Challenge of Cultural Difference' (2008) 4 JILIR 151–198.

appears to be very promising,[25] especially when cultural differences are seen as serious causes for variations in nature and breach of PIL.

e. This problem is in a way solved by the liberal model and the proponents of the notion of 'legalization' to describe the phenomenon of compliance without a central authority. While influenced by the 'internalization model', they have added the concept of judicialization to propose a more compelling explanation for compliance.[26] In this regard, the EU appears to be a typical example of dense institutionalization, allowing patterned interactions and processes of bargaining and resort to legal argumentation. This system is meant to ensure a fair distribution of costs and benefits and to support the reliability of all actors; however, it facilitates the sanctioning of norms violators by independent institutions. Against this backdrop, PIL is considered to be a system of legitimate constraint in which incentives to comply stem from the very fact that actors comply with rules of their own making. In so doing, they have good reasons to expect that abiding by the rules will not be detrimental to their position within the EU.

f. The good record of EU members regarding law compliance therefore is not only due to a certain degree of centralized authority in the hands of supranational institutions, but also to the peculiar mix of monitoring/sanctioning, judicialization/internalization, and participation/acceptance. How States behave depends on how they are internally constituted. Following this logic, liberal States should be more prone to refer to international norms than non-liberal ones, not only because of their cultural and normative backgrounds, but also thanks to their institutional set-up, which enables peaceful resolution of conflicts.[27] Besides, the development of transnational contacts among domestic courts, regulatory agencies, executives, and legislative branches tends to create a transgovernmental order which encourages the development of a truly liberal international

---

25 Jutta Brunnée and Stephen J Toope, 'Constructivism and International Law', in Dunoff and Pollack (n 4) 119–145.

26 Bernhard Zangl, Achim Helmedach, Aletta Mondré, Alexander Kocks, Gerarld Nubauer and Kerstin Blome, 'Between Law and Politics: Explaining International Dispute Settlement Behavior' (2011) 18 Eur J Int Rel 369–401.

27 Kal Raustalia and Anne-Marie Slaughter, 'International Law/International Relations and Compliance', in Carlsnaes, Simmons and Risse-Kappen (n 2) 547; Anne-Marie Slaughter, 'International Law in a World of Liberal States' (1995) 6 EJIL 503–538.

> order, as depicted by neo-Kantians in their writings about the 'democratic peace'. In this scenario, traditional PIL is not the only normative framework for external policies. Since the traditional divide between the domestic and international sphere is vanishing, and since governments have no real monopoly on foreign policy, the set of norms to be referred to by all actors involved in the smooth functioning of this transnational order[28] has to be enlarged to include domestic commercial and constitutional law as well as private transnational law.[29]

Such analyses have certainly paved the way for the surge of works and insights underpinning the PEIL's research agenda. Nonetheless it is still worth considering the ins and outs of this interdisciplinary endeavour, especially with respect to the notion of compliance.

III. PENDING CONTROVERSIES AND AMBIGUITIES

To further elaborate on the possible 'basics' of the PEIL theoretical framework, one has to keep in mind those important debates (among and within IR and PIL) showing that controversies are opportunely instigated by the dual agenda. The following paragraphs do not aim at providing clear-cut answers for an all-embracing range of questions but rather to draw attention to a few issues that the literature on compliance has put to the forefront so far.

III.1. Ontological Issues

All authors dealing with compliance issues develop implicit or explicit views about what PIL is (or what the rules that should be complied with are). These views are not necessarily consistent but surely affect the assessment of compliance records as well as the explanations that their authors provide. The referent object of compliance is not always clearly identified. Especially in IR literature, there are sometimes no clear distinctions between rules, norms and principles. Moreover what is often

---

[28] Joel P Trachtman, 'Open Economy Law', in Dunoff and Pollack (n 4) 544–567.

[29] Nico Krisch and Benedict Kingsbury, 'Introduction: Global Governance and Global Administrative Law in the International Legal Order' (2006) 17 EJIL 1–13.

at stake is the functioning of the regulatory regime, so compliance does not necessarily relate to PIL as such.[30]

First and foremost, it is commonplace to state that positivist, non-positivist, anti-formalist, pluralist conceptions of PIL do affect the way in which compliance is envisaged. Positivists tend to separate law and behaviour to examine the relationship between them, which is the basis for the dominant view of 'compliance'.[31] Anti-formalists, on the contrary, tend to focus on the effects of legitimacy and social practices relating to legal norms. Besides, works inspired by the concept of legalization and those inspired by formalist or post-positivist theories are underpinned by quite different conceptions of law impacting their treatment of the issue of compliance.[32] Broadly speaking, the former tend to focus on treaty-based law or to consider that law is primarily constructed through cases and courts. The latter view law as a broader social phenomenon based on practices and beliefs, and shaped by interactions among societies. They believe that law has creative generative powers in social life. Hence, they criticize legalization-inspired analyses by stating that law cannot be limited to formalized and institutionalized features, which play no significant role in the promotion of compliance, for instance in human rights matters.[33] Summing up, one would conclude sharing the view that 'an emphasis on compliance tends to reinforce the traditional view of law as commands backed by sanctions while overlooking law's aspirational, expressive, constitutive, and learning elements'.[34]

By the same token, some academics like Guzman invite legal scholars to refocus on economic matters and environmental protection, and less on war and peace issues which are, according to him, unlikely to be affected by law. That is a reason why he also suggests adopting a new definition of law that would encompass all sorts of commitments. This invitation has been accepted by several scholars. Although they do not stick to its realist premises, they have developed a study of compliance in regime

---

[30] Richard B Bilder, 'Beyond Compliance: Helping Nations Cooperate', in Dinah Shelton (ed), *Commitment and Compliance. The Role of Non-Binding Norms in the International Legal System* (OUP 2000) 65–73.

[31] Robert Wolfe, 'See you in Geneva? Legal (Mis)Representations of the Trading System' (2005) 11 Eur J Int Rel 344.

[32] Martha Finnemore and Stephen J Toope, 'Alternatives to "Legalization": Richer Views of Law and Politics' (2001) 55 Int Org 743–758.

[33] Ibid 755; Robert Howse and Ruti Teitel, 'Beyond Compliance: Rethinking Why International Law Really Matters' (2010) 1 Global Policy 127–135.

[34] Kenneth W Abbott and Duncan Snidal, 'Law, Legalization, and Politics: An Agenda for the Next Generation of IL/IR Scholars', in Dunoff and Pollack (n 4) 46–47.

reflecting a shift in academic thinking characterized by the decline of national sovereignty and the collapse of the traditional public–private divide. The capacity of international institutions and non-State actors to regulate IR through 'norms' is consequently envisaged with more ease and confidence.[35]

One example of the controversial results that stem from the adoption of a particular conception of PIL is provided by Wolfe's article 'See you in Geneva' (expression used by State officials when they disagree about trade policy).[36] The author proposes a pluralist view considering the WTO to be the proper forum to elaborate a larger legal system resulting from multiple interactions. His main assumption is that law is pervasive in the everyday life of the trading system and not only 'before the court'. He uses the metaphor of the North American family's fridge door: 'The place where everyone posts the relevant textual evidence of our mutual commitments for all to see'.[37] Law is not only what authoritative institutions prescribe, it is what autonomous actors believe they should do. How they act will shape the law or institutions just as those institutions shape them. It follows that codification within the WTO, either through a new agreement or a panel decision that becomes part of the WTO 'acquis', cannot foreclose new bargains that will lead to a different understanding of WTO law. Such a broader view on legal rules entails a different perspective on both the reasons why actors abide by the law and, from a methodological point of view, whose behaviour is going to be scrutinized.[38]

III.2. The Epistemological Debate

The nature and scope of knowledge about compliance has also been under strain. One wonders what is actually at stake: a better knowledge of the determinants of decision-making in foreign policy, a growing

---

[35] Abraham L Newman and David Zaring, 'Regulatory Networks: Power, Legitimacy, and Compliance', in Dunoff and Pollack (n 4) 244–265; Beth A Simmons, 'International Law and State Behavior: Commitment and Compliance in International Monetary Affairs' (2000) 94 Am Pol Sci Rev 819–835.

[36] Wolfe (n 31) 339–365.

[37] Ibid 343.

[38] Kenneth W Abbott and Duncan Snidal signalled that more work on compliance by private actors is needed since they too are subjects of the international legal system. See Abbott and Snidal, 'Law, Legalization, and Politics: An Agenda for the Next Generation of IL/IR Scholars', in Dunoff and Pollack (n 4) 46–47.

efficiency of international institutions, or both?[39] Most scholars are aware of the risks they take when trying to combine legal and social insights. Among them, the risk of theoretical inconsistency is frequently evoked, at least as much as the risk to overestimate the weight of legal rules or of adjudication and enforcement mechanisms. For sure, the risk of over-simplification appears to be a serious concern, notably regarding the bulk of works driven by rationalist thinking.

For some authors, the rational choice model reference is underpinned by a few key factors and assumptions in order to portray itself as a science.[40] Moreover, predictive analyses, which are very welcome in IR literature, imply reducing the complexity of international politics to a limited number of factors but do not always deliver on their promises. As Pulkowski has demonstrated, coercion and reputational costs have proved irrelevant in explaining US (dis)obedience of PIL in the *Avena* case.[41]

Another kind of simplification is also pinpointed by Alvarez: 'Rules *versus* power is a truncated understanding of the institutional choices in the trading system. Expertise is never neutral, every choice of forum privileges some set of actors (something that is rarely envisaged in the compliance literature)'.[42] In other words, predefined categories or opposite terms like 'law' and 'politics/interests', 'legal or illegal' are certainly useful in order to build models of compliance, to estimate the rate of compliant behaviour and to publish in scientific reviews with quantitative

---

[39] See for example Sara McLaughlin Mitchell and Paul R Hensel, 'International Institutions and Compliance with Agreements' (2007) 51 Am J Pol Sci 721–737; Barbara Koremenos, 'Institutionalism and International Law', in Dunoff and Pollack (n 4) 59–82.

[40] According to Robin P Malloy those are the main assumptions:

- All people act in their own self interest
- Each self-interested person acts rationally (this assumption is essential in order to give the model its scientific predictive power)
- People have access to perfect information necessary to make rational decisions in their own self-interest
- People and resources are assumed to be freely movable and transferable (no artificial barriers to market entry or exit).

The model operates in a democratic manner by reacting to wealth-based votes; see chapter 'A New Law and Economics', in Robin P Malloy and Christopher K Braun (eds), *Law and Economics. New and Critical Perspectives* (Peter Lang 1995) 13.

[41] Pulkowski (n 4) 544–546.

[42] Jose E Alvarez, 'Constitutional Interpretation in International Organizations', in Jean-Marc Coicaud and Viejo Heiskanen (eds), *The Legitimacy of International Organizations* (United Nations University Press 2006) 114–115.

methodological orientation. However, if the main challenge is to draw general conclusions about the influence of legal consideration upon foreign policy, one can argue that a State can comply with a rule for reasons that have nothing to do with law. For example, it would be questionable to explain the fact that democracies do not wage war on each other only by referring to the prohibition of war enshrined in the UN Charter. It would similarly be debatable to confer on the European legal system a constraining effect on political decisions taken in certain areas, such as in the single market, and not on others. It could be argued that Member States conform to regulations simply because they are persuaded that liberalization and harmonization in the economic sector are beneficial for their constituents. On the contrary, they appear to be more reluctant with regard to regulations of subsidies and food and in other sectors where the underlying rationale is not shared by all governments. These findings are consistent with some analyses pinpointing the fact that a country's compliance degree may vary depending on which functional area a specific legal instrument pertains to.[43]

It is worth noting that from a PE perspective, authors are also invited to offer solutions for ensuring more compliance; but here again, the cures are heavily dependent on the causes that are identified as the reasons for non-compliance. For instance, in the managerial model, the ambiguity of the treaties, the limited capacity of the State or even uncontrolled economic or social changes are identified as the main causes of non-compliant behaviours. Against this background, technical assistance and the improvement of procedures for dispute resolutions are seen as being relevant. For those who are not convinced by the managerial model, further enforcement mechanisms are required for ensuring compliance precisely because non-compliance is often the result of a calculus made by political elites during critical periods (recession, elections) or result from the design of domestic institutions or international regimes.[44]

In a very corrosive contribution, Lisa Martin states that the problem with the IR literature is that compliance is settled as the dependent variable to measure the influence of international institutions and organizations on State behaviour. Yet, this legal concept is ill-suited to the identification and measurement of institutional effects, notably because the identification of a causal effect needs to be counterfactual: what is the likely outcome in the absence of the institution? She concludes that compliance is not a valid measure of outcomes. Very often, analyses use

43 Delcourt (n 18) at 20.

44 Downs, Rocke and Barsoom (n 8) at 399.

the language of compliance but when they have to measure its implementation, they analyse cooperation or domestic policy change. Other essays confuse compliance with political cooperation, and a third category of scholars, whilst identifying the concept rightly, tells us little about the causal impact of international institutions or agreements.[45]

III.3. Methodological Issues

As already suggested above, the mere fact of embracing a rationalist or a constructivist posture often implies that attention will be focused on different actors, 'rules' and processes. According to Pulkowski, the *Avena* case is a story about a power struggle between various values and identities, and in which a multiplicity of actors (foreign governments, international organizations, courts and pressure groups) played their part. Hence, as it would be surprising to find the same set of actors and interactions in other cases, it would be difficult to draw a more general conclusion on compliance. Based on a comparison of different pieces of literature on the subject, the author's preference is clearly made in favour of a 'one case-study' informed by an in-depth knowledge of facts and rules. But quantification has also proved fruitful in order to 'move beyond the idiosyncrasies of a particular time-period or country'.[46]

A constructivist analysis will probably pay tribute to sociology; the same can be said for those practices that sustain legality (shared understanding, background knowledge, entrepreneurial norms, endeavours of epistemic communities), which in most cases require a combination of the insights provided by Foucault, Giddens and Bourdieu … among many others.[47] Adding more sociological insights does not help much. Indeed, it is quite difficult to operationalize these sociological insights within the PIL domain since this requires very demanding field work to explain a great variety of interactions among a broad range of actors acting in multiple scenarios.

Anyway, discussions about the best methods and tools to address the issue of compliance are more lively and vivid in the field of IR than in legal sciences. Very few legal scholars are willing to embark in such discussions, particularly in Europe. How do we explain (non-) compliance? To what extent do enforcement mechanisms play a role in ensuring

---

45 Martin (n 21) 592–595.

46 von Stein (n 4) 495.

47 Jutta Brunnée and Stephen J Toope, 'Interactional International Law and the Practice of Legality', in Emanuel Adler and Vincent Pouliot (eds), *International Practices* (CUP 2011) 108–135.

compliance? What are the main biases of quantitative studies and the impact of selection on the results of analyses of such phenomenon, considering that compliance is inflated if States only reach agreements that they intend to carry out?[48] Such questions are answered very differently depending on whether this is done by relying on quantitative analysis, on more qualitative analysis, or on both, which is the usual approach.

Such research has attracted heavy criticism from IL scholars.[49] The assumption that conformity and non-conformity are binary does not find an adequate correspondence in international practice. International lawyers experience as interpretation, uncertainty regarding the sources of law, issues of opposability and excuses precluding responsibility must lead to more nuanced conclusions and even scepticism regarding the possibility to elucidate compliance through empirical work alone. But as acknowledged by Dunoff and Pollack,

> the discipline has by now internalized the indeterminacy critique, for example, that legal rules are typically susceptible to more than one reasonable interpretation, and therefore cannot, by themselves, definitively resolve concrete legal controversies. Substantial debate exists over the implication of the indeterminacy critique, but at a minimum it surely problematizes the large body of IR work that foregrounds *compliance* as a central marker for determining international law's impact.[50]

We are thus far from having contributed to common standards in research design on compliance. New methodological controversies have even arisen in this domain, as identified by Jana von Stein.[51] For example, bias and selection effects echo criticism by Finnemore and Sikkink, who argued that behaviouralist and economic approaches favour behaviours that can be easily measured.[52] The controversies surrounding the strength and weaknesses of statistical tools (notably those which test and control for the 'endogeneity and selection' argument) raise even more doubts

---

48 Downs, Rocke and Barsoom (n 8) 382; Dunoff and Pollack (n 5) 17; von Stein (n 4) 491.

49 See for example Benedict Kingsbury (n 6) and Jeffrey L Dunoff and Mark Pollack, 'Reversing Field: What Can International Law Teach International Relations?'(2014) 3 ESIL Refl 5.

50 Dunoff and Pollack (n 49) at 4.

51 Jana von Stein, 'International Law: Understanding Compliance and Enforcement', in Robert A Denemark (ed), *The International Studies Encyclopedia* (Wiley 2010).

52 Martha Finnemore and Kathryn Sikkink, 'International Norm Dynamics and Political Change' (1998) 52 Int Org 887–917.

about the merits of each method. Indeed, Jana von Stein concludes that 'the quantification of the study of international law has been beneficial in a number of ways (...) but has notable drawbacks (...) it leads to a decoupling of methodological and substantive debates and not generated consensus on important issues'.[53]

III.4. Ideological Controversies

The main thesis according to which compliance with legal rules falls along liberal/non-liberal lines has been seriously challenged. Though most of the critics do not intend to reverse this thesis, they somehow cast a doubt on its validity by highlighting the political and methodological bias of this approach. Some critics, notably those emphasizing its prescriptive nature and its alleged collusion with US foreign policy, resonate with slogans such as the one about the New Haven School being a vehicle for the Western liberal hegemonic discourse.[54]

Even the descriptive part of the research undertaken by the liberally-inclined authors is contested. According to José Enrique Alvarez, it appears somehow difficult to demonstrate a causal relationship between treaty compliance or commitment to international arbitration and the political nature of a particular regime.[55] For instance, the record of the US regarding the direct or vertical enforcement of human rights conventions is quite challenging for the liberal thesis. By the same token, it is not obvious that undemocratic countries will be more reluctant to respect their international obligations. What can be perhaps more easily asserted in the field of human rights cannot be proved so easily in other fields.

Ideology is even more obvious in the field of 'Law and Economics', which can be defined as the application of economic theory (micro-economics and the basic concepts of welfare economics) to examine the formation, structure, processes, and economic impact of law and legal institutions. Given economists' concern with efficiency, it is not surprising that many of them started analysing law on the basis of its efficiency properties. Nonetheless, here again there are different visions or ideologies. As Malloy observed:

---

[53] von Stein (n 51).

[54] Philip R Trimble, 'International Law, World Order, and Critical Legal Studies' (1990) 42 Stanford L Rev 811–845.

[55] José E Alvarez, 'Do Liberal States Behave Better? A Critique of Slaughter's Liberal Theory' (2001) 12 EJIL 183–246. See also von Stein (n 4) at 484–485.

> Law and economics provide a process for understanding and engaging in competing discourses concerning power sharing and resource allocation (…). The new law and economics uses economics as a reference point for cross-cultural and ideological mediation in law. It provides a baseline for values and assumptions that allow one to explore shifting norms in alternative systems of social organization. It does this by exploring the connection between legal stories and economic stories that form the basis of alternative rhetoric styles.[56]

Here it is assumed that 'Law and Economics' is subjective and cannot pretend to be both scientific and objective. This is not surprising, since competing discourses are inherent to politics and academic activities, a point which is emphasized in critical American sociology:

> 'The 'career' of an explanation of a problem manifestly hinges in part on the acceptability of the ideological promises it implies. Because a social problem is not a verifiable entity but a construction that further ideological interests, its explanation is bound to be part of the process of construction rather than a set of falsifiable propositions. In a crucial sense problems are created so that particular reasons can be offered for public acceptance (…) so that particular solution can be proposed.[57]

Political economy of law and compliance issues is no exception. It is politically charged and, consequently, debatable.

In this respect, David Kennedy estimates that '[l]aw is the link binding centers and peripheries to one another and structuring their interaction. It is also the vernacular through which power and wealth justify their exercise and shroud their authority'.[58] He suggests then 'rethinking international law as a terrain for political and economic struggle rather than a normative or technical substitute for political choice, itself indifferent to natural flows of economic activity'.[59] To that extent, the PEIL's research agenda could be fruitful if certain conditions are fulfilled, mainly: ending the artificial separation between politics and economics and, at the academic level, spurring international lawyers to understand the PE of the world. This latter task could prove to be far too demanding for international lawyers who do not understand the determinants of compliance.

---

[56] Malloy (n 40) at 3.

[57] Murray Edelman, *Constructing the Political Spectacle* (University of Chicago Press 1988) at 18.

[58] David Kennedy, 'Law and the Political Economy of the World' (2013) 26 Leiden J Int L 7–48.

[59] Ibid at 37.

The ideas developed by Posner in the US in the Seventies are opposite to Kennedy's view. Posner argued that law and courts are more efficient than political institutions for ensuring wealth maximization and that, by the way, wealth maximization is a relatively uncontroversial policy. Politics is conceived as a lower kind of economic transaction, a long-term service used to dupe citizens.[60]

On the contrary, less neo-liberal thinking suggests that wealth redistribution needs political institutions, since judges are not equipped to promote it. Some scholars have indeed demonstrated the limits of rational choice theory and the normative dimensions of a kind of economic theory linked to utilitarian ethics and a blindness towards distributive issues.[61] The New Haven School, for instance, develops greater confidence in government institutions to remedy market failure in society, whereas the Public Choice theory refers to the economic analysis of nonmarket decision-making. Proponents of this latter approach to Law and Economics focus on the creation and implementation of law through the political process.[62]

In the domain of international economic law, dispute settlement is often considered to be the most important feature of the WTO because the rule of law as formal adjudication of explicit texts will ensure liberalization. But according to Wolfe, the narrative that flows from this caricature sees the State as an obstacle to freedom, not the guarantor of democracy.[63] Such controversies explain why some scholars like Martti Koskenniemi estimate that 'compliance comes with dubious politics'.[64] Irrespective of the preferences expressed, it seems that the PEIL will have to deal with such ideological controversies while its proponents should perhaps be invited to show more reflexivity than ever.

---

60 Nicholas Merduro and Steven G Medema, 'Schools of Thought in Law and Economics: a Kuhnian Competition', in Robin P Malloy and Christopher K Braun (eds), *Law and Economics: Critic of Institutions* (Peter Lang Publishers 1995) 65–126 at 74.

61 Niels Petersen, 'How Rational is International Law' (2010) 20 EJIL at 1260–1261.

62 Malloy (n 40) at 13–14; Merduro and Medema (n 60) at 65.

63 A different view about the so-called 'biases' of Law and Economics can be found in Jeffrey L Dunoff and Joel P Trachtman, 'Economic Analysis of International Law' (1999) 24 Yale J Int L 8.

64 Another quite strong criticism against new trends in PIL/IR is to be found in A Claire Cutler, 'Toward a Radical Political Economy Critique of Transnational Economic Law', in Susan Marks (ed), *International Law on the Left. Re-examining Marxist Legacies* (CUP 2008) 199–219.

IV. CONCLUSION

Koskenniemi argues that IR literature about PIL is at best seen as an attempt to appropriate the voice of international legality to a fully instrumentalist discipline dedicated to serving the interests of power.[65] In his view, new words and speakers have become authoritative and the way IR scholars apprehend legal rules by challenging old words is questionable. The new language is tweaked more to management culture, does not refer to sovereignty nor to rules but to governance, objectives, values and interests. Evidence of this can be seen in the shift from institutions to regimes, from rules to regulations, from government to governance, from responsibility to compliance – non-compliance is to be preferred notably because invoking responsibility might be counterproductive for economic treaties[66] from law to legitimacy. As a result, it seems that we are 'lost in translation' so to speak; the terminology of 'consent', 'validity' or 'disputes settlement' is replaced by the social sciences expression of 'explaining behaviour and attaining compliance'.[67] To that extent, the success of 'compliance' is a sign of the times according to which IR experts have won a battle over the monopoly of the interdisciplinary agenda.

Professional and disciplinary competition epitomized by this radical criticism may be a symptom of the enduring difficulty to sustain the very demanding research agenda encompassed in the PEIL. As a matter of fact, Brunnée and Toope also signalled that 'even constructivist IR Scholars have been remarkably uninterested in looking behind the formal account of law to examine how legal obligation arises and influences actors'.[68] Dunoff and Pollack, while acknowledging the added value of IR works, have very recently signed an op-ed in the ESIL newsletter inviting legal scholars to be more pro-active in this field and in rebalancing the dialogue with their own skills and knowledge.

But to a certain extent, we may consider that a focus on compliance is perhaps misplaced if the objective is to foster an interdisciplinary dialogue. As rightly stated by Lisa Martin, we should be more interested

---

[65] Martti Koskenniemi, 'Miserable Comforters: International Relations as New Natural Law' (2009) 15 Eur J Int Rel 395–422.

[66] Ibid 408.

[67] Ibid 410.

[68] Jutta Brunnée and Stephen Toope, 'Constructivism and International Law', in Dunoff and Pollack (eds) (n 4) 109.

in effectiveness and implementation. She encourages quantitative-oriented scholars to rethink the dependent variable and drop the notion of compliance, adding that:

> the way compliance entered IR literature is a cautionary tale about the risks associated with celebrating interdisciplinarity without paying careful attention to the different demands and purposes of various disciplines. (…) Our understanding of the causal effects of institutions and agreements will be much stronger if we focus directly on substantive policies rather than on compliance strategies (…)'.[69]

The conflation of compliance and causal effect, and the danger of inferring causal effect from observed compliance, in not merely an abstract concern. It has confounded many otherwise serious empirical studies on institutional effects.

The PEIL research agenda has the overwhelming advantage, compared to the dual agenda in the Eighties and Nineties, to arise in the midst of an already very mature and sophisticated debate. But it does not mean that the task will be easier; the controversies surrounding the use of the concept of compliance seem to ring a powerful warning signal. We definitively have to elaborate further the kind of 'division of labour' and consistent articulation between different disciplines and paradigms that would be truly beneficial for an interdisciplinary research agenda. Otherwise we run the risk of falling into some sort of sceptical assessment about the incommensurability of paradigms[70] and thereby ruin the perspective of a fruitful dialogue among disciplines.

---

[69] Martin (n 21) 606.

[70] Ole Waever, 'The Rise and Fall of Inter-Paradigm Debate', in Steve Smith, Ken Booth and Marysia Zalewski (eds), *International Theory: Positivism and Beyond* (CUP 1996) 170–173.

8. International Political Economy and the Prisoner's Dilemma: Compliance with International Law

Meredith Kolsky Lewis

I. INTRODUCTION

As the introduction to this Volume ably explains, the relationship between Political Economy (PE) and International Law (IL) has been underdeveloped and underexplored. There is thus much work to be done to examine the ways in which traditional PE tools can be used to help us better understand and theorize Public International Law (PIL). The aim of this Chapter is to advance a small piece of this International Political Economy (IPE) endeavor by exploring the concept of the prisoner's dilemma in the context of compliance with IL.

While the prisoner's dilemma is a concept that has been applied with some regularity in PE literature, it has been used less frequently in the international context and less frequently still as a tool to understand behavior in IL.[1] This Chapter will examine the prisoner's dilemma in a variety of IL contexts, from which we can see IL as *explanandum* in that a prisoner's dilemma sometimes leads to the creation of IL. We will also

[1] Notable exceptions include Joel Trachtman and Andrew Guzman. See, for example, Joel P Trachtman, *The Economic Structure of International Law* (Harvard University Press 2008); Andrew T Guzman, *How International Law Works: A Rational Choice Theory* (OUP 2008). Some, however, believe that IL theorists rely too heavily upon the prisoner's dilemma. See Ian Ayres, 'Playing Games with the Law' (1990) 42 Stanford L Rev 1291, 1294–95; Gregory C Shaffer and Mark A Pollack, 'Hard vs. Soft Law: Alternatives, Complements and Antagonists in International Governance' (2010) 94 Minn Law Review 706 at 731–733; Richard H McAdams, 'Beyond the Prisoners' Dilemma: Coordination, Game Theory, and Law' (2009) 82 Southern Calif L Rev 209, 210–211.

see that IL can serve as *explanans* in the context of the prisoner's dilemma, in that IL has consequences and effects for prisoner's dilemmas while not always resolving them.[2] The Chapter also identifies some limitations of the prisoner's dilemma, in particular by highlighting examples of PE factors that confound the assumptions inherent to a prisoner's dilemma analysis.

II. THE PRISONER'S DILEMMA: OVERVIEW

Although many readers will be generally familiar with the prisoner's dilemma, in this Section it seems important to provide a brief overview of the essential characteristics of this concept.

A prisoner's dilemma is, in its simplest form, a two-player game that is characterized by the following three characteristics:

First, each player has two strategies: to cooperate or to defect.

Second, each player's dominant strategy – the one that will give a party a superior outcome regardless of what the other party does – will be to defect (that is, confessing to the crime in the traditional example).

Third, the dominant solution equilibrium, frequently referred to as the Nash equilibrium, is worse for both players than the nonequilibrium situation in which each plays the dominated strategy of cooperating.[3]

In the classic example, suspects A and B have committed a crime together. They are both brought in for questioning. Each will be interrogated separately and will not know if the other 'cooperates' by keeping quiet, or 'cheats' by confessing A and B's role in the crime. However, A and B both know the payoffs that will result under all of the possible scenarios – both keep quiet; one keeps quiet while the other confesses; or both confess. Table 8.1 below is an example of payoff possibilities that represent a prisoner's dilemma:

---

[2] The *explanandum* and *explanans* concepts are elaborated by Anne van Aaken and Joel P Trachtman, 'Political Economy of International Law: Towards a Holistic Model of State Behaviour', above in this Volume.

[3] Avinash K Dixit and Susan Skeath, *Games of Strategy* (1st edn, W. W. Norton & Co. 1999) at 87.

Table 8.1 The classic prisoner's dilemma

	A keeps quiet	A confesses
B keeps quiet	A gets 1 year in jail/B gets 1 year in jail	A goes free/ B gets 15 years in jail
B confesses	B goes free/A gets 15 years in jail	A gets 5 years in jail, B gets 5 years in jail

Based on these payoff possibilities, both A and B will choose to 'cheat' by confessing. Why is this the case? Let us consider A. A will undertake the following analysis: 'If I keep quiet and B keeps quiet, I get 1 year in jail. If I keep quiet and B tells, I get 15 years in jail. However, if I tell and B keeps quiet, I go free. And if I tell and B tells too, I get 5 years.' The possible payoffs for A if A tells are either going free (when B stays quiet) or five years in jail (if B also confesses). However, the payoffs if A stays quiet are either one year in jail (when B stays quiet) or 15 years in jail (when B confesses). A therefore recognizes that A's payoff possibilities are better if A confesses, *regardless* of what B does. B comes to the same conclusion. Therefore both A and B make the rational decision to cheat, and both confess. This is the Nash equilibrium outcome, but it is not as good an outcome as the parties would have achieved had they both stayed quiet.

Thus the essence of the prisoner's dilemma is that parties act rationally in making the choices they make, given the payoff possibilities, but that this leads to a suboptimal outcome. It is important to emphasize that the parties are making understandable, logical decisions given the payoff possibilities, but that these decisions lead to a suboptimal outcome. The term 'prisoner's dilemma' is often misused to refer to situations where parties make decisions that others do not consider desirable, but which result in outcomes the parties themselves actually wanted.

III. PRISONER'S DILEMMAS IN INTERNATIONAL LAW

There are a number of examples of prisoner's dilemmas in the IL context. Below three different typologies are identified, which illustrate the complexity of the interplay between these dilemmas and IL.

III.1. Prisoner's Dilemma That Has (Largely) Been Solved by International Law

Tendency towards economic protectionism

The prisoner's dilemma can be applied in a variety of trade policy contexts. For example, trade policy generally represents a prisoner's dilemma in that countries are often seen as better off under a system of free trade. Yet the Nash equilibrium finds countries imposing higher tariffs rather than lowering them.[4]

Increases in tariffs make it more expensive for domestic consumers to buy imports; raise costs of imported inputs for domestic producers; and create a comparative disadvantage for domestic producers in their efforts to sell in overseas markets. Accordingly, officials will generally acknowledge that their economies, and therefore their citizens, would be better off if all countries lowered their tariffs.

The maximization of joint welfare is not a Nash equilibrium because, in the absence of international agreements prohibiting such conduct, each country will likely determine that it will be better off if it keeps its tariffs high while the other country lowers its tariffs. Each country will do the best if it alone cheats, while its trading partner cooperates. This of course leads to an equilibrium of both countries cheating by keeping tariffs high.[5] This 'beggar thy neighbor' behavior, most notoriously exemplified by the Smoot-Hawley tariff,[6] indicates that regulation is needed to change the payoff matrix such that countries no longer follow their mercantilist tendencies.[7]

---

[4] Kyle Bagwell and Robert W Staiger, 'Multilateral Tariff Cooperation During the Formation of Free Trade Areas', (1997) 38 Int Econ Rev 291, 297; see also Jeffrey Simser, 'GATS and Financial Services: Redefining Borders' (1996) 3 Buffalo J Int L 33, 40–41.

[5] See Bagwell and Staiger (n 4) 297 n 7.

[6] See US Department of State, Smoot-Hawley Tariff, <http://future.state.gov/when/timeline/1921_timeline/smoot_tariff.html>.

[7] Daniel C Esty and Damien Geradin, 'Regulatory Co-opetition' (2000) 3 JIEL 235, 245. See also Daniel A Farber and Robert E Hudec, 'Free Trade and the Regulatory State: A GATT's Eye View of the Dormant Commerce Clause' (1994) 47 Vanderbilt L Rev 1401, 1405 (arguing that 'an enforcement mechanism is required, not because it is in the interest of each state to defect from the agreement – economists are pretty much united in the view that it isn't – but because the mercantilist perspective that prevails in most political debate makes it seem so.'). See also Andrew T Guzman, 'Why LDCs Sign Treaties That Hurt Them: Explaining the Popularity of Bilateral Investment Treaties' (1998) 38 VJIL 639, 641, 666–667 (least developed country behavior with respect to

Politicians recognize that, while freer trade will help their economies as a whole, there will be segments of society that will be worse off as a result of removing trade barriers. In particular, as shown in Table 8.2, A's producers that do not use significant quantities of inputs subject to tariffs are unlikely to fare well when foreign competition is able, as a result of lower tariffs, to sell more cheaply in country A. Thus the decision to pursue free trade policies is not without risk or consequences, because certain producers will object. This reality creates a temptation for politicians to try to have their cake and eat it too, by agreeing to lower tariffs but then to cheat and actually raise tariffs. If A and only A adopts this strategy, A will have the best of both worlds, with its consumers receiving access to lower-priced goods; its imported input-using producers experiencing lower costs yet remaining shielded from competition; and its exporting producers becoming more competitive as a result of lower tariffs in B. Unfortunately for A, B thinks the same way. As a result, the Nash equilibrium is that both countries will cheat, such that the dominant strategy leads to a suboptimal outcome.

In the absence of IL:

Table 8.2 International trade protectionism payoff matrix (without international law)

	A lowers tariffs	A raises tariffs
B lowers tariffs	Very good outcome for A and B	Best outcome for A/worst outcome for B
B raises tariffs	Best outcome for B/worst outcome for A	Bad outcome for A and B

With respect to international trade protectionism, we can see that this particular prisoner's dilemma should be solvable through the creation of IL. If the politicians in A and B recognize the dynamic for what it is, they should be amenable to entering into agreements that would impose a cost or other negative consequence to cheating. And this is precisely what the WTO and the GATT before it have accomplished. Since countries have committed themselves to tariff ceilings, it is exceedingly rare to

bilateral investment treaties is akin to a prisoner's dilemma in that these countries accept bad terms in order to attract foreign investment even though they could band together with other similarly situated countries to negotiate collectively for better terms).

hear of a WTO member raising tariffs above its bound rates. This suggests that under this typology, the existence of a prisoner's dilemma may have a causal impact on a country's willingness to comply with an associated IL commitment. This would be logical, since part of the impetus for the creation of the IL was to address the problem of the Pareto inefficient outcome.

The creation of IL in this example, shown in Table 8.3, addresses the prisoner's dilemma problem by altering the payoff matrix. Now, if only A cheats, this will not result in the best possible outcome for A. Instead, A will face consequences that mean that cheating is no longer attractive. Under the revised matrix, the equilibrium is to comply with the IL and keep the tariffs lowered.

With international law:

Table 8.3 International trade protectionism payoff matrix (with international law)

	A lowers tariffs	A raises tariffs
B lowers tariffs	Very good outcome for A and B	A faces negative consequences of cheating; less good outcome for A; less good outcome for B (due to A's cheating)
B raises tariffs	B faces negative consequences of cheating; less good outcome for B; less good outcome for A (due to B's cheating)	Worst outcome for A and B

Because there are now consequences attached to cheating, the Nash equilibrium becomes cooperation. In this example, the creation of IL solves the prisoner's dilemma, and the parties are incentivized to comply with the GATT/WTO because there are negative consequences associated with cheating.

Customary International Law – sometimes

Joel Trachtman and others have written about the prisoner's dilemma in the context of Customary International Law (CIL).[8] For example, Trachtman and George Norman have written about the CIL rule of *sic utero tuo* (use your own so as not to injure others) in the context of transboundary pollution as an example of a prisoner's dilemma.[9] I would cast that example differently, and fit it into this typology. The CIL rule is, in this instance, resolving what would otherwise likely be a prisoner's dilemma. Because the equilibrium is largely to follow the CIL rule, CIL is characterized in this situation as resolving a prisoner's dilemma, not as an example of such a dilemma.

III.2. Prisoner's Dilemmas That Have the Potential to be Solved with International Law

A second typology is situations in which we would anticipate IL could resolve a prisoner's dilemma, but in practice, the IL that has been generated has not been fully successful in solving the dilemma. Below two examples of this typology are discussed – climate change remediation and arms races.

Climate change remediation

Climate change remediation presents another context in which a prisoner's dilemma arises in the international arena. Countries are broadly in agreement that measures should be taken to reverse or at least reduce the negative effects of climate change. However, a given country A also recognizes that it would be even better for A if all other countries took the necessary steps to mitigate climate change, allowing A to avoid being fettered by any new restrictions or regulations. Because other countries see the same payoffs as A, the Nash equilibrium is to hope others will act while taking less or no action oneself. The result is less collective climate change remediation than countries feel would be optimal. This dynamic is of course also an example of a tragedy of the commons, a situation widely understood to be one where a collective resource is overused or exploited such that, without regulation, supplies will become exhausted.[10]

In the case of our second prisoner's dilemma example of climate change remediation, we can see that a binding international treaty that

8 For example, George P Norman and Joel P Trachtman, 'The Customary International Law Game' (2005) 99 AJIL 541.

9 Ibid at 563–564.

10 Garrett Hardin, 'The Tragedy of the Commons' (1968) 162 Science 1243.

committed the major emitters to significant emissions reductions would, if complied with, solve the dilemma. However, thus far the IL that has been created to address climate change has been insufficient to achieve this outcome. The most relevant international treaty, the Kyoto Protocol, which extended the United Nations Framework Convention on Climate Change, was itself extended to 2020 from its initial expiration date of December 31, 2012. However, the United States (US) never ratified the original Protocol, and other countries including Japan, Canada and Russia have opted out of the extension. The result is that the developed countries participating in the Kyoto Protocol account for only about 15 percent of global Greenhouse Gas (GHG) emissions.[11] China is also yet to agree to binding reduction commitments. Therefore it appears that in a tragedy of the commons situation, the parties most responsible for consuming the common good may be less willing than other contributors to take the steps necessary to resolve the prisoner's dilemma. This likely relates to the strength of domestic constituencies that would feel the costs of committing to GHG reductions. Because the negotiations have sought to link the amount of GHG emissions to reduction commitments, the worst culprits would have to 'pay' the most. Thus an asymmetry in the costs of changing the payoff matrix may make it more difficult to attain the domestic support necessary for the worst offenders to commit.

Arms races

A similar situation arises in the case of arms races, such as the US and Soviet build-ups of nuclear weapons. Applying our familiar pattern, both the US and Soviet Union considered the best scenario to be the other country reducing nuclear weapons stocks or at least not building any further weapons, with themselves being able to produce more nuclear weapons or at least not having to reduce their own stocks. The worst case scenario would be the reverse situation, where the other party maintained or enhanced its stockpiles in the face of one's own reductions. The costs of arms escalation were significant, and relative positions could have been maintained through mutually agreed reductions. Yet in the absence of an agreement with teeth, the two countries understandably experienced a Nash equilibrium of continued nuclear weapons accumulation – a

[11] Voice of America, 'UN Climate Conference Extends Kyoto Protocol' December 8, 2012 <http://www.voanews.com/content/un-climate-conference-extends-kyoto-protocol/1561253.html>.

suboptimal outcome as both would have preferred that each country engage in a degree of disarmament.[12]

Nonetheless, the parties did manage to reach an agreement on a subset of nuclear weapons capabilities in the 1972 Anti-Ballistic Missile (ABM) Treaty. This treaty imposed various limitations on the production and deployment of ABMs, and provided for verification measures. The treaty was seen as successful for its nearly 30-year duration. However, in December 2001 the US announced its intent to unilaterally withdraw from the treaty, which duly became invalid in June 2002.[13]

The arms race situation is similar to the climate change dilemma in that asymmetries in power and responsibility have likely made it more difficult to maintain an agreement. Tellingly, both the US and USSR were willing to remain committed to the ABM treaty until the collapse of the Soviet Union, at which point the Bush administration in the US likely perceived the US to be in a more advantaged position and thus found the détente less valuable.

III.3. International Law Formation as Creator of Prisoner's Dilemmas

A third typology of prisoner's dilemmas in the IL context features prisoner's dilemmas that are the *result* of IL formation. This Section briefly describes three examples of this typology.

Least-Developed Countries and Bilateral Investment Treaties

Andrew Guzman has documented the phenomenon of Least-Developed Countries (LDCs) entering into Bilateral Investment Treaties (BITs) that provide for broad investor protections, even though LDCs had rejected the Hull Rule of investor protections when acting collectively.[14] Guzman explains this dynamic as a prisoner's dilemma, in which LDCs found it optimal to reject the Hull Rule when acting together, but determined they

[12] For a detailed collection of sources discussing the US–Soviet arms race as a prisoner's dilemma, see Scott Plous, 'The Nuclear Arms Race: Prisoner's Dilemma or Perceptual Dilemma?' (1993) 30 J Peace R 163. Plous, however, argues that the arms race reflected a misperception on both the Soviet and American sides as to what the preferences of the other party were, and as such that it was not a prisoner's dilemma at all. Ibid 166–174.

[13] Space Daily, 'Anti-Ballistic Missile Treaty Between USSR, US in Details' December 16, 2014 <http://www.spacedaily.com/reports/Anti_Ballistic_Missile_Treaty_Between_USSR_US_in_Details_999.html>.

[14] Guzman (n 7).

were better off individually when they 'defected' to form BITs, even when those BITs incorporated the Hull Rule.[15] In this circumstance, the forming of the BITs – a type of IL – creates the prisoner's dilemma.

Developing countries and provisions in Free Trade Agreements

Another iteration of this variety of prisoner's dilemma is the actions of developing countries in Free Trade Agreements (FTAs) as contrasted with their behavior in the WTO. In the WTO, developing countries have banded together and collectively thwarted efforts to include new agreements on certain topics including investment and competition law. Developing countries have also refused to contemplate incorporating environmental or labor standards into the WTO, and are opposed to any intellectual property protections that go beyond those provided for in the TRIPs Agreement. Notwithstanding these collective positions, developing countries have, in their FTA negotiations with developed countries, routinely agreed to TRIPs-plus intellectual property provisions; environment and labor-related coverage; and investment and competition commitments. Again, the ability to form FTAs leads to this dilemma.

The formation of FTAs notwithstanding a preference for the WTO

A final example of this typology is trade ministers' preference for trade liberalization via the WTO rather than via FTAs, contrasted with their decisions to nonetheless pursue FTAs at the expense of the WTO. FTAs have been routinely referred to by government officials as 'second-best'. Many have noted that the resources that go into FTAs divert attention from the WTO and as such are stumbling blocks rather than stepping stones on the path to multilateral trade liberalization. Again, the situation is a prisoner's dilemma in that the participants see the WTO as a better outcome than FTAs, but the 'cheat' option leads to better overall payoffs because the best case is to have other WTO members concentrate on the WTO and provide multilateral benefits, while member A enters into its own chosen FTAs as well. Of course the outcome has been a flood of FTAs and stalemate within the WTO. As with the above examples, the ability to create the FTAs has caused a prisoner's dilemma.[16]

In this set of examples, there are some PE dynamics that may be influencing the preferences of the countries. In particular, path dependence has likely played a role. The actions of those who have acted before

[15] Ibid 666–667.

[16] See generally Meredith Kolsky Lewis, 'The Prisoner's Dilemma Posed by Free Trade Agreements: Can Open Access Provisions Provide an Escape?' (2011) 11 Chi J Int L 631.

serve as an externality that impacts the moves countries feel they need to make. For example, free trade agreements alter comparative advantage, so non-participants feel they must join FTAs as well just to re-establish the status quo ante. Similarly, in bilateral FTA and BIT negotiations, it is difficult for countries to argue against terms that others have already agreed to in other BITs or FTAs.

IV. CHALLENGES IN INVESTIGATING THE INTERPLAY BETWEEN THE PRISONER'S DILEMMA AND IL COMPLIANCE

Before proceeding further with this exploration of the interplay between IL compliance and the prisoner's dilemma, it is necessary to identify some of the limitations and challenges posed by this examination.

IV.1. Challenges in Applying the Prisoner's Dilemma Concept

The first caveat has to do with the prisoner's dilemma examples just discussed. While game theory literature is replete with examples of prisoner's dilemmas along the lines of those identified above, none of those examples are pure prisoner's dilemmas because the players are not kept from communicating with each other, nor playing in one-shot situations. Indeed, government officials may discuss these issues at great length and make numerous policy choices over time. However, even though players have the opportunity to discuss these problems, they do not always do so. And studies suggest that game theory predictions about behavior in prisoner's dilemma situations are borne out even when parties *can* communicate, if they in fact do not *actually* communicate.[17] But when players do manage to interact to discuss the problems, behaviors are more likely to change.[18]

Therefore it is perhaps more appropriate to view these situations as repeated games in which the parties can learn to cooperate rather than as one-off situations in which each party acts in isolation, while recognizing that the opportunity to communicate does not necessarily translate into actual coordination and cooperation. At the same time, 'repeated games' is also not an entirely accurate way to assess these prisoner's dilemmas.

---

[17] Elinor Ostrom, 'Building Trust to Solve Commons Dilemmas: Taking Small Steps to Test an Evolving Theory of Collective Action', in Simon Levin (ed), *Games, Groups, and the Global Good* (Springer 2009) 207–228.

[18] Ibid at 208.

Over time, officials of governments have multiple occasions to interact with officials from other governments to negotiate over these issues, and in that sense the games are repeated. However, the officials within each country change over time, as do domestic interests and constituencies. Most situations involve multiple parties, multiple objectives, and multiple competing domestic interests. And the timing of the compliance is likely separated – sometimes by a very long time period – from the entering into the IL obligation. The actors that need to do the complying may be different (as in the US) from the actors who entered into the commitment. And circumstances may have changed dramatically from the entering into the IL obligation. So it is unlikely any repeated decision about compliance is made with exactly the same objectives, interests to balance, or priorities as any other time. Furthermore, prisoner's dilemmas are seen as a symmetrical game, but outcomes may be experienced asymmetrically. If the US doesn't comply with a WTO decision, retaliation against it will 'hurt' less than retaliation against a smaller economy.

None of this is intended to say the prisoner's dilemma cannot be a useful model, but to acknowledge the limitations of the model as applied to real-world situations.

IV.2. Challenges in Analyzing 'Compliance'

A second challenge is in pinning down what we mean by 'compliance' in the IL context. In Anne van Aaken and Joel Trachtman's chapter in this Volume, they highlight, in the context of IL, that States have a number of different opportunities to take action.[19] First, the State can decide to sign a treaty. Van Aaken and Trachtman call this 'adhering' to IL; in this Chapter it is characterized as 'committing' to IL. Second, the State can take steps that further that commitment. It can ratify the treaty, and then it can act in accordance with the treaty's terms. So we might call this phase 'compliance'. What if the State doesn't ratify the treaty, such as WTO members failing to implement the TRIPS amendment? Is this noncompliance? And there is yet a third opportunity to take action, which is when the State has been deemed to have violated the treaty or other form of IL. At this stage, if the country changes its conduct, this too could be seen as compliance.

To muddy things further, it is not clear whether we should deem a State to be 'complying' when it, in good faith, believes it is complying (though is later deemed not to be), or if it shouldn't matter what the

---

[19] See van Aaken and Trachtman (n 2).

State's intentions are. On the one hand, if we're examining the State's motives in violating international legal obligations, it would seem that an element of scienter is necessary. On the other hand, perhaps what we really care about is that IL is followed, whether accidentally or intentionally. The WTO dispute over the United States' 1916 Act legislation illustrates these difficulties. Should we view the US as not complying with the WTO by having the 1916 Act on the books but never using it or really being much aware of it? Or did it not become noncompliance until the dispute settlement panel and Appellate Body determined the law was a *de jure* violation of the Antidumping Agreement? Does it matter that the US Trade Representative did not care at all about the 1916 Act and would have been happy to have the law repealed? Or is it only relevant that Congress did not in fact repeal the law in a timely fashion? What if there is noncompliance, but no one complains? Does this count as noncompliance?

There is also a range of possibilities within 'compliance'. A government may believe it is complying, but later be adjudged to be in violation. A country can fail to comply without consequences in some situations either because other countries don't care enough to react or aren't in a position to object. For example, it is widely recognized that many FTAs entered into by WTO members would not satisfy the 'substantially all trade' requirement of GATT Article XXIV, if the members were to agree on a definition of 'substantially all'.[20] Because it is understood that there will be no ramifications if members enter into FTAs that are inconsistent with Article XXIV, members can do so without worrying about whether they are complying or not.

It is also possible to take steps to comply but to fall short, or for the executive to want to comply but be unable to do so due to domestic opposition. Furthermore, compliance will entail action by different branches of government, depending on the measure at issue. For example, in a US safeguards action, the executive decides whether to impose, lift or modify a safeguard. But in a dispute involving a congressionally mandated label, for example, the legislature would be the governmental branch that would need to take action to comply with a finding the labeling requirement is inconsistent with WTO rules. Thus it is too simplistic to conceptualize compliance as a decision of 'the State'. Recent research suggests that the most important determinant of compliance with WTO dispute settlement decisions is the branch of government

---

[20] On this issue see Alberta Fabbricotti, 'The Political Economy of Regional Trade Agreements', below in this Volume.

that would need to act to effect compliance. Within the US, the need for Congressional involvement is correlated with a longer time to take steps to comply and less overall likelihood that compliance will occur.[21]

It is also difficult, though, to generalize about the interplay between government and domestic constituencies in the realm of IL compliance. For example, in the *EC – Hormones* dispute,[22] EC officials have appeared to be largely aligned with the populace in opposing the importation of hormone-treated meat, even in the face of negative WTO rulings.[23] However, there are other examples of noncompliance where the respondent government officials have not been opposed to complying, but powerful domestic constituencies have made doing so infeasible. For example, in the *Australia – Apples* dispute,[24] Australia is complying in a slow and incomplete fashion. Nonetheless, New Zealand has not brought a compliance action, likely because New Zealand recognizes that the challenges are in dealing with Australia's apple industry, not with the will of Australian officials to comply.

Compliance is clearly at issue when a country has been deemed to have acted inconsistently with its IL obligations. For example, when a country is caught having produced weapons subject to production bans, or when a State is deemed by an adjudicatory body to have violated international rules. But sometimes a State will have committed to IL and intended to comply with it, even believed it was complying with it, only to be told later it was in fact in violation. In other circumstances, government officials may want to comply, but political realities at a given time may render compliance infeasible.

These situations likely would not be prisoner's dilemmas, because they would not be the equilibrium outcomes, but rather particular outcomes at a given moment in time. Nonetheless, the terminology poses challenges,

---

21 Rachel Brewster and Adam Chilton, 'Supplying Compliance: Why and When the United States Complies with WTO Rulings' (2014) 39 Yale J Int L 201, 203.

22 See Appellate Body Report, *European Communities – Measures Concerning Meat and Meat Products (Hormones)*, WT/DS26/AB/R (Jan. 16, 1998), Panel Report, *European Communities – Measures Concerning Meat and Meat Products (Hormones)*, WT/DS26/R/USA (Aug. 18, 1997).

23 Antonello Tancredi, 'EC Practice in the WTO: How Wide is the "Scope for Manoeuvre"?' (2004) 15 EJIL 933, 934–935 n 4.

24 See Appellate Body Report, *Australia – Measures Concerning the Importation of Apples from New Zealand*, WT/DS367/AB/R (Dec. 17, 2010), Panel Report, *Australia – Measures Concerning the Importation of Apples from New Zealand*, WT/DS367/R (Aug. 9, 2010).

and we should be mindful that 'compliance' could be viewed at various different points of time, either with or without a scienter requirement.

V. THE INTERPLAY BETWEEN INTERNATIONAL LAW COMPLIANCE AND ENFORCEMENT

It is tempting to argue that the solution to prisoner's dilemmas in IL is to ensure the IL includes an enforcement mechanism. As a first step, the solution to a prisoner's dilemma generally involves altering the payoff matrix so that the players will see cooperation and compliance as the rational choice rather than cheating.

And one way to resolve the dilemma is to enter into a binding agreement, such as a treaty, that has an enforcement mechanism.[25] This can turn the game into a cooperative one, which removes the prisoner's dilemma.[26] There are instances in IL where there is an enforcement mechanism and the IL is complied with. However, the story is not quite so simple. For there are also instances where IL is complied with in the absence of enforcement mechanisms, and examples of a lack of compliance even in the presence of enforcement mechanisms. Examples of each of these phenomena are discussed below.

V.1. International Law Compliance without Enforcement Mechanisms

In many instances, IL is created without any mechanism for ensuring compliance with its terms. And much of the time, IL is largely abided by even without the threat of sanction to deter noncompliance. The nuclear nonproliferation treaty could be seen as one such example. Although a few States have violated the treaty, the vast majority of nonnuclear States have remained so. Perhaps this is because most States do not see it as being in their best interests to become nuclear powers. As such, there is no incentive for them to cheat and diverge from an equilibrium of cooperation. Similarly, for the States that do not engage in torture, or that outlaw child labor, their behavior is likely attributable either to domestic preferences against committing torture and child labor or to a belief that entering such treaties will encourage adherence by other countries, rather

25 James D Morrow, *Game Theory for Political Scientists* (Princeton University Press 1994) at 79.

26 Ibid at 111.

than to the creation and existence of international agreements to refrain from such conduct.

Jens Ohlin has argued that IL is, for States with a strong belief in the normative value of law, a Nash equilibrium – meaning that such States tend to gravitate towards forming IL.[27] Instances of compliance with IL even without enforcement could be examples of Ohlin's Nash equilibrium of IL creation. It seems likely that some IL norms such as not committing genocide and not violating international criminal law are followed due to morality and political preferences, and for these issues, there is not an equilibrium of noncompliance but instead an equilibrium of forming IL. For many States and individuals, compliance with these norms is due to factors exogenous to any IL obligation. In other words, countries and their citizens would generally obey these norms even in the absence of any obligation under IL to do so.[28] This is similar to views expressed by Antonia and Abram Chayes, who have argued that States comply with IL because it is efficient to do so; because treaties are bargained for and therefore reflect shared and preferred values; and because officials accept, in a moral sense, that the State is obliged to follow IL.[29]

However, it may be the case that for the types of IL that are created without enforcement mechanisms, the countries that comply would behave in exactly the same way in the absence of the treaty, whereas the countries that violate the treaty feel they can do so because there will not be any consequences. An example is the International Labor Organization treaties. While the US has not ratified the ILO conventions, it nonetheless provides the protections those conventions assure. If the US were to ratify the conventions, its behavior therefore would not change. On the other end of the spectrum, some ILO signatories violate the conventions with impunity. These States apparently do not see sufficient benefit in complying with these unenforceable obligations, though they apparently

---

27 Jens David Ohlin, 'Nash Equilibrium and International Law' (2011) 96 Cornell L Rev 869, 877.

28 This observation lends support to the decision of van Aaken and Trachtman to limit their discussion of compliance to international rules that require conduct that would *not* occur in the absence of such rules. See van Aaken and Trachtman (n 2).

29 See discussion in Tai-Heng Cheng, *When International Law Works: Realistic Idealism after 9/11 and the Global Recession* (OUP 2005) at 102–103. See also in this Volume, Barbara Delcourt, 'Political Economy of International Law: A Convenient Alliance for the Study of Compliance?' (also referring to Chayes and Chayes in discussing the managerial model).

did see some value in committing to the conventions in the first place. In this way, we can see that *complying* with IL must entail additional or different considerations than merely committing to IL.

However, there are situations when States comply with IL even when it might not suit their domestic interests to do so. The GATT method of resolving disputes reflected this dynamic. Even though GATT panel reports were not subject to an enforcement mechanism, and there likely would have been domestic interests within the complainant's country that would have preferred noncompliance, GATT signatories nonetheless largely complied with the reports that found against them. These circumstances are consistent with Ohlin's hypothesis; however, the above discussion demonstrates that there are other contexts in which Ohlin's argument likely goes too far.

V.2. International Law That Achieves Compliance through Enforcement

A second scenario is presented by the instances where IL is created with an accompanying enforcement mechanism, and States comply with the IL. The World Trade Organization's Dispute Settlement Understanding is an example. This variation within IL suggests some difference in States' attitudes towards the conditions under which they will create and comply with IL. In particular, perhaps IL formation is as Ohlin suggests, a Nash equilibrium – in the instances in which it is created. However, IL is not created in all the possible contexts in which it could be.

When IL is not created, the Nash equilibrium is noncooperation. Such circumstances may be examples of a prisoner's dilemma, whereby States would be better off if they created IL obligations, but where the key States nonetheless find it rational not to do so, because the risks associated with noncooperation by others are too high. It may be that these are the circumstances where the noncooperative equilibrium can be overcome by creating IL with an associated enforcement mechanism. In other words, under certain circumstances, the inclusion of an enforcement mechanism is what leads States to be willing to commit to the IL. They perceive the risks of other parties cheating as reduced due to the availability of sanctions, which alters the payoff matrix and resolves the prisoner's dilemma.

One way to accomplish a change in the payoff matrix is to introduce a reciprocity device that removes, or at least lessens, the temptation to unilaterally defect. If a player knows that cheating will lead to a reciprocal move by the other player, the player will realize that it cannot achieve the payoff outcome of 'I cheat/he cooperates'. This will both remove the incentive to unilaterally cheat and to defect as a defensive move.[30]

Posner and Sykes have argued that where IL is created to remedy a prisoner's dilemma, 'it is vital to the preservation of cooperation over time that nations make credible threats to punish deviation from the rules by other nations.'[31] They suggest that noncompliance is not only acceptable but necessary when it is in response to another participant's violation.[32]

In the case of the international trade regime, the creation of the WTO included formalizing the ability to take retaliatory measures in the event a member is deemed not to have complied with a dispute settlement ruling against it. This is, in essence, a reciprocity-style device. While the prevailing party is not 'cheating' in response to the respondent's failure to rectify its breach of the rules, it is able to take a predictable, sanctioned action in response and reaction to the respondent's inaction.

The tool of retaliation is imperfect in that it is neither automatic nor completely reciprocal. With respect to automaticity, there is no automaticity to continuing the WTO dispute settlement process following an adopted panel or Appellate Body report. In practice prevailing parties have not always initiated a compliance proceeding[33] when the respondent member has not complied with an initial panel or Appellate Body report finding against it. In addition, even when the complainant brings a compliance proceeding and prevails, it is not required to suspend concessions in retaliation upon the finding of noncompliance, and in practice, some prevailing parties have not sought to do so. The lack of an automatic, guaranteed retaliatory response to a failure to comply makes the retaliation instrument a less credible threat than if it were always guaranteed to be applied.[34] With regard to reciprocity, it is not feasible to cause precisely the same amount of injury through suspension of concessions as was inflicted by the respondent's initial measure. The

---

30 See Francesco Parisi, 'Sources of Law and the Institutional Design of Lawmaking' (2001) 19 Journal of Public Finance and Public Choice 95, available at <http://ssrn.com/abstract_id=250971> at 29.

31 Eric Posner and Alan O Sykes, 'Efficient Breach of International Law: Optimal Remedies, Legalized Noncompliance, and Related Issues' (2011) 110 Mich L Rev 243–294 at 256.

32 Ibid at 269.

33 Pursuant to Article 21.5 of the WTO Dispute Settlement Understanding.

34 Thomas C Schelling, *The Strategy of Conflict* (Harvard University Press 1970) at 40.

suspension of concessions will be authorized at a dollar amount equivalent to the harm caused by the initial measure. However, the dollar amount of retaliation may be experienced quite differently by a WTO member with a large economy, such as the US, than by the complainant country, which may have experienced injury to a significant sector within its economy.[35]

V.3. International Law That Features Enforcement but does not Achieve Compliance

As a further complicating factor, even when there is an enforcement mechanism, it may not always lead to complete compliance. For example, the WTO Dispute Settlement Understanding (DSU) provides for measures members can pursue if a fellow member fails to comply with a dispute settlement report's recommendations. Such measures are often referred to as retaliation, although that word is not used in the Understanding itself. As discussed above, this mechanism may lead to States complying more often than they otherwise would with decisions against them. However, notwithstanding the 'teeth' present in the DSU, members do not always comply with WTO dispute settlement reports and as a consequence are sometimes subjected to retaliatory measures.

The inclusion of enforcement measures generally goes hand in hand with demands for assurances and safeguards that the rules will be properly interpreted. Thus while the DSU was drafted to include the ability to retaliate for noncompliance, it was also drafted to include a system of appellate review. But even with these safeguards, the rules had to be drafted to still allow for an out. Compliance cannot be forced. The prevailing party can retaliate if the losing party does not comply, but there is no way to force the losing party to change its regulations. It is unlikely that the US among other major economies would have agreed to the DSU without maintaining the option of noncompliance, albeit under the penalty of some consequences.

Why do States fail to comply?

The decision whether or not to comply will involve different considerations for different States. One possible difference is how likely the

---

[35] Some have suggested that members in addition to the complainant party should play a role in retaliation, and that retaliation should be escalated over time in the event of continued noncompliance. See Simon AB Scropp, *Trade Policy Flexibility and Enforcement in the WTO: A Law and Economics Analysis* (CUP 2009) at 320.

country thinks it is that it will be retaliated against. Ohlin posits that stronger States will be less likely to encounter retaliation in their agreements with weaker countries, should they fail to comply, because weaker States will want to form agreements with stronger States notwithstanding possible defections.[36] At the same time, differences in bargaining power will be less relevant when similarly strong or similarly weak States negotiate with each other.[37] This hypothesis does not seem to be borne out in practice, however, at least not in the international trade context.

To test this hypothesis, an examination was undertaken of all of the cases in which one or more complainants sought authorization pursuant to Article 22.2 of the DSU to suspend concessions in disputes featuring the US as respondent and for which a DSU Article 22.6 or the Agreement on Subsidies and Countervailing Measures (SCM) Article 4.11 arbitration had been completed to determine the level of nullification and impairment (Article 22.6) or appropriate countermeasures (SCM Agreement Article 4.11). Two parallel arbitrations that arose out of one initial WTO dispute (*US – Cotton Subsidies*)[38] and a series of simultaneous arbitrations initiated by multiple complainants from a single WTO dispute (*US – Byrd Amendment*)[39] were each treated as single proceedings. Ohlin's argument would suggest that retaliatory measures would primarily be sought in matters between the US and the WTO's other most powerful members because weaker States are less likely to contest the actions of a stronger State. The data however is to the contrary. Utilizing the methodology described above, the US has been the respondent in five proceedings in which the complainants sought to suspend concessions due to noncompliance. The complainant in two of the disputes was the European Communities – EC (*US – FSC*[40] and *US – 1916 Act*[41]).

---

36 Ohlin (n 27) at 894.

37 Ibid.

38 *US – Subsidies on Upland Cotton – Recourse to Arbitration by the United States under Article 22.6 of the DSU and Article 4.11 of the SCM Agreement – Decision by the Arbitrator*, WT/DS267/ARB/1 and WT/DS267/ARB/2 (Aug. 31, 2009).

39 *US – Continued Dumping and Subsidy Offset Act of 2000 – Recourse to Arbitration by the United States under Article 22.6 of the DSU – Decision by the Arbitrator*, WT/DS234/ARB/CAN and WT/DS234/ARB/MEX (Aug. 31, 2004).

40 *US – Tax Treatment for 'Foreign Sales Corporations' – Recourse to Arbitration by the United States under Article 22.6 of the DSU – Decision by the Arbitrator*, WT/DS108/ARB (Aug. 30, 2002).

41 *US – Anti-Dumping Act of 1916 – Recourse to Arbitration by the United States under Article 22.6 of the DSU*, WT/DS162/19 (Jan. 18, 2002) (on

However, in the other three the complainants were either developing countries or a combination of developing and developed countries. Brazil was the complainant in one of the cases (*US – Cotton Subsidies*) and Antigua and Barbuda in another (*US – Gambling*). Eight WTO members brought proceedings against the US relating to the *US – Byrd Amendment* dispute: Brazil, Canada, Chile, EC, India, Japan, Korea and Mexico. This data is broadly consistent with the US experience as a respondent in initial panel proceedings. At the time of this writing, there are 61 panel reports in which the US has been a respondent. The complainants in these disputes could be characterized in different ways depending on one's definition of 'developing' or 'weaker' but regardless of measure the complainants were roughly split between developed countries and developing countries.[42]

These data points suggest that compliance and retaliation cannot be chalked up solely to similarities or differences in bargaining power.[43] In addition, PE factors may lead to noncompliance even under the new payoff. This is not a prisoner's dilemma problem, because it is not an equilibrium outcome, but it is clear that even if payoffs are changed to solve a prisoner's dilemma, circumstances may still lead to noncompliance from time to time. Sometimes, domestic interests at the time of compliance/noncompliance make compliance seem politically infeasible. This may explain why it often takes more than one iteration of domestic action to achieve compliance. For example, Congress amended the US Foreign Sales Corporation tax more than once before the EU was satisfied the US had complied. Posner and Sykes have posited that situations such as these, where domestic preferences for maintaining a WTO-inconsistent policy (or any other breach of IL) are particularly strong, represent instances where noncompliance with IL constitutes efficient breach.[44] Whether it is efficient breach or not, in these contexts the breaches are not the equilibrium outcome, and thus do not represent a prisoner's dilemma.

February 27, 2002, the parties requested that the Arbitrator suspend the arbitration proceeding).

[42] Using OECD membership as a proxy for development yields 34 complaints by developed countries; 25 by developing countries; and two by a mix of developing and developed.

[43] See also Posner and Sykes (n 31) 268–269 (arguing that, contrary to what might be expected, self-enforcement measures do not favor more powerful countries because, in the repeated prisoner's dilemma game, the powerful countries benefit from mutual cooperation just as do the weaker countries).

[44] Ibid at 260.

There is much literature discussing the consequences of cheating, and being perceived as untrustworthy. But what seems clear is that in reality, countries seem to be able to cheat on an exceptional basis with very little damage to their reputations. The EU and US have each had a small number of WTO matters where they haven't complied (for example, the *EC – Hormones* and *United States – Gambling* disputes), but this has not stopped countries from bringing disputes against the US and EU or otherwise saying much about it – presumably because most of the time they do comply and there is a recognition that in exceptional circumstances compliance may not be possible.

VI. CONCLUSION

In considering the many prisoner's dilemma situations discussed in this Chapter, we can see interplays between prisoner's dilemmas and IL, but there is not necessarily a clear linkage to compliance with IL.

It seems that States may find it easier to rise above the prisoner's dilemmas by cooperating in times of shock, crisis, stress and less so when the negative effects of the prisoner's dilemma are experienced incrementally. There are numerous examples of this phenomenon. The GATT was formed following World War II as a part of an effort to avoid a repeat of the pre-war economic mercantilism. More recently, the Philip Morris challenge to Australia's plain-packaging tobacco regime has jolted developed countries into reconsidering investor-State dispute settlement. On the other hand, in the absence of an exogenous shock, we can see PE forces at work keeping the parties on a path of inaction and noncompliance, and prisoner's dilemmas persist. The Doha Round remains unfinished; States keep entering into FTAs; LDCs keep signing BITs; and climate change negotiations are not bearing much fruit.

Changing the payoff to result in an equilibrium of compliance rather than noncompliance may be linked to changing the PE dynamics. In this regard, a sudden, dramatic shock or change may create the necessary impetus. For example, the 9/11 attacks played a role in WTO members agreeing to the Doha Development Agenda. It was suddenly a priority – for political and strategic reasons – to stand together on an economic matter, when it previously had not been. On the other hand, a shock or change can also create a disincentive to continue cooperating, as demonstrated by the US's withdrawal from the ABM treaty after the collapse of the Soviet Union.

In the main, the prisoner's dilemma can help us to understand why States are reaching a suboptimal outcome; however, it is less good at predicting compliance with IL. Many scholars have attempted to resolve various prisoner's dilemmas by extending them into repeated games, in which case it can be shown that parties will learn to cooperate with one another through strategies like tit for tat and the grim trigger. But, as noted in the caveats above regarding the utility of the prisoner's dilemma, the assumptions underlying the game go too far. We are now assuming the same players with the same objectives repeating the same game over time. This is unrealistic in the State context on all levels. States have repeat interactions, but not the same game. The players within the State change, as do motivations.

It is not surprising, therefore, that in practice what we see is not tit for tat, or grim triggers. Instead, solved prisoner's dilemmas look more like Louis Henkin's famous observation – almost all countries comply with almost all their IL obligations almost all of the time.[45] Rather than cheating leading to rampant cheating by others, if the cheating is isolated and in unique circumstances, it seems that countries can get away with it without a real reputational hit and without triggering tit for tat retaliation.

So how can we use prisoner's dilemmas to help improve IL? The different natures of each suggest that the solutions will not be uniform. But in general, the way to encourage compliance and cooperation rather than cheating is to change the payoff matrix so that it is no longer the rational choice to cheat.

How to do this will vary. While it is popular to argue for third party enforcement, we have seen in practice that compliance can occur without enforcement and that enforcement doesn't always guarantee compliance. In the case of the international trade regime, we saw the creation of the GATT. And even though the GATT did not have as strong a dispute settlement mechanism as exists today, countries didn't by and large renege on their tariff cuts. So while having an enforcement mechanism sounds good, it may not always be necessary. Indeed, although the creation of the WTO included a number of changes designed to make the dispute settlement system more attractive to use and easier to enforce, including a retaliatory mechanism for noncompliance, it is not clear that there is less noncompliance now than under the GATT. The *EC – Hormones* case illustrates the point – even with retaliation, the EU never found it politically feasible to comply.

---

[45] Louis Henkin, *How Nations Behave: Law and Foreign Policy* (2nd edn, Columbia University Press 1979) at 47.

Therefore, one PE lesson that can be drawn from prisoner's dilemmas is that there is no 100 percent solution. The prisoner's dilemma assumption that States' preferences are static and in a sense, all or nothing, is too simplistic. Countries may be willing to agree to a principle and to abide by it, but that does not mean an exception will never come up that would make the State go against the general principle.

The interplay between prisoner's dilemmas and compliance with IL merits further study and consideration. For the moment, we can conclude that there is a subset of IL situations that constitute prisoner's dilemmas, and a subset of those dilemmas can be solved by creating IL with which States will comply. More analysis needs to be done to determine whether we can be more categorical as to which situations will be amenable to this solution.

9. The Political Economy of Judicial Production of International Law

Paul B Stephan*

I. INTRODUCTION

Now more than ever, International Law (IL) is judge-made law. Domestic courts increasingly apply and make rules that they attribute to IL.[1] International tribunals proliferate and also generate international rules and norms.[2] What explains this turn to IL, and what kind of IL do these courts produce? In particular, what accounts for divergence in judicial claims about the content of IL?

* I am grateful for comments and criticism from Ashley Deeks, Mila Versteeg, and participants in a workshop at Melbourne University, the 'Economic Foundations of International Law' Conference at the University of Chicago Law School, the 'Political Economy of International Law' Conference at *La Sapienza* University in Rome, the 'Sokol Colloquium on Private International Law' at the University of Virginia School of Law, the 2014 Conference of the American Society of International Law's International Law in Domestic Courts Interest Group, and a Faculty Workshop at the University of Georgia School of Law. Responsibility for errors, omissions and misjudgments remains mine alone.

[1] Eyal Benvenisti, 'Reclaiming Democracy: The Strategic Uses of Foreign and International Law by National Courts' (2008) 102 AJIL 241; André Nollkaemper, *National Courts and the International Rule of Law* (OUP 2011); Anthea Roberts, 'Comparative International Law? The Role of National Courts in International Law' (2011) 60 ICLQ 57.

[2] Robert E Scott and Paul B Stephan, *The Limits of Leviathan – Contract Theory and the Enforcement of International Law* (CUP 2006) at 128–141; Laurence R Helfer, 'Why States Create International Tribunals: A Theory of Constrained Independence', in Stefan Voigt, Max Albert and Dieter Schmidtchen (eds), *International Conflict Resolution* (Moir Siebeck 2006) at 253; Karen J Alter, 'Delegating to International Courts: Self-Binding vs. Other-Binding Delegation' (2008) 71 L Contemp Probs 37; Gary Born, 'A New Generation of International Adjudication' (2012) 61 Duke L J 775.

Simply put, this Chapter shows that claims about the content of IL reflect the kind of court that makes the claims. I draw on Political Economy (PE) to develop a model of judicial structural design.[3] This model predicts that disparities in outcomes among courts and tribunals reflect State and institutional interests, broadly conceived, rather than pure intellectual and ideological commitments. To use the terminology of this book, the model regards the claims about IL recognized by judicial bodies as an *explanandum* of PE.[4]

The Chapter begins with a discussion of the judicial production of IL. An analysis of disputes among courts and tribunals suggests that the structural features of courts do influence judicial decisionmaking in a manner that is consistent with a rational agent-principal account. Courts disagree about the content of IL because the States that design these organs vary their structure for reasons that reflect State interests.

II. DIVERGENT OUTCOMES IN INTERNATIONAL LAW LITIGATION

For purposes of this Chapter, a simple informal model for the production of IL through courts, both international and domestic is proposed. This Chapter assumes that political decisionmakers (that is, lawmakers who are not courts) can make choices about the design and maintenance of judicial bodies. This Chapter further assumes that these actors value judicial bodies for the work that they can do, but also are jealous of their own prerogatives and fear mission creep. Both at the design stage and downstream when making choices that affect a judicial body, the political decisionmakers will seek to balance the benefits they expect to derive from the body's work with safeguards to lower the risk of unwanted outcomes. Put simply, political choices shape judicial structure.[5]

---

[3] See Anne van Aaken and Joel P Trachtman, 'Political Economy of International Law: Toward a Holistic Model of State Behaviour,' above in this Volume, at 9.

[4] Ibid at 13.

[5] This model resembles that offered in Eyal Benvenisti, 'The Political Economy of International Lawmaking by National Courts,' below in this Volume, at 258. I extend the model to the design of international tribunals.

II.1. Why Courts?

PE addresses the question of why individual States create national courts with particular institutional features as well as why multiple States, acting in concert, create international tribunals. At the municipal level, courts may advance an array of interests. They may entrench particular settlements reached through the political process in instances where the benefits from stability outweigh the advantages of flexibility and adjustment. They may serve as a desirable check on political actors. They may allow lawmakers to extend enacted choices into the future through application of statutory commands. They may receive delegations to update and refine enacted choices in light of later developments. Somewhat darkly, they may provide a safe haven for groups that have lost political authority to continue opposition to the programs of new majorities. Even more darkly, political subordinated courts may perform a masquerade to enable autocrats or kleptocrats to disguise their objectionable acts. In most States, they fulfill their functions against a thick historical, social and cultural background, which complicates any rational-actor analysis of their behavior.

PE indicates that States create such bodies because the benefits derived from their operation outweigh the potential costs. They may facilitate the joint production of collective goods, including peace, security, economic liberalism and environmental quality.[6] They may entrench the production of State-specific goods, such as human rights.[7] More darkly, governments may collude in creating an international body that might demand outcomes that the governments may prefer but, at least in some cases, may lack the ability to sell to domestic objectors.[8]

While embracing these benefits, government may worry that tribunals will act in ways that, individually if not collectively, they would prefer to veto. The possibility of not getting all that one wishes is an unavoidable risk of submitting to third-party dispute resolution, of course. States nonetheless will accept some range of disappointments if the benefits from the dispute-settlement commitment are great enough. What States will attempt to do is to keep the tribunal within that acceptable range of discretion.

---

[6] Scott and Stephan (n 2) at 63–70.

[7] Andrew Moravcsik, 'The Origins of International Human Rights Regimes: Democratic Delegation in Postwar Europe' (2000) 54 Int Org 217–251.

[8] Paul B Stephan, 'Accountability and International Lawmaking: Rules, Rents and Legitimacy' (1996–97) 17 Nw J Int L Bus 681 at 697.

As Benvenisti observes, the choices surrounding the creation and design of international tribunals arise out of a two-level game.[9] States both will make choices on the international level that reflect domestic contestation and will pursue international outcomes that may alter domestic politics in favor of the government making the choices. Governments engaged in the creation of international tribunals must both take account of what domestic constituencies will tolerate and will seek features that will benefit the government. Benefits might include national public goods, such as peace and prosperity, or specific rents for members of the executive branch, such as tribunal outcomes that will block the choices of national oppositions.

II.2. Jurisdiction

When designing a judicial organ, a State, acting unilaterally or collectively, must consider the regret contingency of jurisdiction. The State must contemplate the possibility that the organ will claim competence over a matter that the State would wish it to leave alone. If the State attaches sufficient value to this contingency, it can limit the jurisdiction of the organ either *ex ante* or *ex post.*

Ex ante restrictions on jurisdiction can range from a rule requiring State consent as a prerequisite to jurisdiction in all cases, to a limited and precisely delineated consent to particular kinds of cases. The more a judicial body has control over its jurisdiction, the weaker are *ex ante* restrictions. The European concept of *kompetenz kompetenz*, which asserts that the tribunal has the ultimate authority to interpret and apply its jurisdictional limits, represents a weak restriction.[10] Something similar exists in US jurisprudence. The assertion by Chief Justice Marshall that the Supreme Court has the ultimate authority to declare what the law is has the effect of giving that body control over its jurisdiction through the mechanism of establishing what constitutes a legal question.[11]

The International Court of Justice (ICJ) illustrates relatively strong *ex ante* limits on the jurisdiction of an international tribunal. IL imposes no general obligation to submit disputes to that body. Rather, the ICJ's jurisdiction depends on State consent, either given after a dispute arises through a special agreement, or announced in advance by a treaty or

---

[9] Benvenisti (n 5) at 260–261.

[10] See Joseph HH Weiler, 'The Transformation of Europe' (1991) 100 Yale L J 2403 at 2414.

[11] *Marbury v Madison*, 5 US (1 Cranch) 137, 177 (1803).

declaration.[12] Moreover, States can withdraw consent as to disputes with which the ICJ has not yet been seized.

Ex ante restrictions on jurisdiction also can take the form of procedural doctrines that courts and tribunals will accept as defeasing them of the authority to hear a matter. Standing rules, for example, can strip a tribunal of its power to decide a question.[13] Alternatively, allowing States to assert self-judging provisions as a defense to a claim effectively cedes to the State the right to remove a case from judicial review.[14]

Ex post restrictions comprise the measures that States can take to avoid complying with a judicial organ's demand. One must always bear in mind President Andrew Jackson's famous if apocryphal boast, 'John Marshall has made his decision, now let him enforce it!'[15] States can refuse to obey a judgment or simply fail to move quickly enough. Moreover, even if a State honors a particular judicial command, it can withdraw from the ongoing obligation to respect the judicial organ's version of the law. In the case of domestic laws, the State can enact new laws. In the case of an international obligation, the State can denounce the relevant treaty or adopt a superseding international commitment.[16]

The crafters of legal regimes, whether domestic or international, can design them so as to make withdrawal more or less costly, but they cannot eliminate the option altogether.[17] The relevant issue, then, is the

---

12 Statute of the International Court of Justice, Arts 36(2), 40(1).

13 For example, *Case Concerning the Barcelona Traction, Light and Power Company, Ltd* (Belgium v Spain), [1970] ICJ 3 (State lacked standing under doctrine of investor protection to assert interests of shareholders in a company that had suffered an expropriation).

14 For example, Roger P Alford, 'The Self-Judging WTO Security Exception' (2011) Utah L Rev 697. A weaker form of self-judging is the margin-of-appreciation concept, which allows a tribunal to accord a State substantial discretion while retaining ultimate authority to act. For a defense of the concept, see William W Burke-White and Andreas von Staden, 'Private Litigation in a Public Law Sphere: The Standard of Review in Investor-State Arbitrations' (2010) 35 Yale J Int L 283.

15 See Richard P Longaker, 'Andrew Jackson and the Judiciary' (1956) 71 Pol Sci Q 341 at 349.

16 On withdrawal from international obligations, see Curtis A Bradley and Mitu Gulati, 'Withdrawing from International Custom' (2010) 120 Yale L J 202; Eric A Posner and Alan O Sykes, 'Efficient Breach of International Law: Optimal Remedies, "Legalized Noncompliance," and Related Issues' (2011) 110 Mich L Rev 243.

17 Helfer (n 2) at 269–271.

cost of exit. This in turn depends on the extent and depth of the international regime in which a dispute resolution obligation is embedded.

To consider one extreme, many multilateral agreements dealing with what might be broadly understood to be human rights come with separate optional protocols that mandate dispute resolution, typically in the ICJ. Other multilateral agreements, such as Europe's Energy Charter Treaty (ECT), do little more than provide for dispute resolution. A State can denounce this kind of treaty, as the United States (US) did with respect to the optional protocol to the Vienna Convention on Consular Relations (VCCR) and Russia did with respect to the ECT, without losing any other substantive international law benefits.[18] Similarly, States unilaterally and without any direct costs can withdraw *ex ante* declarations to accept ICJ jurisdiction. By contrast, regimes that include extensive free trade commitments and other significant economic benefits, such as the WTO family of treaties or those of the European Union, present large exit costs. A State for the most part cannot pick and choose which parts of the package of international rights and obligations it will accept: it is mostly all or nothing.

As for refusals to comply, the record is more complicated. Some evidence, drawn from Argentina's recent experience, indicates that a State suffers a penalty in terms of increased cost of capital for its refusal to honor arbitral awards arising out of contracts and investor protection treaties.[19] When the judgment involves interests that are less susceptible to quantification, however, only the State's general reputation as a law-abider comes into play. The evidence that this reputation has a decisive effect on State decisionmaking is not clear. The refusal of the US to abide by the ICJ judgment in *Military and Paramilitary Activities In and Against Nicaragua*, for example, had no clear impact on the US, any more than Iran's flouting of the judgment in *Case Concerning United States Diplomatic and Consular Staff in Tehran (United States of America v Iran)* did.[20] In both instances, the disputing States eventually

---

[18] Ibid. Withdrawal might affect the State's general reputation as a good treaty partner, but the scope and salience of such a reputation is debatable. George W Downs and Michael A Jones, 'Reputation, Compliance, and International Law' (2002) 31 J Leg Stud 95; Rachel Brewster, 'Unpacking the State's Reputation' (2009) 50 Harv Int L J 231.

[19] See Benjamin Hébert and Jesse Schreger, 'The Costs of Sovereign Default: Evidence from Argentina' (2015) (working paper).

[20] [1980] ICJ 3.

composed their differences through compacts that bore little relation to the rights delineated by the Court.[21]

II.3. Appointment

One need look no further than the regular dust-ups over appointments to the Supreme Court of the US for evidence that many informed actors believe that the appointment process has some bearing on the subsequent behavior of the appointed. Political scientists have studied the correlation between the voting behavior of US federal judges and the party affiliation of the President who nominated them.[22] Many have detected patterns that would indicate that the method of choosing a judge does influence what kind of judge one gets. Fewer studies have been done on international judges and arbiters, but those that exist indicate that the selection process matters.[23]

To be sure, these studies do not demonstrate that judges serve simply as conduits for the preferences of political masters. Rather, they indicate that those who nominate and confirm appointments have some ability to predict future voting tendencies and do take those tendencies into account. Moreover, the studies tend to confirm the commonsense supposition that those involved in the appointment process do a better job of predicting general positions, such as an inclination to expand or contract judicial discretion, rather than outcomes as to particular issues.[24]

The design of international courts and tribunals also provides indirect evidence that States believe that the appointment power matters. Although some variation exists, in general international judgeships are allocated either to States or groups of States. In many cases the formal appointment power may reside in some collective, but in practice States

---

[21] In the Nicaragua case, the US blocked enforcement through its Security Council veto. A change in regime in Nicaragua led to dropping of the case. Iran and the US settled the embassy crisis through the Algiers Accords, a compact that specifically barred any compensation or recourse for the diplomats who have suffered from the Iranian conduct deemed unlawful by the ICJ.

[22] Richard L Revesz, 'Environmental Regulation, Ideology, and the DC Circuit' (1997) 83 Vanderbilt L Rev 1717; Frank B Cross and Emerson H Tiller, 'Judicial Partisanship and Obedience to Legal Doctrine: Whistleblowing on the Federal Courts of Appeal' (1998) 107 Yale L J 2155.

[23] See Eric Voeten, 'The Politics of International Judicial Appointments: Evidence from the European Court of Human Rights' (2007) 61 Int Org 669.

[24] For discussion of this point in the context of appointments to the Supreme Court of the US, see John C Jeffries, Jr, 'In Memoriam: Lewis F Powell, Jr' (1999) 112 Harv L Rev 597.

choose their own judge with only minimal oversight by their peers. Thus certain powerful States select candidates to the ICJ and the WTO appellate body, while designated blocs choose others. All parties to the EU treaties and the European Convention on Human Rights (ECHR) get to nominate their candidate to the Luxembourg and Strasbourg Courts, respectively.[25] Other regional courts follow the same pattern.

The one categorical exception involves investment and commercial arbitration. They rely on *ad hoc* panels rather than permanent courts. The parties pick the arbiters, with a neutral mechanism in place to break deadlocks over the tie-breaking arbiter. This process allows disputants to avoid unpredictable or idiosyncratic judges. Each side has an incentive not to waste its pick, and the tie-breaker typically gives the parties indirect influence over the choice of the third arbiter.

Eric Posner and John Yoo have presented some evidence that, *ceteris paribus*, States prefer to appear before *ad hoc* tribunals as opposed to bodies with standing membership.[26] Their case is suggestive rather than conclusive, but it does support the intuition that some connection exists between the appointment power, control over decisionmaking, and a State's willingness to submit a matter to a tribunal. After the creation of the ICJ in 1945 and the Strasbourg and Luxembourg Courts in the early 1950s, States for the next three decades largely avoided creating new tribunals with standing judges. They reversed course only during the heady post-Cold War decade of the 1990s, which witnessed the revitalization or creation of a number of multilateral and regional bodies. That boomlet in tribunal creation since has faded.[27] Meanwhile, the adoption of treaties that incorporate *ad hoc* arbitration has proceeded apace, even

---

[25] In the case of the Strasbourg Court, a State puts forward three nominees, diluting its power to control who gets on the tribunal.

[26] Eric A Posner and John C Yoo, 'Judicial Independence in International Tribunals' (2005) 93 Calif L Rev 1, at 51–54. See also Born (n 2) (documenting proliferation of investment and commercial arbitration tribunals).

[27] Aside from the Caribbean Court of Justice, founded in 2001, and the Special Tribunal for Lebanon constituted by SC Res 1757 in 2007, no international tribunal (to my knowledge) has been created in this millennium. The ECOWAS Court was created in 1991 but did not open for business until 2001, and saw its jurisdiction expanded by a 2005 protocol. Laurence R Helfer and Karen J Alter, 'Legitimacy and Lawmaking: A Tale of Three International Courts' (2013) 14 Theo Inq L 479. The Special Court for Sierra Leone, created in 2002, and the Extraordinary Chambers of the Court of Cambodia, created in 2001, are national tribunals that receive significant support from international organs. More generally, one might distinguish criminal tribunals as a special case, inasmuch as they lack the capacity to render judgment on States as such.

though recently a handful of authoritarian regimes (Ecuador, Russia and Venezuela) have pulled back on such commitments.

II.4. Retention

The power to fire, as well as to hire, extends a principal's power over its agent. One of the measures of judicial independence at the national level is the extent to which judges enjoy some form of tenure.[28] The US, which bestows life tenure and a guaranteed level of compensation on its federal judges, represents the extreme end of constraints on retention discretion. States that regularly discharge or punish judges who do not follow directions occupy the opposite extreme.

At the international level, appointments for terms, with the prospect of renewal, are the norm, and life tenure unheard of. Members of the ICJ, the International Tribunal for the Law of the Sea (ITLOS), and the Appellate Body of the WTO dispute settlement body all have limited terms and face the risk of non-reappointment. Similar rules apply to the Luxembourg court. The Strasbourg Court is exceptional inasmuch as its statute forbids reappointment of judges who have been elected to the body.

A subtle constraint on the exercise of the retention power to rein in international judges is a tradition of no public dissent. The Luxembourg Court, for example, produces only one opinion per dispute, whatever the views of the participating judges. Adherence to this custom protects judges from retaliation by diffusing responsibility for unpopular decisions. But it also limits the power of individual judges to shape debates and influence future decisions.

The strongest example of retention power built into international tribunals is *ad hoc* arbitral tribunals. Because appointments do not outlast the term of the dispute, arbiters must know that their performance in the present case may affect their prospects for future work. They are, in effect, employees at will.

If arbiters prefer re-employment to rejection, and if they believe that their current performance can be observed and taken into account in later re-employment decisions, then they will be reluctant to vote and write in a way that will reduce their future prospects. This presents interesting branding problems. On the one hand, arbiters should avoid seeming idiosyncratic and unpredictable. On the other hand, they presumably

---

28 See, for example, Lars P Feld and Stefan Voigt, 'Economic Growth and Judicial Independence: Cross-country Evidence Using a New Set of Indicators' (2003) 19 Eur J Pol Econ 497.

should not want to seem too predictable, in the sense that their peers would consider them an unabashed and unreconstructed agent for particular interests. Instead, they are more likely to shade toward doctrinal conservatism (no bold new claims) with discernible but not overwhelming bias in favor of a particular, relatively numerous class of parties. In the case of investor-State arbitration, for example, one would expect arbiters generally to mix a reputation for accommodation and persuasiveness with inclinations, but not inflexible commitment to, arguments that favor either investors or States.

II.5. The Effect of Structural Variation

To test the claim that States seek to constrain the actions of international courts and tribunals, four hypotheses as to how particular constraints might affect outcomes are proposed here below.

National courts will demonstrate a significant variation in claims about International Law

This hypothesis reflects three observations: Great variation exists among States in the nature of constraints imposed on domestic courts; national courts engage their political systems in a variety of ways; and various issues have different salience in different countries. To take one extreme, courts that are subservient to their national leaders are unlikely to recognize any IL claim that constrains their political masters, but might invoke IL to undo inconvenient impediments to those masters.[29] Alternatively, a national judiciary might have strong political ties to one party or faction in a contested polity and use IL to bolster rulings that favor that party. Or the judiciary might invoke IL to launch a law reform project that it favors more than the political authorities do, much in the style of (some) US constitutional adjudication.[30]

Because any of these scenarios, as well as variations and refinements, might describe particular national judiciaries, one should expect wide disagreement about both what IL encompasses and what it does when it

---

[29] For example, *Gramara (Pvt) Ltd. v Zimbabwe*, HH 169-2009, HC 33/09 (Zimbabwe High Ct. 2010) (refusing to recognize discriminatory expropriation as illegal); Judgment No 504 of Oct. 19, 2009, Constitutional Chamber of the Supreme Court of Nicaragua, published at <http://librepenicmoncjose.blogspot.com/2009/10/exp-no-602-09-sentencia-no-504-corte.html> (2009 ruling of Nicaraguan Supreme Court invoking human rights law to overturn constitutional term limits so as to allow President Daniel Ortega to retain power).

[30] Benvenisti (n 5).

applies. Moreover, in a world where the corpus of IL is widely seen as undergoing progressive development, innovative claims are not for that reason alone out of bounds. Accordingly, national courts can invoke IL, or ignore it, in many contexts and for many purposes. Because the structure of national courts differs so widely, then claims also should vary, if structure has an impact on product.

The responsiveness of international tribunals to State interests will reflect the jurisdiction, appointment, and retention constraints that apply to them

This hypothesis rests on the premise that States will adjust jurisdiction of international tribunals, appoint judges, and make retention decisions in ways that further their national interests, rather than those of humanity as a whole. The hypothesis does not assume that States choose judges that will act simply as conduits for the foreign office, essentially for the same reasons that arbiters will not try to develop reputations as intractable advocates of particular interests. Rather, the organization of an international tribunal presents a State with a collective action problem. If one State can assign a conduit to the body, while others appoint more independent actors, it would do so. But if all States send conduits, the tribunal would provide no advantages over a diplomatic conference. In the face of this dynamic, States are more likely to further their interests by appointing judges who are influential, which would require some separation between the judge's behavior and the immediate short-term interests of the sending State.

What follows from this analysis is a conjecture that States will set boundaries on what international tribunals will do, rather than procure specific outcomes in particular cases. Because of the collective action aspect of tribunal organization, States normally cannot count on commanding outcomes. They can, however, send representatives who will check tendencies that might lead States to regret creation of the tribunal. States also can select representatives based on second-order characteristics that, over the long run, will match the sending State's preferences. Thus Eric Voeten has demonstrated a statistically significant relationship between the votes of Strasbourg Court judges regarding expansion or constriction of the Court's jurisdiction and the orientation of the sending governments in favor of greater or lesser European integration.[31]

---

31 Eric Voeten, 'The Politics of International Judicial Appointments: Evidence from the European Court of Human Rights' (2007) 61 Int Org 669. But cf

Regional international tribunals will reflect regional interests more often than will multilateral tribunals

Regional tribunals generally are subject to the same political economy as multilateral tribunals. What distinguishes them are the distinctive shared interests of the States that choose the judges. To the extent that regional interests differ from global ones, one would expect that the States selecting judges will seek systematically to advance those regional interests.

The phenomenon documented by Voeten illustrates this hypothesis. One might plausibly assume (and I will argue below) that in general States oppose novel jurisdictional arguments, including those over the scope of IL, that allow an international tribunal to expand its authority at the expense of State autonomy. A regional unification project, however, might alter those preferences, at least where jurisdiction expansion coincides with an increase of the authority of regional institutions that benefits some coalition of States.

Special purpose international tribunals will expand their jurisdiction more frequently than will general purpose tribunals

Tribunals created to process disputes arising from a specific set of events know that their rulings will have limited scope. Because their jurisdiction is limited as to parties, subject matter, and time period, the impact of their decisions is circumscribed. Members of the tribunal will have some incentive to prolong the life of the organ so as to extend their (presumably desirable) employment, and States will not resist because of the limited impact of the tribunal's work. But such tribunals can make idiosyncratic, jurisdiction-expanding claims with greater frequency than permanent tribunals can. Put simply, the damage to State interests from such claims will be less because of the clear limits of the tribunal's powers.

III. THE CASE STUDIES

To test these hypotheses, I consider six issues of general IL in which courts and tribunals have reached divergent outcomes. In five instances, this divergence emerged in a single dispute. In the remaining instance, different international tribunals as well as national courts reached different conclusions about a fundamental principle of IL.

Helfer and Alter (n 27) (arguing that the evidence indicating a link between judicial activism and loss of legitimacy is problematic).

III.1 Sovereign Immunity and Grave Human Rights Abuses

Over the last decade, multiple national courts and two international tribunals have considered whether to recognize a human rights exception to sovereign immunity. The most complex of the cases involved two levels of the Italian judicial system, two levels of the Greek system, and the ICJ. The Greek courts split in a claim based on responsibility for grave war crimes during World War II, with a higher level special court rejecting the exception. The highest level Italian civil court recognized the exception in another war crimes claim, leading Germany, the defendant State, to seek a ruling from the ICJ. The ICJ determined that customary IL required Italy to respect Germany's immunity from suit, even though Germany's army stood accused of committing grave violations of international human rights law on Italian territory. The Italian Constitutional Court in turn struck down the legislation that Italy enacted to implement the ICJ judgment, ruling that the UN Charter and the authority of the ICJ could not override the national constitutional right of access to justice with respect to core human rights.[32]

That one case aside, multiple national courts and the Strasbourg Court also have addressed the issue. Most of the decisions involved the interpretation of national legislation or the ECHR, rather than Customary International Law (CIL).[33] One could therefore distinguish them all as representing *lex specialis* rather than as interpretations of a general international legal obligation. But each of these instances provides evidence that, as the ICJ determined, State practice does not support a rule of CIL carving an exception from State immunity for lawsuits based on grave human rights abuses.

The State immunities episode reveals deep divergence both among national courts and between the ICJ and national courts on a matter of fundamental importance to IL. At the level of substantive law, these judicial organs disagree as to whether civil suits against States and their

---

32 Italian Constitutional Court, Judgment n. 238 of October 22, 2014. Unofficial English translation by Alessio Gracis, available at <http://italyspractice.info/judgment-238-2014>. For more on that case, see Paul B Stephan, 'The Political Economy of *Jus Cogens*,' above in this Volume, at 75.

33 *Princz v Federal Republic of Germany*, 26 F3d 1166 (DC Cir 1994); *Al-Adsani v United Kingdom*, (2001) 34 EHRR 273; *Bouzari v Islamic Republic of Iran*, (2004) 71 OR3d 675 (Canada); *Fang v Jiang*, (2006) 30 TCL 7/8 (New Zealand); *Jones v Ministry of Interior of Saudi Arabia*, [2006] UKHL 26; *Zhang v Zemin*, [2010] NSWCA 255, 243 FLR 299 (Australia); *Jones et al. v United Kingdom*, (2014) 59 EHRR 1.

agents for violations of core human rights themselves violate international law. At a deeper level, they disagree about the hierarchy and fundamental structure of IL. The highest civil court in Italy embraced the conception, popular in academic circles, that human rights, derived from first principles rather than from national enactments, trump all other aspects of IL. The Italian Constitutional Court interpreted national law to achieve the same outcome. The ICJ, the Strasbourg Court and many national courts instead envision IL as a product of State consent, without any exceptions.

III.2. Taxation as Expropriation: The *Yukos* Case

One of the most important international legal developments in the last half-century has been the transformation of investor protection from a matter of diplomacy based largely on claims about international custom to a treaty system that provides for direct arbitration between investors and States.[34] As the system developed, focus shifted from outright seizures of property by the State to regulatory measures that impair the value of an investment. Proponents of the contemporary regime argue that it encourages development and thus improves the life prospects of the poorest of humanity. Critics argue that the system compromises national sovereignty and enriches powerful multinational corporations at the expense of essential regulatory policies, including environmental protection, worker rights, and basic law enforcement.[35]

One of the more remarkable recent disputes involved the Yukos energy conglomerate, a Russian firm that, in its heyday, was that country's largest oil producer.[36] In 2004 the tax authorities levied a massive assessment on the company, immediately obtained a judicial order freezing the firm's property, rejected several overtures to settle the dispute, and then auctioned off the company's principal production assets

---

[34] O Thomas Johnson Jr and Jonathan Gimblett, 'From Gunboats to BITs – The Evolution of Modern International Investment Law' (2010/2011) Yb Int Invest L Pol at 646.

[35] A secondary set of arguments dispute whether international investment law enhances or diminishes the domestic rule of law. Paul B Stephan, 'International Investment Law and Municipal Law: Substitutes or Complements?' (2014) 9 Cap Mkts L J 354.

[36] For details of the dispute and its background, see Paul B Stephan, 'Taxation and Expropriation: The Destruction of the Yukos Oil Empire' (2013) 35 Houston J Int L 1. Between 2008 and the present, this author advised Yukos shareholders in connection with the dispute and testified as an expert witness on behalf of Yukos in the Quasar de Valores proceeding discussed below.

to a conduit entity that passed them on to Rosneft, a State-owned company. A bankruptcy administrator took over management of the company, and three years later procured the dissolution of the firm and the transfer of most of its remaining assets to Rosneft and its affiliates.

Russian courts participated in the assessment of Yukos's tax liability. Because Yukos had substantial overseas assets and operations and several of its officials fled the country, national courts in Armenia, Cyprus, Lithuania, the Netherlands, Switzerland, the United Kingdom (UK) and the US all entertained suits either to enforce or challenge the Russian judicial decisions. Aside from Armenia, each of these national courts refused to further the Russian government's effort to gather in the overseas assets and personnel, but none directly challenged the legality of the Russian assessment and collection proceedings.[37]

Four treaties gave Yukos or its investors a right to challenge the Russian government through international litigation. Three provide for *ad hoc* arbitration, while the fourth, the ECHR, gives jurisdiction to the Strasbourg Court, a permanent tribunal. Arbitral bodies formed by the Swedish Chamber of Commerce pursuant to the UK and Spanish Bilateral Investment Treaties (BITs) and by the Permanent Court of Arbitration pursuant to the multilateral ECT ordered Russia to compensate the investors for the destruction in value of their investment.[38] The Strasbourg Court ruled that the assessment of Yukos's tax liability did not violate the ECHR, aside from certain procedural irregularities, but that the enforcement process failed adequately to account for Yukos's interest in remaining a viable entity.[39]

The divergence between the three investment tribunals and the Strasbourg Court on the legality of the assessment is striking. All these bodies considered essentially the same evidence. The legal standards articulated by the relevant treaties were substantially the same: The investment treaties require compensation in the case of an expropriation, while the First Protocol of the ECHR mandates that a State may not deprive

[37] For a full description, see ibid at 30–34.

[38] *Rosinvest Co UK Ltd v Russian Federation*, Final Award, (2010) SCC Case No 075/2008, IIC 471, ¶ 495; *Quasar de Valores SICA V S.A. v Russian Federation*, (2012) SCC Case No 24/2007, Award, IIC 557; *Yukos Universal Ltd v Russian Federation*, (2014) PCA Case No AA 227, IIC 652.

[39] *OAO Neftyanaya Kompaniya Yukos v Russia*, (2011) ECHR 14902/04, 54 EHRR 19 ¶ 597. The Strasbourg Court's subsequent award of damages for the violations that it recognized was substantial, but far less than those recognized by the BIT tribunals. *OAO Neftyanaya Kompaniya Yukos v Russia*, (2014) ECHR 14902/04, Jul 31, 2014.

anyone of the peaceable enjoyment of property 'except in the public interest and subject to the conditions provided for by law and by the general principles of IL.'[40] Essentially, each had to determine whether the legal basis of Russia's actions were 'sufficiently accessible, precise and foreseeable.'[41] Yet their assessments of the Russian administrative actions and the behavior of the reviewing courts were radically different.

III.3. Retroactivity and International Crimes

Certain grave international crimes, established by treaty, come with an obligation to extradite or prosecute (*aut dedere aut judicare*). This obligation reduces the risk of impunity by providing a path to prosecution for all wrongdoers, as long as that person can be found within any State party. While a number of treaty regimes employ this device, the Convention Against Torture (CAT), the Genocide Convention and the 1949 Geneva Conventions are especially salient because nearly every State has joined them.

The principle of legality, however, complicates the development of international criminal law. This rule requires that criminal liability rest on the prior enactment of a proscription of the conduct in question (*nullum crimen, nulla poena sine lege*). The Nuremberg tribunal punished its subjects based on legal concepts that had no formal legislative basis, either through statute or treaty. The framers of the International Covenant on Civil and Political Rights (ICCPR), two decades later, acknowledged the problematic nature of international criminality through its adoption of a dual formulation. On the one hand, criminal punishment without prior authoritative proscription is forbidden: 'No one shall be held guilty of any criminal offence on account of any act or omission which did not constitute a criminal offence, under national or IL, at the time when it was committed.'[42] On the other hand, 'general principles of law recognized by the community of nations' justify criminal punishment, even if the recognition of these principles had not taken the form of legislation or treaty.[43] In effect, unwritten 'general principles of law' provide an exception to the principle of legality.

What happens when a State under a duty to extradite or prosecute has not yet enacted a law covering the crime in question? Extraterritoriality is exceptional in criminal law, which means that most States, before joining

---

40 ECHR, Protocol 1, Art 1.

41 *OAO Neftyanaya Kompaniya Yukos* (n 39) at ¶ 595.

42 ICCPR, Art.15(a).

43 Ibid, Art 15(b).

a treaty related to international crimes, do not have on their books statutes governing atrocities undertaken by persons with no relation to that State who commit offenses on the territory of other States. If a State adopts such a statute after the atrocity in question, may it apply that statute retroactively to someone who later comes into its territory?

Two international tribunals came to opposite conclusions on this issue with respect to the same accused. Hissène Habré, the dictator of Chad, fled to Senegal in 1990 after eight years in power. Persons claiming to have suffered torture at his hands sought to initiate criminal charges against him first in Senegal, then in Belgium. The Senegalese courts determined that they lacked jurisdiction to proceed because at the time of Habré's crimes Senegal had no law that covered such cases. Belgium's court determined that it did have jurisdiction, and Belgium requested that Senegal fulfill its obligation to extradite or prosecute.

When Senegal subsequently adopted new laws and proceeded to organize a prosecution, Habré appealed to regional tribunals to challenge the legality of this step. The African Court on Human and People's Rights rejected the filing on the ground that Senegal had not accepted its jurisdiction, but the Court of Justice of the Economic Community of West African States (ECOWAS Court) did take the case. In 2010, it ruled that the non-retroactivity principle of the ICCPR barred Senegal from prosecuting Habré. Rather, the Court determined, Senegal would have to hand over Habré to an international tribunal, which alone could try him for violations of the CAT.[44]

Meanwhile, Belgium sought the assistance of the ICJ. That body ruled that, even though the prohibition against torture had become a peremptory norm of IL, the obligation to prosecute or extradite extends only to acts alleged to have occurred after a State had joined the CAT.[45] Senegal still had to act on Habré's case, because he faced charges of violations that occurred after Senegal had joined the treaty. Somewhat cryptically, the ICJ stated that 'Senegal's duty to comply with its obligations under the Convention cannot be affected by the decision of the ECOWAS Court of Justice.'[46]

The ICJ did not address the non-retroactivity issue directly, but did conclude that 'Senegal has breached and remains in breach of its obligations.'[47] As for a remedy, it demanded that 'Senegal must therefore

---

44 *Habré v Senegal*, (2010) Judgment No ECW/CCJ/JUD/06/10.

45 *Questions Relating to the Obligation to Prosecute or Extradite* (Belgium v Senegal), [2012] ICJ 422 ¶¶ 99, 102.

46 Ibid at ¶ 111.

47 Ibid ¶ 117.

take without further delay the necessary measures to submit the case to its competent authorities for the purpose of prosecution, if it does not extradite Mr. Habré.'[48] This demand certainly implies that, as a matter of IL, Senegal faces no barrier to proceeding with a prosecution. This strongly suggests that the ICJ did not believe that the non-retroactivity requirements of the ICCPR prevented Senegal from prosecuting domestically.

Scoring this episode as a clear conflict between international tribunals is not self-evident. The ICJ's summary dismissal of the ECOWAS Court is so cryptic as to admit multiple interpretations, not all requiring a substantive disagreement. But, at the end of the day, the two tribunals seem to have taken a decidedly different view of the relationship between the non-retroactivity principle and the principle of impunity for international crimes. This divergence in turn indicates a fundamental disagreement about the nature of international obligations and the balance of human rights enshrined by IL.

III.4. Consular Notification and Post-Conviction Remedies

For more than a decade, the ICJ and the Supreme Court of the US have disputed the process due to a person convicted of a crime where the initial arrest entailed violation of the treaty obligation to notify foreign nationals of their right to seek assistance from their consulates. In four instances, a US State executed persons while the ICJ was seized of a dispute regarding their fate.[49]

The VCCR, to which almost every State in the world is a party, requires authorities who arrest a foreign national to advise that person 'without delay' of his or her right to contact consular officials to obtain assistance.[50] The several cases that prompted proceedings in the ICJ as well as US litigation all had a common pattern. Local authorities arrested a foreign national without providing the requisite consular notice. The accused, represented by competent counsel, went to trial and never raised the VCCR issue. After conviction and exhaustion of all ordinary appeals, the accused brought a collateral challenge to his sentence based on the treaty violation. In every case, the local law pertaining to post-conviction

---

48 Ibid ¶ 121.

49 *Leal Garcia v Texas*, 131 S Ct 2866 (2011); *Medellín v Texas*, 552 US 491, 554 US 660 (2008); *Federal Republic of Germany v United States*, 526 US 111 (1999); *Breard v Greene*, 523 US 371 (1998).

50 See VCCR, Art 36(1)(b).

remedies treated the VCCR claim as barred because of counsel's failure to raise it in a timely fashion.

At bottom, the disagreement between the ICJ and the Supreme Court reflects different understandings of the relationship of international and domestic law. The ICJ, despite the 'conformity' language of the Convention, indicated deep suspicion of a local rule that seemed to frustrate fulfillment of an international obligation. The Supreme Court, by contrast, expressed incredulity that a treaty right would enjoy a higher level of protection than those guaranteed by the Constitution, which ubiquitously are subject to procedural default.[51] The ICJ believed that the consular notification right survives a competent advocate's decision not to assert it; the Supreme Court did not.

III.5. Hearsay and Human Rights

National judicial resistance to an international tribunal is not confined to the US. Because the process of ascertaining criminal guilt varies significantly among States, and in particular because of the gulf between the common law and civilian worlds in criminal trials, the development and application of international standards to specify minimum requirements is challenging. The British courts and the Strasbourg Court have fought over the meaning of the fair trial guarantee embodied in Article 6(3)(d) of the ECHR with respect to the use of hearsay evidence in criminal trials. The British Supreme Court, like its US counterpart, believes that IL does not forbid traditional criminal justice practice; the Strasbourg Court, like the ICJ, would extend IL into the domain of mainstream common law criminal procedure.

In England and Wales, the Criminal Justice Act 2003 generally forbids the use of hearsay evidence. It does contain exceptions, however, where the inability to produce a witness to testify rests on compelling considerations. In such cases, the defense has greater leeway to challenge the evidence than it normally would; the judge may stop a trial upon conviction where the evidence is insufficiently reliable to justify a guilty verdict; and the judge must give the jury careful instructions indicating that the inability of the defense to confront the witness in question should affect the weight given to the evidence. The Act rejected the former collaboration rule, which had rendered all hearsay evidence going to an

51 *Sanchez-Llamas v Oregon*, 548 US 331, 358–359 (2006).

element of an offense to be inadmissible in the absence of some collaborating evidence.[52]

Significantly, in a common law system inadmissibility means that the court must keep the evidence from the jury, while in a civil law system the criminal tribunal knows the contested evidence but may not rely on it. This distinction affects sequencing: a civil law court can wait until it has received all the evidence before determining whether other evidence adequately corroborates the hearsay material. A common law court does not have that luxury. The practical impact of a rule linking admissibility to the adequacy of collaborative evidence thus differs significantly in the two systems.

In 2009, a chamber of the Strasbourg Court ruled in *Al-Khawaja and Tahery v United Kingdom*,[53] that British practice under the Criminal Justice Act 2003 violated the Covenant. The Supreme Court responded to Strasbourg the following year. In *Regina v Horncastle*, it observed that while an Act of Parliament had obligated British courts to try to conform to Strasbourg jurisprudence, judgments of the Strasbourg Court did not bind them as a matter of precedent and did not relieve them of their obligation independently to determine the meaning of the ECHR in cases before them.[54] It attributed the Chamber decision to a failure to appreciate the mechanics of a criminal justice system that treats the court and the trier of fact as separate and independent decisionmakers. Compliance with the Act, the Court held, satisfied the requirements of the European Convention, even when the evidence in question was crucial to the outcome of a criminal trial.[55]

Strasbourg responded in turn. The Grand Chamber took up *Al-Khawaja* and, at the end of 2011, made a few adjustments in the ruling.[56] It explained that the 'sole or decisive' standard is not absolute. All the same, 'where a conviction is based solely or decisively on the evidence of absent witnesses, the Court must subject the proceedings to the most searching scrutiny.'[57] It concluded that the safeguards contained in the 2003 Act were 'in principle' strong and designed to ensure fairness.[58] Specific instances of its application, however, violated the Convention. The opportunity to challenge that witness's credibility by

---

52 *Regina v Horncastle*, [2009] UKSC 14 ¶¶ 6–17.

53 *Al-Khawaja and Tahery v United Kingdom*, (2009) 49 EHRR 1.

54 Horncastle (n 52) at ¶ 20.

55 Ibid ¶¶ 79–81.

56 *Al-Khawaja and Tahery v United Kingdom*, (2012) 54 EHRR 23.

57 Ibid ¶ 147.

58 Ibid ¶ 151.

means other than cross-examination, and the judge's warning to the jury that the hearsay nature of the evidence weakened its force, did not suffice to ameliorate the Article 6 violation.[59]

Although the Grand Chamber moved in the direction of the Supreme Court, a gap remains. The Supreme Court asserts that the fundamental issue is fairness, and that the admission of hearsay evidence is not inherently unfair. With sufficient safeguards and attention to the circumstances that produced the out-of-court statement, it is willing to base a conviction largely on such evidence. The Grand Chamber, by contrast, seems to require some corroboration, a rule that would revive the practice that the British authorities had abandoned in 2003.[60]

III.6. Imputed Responsibility for International Crimes

International criminal law proscribes conduct such as genocide, torture, and grave war crimes, but no treaty specifies the rules for imputing responsibility for these offenses. Crimes that occur in the course of armed conflict often implicate complex organizations with blurred lines of authority, especially if informal militias rather than conventional uniformed military formations do the dirty work. Two international tribunals, as well as several US domestic courts, have struggled with the issue.

The ICJ confronted the problem in *Military and Paramilitary Activities In and Against Nicaragua (Nicaragua v United States)*.[61] The Court found that the US had given substantial assistance to the irregular forces opposing the Nicaraguan government, thereby violating an international legal obligation not to use force against the territorial integrity of another State. The Court determined, however, that the US was not separately liable for acts committed by the irregulars. To impute responsibility to the US for those acts, the Court held, one would have to establish sufficient 'dependence on the one side and control on the other that it would be right to equate the [irregulars], for legal purposes, with an organ of the US Government, or as acting on behalf of that Government.'[62]

Some years later, the Appeals Chamber of the International Criminal Tribunal for the Former Yugoslavia (ICTY) addressed a challenge to its

---

59 Ibid ¶ 161-62.

60 See also *Moohan v Lord Advocate*, [2014] UKSC 67 (rejecting position of Strasbourg Court on voting rights of convicts).

61 [1986] ICJ 14.

62 Ibid at ¶ 109.

jurisdiction over acts by the Bosnian Serb militia. The appellant had been prosecuted for grave war crimes under the 1949 Geneva Conventions, which apply only if the accused's conduct occurred in an international armed conflict.[63] The prosecutor thus needed to bring Serbia into the narrative to satisfy a jurisdictional element of the offense. Breaking with the ICJ, the Appeals Chamber ruled that it sufficed to show 'that the group as a whole be under the overall control of the State.'[64] A general role in the organization and support of the militia, rather than direct operational control, sufficed to establish State responsibility. The ICTY found the ICJ approach unpersuasive, both because it lacked flexibility and, in the view of the Court, departed from existing State practice.

In the US, the questions of imputed liability under IL arises most often in civil cases seeking to hold non-State actors liable in tort for their involvement in international crimes carried out by States. At least for now, their decisions reflect the disorder in the international sphere. Two circuits have expressly or implicitly embraced the ICJ standard by holding that imposition of liability requires proof that the private actor was under the effective control of a State or otherwise purposively cooperated with a State.[65] The District of Columbia Circuit disagreed and aligned itself with the ICTY.[66]

---

[63] Common Article 3 of the Geneva Conventions deals separately with non-international armed conflicts, and imposes fewer and less specific constraints on States in such circumstances.

[64] *Prosecutor v Tadić*, (1999) Case No. IT-94-1-A at ¶ 120.

[65] *Ford v Garcia*, 289 F3d 1283, 1290 (11th Cir 2003); *Presbyterian Church of Sudan v Talisman Energy*, 582 F3d 244, 257–59 (2d Cir 2009). A related question is whether the customary international law of armed conflict proscribes material contributions to, as opposed to direct participation in, illegal activity. The DC Circuit has ruled that it does not. *Hamdan v United States*, 696 F3d 1238 (DC Cir 2012).

[66] *Doe v Exxon*, 654 F.3d 11, 33–39 (DC Cir 2011). The Ninth Circuit avoided taking a stand on the issue. *Sarei v Rio Tinto*, PLC, 671 F3d 736, 765–766 (9th Cir 2011), vacated, 133 S C. 1995 (2013), dismissed, 722 F3d 1109 (9th Cir 2013). Plaintiffs and academics have tried to avoid the problem by arguing that a more encompassing domestic law, rather than IL, should apply to this issue. Chimène I Keitner, 'Conceptualizing Complicity in Alien Tort Cases' (2008) 60 Hastings L J 61; Ingrid Wuerth, 'The Alien Tort Statute and Federal Common Law: A New Approach' (2010) 85 Notre Dame L Rev 1931. To date, however, the argument has not gotten much traction in the courts.

IV. JUDICIAL BEHAVIOR UNDER STRUCTURAL VARIATION: A REVIEW OF THE CONFLICTS

The six case studies invoked in Part III of this Chapter conform to the four hypotheses advanced in Part II. Where courts and tribunals diverge in their interpretations of IL, their divergences are consistent with the different institutional characteristics of the judicial bodies that produce the interpretations. Conformity is not, of course, proof of causation.

IV.1. Sovereign Immunity

Judicial creation of an exception to traditional sovereign immunity for grave human rights violations has several consequences. First, it permits litigation that may irritate the government of defendant States, leading to complications for the forum State's government. Second, it destabilizes an established body of law, and thus implies that further disruptions may occur down the road. Third, it establishes the capacity of the court to invoke an open-ended set of rules to reach outcomes it regards as desirable, without tying the provenance of the invoked rule to any actions by responsible State actors. Each of these effects, which result from the process of invoking a new, 'progressive development' of IL arising independent of State consent, come with costs, whatever the desirability of the substantive outcomes.[67]

In general, governments have three reasons to dislike this state of affairs. First, when their courts recognize the exception, this act creates diplomatic problems with few if any direct benefits. Second, the precedent exposes them to potential liability in foreign and international tribunals. Third and most significantly, it bolsters the argument that rules of IL can emerge without State participation in their formation and that an independent tribunal can invoke such rules to reach outcomes that the State would rather avoid. Governments normally would prefer not to open such a Pandora's box.

Among national courts, most recognize the difficulty of creating a new exception to immunity and have declined to do so. The two national courts that broke ranks, Greece and Italy, operate in complex, and to some extent dysfunctional, political environments that sometimes draw in the judiciary as an alternative source of authority and legitimacy. As the first hypothesis predicts, national courts as a whole have reached a wide

---

[67] Paul B Stephan, 'Privatizing International Law' (2011) 97 Virginia L Rev 1573.

range of answers to this particular legal question, with a few outliers producing unusual and potentially destabilizing results.

As for the ICJ, the second hypothesis predicts that States are not likely to appoint judges who treat State consent as irrelevant to the formulation of rules that constrain State behavior. Sovereign immunity helps governments by making troublesome disputes go away, or more precisely by ensuring that governments, rather than courts, raise and resolve these issues. A fundamental human rights exception to immunity, whatever its merits, cannot be derived from State consent, and most governments would not like a rule that complicates their jobs and that they did not have a chance to veto.

Complementing this effect is a particular constraint on the ICJ, namely its fragile jurisdiction. As noted above, States can withdraw general consent to ICJ jurisdiction, as both the US and France have done, or not grant such consent *ab initio*, as in the case of China, Russia and, for all practical purposes, India. States also can denounce treaties that provide specific consent, as the US did with the optional protocol to the VCCR. If members of the ICJ value the breadth of its authority, they would tend not to take steps that increase uncertainty about their future actions. Adhering to a methodology that limits the set of rules they can access, as a State-consent approach does, provides some reassurance to the audience of States.

The third hypothesis might explain why the Strasbourg Court was so sharply divided on the issue when it first considered it, in contrast to the ICJ's near unanimity. A number of States that appoint judges to that court typically are willing to support European unification at the price of national autonomy. Expanding the set of rules that the Court can access by disregarding State consent furthers that project. Moreover, the Strasbourg Court was designed to minimize constraints on its judges. The dilution of States' selection power, the absence of retention checks and the high barriers to exit from its jurisdiction give its members greater freedom from accountability, compared to members of other tribunals.

IV.2. Taxation as Expropriation

The Yukos saga has not generated enough investment arbitration decisions to justify any firm conclusions about the distinct incentives of these tribunals. The most one can suggest is that investment arbiters typically are drawn from a pool of lawyers with some business law experience, and hence some capacity to analyze and assess business regulation. The findings against the Russian government in these cases did demand an ability to distinguish normal from abnormal tax assessments and to appreciate how tax recharacterization of business transactions typically works.

The Strasbourg Court is not a special purpose court within the terms of hypothesis four, because it has jurisdiction over a wide range of actors within its region and faces no time cut-offs on its jurisdiction. It is, however, a special subject matter court, inasmuch as its mandate is limited to human rights violations. For historical and cultural reasons, human rights specialists tend not to come from the business world. Especially in Europe, their training and career paths are departmentalized. Thus it is not surprising that a court staffed by human rights specialists would display considerable diffidence towards the project of reconstructing national tax laws and their administration.

Moreover, in accordance with the third hypothesis, the States that have signed up to the ECHR on average accept a larger role for State involvement in business matters than, say, the US or most Commonwealth countries, even though that involvement may lead to rent-seeking and wasteful redistribution.[68] The Convention itself suggests a lower level of protection for property rights than, say, that provided by most BITs, the ECT or the US Constitution's Takings and Due Process Clauses. The members of the Strasbourg Court might believe that, while they may interfere in police affairs and the criminal justice system without facing much resistance from the States subject to their jurisdiction, meddling with business regulation will elicit concern, resistance, and retaliation. In such circumstances, the Court might be willing to allow formal categorization of an action as tax enforcement to foreclose any serious look behind the measure, lest even a minimal review suggest that other measures also might face scrutiny.

---

[68] According to the International Finance Corporation (IFC)'s most recent study of business regulations for domestic companies, half of the 44 ECHR parties studied fell out of the top 35 countries in terms of ease of doing business, with four in the bottom 100. The IFC did not rate Andorra, Lichtenstein and Monaco. By contrast, New Zealand, the US, the UK, Australia and Canada came in third, fourth, seventh, tenth and seventeenth, respectively. International Finance Corporation, Doing Business 2013 – Smarter Regulations for Small and Medium-Size Enterprises 3 (10th edn, 2012).

IV.3. Retroactivity and International Crimes

The difference between the ECOWAS Court and the ICJ on the applicability of international criminal law to pre-enactment conduct is consistent with the third hypothesis. For the ICJ, the formulation that a country cannot use a failure to act domestically as a defense to a violation of its international obligation breaks no new ground and thus did not expand the reach of IL at the expense of State autonomy. In particular, the majority was careful not to address the question of whether a State had an obligation to prosecute grave human rights abuses in advance of assuming a treaty obligation, thus keeping the focus of IL formation on State consent.

One can explain the ECOWAS Court decision as reflecting a common apprehension by West African States that recolonialization might come garbed in the raiment of IL. They thus might choose judges that systematically fight harder to preserve State sovereignty against assertions resting on European-origin international rights. For these judges, IL, in the form of the ICCPR and its rule of non-retroactivity, becomes a shield to protect a State from international (that is, Western Power) accountability.

IV.4. Consular Notification and Post-Conviction Remedies

The puzzle presented by the consular notification imbroglio is the willingness of the ICJ persistently to challenge a hegemon State as to an issue seen by US lawyers and judges as having some importance. One relevant factor might be the uniqueness of US post-conviction remedies. Other countries engage in post-conviction review more rarely and less comprehensively, making it easier to maintain flexibility in the rare case where a change in circumstances justifies revisiting a conviction. Thus, as a practical matter, the VCCR issue had a unique context in the US. No other country combines broad but formalized post-conviction review with resort to capital punishment. The ICJ decision thus had no ramifications beyond the US.

Consistently with the second hypothesis, the ICJ may have found it easier to maintain its course. Whatever the throw-weight of the US in international politics generally, on the ICJ its particular influence does not extend beyond the one judge that it selects for that body. The other judges confronted a national practice – capital punishment – that they found extremely distasteful even if they lacked a sound basis to declare it categorically illegal, and a supposed procedural bar to the international legal claim that had no counterpart in most other national criminal justice regimes. The ICJ rulings expanded the scope of an international treaty at the expense of national autonomy, but in a context where only one State would suffer the loss.

IV.5. Hearsay and Human Rights

The Strasbourg-British conflict over hearsay evidence presents essentially the same puzzle as does the VCCR episode. The UK is not the most important country in Europe (that would be Germany), but it is influential and its legal practices and respect for human rights are well known. Why did the Strasbourg Court choose to fight this battle? Again, nearly unique institutional features, consistent with the second hypothesis, may provide an answer.

Very few countries in Europe employ the common law jury, which the British see as a fundamental aspect of their legal system. Rather, lay persons sit with professional judges on the tribunal. As noted above, exclusion of evidence functions very differently in a common law process, because the decision to admit is irreversible and may arise early in a proceeding. The Strasbourg ruling, consistent with the second and third hypothesis, ignored this distinction. As a practical matter its approach affects, at most, only the UK and Ireland.

IV.6. Imputed Responsibility for International Crimes

The divide between the ICJ and the ICTY on the legal standard for holding a State accountable for the actions of private persons conforms to the second and fourth hypotheses. As already discussed, the ICJ faces substantial constraints that induce caution in the imposition of obligations on States. The ICJ's formulation of the standard for imputing responsibility, an issue that might arise in a wide range of contexts and thus affect many States, limits the risk of liability.

The ICTY faced very different incentives. Because its jurisdiction extends only to persons in and around the former Yugoslavia and events tied to a specific time period, any rules it ascribes to IL present no risk of application to States generally. Moreover, its remit is limited to international crimes, which for the most part (genocide excepted) require a nexus between individual actors and States. Asserting a more encompassing standard thus bolstered its jurisdiction without risking any retaliation from interested States.

The disarray among US domestic decisions suggests a largely instrumental approach to the issue, thus bolstering the first hypothesis. Courts that favor the expansion of a regulatory regime, such as Alien Tort Statute

(ATS) litigation, adopt a liberal rule of imputation, while those skeptical of the regime do the reverse. Indeed, one court, the DC Circuit, has taken both approaches, one to advance ATS litigation, the other to limit the use of military commissions to dispose of accused terrorists.

V. CONCLUSION

A view of the world that explores judicial behavior through the lens of a rational-actor model can help unpack the messy new world of IL. Like all models, this approach makes choices about the relevance of data and thus excludes potentially valuable information.[69] The cost may be worth it, however, if the resulting insights make the complex social phenomena under observation more tractable. Moreover, a focus on rationality and interest may serve as an antidote to the unreflective normativity that for so long has made it difficult for outsiders to take IL seriously.

One consequence of this approach is a shift of metaphors. When talking about judges, both generally and in the international legal system in particular, Ulysses, not Hercules, becomes the better model.[70] The evidence suggests that judges are cagey in many respects, including respecting the limits that political decisionmakers impose on them. While they have a range of discretion, the range has boundaries that reflect State interests.

This Chapter argues that the present state of the world of judicially produced IL is one of dissensus, and that reasons exist to expect this state to continue indefinitely. If this is so, then judicial claims about the content of IL will continue to diverge, reasoned dialogue notwithstanding.

---

[69] 'Essentially, all models are wrong, but some are useful.' George EP Box and Norman R Draper, *Empirical Model-Building and Response Surfaces* 74 (Wiley 1987) at 424.

[70] Cf Ronald Dworkin, *Law's Empire* (Harvard University Press 1986).

10. The Political Economy of the (Non-)Enforcement of International Human Rights Pronouncements by States

Andreas von Staden

I. INTRODUCTION

Human rights are protected by a large number of global and regional agreements, partly of a general character, partly focused on select rights, and partly addressing human rights incidentally in the context of other issue areas. In addition to laying down primary rules, many agreements also provide for the establishment of supervisory bodies and a range of mechanisms to monitor the extent to which States abide by the obligations they have accepted under these agreements and to settle disputes on their interpretation and application. A few supervisory bodies, all situated at the regional level, are constituted as courts[1] that have been authorized to issue legally binding judgments, with the attendant obligation to comply with them. By contrast, the ten bodies established to monitor and solve disputes regarding the nine principal UN human rights treaties[2] are

[1] They are the European Court of Human Rights (ECtHR), the Inter-American Court of Human Rights (IACtHR), and the African Court of Human and Peoples Rights (AfrCtHPR). The American and African systems also include Commissions of Human Rights and of Human and Peoples Rights, respectively, whose decisions are legally non-binding. Originally, the ECHR also provided for a commission and binding decision-making authority of the Council of Europe's Committee of Ministers; both were abolished with entry into force of Protocol no 11 (1 Nov 1998).

[2] For basic information on each of these, see Monitoring the Core International Human Rights Treaties <http://www.ohchr.org/EN/HRBodies/Pages/TreatyBodies.aspx> accessed 10 Sep 2015.

'committees' whose make-up and procedures evince some judicial elements without, however, being fully judicialized.[3] All of the treaty bodies have (by now) been given the optional competence to receive and respond to 'communications' from States and/or individuals claiming violations of the legal instrument in question. In addition to dispute settlement decisions and some other types of output, the treaty bodies in particular review and provide so-called 'concluding observations' on the periodic reports that States are required to submit and in which they are expected to comment on the laws, policies and other practical measures they have adopted to give effect to the treaties domestically. This rich set of monitoring and dispute settlement institutions and mechanisms has produced a wealth of pronouncements on the human rights obligations of States under the various international legal instruments. These pronouncements, despite the absence of formal legal bindingness of much of the supervisory bodies' output, nonetheless have a normative quality in that they articulate, albeit with different degrees of specificity and persuasiveness, how States ought to behave in light of the human rights obligations they have accepted by ratifying the relevant treaties. This normative component raises the twin questions of, on the one hand, the extent to which States actually comply with the supervisory bodies' normative output,[4] and, on the other, whether and how compliance[5] can be enforced when States fail to comply.

This Chapter addresses the second question. While existing assessments of (non-)compliance rates suggest that there is a broad 'opportunity space' and need for enforcement, there is very little enforcement activity actually in evidence at the international level: While the treaty regimes create supervisory bodies, they do not provide for institutionalized enforcement mechanisms – beyond opportunities for naming-and-shaming – that could be employed in response to cases of intentional or grossly negligent non-compliance with supervisory body pronouncements, that is, in cases where enforcement, rather than management

[3] The only global court with potentially comprehensive jurisdiction over human rights obligations (but no standing for individual claimants) is the International Court of Justice (ICJ); see generally Shiv Bedi, *The Development of Human Rights Law by the Judges of the International Court of Justice* (Hart 2007).

[4] For a review of the main theories of State compliance with IL, see Ulyana Kohut, below in this Volume.

[5] On the concept of compliance see Barbara Delcourt, above in this Volume.

techniques,[6] appears to be suitable and likely more effective. In the absence of institutionalized enforcement, States have to engage in enforcement on an individual or collective basis, using strategies and techniques that are available in the international law (IL) and politics toolkit, but here as well, we do observe very little enforcement activity empirically. As Louis Henkin noted, '[f]or most international norms or obligations there is no judgment or reaction by the community to deter violation' and, indeed, 'it is unusual for States not directly involved to respond to a violation even of a widely accepted norm [...].'[7] Human rights advocates may bemoan the lack of compliance with human rights obligations and the unwillingness of other States to step up and provide enforcement either individually or collectively, but a sober look from a Political Economy (PE) perspective that foregrounds the strategic environment in which States assess the expected costs and benefits of the enforcement of human rights pronouncements[8] makes clear that non-enforcement is indeed the outcome to be expected and enforcement the atypical course of action.

The next Section provides an overview of the output generated by the principal regional and global treaty-based human rights supervisory bodies to show the rich landscape of normative pronouncements on the contents of international human rights law. After this overview, I address the significance of legal status for the question of enforcement, arguing that a pronouncement's legal status affects the available, legally permissible means to enforce that pronouncement, but not the possibility of enforcement as such. I then turn specifically to the conditions under which enforcement of human rights pronouncements by States that are assumed to act rationally may be expected to occur, and when not. The last Section summarizes and concludes.

---

[6] On 'enforcement' vs 'management' in ensuring compliance, see Abram Chayes and Antonia Handler Chayes, *The New Sovereignty: Compliance with International Regulatory Agreements* (Harvard University Press 1995).

[7] Louis Henkin, *How Nations Behave: Law and Foreign Policy* (2nd edn, Columbia University Press 1979) 58.

[8] For a different PE approach to human rights enforcement employing Marxist methodology, see Ivan Manohka, *The Political Economy of Human Rights Enforcement* (Palgrave Macmillan 2008).

II. THE UNIVERSE OF PRONOUNCEMENTS ON THE HUMAN RIGHTS OBLIGATIONS OF STATES

The monitoring and dispute settlement activities of the set of five regional judicial and quasi-judicial human rights institutions and the ten UN human rights treaty bodies[9] have produced a voluminous body of normative pronouncements on State behaviour in the field of human rights that articulate, with varying degrees of specificity, expectations as to appropriate behaviour under the human rights norms over which these bodies' subject matter jurisdiction extends. Table 10.1 below provides an overview of the number of States subject to the supervisory bodies' jurisdictions as well as of the quantitative dimension of some of their output as of late 2014.

II.1. Types of Pronouncements

Dispute settlement decisions (judgments, views, reports)

Both the regional courts and commissions as well as all of the nine principal UN human rights treaties, or their protocols, provide for individual complaints mechanisms, and most, except for the Convention on the Elimination of all Forms of Discrimination against Women (CEDAW) and Convention on the Rights of Persons with Disabilities, also for inter-State complaints.[10] Only in the case of the European Court of Human Rights (ECtHR) are both individual and inter-State complaints automatically accepted as part of the ratification of the European Convention on Human Rights (ECHR).[11] In the American system,

---

[9] Many other international bodies here omitted address human rights directly or incidentally, such as the International Labour Organization, the European Committee for the Prevention of Torture and Inhuman or Degrading Treatment or Punishment, the European Committee of Social Rights, the Arab Human Rights Committee, and various UN-Charter-based organs and UN specialized agencies; on the latter two, see Michael Haas, *International Human Rights: A Comprehensive Introduction* (Routledge 2008) ch 9.

[10] Nigel Rodley, 'The Role of and Impact of Treaty Bodies', in Dinah Shelton (ed), *The Oxford Handbook of International Human Rights Law* (OUP 2013) 633–634.

[11] ECHR arts 33 and 34. This is the case since the entry into force of Protocol no 11 on 1 Nov 1998. Before that, individual complaints and the Court's jurisdiction were optional, requiring separate declarations of acceptance.

Table 10.1 Output of main regional and global human rights supervisory bodies[a]

	Supervisory Body	Operational since:	Number of States subject to supervisory body's jurisdiction (as of December 2014)	Number of States accepting competence to receive individual complaints (as of December 2014)	Country Reports / (sets of) Concluding Observations (as of ...)	Number of judgments/ views/ reports on the merits (as of ...)	Thereof: Judgments finding at least one violation
Regional Bodies	European Court of Human Rights	1959	47	47	N/A	15,277 (2013)	14,121
	Inter-American Court of Human Rights	1979	20	20[b]	N/A	184 (2013)	≥ 169[c]
	Inter-American Commission of Human Rights	1960	35	20/35[d]	64	370 (1997-2013)	*No summary statistics available*
	African Court on Human and Peoples' Rights	2006	26	7	N/A	2 (2014)	2
	African Commission on Human and Peoples' Rights	1987	53	53	40	83 (2013)	*No summary statistics available*

UN Treaty Bodies	Human Rights Committee	1976	168	115	~420 (24/07/2014)	1,008 (03/2014)	850
	Committee on Economic, Social and Cultural Rights	1985	162	17	~424 (18/06/2014)	– (2013–)	–
	Committee on the Elimination of Racial Discrimination	1970	177	55	~684 (25/09/2014)	30 (05/2014)	15
	Committee on the Elimination of Discrimination Against Women	1982	188	105	~614 (24/07/2014)	16 (2014)	15
	Committee Against Torture	1988	156	65	~341 (23/01/2014)	238 (08/2014)	88
	Subcommittee on Prevention of Torture	2007	76	N/A	11 (25/08/2014)	N/A	N/A
	Committee on the Rights of Persons with Disabilities	2009	151	85	~20 (31/10/2014)	5 (05/2014)	–
	Committee on Enforced Disappearances	2011	43	17	~8 (22/04/2014)	–	–
	Committee on the Rights of the Child	1991	194	14	~633 (09/19/2014)	–	–
	Committee on Migrant Workers	2004	47	Indiv. complaint mechanism not yet in force	~36 (05/01/2014)	–	–

Sources: [a] Ratifications/declarations: UN treaty collection <treaties.un.org/Pages/Treaties.aspx?id=4&subid=A&lang=en> and UNHCHR status of ratification database <indicators.ohchr.org/>; Annual Reports of courts, commissions, and committees; African Human Rights Case Law Analyser <caselaw.ihrda.org/acmhpr/>; concluding observations and views: entries in database (not verified for uniqueness, numbers should only be taken to indicate magnitude) and statistical surveys on individual complaints available through UNHCHR at <www.ohchr.org/EN/HRBodies/Pages/HumanRightsBodies.aspxand> all accessed 15 Dec 2014.

[b] Equals number of States that accept the Court's jurisdiction (complaints, however, can be referred to the Court only by States or the Inter-American Commission on Human Rights).

[c] Includes friendly settlements.

[d] The two figures represent the number of States subject to the Commission's jurisdiction under the American Convention on Human Rights (= all ACHR parties) and under the American Declaration of Human Rights (= all OAS member States), respectively.

individual complaints are automatically accepted, but inter-State complaints are optional,[12] while in the African system, the African Commission of Human and Peoples' Rights (AfrCmHPR) can receive communications from both States and individuals, but the African Court's competence with respect to the latter is optional.[13] In all of the UN human rights treaties, both types of complaints proceedings are optional, requiring either a separate declaration under the treaty or the ratification of an additional protocol. Except for a few instances in the European and the American human rights systems,[14] the inter-State procedures have so far not been used.[15]

Interim measures

When it appears during dispute settlement proceedings that an applicant's rights might be irreparably damaged prior to a decision on the merits, most of the courts, commissions, and committees have 'ordered' the respondent State, often without explicit authorization in the relevant treaty, to take interim measures to protect the applicant's legal position (for example, through staying an execution or deportation).[16]

Concluding observations

All UN human rights treaties require States to periodically submit reports to the committees in which they are to describe, as, for example, in the

---

[12] American Convention on Human Rights (ACHR) arts 44 and 45 (1); IACmHR Rules of Procedure art 51.

[13] African Charter on Human and Peoples' Rights (AfrChHPR) arts 47–54 and 55–59 (note that the African Commission's competence with respect to communications other than from States was intended to identify repeated, widespread violations, not to settle individual disputes); Protocol to the AfrChHPR on the Establishment of an African Court of Human and Peoples' Rights art 34 (6).

[14] As of late 2014, only 24 inter-State applications, several relating to the same situation, had been lodged with the Convention organs, and only four of these have so far resulted in judgments of the Court; Inter-State Applications <www.echr.coe.int/Documents/InterStates_applications_ENG.pdf> accessed 14 Sep 2015. In the Inter-American system, a mere two applications have been lodged, one of which was found to be inadmissible; see Jo Pasqualucci, *The Practice and Procedure of the Inter-American Court of Human Rights* (2nd edn, CUP 2013) 136–137.

[15] Rodley (n 10) 633; Office of the High Commissioner of Human Rights, Human Rights Bodies (OHCHR): Complaints Procedures <www.ohchr.org/EN/HRBodies/TBPetitions/Pages/HRTBPetitions.aspx> accessed 14 Sep 2015.

[16] See generally Jo Pasqualucci, 'Interim Measures in International Human Rights: Evolution and Harmonization' (2005) 38 Vanderbilt J Transnatl L 1.

case of the International Covenant on Civil and Political Rights (ICCPR), 'the measures they have adopted which give effect to the rights recognized and [...] the progress made in the enjoyment of those rights.'[17] The treaty bodies then review the reports and articulate so-called 'concluding observations' which include the committees' assessments, concerns and recommendations. The latter are frequently of a more general character than findings in case-specific judgments and views,[18] but are normative nonetheless, telling States what they should do to bring their conduct into conformity with the requirements under the respective treaty, as interpreted by the competent committee.

A random selection reveals this normative character as, for example, when the Human Rights Committee (HRC) concludes that Ireland 'should [*inter alia*] revise its legislation on abortion, including its Constitution, to provide for additional exceptions in cases of rape, incest, serious risks to the health of the mother, or fatal foetal abnormality';[19] when the Committee against Torture (CmAT) recommends that Ecuador 'should ensure that torture is considered an offence in its domestic law and should adopt a definition of torture that includes all the elements contained in article 1 of the Convention. The State party should also ensure that such offences are made punishable by appropriate penalties [...]';[20] or when the Committee on the Elimination of all Forms of Discrimination against Women (CmEDAW) 'invites [the Indian] parliament to take the necessary steps regarding the implementation of the present concluding observations between now and the next reporting period under the Convention.'[21] All of these pronouncements articulate general, but clear behavioural expectations that are amenable to assessment in terms of compliance and non-compliance.

---

[17] ICCPR art 40 (1).

[18] During the Cold War some State representatives argued (with some success due to the culture of consensus) that the HRC should not assess performance by States at all; see Michael O'Flaherty, 'The Concluding Observations of United Nations Human Rights Treaty Bodies' (2006) 6 HR L Rev 28–29.

[19] HRC, *Concluding Observations on the Fourth Periodic Report of Ireland*, UN Doc CCPR/C/IRL/CO/4 (19 Aug 2014) 3 (para 9).

[20] CmAT, *Concluding Observations on the Combined Fourth to Sixth Reports of Ecuador*, UN Doc CAT/C/ECU/CO/4-6 (7 Dec 2010) 3 (para 10).

[21] CmEDAW, *Concluding Observations on the Combined Fourth and Fifth Periodic Reports of India*, UN Doc CEDAW/C/IND/CO/4-5 (24 July 2014) 2 (para 7).

General Comments

Some committees occasionally adopt so-called 'General Comments' which are intended to provide interpretive guidance to Convention law; suggest policies to be adopted by States, in part based on best practices; and indicate the pieces of information that States should include in their periodic reports.[22] Because they 'clarify [...] expectations of what the conventions demand of State parties',[23] using the signal words 'obligation', 'require', 'should' and 'must', they form part of the committees' normative output. The HRC, for example, has explicated in its General Comments the conditions under which States may derogate from ICCPR provisions in states of emergency and the requirements under the substantive provision on freedom of opinion and expression;[24] the Committee on the Rights of the Child (CmRC) has detailed the obligations of States to prevent, or remedy the consequences of, violence against children;[25] and CmEDAW has articulated guidelines for assuring the economic rights of women 'in all matters relating to marriage and family relations' under art 16 of the Convention.[26]

Inquiries and urgent actions

Some committees can initiate inquiries and reports independent of specific complaints or State-submitted self-assessments that can have a normative quality. The CmAT, the Sub-Committee on the Prevention of Torture (SPT), and CmEDAW, amongst others, have been given this mode of operation by treaty, and the HRC claimed the authority on its own behalf.[27] The Inter-American and the African Commissions can likewise initiate reports and studies on their own. In addition to its individual complaints procedure, the Committee on Enforced Disappearance (CED) has been given the authority to initiate 'Urgent Actions' with

---

22 Helen Keller and Leena Grover, 'General Comments of the Human Rights Committee and Their Legitimacy', in Helen Keller and Geir Ulfstein (eds), *UN Human Rights Treaty Bodies: Law and Legitimacy* (CUP 2012) 124–126.

23 Rodley (n 10) 631.

24 HRC, *General Comment no 29: States of Emergency (Article 4)*, UN Doc CCPR/C/21/Rev.1/Add.11 (31 Aug 2001); *General Comment no 34: Freedoms of Opinion and Expression (Article 19)*, UN Doc CCPR/C/GC/34 (12 Sep 2011).

25 CRC, *General Comment no 13: The Right of the Child to Freedom From all Forms of Violence*, UN Doc CRC/C/GC/13 (18 April 2011).

26 CmEDAW, *General Recommendation on Article 16 of the Convention on the Elimination of All Forms of Discrimination against Women* (Economic Consequences of Marriage, Family Relations and Their Dissolution), UN Doc CEDAW/C/GC/29 (30 Oct 2013).

27 Rodley (n 10) 629 and 636.

the objective 'that a disappeared person should be sought and found [...] as matter of urgency', in the course of which the CED 'may transmit recommendations to the State Party, including a request that the State Party should take all the necessary measures, including interim measures, to locate and protect the person concerned.'[28]

Other normative output

Casting an even wider net, there are many further types of pronouncements that also exhibit a normative quality of 'ought-ness': Like General Comments above, advisory opinions also clarify aspects of the law that may have behavioural implications. Friendly settlements, where provided for and formally recognized, contain commitments of a usually monetary, but sometimes also substantive nature. Even decisions of a procedural nature, such as those on admissibility, have normative import and can trigger non-compliance, for example, when a State disregards a positive admissibility decision and refuses to participate in the proceedings.

II.2. The Legal Status of Pronouncements

Only a few of these pronouncements are expressly recognized as legally binding. In the case of the three regional courts, their statutes affirm the legally binding status of their judgments.[29] While the reports of the two regional commissions in individual complaints cases are not so characterized, they do monitor compliance with them and with friendly settlements,[30] and have reported instances of non-compliance to the general assemblies of their regional umbrella organization.[31] This indicates that despite the absence of express legal bindingness, there is an expectation that these decisions are responded to in an appropriate manner.

In the UN human rights treaties and protocols, no mention is made of the legal status of the supervisory bodies' output. This silence, plus the choice of terminology (for example, 'views', 'concluding observations',

---

[28] CED art 30 (1) and (3).

[29] ECHR art 46 (1); ACHR art 68 (1); Protocol on AfrCtHPR art 30.

[30] In the case of the IACmHR provided for in its Rules of Procedure arts 47 (3) and 48 (1).

[31] See for example, Combined 32nd and 33rd Activity Rep AfrCmHPR, AU Doc EX.CL/782(XXII) Rev.2 (Jan 2013) 9 (para 24), <www.achpr.org/files/activity-reports/32-and-33/achpr5152_actrep32and33_eng.pdf>; IACmHR, Annual Report 2013, 74–330, <www.oas.org/en/iachr/docs/annual/2013/docs-en/AnnualReport-Chap2-D.pdf> accessed 14 Sep 2015.

and 'recommendations', instead of 'decisions' or 'judgments') strongly suggests that compliance with their pronouncements was not intended to be a legal obligation. Subsequent practice also provides evidence for the 'general perception of States that Views do not impose legal obligations on them. [...] At best, [States] acknowledge that their acceptance of the individual communication procedure entails an obligation to review their position, or [...] "to address the conclusions of the Committee".'[32] The same lack of a legal obligation to comply is generally recognized as applying to concluding observations 'by virtue of their recommendatory character'.[33]

The fact that a committee pronouncement is not legally binding does not mean, however, that it is normatively irrelevant or without effect. As the legalization literature has highlighted, normativity and obligation are not binary in nature, but come in degrees, and even 'soft commitments may [...] implicate the legal principle of good faith compliance'[34] with the underlying treaties which, after all, remain legally binding instruments.[35] In the HRC's own opinion, 'the views of the Committee under the Optional Protocol represent an authoritative determination by the organ established under the Covenant itself charged with the interpretation of that instrument'; the customary obligation of States to perform treaties in good faith is thus said to result in 'a duty to cooperate with the Committee'.[36] In the case of interim measures, the HRC has even asserted their legally binding quality, as '[f]ailure to implement such

---

[32] Rosanne van Alebeek and André Nollkaemper, 'The Legal Status of Decisions by Human Rights Treaty Bodies in National Law', in Helen Keller and Geir Ulfstein (eds), *UN Human Rights Treaty Bodies: Law and Legitimacy* (CUP 2012) 372 and 373.

[33] Walter Kälin, 'Examination of State Reports', in Helen Keller and Geir Ulfstein (eds), (n 32) 31; Jasper Krommendijk, *The Domestic Impact and Effectiveness of the Process of State Reporting under UN Human Rights Treaties in the Netherlands, New Zealand, and Finland: Paper-Pushing or Policy Prompting?* (Intersentia 2014) 9–11.

[34] Kenneth Abbott, Robert Keohane, Andrew Moravcsik, Anne-Marie Slaughter and Duncan Snidal, 'The Concept of Legalization', in Judith Goldstein, Miles Kahler, Robert Keohane and Anne-Marie Slaughter (eds), *Legalization and World Politics* (MIT Press 2001) 24–28.

[35] For the ICCPR, see HRC, *General Comment no 31: The Nature of the General Legal Obligation Imposed on States Parties to the Covenant*, UN Doc CCPR/C/21/Rev.1/Add. 13 (26 May 2004).

[36] HRC, *General Comment no 33: The Obligations of States Parties under the Optional Protocol to the International Covenant on Civil and Political Rights*, UN Doc CCPR/C/GC/33 (5 Nov 2008) paras 13 and 15.

interim or provisional measures is incompatible with the obligation to respect in good faith the procedure of individual communication [...].'[37] While the specific content of State obligations under non-binding pronouncements remains subject to debate, many commentators agree that States, at a minimum, have to engage seriously with the arguments and conclusions advanced by the treaty bodies and give them some weight in their decision-making.[38] In any event, the output of the committees, even if formally non-binding, may have effects simply by engendering expectations and being invoked by other actors. Michael Reisman's comment, made in the context of the International Court of Justice (ICJ)'s advisory opinions, that the lack of legal bindingness does not by itself negate the 'political or even legal force' of such pronouncements applies here as well.[39]

III. THE SIGNIFICANCE OF LEGAL STATUS FOR ENFORCEMENT

In a basic sense, 'enforcement' is simply '[t]he act of putting something such as a law into effect' and 'the carrying out of a mandate or command.'[40] Under that definition, compliance with an obligation, whatever its cause, would always also count as 'enforcement' of that obligation simply by virtue of giving effect to it. Similarly, the legal literature often refers to the recognition and application of norms, or specific interpretations thereof, by judicial bodies as 'enforcement' of those norms or interpretations.[41] In the social sciences, however, the term 'enforcement' has a more circumscribed meaning. Here, enforcement is commonly understood as a specific type of response to situations in

---

37 Ibid para 19.

38 O'Flaherty (n 18) 34–36; Henry Steiner, 'Individual Claims in a World of Massive Violations: What Role for the Human Rights Committee?', in Philip G Alston and James R Crawford (eds), *The Future of UN Human Rights Treaty Monitoring* (CUP 2000) 30; Geir Ulfstein, 'Individual Complaints', in Helen Keller and Geir Ulfstein (eds), *UN Human Rights Treaty Bodies: Law and Legitimacy* (CUP 2012) 92–100.

39 W Michael Reisman, 'The Constitutional Crisis in the United Nations' (1993) 87 AJIL 92.

40 *Black's Law Dictionary* (6th edn, West 1990) 528.

41 See only Mary Ellen O'Connell, *The Power and Purpose of International Law: Insights from the Theory and Practice of Enforcement* (OUP 2008) chs 8 and 9 (addressing 'International' and 'National Court Enforcement', respectively).

which an actor under an obligation to perform some act (or refrain from performing it, as the case may be) does not comply with that obligation. Enforcement (or the credible threat thereof) seeks to bring about compliance by so affecting the cost-benefit calculations of an actor that compliance becomes the preferred course of action in comparison to non-compliance. Conversely, where compliance is voluntary, for example, based on self-interest, there is no need for enforcement. On this view, then, judicial decisions may apply, clarify and develop the law, but they do not as such enforce it (although their decisions may constitute precursors to enforcement).[42]

Enforcement always works through the imposition of costs on the non-complying actor (and usually generates costs for the enforcer as well): These may either be costs that are actually incurred, or they may be opportunity costs in the form of the conditional withholding of benefits, subject to the performance of the desired behaviour.[43] The nature of these costs may differ: They can be material in kind, such as in the case of economic or military sanctions; political, as in the suspension of voting rights in international organizations or diplomatic isolation; or social and psychological, as with naming and shaming; or a combination of these three. Any type of obligation can in principle be made subject to enforcement, irrespective of whether it is legally binding or not; for enforcement as a technique it does not matter from what source an obligation originates, as long as someone with the power to enforce recognizes it as an enforceable obligation and acts accordingly. And indeed, violations of many non-legal norms – social, cultural, religious, or political – are regularly sanctioned by other actors,[44] often with a view to compelling a return to more acceptable behaviour. In the context here under consideration, the principal difference between legally binding and non-binding pronouncements is not that only the former are subject to

[42] See similarly Clifford Carruba and Matthew Gabel, 'Courts, Compliance, and the Quest for Legitimacy in International Law' (2013) 14 Theo Inq L 506–507.

[43] The granting of benefits *ex ante* as a type of payment in expectation of subsequent compliance would, by contrast, usually be classified as an inducement ('carrot'), rather than enforcement ('stick'), but also contains an element of the latter in that failure to perform in accordance with the conditions of the reward will likely generate opportunity costs with respect to future cooperation and benefits. On rewards in the enforcement context, see Anu Bradford and Omri Ben-Shahar, 'Efficient Enforcement in International Law' (2012) 12 Chi J Int L 375, 382–383 and 391–393.

[44] Cf Geoffrey Brennan, Lina Eriksson, Robert Goodin and Nicholas Southwood, *Explaining Norms* (OUP 2013) 43–46.

enforcement, but rather that the legally available options (may) differ: State behaviour in response to legally binding decisions by international courts is subject to the secondary rules of the IL of State responsibility, whereas the legally non-binding output of human rights treaty committees is not.

As formulated by the International Law Commission (ILC), a State's responsibility is engaged if it has committed an internationally wrongful act, that is, if conduct attributable to the State breaches, or has breached, an international obligation incumbent upon it.[45] A breach occurs 'when an act of that State is not in conformity with what is required of it by that obligation, regardless of its origin or character', including obligations that arise from the decisions of international organizations, such as courts.[46] Although not expressly stated in the draft articles, it is made clear throughout the commentaries that 'obligation' there always means legally binding obligations under IL.[47] Two consequences of responsibility for an international wrongful act are important here: *First*, such responsibility triggers the threefold secondary obligation to end conduct in violation of the primary obligation, to prevent its recurrence, and to make reparation for any injury caused;[48] *Second*, an injured State may take countermeasures against the offending State that are themselves in breach of international legal obligations, subject to certain restrictions.[49]

In the case of human rights obligations, the injured party is normally not a State, but individuals or corporate non-State actors to whom the obligations in question are primarily owed. At the same time, human rights are an exemplary instance of 'community norms' in IL that are said to operate *erga omnes*, in the case of the most basic physical integrity rights that have become part of custom, or *erga omnes partes*, in the case of rights which are rooted in treaty law or regional custom. For such *erga omnes* obligations, the draft articles, building upon the ICJ's *Barcelona Traction* jurisprudence, provide that any State with a legal stake in them may invoke the responsibility of another State that has breached such an obligation and may demand the cessation and non-repetition of the violation.[50]

---

[45] ILC, Draft Articles on the Responsibility of States for Internationally Wrongful Acts (ARSIWA), with Commentaries arts 1 and 2 (2001) ILC Yb, vol. II, Part Two.

[46] Ibid arts 12 and 55.

[47] Ibid *passim.*

[48] Ibid arts 30 and 31.

[49] Ibid arts 22 and 49 ff.

[50] Ibid art 48 (1) and (2).

The thornier issue, of course, is whether this entitlement also results in the right to take countermeasures. While it is clear that States are not generally obligated to engage in enforcement or other action in response to non-compliant behaviour by other States – except in narrowly circumscribed circumstances concerning grave human rights violations[51] and *ius cogens* norms[52] – and that such a general positive obligation would also not necessarily be desirable, if only for practical reasons,[53] the question is whether a State would be legally permitted to do so if it held a preference for such a course of action. Some have discerned in State practice support for the proposition that countermeasures by non-injured States would be permissible under customary law at least in the case of 'large scale or systematic breaches of obligations *erga omnes*'.[54] The ILC, however, decided that State practice was too 'embryonic' to identify an existing rule and that the issue was too controversial politically to develop this area of the law through the draft articles.[55] These considerations resulted in a compromise 'saving clause' that merely notes that the chapter on countermeasures 'does not prejudice the right of any other State, entitled under article 48, paragraph 1, to invoke the responsibility of another State, to take lawful measures against that State to ensure cessation of the breach and reparation in the interest of the injured State or of the beneficiaries of the obligation breached'.[56] Whether such lawful measures also include countermeasures that would, in the absence of a foregoing breach against which they are directed, be unlawful, is thus expressly left open. While countermeasures might thus at least potentially be available with respect to the enforcement by non-injured States of some legally binding *erga omnes* obligations, they are not available as a 'circumstance precluding wrongfulness' with respect to legally non-binding pronouncements, simply because the State responsibility regime does not formally apply to them.

While some regimes provide for enforcement mechanisms with respect to non-compliance with the decisions of their judicial institutions, at least

---

[51] Monica Hakimi, 'State Bystander Responsibility' (2010) 21 EJIL 342–344.

[52] ARSIWA (n 45) art 41.

[53] Lea Brilmayer and Isaias Yemane Tesfalidet, 'Third State Obligations and the Enforcement of International Law' (2011) 44 NYU JILP 37 ff.

[54] Christian Tams, *Enforcing Obligations* Erga Omnes *in International Law* (CUP 2005) 250.

[55] James Crawford, *State Responsibility: The General Part* (CUP 2013) 703–706.

[56] ARSIWA (n 45) art 54.

in principle,[57] no such institutionalized enforcement mechanisms, either globally or regionally, exist with respect to international human rights pronouncements.[58] Under the ECHR, the Council of Europe's Committee of Ministers is charged with supervising the execution of the judgments of the ECtHR, but it has no material means at its disposal to enforce compliance where it is not forthcoming; the most it can do is publicize instances of non-compliance, bring them before the Court again under art 46 (4) ECHR, or, as a last step, expel a recalcitrant member State from the Council. In most of the other regimes, the treaties do not even provide for a follow-up procedure on compliance with judgments, reports, or views;[59] what follow-up has emerged has been pursued at the supervisory bodies' own initiative.[60] While many supervisory bodies issue reports to the relevant assemblies of States,[61] the latter likewise have no formal enforcement powers beyond naming-and-shaming in this respect. In the absence of institutionalized enforcement mechanisms – an absence that itself can be taken to indicate the treaty parties' general disinclination to enforce human rights commitments[62] – States willing to enforce non-binding obligations would thus either have to use lawfully available means – such as diplomatic and public censuring, postponing

---

[57] For the ICJ, see UN Charter art 94 (2) and Karin Oellers-Frahm, 'Article 94', in Bruno Simma et al. (eds), *The Charter of the United Nations: A Commentary* (3rd edn, OUP 2012) 1966–1968; for the WTO, see Understanding on Rules and Procedures Governing the Settlement of Disputes, Annex 2 of the Agreement Establishing the World Trade Organization (WTO) art 22 (2); for the EU, see Treaty on the Functioning of the European Union (TFEU) art 260 (2).

[58] Or with respect to most *erga omnes* obligations, for that matter; cf Karl Zemanek, 'New Trends in the Enforcement of Erga Omnes Obligations' (2000) 4 Max Planck UN Yb 16.

[59] Cf Bas de Gaay Fortman, *Political Economy of Human Rights: Rights, Realities and Realization* (Routledge 2011) 46–47 (noting that 'there is remarkably little attention [in the global human rights system] to the follow-up of cases in which evident violations of human rights were established').

[60] See Rodley (n 10) 638–639; Kälin (n 33) 27–28 (follow-up to concluding observations); Ulfstein (n 38) 106–107 (follow-up to Views); Pasqualucci (n 14) 303 ff. (IACtHR monitoring of compliance with its judgments).

[61] For example, the UN human rights treaty bodies submit annual reports on their work to the UN General Assembly (see only ICCPR art 45 and ICCPR-OP art 6), while the IACmHR and the IACtHR submit reports to the OAS General Assembly (ACHR art 65; Statute of the IACmHR art 18 lit f).

[62] As sometimes also documented in the *travaux préparatoires*; see for example, with respect to the HRC, Makau wa Mutua, 'Looking Past the Human Rights Committee: An Argument for De-Marginalizing Enforcement' (1998) 4 Buffalo HR L Rev 218–219.

cooperative arrangements with the target State, or adding conditionalities as part of trade policy[63] – or decide that violations of other obligations, and any possible consequences thereof, are costs they are willing to bear to enforce compliance with the obligation in question.

IV. ENFORCING HUMAN RIGHTS PRONOUNCEMENTS

Despite ample opportunity and demand (by the prospective beneficiaries) for the enforcement of human rights pronouncements that are not voluntarily complied with, however, empirically observable enforcement of human rights obligations in general, and of human rights pronouncements by monitoring and dispute settlement bodies specifically, is rare. The remainder of this Chapter discusses why this under-supply of enforcement is not an unintended systemic aberration, but, assuming rational State actors, the predictable[64] outcome that follows from weighing the relative costs and benefits of enforcement and non-enforcement.

IV.1. The Demand Side: The Incidence of Non-Compliance

As noted, enforcement is a response to threatened or actual non-compliance, so that the need for it dwindles as voluntary compliance becomes prevalent. While the compliance record with respect to some types of pronouncements and measures in some regions and some types of States is solid and of a reasonably high standard,[65] for all treaties and State parties as a whole it is clearly neither perfect nor even satisfactory: As regards adverse views of treaty bodies, the rate of compliance has been estimated to range between 10% and 30%;[66] similarly, a recent

---

[63] See for example, Chayes and Handler Chayes (n 6) 88; Emily Hafner-Burton, *Forced to be Good: Why Trade Agreements Boost Human Rights* (Cornell University Press 2009).

[64] Beth Simmons, *Mobilizing for Human Rights: International Law in Domestic Politics* (CUP 2009) 115.

[65] With respect to the ECHR and ECtHR, see Andreas von Staden, *Shaping Human Rights Policy in Liberal Democracies: Assessing and Explaining Compliance with the Judgments of the European Court of Human Rights* (PhD dissertation, Princeton University 2009).

[66] Ulfstein (n 38) 104–106; van Alebeek and Nollkaemper (n 32) 357; Open Society Justice Initiative, *From Judgment to Justice: Implementing International and Regional Human Rights Decisions* (Open Society Foundations 2010) 118–121.

study on the effectiveness of concluding observations found that 'most of [them] have remained ineffective in terms of leading to or influencing actual policies and legislation'[67] (indeed, many States fail to comply with their treaty-based obligation to submit initial and periodic subsequent reports in the first place);[68] at the end of 2013, the IACtHR still monitored compliance with 148 out of its 184 judgments;[69] and even in the case of the presumably most effective human rights regime in the world, the ECHR and ECtHR, close to 11,000 judgments were still being monitored by the Committee of Ministers at the end of 2014, some of them nearly 20 years old.[70] Compliance with pronouncements that require States to change their ways almost always involves material and/or political adjustment costs – sometimes more, sometimes less, depending on the scope and depth of the necessary changes – and thus creates incentives to avoid them through non-compliance. Where such incentives exist, enforcement is one potential instrument to deter or correct non-compliant behaviour that, in order to be effective, must impose costs for non-compliance that are at least of the same magnitude as the benefits of avoiding the costs of compliance so as to neutralize them.[71]

IV.2. The Supply Side: The Rational Choice Calculus

Enforcement always involves costs: It imposes real or opportunity costs on the actor against which an obligation is enforced, but also generally creates costs for the enforcer. This is obviously the case in circumstances where the imposition of sanctions requires the deployment of a State's own resources ('retaliation', in Andrew Guzman's typology of the 'three Rs of compliance'),[72] but also applies to circumstances of withholding benefits, such as when blocked market access denies people in the enforcing State the benefit of being able to buy goods produced in the targeted State which might be available at lower prices, higher quality, or

---

67 Krommendijk (n 33) 372.

68 Cf Reporting Status of Human Rights Treaty Bodies (13 Feb 2013), <lib.ohchr.org/HRBodies/TreatyBodies/Documents/ReportingStatus2013.xls> accessed 10 Sep 2015.

69 IACtHR (2013) Ann Rep 71.

70 Committee of Ministers, Supervision of the Execution of Judgments and Decisions of the ECtHR (2014) 8th Annual Report 30.

71 George Downs, David Rocke and Peter Barsoom, 'Is the Good News about Compliance Good News about Cooperation?' (1996) 50 Int Org 386.

72 Andrew T Guzman, *How International Law Works: A Rational Choice Theory* (OUP 2008) 46–48.

otherwise be essential for the domestic economy; in addition, the targeted State may retaliate in turn.[73] Because enforcement is costly, it will not be provided freely, but, assuming rational decision-making, only if it promises expected benefits that over some specified time horizon exceed the expected costs incurred by engaging in the necessary level of enforcement activity. As a corollary, where the costs, or lack of benefits, incurred by the potential enforcer due to the non-compliant behaviour of another State (and thus the expected benefits of returning that actor to compliant behaviour) are negligible, or the costs for the necessary level of enforcement are too big in relation to the expected benefits, or the likelihood of success, given the sources of non-compliance and the circumstances of the target, is too small,[74] the rational choice will be to abstain from enforcement.

Importantly, the calculus for or against enforcement, to be complete, must not only include the direct costs and benefits of engaging in, or abstaining from, enforcement, but also the effects that such action may generate among relevant audiences beyond the immediate enforcement dyad, most notably other States and domestic constituencies. These two audiences may show no interest in the issues at stake in a given enforcement situation in which case they can be ignored, but they might also either approve or disapprove of such action and as a result generate benefits or costs, respectively, of their own. Because other States usually lack complete information about the true motives of the enforcing State, they may view its behaviour as aggressive and guided by self-interest, rather than as the good faith enforcement of legal obligations, and may impose costs of their own in response.[75] Domestic audiences may likewise applaud or criticize the government's conduct and may reward or punish it accordingly at the polls, through public opinion, and other expressions of (lack of) support.

Figure 10.1 shows the key variables in a potential enforcer Y's comparison of the payoffs of the two principal options in response to non-compliance by State X. State Y has a general preference in favour of compliance with a particular human rights standard by State X and must now assess whether the sum of the expected costs and benefits of engaging in enforcement is positive or negative. Enforcement will

---

[73] For a discussion of costs associated with different sanctions, see Bradford and Ben-Shahar (n 43) 385–389.

[74] Cf ibid 383–384 and 389–390.

[75] Alexander Thompson, 'The Rational Enforcement of International Law: Solving the Sanctioner's Dilemma' (2009) 1 Int Theo 311–312.

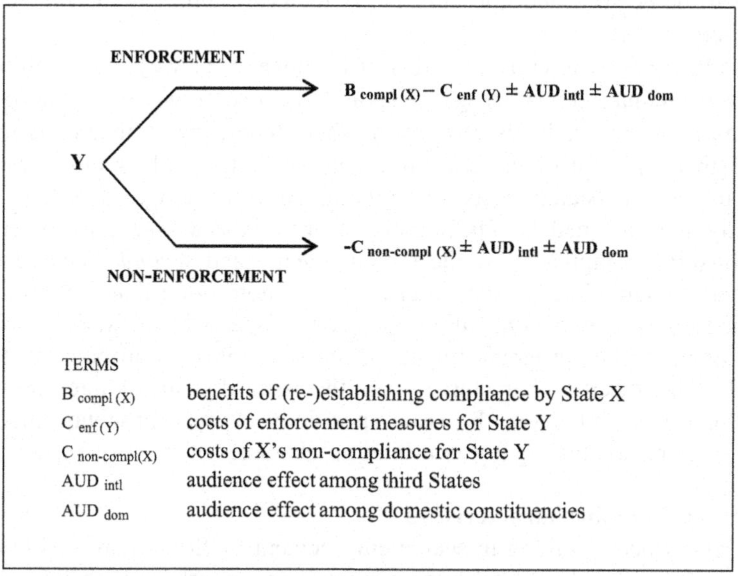

Figure 10.1 The potential enforcer's cost-benefit calculations

normally be motivated primarily by the expected benefits of (re)establishing compliance by X ($B_{compl(X)}$), but also creates enforcement costs for Y ($C_{enf(Y)}$). In addition, Y will have to take into account the expected effect among relevant audiences, namely, on the one hand, other States (AUD_{intl}), and, on the other, domestic audiences (AUD_{dom}). This effect can be positive, and hence a benefit, or negative, and thus a cost. In the case of abstaining from enforcement, State Y would suffer the externalities of non-compliance with an obligation by State X ($C_{non\text{-}compl(X)}$), if any, but would not incur direct enforcement costs. Still, abstaining from enforcement may also have audience effects, both internationally and domestically, as other States or domestic interest groups may, for example, prefer to see enforcement by State Y and withhold support for it as a result of its decision not to provide enforcement; alternatively, abstention from enforcement may be viewed as the appropriate course of action and either receive a neutral response or even be rewarded. The expected audience effects for enforcement and non-enforcement should be logically consistent among the two options, so that if an audience effect is a cost in the case of enforcement, that audience should either be neutral or bestow a benefit in the case of non-enforcement, and vice versa. For State Y to engage in enforcement, the sum of the terms under 'enforcement' will have to be positive and normally larger than the sum of the terms under 'non-enforcement'.

Given these basic considerations, it becomes clear why State enforcement of human rights obligations (and of other *erga omnes* (*partes*) norms more generally) is rare, even when bracketing further complications that arise out of the collective nature of these obligations:[76] *First*, because the expected costs of enforcement for individual States are mostly not matched by sufficiently sizable expected benefits of (re-) establishing compliance by the targeted State; and *second*, because the expected international audience effects will more often than not tend to be negative and thus constitute costs. Three aspects of the various types of human rights pronouncements discussed above contribute to this result: The specific characteristics of the issue domain of international human rights protection; the issue specificity of most pronouncements; and – after all – the legally non-binding character of most of them.

Effects of domain characteristics

The first aspect resulting in scarce enforcement by States is rooted in the very nature of international human rights law and affects both first- and second-order compliance.[77] As has been pointed out before, unlike some other areas of IL, such as trade or security, norms for the international protection of human rights are, by their very nature, intended to have effects almost entirely domestically and lack the element of reciprocity:[78] their purported benefits do not require the cooperation of States in order to realize joint gains that would be unavailable otherwise. To the contrary, and leaving aside for the moment constraints imposed by limited resources, each State party to a human rights treaty can generate the benefits of that treaty and work towards achieving its object and purpose independent of what other States are doing. As a corollary,

---

[76] While the number of States that could legitimately engage in enforcement increases with the qualification of an obligation as *erga omnes*, so does arguably the free-rider problem; see, respectively, Eric Posner, 'Erga Omnes Norms, Institutionalization, and Constitutionalism in International Law' (2008) University of Chicago Law & Economics Working Paper no. 419 <http://ssrn.com/abstract=1211424> accessed 14 Sep 2015, and Alexander Stremitzer, 'Erga Omnes Norms and the Enforcement of International Law' (2009) 165 JITE 29.

[77] First-order compliance refers to compliance with primary treaty norms, whereas second-order compliance addresses compliance with the output of third-party dispute settlement and monitoring bodies; see Roger Fisher, *Improving Compliance with International Law* (University Press of Virginia 1981).

[78] Louis Henkin, 'International Law: Politics, Values and Functions' (1989) 216 Recueil des Cours 250; Simmons (n 64) 123.

compliance with human rights obligations by one State does not, for the most part, create direct benefits for other States, nor do human rights violations, again, for the most part, generate negative externalities that impose a burden on the other parties to the treaty regime in question. In other words, in the great majority of cases, the direct benefits of compliance ($B_{compl(X)}$) as well as the direct costs of non-compliance ($-C_{non\text{-}compl(X)}$) with human rights, both materially and politically, for State Y (and other third States) are zero, or close to zero, taking a key argument in favour of enforcement out of the cost-benefit calculation.

In only a limited set of circumstances is it plausible to expect tangible positive or negative externalities beyond moral indignation due to (non-) compliance with human rights norms by other States. This is, for example, the case where a deteriorating human rights situation in a country triggers refugee flows across its borders which impose material costs on neighbouring countries (and beyond). While any enforcement action in response to such costs may also aim at increasing compliance with basic human rights obligations, the fact that such dire human rights situations often result from armed conflicts and/or failing Statehood make this as much a case of re-establishing peace, security, and stability as one of human rights enforcement. In such situations, humanitarian justifications will usually be only one among several motivations of the intervening State, and have in the past often been met with scepticism and criticism by other States,[79] which may turn AUD_{intl} into a cost, at least politically. Another set of circumstances involving non-compliance with human rights that could be characterized as creating direct social and political costs is one where an ethnic group is separated by State borders and the human rights of one part of the group are being violated.[80] Such a situation may make AUD_{dom} positive in case of enforcement action and

---

[79] Examples include India's 1971 war with Pakistan concerning what later became Bangladesh, and Vietnam's 1979 intervention in Cambodia to end the reign of the Khmer Rouge; cf Mark Weisburd, *Use of Force: The Practice of States Since World War II* (Pennsylvania State University Press 1997) 42–44 and 146–150.

[80] The protection of ethnic minorities is a recurrent issue in human rights jurisprudence; see for example, Alexander Morawa, 'The United Nations Treaty Monitoring Bodies and Minority Rights, with Particular Emphasis on the Human Rights Committee', in Alexander Morawa and Mark Weller (eds), *Mechanisms for the Implementation of Minority Rights* (Council of Europe 2005) 29; Dia Anagnostou and Evangelia Psychogiopoulou (eds), *The European Court of Human Rights and the Rights of Marginalised Individuals and Minorities in National Context* (Martinus Nijhoff 2010).

negative in the case of abstention, thus adding to the case for enforcement. A third constellation in which the human rights practices in another State create externalities for other States exists where a State is requested, or under a legal obligation, not to implement domestic decisions on extradition, expulsion, or repatriation of non-citizens due to the threat of maltreatment in the receiving State, a situation that has yielded a sizable number of pronouncements.[81]

Effects of issue specificity

A second aspect that reduces the inclination of States to enforce human rights pronouncements has to do with their 'issue specificity', that is, the fact that such pronouncements tend to address quite specific issues, often concerning individual instances of violation, that, if not complied with, make it difficult to conceive appropriately targeted enforcement measures and to rouse sufficient support for enforcement by relevant audiences. Moreover, while much of the human rights literature has traditionally focused on violations of physical integrity rights, a good deal of the output of the human rights supervisory bodies addresses rights other than the right to life, freedom from torture, and security of the person, and violations of these other rights – for example, right to privacy, protection of property, freedom of speech, right to proceedings in a reasonable time, or social and economic rights – tend to be less prone to 'shock' audiences into supporting costly enforcement action.

Because it is difficult – even when leaving practical issues aside – to devise and implement efficient and proportionate enforcement measures to compel compliance with, for example, judgments requiring the investigation and prosecution of those responsible for human rights violations,[82] the concluding observation that Finland should 'find an adequate solution to the question of the ownership and use of land in the Sámi Homeland in close consultation with all parties concerned, including the Sámi Parliament, and then ... ratify ILO Convention no 169 concerning Indigenous and Tribal Peoples in Independent Countries as a matter of priority',[83] or an interim measure requesting that the applicants

---

[81] See for example, ECtHR Factsheet: Expulsions and Extraditions (July 2013) <www.echr.coe.int/Documents/FS_Expulsions_Extraditions_ENG.pdf>; Expulsions of Aliens in International Human Rights Law, OHCHR Discussion Paper (Sep 2006) <www2.ohchr.org/english/issues/migration/taskforce/docs/Discussion-paper-expulsions.pdf> accessed 10 Sep 2015.

[82] See examples in Pasqualucci (n 14) 325–328.

[83] CESCR, *Concluding Observations on Fifth Periodic Report by Finland*, UN Doc E/C.12/FIN/CO/5 (16 Jan 2008) 4 (para 20).

are not handed over to authorities of another State while proceedings in their case are pending,[84] States for the most part resort to expressions of diplomatic disapproval as a form essentially of social enforcement[85] and usually the least costly response – if, indeed, any response is forthcoming at all. Since re-establishing compliance in these and other structurally similar instances does not create direct benefits for other States, any costs incurred for enforcement action would have to be compensated with positive international or domestic audience effects; these however, will usually not be sufficiently generated by unremedied individual, or even repeat, violations of this sort.

No State is known to have considered responding through enforcement, for example, to the long-lasting non-compliance with ECtHR judgments finding the systemic violation of prisoners' right to vote in the UK[86] or of the right to proceedings within a reasonable time in Italy.[87] The 'enforcement' action that has occurred in these cases has been limited to expressions by the Council of Europe's Committee of Ministers of 'serious concern', 'urg[ing] the [UK] to rapidly adopt the [necessary] measures',[88] and 'urg[ing] the Italian authorities at the highest level strongly to hold to their political commitment to resolving the problem of the excessive length of judicial proceedings and to take all necessary technical and budgetary measures accordingly'.[89] What further weakens the case for enforcement in these instances is the fact that neither the UK (at least for many years) nor Italy (nor many other States with compliance issues) have expressly rejected the duty to comply, but instead undertook steps or adopted measures in the past that *prima facie* suggested some reasonably meaningful (if eventually still insufficient) progress toward full compliance (such as partial reforms, provision of resources at an insufficient level, domestic consultations etc). Where non-compliance results from the attempt to minimize political and

---

[84] For example, (admittedly in unique circumstances) in *Al-Saadoon and Mufdhi v UK* ECHR 2010-II 61, 69 (para 4).

[85] Cf Brennan et al. (n 44) 45.

[86] *Hirst v UK* (no 2) ECHR 2005-IX 187; *Greens and MT v UK* ECHR 2010-VI 57.

[87] See only *Ceteroni v Italy* ECHR 1996-V 1756 and the list of over 2,000 related length of proceedings cases attached to Committee of Ministers Interim Res CM/ResDH(2010)224 (2 Dec 2010).

[88] Interim Res CM/ResDH(2009)160 (3 Dec 2009) (relating to *Hirst* (no 2) judgment).

[89] See Interim Res CM/ResDH(2010)224 (n 87).

material compliance costs, not outright defiance, action exceeding diplomatic nudging is likely seen as an inappropriate response, by both the target State and third States.

Even in cases where enforcement, rather than dialogue and management, appears appropriate, the findings and specified obligations are usually of a nature that discourage enforcement because both sources of benefits – direct benefits ($B_{compl(X)}$) as well as indirect ones (AUD_{intl} and AUD_{dom}) – are at best quite small and do not outweigh the costs of enforcement beyond statements of disapproval. The situation becomes different only when violations occur on a sufficiently large scale and either concern certain types of rights, especially physical integrity rights, or rights that are linked with other interests (such as peace and security). While no ECHR State is known to have contemplated enforcement action against Italy for the protracted non- or partial compliance with respect to the systemic length of proceedings problems of its domestic judiciary (probably in part because almost all ECHR parties suffer from the same problem, if on a lesser scale), the situation might have been different if the same number of judgments had revealed the systematic use of torture in violation of art 3 ECHR. At the same time, rights other than physical integrity rights may be subject to enforcement: The European Union, for example, has included in its accession partnership agreements with Turkey express provisions that call on Turkey to 'ensure full execution of the judgments of the ECtHR',[90] a provision first included in response to Turkey's refusal to comply with the 1998 *Loizidou* just satisfaction award[91] which concerned property-related consequences of the Turkish invasion of the northern part of Cyprus in 1974.[92] Because the partnership agreements were already in place, adding this conditionality was effectively costless for the EU and its member States.

---

[90] Turkey 2007 Accession Partnership annexed to Council Decision 2008/157/EC of 18 Feb 2008 on the Principles, Priorities and Conditions Contained in the Accession Partnership with the Republic of Turkey and Repealing Decision 2006/35/EC [2008] OJ L51/4, 18.

[91] *Loizidou v Turkey* (Article 50) ECHR 1998-IV 1817.

[92] In June 2001, the Committee of Ministers had 'call[ed] upon the authorities of the member States to take such action as they deem appropriate' to achieve compliance with the judgment; CM Interim Res DH(2001)80 (26 June 2001). This was understood by EU member States as a 'request to include in Turkey's partnership agreement with the European Union a clause requiring Turkey to respect the [ECtHR's] judgments' (Clare Ovey and Robin White, *Jacobs and White: The European Convention on Human Rights* (4th edn, OUP 2006) 505). The March 2001 Accession Partnership Document (APD) had already featured Turkey's human rights performance under the Convention

Effects of legal status

Above, this Chapter argued that the legal status of an obligation – whether 'hard' or 'soft' law – does not by itself prejudice the question of the possibility of enforcement. Legally non-binding pronouncements also articulate behavioural obligations to which some expectation of compliance is attached, and such compliance, where not forthcoming voluntarily, could be made subject to enforcement. At the same time, one has to recognize that States themselves *do* attach meaning and significance to the distinction between legally binding and legally non-binding obligations and generally choose deliberately whether the agreements and arrangements they make and accept shall belong to the first or to the second category. Among several considerations,[93] one of the reasons why States opt for legally non-binding rather than legally binding supervisory mechanisms is precisely because they expect that they will either not be able to, or may prefer not to, comply with at least some of the normative claims on their behaviour that might be articulated by these mechanisms in the future.[94] In other words, States seek to limit (especially unanticipated) sovereignty costs,[95] including those that are linked to the expected probability of future enforcement action. This does not mean that soft law cannot have significant consequences and effects,[96] nor that States

(Turkey: 2000 Accession Partnership, annexed to Council Decision 2001/235/EC on the Principles, Priorities, Intermediate Objectives and Conditions Contained in the Accession Partnership with the Republic of Turkey [2001] OJ L 85/13), but had not yet referred to the Court's judgments. The 2003 APD, however, expressly included as a priority Turkey's compliance with the ECHR, 'including respect of the judgments of the European Court of Human Rights (section II of the Convention)' (Turkey: 2003 Accession Partnership annexed to Council Decision 2003/398/EC on the Principles, Priorities, Intermediate Objectives and Conditions Contained in the Accession Partnership with Turkey [2003] OJ L145/43). ECHR sec II contains, *inter alia*, the obligation to abide by the Court's judgments (ECHR art 46 para 1).

[93] Cf Charles Lipson, 'Why are Some Agreements Informal?' (1991) 45 Int Org 495.

[94] Dinah Shelton, 'Introduction: Law, Non-Law and the Problem of Soft-Law', in Dinah Shelton (ed), *Commitment and Compliance: The Role of Non-Binding Norms in the International Legal System* (OUP 2000) 12.

[95] Kenneth Abbott and Duncan Snidal, 'Hard and Soft Law in International Governance', in Goldstein et al. (n 34) 52–60.

[96] The 1975 Helsinki Final Act's non-binding human rights provisions for example, triggered socio-political processes in the Warsaw Pact countries that eventually contributed to ending the Cold War; see Daniel Thomas, *The Helsinki Effect: International Norms, Human Rights, and the Demise of Communism* (Princeton University Press 2001).

may not voluntarily comply with it, but it does mean that they do not expect to be held to a strict standard of required compliance and to be subject to legal responsibility in case of non-compliance.

Because this intention when choosing 'soft' rather than 'hard' obligations is shared knowledge among States, it has implications for the enforcement calculus. While domestic audiences, especially the general public, will often make fewer strict distinctions between enforcement of legally binding versus non-binding human rights decisions and bestow approval or disapproval based on substantive content and their own preferences, governments are more discriminating and will tend to view any action to enforce non-binding human rights pronouncements, given the shared knowledge that the non-binding form was intentionally chosen, sceptically. For legally binding *erga omnes* (*partes*) norms, the hurdle to convince other States that such action is norm enforcement, and not action undertaken for ulterior, purely self-interested reasons, is already high, and in instances of the enforcement of legally non-binding norms it can be expected to be even higher. Enforcing what by common understanding was not meant to be enforced would thus itself likely be seen as the violation of an underlying political norm.

V. CONCLUSION

Inter-State enforcement of human rights obligations generally, and of the concrete interpretations given to them by the various regional and global human rights supervisory bodies specifically, whether formally binding or not, might be seen as a promising option in light of the absence of institutionalized multilateral enforcement mechanisms. Assuming rational governmental decision-makers, and taking into account the principal costs and benefits that go into the calculation for and against enforcement, reveals, however, that these cost-benefit calculations will predictably and overwhelmingly come out against inter-State enforcement. Even if a State has a preference for compliance with a particular pronouncement by one of the human rights dispute settlement and monitoring bodies, the expected material and political costs of engaging in enforcement are generally not matched by the expected direct or indirect benefits. In addition, States may also simply not want to create precedents that other States could subsequently invoke against themselves with respect to their own non-compliance with binding or non-binding pronouncements in the human rights domain and elsewhere; while desirable (and often necessary) for reaping mutual benefits in cooperative relationships, reciprocity becomes a disincentive when applied to adverse conduct that threatens to impose costs. Recognition of the systematic biases against inter-State enforcement of human rights obligations (as well as of some other areas of IL) has thus led political scientists to look for the principal levers and mechanisms for inducing and compelling human rights compliance in domestic politics.[97] In either case, as long as the decision whether to enforce or not is governed by the logic of rational choice, then the provision of enforcement of human rights obligations requires that actors with pro-compliance preferences face expected material benefits and positive audience effects that exceed the costs of enforcement, with the sign and magnitude of the audience effects being affected, *inter alia*, by the legal status of the obligations in question.

[97] See for example, Simmons (n 64) ch 4; Xinyuan Dai, *International Institutions and National Policies* (CUP 2007) ch 4; Courtney Hillebrecht, *Domestic Politics and International Human Rights Tribunals: The Problem of Compliance* (CUP 2014); Heather Smith-Cannoy, *Insincere Commitments: Human Rights Treaties, Abusive States, and Citizen Activism* (Georgetown University Press 2012).

11. The Political Economy of International Lawmaking by National Courts

Eyal Benvenisti

I. INTRODUCTION

Many scholars who sought to expand the discretion of international courts, and thereby, presumably, to limit State sovereignty above and beyond the original intent of State executives, luminaries such as Scelle,[1] Lauterpacht[2] and Conforti,[3] as well as the members of the *Institut de Droit International* (IDI),[4] have prodded national courts (referred to as 'municipal' or 'domestic' courts) to accept their role as local agents of the international legal system. The IDI Resolution from 1993, while acknowledging that a national court has to apply International Law (IL) 'through its own methods of interpretation within each State', urges national courts to 'bas[e] themselves on the methods followed by international tribunals' and 'mak[e] every effort to interpret it as it would be interpreted by an international tribunal and avoid [...] interpretations influenced by national interests.'[5]

[1] Georges Scelle, *Précis de droit des gens: Principes et systématique*, 2 volumes, Dalloz 1932 and 1934 (reprint 2010) (on dédoublement fonctionel).

[2] Hersch Lauterpacht, 'Decisions of Municipal Courts as a Source of International Law' (1929) 10 BYIL 65, 93.

[3] Benedetto Conforti (Rapporteur), 'The Activities of National Judges and the International Relations of their State, Final Report' (1993) 65 Ann IDI, Part L 42.

[4] Institut de Droit International (IDI), 'The Activities of National Judges and the International Relational of their State' (Milan, 7 September 1993), www.idi-iil.org/idiE/resolutionsE/1993_mil_01_en.PDF (last visited 20 Aug. 2015).

[5] Ibid, in the Preamble (4th consideration), and article 1, par. 2. For a critical assessment of this thesis see Helmut Philipp Aust, Alejandro Rodiles and Peter Staubach, 'Unity or Uniformity? Domestic Courts and Treaty Interpretation'

But insights from Political Economy (PE) suggest that this promise faces serious challenges.[6] National constitutions and domestic politics heavily shape the scope of discretion that national courts enjoy. Throughout the twentieth century, domestic pressures led national courts to adopt a deferential attitude towards their respective executive branches. And when, since the early 2000s, national courts of key countries in Europe and Asia have begun to change course, they have sought to chart their own courses and explored unique trajectories for the development and implementation of IL rather than simply mimicking international courts.[7] As this Chapter will suggest, insights from PE can offer an explanation.

II. THE MOTIVATIONS FOR INTERNATIONAL LAWMAKING BY NATIONAL COURTS

A PE explanation for the recent embrace of IL by national courts would focus on the economic and political dynamics of globalization. The traditional judicial policy of ensuring that the State speak 'in one voice', that is, the voice of the government, rested on three premises.[8] First was that the murky world of diplomacy is detached from the domestic one,

---

(2014) 27 Leiden J Int L 75 (demonstrating the diversity in the interpretative approaches of IL by the Supreme Court of the United States, the Mexican Supreme Court, and the European Court of Justice).

[6] Several suggestions were put forward over the years, all based on the somewhat naïve assumption that the causes of judges' hesitance in applying IL is their lack of knowledge of IL, or the existence of certain limitations on their independence which can be overcome with legal education and perhaps appeal to their conscience. More radical proposals, such as the call for changing the Statute of the International Court of Justice in order to permit national courts to refer a question for its interpretation were fortunately not pursued. Conforti (n 3) at 435.

[7] Eyal Benvenisti, 'Reclaiming Democracy: The Strategic Uses of Foreign and International Law by National Courts' (2008) 102 AJIL 241.

[8] Harold Hongju Koh, 'Transnational Public Law Litigation' (1990–1991) 100 Yale L J 2347, at 2383–2394, distinguishes between three types of judicial concerns: separation of powers concerns, judicial competence concerns, and comity concerns. The more frank judicial statements doubt whether their 'engagement in the task of passing on the validity of foreign acts of state may hinder rather than further [their] country's pursuit of goals' *Banco Nacional de Cuba v. Sabbatino*, 376 U.S. 398, 423 (1963), and mention '[t]he advantage of the diplomatic approach to the resolution of difficulties between two sovereign nations, as opposed to the unilateral action by the courts of one nation', *United States v. Alvarez-Machain*, 504 U.S. 655 (1992), fn. 16.

where the rule of law should prevail. The second assumption was that the government adequately represents the interests of its domestic constituency in its foreign diplomacy. The third premise was that the government can better conduct diplomatic affairs without the intervention of the judiciary.

None of these assumptions can be claimed to be valid today. The spheres of global regulation increasingly potentially affect the lives of all citizens; national governments are even more captured than ever by narrow domestic interests and, hence, unable to represent broad constituencies; and lastly, the contemporary world of diplomacy exposes governments to increasing pressure, where – counterintuitively – quite a few would actually benefit from domestic legal constraints that would tie their hands in the international bargaining process. National courts are left with only limited opportunities to restrain or at least slow down the drain of power from domestic to global institutions, which includes judicial bodies that could overshadow national courts. The newly evolving judicial approach may be interpreted, therefore, as aimed at facing up to globalization and revitalizing the authority of the national institutions.

With the advent of globalization, national courts have come to realize that, under conditions of increased external pressures, allowing the government *carte blanche* to act freely in world politics actually impoverishes the domestic democratic and judicial processes and reduces the opportunity of most citizens to use these processes to shape outcomes. These courts, better insulated from external pressures, may have concluded that, by aggressively restricting their government, they can actually revive the domestic democratic processes and secure their own autonomy. The courts may have also concluded that making stricter demands of the government does not necessarily jeopardize the latter's bargaining position vis-à-vis its negotiating partners (nor, hence, are national interests compromised and thus the government will not protest too strongly). In fact, under certain circumstances, a persistent court could actually strengthen its government's bargaining position.

The logic of international negotiations clarifies this point. As is well illustrated in the introductory Chapter above in this Volume,[9] the complex interaction between domestic and international politics has been described as a 'two-level game', namely, a game played simultaneously at the first, international level between a national government and

---

[9] See the introductory Chapter by Anne van Aaken and Joel P Trachtman, 'Political Economy of International Law: Towards a Holistic Model of State Behaviour', above in this Volume.

representatives of a foreign State and at the second, domestic level, amongst representatives of domestic interest groups. Second-level negotiations are necessary to secure domestic ratification for international agreements negotiated at the first level. This game produces a paradox: all things being equal, the stronger the domestic support for Government A's policies, the weaker it is at the international level because its negotiations adversary, Government B, then knows it can play tougher and demand more and more concessions, which would still be acceptable to Government A's supporters at home. In view of these dynamics, negotiating governments often 'compete' over who is more vulnerable domestically.[10] Accordingly, all other things being equal, Government A will be in a weaker bargaining position vis-à-vis Government B if its national court is expected to remain deferential in the process. For example, were the court in Country A to intervene, say, by declaring (or hinting at its intention to declare) the negotiated treaty as impinging excessively on citizen rights, then presumably Government B would be prepared to concede in the negotiations so as to ensure ratification and implementation of the agreement by Country A. Thus, pressure from a disapproving court can, in fact, result in greater bargaining leeway for its government, as a constrictive court decision can be used to explain why it is prevented from bowing to the external pressure in the bargaining process. Needless to say, these dynamics rest on the assumption that B would still be interested in the agreement with A under the terms acceptable to the court. If B can find an alternative to A, the leverage facilitated by A's court will be limited.

Not all courts need to be equally assertive in safeguarding the domestic political process. Courts in more powerful countries with relatively robust domestic democratic processes can be expected to show greater deference to their governments. As long as the US maintains dominance in setting global standards, we can anticipate (and explain) limited involvement by the US federal courts in the President's conduct of diplomacy.[11]

---

10 Robert D Putnam, 'Diplomacy and Domestic Politics: The Logic of Two-Level Games' (1988) 42 Int Org 427; Helen Milner, *Interests, Institutions and Information: Domestic Politics and International Relations* (Princeton University Press 1997).

11 As Curtis Bradley observes, the three branches of the US government have kept the domestic political and legal processes insulated from the direct influence of external policy and lawmaking through a variety of 'non-self-execution filters'. See Curtis A Bradley, 'International Delegations, the Structural Constitution, and Non-Self-Execution' (2003) 55 Stanford L Rev 1557, at 1587–1595. Consider, however, the US Supreme Court's jurisprudence on the treatment of

An assertive national court will bolster not only the domestic democratic processes but also its own authority to interpret and apply national and international law. For national courts, the new international judicial forums challenge their own authority as interpreters of the law and balancers of competing State interests against rights grounded in constitutional or international law. The most effective way to respond to this challenge is to engage in a dialogue with international tribunals, for two reasons. As a purely doctrinal matter, national courts are directly and indirectly engaged in the evolution of Customary International Law (CIL): their decisions that are based on IL are viewed as reflecting CIL,[12] and their governments' acts in compliance with their decisions will constitute State practice coupled with *opinio juris*. As such, international tribunals will have to pay heed to national courts' jurisprudence. Hence, the more national courts engage in applying IL, the more their jurisprudence constrains the choices available to the international courts when the latter deal with similar issues. Moreover, from the perspective of the complex interplay between international and national courts, the international tribunals are, to a certain extent, dependent on national courts, because they need the latter's cooperation for implementation of their decisions.[13] A national court that engages in a serious application of IL

---

post 9/11 detainees in Guantanamo and elsewhere. Referral back to the executive or legislature was the first stage of the Court's involvement in this matter. The *Rasul* and *Hamdi* decisions asserted the Court's jurisdiction to review executive action with respect to unlawful combatants held on US territory or territory under US administration, and required the president to clarify the executive's authority to act. The second round came two years later with the *Hamdan* decision, which rejected the president's response to the previous judgments. In *Hamdan*, the majority relied on IL as the standard for assessing the legality of the military commissions established by the president to determine the status of Guantanamo detainees. In its judgment, the Court diverged from the executive's position in two important aspects: first, that common Article 3 of the 1949 Geneva Conventions applied to the conflict with *Al Qaeda* and, second, that the standards set by that article were not met by the commissions. *Rasul v. Bush*, 542 U.S. 466 (2004); *Hamdi v. Rumsfeld*, 542 U.S. 507 (2004); *Hamdan v. Rumsfeld*, 548 U.S. 557 (2006).

[12] See, for example, the International Court of Justice (ICJ) judgment in *Arrest Warrant of 11 April 2000* (*Democratic Republic of the Congo v. Belgium*), 2002 ICJ Reports 3, available at <http://www.icj-cij.org/docket/files/121/8126.pdf> (last visited 13 Oct. 2014) (examining national courts' jurisprudence to assess the extent to which heads of State enjoy immunity in foreign courts).

[13] On the interplay between a supreme court (as the principal) and lower courts (as its agents), see McNollgast, 'Conditions for Judicial Independence' (2006) San Diego Legal Studies Paper No. 07-43, 26 <http://ssrn.com/abstract=

sends a strong signal to international courts, that the national court regards itself an equal participant in the transnational lawmaking process and will not accept just any decision rendered by an international tribunal. Since the effectiveness of international tribunals depends on compliance with their decisions, they must anticipate the reaction of the national courts to those decisions and come to terms with their jurisprudence. In this sense, assertive national courts invoking IL – or even invoking their own constitutional law as pre-empting IL, and potentially prodding a modification of IL through new CIL[14] – can effectively limit the autonomy of international tribunals.

But this strategy lacks one crucial element for it to have effective impact: a united, coordinated judicial front. If only one national court were to adopt assertive policies, it would face the danger of being singled out as the individual troublemaker, whose jurisprudence does not reflect general State practice. Its government could, therefore, be sidestepped when global forces seek out other governments, those unconstrained by their courts and, hence, more vulnerable to external pressure. Thus, courts seeking to enhance domestic institutions and processes must try to ensure a common interjudicial stance.

895723>; McNollgast, 'Politics and the Courts: A Positive Theory of Judicial Doctrine and the Rule of Law' (1995) 68 Southern Calif L Rev 1631. The dependence of an international tribunal on national courts that are not formally bound by its decisions is even greater. The tense relations that developed between the European Court of Justice and some of the national courts, in particular the German and the Italian courts, confirm this theoretical observation. Bruno de Witte, 'Direct Effect, Supremacy, and the Nature of the Legal Order', in Paul Craig and Grainne de Burca (eds), *The Evolution of EU Law* (OUP 1999), 177. According to Juliane Kokott, Germany tried to shape European integration through the jurisprudence of the German Constitutional Court, See Juliane Kokkot, 'Report on Germany', in Anne-Marie Slaughter, Alec Stone Sweet and Joseph HH Weiler (eds), *The European Court and National Courts – Doctrine and Jurisprudence* (Hart 1998) 77; Wojciech Sadurski noted that the newly formed constitutional courts in Central and Eastern Europe emulated the German court's approach to EU law as a way of strengthening their position vis-à-vis other national political actors. See Wojciech Sadurski, 'Solange, chapter 3': Constitutional Courts in Central Europe – Democracy – European Union' (2008) 14 ELJ 1.

[14] See most recently, the Italian Constitutional Court's judgment which rejected the effects of the 2012 International Court of Justice's decision in Jurisdictional Immunities of the State within the Italian legal order on the basis of incompatibility with the Italian Constitution. See Corte Costituzionale, Sentenza N. 238, del 22 ottobre 2014, available at <http://www.foroitaliano.it/wp-content/uploads/2014/10/Corte-cost-238-141.pdf>.

As noted, a court that ties its government's hands in international negotiations will not strengthen the latter's position if its counterparts have viable alternatives. The example of the intervening court in Country A sought to illustrate that, presumably, Government A's partners in its international dealings will be prepared to concede to A's demands but only if they can find no alternative partner. Thus, the court's assertiveness will assure a strengthened position for Government A only if similarly situated governments are similarly constrained by their courts. For example, governments in developing countries will hardly be able to withstand external pressure to maintain low environmental standards for dumping hazardous wastes in their territories unless they coordinate their activities or – if not – benefit from coordinated assertiveness on the part of their respective courts. Likewise, in the context of the fight against terrorism, constraints on counterterrorism measures imposed by a court in Country A but not by courts in other countries may expose A's citizens to an increased risk of terrorist attack. A country that refrains from deporting foreign citizens due to concerns regarding torture, or a country in which privacy rights are more strictly upheld, could become (or could be seen as having the potential to become) a haven for terrorists if other countries are less tolerant to migrants or have laxer privacy rights. Another factor is the international pressure that could be brought to bear on a government to circumvent its court's decisions, or force it into compliance, or else risk the loss of peer protection for failing to comply with the group's demands. The optimal response to all these possibilities is coordination amongst national courts. A transnational united front amongst the highest domestic courts would ensure that no country will become the dumping ground for imported waste or a terrorist haven or face collective sanctions and that less peer pressure will be exerted on governments to ignore their courts' judgments.

National courts are the prisoners in the classic prisoner's dilemma.[15] If they could have been assured that courts in other jurisdictions would similarly enforce IL, they would have been more willing to cooperate. They might have been ready to restrict their government's free hand, had they been reassured that other governments would be likewise restrained. But in the current status of international politics, such cooperation is

[15] A comprehensive analysis of the prisoner's dilemma theory and applications is offered by Meredith Kolsky Lewis, 'International Political Economy and the Prisoner's Dilemma: Compliance with International Law', above in this Volume.

difficult to achieve, and rational judges act like the prisoner who cannot be sure that his or her fellow prisoner will cooperate.[16]

While this is a theoretical model that suggests that judges would be behaving consistently with it even if they may not in fact be consciously following the logic of it, one finds several judicial remarks indicating that national courts are acutely aware of the need for a coordinated stance.[17] Even the courts of the most powerful nations are concerned that 'unilateral action by the courts of one nation'[18] would not produce the desired outcomes. The House of Lords, for example, has first stated that 'international treaties should, so far as possible, be construed uniformly by the national courts of all States'[19] and afterwards even asserted that 'it is not for a national court to "develop" IL by unilaterally adopting a version of that law which, however desirable, forward-looking and reflective of values it may be, is simply not accepted by other States.'[20] In the context of coordinating migration policies, in particular the administration of the dramatically increasing number of asylum seekers, judges from several developed countries went beyond statements and established an institution to ensure uniformity.[21] Courts need assurances that courts in other jurisdictions will enforce similar rules.

---

[16] Eyal Benvenisti, 'Judicial Misgivings Regarding the Application of International Law: An Analysis of Attitudes of National Courts' (1993) 4 EJIL 159, at 175.

[17] The lack of certainty regarding any such coordination lay at the basis of their earlier attitude of deference towards their respective executive branches, see above in the introduction.

[18] Note the quote from the already mentioned *Alvarez-Machain* judgment, about the 'advantage of the diplomatic approach … as opposed to the *unilateral action* by the courts of one nation' (emphasis added). See *United States v. Alvarez-Machain* (n 8).

[19] *R v. Bow St. Metro. Stipendiary Magistrate & Others, ex parte Pinochet Ugarte* (No. 3), [2000] 1 AC 147, 244 (HL) (per Lord Hope of Craighead). See also Lord Hobhouse of Woodborough in *R v. Secretary of State for the Home Department, ex parte Adan*; *R v. Secretary of State for the Home Department, ex parte Aitseguer*, [2001] 1 All ER 593, 616.

[20] *Jones* (Respondent) *v. Ministry of Interior* (Kingdom of Saudi Arabia) (Appellants), 2006 UKHL 26 para. 63 (HL) (per Lord Hoffmann).

[21] The formulation of national migration policies has been high on the political agenda of many destination countries. The political branches expected the courts to respect domestic political processes and uphold both the results of sustained deliberation and public opinion. Defying the popular will by abiding by the demands of IL might incur more than heavy criticism. A court that 'cooperated' with the strict requirements of IL would channel refugees to its country's shores if other courts 'defected' by interpreting the IL concerning

Establishing a higher court to whose decisions national courts must adhere, such as the Court of Justice of the European Union (CJEU), is surely one effective avenue for forging common judicial ground[22] (or, in more sinister scenarios, a means to curtail national courts' authority). But this is not a prerequisite for transnational judicial coordination. Cooperation can evolve endogenously also amongst courts, even when they seek to promote national interests rather than global justice. Game theory demonstrates that indefinitely iterated prisoner's dilemma games between two players are likely to induce cooperation, even absent external intervention. If the number of iterations is indefinite and the 'shadow of the future' high enough (namely, the players assign a sufficiently high value to the expected payoffs from future iterations of the game), then each player is expected to choose the strategy of conditional cooperation in a 'friendly tit for tat'. Using the implicit threat of retaliation against defection, the players can elicit cooperation. The same tit for tat strategy will produce cooperation also in a game played by a group larger than two players and even when some of the players choose to defect unconditionally. Such situations, which are the least likely to generate cooperation when played only once, are in fact

refugees less generously. On the modifications introduced by destination States since the early 1990s, see Jane McAdam, *Complementary Protection in International Refugee Law* (OUP 2007). The Schengen Treaties (1985 and 1990), concerning the abolition of common border controls and a common visa policy and the Dublin Convention (1990) setting the criteria for determining the contracting party responsible for examining an asylum application lodged in one of the contracting parties by a third-country national are legal frameworks for inter-judicial cooperation in migratory matters. Prior to 1999, these treaties and the rules adopted under them operated independently from the European Union, as intergovernative tools. The Amsterdam Treaty however incorporated them into EU law, while providing opt-outs for the only two EU member States which had remained outside the Area. The Lisbon Treaty confirmed the migration and refugee law policies as being within of the EU (though not exclusive) competences. Marleen Maes, Marie-Claire Foblets and Philippe De Bruycker (eds), *External Dimensions of EU Migration and Asylum Law and Policy* (Bruylant 2011). For a comprehensive assessment of regional responses to the crisis in the asylum/refugee system and a critical exam of how different regions tackle the problem see Ademola Abass and Francesca Ippolito (eds), *Regional Approaches to the Protection of Asylum Seekers: An International Legal Perspective* (Ashgate 2014).

[22] For an analysis of the active role played by national courts in strengthening the EU, see Joseph HH Weiler, 'A Quiet Revolution: The European Court of Justice and its Interlocutors' (1994) 26 CPS 510.

potentially cooperative games when the players remain in the game for an indefinite period of time.

III. THE PRESSURE TO DEVELOP TOOLS FOR ENHANCING AND STABILIZING COMMUNICATIONS AMONG NATIONAL COURTS

For courts to bolster their governments by restraining them and asserting their own authority, they must initiate cooperation with similarly situated courts. The only effective way for courts in developing countries to put a stop to the intensifying levels of pollution, environmental degradation, and imported waste is to take a united stand against external interests shopping for less restrictive jurisdictions. Courts that wish to maintain a higher level of human rights protection within their jurisdiction but without turning into a terrorist haven or target, or without diverting the world's asylum seekers to their shores, should also strive to forge a united front with their counterparts in other countries. In other words, inter-judicial cooperation can be a strategic choice for national courts determined to protect their own authority and to reclaim domestic democratic processes.

The optimal way for courts to initiate and maintain cooperation is through mutual exchange of information. Their judicial reasoning and outcomes convey information about their commitment to cooperating. More specifically, their reliance on the same or similar legal sources facilitates this communication and, to a considerable extent, signals their commitment. Both positive as well as negative messages can be communicated in this framework. Cooperative courts will be cited with approval and approbation by their counterparts, whereas courts that step out of line by either refusing to give force to a new standard or by setting a different standard will be criticized, sometimes quite severely, in judgments.[23] In other words, one court's decisions function as signals to other courts about the former's commitment to cooperation. These signals can

---

[23] For example the Italian Court of Cassation criticized in 2004 (*Ferrini v. Federal Republic of Germany*, Judgment No. 5044/2044, 11 March 2004 (2004) 87 RDI 539; 128 ILR 659; Annex 1) a decision of the Greek Court of Cassation of 2000 (*Prefecture of Voiotia v. Federal Republic of Germany*, Case No. 11/2000, 129 ILR 513), while the House of Lords criticized, in turn, the *Ferrini* judgment (see above Jones (n 20) at paras 22, 63). See Pasquale De Sena and Francesca De Vittor, 'State Immunity and Human Rights: The Italian Supreme Court Decision on the *Ferrini* Case' (2005) 16 EJIL 89, 101–102.

embolden the other courts or weaken their resolve in the face of the same dilemmas. At times, specific judgments will have novel and eminently compelling statements that resonate amongst courts in other jurisdictions. One such example is the landmark *Minors Oposa* judgment rendered by the Philippines Supreme Court, which recognized the stake of future generations in a healthy environment.[24] The same practice is discernible in the field of cultural heritage.[25] A court in one jurisdiction can serve as the beacon for other courts, as has the Indian Supreme Court for the Indian subcontinent and elsewhere in the developing world in the area of environmental protection.[26]

Courts that wish to signal readiness to cooperate will tend to use the language other courts understand: comparative law (primarily comparative constitutional law) and IL.[27] The use of comparative analysis is a signal that courts are willing to learn from one another, or are seeking support from other jurisdictions for their judgments, or both. More significantly, they learn from each other's legal systems how to balance amongst the competing common interests and how to manage the conflicting common risks to their societies. They can compare statutory arrangements, such as, for example, conditions for detaining suspected

---

24 *Minors Oposa v. Sec'y of Dep't Env't & Natural Res.*, 33 ILM 174 (1994). This celebrated case was cited by the Bangladeshi and Indian courts, *Farooque v. Gov't of Bangladesh*, 17 BLD (AD) 1 (Bangladesh Appellate Division 1997), available at <http://www.elaw.org/node/6126> (last visited 17 Oct. 2014); *A.P. Pollution Control Bd. (II) v. Nayudu,* [2001] 2 SCC 62 (Indian Supreme Court), available at <http://www.ielrc.org/content/e0010.pdf> (last visited 17 Oct. 2014) and in numerous scholarly articles from across the globe.

25 Alessandro Chechi, 'The Role of Domestic Courts in Resolving Restitution Cases: Unveiling Judicial Strategies for Culture-Sensitive Settlements', in Marc-André Renold, Alessandro Chechi and Anne Laure Bandle (eds), *Resolving Disputes in Cultural Property* (Schultess 2012) 147–173, at 159.

26 See Benvenisti (n 7) at 251.

27 The discord within the US Supreme Court towards comparative constitutional law and its relative reticence to cite IL may perhaps be influenced by the relative robustness of the domestic processes in the US, which currently do not require judicial support. On the debate in the US on this matter see for example, the articles by Harold Hongju Koh (at 43), Roger P Alford (at 57), Gerald L Neuman (at 82), T Alexander Aleinikoff (at 91), in the (2004) 98 AJIL, under the Agora: *The United States Constitution and International Law;* the articles by Richard A Posner (at 32), Vicki Jackson (at 109), Jeremy Waldron (at 129) and Ernst A Young (at 148), published in the (2005) 119 Harv L Rev, under the heading: *The Supreme Court – 2004 Term*; Melissa A Waters, 'Creeping Monism: The Judicial Trend Toward Interpretive Incorporation of Human Rights Treaties' (2007) 107 Colum L Rev 628.

terrorists, seeking the arrangement that minimally impinges on constitutional rights.[28] Even more accessible than specific statutes are the constitutional texts, which often have similar provisions regarding such issues as the right to life, due process, equality, and fundamental political rights. And indeed, courts seeking cooperation do engage in comparative analysis in their judgments. But even more significantly, IL, the source of collective standards, has become a most valuable coordination tool for national courts. The ability of these courts to rely on the same or similar legal norms (international treaties like the 1951 Geneva Convention Relating to the Status of Refugees – CRSR, or human rights treaties) facilitates harmonization amongst them.[29] By making references to each other's interpretation of a shared text they not only signal readiness to cooperate, but also to a certain extent impede the future retreat of one of them from the shared interpretation: As courts carefully watch each other, the one that backs away has to offer an explanation to its peers.

However, the fact that the same norm is being applied does not render its implementation unproblematic for the relevant court. First, the norm's content may entail deference to the national governments, the drafters of the international text in which the norm is anchored. Second, there is a significant variance amongst jurisdictions with respect to the status of IL

---

[28] See for example, the decision of the Canadian Supreme Court in a terrorism-related matter, the *Charkaoui* decision of February 2007 (*Charkaoui v. Canada* (Minister of Citizenship and Immigration), (2007) SCC 9, 2007 – 1 SCR 350), available at <http://www.lexisnexis.ca/documents/2008scc38.pdf> (last visited 17 Oct. 2014). The Court declared unanimously that the procedures allowing for the deportation of noncitizens suspected of terrorist activities on the basis of confidential information, as well as the denial of a prompt hearing to foreign nationals, are incompatible with the Canadian Charter of Rights and Freedoms. This bold decision was replete with comparative references to foreign and international statutory and case law. The Court referred specifically to the British Anti-terrorism Act as an example of hearing procedures for suspected terrorists that the Canadian legislature should consider adopting. This emerging judicial dialogue has not been confined to the British and Canadian courts. It currently includes courts in several other jurisdictions, including France, Germany, Hong Kong, India, Israel, and New Zealand, all in the context of limiting counter-terrorism measures. Benvenisti (n 7) at 255.

[29] In the area of refugee law, national courts dealing with asylum seekers long since began citing each other's interpretation of the 1951 Geneva Convention relating to the Status of Refugees. For example, in 1993 the Canadian Supreme Court cited a 1985 decision of the US Board of Immigration Tribunal, which was later cited by the High Court of Australia (1997), by the New Zealand Refugee Status Authority (1998) and by the House of Lords (1999). *R v. Immigration Appeal Tribunal, ex parte Shah*, [1999] 2 AC 629, para. 643.

within the domestic legal hierarchy. Third, the language of the domestic statute that incorporated the specific international treaty may have modified the specific obligation. But courts have devised ways to overcome these hurdles, if they so wish. They tap into the rich jurisprudence developed by international tribunals concerning 'effective',[30] 'evolutive',[31] or 'systemic'[32] interpretation of treaties or rely on the tribunals' unsystematic ways of identifying customary norms.[33] Moreover, they interpret domestic legislation based on the premise that the legislature does not intend to contravene international obligations. Finally, even domestically unincorporated treaties and custom are often treated as a relevant consideration for the executive when exercising its discretion under domestic authorizing statutes.

IV. THE POSITIVE EXTERNALITIES OF INTERNATIONAL LAWMAKING BY NATIONAL COURTS

In addition to protecting domestic interests, the independent stance of national courts promoted them to become key actors in indirectly reviewing decision-making at the global level, using their 'gatekeeping' opportunity to reject global policies that they regard as incompatible with domestic law.[34] National courts can invoke several legal sources and

---

[30] Hersch Lauterpacht, *The Development of International Law by the International Court of Justice* (Stevens and Sons 1958) 227–228, 267–293.

[31] See Rudolf Bernhardt, 'Evolutive Treaty Interpretation, Especially of the European Convention on Human Rights' (1999) 42 GYIL 11.

[32] Campbell MacLachlan, 'The Principle of Systemic Integration and Article 31(3)(c) of the Vienna Convention' (2005) 54 ICLQ 279; Duncan French, 'Treaty Interpretation and the Incorporation of Extraneous Legal Rules' (2006) 55 ICLQ 281.

[33] See, for example, Theodor Meron, 'Revival of Customary Humanitarian Law' (2005) 99 AJIL 817, 819–820. Meron comments on the ICJ's 'complete failure to inquire whether *opinion iuris* and practice support the crystallization of [the relevant Articles] into customary law.' Meron salutes this 'more relaxed approach' and views it as 'essential … to the effectiveness of customary law.'

[34] See Eyal Benvenisti and George W Downs, 'Court Cooperation, Executive Accountability and Global Governance' (2009) Tel Aviv University Law Faculty Paper 108, 29 <http://papers.ssrn.com/sol3/papers.cfm?abstract_id=1409406> (last visited 17 Oct. 2014). See also Benedict Kingsbury, 'Weighing Global Regulatory Rules and Decisions in National Courts: Definitional Issues in Global Administrative Law' (2009) Acta Juridica 90.

doctrines. The ubiquitous response is to rely on the domestic constitution or on a statutory text, but courts have also used IL principles to narrowly interpret the immunities of international organizations[35] or the text of the international standard.[36] For example, in one case a US court found that an international claims commission did not offer adequate protection for a claimant and therefore refused to block her suit based on the private law procedural doctrine of *forum non conveniens*.[37]

The assertiveness of the national courts offers 'cover' to international tribunals who worry about compliance with their judgments and about retaliation from key member States. If national courts are expected to rule against the intergovernmental organizations, State executives may be more inclined to tolerate a ruling by the international tribunal to the same effect. Three examples demonstrate the potential of such 'bottom-up' cooperation between national and international courts.

The *Kadi* judgment[38] might not have been written without the cue provided by some European national courts. In the post 9/11 era, several prominent national courts appear to have realized that Security Council resolutions related to counterterrorism posed a potential threat to their own standing as institutions that are constitutionally empowered to determine the balance between security and liberty.[39] They responded by asserting their authority to interpret such resolutions narrowly, or limit their domestic applicability, in line with the principles of their national constitutions.

---

[35] Antonios Tzanakopoulos, 'Domestic Court Reactions to UN Security Council Sanctions', in August Reinisch (ed), *Challenging Acts of International Organizations Before National Courts* (OUP 2010) 54; August Reinisch (ed), *The Privileges and Immunities of International Organizations in Domestic Courts* (OUP 2013).

[36] Case T-727-08, *Abdelrazik v. Minister of Foreign Affairs and Attorney General of Canada* (2009) FC 580.

[37] *Nemariam v. Federal Democratic Republic of Ethiopia*, 315 F.3d 390 (D.C. Cir.), cert. denied, 124 S. Ct. 278 (24 January 2003).

[38] On this litigation – that we have discussed in several places – see for example, Lisa Ginsborg and Martin Scheinin, 'Judicial Powers, Due Process and Evidence in the Security Council 1267 Terrorist Sanctions Regime: The Kadi II Conundrum' (2011) EUI Working Papers RSCAS 2011/44 <http://www.eui.eu/Projects/GGP/Documents/Publications/WorkingPapers/RSCAS201144-LGinsborgMScheinin.pdf>; Peter Hipold, 'UN Sanctions Before the ECJ: the Kadi Case', in Reinisch (ed), *Challenging* (above n 35) 18.

[39] Eyal Benvenisti and George W Downs, 'Democratizing Courts: How National and International Courts are Promoting Democracy in an Era of Global Governance' GlobalTrust Working Paper 5/2013 <http://globaltrust.tau.ac.il/publications> (last visited 17 Oct. 2014) at 17.

In 2006 the French Court of Cassation declared that in France Security Council resolutions had no direct effect until incorporated into national law by domestic measures that would be subject to judicial review.[40] In 2007 the House of Lords was faced with the claim that a Security Council resolution limited its authority to review the implementation of the European Convention on Human Rights (ECHR).[41] Like the French court, the British court, too, interpreted the Security Council resolution narrowly and subjected compliance with it to a proportionality analysis. It found that the Security Council resolution qualified but did not displace the obligation of UK forces to comply with the ECHR, unless it was 'necessary for imperative reasons of security' to deviate from it.[42] To these judgments one could add the 'Solange'[43]-type judgments of courts in Europe that have kept European institutions mindful of their dependence on domestic implementation. More specifically, a few national courts have upheld indirect challenges to the 'targeted sanctions' regime.[44] It is quite likely that these judgments had an impact on the Grand Chamber of the CJEU in *Kadi*.[45] On appeal, the court's advocate general, Miguel Maduro, outlined a way for the court to overcome the apparent obligatory compliance with Security Council resolutions, which the court endorsed. In particular, Maduro's suggestion to the court – that national courts had both the authority and the willingness to step in if the CJEU would not, and that it was 'very unlikely that national measures for the implementation of [Security Council resolutions] would enjoy

---

[40] *Iraqi State v. Corporation Dumez GTM* (SA), Appeal (Cassation) judgment, Cour d'appel [CA][regional court of appeal] Paris, 1e civ, Apr. 25, 2006, ILDC 771.

[41] *R v. Secretary of State for Defence* (2007) UKHL 58.

[42] See *A, K, M, Q & G v. HM Treasury* (2008) EWHC 869 (Admin).

[43] *Solange I – Internationale Handelsgesellschaft von Einfuhr- und Vorratsstelle für Getreide und Futtermittel*, Decision of 29 May 1974, BVerfGE 37, 271 (1974) CMLR 540. *Solange* ('as long as') stands for the assertion by European constitutional national courts resisting a surrender of their authority to the CJEU, and insisting on their role as guardians of their national constitutions. See above (n 13).

[44] For a review of these and other judgments of national courts, see Tzanakopoulos (n 35).

[45] CJEU (Grand Chamber), *Kadi and Al Barakaat International Foundation v. Council and Commission,* Joined Cases C-402/05 P and C-415/05 P, Judgment of 3 September 2008, Reports of Cases 2008 I-06351, available at <http://curia.europa.eu/juris/celex.jsf?celex=62005CJ0402&lang1=en&type=TXT&ancre=>.

immunity from [national] judicial review'[46] – appears to have been determinative.

After the Court of First Instance (CFI) rendered its *Kadi* judgment (2005), the president of the Security Council mentioned that '[I]nternational, national and regional courts must review Security Council Resolutions to ensure that they comply fully with internationally recognized human rights norms and the principles and purposes of the United Nations Charter.'[47] The chair of the Sanctions Committee admitted that '[o]ne cannot ignore the international context … [the Security Council] sanctions regimes find themselves increasingly under pressure and have recently been questioned, especially in light of the need for fair and clear procedures for listing, de-listing and the granting of humanitarian exemptions.'[48] Indeed, it was 'European pressure' that in 2008 compelled the Security Council's committee to 'identify formal guidelines or evidentiary standards for States to follow in proposing names, and to incorporate humanitarian exceptions and a de-listing procedure.'[49] By that time the *Kadi* case was already in appeal before the CJEU, and the Security Council's Sanctions Committee expressly stated its concern that the Court would undermine the targeted sanctions regime by holding the implementation regulation invalid, warning that 'it would trigger similar challenges that could quickly erode enforcement'.[50] As a result, '[t]he Committee has made a series of incremental improvements to its procedures'.[51] After the adoption of Security Council Resolution 1904, in

---

[46] Opinion of Advocate General Poiares Maduro, Case C-402/05 P, delivered on 16 January 2008, at 12, note 34, available at <http://blogeuropa.eu/wp-content/2008/02/cnc_c_402_05_kadi_def.pdf>.

[47] Security Council 5599th Meeting Record, UN Doc. S/PV.5599, at 3 (19 Dec. 2006), available at <http://www.un.org/ga/search/view_doc.asp?symbol=S/PV.5599>.

[48] Security Council 6043rd Meeting Record, UN Doc. S/PV.6043, at 9 (15 Dec. 2008).

[49] José E Alvarez, 'Contemporary International Law: An "Empire of Law" or the "Law of Empire"?' (2009) 24 Am U Int L Rev 811, 830.

[50] Chairman of the Security Council, Letter dated 13 May 2008 from the Chairman of the Security Council Committee established pursuant to resolution 1267 (1999) concerning Al-Qaida and the Taliban and associated individuals and entities addressed to the President of the Security Council, 40, UN Doc. S/2008/324 (14 May 2008), available at <http://www.un.org/ga/search/view_doc.asp?symbol=S/2008/324> (last visited 17 Oct. 2014).

[51] Ibid.

December 2009,[52] U.S. Ambassador Rice explained the measure as 'address[ing] concerns that have been expressed by some European courts'.[53]

The second example of national courts contributing to strengthening the rule of law at the intergovernmental organization level comes from the area of employment standards within intergovernmental organizations, another key area of global governance.[54] Whereas initially several intergovernmental organizations sought to insulate themselves from judicial supervision of their employment conditions, they have eventually had to heed the pressure brought to bear by national courts. The World Bank established its Administrative Tribunal (WBAT) only after it became clear that the Bank's employment policies could be subjected to challenges in national courts.[55] And in Europe, the famous *Waite and Kennedy* decision of the ECtHR[56] was preceded by judgments by national labor courts that rejected the immunity of intergovernmental organizations to national labor standards. After initial remarks by the French Court of Cassation in 1995 that raised the concern that such immunity could amount to a denial of justice, a French appellate court in 1997 rejected UNESCO's plea of immunity by directly invoking the ECtHR.[57] The ECtHR's expectation that intergovernmental organizations

---

[52] Security Council Res. 1904, UN Doc. S/RES/1904 (17 Dec. 2009), available at <http://www.un.org/ga/search/view_doc.asp?symbol=S/RES/1904 (2009)> (last visited 17 Oct. 2014).

[53] Susan E Rice, *Remarks by Ambassador Susan E. Rice, U.S. Permanent Representative to the United Nations, on Security Council Resolution 1904, Sudan, and the Middle East, at the Security Council Stakeout* (17 Dec. 2009), available at <http://usun.state.gov/briefing/statements/2009/133836.htm> (last visited 17 Oct. 2014).

[54] There are a few other examples of national courts indirectly reviewing intergovernmental organizations' policies. See (n 36).

[55] On the events leading up to the establishment of the WBAT, see Theodor Meron and Betty Elder, 'The New Administrative Tribunal of the World Bank' (1981) 14 NYU JILP 1; Chittharanjan Felix Amerasinghe, 'The World Bank Administrative Tribunal' (1982) 31 ICLQ 748.

[56] ECtHR, *Waite and Kennedy v. Germany*, App. No. 26083/94, Judgment of 18 February 1999, available at <http://hudoc.echr.coe.int/sites/eng/pages/search.aspx?i=001-58912> (last visited 17 Oct. 2014); *Beer and Regan v. Germany*, App. No. 28934/95, Judgment of 18 February 1999, available at <http://hudoc.echr.coe.int/sites/eng/pages/search.aspx?i=001-58299> (last visited 17 Oct. 2014).

[57] August Reinisch, 'The Immunity of International Organizations and the Jurisdiction of their Administrative Tribunals' (2008) 7 Chinese J Int L 285 (on national court review of employment conditions in international organizations).

offer equivalent protection to their employees was soon echoed by the courts in Belgium, France and Italy. The latter set aside the immunities of those intergovernmental organizations and critically reviewed their procedures for resolving disputes with their employees.[58]

The third example comes from the EU.[59] One way to explain the heroic *Van Gend en Loos* judgment[60] is to note the backing it received from the national courts of the three smaller members of the original EEC. That the Benelux countries were keen to embrace the EC Treaty and give it legal effect was already reflected in their national laws. The Dutch Constitution of 1953 provided for the supremacy of international treaties over domestic statutes.[61] The Luxembourg Court of Cassation (in 1950) and its Conseil d'État (in 1951) acknowledged the supremacy of treaty obligations over local laws.[62] In Belgium, 'the van Gend en Loos decision, though revolutionary, created hardly a ripple at the time',[63]

---

[58] See *Western European Union v. Siedler*, Appeal judgment, Cass No S 04 0129 F, ILDC 1625 (BE 2009), 21 December 2009, Court of Cassation (Belg.); *African Development Bank v. X*, Appeal judgment, 04-41012, ILDC 778 (FR 2005), 25 January 2005, Court of Cassation (Fr.); *Pistelli v. European University Institute*, Appeal judgment, No 20995, Guida al diritto 40 (3/2006), ILDC 297 (IT 2005), 28 October 2005, Supreme Court of Cassation (Italy). On these cases see, respectively, Cederic Ryngaert, 'Belgium', Genevieve Bastid Burdeau, 'France', Riccardo Pavoni, 'Italy', in Reinisch, *Privileges* (n 35) at 61–69, 118–119 and 166 respectively; Cedric Ryngaert, 'The Immunity of International Organizations Before Domestic Courts: Recent Trends' (2010) 7 Int Org L Rev 121.

[59] Eyal Benvenisti and George W Downs, 'The Premises, Assumptions, and Implications of Van Gend en Loos: Viewed from the Perspectives of Democracy and Legitimacy of International Institutions' (2014) 25 EJIL 85.

[60] EEC Court of Justice (CJEU), *van Gend en Loos*, Case 26/62, Judgment of 5 February 1963.

[61] The Dutch constitution of 1953 was designed to provide supremacy to EC law (including CJEU decisions). As Daniel Halberstam observed, the reference in the *van Gend* case came from the Netherlands, which already had adopted monism: Daniel Halberstam, 'Constitutionalism and Pluralism in Marbury and Van Gend', in Miguel Poiares Maduro and Loïc Azoulai (eds), *The Past and the Future of EU Law: Revisiting the Classics on the 50th Anniversary of the Rome Treaty* (Hart 2010) 26.

[62] As the Luxembourg Court of Cassation later explained in its *Pagani* judgment of 14 July 1954, 'a treaty is a law of a superior nature [essence] having a superior origin than the will of an internal [national] organ' (quoted, together with the other cases, in Jorg Polakiewicz and Valerie Jacob-Foltzer, 'The European Human Rights Convention in Domestic Law' (1991) 12 HRLJ 125, 126).

[63] Hjalte Rasmussen, *On Law and Policy in the European Court of Justice: A Study in Comparative Judicial Policy-Making* (Martinus Nijhoff 1986) at 334 (citing Ivan Verougstraate's unpublished paper from 1981).

given the pro-integration attitude of the 'most outstanding' members of the Belgian judiciary.[64] The Belgian Procureur Général Ganshof van der Meersch stated that the Rome Treaty created a common legal order whose subjects are not only States but also their citizens.[65] The celebrated judgment of the Belgian Court of Cassation in its 1971 *Le Ski* decision,[66] which endorsed monism and accepted the primacy of EEC law, was considered a 'logical and easy'[67] application of the principle of direct effect. These three small States fully grasped the benefits of international cooperation and that arguing in favor of the EC Treaty was clearly within their self-interest. They, the Netherlands in particular, signaled to the CJEU that they would accept and follow its judgments whatever they might be. In the event that France or Germany did not accept its rulings,[68] they would be the ones to be regarded as the violators of the Treaty, whereas the CJEU would be deemed its guardian.[69]

National courts also have tools for addressing global private regulation. Since several of the private regulators[70] refer to private arbitration procedures, the courts have an opportunity both to control the private bodies' demand to commence arbitrations and to review the legality of the award. For example, in *Lance Armstrong v. Tygart and U.S. Anti-Doping Agency* (USADA) a US court reviewed the decision made by USADA, a nongovernmental organization, to charge Armstrong with violating various anti-doping rules, and to give him the option of either contesting the charges through arbitration or accepting sanctions. Armstrong challenged USADA's authority to bring such charges against him, and alleged that USADA's charging and arbitration procedures violated

[64] Ibid at 333 and 370.

[65] Ibid at 333.

[66] *Minister for Economic Affairs v. Fromagerie Franco-Suisse 'Le Ski'*, Belgian Cour de Cassation, First Chamber [1972] CMLR 330 (Belg.).

[67] Cited in Rasmussen (n 63) at 334.

[68] On the resistance of the French, German and Italian courts to the reference to the CJEU, see Karen J Alter, *Establishing the Supremacy of European Law: The Making of an International Rule of Law in Europe* (OUP 2001) Chapters 3 and 4; Rasmussen (n 63) at 307–325.

[69] As Geoffrey Garrett, R Daniel Kelemen and Heiner Schulz noted, 'the Court cannot afford to make decisions that litigant governments refuse to comply with or, worse, that provoke collective responses from the EU governments to circumscribe the Court's authority': Geoffrey Garrett, R Daniel Kelemen and Heiner Schulz, 'The European Court of Justice, National Governments, and Legal Integration in the European Union'(1998) 52 Int Org 149, 174.

[70] On these bodies see Benvenisti, *The Law of Global Governance* (Brill 2014) Chapter 2.

his due process rights.[71] On the other hand, in *Gatlin v. U.S. Anti-Doping Agency, Inc.*,[72] a federal district court found a CAS arbitration panel decision to be 'arbitrary and capricious', but nonetheless one that did not 'rise to the level of moral repugnance' which would justify refusal to recognize the CAS award. These judgments could suggest that in relation to the workings of private regulators of sports, national courts still hesitate to challenge the global actors, leaving the athletes to rely on the CJEU to protect their rights.[73]

V. CONCLUSION

There are obviously different ways to explain the crystallization of judicial approaches. Was it better education in IL that prompted judges to embrace IL, or a sense of global solidarity? Perhaps. The PE explanation provided here offers one explanation out of many, without disputing the plausibility of additional explanations.

It is likely that judges that pioneered the new approach to IL were not fully cognizant of the underlying PE motivations for their new strides in international lawmaking. But PE explanations do not need to prove that actors were aware of the pressures that influenced their choices. As Gary Becker said, 'the economic approach does not assume that economic units are necessarily conscious of their efforts to maximize or can verbalize or otherwise describe ... reasons for the systematic pattern of their behavior.'[74]

---

71 *Lance Armstrong v. Tygart and USADA*, Order of 20 August 2012 (Fed. D.C. W. Tex. 2012).

72 *Gatlin v. United States Anti-Doping Agency*, Inc., No. 3:08-cv-241/LAC/EMT, 2008 WL.

73 See EC Court of Justice (CJEU), *Meca-Medina and Majcen*, Case C-519/04 P, Judgment of 18 July 2006, <http://curia.europa.eu/juris/showPdf.jsf?text=&docid=57022&pageIndex=0&doclang=EN&mode=lst&dir=&occ=first&part=1&cid=10773>; Case C-415/93, *Bosman*, Judgment of 15 December 1995, <http://eur-lex.europa.eu/legal-content/EN/TXT/PDF/?uri=CELEX:61993CJ0415&from=EN>.

74 Gary S Becker, *The Economic Approach to Human Behavior* (University of Chicago Press 1976) 7 ('the economic approach does not assume that economic units are necessarily conscious of their efforts to maximize or can verbalize or otherwise describe ... reasons for the systematic pattern of their behavior.').

12. Political Economy and the Responsibility of States: The Problem of Many Hands in International Law

André Nollkaemper*

I. INTRODUCTION

This Chapter examines the phenomenon of diffusion of responsibility from a Political Economy (PE) perspective. It is argued that concerted actions that lead to harmful outcomes may trigger a diffusion of responsibility between States, International Organizations (IOs) and other actors involved in the concerted action. Such diffusion may bring both costs and benefits for relevant actors. The Chapter construes diffusion as a political process, of which International Law (IL) is an integral part, and exposes the costs and benefits involved.

Up front, we have to define what we mean with the concept 'diffusion'. In sociology, diffusion refers to the spread of ideas, policies and practices.[1] This concept can also be applied to legal phenomena. For instance, we can say that the notion of the 'rule of law' is diffused across levels of governance. A notion that originally was connected to national legal orders, spreads to international institutions and more generally the

* The research leading to this Chapter has received funding from the European Research Council under the European Union's Seventh Framework Programme (FP/2007–2013)/ERC grant agreement no 249499, as part of the research project on Shared Responsibility in International Law (SHARES), carried out at the Amsterdam Center for International Law (ACIL) of the University of Amsterdam.

[1] Frank Dobbin, Beth Simmons and Geoffrey Garrett (eds), *The Global Diffusion of Markets and Democracy* (CUP 2008); Katharina Holzinger, Helge Jörgens and Christoph Knill, *Transfer, Diffusion und Konvergenz: Konzepte und Kausalmechanismen* (Springer 2007).

international legal order.[2] Likewise, we can say that responsibility is diffused, if, rather than resting on one person, it is spread over a multitude of persons.

Diffusion of responsibility occurs in particular in the context of concerted action. It is clear that diffusion also may occur in situations where multiple actors do not act in concert, yet where parallel actions cause a single harmful outcome. However, it is submitted that in situations of concerted action, diffusion of responsibility is especially likely to occur and, where it does, it has particular manifestations that differ from non-concerted action. This is in particular due to the relations between the actors. A key characteristic of the type of concerted action in which I am interested is that the concerted action involves interaction or coordination of conduct between the participating actors. This means that outcomes cannot be explained by individual conduct of individual actors. By engaging in cooperation, States bring about results that they could not have brought about on their own.

Diffusion of responsibility in situations of concerted action may (but need not) imply that the actual share of responsibility of each person involved becomes smaller.[3] This dimension of diffusion is well captured in Mark Bovens' observation that '[a][a]s the responsibility for any given instance of conduct is scattered among more people, the discrete responsibility of every individual diminishes proportionately'.[4] Moreover, the plurality of contributions, and their interrelationship, may make it difficult, and sometimes impossible, to determine individual causes and thus to determine who is responsible for what.[5]

This dimension of the diffusion of responsibility in cases of concerted action is a manifestation of the so-called 'problem of many hands'. This problem (TPMH) is commonly attributed to a 1980 article by Dennis Thompson; *Moral Responsibility of Public Officials: The Problem of*

---

[2] Michael Zurn, André Nollkaemper and Randy Peerenboom (eds), *The Rule of Law Dynamics in Rule of Law Dynamics in an Era of International and Transnational Governance* (CUP 2014).

[3] Andrew Linklater, *The Problem of Harm in World Politics: Theoretical Investigations* (CUP 2011) 57, 225.

[4] Mark Bovens, *The Quest for Responsibility: Accountability and Citizenship in Complex Organizations* (CUP 1998) 46.

[5] In this respect the problem of many hands is closely related to the concept of shared responsibility as used for instance by Larry May, who argues that shared responsibility arises when there is no effective possibility to determine causal contributions. See Larry May, *Sharing Responsibility* (University of Chicago Press 1996).

Many Hands.[6] Thompson argued that assigning responsibility in the framework of governmental organizations becomes more difficult when more persons – 'many hands' – are involved in the process that caused harm. Though TPMH has been applied in a variety of different theoretical contexts, such as agency theory,[7] the collective responsibility,[8] and public goods,[9] its prime application is in the sphere of responsibility. TPMH can help to explain and understand the difficulty of determining and implementing responsibility in collective settings. It may allow us to identify the conditions and processes that explain when diffusion of responsibility occurs and to assess its benefits and costs.

While the notion of TPMH mostly has been applied in a domestic context, it is highly relevant in the international sphere. Examples of cases of diffusion of responsibility are the *Legality of the Use of Force* cases in the International Court of Justice (ICJ)[10] or the *Saddam Hussein* case before the ECtHR,[11] in which plaintiffs did not succeed in successfully bringing claims against a multitude of (allegedly) responsible parties. Further examples can be drawn from other issue-areas. If States cooperate to conserve fish stocks beyond their Exclusive Economic Zone (EEZ) but fail to realize agreed objectives, distribution of responsibility among the States and institutions involved likewise will be difficult.[12] If States or IOs fail to live up to the collective 'responsibility to protect'

---

[6] Dennis F Thompson, 'Moral Responsibility of Public Officials: The Problem of Many Hands' (1980) 74 Am Pol Sci Rev 905.

[7] Kathleen M Eisenhardt, 'Agency Theory: An Assessment and Review' (1989) 14 AMR 57.

[8] David Miller, 'National Responsibility and Global Justice' (2008) 11 Crit Rev Int Soc Polit Philos 383.

[9] Mancur Olson, *The Logic of Collective Action: Public Goods and the Theory of Groups* (Harvard University Press 1971); Thomas C Schelling, *Micromotives and Macrobehavior* (WW Norton & Company 1978).

[10] *Legality of Use of Force (Yugoslavia v United States)* (Provisional Measures: Order) [1999] ICJ Rep 916 (nine similar cases were brought by Yugoslavia against other NATO Member States).

[11] *Hussein v Albania* App no 23276/04 (ECtHR, 14 March 2006) para 1.

[12] See for example, 'Agreement for the Implementation of the Provisions of the United Nations Convention on the Law of the Sea of 10 December 1982 Relating to the Conservation and Management of Straddling Fish Stocks and Highly Migratory Fish Stocks' UN Conference on Straddling Fish Stocks and Highly Migratory Fish Stocks (New York 24 July–4 August 1995) (8 Sept. 1995) UN Doc A/CONF. 164/37. In 2013, the Sub-Regional Fisheries Commission asked an Advisory Opinion to ITLOS, with an aim of clarifying the responsibilities of multiple actors engaged in illegal fisheries, see *Request for an Advisory Opinion Submitted by the Sub-Regional Fisheries Commission (SRFC) Case No.*

human populations from mass atrocities[13] – a responsibility that rests in part on obligations that are binding on a plurality of States or organizations[14] – it likewise may be difficult to determine which of the actors is responsible.[15]

In all such situations, contributions are spread over several actors, so that it may become difficult to determine that the conditions of responsibility are satisfied; sometimes that will be impossible, with the result that no responsibility can be determined.

In this Chapter I will first set out the dynamics of cooperation that help to understand the situations in which diffusion occurs (Section II). In Section III, I will zoom in on situations in which diffusion may lead to responsibility gaps. I then will discuss what I will call the politics of diffusion. Diffusion is not an autonomous effect of wider changes in global governance, but may be an intended consequence of strategic choices by actors participating in a concerted action (Section IV). Finally, I will discuss the benefits and costs of diffusion and argue that while such gaps in particular cases may be inevitable and may even be preconditions for getting relevant actors to agree on action, they raise fundamental normative and institutional challenges for the organization and implementation of concerted action (Section V).

II. UNDERLYING DYNAMICS

This Section will explain that the trend towards concerted action is of a structural nature (II.1) that is reinforced by acceptance of 'shared responsibilities' (II.2).

---

21 (Request to Render an Advisory Opinion, Order of 24 May 2013) ITLOS Rep 2013, 2.

[13] Report of the Secretary-General 'Implementing the Responsibility to Protect' (2009) UN Doc A/63/677 [hereinafter R2P Report].

[14] Monica Hakimi, 'State Bystander Responsibility' (2010) 21 EJIL 342–343, 342 n 5; Arne J Vetlesen, 'Genocide: A Case for the Responsibility of the Bystander' (2000) 37 J Peace R 529.

[15] This question has been considered to some extent by the International Court of Justice (ICJ), *Case Concerning Application of the Convention on Prevention and Punishment of Crime of Genocide (Bosnia and Herzegovina v Serbia and Montenegro)* (Judgment) [2007] ICJ Rep 43, 379. See also James Pattison, 'Assigning Humanitarian Intervention and the Responsibility to Protect', in Julia Hoffman and André Nollkaemper (eds), *Responsibility to Protect: From Principle to Practice* (Amsterdam University Press 2012) 173.

II.1. Dynamics

Concerted action is not an incidental phenomenon in international affairs that can be expected to give way to the traditional pattern of individualism. It rather reflects fundamental developments in international society and the international legal order that are bound to persist. Three trends that contextualize the phenomenon of shared responsibility are here identified: interdependence, moralization and heterogeneity.[16] These trends influence each other in an intertwined way.

The *first trend* that drives concerted action is interdependence, underlying the passage from a 'society' mainly characterized by coexistence to one also characterized by cooperation.[17] This trend is easily overstated, and in many situations, in particular relating to territory, boundaries, use of force and (non-)intervention the prime function of IL continues to be secure coexistence between States.[18] Nonetheless, it seems incontrovertible that in many areas, States have become dependent on each other to pursue common goods, and indeed have felt compelled to address them jointly.

The interdependencies are both of an objective and a subjective nature. As to the former, in certain areas, factual effects extend across borders, creating interdependencies when States wish to address such effects. Transboundary environmental effects, depletion of natural resources, trade in endangered species, piracy, refugee flows, human trafficking, arms trade, and transboundary crime are examples.

In other areas it is merely the perception that has changed, rather than a reality. The recognition that it is no longer acceptable that genocide or mass killings within a particular State be committed is an example.[19] The interdependence here does not necessarily arise from a physical cross-border dimension, but rather from a shared perception that there is a

---

[16] See for earlier discussion André Nollkaemper and Dov Jacobs, 'Shared Responsibility in International Law: A Conceptual Framework' (2013) 34 Mich J Int L 359, 370–372.

[17] See Wolfgang Friedman, 'General Course in Public International Law' (1969) 47 Recueil des Cours 127. Specifically on interdependence, see for example, Ernst-Ulrich Petersmann, 'International Economic Law, "Public Reason", and Multilevel Governance of Interdependent Public Goods' (2011) 14 JIEL 23.

[18] George M Abi-Saab, 'Whither the International Community?' (1998) 9 EJIL 248; Pierre-Marie Dupuy, 'International Law: Torn between Coexistence, Cooperation and Globalization. General Conclusions' (1998) 9 EJIL 278.

[19] See generally Yuval Shany, 'The Road to the Genocide Convention and Beyond', in Paola Gaeta (ed), *The Genocide Convention – A Commentary* (OUP 2009) 3.

problem to be solved, combined with the fact that individual actors will not be able to effectively prevent genocide or effectively respond to it when it occurs.

Responding to situations of interdependence by concerted action primarily seeks to enhance the efficiency and effectiveness of such action. In the areas indicated above – environmental cooperation, trans-border criminal cooperation, and responding to genocide and mass killings – individual States often will be powerless to make a fundamental difference. However, interdependence may also stem from the perceived need to enhance legitimacy of policies. While multilateralism surely does not guarantee legitimacy,[20] when the legality of State action may be contested, acting together may help build an argument that the action is legitimate and perhaps even legal. A State acting on its own will more easily be open to the criticism of acting for its own interests.[21] This seems to underlie, for instance, the concerted action in relation to ISIL in Iraq and Syria in 2014–2015.

Interdependence in any of the above ways can drive a variety of forms of cooperation – from loose agreement on objectives to action through a common organ of an IO. But in a sizeable number of cases, it has led to cooperation that would fall into the category of concerted action, where States and other actors closely coordinate their policies in pursuit of a common aim. Examples are the concerted action in relation to ISIL, through 'coalitions of the willing' in Libya,[22] in AU peacekeeping operations,[23]

---

[20] José E Alvarez, 'Multilateralism and its Discontents' (2000) 11 EJIL 393.

[21] Pierre Buhler, 'Military Intervention and Sources of Legitimacy', in Gilles Andréani and Pierre Hassner (eds), *Justifying War? From Humanitarian Intervention to Counterterrorism* (Palgrave Macmillan 2008) 167; Nicholas Tsagourias, 'Cosmopolitan Legitimacy and UN Collective Security', in Roland Pierik and Wouter Werner (eds), *Cosmopolitanism in Context: Perspectives from International Law and Political Theory* (CUP 2010) 129.

[22] See Jeffrey H Michaels, 'Able But Not Willing: A Critical Assessment of NATO's Libya Intervention', in Kjell Engelbrekt, Marcus Mohlin and Charlotte Wagnsonn (eds), *The NATO Intervention in Libya: Lessons Learned from the Campaign* (Routledge 2014) 17.

[23] See for example, Paul D Williams and Arthur Boutellis, 'Partnership Peacekeeping: Challenges and Opportunities in the United Nations–African Union Relationship' (2014) 113(451) Afr Aff 254.

in relation to piracy in the horn of Africa,[24] and in international fisheries policy.[25]

The *second trend*, directly related to the above noted subjective dimension of interdependence, is 'moralization'. Seeking to distance themselves from the realist view of international relations in which States seek the protection of their own interests, a variety of actors (including notably European States, IOs, NGOs and scholars) have construed the international legal order in the direction of an increased 'moralization'. They thereby contribute to a paradigm shift from State sovereignty as the cornerstone of the legal order, to a paradigm based on rights of the individual,[26] on the one hand, and the values and interest of international community, on the other.[27] This trend of moralization is far from being universally accepted[28] and can be critiqued on the ground that it in fact amounts to an effort of a limited number of actors to impose their understanding of community interests on others.[29] Nonetheless, the trend is pervasive and has propelled concerted action in a wide variety of situations.

IL incorporates and reflects this trend, as it highlights community interests over individual action and individual interests. This is reflected

---

[24] Laurie R Blank, 'Rules of Engagement and Legal Framework for Multinational Counter-Piracy Operations' (2013) 46 Case W Res J Int L 397. See also James Kraska and Brian Wilson, 'Combating Pirates of the Gulf of Aden: The Djibouti Code and the Somali Coast Guard' (2009) 45 Stanford J Int L 243.

[25] Oran R Young, *International Cooperation: Building Regimes for Natural Resources and the Environment* (Cornell University Press 1989).

[26] And, by extension, the 'peoples', see *Accordance with International Law of the Unilateral Declaration of Independence in Respect of Kosovo* (Advisory Opinion) [2010] ICJ Rep 403, separate opinion of Judge Antonio A Cançado Trindade. Other authors have referred to this trend as 'humanization' of international law: Theodor Meron, *The Humanization of International Law* (Martinus Nijhoff 2006); Anne Peters, 'Humanity as the A and Ω of Sovereignty' (2009) 20 EJIL 513.

[27] Augusto A Cançado Trindade, *International Law for Human Kind: Towards a New Jus Gentium* (Martinus Nijhoff 2013); Sienho Yee, 'Towards a Harmonious World: The Roles of the International Law of Co-progressiveness and Leader States' (2008) 7 Chinese J Int L 99, 102.

[28] See for example, Jean d'Aspremont, 'The Foundations of the International Legal Order' (2007) 18 Finnish Yb Int L 219; Yasuaki Onuma, 'In Quest of Intercivilizational Human Rights: "Universal" vs. "Relative"' (2000) 1 Asia-Pac J Int L 53.

[29] See Antony Anghie, *Imperialism, Sovereignty and the Making of International Law* (CUP 2012).

in a hierarchy of norms;[30] and affects the operation of particular rules of interpretation,[31] and the law of responsibility.[32]

According to one argument, the moral weight of this set of norms (notably the protection of individuals and individual rights) would not only require and justify the action of single States to try to protect such rights, but would require States to act together.[33] Such normative claims may be contested. While it may be relatively easy to articulate the negative implications of hierarchically higher values (for example, in terms of the invalidity of treaties that deviate from them), it is less easy to explain why they would call for concerted action. However, it is precisely in relation to *ius cogens* norms, that the ILC has accepted an obligation to cooperate.[34] In any case, as an empirical matter it can be observed that concerted action frequently arises in areas that carry heavy moral undertones, such as responsibility to protect, protection of civilians during armed conflict, protection of populations from climate change, and so forth. Similar to the trend of interdependence, this dimension of

---

[30] Alain Pellet, 'Can a State Commit a Crime? Definitely, Yes!' (1999) 10 EJIL 425; Dinah Shelton, 'Righting Wrongs: Reparations in the Articles on State Responsibility' (2002) 96 AJIL 833, 841; Eric Wyler, 'From "State Crime" to Responsibility for "Serious Breaches of Obligations under Peremptory Norms of General International Law"' (2002) 13 EJIL 1147; Pierre Klein, 'Responsibility for Serious Breaches of Obligations Deriving from Peremptory Norms of International Law and United Nations Law' (2002) 13 EJIL 1241.

[31] Ineta Ziemele (ed), *Reservations to Human Rights Treaties and the Vienna Convention Regime: Conflicts, Harmony or Reconciliation* (Martinus Nijhoff Publishers 2004).

[32] For an overview of the historical evolution towards the taking into account of community interests in the law of State responsibility, see Georg Nolte, 'From Dionisio Anzilotti to Roberto Ago: The Classical International Law of State Responsibility and the Traditional Primacy of a Bilateral Conception of Inter-State Relations' (2002) 13 EJIL 1083. See also Santiago M Villalpando, *L'émergence de la communauté internationale dans la responsabilité des Etats* (PUF 2005).

[33] Toni Erskine, '"Coalitions of the Willing" and the Shared Responsibility to Protect', in André Nollkaemper and Dov Jacobs (eds), *Distribution of Responsibilities in International Law* (CUP 2015).

[34] Articles on Responsibility of States for Internationally Wrongful Acts (ARSIWA), ILC Yb 2001/II(2), art 41; 2011 Draft Articles on the Responsibility of International Organizations (ARIO), ILC Report on the work of its sixty-third session, UNGAOR 66th Sess, Supp No 10, UN Doc A/66/10 (2011) (ARIO), art 42.

moralization thus propels the number of situations where *ex post facto* questions of shared responsibility may arise.

The *third trend* relevant to concerted action is the multiplication of actors that participate in international society.[35] In some situations actors other than States are a relevant factor because they themselves contribute to harmful outcomes, and their cooperation thus is relevant for addressing such harm. In other cases they may not as such be a cause of harm, but they are relevant in terms of their ability to contribute to a solution.

This is most immediately obvious for IOs. The fact that States now regularly defer to IOs to 'legislate' on a wide-ranging array of topics, from cultural heritage to health and environmental law, can, given the continuing role of States in the development and implementation of decisions of IOs, result in concerted action between multiple organizations and/or between organizations and States. The layered nature of IOs, which are legal persons but at the same time consist of sovereign States and members, facilitates the construction of responsibility for wrongdoing as a shared responsibility between the organization and member States.[36] The 2011 Draft Articles on the Responsibility of International Organizations (ARIO) indeed envisage that an organization can be responsible in connection with the wrongful acts of States, for instance on the ground that an organization is responsible for adopting decisions that require States to commit acts that contravene international obligations.[37] Significantly, these Articles acknowledge that in such situations both the organization and the State can be responsible, resulting in a situation of shared responsibility.[38]

In addition to international institutions, the increased role of private actors in international relations can lead to situations of concerted action. The practice of States of delegating powers to private entities (the use of private military contractors by States is an obvious example) leads to

---

[35] Generally: Rosalyn Higgins, *Problems and Process: International Law and How We Use It* (OUP 1995) ch 3; Andrea Bianchi (ed), *Non-State Actors and International Law* (Ashgate 2009); Jean d'Aspremont (ed), *Participants in the International Legal System: Multiple Perspectives on Non-State Actors in International Law* (Routledge 2011).

[36] See generally on the layered nature of IOs Catherine Brölmann, *The International Institutional Veil in Public International Law. International Organisations and the Law of Treaties* (Hart Publishing 2007).

[37] ARIO (n 34), art 17.

[38] ARIO (n 34), art 19.

forms of concerted action.[39] The same holds for international institutions that rely on public–private partnerships.[40]

The combined effect of these three trends is that States, international institutions and increasingly other actors increasingly cooperate in response to perceived common problems, thus proportionately increasing the situations where harmful outcomes may result from such cooperation.

II.2. The Multiplier Effect of 'Shared Responsibilities'

The practice of States and other actors to engage in concerted action is further strengthened by recognition of moral, political and legal responsibilities to do so. In relation to many of the areas identified above, States and other actors that engage in concerted action do so in recognition of a 'shared responsibility' that they would have in relation to that particular issue. For instance, in December 2014, the Security Council adopted a resolution prompted by the ties between cross-border crime and terrorism and stressed the importance of strengthening trans-regional and international cooperation on a basis of 'a common and shared responsibility to counter the world drug problem and related criminal activities'.[41]

Speaking of 'shared responsibilities' in this sense means something different than international lawyers generally mean when they speak of responsibility for internationally wrongful acts. In the examples given above, saying that two persons share a responsibility in relation to a particular situation then may mean that these persons both have to take care of that situation. It then concerns an *ex ante* rather than an *ex post* responsibility. Responsibility in this sense is essentially forward looking, rather than relating to a sharing of harm that already has been caused.

The recognition of shared responsibilities in this *ex ante* sense is highly relevant for our topic. They provide a normative underpinning that sustains and propels concerted action. They transform concerted action

---

[39] For example, Nigel D White and Sorscha MacLeod, 'EU Operations and Private Military Contractors: Issues of Corporate and Institutional Responsibility' (2008) 19 EJIL 965.

[40] Lisa Clarke, 'Responsibility of International Organizations under International Law for the Acts of Global Health Public-Private Partnerships' (2011) 12 Chi J Int L 55; Laurence Boisson de Chazournes, 'United in Joy and Sorrow: Some Considerations on Responsibility Issues Under Partnerships Among International Financial Institutions', in Maurizio Ragazzi (ed), *Responsibility of International Organizations: Essays in Memory of Sir Ian Brownlie* (OUP 2013) 211. See also the Chapter by Ramses A Wessel and Evisa Kica, in this Volume.

[41] UNSC Res 2195 (19 December 2014) UN Doc S/RES/2195.

from ad hoc cooperation, depending on the will and perceived interests of the actors involved, in a cooperation that is expected or required.

We can identify three different strands of these '*ex ante*' shared responsibilities: moral, political and legal. The moral, or philosophical, strand has been articulated in the scholarship of such authors as Larry May,[42] David Miller,[43] Seumas Millar[44] and Samantha Besson.[45] In this body of literature, speaking of a shared responsibility for say, human rights (HR), refers to moral requirements of individuals, States or organizations to act for the protection of HR.[46] The political dimension of shared responsibility refers to situations where actors at a political level agree that they share a responsibility to act in relation to a common interests. Examples are the sharing of responsibility between the US and European partners in NATO,[47] or the sharing of responsibility between European States in regard to refugee flows from Northern Africa.[48] In addition to the moral and the political dimension of shared responsibility, there also is a distinct legal dimension. An example is Principle 21 of the 1972 Stockholm Declaration that confirms the responsibility of all States to prevent transboundary environmental harm.[49]

The moral, political and legal dimensions of shared responsibility will often intertwine, and the same shared responsibility that in scholarship may be advanced on moral grounds, may be accepted by actors and be transformed into a political and/or a legal principle. The 'responsibility to

---

42 Larry May, *Sharing Responsibility* (University of Chicago Press 1996).

43 David Miller, *National Responsibility and Global Justice* (OUP 2007).

44 Seumas Miller, 'Collective Responsibility' (2001) 15 Pub Aff Q 65.

45 Samantha Besson, 'La pluralité d'États responsables: vers une solidarité internationale?' (2007) 17 SZIER/ RSDIE 13.

46 Samantha Besson, 'The Allocation of Anti-Poverty Rights Duties: Our Rights, But Whose Duties?', in Krista Nadakavukaren Schefer (ed), *Poverty and the International Economic Legal System: Duties to the World's Poor* (CUP 2013) 408, 424. See also ibid 426 on the shared nature of such responsibility.

47 Peter K Foster and Stephen J Cimbala, *The NATO, US and Military Burden Sharing* (Routledge 2005).

48 Steve Scherer and Ilaria Polleschi, 'Italy in Talks with EU to share responsibility for boat migrants' (*Reuters,* 8 July 2014) <http://www.reuters.com/article/2014/07/08/us-eu-italy-migrants-idUSKBN0FD1YL20140708> accessed 17 March 2015.

49 UN Environment Programme, 'Declaration on the United Nations Conference on the Human Environment' (1972), principle 21.

protect' is an example of this cooperation-propelling potential of a mixed moral-political-legal concept of shared responsibility.[50]

III. RESPONSIBILITY GAPS

Diffusion of responsibility, which means that in situations of concerted action responsibility is spread over this multiplicity of actors, does not adversely affect the possibility to determine responsibility. Individual actors retain their individual obligation, even when they act in concert. Moreover, the fact that more than one actor is engaged in a particular wrongful act, does not release each individual actor from its responsibilities. This was recognized in the *Corfu Channel* case, where the ICJ was apparently faced with a harm caused by two parties, but only one appeared before it as a defendant, and it decided to neglect the other party and put all responsibility and all compensation on Albania.[51]

However, in particular situations, diffusion may lead to the undermining of responsibility. This Section will identify three reasons that help explain why this can be the case: the normative problem of determination of obligations and attribution in collective settings (III.1), institutional gaps in situations of concerted action (III.2) and informational gaps (III.3).

III.1. The Normative Gap

In its original formulation, TPMH was framed as a normative problem. Thompson developed his theory of TPMH from the viewpoint of moral responsibility.[52] TPMH arose from the fact that it is morally problematic to attribute responsibility to individuals where that could not be justified on moral grounds.[53] This normative condition of diffusion of responsibility can be transposed to the legal domain. Diffusion of responsibility

---

[50] Luke Glanville, *Sovereignty and the Responsibility to Protect: A New History* (University of Chicago Press 2013).

[51] *Corfu Channel Case (United Kingdom v Albania)* (Judgment) [1949] ICJ Rep 244.

[52] Thompson (n 6).

[53] Dennis F Thompson, 'Designing Responsibility: The Problem of Many Hands in Complex Organizations', in Jeroen van den Hoven, Seumas Miller and Thomas Pogge (eds), *The Design Turn in Applied Ethics* (CUP, forthcoming); Ibo van de Poel, Jessica Nihlén Fahlquist, Neelke Doorn, Sjoerd Zwart and Lambèr Royakkers, 'The Problem of Many Hands: Climate Change as an Example' (2012) 18 Sci Eng Ethics 49, 64.

arises when responsibility cannot be assigned or determined because the *legal* conditions for responsibility (in particular breach of an international obligation and attribution of the conduct in question) have not been (fully) met.[54]

This will in particular be the case when it cannot be determined who is responsible for what and/or because the conditions for such responsibility are not satisfied. Another way of saying this is that the conditions that have been specified are not attuned to the specific nature of concerted action. In this respect it is relevant to recall that in several other systems of law, such as tort law[55] and international criminal law,[56] specific conditions have been developed seeing the multiple wrongdoers. If these sets of principles would not exist, clearly a gap would arise, that would feed back on the nature of the obligation themselves. In IL such principles are virtually absent,[57] making it less likely that the existing principles are well attuned to the determination of responsibility in situations of concerted action.

The difficulty of identifying who is responsible for a harmful outcome in a collective setting then may be due to the fact that individual contributions may be too small or otherwise be insufficient to meet criteria for responsibility. The principle of independent responsibility dictates that responsibility is only assigned to actors whose individual contributions to the harm are sufficiently significant to pass the threshold that is required for responsibility. However, in situations of many hands, tasks may be chopped up, so that multiple actors perform small tasks which combine to larger (harmful) outcomes.[58] Individual actors then may not meet the conditions for responsibility.

Three situations in particular can be identified where a normative gap may arise that leads to diffusion of responsibility. A first situation in which diffusion may lead to a responsibility gap arises when not all

---

[54] ARSIWA (n 34), art 1-2; ARIO (n 34), art 1-2.

[55] European Group on Tort Law, 'Principles of European Tort Law' (2005) available at <http://civil.udg.edu/php/biblioteca/items/283/PETL.pdf> accessed 28 September 2015.

[56] HG van der Wilt, 'The Continuous Quest for Proper Modes of Criminal Responsibility' 2009 7 J Int Crim Just 307; Koi Ambos, 'Joint Criminal Enterprise and Command Responsibility' (2007) 5 J Int Crim Just 159; Elies van Sliedregt, 'Joint Criminal Enterprise as a Pathway to Convicting Individuals for Genocide' (2007) 5(1) J Int Crim Just 184.

[57] Roger P Alford, 'Apportioning Responsibility Among Joint Tortfeasors for International Law Violations' (2011) 38 Pepp L Rev 233.

[58] Larry May, *Sharing Responsibility* (University of Chicago Press 1996) 7, 8 and 73.

actors involved are bound by primary obligations. This is in particular relevant for concerted action involving IOs, which may not in a similar degree as States be bound by treaty or customary obligations. It is precisely this feature that has given rise to the idea of circumvention: the possibility that States circumvent their own obligations by acting through an international organization, as a result of which their own responsibility may be mitigated or precluded. Article 61 of the ARIO, which seeks to assign (shared) responsibility to States that so seek to circumvent their responsibility, is a somewhat ill-conceived attempt to preclude such diffusion of responsibility.[59]

Similar normative gaps may occur when States act with or through other non-State actors that may not at all be bound by international obligations, for instance paramilitary groups, private military contractors or security firms that are hired to protect ships against piracy.[60] While the fact that these actors are not similarly bound by international obligations need not be the motive for States to engage in such concerted action, the result of such 'acting through others' may well be a diffusion of responsibility. This indeed appears to be a fundamental feature of partnerships among international institutions, such as UN Aids, where not all partners in the partnership will be bound by the same obligations.[61]

The second cause of a normative gap is when secondary obligations are unassigned. Diffusion of responsibility can undermine the forward-looking potential of the law of responsibility by making it unclear who is to respond to a breach. This is in particular relevant for obligations to prevent[62] and obligations of result which may be structured in a way that makes it difficult to determine who is responsible for what, and may

---

[59] See for example, Ana Sofia Barros and Cedric Ryngaert, 'The Position of Member States in (Autonomous) Institutional Decision-Making: Implications for the Establishment of Responsibility' (2014) 11 Int Org L Rev 53; Jean d'Aspremont, 'Abuse of the Legal Personality of International Organizations and the Responsibility of Member States' (2007) 4 Int Org L Rev 91.

[60] Jessica NM Schechinger, 'Responsibility for Human Rights Violations Arising from the Use of Privately Contracted Armed Security Personnel against Piracy: Re-emphasizing the Primary Role and Obligations of Flag States' (2014) Amsterdam Center for International Law SHARES Research Paper No 58, <http://www.sharesproject.nl/wp-content/uploads/2014/11/ACIL-2014-30-Responsibility-for-Human-Rights-Violations-JS.pdf> accessed 2 August 2015.

[61] Boisson de Chazournes (n 40); Davinia Aziz, 'Global Public-Private Partnerships in International Law' (2012) 3 Asian J Int L 339.

[62] Orna Ben Naftali, 'The Obligation to Prevent and to Punish Genocide', in Paola Gaeta (ed), *The UN Genocide Convention: A Commentary* (OUP 2009) 27.

allow States to escape their responsibility by pointing to the non-performance of obligations by others.[63] David Miller's observation that, 'an undistributed duty [...] to which everybody is subject is likely to be discharged by nobody unless it can be allocated in some way',[64] is relevant for diffused responsibility. In effect, this may lead to a bystander effect.[65]

The third situation arises when the conditions for responsibility cannot be met, because tasks and conduct are chopped up. While harmful outcomes may occur, no single actor may be held responsible. Partners can then together produce a result that would have been wrongful if it had been produced by one of them. An example is the ECtHR's judgment in *Sari v Turkey and Denmark*. The case concerned the length of criminal proceedings which were consecutively instituted in Denmark and Turkey against a Turkish national for crimes committed in Denmark. Mr. Sari complained that the criminal proceedings were not settled within reasonable time: eight years, seven months and twenty-two days had lasted between the indictment by a Danish Court and the sentence delivered by the Turkish Court. Although the Court held the length of the proceedings to fall under the 'joint responsibility' of Denmark and Turkey, the Court did not find a violation of Article 6 on the part of either State. The Court reasoned that the delays could not be attributed to either State, because they resulted, rather, from 'a system of mutual assistance under which the requesting State is dependent on the co-operation of the other State'.[66]

It is relevant to recall that under the principle of independent responsibility, the State, or international organization, as the case may be, is responsible for its *own* conduct and its *own* wrongs.[67] It is not responsible for the conduct of someone else. The principle of independent responsibility is firmly established in the ARSIWA[68] and in the relatively

[63] More generally; responsibility as obligations may directly influence 'responsibility-as-blameworthiness', see van de Poel (n 53) 52.

[64] David Miller, *National Responsibility and Global Justice* (OUP 2007) 99–100.

[65] See John M Darley and Bibb Latané, 'Group Inhibition of Bystander Intervention in Emergencies' (1968) 10 J Pers Soc Psychol 215, 215.

[66] *Sari v Turkey and Denmark* App no 21889/93 (ECtHR, 8 November 2001) para 92.

[67] See ARSIWA Commentary, ILC Yb 2001/II(2), commentary to art 47, para 8.

[68] The basic principle embodied in arts 1 and 2 ARSIWA ('Every internationally wrongful act of a State entails the international responsibility of that State' and 'There is an internationally wrongful act of a State when conduct consisting of an action or omission' is attributable to the State and constitutes a

scarce case law, such as the *Corfu Channel*,[69] the *Certain Phosphate Lands in Nauru* case,[70] *M.S.S. v Belgium and Greece*[71] and the *Eurotunnel* case.[72] While independent responsibility certainly can be relevant in situations of concerted action, reducing complex relationships to the responsibility of an individual State may be unlikely to result in a satisfactory outcome. In combination with the procedural limitations of dispute settlement, the concept of individual responsibility of States has led courts to reduce complex cooperative schemes to binary categories, without resulting in principled discussions of the shared nature of responsibility.[73] This becomes particularly problematic when conduct is attributed to one actor only. Dual attribution is very rare. Although a few scholars have defended the possibility of dual attribution, in particular in the context of peacekeeping operations,[74] practice remains rare.[75]

---

breach of an obligation of the State) underlies the ARSIWA as a whole. ARSIWA (n 34), arts 16–18 to some extent form an exception.

69 *Corfu Channel Case (United Kingdom v Albania)* (Judgment) [1949] ICJ Rep 244.

70 *Certain Phosphate Lands in Nauru (Nauru v Australia)* (Preliminary Objections, Judgment) [1992] ICJ Rep 240.

71 *M.S.S. v Belgium and Greece* [GC] App no 30696/09 (ECtHR 21 January 2011).

72 *Channel Tunnel Grp. Ltd. v United Kingdom*, Partial Award (Perm. Ct. Arb. 2007) para 187.

73 *Corfu Channel* (n 69); *Military and Paramilitary Activities in and against Nicaragua* (*Nicaragua v United States of America*), Judgment, ICJ Rep 1986, 14; *Nauru* (n 70); *East Timor* (*Portugal v Australia*), Judgment, ICJ Rep 1995, 90; and *Legality of Use of Force* (*Serbia and Montenegro v United Kingdom*), Provisional Measures, Order of 2 June 1999, ICJ Rep 1999, 826.

74 Luigi Condorelli, 'Le statut des forces de l'ONU et le droit international humanitaire' (1995) 78 RDI 881 and Luigi Condorelli, 'Le statut des forces des Nations Unies et le droit international humanitaire', in Claude Emmanuelli (ed), *Les casques bleus: policiers ou combatants?* (Wilson and Lafleur 1997) 87; Nicholas Tsagourias, 'The Responsibility of International Organisations for Military Missions', in Marco Odello and Ryszard W Piotrowisz (eds), *International Military Missions and International Law* (Martinus Nijhoff 2011) 245; Karl T Dannenbaum, 'Translating the Standard of Effective Control into a System of Effective Accountability: How Liability Should be Apportioned for Violations of Human Rights by Member State Troop Contingents Serving as United Nations Peacekeepers' (2010) 51 Harv Int L J 113; Aurel Sari, 'Jurisdiction and International Responsibility in Peace Support Operations: The Behrami and Saramati Cases' (2008) 8 HR L Rev 151.

75 See for example, *HN v Netherlands* (Ministry of Defence and Ministry of Foreign Affairs), First instance judgment of 10 December 2008, District Court of the Hague, ILDC 1092 (NL 2008) paras 47–49. However, the Court of Appeal

Illustrative is the *Saddam Hussein* case before the ECtHR,[76] in which Saddam Hussein brought a case against twenty-one States that were allegedly implicated in the invasion of Iraq and that were responsible for his arrest, detention and ongoing trial.[77] The ECtHR considered that the responsibility of any of the respondent States could not be invoked 'on the sole basis that those States allegedly formed part (at varying unspecified levels) of a coalition with the US, when the impugned actions were carried out by the US, when security in the zone in which those actions took place was assigned to the US and when the overall command of the coalition was vested in the US.'[78] Another noteworthy example is the decision of the ECtHR in *Behrami*. The Court attributed all acts and omissions relating to the failed demining operations in Kosovo exclusively to the UN, and not to its member States, without considering the possibility of a more nuanced solution in which responsibility would be shared.[79] Also in relation to the role of the UN Interim Administration Mission in Kosovo (UNMIK), responsibility was channelled to the UN rather than (also) Kosovo, effectively undermining a role of Kosovo in the eventual rebuilding process.[80]

The common element of the above examples is that IL structures its primary and secondary rules in a way that makes it relatively easy for each of multiple parties to contribute to a wrong, yet remain below the threshold where its responsibility would be engaged.

III.2. The Institutional Gap

A second cause that may contribute to diffusion of responsibility is the institutional setting in which concerted action is embedded. Particular

---

departed from this holding, and found that one act could both be attributed to the Netherlands and the UN. See *Nuhanović v Netherlands,* Gerechtshof, 5 July 2011, LJN BR 0133; and André Nollkaemper, 'Dual Attribution: Liability of the Netherlands for Conduct of Dutchbat in Srebrenica' (2011) 9 J Int Crim Just 1143.

[76] *Hussein v Albania* (n 11) para 1.

[77] *Hussein v Albania* (n 11) para 1.

[78] *Hussein v Albania* (n 11) para 1. See Maarten den Heijer, 'Issues of Shared Responsibility Before the European Court of Human Rights' (2013) 60 NILR 411.

[79] *Behrami v France* App nos 71412/01 and 78166/01 (ECtHR, 2 May 2007).

[80] Matthew W Saul, 'Internationally Administered Territories', in André Nollkaemper (ed), *The Practice of Shared Responsibility in International Law* (CUP 2015).

institutional structures may not be attuned to a diffusion of responsibility, and may sustain responsibility gaps by making it difficult to identify who did what and who was responsible for what.

One problem relates to the set-up of international adjudication. Though questions of responsibility are not typically brought in international courts (but rather are settled in negotiations), there is a not insignificant body of case law on questions of international responsibility involving multiple responsible parties, in particular in the ICJ[81] and the ECtHR.[82] However, the present system of international dispute settlement is not well designed to deal with multilateral disputes.[83] This has relevance for adjudication of questions of harm arising out of concerted action. For instance, given that international dispute settlement mechanisms are based on the consent of States, the mere fact that one responsible State has not consented to the judicial process may suffice to exclude a case of harm arising from concerted action from judicial scrutiny. Likewise, if one of the wrongdoing actors is an IO other than the EU or the Seabed Authority, questions of shared responsibility may be deemed inadmissible before the ICJ, the WTO Dispute Settlement Understanding (DSU), the Convention on the Law on the Sea (LOSC) Dispute Settlement Procedure (DSP) and the ECtHR, which do not have jurisdiction over (other) IOs.

Perhaps the most visible barrier to adjudication of claims arising out of concerted action is that a court may not be able to proceed against one actor, if the other actors involved in the concerted action are not part of the litigation. A court may be required to protect the interests of co-responsible parties who are not party to the dispute, by deciding that it has no jurisdiction over the claim against the actor over which it

[81] See Martins Paparinskis, 'Procedural Aspects of Shared Responsibility in the International Court of Justice' (2013) 4 J Int DS 295; André Nollkaemper, 'Issues of Shared Responsibility before the International Court of Justice', in Eva R Rieter and Henri de Waele (eds), *Evolving Principles of International Law – Studies in Honour of Karel C Wellens* (Martinus Nijhoff 2011) 199.

[82] See Marteen den Heijer, 'Procedural Aspects of Shared Responsibility in the European Court of Human Rights' (2013) 4 J Int DS 363.

[83] Lori F Damrosch, 'Multilateral Disputes', in Lori F Damrosch (ed), *The International Court of Justice at a Crossroads* (Dobbs Ferry 1987) 376.

otherwise would have jurisdiction. The *Monetary Gold* principle, as it operates in the practice of the ICJ, is the prime manifestation of this rule.[84]

Institutional limitations may also apply in respect of supervisory mechanisms, outside the sphere of international adjudication. Problems of many hands may be counteracted by monitoring and supervision arrangements that make it possible to identify the contribution of each actor. An example is the detailed reports compiled within the framework of the 1973 Convention on International Trade in Endangered Species (CITES) on the roles and infractions by individual parties who, collectively, contribute to the extinction of particular species.[85] However, there are considerable differences in the existence of such mechanisms and their ability to obtain the relevant information, with direct consequences for diffusion of responsibility. In situations where no institutional mechanisms have been set up to determine relevant fact and to identify who did what, this will increase the possibility of diffusion of responsibility.

III.3. The Information Gap

A directly related third cause of diffusion of responsibility is that 'many hands' make it difficult to identify who did what. For outsiders, 'it is usually very difficult, if not impossible, to know who contributed to, or could have prevented, a certain action, who knew or could have known what.'[86] It even 'may not be clear "even to the members of the collective itself who is accountable".'[87] So conceived, the problem of many hands is an epistemological problem: the problem of identifying who is responsible for what arises from a lack of knowledge, or information.[88]

The practical problem arose clearly in *Legality of the use of force* cases[89] and in the *Saddam Hussein* case[90] where it was next to impossible for the plaintiffs to identify who did what. It also is well

---

[84] Alexander Orakhelashvili, 'The Competence of the International Court of Justice and the Doctrine of the Indispensable Party: from Monetary Gold to East Timor and Beyond' (2011) 2 J Int DS 373.

[85] CITES, 993 UNTS 243.

[86] van de Poel et al. (n 53) 61.

[87] Helen Nissenbaum, 'Accountability in a Computerized Society' (1996) 2 Sci Eng Ethics 25, 29.

[88] van de Poel et al. (n 53) 61.

[89] *Legality of the Use of Force (Serbia and Montenegro v Belgium)* (Judgment) [2004] ICJ Rep 279.

[90] *Hussein v Albania* (n 11) para 1.

illustrated by the fact that painstaking research made clear that fifty-four States participated in the US rendition policy.[91]

This problem is increased by the informal nature of arrangements in collaborative action. Informality leads to responsibility gaps. Examples abound, including transborder police cooperation,[92] financial arrangements within the Basel committee,[93] the rules of the nuclear suppliers group, and command and control structures in military operations.[94] Information gaps also may exist in relation to joint action on piracy, where rules of engagement usually will be beyond the reach of plaintiffs and cross-border joint policy operations.

IV. THE POLITICS OF DIFFUSION

Diffusion, and its possible effects on responsibility gaps, is not a phenomenon that is 'out-there', but rather a manifestation of conduct and strategies of relevant actors.

This Section will first identify the essential political nature of the law of responsibility (and of particular choices on the assignment of responsibility) (IV.1) and then identify particular strategies for diffusing responsibility (IV.2).

IV.1. The Political Nature of Responsibility-Design

The form and content of any scheme of responsibility does not automatically follow on the substantive law but is a matter of conscious design, mostly by States or IOs but also by international courts. Indeed,

---

91 Open Society Justice Initiative, 'Globalizing Torture: CIA Secret Detention and Extraordinary Rendition' (Open Society Foundation, 2013) <http://www.opensocietyfoundations.org/sites/default/files/globalizing-torture-20120205.pdf> accessed 24 February 2015. Dick Marty report 'Secret Detentions and Illegal Transfers of detainees involving Council of Europe Member States', Doc 11302 rev, 11 June 2007 'CoE Rendition Report (2007)'.

92 Saskia Hufnagel, *Policing Cooperation Across Borders: Comparative Perspectives on Law Enforcement within the EU and Australia* (Ashgate 2013).

93 David Zaring, 'Informal Procedure, Hard and Soft, in International Administration' (2004) 5 Chi J Int L 547.

94 Matteo Tondini, 'The "Italian Job": How to Make International Organizations Compliant with Human Rights and Accountable for Their Violation by Targeting Member States', in Jan Wouters, Eva Brems and Stefaan Smis (eds), *Accountability for Human Rights Violations of International Organizations* (Intersentia 2010) 169.

rules on responsibility are as much a result of a political choice, as primary rules of conduct pertaining to, say, environmental law, trade law or military matters. The normative and institutional choices reflect 'productive power' of relevant actors over others.[95] States exercise power over IL-making or over particular international institutions, in a way that serves their interests. Thereby, they can influence the rules of responsibility that determine whether or not a particular type of conduct (including participation in concerted action) does or does not engage the responsibility of a State.

Power, from this perspective, may not only breed responsibility, but may also shield actors from responsibility. The law of responsibility, and the institutions and processes in which it is embedded, in itself is the result of choices and practices of States. The ineptitude of IL for dealing with harmful consequences of concerted action serves States and other actors well, by allowing them to engage in blame-avoidance and blame-shifting, thus shielding themselves from responsibility.

IL is for instance agnostic in regard to the exercise of soft power, by which States can affect others 'through the effective means of framing the agenda, persuading, and eliciting positive attraction in order to obtain preferred outcomes'.[96] The same holds when States exercise 'overall control' over other actors. It was precisely the concern over the range of power not covered by effective control that prompted the International Criminal Tribunal for Yugoslavia (ICTY) to opt for the less demanding standard of overall control in *Tadic*.[97] The fact that the ICJ in the *Bosnian Genocide* reconfirmed effective control as the appropriate standard,[98] confirms the shielding function of the standard of attribution, working against the proposition that power breeds responsibility. The high thresholds set by the ARSIWA and the ARIO make it perfectly possible that a State exercises (soft) power to influence, in a concerted action, private actors or other States, without this leading to attribution of such acts to

---

95 Michael N Barnett and Raymond Duvall, 'Power in Global Governance', in Michael N Barnett and Raymond Duvall (eds), *Power in Global Governance* (CUP 2005) 18.

96 Joseph S Nye, *The Future of Power* (Public Affairs 2011) 20–21.

97 *Prosecutor v Tadic* (Judgment) ICTY-94-1 (26 January 2000).

98 *Application of Convention on Prevention and Punishment of Crime of Genocide* (Bosnia and Herzegovina v Serbia and Montenegro), Judgment, 2007 ICJ Rep 43, paras 402–406.

the State and thus without leading to (shared) responsibility.[99] The result may be that responsibility is shifted to other actors.

A related point is that the law of responsibility, itself the product of power, feeds back to constitute and legitimize particular exercises of power. International obligations do not only prohibit but also legitimize doing what is not prohibited.[100] This applies equally to rules of responsibility. The prohibition on aid and assistance with regard to the commission of a wrongful act may, for instance, legitimize more than it prohibits.[101]

IV.2. Diffusion Strategies

To some extent, concerted action in itself can be considered as a diffusion strategy. From the perspective of the participants in a particular concerted action, adding more 'hands' to the concerted action can be necessary as drawing in outside actors may increase the chances of success of cooperation (for instance in the case of climate change). However, adding more partners also may increase the possibility of diffusion, and thus may shield participants from responsibility. Partnerships between international institutions and other actors are an example. Partnerships engaged by the WHO or the World Bank involve a great many different actors. When no clear arrangements have been made on the assignment of responsibility, it becomes difficult to determine who is responsible for what.[102]

International practice shows a variety of other strategies by which States can diffuse (or shift) responsibility to other actors. In relation to IOs, the concept of 'circumvention' represents a strategy by which IOs can work through States,[103] or, conversely, by which States can act, in a concerted action, through IOs.[104]

---

[99] Christine Chinkin, 'A Critique of the Public/Private Dimension' (1999) 10 EJIL 387.

[100] This is the argument in Antony Anghie, *Imperialism, Sovereignty and the Making of International Law* (CUP 2005).

[101] Vladyslav Lanovoy, 'Complicity in an Internationally Wrongful Act', in André Nollkaemper and Ilias Plakokefalos (eds), *Principles of Shared Responsibility in International Law* (CUP 2014) 134.

[102] Boisson de Chazournes (n 40) 215–216.

[103] ARIO (n 34), art 17.

[104] ARIO (n 34), art 61.

Yet another alternative concept is orchestration – a term that has been conceptualized as referring to indirect and soft ways in which international institutions act through intermediaries.[105] Orchestration need not be (and commonly will not be) a strategy expressly aimed to achieve diffusion, but this may well be the result. In particular cases, the result may well be intended.

Delegation presents another strategy. By delegation States and international institutions can act with and through others, with potential limiting effects on the scope of their own responsibility.[106] A variant is the phenomenon of 'outsourcing' of tasks, possibly with accompanying responsibility, to other actors, such as private security corporations.[107]

The strategies identified above need not be designed to evade responsibility or shift it to other actors. However, in some cases it may be the intention of actors that seek to diffuse responsibility to ensure that they themselves are protected from claims. Diffusion strategies then may take the form of blame games, a term referring to situations 'where multiple players are trying to pin the responsibility on one another for some adverse event, acting as blamers to avoid being blamees'.[108]

Two main blame game strategies can be distinguished. A first strategy is to 'blunt' responsibility by collectivizing it.[109] The relevant actor structure powers and tasks in such a way that they are spread over multiple actors, as a result of which in the outside actors cannot easily identify who is to blame for any particular event. Partnerships between international institutions and other actors may have this effect. It may be unclear whether diffusion of responsibility, and deflection of blame is an intended aim of such partnerships, or simply an unintended consequence. However, if no clear arrangements have been made on the assignment of responsibility, responsibility rests on all, and as a result perhaps on no one. Such strategies do not make the call for responsibility (or 'blaming') in situations of harmful outcomes disappear, but they do make it unclear

---

[105] For example, Kenneth W Abbott et al., 'Orchestration: Global Governance Through Intermediaries', in Kenneth W Abbott et al. (eds), *International Organizations as Orchestrators* (CUP 2014) 3.

[106] See for example, Dan Sarooshi, 'Conferrals by States of Powers on International Organizations: The Case of Agency' (2004) 74 BYIL 291.

[107] Corinna Seiberth, *Private Military and Security Companies in International Law* (Intersentia 2013); Simon Chesterman and Angelina Fisher, *Private Security, Public Order: The Outsourcing of Public Services and Its Limits* (OUP 2009).

[108] Christopher Hood, *The Blame Game. Spin, Bureaucracy and Self-Preservation in Government* (Princeton University Press 2011) 7.

[109] Ibid 100.

who did what 'and leave potential blamers nonplussed by the complexity of the organizational arrangements.'[110]

An alternative strategy is individualizing blame.[111] Rather than collectivizing blame (and extending it all), blame is then shifted to one or a few actors, in effect shielding the blamers. As noted by Hood, this strategy 'is about shifting rather than reducing or preventing blame.'[112] In the Srebrenica cases, which sought to hold the Netherlands and the UN responsible in relation to the eviction of persons from the UN compound in Srebrenica, both defendants denied responsibility; they thus effectively placed the blame on each other, and they both attempted to shift blame onto the Bosnian Serbs and the FRY.[113]

In international affairs blame shifting is not a regular practice, at least not between allies. Blame avoidance may be politically more attractive.[114] This may be different, however when there are alternative actors to whom blame can be shifted without the accompanying risk that this practice may at one point backfire.

V. BENEFITS AND COSTS OF DIFFUSION

Having set out the factors that contribute to diffusion of responsibility, the question now can be addressed how we normatively should assess this phenomenon. Is diffusion of responsibility a problem we should care about, and that would call for a reconsideration of the role and contents of responsivity in situations of concerted action? Or is it a regular part of responsibility processes that simply reflects the nature and loci of international governance? In other words: is 'the problem of many hands' really a problem?

Diffusion in itself is a neutral term that frames and describes the spread of ideas, institutions or, as in the case of responsibility, legal

---

110 Ibid 83

111 Ibid 100.

112 Ibid. See also Christopher Hood, 'The Risk Game and the Blame Game' (2002) 31 Government and Opposition 15.

113 See generally André Nollkaemper, 'Multilevel Accountability in International Law: A Case Study of the Aftermath of Srebrenica', in Yuval Shany and Tomer Broude (eds), *The Shifting Allocation of Authority in International Law: Considering Sovereignty, Supremacy and Subsidiarity* (Hart 2008).

114 This is also the conclusion in Sara B Hobolt and James Tilley, *Blaming Europe? Responsibility Without Accountability in the European Union* (OUP 2014) 101. See also Kent R Weaver, 'The Politics of Blame Avoidance' (1986) 6 JPP 371.

principles and processes. Even the fact that responsibility gaps may occur in principle does not strip diffusion of its neutral nature. Whether diffusion with its resulting gaps is a good development depends on several questions: is responsibility in itself a positive value; does it fit in the variety of other contexts to which it is diffused;[115] if not, are there proper alternatives, and so on. Saying that 'responsibility' is diffused in itself is just a way of framing and describing processes of governance that may or may not be evaluated in positive terms.

I will separately identify a number of benefits (V.1) and costs (V.2) of diffusion and related responsibility gaps. Articulating the benefits and costs also helps us understand better the strategic choices of relevant actors to engage in politics of diffusion, as discussed in the previous section.

V.1. Benefits

Responsibility fulfils important, positive functions – both in domestic societies and in IL. If responsibility indeed is a positive value, it follows that diffusion of responsibility in principle is a positive development. It allows responsibility to be better attuned to processes of governance which have become diffused or, as coined by Nico Krisch, become 'liquid'.[116] The fact that responsibility also becomes diffuse may match better the places where decisions are actually made.

Perhaps somewhat counterintuitively, also when diffusion leads to responsibility gaps, this may serve positive functions. This is in particular due to the fact that responsibility can have a chilling effect. If so, a designed problem of many hands, that leads to such absence of responsibility, may well have benefits. The willingness of States to accept obligations may be dependent on their ability to prevent responsibility. One option for doing so is diffusion. If they are unable to do so, they may be unwilling to engage in cooperation in the first place. Cole notes with reference to climate change that using liability to promote mitigation of greenhouse gas emissions could prove counterproductive; rather

---

[115] Cf, for the international rule of law, Jeremy Waldron, 'The Rule of International Law' (2006) 30 Harv JLPP 15.

[116] Nico Kirsch, 'The Structure of Postnational Authority' (2015) SSRN Working Paper available at <http://papers.ssrn.com/sol3/Papers.cfm?abstract_id=2564579>.

than inducing cooperation, it might reduce incentives for States to participate in international regimes, that is, to share responsibility.[117]

In terms of costs-benefit assessment, diffusion of responsibility then may be beneficial: action without, or with 'diluted' responsibility may produce better outcomes than no action at all.[118]

Whether States indeed would make their willingness to engage in cooperation conditional on their ability to escape responsibility is easier raised then answered. In many of the examples where diffusion occurs, it remains somewhat speculative whether or not such diffusion actually matters in terms of the incentives of relevant actors to agree to ambitious international obligations. Do we know whether States now set ambitious targets (for example, in fisheries, pollution control etc.) that they would not normally do if there would be a risk of responsibility upon breach? To answer this question affirmatively it would not only need to be demonstrated that the risk of responsibility is a consideration that is relevant to State conduct at all, but also that the prospect of diffusion of responsibility is a relevant consideration for States to engage in cooperative action, in which they would not engage without such diffusion. The point is not entirely implausible. There are ample indications that suggest that States care about preventing responsibility (and partly for that reason opt for modes of governance and substantive obligations that reduce the chance of being held responsible), and it is plausible that the higher the risk of responsibility in case of non-performance, the more cautious they will be in accepting obligations. If so, we should be cautious in adopting a one dimensional critique on diffusion, and not uncritically resort to antidotes (such as joint and several responsibility) that may improve responsibility in situations of concerted action, yet undermine such action in the first place.

V.2. Costs

Benefits of diffusion of responsibility and in particular of responsibility may be partially or wholly outweighed by costs of diffusion. Two such costs are particularly relevant: costs in terms of the performance of obligations and in terms of injured parties.

---

[117] Daniel H Cole, 'The Problem of Shared Responsibility in International Climate Law', in André Nollkaemper and Dov Jacobs (n 33).

[118] Obviously, this potential benefit of diffusion only applies in relation to situations in which States and other actors engage in concerted action for beneficial purposes. It does not apply to situations where actors intentionally cause harm.

Impact on performance of obligations

A first angle for assessing the impact of diffusion is that responsibility is a central element of international obligations and their performance. Diffusion of responsibility can undermine the assignment and performance of obligations and thereby the achievement of objectives. The objectives may relate to specific interests of the actors involved, but may also represent broader public goods.

It is a plausible proposition that diffusion of responsibility can undermine incentives for action. If no one can be meaningfully called to account after the event 'no one need feel responsible beforehand'.[119] This may reduce the possibility that individual actors perform obligations and that the interests that the law seeks to protect are actually protected.

Whether diffusion indeed will undermine the incentives of actors to perform their obligations presumes, as a first step, that obligations matter at all for the conduct of relevant actors[120] and, as an extension, that the perspective of being held responsible is a relevant factor in changing the conduct of States and international institutions. Thus, while responsibility presumes the existence of obligations, it also is more than that, and its incentives-effects may go beyond those of obligations.

Three more specific reasons can be identified that would support such an impact. One is that responsibility may strengthen the internalization of obligations – one of the main factors that supports compliance with international obligations.[121] A second factor is that responsibility may impact on the reputational impact of IL.[122] States may care about the reputational effects of non-compliance, but may do so even more when such non-compliance may trigger their international responsibility. A third factor is that reparation, notably obligations of restitution and

---

[119] Mark Bovens, *The Quest for Responsibility: Accountability and Citizenship in Complex Organisations* (CUP 1998); Michael A Wallach, Nathan Kogan and Daryl J Bem, 'Group Influence on Individual Risk Taking' (1962) 65 J Abnorm Soc Psychol 75; Michael A Wallach, Nathan Kogan and Daryl J Bem, 'Diffusion of Responsibility and Level of Risk Taking in Groups' (1964) 68 J Abnorm Soc Psychol 263.

[120] Eric A Posner and Alan O Sykes, *The Economic Foundations of International Law* (Harvard University Press 2013); Andrew T Guzman, *How International Law Works: A Rational Choice Theory* (OUP 2008).

[121] Ryan Goodman and Derek Jinks, 'How to Influence States: Socialization and International Human Rights Law' (2004) 54 Duke L J 622.

[122] Andrew T Guzman, 'Reputation and International Law' (2005) 34 Georgia J Int Comp L 379.

compensation, provides incentives for compliance.[123] The two last mechanisms may be supported by scholarship that is premised on theories of rationality which somehow seems to presume that States make calculating decisions in their own self-interest.[124]

This impact of diffusion on incentives may have wider ramifications in the form of collective action problems. If actors do not individually feel the consequences in terms of being held responsible, they may be tempted to look for others to do the job. This will be particularly relevant when the participation of multiple States is necessary for addressing a perceived problem and for producing a common good, for instance in situations involving transborder effects in areas such as global health, financial markets, the environment, or organized crime, where any single State is quite powerless to provide answers. Because obligations and responsibilities are not specifically assigned, and responsibility is not likely to be forthcoming, actors may be inclined to wait for each other, with the result that nothing happens. One can recall Olson's argument, which developed the theory in the economic context of public goods, that as members of a large group generally hold the assumption that someone else in the group can and will provide the public good, the incentives for these members to provide for it themselves are weakened.[125] This will in particular affect 'aggregate-effort' goods, which require action by all actors involved.[126] In these areas, 'the outcome that each agent desires cannot be achieved unless everyone performs his or her contributory action. Here the action of each agent is directly causally necessary for realization of the desired outcome, so the outcome is of necessity aimed at qua collective end.'[127] Diffusion then may undermine the actual realization of the common aims.

---

123 Eric A Posner and Alan O Sykes, 'An Economic Analysis of State and Individual Responsibility Under International Law' (February 2006) U Chicago Law & Economics Olin Working Paper No. 279 available at <http://ssrn.com/abstract=885197>.

124 Eric A Posner and Alan O Sykes (n 120); Guzman (n 120).

125 Mancur Olson, *The Logic of Collective Action: Public Goods and the Theory of Groups* (Harvard University Press 1968) 44.

126 Jack Hirshleifer, 'From Weakest-link to Best-shot: The Voluntary Provision of Public Goods' (1983) 41 Public Choice 371, 372; Scott Barrett, *Why Cooperate? The Incentive to Supply Global Public Goods* (OUP 2007) 74.

127 Seumas Miller, 'Collective Responsibility' (2001) 15 Pub Aff Q 65, 73.

Private costs

Diffusion can undermine a key function of attributing responsibility: to ensure justice to victims.[128] This holds both for injured States and injured individuals. If harm is caused, yet the conditions for individual responsibility are not satisfied or responsibility cannot be determined for other reasons, and it also is not possible to bring an effective claim against the collectivity as such, injured parties will be without redress.[129] In effect, the loss will then be left where it falls – with the victim, rather than being transferred back to one or more responsible actors.[130]

One reason why the position of victims tends to be weaker in situations of concerted action is that it may be more difficult for private parties to determine which actors play which role in a particular concerted action. This is particularly the case where information is spread over many actors and moreover of an informal nature – for instance in the case of partnerships between international institutions and private parties.[131]

The effect on injured parties has both a procedural and a substantive dimension. As to the former, diffusion of responsibility over multiple parties will limit access of injured parties to courts in relation to all or the main actors involved in a concerted action. There often is a mismatch between the concerted nature of action, on the one hand, and the available remedies against the actors involved in that action, on the other. The principles of individual responsibility are accompanied by processes for implementation and enforcement that match the characteristics of individual rather than shared responsibility.[132] However, in the increasingly complex character of international relations, 'legal disputes between States are rarely purely bilateral'.[133] The present system of

---

[128] van De Poel et al. (n 53) 49, 64; Mark Bovens (n 4) 49.

[129] See for example, Philipp Stöckle, 'Victims Caught Between a Rock and a Hard Place: Individual Compensation Claims against Troop-Contributing States' (2013) 88 Die Friedens-Warte: Journal of International Peace and Organization 19.

[130] James Crawford and Jeremy Watkins, 'International Responsibility', in Samantha Besson and John Tasioulas (eds), *The Philosophy of International Law* (OUP 2010) 286.

[131] Boisson de Chazournes (n 40) 211.

[132] See, on the connection between substance and procedure, Jenny S Martinez, 'Process and Substance in the "War on Terror"' (2008) 108 Colum L Rev 1013; Markus Benzing, 'Community Interests in the Procedure of International Courts and Tribunals' (2006) 5 L Prac Int Cts Tribs 369.

[133] Separate Opinion Judge Shahabuddeen in Nauru (n 70), 270.

international dispute settlement is hardly designed to deal with multilateral disputes.[134] Procedures may not be able to capture all parties involved and may not do justice to the complexity of a context consisting of multiple responsible actors. For instance, given that international dispute settlement mechanisms are based on the consent of States, the mere fact that one State involved has not consented to the judicial process may suffice to exclude any case of shared responsibility from judicial scrutiny. Likewise, if one of the wrongdoing actors happens to be an IO, questions of shared responsibility will be deemed inadmissible before most international judicial bodies given that acts of IOs are not judiciable before them.

Diffusion of responsibility also may affect substantive entitlements. If contributions are spread over multiple actors, relative contributions of individual actors will be relatively small. In the absence of a principle of joint and several responsibility, individual actors may not be able, or may not be required, to provide a full remedy. When reparation consists of restitution or specific performance, individual responsible actors may not be able to provide the remedy that is required.

VI. CONCLUSION

This Chapter has demonstrated that diffusion of responsibility may result in responsibility gaps and that such gaps in part are explained by the dominant paradigm of individual responsibility. This process of diffusion should be understood as a political process, that is sustained and driven by IL, which in itself is a reflection of that political process. Diffusion may bring both benefits and costs, in terms of the accountability of the exercise of public authority, in terms of performance of international obligations, and in particular in terms of the protection of the rights of injured parties. How these benefits and costs will be evaluated depends on a contextual analysis and cannot be answered in the abstract. What can be concluded at a general level, though, is that while diffusion as such may help connect responsibility to a diversity of actors, it also may lead to responsibility gaps that undermine the value and role of responsibility in the international legal order.

---

[134] Damrosch (n 83).

PART IV

Political Economy and Substantive Fields of International Law

13. The Political Economy of Regional Trade Agreements

Alberta Fabbricotti

I. INTRODUCTION

The proliferation of Regional Trade Agreements (RTAs) – as a common phraseology to indicate the increasing number of RTAs being recorded in the last 20–25 years – has captured the attention of a huge number of scholars from very different disciplines for decades. In particular, this phenomenon represents a conundrum under both a Political Economy (PE) and an International Law (IL) – to be precise an International Economic Law (IEL) – point of view.

From a PE perspective, the proliferation of RTAs is somehow rationally absurd since it reduces or impairs the benefits that States would gain if they were otherwise to pursue world free trade exclusively on a larger multilateral scale.

From an IEL perspective, RTAs are international treaties ostensibly conflicting with the non-discriminatory trade rules under the multilateral World Trade Organization (WTO) treaty. Since the latter should prevail according to IL rules, IEL scholars are unprepared to answer the question: how RTAs not only continue to be operational but also continue proliferating in number and scope.

This Chapter explores these two perspectives and sees them as complementary. The aim is to ascertain whether PE and IEL can interact in a way which opens new grounds for the elaboration of viable answers and solutions.

Some of the conceptual tools highlighted in the above general introduction by Anne van Aaken and Joel Trachtman[1] are developed here. This Chapter mainly follows an International Political Economy (IPE)

[1] Anne van Aaken and Joel P Trachtman, 'Political Economy of International Law: Towards a Holistic Model of State Behaviour', above in this Volume.

rather than a PE approach, focusing on States' attitudes and behaviours on the international economic plane rather than on identifying domestic interests and stakeholders which impact States' international policies from behind the scenes. However, since the two approaches often appear to be inextricably intertwined, PE considerations will occasionally arise in this Chapter.

The central issue here is adherence, not compliance. Indeed, the aim of this Chapter is to investigate why States enter RTAs, not whether States comply with RTAs once they are on board. Compliance is nevertheless also at stake in this Chapter because, in turn, RTAs have to meet the requirements of GATT Article XXIV. As explained in Section IV below, compliance with art. XXIV stands for the IL argument regarding RTAs.

Finally, the present Chapter depicts IL as *explanandum* vis-à-vis IPE considerations, since the latter are considered to be the determinants of the States' decision to adhere to RTAs. This does not entirely exclude the fact that IL will come up incidentally as *explanans* since, as described in the next Section, the formation of an RTA is likely to create new RTAs following a domino effect.

Section II below provides a thorough empirical description of the RTA landscape. Section III reviews the PE theories on the conclusion of RTAs. Section IV introduces the IL argument regarding RTAs. Section V explores the interfaces and possible interactions between PE and IL regarding the proliferation of RTAs. Section VI provides a conclusion.

II. THE CHANGING LANDSCAPE OF REGIONAL TRADE AGREEMENTS

As noted above, the number of RTAs has grown enormously over the last two decades. As of 1 February 2016, RTAs having been notified to the WTO and still in force amount to 267.[2]

Any empirical description of the RTA landscape must start from a clear-cut definition of what the word or acronym 'RTA' means. It would however be deceptive to pretend to give a univocal meaning in the present context as this is obviously understood in a completely different way whether viewed under the lenses of PE or of IL.

From a PE perspective, an RTA is an arrangement among more than two countries aiming at directing international trade towards given

2 Counting RTAs covering trade in goods, those covering trade in services and accessions together. Source: WTO. See <https://www.wto.org/english/tratop_e/region_e/region_e.htm> (accessed 11 March 2016).

outcomes and achievements in the interest of its participants. Relying on economic models, PE classifies RTAs as a hierarchy that runs bottom-up from free trade areas to economic unions (the intermediate stages being customs unions and common markets).[3] The terminology of 'hierarchy' is used to clarify that each level incorporates all the provisions and achievements of the lower level of integration. However, these categories never come up in practice as being exactly true as they have been conceived in the economic and PE literature.[4]

From an IL perspective, an RTA is an international treaty among a relatively small group of States for the regulation of their trade. Being an international treaty, an RTA is first of all a source of rights and obligations for its contracting parties, provided the RTA is in force.[5] Considering its regional scope, any RTA is potentially in conflict with the international treaty establishing the WTO, which covers the same subject matter even though it has a universal vocation in terms of number of participant States. The issue of the normative (and often jurisdictional) conflict between these international treaties – regional and universal – is at the core of IL literature.

Generally speaking, the label 'regional' in the acronym RTA can be misleading since, contrarily to the post-war period when the concept of 'RTA' was associated with the grouping of no less than three contiguous States, in more recent years a great number of free trade agreements have been concluded by States that are not even geographically close. Moreover, a large proportion of these agreements are bilateral, in that they are concluded between only two countries (for example, the US and Israel), and more and more often they are inter-regional, since they join two already existing regional arrangements (for example, the trade agreement between the EU and the MERCOSUR).

Whilst, as is illustrated below, the phenomenon of 'regional' economic integration shows very different features, one (perhaps the only) common denominator of all RTAs is their preferential nature. To a major or minor extent, RTAs are instrumental to the mutual concession of trade preferences among participant States, to the exclusion of all the other States. This is the most typical feature of RTAs and opposite to the WTO

---

[3] John Ravenhill, 'Regional Trade Agreements', in John Ravenhill (ed), *Global Political Economy* (3rd edn, OUP 2011) at 175.

[4] Alberta Fabbricotti, *Gli accordi di integrazione economica regionale e il diritto dell'Organizzazione Mondiale del Commercio* (2nd edn, Aracne 2009) at 435–436.

[5] The entry into force of treaties is dealt with in VCLT Article 24.

non-discriminatory system.[6] This said, the present Chapter uses the adjective 'regional' instead of 'preferential' just conventionally, without entering into any further theoretical discussion about its appropriateness.[7]

Mapping the proliferation of RTAs and identifying its trends and characteristics is particularly challenging because of the fast pace and random nature of this proliferation. To sum up, four main trends have emerged in the last two decades.[8] *First*, as noted above, the classical model of RTAs is always more frequently either split into several bilateral arrangements or, on the contrary, expanded as inter-regional. *Second*, an increasing number of RTAs are now North-South, involving both developed and developing countries (for example the NAFTA, concluded between two G8 members, and Mexico, a developing country) on a reciprocal basis, or South-South, among key developing countries (for example, MERCOSUR or ASEAN Free Trade Agreement – AFTA). *Third*, RTAs are becoming increasingly complex and comprehensive, creating cohesion among participant States toward common goals and areas which go well beyond the liberalization of trade, for example investments and the environment.[9] *Fourth*, the ongoing negotiations of the Trans-Pacific Partnership (TPP) and the Transatlantic Trade and Investment Partnership (TTIP) show an even greater recent shift toward cross-polar RTAs forming extra large two-by-two coalitions between geographical and economic areas, nearly coinciding with the three pillars of the actual multipolar economic world, notably the EU, the US and the Asia Pacific.[10]

---

[6] As discussed below in this Chapter, at Section IV.

[7] It is to be noted that, according to the WTO language, 'preferential trade arrangements' means something different from RTAs, namely unilateral trade preferences, such as those preference schemes under which developed countries grant preferential tariffs to imports from developing countries on a non-reciprocal basis.

[8] This list takes the cue from Roberto V Fiorentino, Jo-Ann Crawford and Christelle Toqueboeuf, 'The Landscape of Regional Trade Agreements and WTO Surveillance', in Richard E Baldwin and Patrick Low (eds), *Multilateralizing Regionalism: Challenges for the Global Trading System* (CUP 2009) 28–64.

[9] For a thorough review of the new areas now covered by RTA rules, see Antoni Estevadeordal, Kati Suominen and Robert Teh (eds), *Regional Rules in the Global Trading System* (CUP 2009); Simon Lester and Bryan Mercurio (eds), *Bilateral and Regional Trade Agreements: Commentary and Analysis* (CUP 2009) part IV.

[10] There is already a huge literature about these negotiations. See recently Gary Clyde Hufbauer and Cathleen Cimino-Isaacs, 'How will TPP and TTIP Change the WTO System?' (2015) 18 JIEL 679–696; Bernard M Hoekman and

The participation of each country or RTA in more than one (other) RTA and the overlapping of a great number of such free trade arrangements in several intersecting areas have created a very complex framework which, in turn, has given rise to evocative theories and models in economics and politics. Two of these have become very popular. In 1995 Bhagwati introduced the phraseology 'spaghetti bowl' to describe the entanglement of criss-crossing RTAs.[11] In 1996 Wonnacott injected the terminology of 'hubs and spokes' within the debate over RTAs.[12] A hub exists where one country or RTA is a member of two (or more) distinct bilateral or plurilateral RTAs. It follows that a country is a spoke in today's uncommon situation in which such a country or RTA participates in only one RTA, bilateral or plurilateral as it may be. Hubs and spokes depict a negative feature of the proliferation of RTAs as they create multi-layered preference schemes. Obviously, spokes have less market access than the hub since the latter enjoys preferential access to all spokes but a spoke has preferential access to the hub only. A spoke country can avoid this limitation by entering into its own set of bilateral or plurilateral RTAs and thus becoming a hub. If exponentially multiplied, this reaction explains the acceleration in bilateral agreements which is occurring today.

Economists consider RTAs with scepticism since they undermine the efficiency and growth that trade liberalization can bring. Policy makers are concerned with the many geopolitical implications deriving from the patchwork of economic preferences that RTAs create. Over the past two decades, both categories of scientists have worried about the phenomena

---

Petros C Mavroidis, 'WTO "à la carte" or "menu du jour"? Assessing the Case for More Plurilateral Agreements' (2015) 26 EJIL 319–343.

[11] The term was first used by Jagdish Bhagwati in 'U.S. Trade Policy: The Infatuation with Free Trade Agreements', in Jagdish Bhagwati and Anne O Krueger, *The Dangerous Drift to Preferential Trade Agreements* (AEI Press 1995) 1–18. In that first essay Bhagwati was probably referring exclusively to the problem of the different rules of origin in RTAs, that is to say to the manner in which half-finished products and parts go around various FTA networks using tariff differentiation in an effort to export finished products to the consumer countries at the lowest price. He represented this as crisscrossing lines and likened these strings of lines to strands of spaghetti tangled in a bowl. But the 'spaghetti bowl' phenomenon is certainly meant to refer more generally to the chaos of domestic rules and trade regulations created by different RTAs. On the origin of this phraseology see Jagdish Bhagwati, *Termites in the Trading System: How Preferential Agreements Undermine Free Trade* (OUP 2008) 61 ff.

[12] Ronald J Wonnacott, 'Trade and Investments in a Hub-and-Spoke System versus a Free Trade Area' (1996) 19 World Econ 237–252.

caused by the proliferation of RTAs which are increasingly difficult to reconcile with overall economic openness and liberal global trading. All of this helps explain why 'trade, and regionalism specifically, is the quintessential international political economy (IPE) topic pitting the efficiency models of economists against the political imperatives of those implementing policy'.[13]

III. WHY DO STATES CONCLUDE REGIONAL TRADE AGREEMENTS?

Clearly, the 'why' question – the reasons why States enter into RTAs – is unavoidable by those scholars who investigate the proliferation of RTAs from an IPE perspective. Some of these reasons impinge on the States' domestic backstage, yet PE considerations are also relevant. From an IL point of view, the 'entering' of a State into an RTA assumes that this State either negotiated it originally and thus concurred in the creation of the RTA, or joined the other contracting parties at a later stage, while the RTA was already in force (accession).[14] In IL language, 'adherence' is used to identify this second way of entering into a treaty. In this Volume, however, this term applies to becoming an RTA contracting party, regardless of the way and procedure used.

Economists formulate that an economy's welfare can be maximized if governments lower trade barriers, for example, reducing or removing tariffs, on a non-discriminatory basis (either through unilateral action or through WTO negotiations). Why, then, do States conclude RTAs? As there are both fervent opponents and supporters of RTAs among economists, it is unclear which economic theory to turn to.[15] The most

---

13 Cp Greg Anderson, 'Regionalism's Past, Present and Future', in David A Deese (ed), *Handbook of International Political Economy of Trade* (Edward Elgar 2014) at 227.

14 VCLT Articles 11–15.

15 A selection of economic literature might possibly include Bela Balassa, *The Theory of Economic Integration* (Allen and Unwin 1961; reprinted Routledge 2011); Jeffrey A Frankel, *Regional Trading Blocs in the World Economic System* (Institute for International Economics 1997); Richard Pomfret, *The Economics of Regional Trading Arrangements* (Clarenson 1997); Arving Panagariya and T N Srinivasan, 'The New Regionalism: A Benign or Malign Growth?', in Jagdish Bhagwati and Mathias Hirsch (eds), *The Uruguay Round and Beyond: Essays in Honour of Arthur Dunkel* (Springer 1998) 221–240; Walter Mattli, *The Logic of Regional Integration: Europe and Beyond* (CUP 1999); Kyle Bagwell and Robert W Staiger, *The Economics of the World Trading System* (MIT 2002) 111–123; Viet

influential contribution to the debate has probably been Viner's 1950 distinction between 'trade creation' and 'trade diversion'.[16] Viner assessed the economic costs and benefits of RTAs (customs unions) and demonstrated, contrary to the then conventional wisdom, that a selective removal of tariffs within the RTA area might not enhance welfare. The tariffs removal process would indeed unleash two opposite forces: 'trade creation', occurring when imports from a regional partner supplant goods which so far had been produced domestically at higher costs and yet had become uncompetitive; and 'trade diversion' occurring when imports from a regional partner replace those previously originating outside the RTA because the extra-regional imports are no longer price competitive compared to imports from within the RTA area. In Viner's view, an RTA yields more economic benefit than harm (trade creation overcoming trade diversion) only if it brings together sizable countries and has an almost comprehensive coverage in terms of goods and productive sectors traded.[17] Much of the literature that flourished since Viner's contribution was concerned with economic conditions and criteria inducing the effects of trade creation to outweigh those of trade diversion. However, since RTAs continue to be concluded by disregarding any such condition or parameter – for example, they join countries of different sizes and exclude sensitive sectors – it has finally become clear that they are not entirely driven by economics.[18]

Actually, it is now widely recognized that the PE of RTAs 'revolves more around politics than economics'.[19] It seems therefore convenient to turn the discussion to politics.

This Section expands upon Ravenhill's seminal classification of political motivations for RTAs[20] also through its pointed rereading provided by Chad Damro.[21] The conclusion of RTAs may be pursued because:

(1) States fear remaining marginalized in the world trade arena (marginalization syndrome);

D Do and William Watson, 'Economic Analysis of Regional Trade Agreements', in Lorand Bartels and Federico Ortino (eds), *Regional Trade Agreements and the WTO Legal System* (OUP 2006) 7–22; Bhagwati, *Termites* (n 9).

[16] Jacob Viner, *The Customs Union Issue* (Stevens and Sons 1950).

[17] Ibid at 44.

[18] Olivier Cattaneo, 'The Political Economy of PTAs', in Lester and Mercurio (eds) (n 9) 28–51, 39.

[19] Cp ibid at 50.

[20] Ravenhill (n 3) 177 ff.

[21] Chad Damro, 'The Political Economy of Regional Trade Agreements', in Lorand Bartels and Federico Ortino (eds) (n 13) 23–42, at 29.

(2) States aim at creating confidence within their region in order to prevent security problems through the enhancement of economic cooperation (security via economic means);
(3) States indirectly address security threats that are not traditional military threats, such as environmental hazards, illegal migration, organized crime, drugs smuggling and international terrorism ('new security' needs);
(4) States seek to increase their bargaining power in international negotiations (increase in negotiating leverage);
(5) States attempt to lock in liberalizing trade reforms (lock-in domestic reforms);
(6) States satisfy domestic constituents (accommodating domestic constituents);
(7) States find it easier to negotiate RTAs than to negotiate multilateral trade liberalization (ease of regionalism).[22]

It seems unnecessary to explain the above political motivations in detail as they are rather intuitive. Each is sufficient to explain why States may enter RTAs. More likely, adherence to an RTA is an outcome resulting from the combined operation of more than one of these motivations.

There is a mixture of IPE and PE arguments in the above motivations. This is quite obvious, considering that IPE and PE are interconnected vessels and that the distinction between them depends also on the subject area concerned. Van Aaken and Trachtman, in their contribution to the present Volume, argue that IPE is largely confined to international economic relations as a subject matter, whilst PE applies to all substantive matters.[23] Yet, the 'security issues' listed above at (2) and (3) clearly originate in the realm of PE while the others preferably fall within the IPE area.

Moreover, a different method of analysis has been used to identify the above motivations. In general, the list adopts a 'statist' mode of analysis in which the State is seen as a unified rational actor pursuing some well-defined objective (as a 'black box'[24] or as a 'billiard ball'[25]). Only two motivations – (5) lock-in domestic reform and (6) accommodating

[22] On this point, Alberta Fabbricotti, 'Universalisme et régionalisme dans le domaine des échanges commerciaux internationaux', in James Crawford and Sarah Nouwen (eds), *Select Proceedings of the European Society of International Law – ESIL* (Hart 2012) at 306.

[23] van Aaken and Trachtman (n 1) para I.

[24] Anne van Aaken, 'Rational Choice Theory' (23 March 2012) in *Oxford Bibliographies Online* <http://www.oxfordbibliographies.com/view/document/

domestic constituencies – have been detected through a two-level investigation since, as Robert Putnam puts it,[26] the identification of States' preferences on the international plane assumes that the determination of a government's best policy option in the light of inter-State negotiations be (re)balanced according to the prevailing interests of domestic lobby groups and stakeholders.

According to Anne van Aaken and Joel Trachtman, among the factors within the domestic politico-legal sphere that may cause States to adhere to IL, domestic interests and partisan politics or preferences, which are listed at (6) in Ravenhill's list above, are the most representative because a preference-based explanation of entry into law will generally be more powerful.[27] The model of adherence to IL provided in their Chapter in this Volume,[28] as well as other models more specifically designed in connection with international trade negotiations and trade agreements such as the Grossman-Helpman model,[29] all focus indeed on the pressure exercised on incumbent governments by domestic political interest groups and lobbies to adhere or not to IL (an RTA, in the present context).

In conclusion, it is important to address briefly those theories linking the adherence to RTAs to collective action (and reaction) problems. These problems reveal situations in which the decision of a State to adhere to an RTA is not driven by a balanced self-assessment of its best interests because it is trapped by a collective fear or strategy of States or of domestic companies. Two of these theories or games are particularly emphasized in PE literature: the 'domino effect' and the 'prisoner's dilemma'.

As already noted, RTAs' common denominator is discrimination through preferential treatment: non-member States do not share the benefits they provide. Companies located in non-member States find that RTAs place them at a competitive disadvantage. Therefore, they start

---

obo-9780199796953/obo-9780199796953-0051.xml?rskey=IGLEI7&result=2&q=rational+choice+theory#firstMatch> (accessed 29 August 2015).

[25] Jack L Goldsmith and Eric A Posner, *The Limits of International Law* (OUP 2008); Joel P Trachtman, *The Economic Structure of International Law* (Harvard University Press 2008).

[26] Robert D Putnam, 'The Logic of Two-Levels Game' (1988) 42 Int Org 427–460.

[27] van Aaken and Trachtman (n 1) para IV.2.

[28] Ibid part V.

[29] Gene M Grossman and Elhanan Helpman, 'The Politics of Free-Trade Agreements' (1995) 85 Am Econ Rev 667–690. This model is also described in van Aaken and Trachtman (n 1) part V.

lobbying their governments to conclude RTAs (either acceding to an existing agreement or negotiating a new one) that will provide them with equivalent access. This incentive towards RTAs' adherence will produce what Baldwin called a 'domino effect' in regionalism, which results in either multiplying RTAs or broadening the scope of liberalization.[30]

The fact that, in concluding RTAs, States do not pursue their best interests (which would on the contrary be lowering trade barriers on a non-discriminatory basis) has led some authors to argue that States are experiencing a prisoner's dilemma. As this game theory is exhaustively discussed by Meredith Kolsky Lewis, in Chapter 8 in this Volume,[31] it will not be described here in detail. In the present context it is sufficient to resume the prisoner's dilemma's paradox by applying it to explain the reasons for RTA proliferation. States can either opt to cooperate by pursuing their first best strategy, that is lowering their trade barriers on a multilateral non-discriminatory basis, or to defect, focusing their energies on preferential RTAs.[32] The States' dominant strategy appears to be defection. If a first group of other States with whom they are competitive in export markets decides to reject RTAs and only liberalize through the multilateral negotiations, they will do better to defect, adhering to RTAs with a different group of States, since they will have either the benefit of lower tariffs from this second group or a comparative advantage over their competitors in select key markets. The same is true if the first group of competitor countries decides to shift toward RTAs; the States considered will do better to act as well, otherwise the competitors will improve their comparative advantage in the markets of their partners in RTAs and they will miss the chance. Yet, the overall result seems to produce exactly the dynamics of the RTA proliferation, which has occurred in the last decades.

---

[30] Richard E Baldwin, *A Domino Theory of Regionalism*, Working Paper 4465, National Bureau of Economic Research (1993), 'The Causes of Regionalism' (1997) 20 World Econ 865–888, and 'Multilateralising Regionalism: Spaghetti Bowls as Building Blocs on the Path to Global Free-Trade' (2006) 29 World Econ 1451–1518.

[31] Meredith Kolsky Lewis, 'International Political Economy and the Prisoner's Dilemma: Compliance with International Law', above in this Volume.

[32] This part of the Section draws heavily on Meredith Kolsky Lewis, 'The Prisoners' Dilemma and FTAs: Applying Game Theory to Trade Liberalization Strategy', in Ross Buckley, Vai Io Lo and Laurence Boulle, *Challenges to Multilateral Trade: The Impact of Bilateral, Preferential and Regional Agreements* (Wolters Kluwer 2008) 21–39.

IV. THE INTERNATIONAL LAW ARGUMENT OVER REGIONAL TRADE AGREEMENTS

From an IL perspective, RTAs are viewed as international treaties; as such, RTAs are the expression of the States' consent to be bound by obligations, regardless of how and by whom this consent has been generated or influenced. Therefore, RTAs are the sources of norms providing rights and duties which are binding for participant States.

The main IL concern regarding RTAs is not their mutual coexistence but first and foremost their overall coexistence with the multilateral trade agreements which go under the name of the WTO treaty. Since RTAs and the WTO treaty relate to the same subject matter, specifically trade, though from the perspective of divergent interests, their coexistence clearly poses a problem of compatibility (that is, conflict) between them. Article 30 VCLT is devoted to disentangling the complex issue of successive conflicting treaties when no provision conferring the primacy to one of them is traceable within the treaty texts themselves.

This is not the case of the alleged RTAs–WTO conflict. The WTO legal system is indeed equipped with a coordination regime laying down the legal parameters within which RTAs are not only tolerated but even welcomed.[33] Compliance with these parameters implies the disappearance of any treaty conflict issue (actually the issue does not even arise) and, therefore, that WTO members which become also contracting parties in compliant RTAs do not incur a WTO law (and thus IL) violation. The contrary applies if RTAs do not comply with the parameters.

GATT Article XXIV is the main WTO provision which acts as a coordination regime for RTAs,[34] meaning that it sets down the substantial and procedural requirements that RTAs should fulfil.[35] Substantial

33 As the text of Article XXIV para 4 suggests: '[t]he contracting parties recognize the *desirability* [...] through voluntary agreements, of closer integration between the economies of the parties [...]' (emphasis added).

34 Other WTO provisions addressing, either expressly and directly or implicitly and indirectly, the formation of RTAs are to be found in Article V GATS, in the 1979 Decision on Differential and More Favourable Treatment, Reciprocity and Fuller Participation of Developing Countries (the so-called 'Enabling Clause'), in Article 6.3 of the Agreement on Technical Barriers to Trade (TBT), Article 4.2 of the Agreement on Sanitary and Phytosanitary Measures (SPS), Article 5.2(b) of the Agreement on Safeguards. For a detailed analysis of these provisions, see Fabbricotti (n 4).

35 The literature focusing on GATT Article XXIV is immense; it is impossible here to cite even a selection of it.

requirements are essentially two. In synthesis, the first (so-called 'internal requirement') commits the WTO members, on entering a RTA, to abolish or diminish approximately to zero the tariffs and other commercial regulations in respect of nearly all (the text uses the expression 'substantially all') trade originating from one of their regional partners, while the second ('external requirement') imposes upon RTA members the obligation, regarding their trade with third States, to apply 'substantially the same' tariffs and other regulations of commerce. These should also not be increased or aggravated when compared to the duties applied prior to the RTA formation. The procedural requirements concern the duty to notify the text of the RTA and any subsequent change to it to the relevant WTO political bodies. It is noteworthy that Article XXIV was drafted having in mind Viner's theory on 'trade creating' and 'trade diverting' effects of RTAs.[36]

As clarified by the WTO Appellate Body, GATT Article XXIV provides WTO members which are also parties in an RTA (which complies with its requirements) with a 'defence' – that is to say a justification – against any charge of having violated other WTO provisions.[37] Without the coverage of such a defence, an RTA would clearly incur the infringement of a great number of WTO principles and norms, and primarily of the non-discriminatory Most Favoured Nation (MFN) and national treatment rules.

It is beyond the scope of this Chapter to analyse Article XXIV thoroughly.[38] Also, this would probably be a fruitless exercise as it is impossible to ignore or underestimate what is abundantly evidenced by facts, that is, that RTAs' behaviour quite systematically diverges from the requirements of Article XXIV, either directly or, more often, disguisedly. Most frequently and noticeably, RTAs exclude a number of sensitive sectors from their liberalization plans, thus failing to meet the internal

---

36 See Section III above.

37 See Appellate Body Report, *Turkey – Restrictions on Imports of Textile and Clothing Products*, WT/DS34/AB/R, adopted 19 November 1999.

38 This Section of the present Chapter draws on Alberta Fabbricotti, *The Interplay Between the WTO and the RTAs: Is It A Question of Interrelation Between Different Sources of International Law?*, Society of International Economic Law Inaugural Conference, Geneva, 15–17 July 2008, SIEL Online Proceedings Working Paper No. 12/08, <http://ssrn.com/abstract=1151386>; Alberta Fabbricotti, 'The WTO and RTAs: A "Bottom-Up" Interpretation of RTAs' Autonomy over WTO Law', in Susan Frankel and Meredith Kolsky Lewis (eds), *International Economic Law and National Autonomy: Convergence or Divergence?* (CUP 2010) 116–140.

requirement, or increase trade barriers towards non-partners' exports, thus disregarding the external requirement.

Partly, the inefficiency of Article XXIV rests with its outdated text which does not envisage RTAs other than free trade areas and customs unions, ignoring more complex models of economic integration such as common markets and economic unions.[39] Furthermore, it is the language of Article XXIV itself which is repeatedly circumlocutory and unclear. This has led to a number of controversial interpretative issues which still remain largely unsolved and, consequently, to legal uncertainty regarding the scope and stringency of its provisions.

WTO members are extremely reluctant to modify the provisions of Article XXIV, no matter if the proposed change has the purpose of strengthening the rules or has only clarifying and explanatory intents. For example, notwithstanding its renowned inefficiency, Article XXIV was used as a model for the drafting of para. 2(c) of the Enabling Clause and of Article V of the GATS. New evidence of this reluctance, if necessary, is provided by the very modest *Transparency Mechanism for Regional Trade Agreements* which resulted from the Doha Round negotiations[40] compared to the original mandate of the Ministerial Conference which was to clarify and improve disciplines and procedures applying to RTAs under the existing WTO provisions.[41]

Besides, not only have the WTO members persistently failed to check RTAs in the framework of the pertaining WTO political bodies, primarily the Committee on Regional Trade Agreements (CRTA), they have also often avoided challenging RTAs judicially.[42]

---

[39] On this hierarchy see Section II above.

[40] General Council Decision, WT/L/671 of 14 December 2006. Emblematic of the shortcomings of the Transparency Mechanism is its para. 10: 'The WTO Secretariat's factual presentation shall not be used as a basis for dispute settlement procedures or to create new rights and obligations for Members'.

[41] Para. 29 of the Doha Ministerial Declaration adopted on 14 November 2001.

[42] On this issue, Frieder Roessler, 'The Relationship between Regional Integration Agreements and the Multilateral Trade Order', in Kym Anderson and Richard Blackhurst (eds), *Regional Integration and the Global Trading System* (Harvester-Wheatsheaf 1993) at 322, observes that: 'For a third party to insist that a regional agreement meet the substantially-all-trade requirement means therefore in practice to insist that the countries forming a customs union or free trade area extend it to substantially all trade, which in turn means that the third party asks that the discrimination against it be broadened.' But WTO members refrain from challenging RTAs before a panel also because they are not willing for the panel to strengthen or clarify the provisions of Article XXIV as this might

Last but not least, in those instances where Article XXIV is invoked as a defence to justify otherwise non-permitted deviations from other WTO provisions, the panels and the Appellate Body usually avoid scrutinizing either the RTA in its entirety or the specific regional measure at issue.

Hence, there are plenty of reasons to doubt the legal status of Article XXIV, since this provision has always been largely inoperative as a legal discipline.[43]

V. INTERFACES BETWEEN POLITICAL ECONOMY AND INTERNATIONAL LAW REGARDING THE PROLIFERATION OF REGIONAL TRADE AGREEMENTS

In the light of the two preceding Sections it is now possible to explore the interactions between PE and IL regarding their approaches and solutions to the issue of the RTA proliferation. The latter phenomenon seems to have blown all theoretical paradigms away. As already noted in the introduction to this Chapter, the proliferation of RTAs finds no adequate rational explanation under both PE and IL, because it follows some kind of anarchical logic escaping concepts and classifications which are deeply rooted in these scientific areas (suffice it to think about economic theories such as 'comparative advantage' and 'welfare maximization' or of IL concepts such as '*pacta sunt servanda*' or 'conflicting treaties').

Since this Chapter perceives IL as *explanandum* vis-à-vis IPE considerations, what is explained here is the rationale of the persistent infringement of GATT Article XXIV by RTAs. The proliferation of RTAs does not, per se, pose problems under IL because the formation of new

---

compromise the claimant's own regional plans and because they do not trust panels to adopt binding decisions on the economically and technically complex question of compliance to Article XXIV. For this view, see for example Petros C Mavroidis, 'If I Don't Do It, Somebody Else Will (Or Won't): Testing the Compliance of Preferential Trade Agreements with the Multilateral Rules' (2006) 40 JWT 187–214.

[43] John H Jackson, *World Trade and the Law of GATT* (Bobbs-Merrill 1969) at 621: 'It is apparent that the criteria for permissible regional arrangements under GATT are ambiguous and difficult to apply […]. The preparatory work of GATT suggests that at least two goals were desired by various factions of the draftsmen of GATT […]. It is probable that these two goals are inconsistent when applied to specific cases.'

economic groupings is legitimized by Article XXIV, however provided that certain requirements are fulfilled. The IL issue is rather why there is an RTA proliferation in blatant disregard of Article XXIV requirements.

This question can first be addressed straightforwardly by pointing one's finger to Article XXIV loopholes.[44] Since it is unlikely that the problematic text of Article XXIV is the result of the incompetence or naïvety of the GATT drafters, the only explanation of the vagueness and scarce clarity of this text remains the intention of the GATT negotiators to leave the GATT contracting parties a wide 'margin of appreciation' regarding the ways to create RTAs and make them function. The margin of appreciation consists in a methodological approach or a standard of review which introduces a degree of flexibility into the operation of IL. Among the criteria allowing for the application of the margin of appreciation is of course the degree of uncertainty of the norm, as uncertainty may well have been intentionally built into the text by the parties.[45]

What matters in the present analysis is that, through the tool of the margin of appreciation, PE appraisals swarm into IL implementation outcomes and, vice versa, IL gives a legal brand or status to PE values and considerations. Since, as Pauwelyn argues,[46] the WTO/RTAs relationship is governed by politics, this tool obviously plays a major role in the application of Article XXIV.

At this point, the analysis should address the question: is the margin of appreciation left to the discretion of WTO/RTAs members under Article XXIV just a methodological approach under a treaty provision or is it the symptom of a wider and deeper freedom (or absence of legal engagements) the States perceive themselves as being entitled to? The IL argument set down by the present author in previous essays is the existence, in international trade relations, of a customary 'regional exception' rule,[47] in other words, an unwritten right or freedom to prefer

---

[44] Already in 1963, Kenneth W Dam had remarked: 'Article XXIV appears, on first impression, to set forth a precise set of rules for determining the circumstances under which regional arrangements will be permitted. The apparent precision is quite illusory.' See Dam, 'Regional Economic Arrangements and the GATT: the Legacy of a Misconception' (1963) 30 U Chi L Rev 615, at 619.

[45] Jean-Pierre Cot, 'Margin of Appreciation', in Rüdiger Wolfrum (ed), *Max Planck Encyclopedia of Public International Law* (OUP 2012) paras 1, 2 and 13.

[46] Joost Pauwelyn, 'Legal Avenues to "Multilateralizing Regionalism": Beyond Article XXIV', in Baldwin and Low (eds) (n 8) 368.

[47] On the relationship between PE and customary IL, see Niels Petersen, 'The Political Economy of Customary International Law', and Alessandra

materializing as a right or freedom to conclude RTAs and, of course, to continue to take part in these preferential arrangements.[48]

It does not appear useful to reword the idea of a customary regional exception here but rather to put this idea in practical terms. Empirical observation shows that RTAs behave with large autonomy in respect to the WTO legal system (as a result but also regardless of Article XXIV loopholes) and that, thanks to the fragmentation produced by RTA proliferation, the MFN treatment is no longer the main discipline regulating trade relations among WTO member States, but the exception. Provocatively, it was even suggested that the MFN treatment be defined as that of the least-favoured-nation![49]

Regarding this sort of anarchical situation, it has been noted that the point has already been reached where it is not the WTO which determines and enforces the legitimacy of the RTAs but it is the RTAs themselves which determine the degree of their adherence to the WTO law, through their concrete behaviour.[50] Therefore, it has been suggested to overturn the perspective from which the issue of WTO–RTAs relationship is usually approached under IL, switching from a 'top-down' approach (maintaining the idea of the primacy of the WTO over the RTAs), to a 'bottom-up' approach (asserting the somewhat contractual nature and variable scope of the obligations undertaken by the RTAs).[51]

This 'bottom-up' approach seems to be supported also by a particular sociological perspective, defined as 'symbolic-interactionist',[52] as applied to the WTO–RTAs debate, according to which, since 'the need to

---

Gianelli, 'Can Political Economy Help Solve the Riddle of Customary International Law?', above in this Volume.

[48] Fabbricotti (n 36).

[49] See Report by the Consultative Board to the Director-General Supachai Panitchpakdi, *The Future of the WTO – Addressing Institutional Challenges in the New Millennium*, 2004, p. 19, para. 60.

[50] Fabbricotti (n 36).

[51] Ibid.

[52] According to Moshe Hirsch, 'The Sociology of International Economic Law: Sociological Analysis of the Regulation of Regional Agreements in the World Trading System' (2008) 19 EJIL 277–299, at 299: 'The sociological analyses reveal that the major sociological perspectives suggest different answers to the question of the desirable relationship between the WTO and RTAs […]. [T]he particular virtues of the symbolic-interactionist approach justify a presumption in favour of this approach to RTAs. The contribution of RTAs to socio-economic pluralism in the international system and the accompanying benefits to IEL indicate that the relevant WTO legal rules should be interpreted in a liberal manner.'

generate shared social understandings in the international economic system cannot be effectively fulfilled by the imposition of external, global rules [...] [c][c]ommon norms that embody common understandings on the global level should emerge "from below", in other words, from the interaction among states and societies in smaller regional groups'.[53]

Structurally, this kind of 'Copernican revolution' would presuppose the absolute groundlessness of a system based on an automatic MFN general rule with certain exceptions to its operation, 'with "regionalism" being totally subordinated to the general principles of "internationalism" and made an instrument for indiscriminate and world-scale liberalizing of trade'.[54]

It is difficult to imagine how what has just been described as the real dynamics of the relationship between the RTAs and the WTO – with the regional preferences being the Sun and the MFN principle the Earth (to continue the parallel with the Copernican paradigm) – could ever turn into the treaty content and language of the WTO. This would be tantamount to founding a completely new multilateral trade legal order!

On the contrary, a bottom-up approach of the WTO–RTAs relationship as is described above seems to square up perfectly with an IPE perspective. WTO members associated in regional groupings shape their WTO commitments depending on their trade interests and needs as the latter arise. Possibly, but not necessarily, they determine the formulation of new rules or the amendment of previous ones accordingly.

VI. CONCLUSIONS

RTAs are a phenomenon continually evolving and unlikely to fit PE and IL yardsticks.

This Chapter puts PE and IL in a complementary relationship in order to suggest new grounds for analysis and explanation. Under both PE and IL the dominant question is: why do States adhere to RTAs? It was preliminarily decided, as a matter of method, to face the IL issue through the lenses of PE and not vice versa – thus viewing IL as *explanandum*

---

[53] Ibid at 293.

[54] See Ennio Triggiani, 'Some Thoughts on the Most-Favoured-Nation Treatment' (1985) Italian Yb Int L 124–144, at 132. For a criticism regarding the 'exception approach' see also Sungjoon Cho, 'Breaking the Barrier Between Regionalism and Multilateralism: A New Perspective on Trade Regionalism' (2001) 42 Harv Int L J, at 451–452.

and not as *explanans* – and to opt for an IPE rather than a PE approach, while at the same time accounting the States as decision-making units or, to use a popular terminology, as 'black boxes'.

In IL language the above dominant question turns into: why do States adhere to RTAs in patent disregard of the WTO requirements of GATT Article XXIV? The present Chapter answers this question in three steps. *First*, what at first sight appears to be an attitude of patent disregard of rules by WTO members may be only ostensibly so; when rules are neglected in such a widespread and general way, one would better start doubting the existence of the rule itself. *Second*, the text of Article XXIV was intentionally drafted in a vague and flexible way in order to leave a wide margin of appreciation to the GATT/WTO contracting parties willing to create or adhere to RTAs; it is unlikely that the RTA phenomenon may be stopped or reduced by making the provisos of Article XXIV more strict or meticulous as this result is ultimately unpopular among WTO members. *Third*, the wide margin of appreciation left to the WTO members can be interpreted not only as an end in itself but also as a result of the pervasion or predominance of mere IPE considerations over the IL role within the WTO order; thanks to the loopholes for RTAs in Article XXIV WTO members are allowed to choose, through a bottom-up approach, the degree of their adherence to the WTO commitments depending on their own trade and other interests (in the face of a top-down approach which would have upheld the primacy of the WTO over the RTAs and the major role of IL within the WTO system).

14. Political Economy and International Investment Law: The Conclusion of IIAs by Developing Countries during the Twentieth Century

Tobias A Lehmann

I. INTRODUCTION

International Investment Agreements (IIAs) are treaties between sovereign States in which each State agrees to grant certain material and/or procedural rights to investors from the other contracting States.[1] These agreements usually provide foreign investors with the procedural right to directly file a claim against the host State before an international dispute resolution institution based on an alleged violation of the relevant IIA's material obligations by the host State (a so-called 'investor State dispute settlement provision'). Such IIAs, most notably in the form of bilateral investment treaties (BITs), have been concluded since the late 1950s, but their number has only exploded in the 1990s.[2]

This Chapter advances a descriptive (positive) theory of the adherence of developing countries (DCs) to IIAs that is, a theory of the causal factors underlying a DC's decision to conclude an IIA. Knowledge of such causal factors is important for several reasons.[3] First, such a theory is necessary in order to make sound predictions on how DCs are likely to

[1] IIAs' material/substantive norms, most notably, include standards of compensation in the event of direct or indirect expropriations, standards for capital repatriation, national-treatment requirements, and most-favoured-nation requirements.

[2] See for example, UNCTAD, *World Investment Report: Global Value Chains: Investment and Trade Development* (United Nations 2013) 101 ff.

[3] Joost Pauwelyn, 'At the Edge of Chaos? Foreign Investment Law as a Complex Adaptive System, How It Emerged and How It Can Be Reformed' (2014) 29 ICSID Review 372, 374 et seq.

behave in the future in the context of the conclusion of IIAs and therewith for machining sound predictions on where the contemporary international investment law regime (especially its 'investor State dispute settlement' component) is likely heading. In so doing, the theory may for instance be used to assess the possible consequences of the recent 'backlash' by DCs against IIAs, in particular, against investor-State dispute-settlement institutions.[4] Second, such a theory is necessary to make realistic prescriptions on how to reform the regime since a thorough understanding of the functioning of DCs' decision-making allows one to better assess whether one's prescriptions are actually likely to be implemented by the DCs when concluding future IIAs (the theory provides one with 'feasibility bounds' if you will). Third, such a theory may also be of direct relevance to investment arbitral tribunals. On the one hand, the theory may be of interest to the tribunal when it decides on the question of 'admissibility';[5] such a question should be answered by considering the whole set of circumstances within which the dispute is taking place,[6] which arguably includes the consideration of the likely consequences of a decision on the international investment law regime as a whole (which includes the consequences thereof on the conclusion of future IIAs by DCs). On the other hand, the theory may be of interest to the tribunal when it interprets IIA's norms; knowledge of the underlying (causal) factors which drove DCs to conclude this IIA in the first place

---

[4] We have recently experienced a backlash by States against international investment law in its current form. See seminally, Anne van Aaken, 'Perils of Success? The Case of International Investment Protection' (2008) 9 JIEL 1–27; see also the contributions in Michael Waibel et al. (eds), *The Backlash against Investment Arbitration: Perceptions and Reality* (Kluwer Law International 2010). States have negatively reacted to the existing regime of international investment law. Think, for instance, of the withdrawal from the ICSID Convention by the plurinational State of Bolivia (3 November 2007), Ecuador (7 January 2010), and Venezuela (25 July 2012). Or of Australia's announcement in April 2011 that it would no longer include investor State dispute settlement provisions in its future IIAs and FTAs. The plurinational State of Bolivia, Ecuador, South Africa or Venezuela all have withdrawn or terminated multiple IIAs since 2008.

[5] Jan Paulsson, 'Jurisdiction and Admissibility', in Gerald Aksen et al. (eds), *Global Reflections on International Law, Commerce and Dispute Resolution: Liber Amicorum in Honour of Robert Briner* (ICC Publishing 2005) at 617.

[6] Shabtai Rosenne, 'International Courts and Tribunals, Jurisdiction and Admissibility of Inter-State Applications', in Rüdiger Wolfrum (ed), *Max Planck Encyclopedia of Public International Law* (OUP 2006) at para 2.

(that is, of the countries' underlying motivations) may be relied upon in a teleological interpretation perspective or a historical interpretation perspective.[7]

This Chapter suggests that such a descriptive theory should take a non-unitary State perspective – that is, it should explicitly build upon country-internal dynamics. Such an approach is in contrast with the existing scholarly theoretical international investment law literature which has almost exclusively taken a unitary State perspective.[8] To develop this descriptive non-unitary State theory, this Chapter adopts a political economy approach: it relies upon the economic methodology, and thus uses rational choice theory to capture/model decision-making as well as equilibrium theory to model the outcome of strategic interactions between several decision-makers.[9] Amongst the many non-unitary State theories available, this Chapter proposes to take country-internal dynamics into account by relying upon the conceptual framework known as

---

[7] These perspectives are captured in articles 31 and 32 of the 'Vienna Convention on the Law of Treaties' (23 May 1969 (entered into force 27 January 1980), 1155 UNTS 331, 114 members by the end of 2013).

[8] Seminal within that literature is Andrew T Guzman, 'Why LDCs Sign Treaties That Hurt Them' (1998) 38 VJIL 639. See also Zachary Elkins, Andrew T Guzman and Beth A Simmons, 'Competing for Capital: The Diffusion of Bilateral Investment Treaties, 1960-2000' (2006) 60 Int Org 811–846. Exceptions (adopting a non-unitary State perspective) are: Anne van Aaken and Tobias A Lehmann, 'Sustainable Development and International Investment Law: A Harmonious View from Economics', in Roberto Echandi and Pierre Sauvé (eds), *Prospects in International Investment Law and Policy* (CUP 2013) 323 ff., they sketch the skeleton of a political-economy model of IIA conclusions which builds upon country-internal dynamics; and the recent 'partisan theory of FDI', developed in most detail in Pablo M Pinto, *Partisan Investment in the Global Economy: Why the Left Loves Foreign Direct Investment and FDI Loves the Left* (CUP 2013), which holds that the partisan alignment of a State's government, namely whether it is pro-capital or pro-labour, strongly influences a State's FDI policies. This situation is in stark contrast with the scholarly theoretical trade law literature which, for decades now, has accepted country-internal dynamics as central elements of a theory of State decision-making in the context of trade policies; also observing so is UNCTAD (n 2).

[9] Barry R Weingast and Donald A Wittman, 'The Reach of Political Economy', in Barry R Weingast and Donald A Wittman (eds), *The Oxford Handbook of Political Economy* (OUP 2006) 3: 'In our view, political economy is the methodology of economics applied to the analysis of political behavior and institutions.' Gary S Becker, *The Economic Approach to Human Behavior* (University of Chicago Press 1976) 5: 'The assumptions of maximizing behavior, [...] equilibrium, [...] form the heart of the economic approach as I see it.'

'selectorate theory'– namely, this Chapter develops a *selectorate theory* of DCs' adherence to IIAs.

This Chapter finds that even though a non-unitary State theory is by definition less parsimonious than a unitary State theory, the proposed selectorate theory remains nonetheless easy to understand and to use by a wide audience (that is, it remains 'tractable').[10]

This Chapter furthermore finds that the proposed selectorate theory is empirically consistent. Additional empirical support for the proposed selectorate theory is provided by the finding that a unitary State perspective has difficulties in fully explaining several observed behaviours which the proposed selectorate theory is able to explain (and thus to predict).[11]

A non-unitary State perspective is finally shown to be valuable when interpreting the empirical data. The proposed selectorate theory makes it clear that the common interpretation of one of the central empirical findings within international investment law scholarship – that there exists a positive statistical association (that is, statistically significant correlation) between the probability of a DC stipulating a BIT and the conclusion of BITs by its FDI-inflow competitors[12] – does actually not readily follow. Specifically, it shows that, contrary to what is generally held, this positive association does not necessarily imply that DCs concluded IIAs during the twentieth century to 'compete for capital'; namely, it shows that DCs concluding IIAs were not necessarily driven by an increased FDI-inflow motivation.

A few important remarks are to be made here. *First*, contrary to the existing IIA literature, this Chapter explicitly focuses on explaining the conclusion of (that is, the ratification of) IIAs;[13] because the majority of

---

[10] Eddie Dekel and Barton L Lipman, 'How (Not) to Do Decision Theory' (2010) 2 Ann Rev Econ 257, 262: 'because models do not simply sit on a shelf but are to be used, tractability is valuable'. This point is important as a lack of tractability has often been advanced to reject the usage of a non-unitary State perspective; See for example, Andrew T Guzman, *How International Law Works: A Rational Choice Theory* (OUP 2008) 19.

[11] Empirical support for a theory coming from the empirical inconsistency of that theory's rival alternative theories is known as 'lateral (empirical) support', see Jon Elster, *Explaining Social Behavior: More Nuts and Bolts for the Social Sciences* (CUP 2007) 20.

[12] This positive association was first observed by Elkins, Guzman and Simmons (n 8).

[13] The existing theoretical and empirical IIA literatures have mainly focused on IIA signings. Seminal in the theoretical literature is Guzman (n 8).

signed IIAs have been ratified,[14] the present selectorate theory can in general also be applied to the signature of IIAs.[15] *Second*, even though this Chapter only tests the proposed selectorate theory against DCs' behaviours during the twentieth century, it can readily be relied upon to analyse contemporary IIA issues, for both developed and DCs, because the theory's underlying causal factors (that is, country-internal dynamics) are relevant over time and across development levels. *Third*, this Chapter does not explicitly consider negotiations; as such, it is not interested in the precise content of IIAs, but with whether a State is fundamentally willing to conclude IIAs. *Fourth*, this Chapter does not provide a complete theory because it does not explicitly propose a theory of the organisability of interest groups;[16] the theory is meant to serve as a guide for what factors one should take into account (read: a guide for where to look) when trying to understand past or to predict future IIA conclusions. *Fifth*, this Chapter does not explicitly address the question of whether DCs faced a voluntary contributions game (of which the popular prisoner's dilemma is a special case); that is, it does not explicitly consider whether DCs ended up worse off by concluding IIAs on a bilateral basis.[17]

The remainder of this Chapter is organised as follows. Section II presents a theory of State decision-making which builds upon country-internal dynamics – this theory is known as the 'selectorate theory'. Section III applies this theory to the conclusion of IIAs by DCs during the twentieth century. Section IV discusses empirical support of that theory. Finally, Section V concludes.

---

[14] By 2014, 2250 out of 3084 signed IIAs had been ratified. For the data, see UNCTAD's 'International Investment Agreement Navigator' (available at <http:// investmentpolicyhub.unctad.org>). A notable exception that confirms the rule is Brazil which has not ratified a single one of its signed IIAs (Section IV.2).

[15] 'In general' because if the agency responsible for signing IIAs is under weak political oversight by the entity (typically the legislative body) responsible for ratifying IIAs, then a State may at some given point in time have a preference for signing an IIA but not for concluding that IIA. Consequently, although it can be expected to hold on average (in other words, 'in general'), it need not hold for a specific State. Brazil is a case in point, see Section IV.2.

[16] Whether some potentially relevant IG is organised, and thus has the capacity to provide political support, must therefore be assessed by looking at historical data; namely, 'organisability' is an empirical question. See below (n 33 and the text preceding it).

[17] Seminal for such an analysis is Guzman (n 8); see also Ryan J Bubb and Susan Rose-Ackerman, 'BITs and Bargains: Strategic Aspects of Bilateral and Multilateral Regulation of Foreign Investment' (2007) 27 IRLE 291.

II. CONCEPTUAL FRAMEWORK: THE SELECTORATE THEORY OF STATE DECISION-MAKING[18]

Every leader answers to some group that retains her in power

– Bruce Bueno de Mesquita, Alastair Smith, Randolph M. Siverson, and James D. Morrow[19]

The 'selectorate view of politics' starts from the observation that every leader requires the support of some group of people in order to remain in office. The concept of 'leader' (or 'State managers' if you prefer) describes the entities whose behaviours amount to State decision-making.[20] Such an entity may amount to a single individual (for example, in a dictatorship or in an absolute monarchy) or it may amount to a set of individuals (for example, the parliament).[21] Since every leader faces rivals (called 'challengers') which are willing to challenge the leader's position in office, the leader requires the support of some group of people to stay in office.[22]

The theory's central assumption is that leaders are primarily motivated by *political survival* and therefore behave so as to maximise the satisfaction of this motivation; namely, that State decision-making is primarily driven by a political survival motivation.[23] This assumption is reasonable because the process underlying the road one has to travel to become and to stay a leader amounts to an evolutionary selection

---

[18] The core structure of the conceptual framework commonly referred to as 'selectorate theory' was developed in Bruce Bueno de Mesquita et al., 'Political Institutions, Policy Choice and the Survival of Leaders' 32 British J Pol Sci 559 and Bruce Bueno de Mesquita et al., *The Logic of Political Survival* (MIT Press 2003).

[19] Bueno de Mesquita et al., *The Logic of Political Survival* (ibid) 7.

[20] The concept of 'leader' therefore, most notably, captures: dictators, (public) judges, monarchs, and politicians. The usage of entities in plural is to allow for the fact that different entities may act on the State's behalf in different instances (in other words, separation of powers).

[21] Bueno de Mesquita et al., *The Logic of Political Survival* (n 18) 38.

[22] Ibid 28 ff.: 'Make no mistake about it, no leader rules alone. Even the most oppressive dictators cannot survive the loss of support among their core constituents.'

[23] Ibid 9.

mechanism, selecting at each step on the road the individual (consciously or unconsciously) maximising their political survival.[24]

A leader's subsidiary motivations are thus assumed to only dictate State decision-making if political survival is not affected; that is, subsidiary motivations determine the choice amongst several available options which all yield the same (or similar) probabilities of political survival. Therefore, although leaders are assumed to be homogeneous with respect to their primary motivation, the theory sets no restrictions on subsidiary motivations. These subsidiary motivations can be mapped onto a line going from a self-interested motivation (private interest theories) to a political ideology motivation (public interest theories). The widespread existence of corruption suggests that there are indeed leaders out there who are driven by a self-interested motivation.

II.1. Potentially Relevant Influencers: The Causal Factors

Political survival requires *political support*.[25] The concept of *selectorate* describes the set of (natural and juridical) persons which have the capacity to provide political support; that is, those persons having the power to influence political survival.[26] Political support includes, amongst others, voting, political contributions,[27] peaceful demonstrations,

---

[24] Similarly, ibid 23: 'We have no doubt that many people value other things above political survival. It is just that such people are not likely to find themselves in high office and so need not overly occupy our interest.'

[25] The modern focus on political support to describe State decision-making has its source in the seminal book by Anthony Downs, *An Economic Theory of Democracy* (Harper & Row 1957) 52: '[leaders adopt] those acts of spending which gain the most votes by means of those acts of financing which lose the fewest votes'.

[26] The concept of 'selectorate' was introduced in Susan Shirk, *The Political Logic of Economic Reform in China* (University of California Press 1993). I depart from the selectorate theory's original formulation which restricts the selectorate to those individuals having a say under the State's formal (political selection) institutions (Bueno de Mesquita et al., *The Logic of Political Survival* (n 18) 42 ff.). Remark that by not restricting the selectorate to residents, the approach adopted herein implicitly allows for 'foreign selectors' to influence State decision-making, either directly or indirectly through their own home State.

[27] Seminally, Uri Ben-Zion and Zeev Eytan, 'On Money, Votes and Policy in Democratic Society' (1974) 17 Public Choice 1; for an extensive treatment, see Gene M Grossman and Elhanan Helpman, *Special Interest Politics* (MIT Press 2001) Ch. 10.

and violent protests (brute force).[28] The selectorate amounts to a heterogeneous group, wherein selectors vary in terms of the strength and type(s) of their political support.[29] Clearly, not all selectors fundamentally have the capacity to vote in democracies (think of firms and foreign residents) and not all selectors fundamentally have the capacity to make political contributions (for example, due to their lack of financial resources), engage in street protests, strike, and/or provide brute force.

If a leader exhibits a self-interested subsidiary motivation, then non-selectors may also influence State decision-making by providing *(non-political) support* in the form of private benefits (read: bribery) through immediate material benefits or the promise of future material benefits (revolving doors).[30] Clearly, not all persons fundamentally have the capacity to engage in this type of support.

Even where a person fundamentally has the capacity to provide (political or non-political) support, if that person views itself as part of a larger group of persons which are similarly affected by State decision-making – namely, if it views itself as part of an *Interest Group* (IG)[31] – then that group must overcome a collective action problem for any of its members to actually provide any type of support and thus to influence State decision-making.[32] An IG which is able to overcome this problem is called an Organised Interest Group (OIG); namely, an OIG's members amount to influencers. It is important to remark that the theory presented in this Chapter says nothing about the organisability of some IGs. This Chapter refrains from including such a theory because it is not believed that there exists a satisfactory theory out there – whether some IG is

---

28 This may take the form of military coups, revolutions, inter-State wars, or covert foreign interventions.

29 This Chapter departs from the selectorate theory's original formulation wherein all selectors were assumed to be equal in terms of political support (Bueno de Mesquita et al., *The Logic of Political Survival* (n 18) 77).

30 The concept of 'revolving door' captures the idea that political support also results from back and forth employments between the private and the public sector.

31 This definition of 'interest group' follows Grossman and Helpman (n 27) 1.

32 They face a so-called 'collective-action problem' because State decision-making (in other words, the policies) amount to 'public goods' or 'club goods', so that the game in material terms which each member of the group is facing amounts to a 'voluntary-contributions game' (of which the famous 'prisoner's dilemma' is a special case). If the members are motivated by self-interest, then each member may have an incentive to free-ride on the other members' contributions – making the provision of the public good uncertain.

organised therefore requires one to consider historical data and make an inference thereupon (that is, organisability in this theory is therefore an empirical question).[33] Because of this lack of satisfactory theory, a person which fundamentally has the capacity to provide some form of support is hereinafter referred to as a *potential influencer*.

Since virtually all State decision-making affects different persons similarly, to simplify the conceptual framework, we will henceforth be thinking in terms of IGs rather than in terms of individual persons.[34]

The selectorate theory emphasises the expected distributional consequences of policies – namely, that policies create both winners and losers.[35] The well-beings of different IGs are, however, not only differently affected by State decision-making (for example, foreign investor protection policies), they are also affected with varying intensity. Under the reasonable assumption that substantially affected IGs are likely to react most strongly (in other words, likely to provide most support either to the leader or its challengers),[36] an instrumentally rational leader will primarily aim at satisfying the preferences of substantially affected OIGs when making policies so as to 'ensure' the future support of those IGs in exchange. These substantially affected IGs are hereinafter referred to as *potentially relevant influencers*. Importantly, the set of potentially relevant influencers may vary (i) over time as well as (ii) across policies.[37] To simplify the conceptual framework further, we will henceforth restrict the analysis to potentially relevant influencers.

Note finally that the focuses (read: simplifying assumptions) on IGs as well as on substantially affected ones are in any event desirable because they guarantee the tractability of the theory.

---

[33] Seminal for proposing a theory of the organisability of IGs is Mancur Olson, *The Logic of Collective Action: Public Goods and the Theory of Groups* (Harvard University Press 1965); roughly speaking, he theorised that smaller groups are more likely to organise than larger ones. For a recent critic of Olson's theory based on empirical data, see Steven Croley, 'Interest Groups and Public Choice', in Daniel A Farber and Anne Joseph O'Connell (eds), *Research Handbook on Public Choice and Public Law* (Edward Elgar 2010).

[34] In the special case wherein a single person is differently affected than everybody else, that person's interest group would simply be composed of one person (itself).

[35] Daaron Acemoglu and James A Robinson, *Economic Origins of Dictatorship and Democracy* (CUP 2006) 20.

[36] Clearly, whether they can react at all depends on whether that interest group is organised.

[37] Namely, the set of relevant influencers may not be the same for trade policies than say for foreign investment protection policies.

II.2. Empirical Consistency of the Selectorate Theory Beyond the Realm of IIA Conclusions

This Section presents evidence of a non-unitary State perspective's empirical consistency in other areas of State decision-making (such as in trade law or in foreign direct investment (FDI) regulation more generally).

Importantly, however, although such empirical consistency may increase our confidence that the said non-unitary State perspective should also be used when studying IIA conclusions, it provides no certainty and therefore we must still complement it with a systematic study of the said non-unitary State perspective's empirical consistency in the context of IIA conclusions (Section IV).

Causal mechanisms

The following observations provide empirical support for some of the conceptual framework's underlying causal mechanisms. They provide empirical support that that (political and non-political) support influences State decision-making – namely, that State decision-making is influenced by country-internal dynamics and therefore that a non-unitary State perspective is called for.

Political contributions appear to be substantial in democracies. Take for instance the United States (US). Campaign contributions in the US increased from 159.3 million USD in 1990 to 454.3 million USD in 2012;[38] also, they tend to significantly increase in the weeks surrounding US congressional votes.[39] Lobbying in the US increased from 1.45 billion USD in 1998 to 2.38 billion USD in 2013 (reaching a peak at 3.55 billion USD in 2010);[40] lobbying involves the transmission of information to the leader about the consequences of its policies,[41] which includes, for instance, informing a leader that some policy will make the lobbyist's principal willing to build a new factory (that is, job prospects) within the leader's territory. Under the reasonable assumption that firms are instrumentally rational and motivated by material self-interest (in other words, that they amount to profit maximisers), they would not

---

38 According to <http://www.opensecrets.org/lobby>.

39 Thomas Stratmann, 'The Market for Congressional Votes: Is Timing of Contributions Everything?' (1998) 41 J L Econ 85.

40 According to <http://www.opensecrets.org/lobby>.

41 Grossman and Helpman (n 27) 4: 'those [activities] intended to educate and persuade lawmakers'; David P Baron, 'Review of Grossman and Helpman's Special Interest Politics' (2002) 40 J Econ Lit 1221, 1224: 'Lobbying is the strategic presentation of information'.

make political contributions if they were not to expect a return on such investments: we should therefore understand the real world observation of substantial political contributions as evidence that political contributions influence State decision-making. Further support for this causal mechanism is provided by the fact that leaders and challengers spend most of their campaign contributions on television advertising (that is, on issue framing),[42] and that there is widespread empirical support that the opinion of the masses about an issue depends on how the issue is framed.[43]

An ingenious empirical study analyses the impact of the size of a protest on State decision-making by using the weather as an exogenous variation thereupon; namely, that rainfall yields less attendance. The study finds that good weather is associated with significantly more favourable State decision-making.[44] This study suggests that *peaceful demonstrations* may influence State decision-making. As such, the average resident may amount to an influencer even when they do not act as 'voters'.

Influence through voting and brute force is trivial and will not be discussed here. Empirical support for influence through revolving doors is difficult to come by and is likely to be more anecdotal than systematic.

FDI-related policy making

Several quantitative and qualitative empirical studies find that a State's FDI policies reflect the interests of that State's potentially relevant influencers weighted by the strength of their respective political support. These studies therefore provide empirical support that State decision-making is influenced by country-internal dynamics and thus that a non-unitary State perspective is called for.

---

42 Andrea Prat, 'Rational Voters and Political Advertising', in Weingast and Wittman (eds) (above n 9) 50.

43 James N Druckman, 'Public Opinion: Stunted Policy Support' (2013) 3 Nature Climate Change 617, 617. For an extensive review, see for example, Brian F Schaffner and Patrick J Sellers (eds), *Winning with Words: The Origins and Impact of Political Framing* (Routledge 2010).

44 Andreas Madestam et al., 'Do Political Protests Matter? Evidence from the Tea Party Movement' (2013) 128 Q J Econ 1633, 1633, find, based on cross-sectional data of the coordinated rallies by the Tea Party movements across the United States on Tax Day (15 April 2009), that good weather in a district increases the likelihood of its current congressmen to vote more in accordance with the Tea Party's ideology; it furthermore finds support for the causal mechanism: good weather increases the likelihood of the masses voting for the Tea Party.

Quantitative studies find a strong and robust correlation between whether a State is pro-labour or pro-capital and that State's FDI policies: a pro-labour leader (in other words, a State whose strongest influencers amongst the potentially relevant influencers are those who care for employment and wages) is more likely to adopt FDI-inflow-friendly policies; and that this pattern is strongest in manufacturing.[45] Case studies of Argentina's and South Korea's FDI-inflow policies during the twentieth century also suggest that a pro-labour leader is more likely to adopt FDI-inflow-friendly policies.[46] Case studies furthermore point out that a pro-capital leader is likely to adopt FDI-friendly policies when FDI inflows can be anticipated to increase the profits of domestic firms (for example, because of technology transfers).[47]

III. THE CONCLUSION OF IIAS BY DEVELOPING COUNTRIES DURING THE TWENTIETH CENTURY

III.1. Potentially Relevant Influencers[48]

Even though the conclusion of IIAs generally occurred under the radars of public discourse in DCs,[49] a State's leader is likely to consider the respective position of the masses, labour unions, and domestic firms

---

[45] Pinto (n 8) 98 ff., finds, based on a panel-data analysis of FDI regulation for a subset of 27 OECD States between 1980 and 2000 (96 observations), that 'partisanship is correlated with the measure of investment policy orientation [capturing a State's openness to FDI inflows] in the direction predicted'; and at 113, footnote 24, finds, based on cross-section data of FDI regulation at the sectoral level for a subset of 28 OECD States for the year 2000, that '[a pro-labour government] is associated with lower restrictions across the board, but especially in manufacturing'.

[46] Ibid 142 ff. and 205 ff.

[47] Take for instance pro-capital South Korea (arguably captured by the chaebols): 'The chaebols were interested in acquiring technology but worried about foreign firms competing with them in the Korean product and factor markets. Foreign investment was thus [desired, but] limited [by law] in form to minority joint ventures followed by divestment after technology had been transferred to the local partner.' (Ibid 24).

[48] See also Roberto Echandi, 'What Do Developing Countries Expect from the International Investment Regime', in José E Alvarez et al. (eds), *The Evolving International Investment Regime* (OUP 2011) 13.

[49] See for example, Lauge N Skovgaard Poulsen, 'Bounded Rationality and the Diffusion of Modern Investment Treaties' (2014) 59 Int Stud Q 1, 2.

when deciding whether to conclude an IIA because of a latent revelation risk: a challenger may decide to reveal the conclusion of an IIA to the public so as to decrease the leader's political survival; in other words, these IGs amount to potentially relevant influencers whether or not they actually had knowledge of the conclusion of such an IIA.

Let us first consider the position of *the masses* which may influence State decision-making through peaceful demonstrations, brute force (read: revolutions), and additionally, in democracies, through the act of voting. We can expect that the masses generally believe that IIAs have the potential to increase FDI inflows because an IIA reduces foreign investors' political risk of investing in the DC party to the IIA (that is, they increase the expected profits of investing therein), which may increase their willingness to invest in that DC, and which may hence increase FDI inflows.[50]

Before 1990, we can reasonably expect the masses to have been opposed to FDI inflows and therefore opposed to the conclusion of IIAs. The post World War II period was arguably characterised by an opposition to FDI inflows from developed countries because of a combination of two beliefs: the period was marked by decolonisation, and these newly independent States arguably perceived such foreign investments as yet another form of colonialism by foreign States through the control of the means of production;[51] and the Soviet model of centralised economic organisation provided for a credible alternative to capitalism (and its free investment flows).

After 1990, however, we can expect the masses to have switched their views regarding FDI inflows and being supportive of IIAs. Indeed, even though the masses may still have been concerned by a neo-colonialism threat, and even though they may have been concerned that the conclusion of IIAs may increase the costs of future policies (that is, sovereignty restriction risk),[52] they can be expected to have taken their chances

---

[50] See seminally Guzman (n 8), for a more detailed exposition of this rationale.

[51] See for example, Kenneth J Vandevelde, 'A Brief History of International Investment Agreements', in Karl P Sauvant and Lisa E Sachs (eds), *The Effect of Treaties on Foreign Direct Investment: Bilateral Investment Treaties, Double Taxation Treaties, and Invesmtent Flows* (OUP 2009) 11; see also Kenneth J Vandevelde, 'The Political Economy of a Bilateral Investment Treaty' (1998) 92 AJIL 621, 625.

[52] In any event, however, we can expect them to have perceived such a risk to be quite small insofar as their respective home States' were switching to

because of the dire economic prospects they were facing and the economic benefits which the conclusion of IIAs were promising.[53]

In Latin America, for instance, these dire economic prospects resulted from the following facts. Latin America had experienced its most serious debt crisis in 1982 which led to an economic downturn, reduced income and increased unemployment to high levels. Also, traditionally relied upon financial sources disappeared as (private and official) lending as well as financial assistance from official aid institutions dropped in the aftermath of the debt crisis. Furthermore, the collapse of the Soviet Union meant the disappearance of yet another source of financial aid flow.[54]

The perceived economic benefits promised by IIAs resulted from the following facts. IIAs have the potential to increase FDI inflows. Contemporary economic growth theories held that higher investments, whatever their origin (in other words, independently of whether they come

---

decentralised/liberal economic systems (as exemplified by the massive privatisations that took place during the 1990s in developing countries around the world) since such an economic organisation is likely to have been perceived as not entailing behaviours which would violate IIAs. Since not even the United States anticipated how broadly IIAs' provisions could/would be interpreted (Kenneth J Vandevelde, 'A Comparison of the 2004 and 1994 U.S. Model BITs: Rebalancing Investor and Host Country Interests', in Karl P Sauvant (ed), *Yearbook on International Investment Law and Policy 2008–2009* (OUP 2009) 285) we can reasonably expect developing countries not to have anticipated this either. The experimental sciences even suggest that they may have perceived the small probability of sovereignty restriction to be zero: individuals seem to either exaggerate or ignore low probability States of the world (even if they are high impact states of the word); for a review of the experimental literature, see Paul Slovic, *The Perception of Risk* (Earthscan 2000).

[53] Because of these dire prospects, the masses were arguably perceiving the world through a so-called 'loss frame' and therefore were exhibiting risk-loving preferences. Experimental studies have repeatedly found that participants tend to be risk averse when they face a choice between gains (in other words, a choice framed in terms of gains) and to be risk loving when they face a choice between losses (in other words, a choice framed in terms of losses). Seminal for the frame dependence of risk preferences are Amos Tversky and Daniel Kahneman, 'The Framing of Decisions and the Psychology of Choice' (1981) 211 Science 453, and Daniel Kahneman and Amos Tversky, 'Choices, Values, and Frames' (1984) 39 Am Psychol 341. Noting that there was a belief that IIAs increase FDI flows and that FDI was vital for development: Antony Anghie, *Imperialism, Sovereignty and the Making of International Law* (CUP 2004) 223.

[54] See for example, Vandevelde (2009) (n 51) 21.

from abroad), increases economic growth.[55] Asian economies, fuelled by private foreign investments, provided support for these theories as they had been experiencing growth rates three times higher than Latin American and sub-Saharan African economies.[56] And the failure of the Soviet model of centralised economic organisation made the decentralised model, including free investment flows, appear as the only viable alternative for economic growth.

Labour unions may influence State decision-making with peaceful demonstrations, strikes, and brute force. The position of labour unions in DCs is similar to the position of the masses.

Domestic firms (or 'capital holders' if you prefer), which arguably amounted mainly to non-foreign investment-making firms during the twentieth century, may influence State decision-making through political contributions and bribery. Domestic firms can also be expected to have believed that IIAs have the potential to increase FDI inflows.[57] For the same reasons as for the masses,[58] we can expect them to have been generally opposed to FDI inflows before 1990. Even if they believed after 1990 that increased FDI inflows would further economic growth,[59] their position vis-à-vis the conclusion of IIAs would depend on whether they expected FDI inflows into their own sector or not. Because the destination of FDI inflows is somewhat uncertain *ex ante*, we can generally expect domestic firms for have opposed IIA conclusions.

We can expect (foreign investment-making) *foreign firms*, which may also influence State decision-making through political contributions and bribery, to have been supportive of IIAs because they are likely to have perceived a DC as exhibiting a high political risk and IIAs to be able to reduce this political risk.[60]

---

55 Theodore H Moran, *Harnessing Foreign Direct Investment for Development: Policies for Developed and Developing Countries* (Center for Global Development 2006) 1 ff.: 'During the heyday [read: 1980s and 1990s] of the "Washington consensus," conventional wisdom held that foreign direct investment was "good" for development (as long as the foreign firms did not engage in flagrant worker abuse or environmental pollution), and the more the better'.

56 Vandevelde (2009) (n 51) 21.

57 Above (n 50).

58 Above (text surrounding n 51).

59 For the reasons, see above (text surrounding n 55).

60 This follows directly from the observation that foreign investment-making firms in developed countries strongly supported the conclusion of IIAs in their own home States; see Vandevelde (2009) (n 51) 32.

III.2. Underlying Cognitive Process: Rational Cost-Benefit Calculus and Imitation

The previous discussion of potentially relevant influencers' positions vis-à-vis the conclusion of IIAs implicitly assumed that their respective position results solely from a rational weighing of the pros and cons – namely, from a rational cost-benefit calculus – regarding variations in FDI flows. Clearly, however, other pros and cons as well as other underlying cognitive processes, such as 'imitation', could be driving their respective positions – especially the position of the masses.[61] The selectorate theory presented herein does neither presume any specific weighing of pros and cons nor any specific underlying cognitive process. The focus on variations in FDI flows was motivated by the existing literature's focus thereon.

The following brief presentation of empirical studies suggests that a lot of DCs' IIA conclusions were driven by rational calculus, and not simply with respect to variations in FDI flows, as well as that some IIA conclusions by DCs appear to have been driven by imitation.

Rational calculus

National treatment clauses and transfer clauses are less constraining in developing-developing IIAs than in developed-developing IIAs.[62] This finding suggests rational calculus.

Before 1990, a DC's probability of signing (and arguably of concluding) a BIT is on average positively influenced by its FDI-inflow competitors' BIT signings.[63] This finding suggests rational calculus.

DCs are more likely to sign (and arguably to conclude) an IIA with the United States, the higher the military aid received by the United States.[64] This finding suggests rational calculus.

Empirical studies suggest that the probability that a DC signs (and arguably concludes) a BIT during a given year increases on average if the

---

[61] Identically: 'We do not doubt that multiple motives exist for the spread of this form of protection for foreign investors [read: BITs].' (Elkins, Guzman and Simmons (n 8) 842).

[62] See below (n 89 and the text preceding it).

[63] See Section IV.3.

[64] See below (n 77).

country receives credits from the IMF during that year.[65] This finding suggests rational calculus.

Several observations suggest that the presence of foreign investments that could be expropriated on average negatively influenced a DC's signing (and arguably conclusion).[66] This finding suggests rational calculus.

Finally, an empirical study finds that during the 1990s, the probability that a DC signs (and arguably concludes) a BIT was on average substantially reduced if that country experienced a BIT claim in the recent past.[67] This finding suggests rational calculus.

Imitation

An empirical study finds that the probability that a DC signs (and arguably concludes) a BIT during the 1990s on average increases with the number of BITs signed by its 'peers'; it finds no statistically significant relation for the period between 1970 and 1990.[68] These findings may be interpreted as evidence that during the 1990s imitation

---

65 See Elkins, Guzman and Simmons (n 8) 840; and Srividya Jandhyala, Witold J Henisz and Edward D Mansfield, 'Three Waves of BITs: The Global Diffusion of Foreign Investment Policy' (2011) 55 JCR 1047, 1067.

66 Bubb and Rose-Ackerman (n 17) 306 ff., noting that, on average, developing countries seem to have started signing BITs at the same time as expropriations in those countries became increasingly rare in the 1970s and observing that '[a]lmost all early treaties were signed between Germany and Switzerland, on the one hand, and poor countries, mostly in Africa. Of the 56 BITs signed between 1959 and 1967, 45 were signed by either Germany or Switzerland. Neither was a major colonial power, and they signed BITs with countries that would not have had much German or Swiss capital to expropriate.'

67 Lauge N Skovgaard Poulsen and Emma Aisbett, 'When the Claim Hits: Bilateral Investment Treaties and Bounded Rational Learning' (2013) 65 World Politics 273, 299 ff., based on the data set (updated to include BIT claims) from Elkins, Guzman and Simmons (n 8), but restricted to the 1990s because BIT claims only really occurred since the middle of the 1990s; see below (n 91) for a brief description of their data set. This finding seems robust because Poulsen and Aisbett 292 ff. (Tables 3, 5 and 6), based on a panel data analysis of all BITs signed by developing countries between 1990 and 2009 and ratified within three years of being signed, also find such a negative effect on the probability of signing a BIT.

68 Jandhyala, Henisz and Mansfield (n 65) 1063. They find a statistically significant positive relation, while amongst others controlling for 'FDI-inflow competitors' BIT signings', for the following definitions of 'peers': according to bilateral trade relations, common language, common colonial history, common participations in international organisations; or common region.

was a driver of IIA conclusions. This interpretation is further supported by the fact that DCs increasingly signed and concluded IIAs with other DCs since 1990 (they amounted to around half of the BITs signed during that period).[69] Indeed, since these countries had no existing FDI flows amongst themselves and no prospects thereof in the near future, these findings do not seem to be driven by rational calculus and therefore suggest imitation.[70]

III.3. Explanatory Relevance of Potentially Relevant Influencers

A selectorate theory allows for the possibility that a leader does not consider potentially relevant influencers when the leader's political survival is not affected by such negligence.

There indeed exists some evidence that leaders in DCs sometimes concluded IIAs merely to provide themselves with photo opportunities.[71] However, the empirical evidence just discussed (Section III.2) suggests that DCs also concluded IIAs after engaging in a rational cost-benefit calculus, which prevents us from excluding at the outset the causal/explanatory relevance of at least some of the previously identified potentially relevant influencers – and therewith the explanatory relevance of how IIA conclusions affect these potentially relevant influencers.

III.4. Notable Implication

Remarkably, a selectorate theory implies that DCs, even though they had virtually no capital-exporting capacity, may have concluded IIAs solely to protect foreign investment (that is, out of a 'foreign investment protection motivation').[72] Indeed, assume that nobody believes that IIAs increase FDI flows or that nobody believes that IIAs will further

---

[69] UNCTAD, *Bilateral Investment Treaties, 1959–1999* (United Nations 2000) 4.

[70] Elkins, Guzman and Simmons (n 8) 818 ff.

[71] Researchers have come across government files stating so. For Pakistan, for instance, see for example, Poulsen and Aisbett (n 67) 280.

[72] This theoretical possibility is generally not recognised by scholars (who implicitly/unconsciously reason within a unitary State framework). Instead of many, Omar E García-Bolívar, *Defining an ICSID Investment: Why Economic Development Should be the Core Element* (Investment Treaty News Quartely 2(3), April 2012) 3: 'it is clear that states enter into IIAs with the expectation that this will enhance the chances of attracting capital, and that this will, in turn, promote their economic development.'

development;[73] in this situation, a DC may still conclude IIAs if foreign firms' influence on the said country's decision-making is strong enough.[74] Since foreign firms are only interested in protecting their foreign investments, that DC, by extension, would conclude those IIAs solely to protect foreign investments – and not out of an increased FDI-inflow motivation (that is, not to compete for capital).

IV. EMPIRICAL SUPPORT

IV.1. General Predictions

Without additional assumptions about the relative strength of the different potentially relevant influencers, a selectorate theory is indeterminate on whether DCs conclude IIAs at all. This is ultimately an empirical question as it requires a detailed study (read: a case study) of the said country's internal dynamics. The raw theory, however, makes some general predictions which seem to be supported by the data.

First, it predicts that IIAs concluded by DCs are likely to have significantly increased since 1990 because the masses are likely to have supported IIA conclusions after that date, in both young democracies and military dictatorships.[75] This prediction is consistent with the data: the number of concluded IIAs exploded after the Cold War.[76]

Second, it predicts that if a DC did not conclude IIAs after 1990, it is most likely because domestic firms (which may oppose IIAs) amounted to powerful relevant influencers. This prediction appears consistent with the dynamics which were at play in Brazil for instance.

---

[73] In such conditions, we can expect that domestic firms will not oppose the conclusion of IIAs, and that the masses will either be indifferent vis-à-vis the conclusion of IIAs (if they believe that IIAs do not impact development; for example, because they underestimate IIAs' sovereignty-restriction risk) or they will oppose it (if they anticipate IIAs' sovereignty-restriction risk).

[74] This situation is, obviously, most likely in non-democratic developing countries wherein the (military) government primarily requires financial and/or military resources to secure its political survival. Foreign investors may provide that government with financial resources (bribery), foreign aid (through their home States), and/or military aid (through their home States).

[75] Even military dictators face the threat of revolutions and therefore respond – to some degree – to the preferences of non-military relevant influencers; most notably, to the preferences of the masses.

[76] See above (n 2).

Third, it predicts that foreign firms may pressure their own home States to put pressure on the host State to conclude IIAs. This prediction appears consistent with the data: a recent empirical study of the concluded BITs by the United States finds that if a DC received military aid from the US, that DC was significantly more likely to conclude a BIT with the US.[77]

IV.2. Short Case Studies

The following two short case studies strongly suggest that a selectorate theory (that is, a non-unitary State perspective) is better suited than a unitary State theory to account for some of the IIAs. Because both studies deal with countries having quite large economies, one may feel that there exists a case selection bias – namely, that the superiority of the selectorate theory only exists for countries exhibiting large economies.[78] Although case studies of smaller economies are ultimately needed to resolve this issue, the goal of this Section is more modest: it only understands those two studies to suggest that such a superiority may exist more generally and that, until proven otherwise, it is worthwhile for a researcher to keep a selectorate theory in mind when thinking about the conclusion of IIAs.

The case of Brazil

Brazil is one of a couple of countries which have no IIA in force. Actually, Brazil signed fourteen BITs during the 1990s, but did not conclude (ratify) a single one of them.

The following explanations for Brazil's non-ratification are generally advanced – none of which appears convincing. *First*, although the existence of general opposition in Brazil against FDI inflows from developed countries cannot generally be rejected,[79] the case for it is rather weak during the 1990s: there seems to be no general opposition

---

[77] Adam Chilton, 'The Politics of the United States' Bilateral Investment Treaty Program' Working Paper, January 2014 [On file with the author], 19 ff., based on the United States 46 BITs that are in force today (45 of which entered into force during the twentieth century). Since the only reason for the United States to make such a threat would have been the influence of its (foreign investment-making) domestic firms, we may reasonably interpret this statistical finding as evidence that foreign firms influenced the conclusion of IIAs by developing countries (through their home State).

[78] I thank Eyal Benvenisti for suggesting this potential case selection bias.

[79] See above (n 51 and the text preceding it) for the arguments underlying the view that such an opposition may have existed.

against the conclusion of international treaties (in other words, against binding oneself under public international law) as Brazil concluded multiple ones during the 1990s;[80] and there seems to be no general opposition against FDI inflows because Brazil enacted multiple domestic investor-friendly laws since the middle of the twentieth century,[81] and because Brazil's media aggressively supported investor-friendly policies during the 1990s.[82] *Second*, the argument that IIAs were not concluded because they were perceived as violating the Brazilian constitution is also weak: the Brazilian constitution (enacted 5 October 1988) does not appear to represent a real barrier as it was amended over sixty-four times between 1988 and 2010.[83] *Third*, the argument that Brazil thought that it did not have to conclude IIAs because it already enacted domestic investor-friendly laws is also unconvincing: this argument misses the point of IIAs which is either to reduce political risk by imposing public international legal obligations on States (domestic legislations, by definition, do not create such obligations) or to imitate other States' behaviours. *Fourth*, the argument that Brazil thought that a reduction of its

---

80 Including, most notably perhaps, double tax treaties (Leany Lemos and Daniela Campello, 'The Non-Ratification of Bilateral Investment Treaties in Brazil: A Story of Conflict in a Land of Cooperation' Working Paper, April 2013, available at SSRN: <http://ssrncom/abstract=2243120> 12), and Brazil's membership to the WTO on 1 January 1995.

81 Brazil encouraged foreign investments in most manufacturing sectors during most of the second half of the twentieth century; see for example, Ben Ross Schneider, 'Big Business in Brazil: Leveraging Natural Endowments and State Support for International Expansion', in Lael Brainard and Leonardo Martinez-Diaz (eds), *Brazil as an Economic Superpower? Understanding Brazil's Changing Role in the Global Economy* (Brookings Institution Press 2009) 177. It is important to observe that such domestic laws do not alter Brazil's perceived relevant political risk. We can consequently expect domestic firms not to have opposed such domestic legislations.

82 See for example, Lemos and Campello (n 80) 8: 'News in the early 1990s often urged Brazil to move fast to attract investors, in face of the competition entailed by the transition to capitalism of former communist countries and China. Argentina's privatization process was also extensively reported and used as justification for the need to adopt market friendly policies designed to attract investment.'

83 For a detailed description of those amendments, see Chamber of Deputies, *Constitution of the Federal Republic of Brazil: Constitutional text of October 5, 1988, with the alterations introduced by Constitutional Amendments N. 1/1992 through 64/2010 and by Revision Constitutional Amendments N. 1/1994 through 6/1994* (Documentation and Information Center, Publishing Coordination, Chamber of Deputies 2010).

political risk through the conclusion of IIAs would not impact FDI inflows because of its large market and/or natural resources is also unconvincing: if the pool of foreign investments was not perceived as fully inelastic, which we can reasonably expect,[84] then concluded IIAs would have been perceived as potentially the total amount of FDI inflows. In consequence, a unitary State perspective does not seem to be able to explain Brazil's behaviour with respect to the conclusion of IIAs.

A selectorate theory suggests another explanation: domestic firms had substantial influence on State decision-making in the context of IIAs and were therefore able to oppose their conclusion. There appears to be some evidence supporting the claim that big domestic firms had a strong influence on State decision-making in Brazil during the twentieth century,[85] and thus providing some preliminary support for the selectorate theory explanation of Brazil's non-ratification attitude. Further empirical research is required to confirm this explanation.

The case of South Africa

South Africa started concluding IIAs in the middle of the 1990s, that is, during the decade marked by the disintegration of the Apartheid regime. Arguably in order to encourage affirmative action measures aimed at increasing the black population's ownership and participation in the economy, the new Constitution, although promising compensation for

---

[84] Evidence that the inelasticity view was not widespread is given by 'four treaties were tabled together at the threshold committee on November 1996 [...] The rapporteurs were all members of the governing coalition, and their drafts received full approval. They revealed a pervading positive view of the treaties, which were expected not only to make Brazil more competitive vis-à-vis competing Asian countries (especially China)' (Lemos and Campello (n 80) 18).

[85] Prior to the 1990s, Brazil's big domestic businesses had close ties to the government and tended to benefit from significant government support; see for example, Schneider (n 81) 160, '[big domestic businesses] enjoyed protection (banking, steel, telecommunications, and transport) or received [...] sustained state assistance (construction and petrochemicals)'.

Brazil's corporate law revision in 2001 (Corporate law, Nr 6.404/1976, was amended, Nr 10.303/2001), in which it insufficiently increased the protection of minority shareholders by international standards and according to economic development theories, may be understood as evidence that big domestic firms influence State decision-making. Actually even those political scientists who are generally sceptical about the business sector's substantial influence on State decision-making in Latin America tend to interpret this rejection in this way; see, perhaps most notably, Ben Ross Schneider, 'Economic Liberalization and Corporate Governance: The Resilience of Business Groups in Latin America' (2008) 40 Comparative Politics 379, 397, endnote 50.

expropriation, did not promise compensation at the 'fair market value' and only promised compensation for direct expropriation.[86] These standards were in clear opposition to the BITs South Africa started to conclude with developed countries during that period, as these treaties required compensation amounting to the 'genuine value of the investment' (read: fair market value) for both direct and indirect expropriations.

In 1995, South Africa signed a BIT with Canada (note: this BIT was never ratified) which included preferential measures towards Canada's aboriginal people, yet did not include any exclusion for affirmative action measures in South Africa.[87]

It has been held that South Africa simply did not properly understand the norms it was agreeing upon.[88] There is, however, some evidence suggesting that DCs generally, including South Africa, actually did understand quite well the norms they were signing: developing-developing BITs seem to exhibit significantly and substantially less constraining (that is, restricting State behaviour less) 'national-treatment clauses' and 'transfer clauses' than developed-developing BITs;[89] this variation strongly suggests an understanding of these norms by DCs.[90]

A selectorate theory proposes an alternative explanation (an explanation which does not require one to assume an ignorant South Africa): foreign firms may influence State decision-making in South Africa in the context of the conclusion of IIAs. Since such influence is especially likely for developed-developing IIAs because developed countries exhibited powerful (foreign-investment-making) firms, we should expect developed-developing IIAs to be more constraining for DCs than

---

[86] See Skovgaard Poulsen (n 49) 7.

[87] Ibid at 9.

[88] For such a (bounded-rationality) explanation, see ibid at 7 ff.

[89] Lauge N Skovgaard Poulsen, 'The Politics of South-South Bilateral Investment Treaties', in Tomer Broude, Marc L Busch and Amelia Porges (eds), *The Politics of International Economic Law* (CUP 2011) 192 ff. and 201, based on a statistical analysis of a random sample of BITs signed by developing countries between 1994 and 2006 (303 BITs; 191 of which were signed between 1994 and 2000; and 124 of which amount to developing-developing BITs). Although one may hold that the difference is solely driven by the BITs signed after 2000 (once the potential of BITs became widely known due to the rise of investment claims), this is unlikely: developing countries already argued for such less-constraining clauses during the multilateral discussions on the 'UN Draft Code on Transnational Corporations' in the 1980s (see for example, ibid 191 and 194).

[90] I am not saying, however, that they correctly anticipated how investment arbitral tribunals would interpret these norms.

developing-developing IIAs; this is consistent with the data. Furthermore, since we can expect foreign firms to have only focused on influencing State decision-making in the context of the conclusion of IIAs (and not on constitutional issues) as only IIAs allow to decrease South Africa's political risk, we should expect IIAs to be more constraining than South Africa's constitution; this is again consistent with the data.

IV.3. Positive Statistical Association between the Conclusion of BITs and the Conclusion of FDI-Inflow Competitors' BITs

Empirical studies of BITs during the twentieth century find a statistically significant positive association (that is, positive correlation) between the probability that a DC concludes a BIT and the conclusion of BITs by its FDI-inflow competitors; an FDI-inflow competitor is defined as a country whose export markets are similar and/or which exports the same basket of goods.[91] Importantly, when BITs are analysed only during the 1990s, empirical studies find that the strength of this positive association becomes substantially smaller (some studies even find that it becomes statistically insignificant).[92] Note that we can arguably expect the probability of a DC concluding an IIA to also be positively related to FDI-inflow competitors' IIAs.

Traditional interpretation

This positive statistical association tends to be interpreted as evidence that DCs 'competed for capital' and thus that DCs on average concluded IIAs during the twentieth century to, amongst others, 'compete for capital'; that is, because they exhibited an increased FDI-inflow motivation (that is, a competition-for-capital motivation).[93] A selectorate

---

[91] Seminally, Elkins, Guzman and Simmons (n 8) 811, based on a panel data analysis of all BITs signed between 1958 and 2000 (except developed-developed BITs): 'The evidence suggests that potential hosts are more likely to sign BITs when their competitors have done so'; Jandhyala, Henisz and Mansfield (n 65) 1063, based on a panel-data analysis of all BITs signed between 1970 and 2000.

[92] See respectively Jandhyala, Henisz and Mansfield (n 65) 1063; and Poulsen and Aisbett (n 67) 300 (using the dataset from Elkins, Guzman and Simmons (n 8)).

[93] Seminal for spreading such an interpretation are the authors of the first empirical study testing this association: Elkins, Guzman and Simmons (n 8) 825 and 836, 'The possibility of investment diversion means that governments may have competitive reasons to implement BITs [...] [we interpret the data as] fairly convincing evidence of the importance of competition for capital among developing countries in explaining the proliferation of BITs'. 'Amongst others'

theory, however, points out that such an interpretation does not readily follow from this positive statistical association.[94]

Selectorate theory interpretation

Think of a world wherein the only relevant influencers supporting the conclusion of IIAs are foreign firms. Assume that it is generally believed that IIAs increase FDI flows, but that nobody believes that IIAs further development. If either the masses or domestic firms amount to relevant influencers and if both oppose IIAs, then DCs' IIA-signing patterns may still exhibit such a positive statistical association. Indeed, on the one hand, FDI-inflow competing countries' IIAs do not affect the strength of the foreign firms' political support since those signings do not affect the political risk to which their foreign investments are exposed. On the other hand, FDI-inflow competitors' IIAs reduce the strength of the masses' and domestic firms' opposition because those agreements reduce the expected increase in FDI inflows (and thus reduce the expected negative consequences) that the conclusion of IIAs may potentially yield. In this

---

because nothing of what I am saying excludes that other motivations were also driving developing countries' conclusions of IIAs. See Section III.2 for a discussion of other potential underlying motivations.

[94] The competition-for-capital motivation interpretation has also been attacked from a unitary State perspective. None of these attacks appears, however, to be convincing. First, it has been argued that if such a motivation had existed, then we would have observed more investor-friendly IIAs (Santiago Montt, *State Liability in Investment Treaty Arbitration: Global Constitutional and Administrative Law in the BIT Generation* (Hart 2009) 110: 'there were more preferable alternatives for investors [...] that is, treaties that could have offered more convenient standards to foreign investors'). This argument is flawed for at least two reasons. On the one hand, the conclusion of IIAs by developing countries may be driven by a development motivation which may prevent them from offering better conditions to foreign investors. On the other hand, developed countries may face domestic opposition to conclude IIAs by the masses; consequently, if more investor-friendly conditions would have led to domestic opposition (due to a threat of higher FDI outflows and/or a threat to their home State's sovereignty), then they would never have been on the table. Second, it has been argued that if a competition-for-capital motivation had existed, then 'their content should have become progressively more investor-friendly over time' (Poulsen (n 49) 4). This argument is unconvincing. We can reasonably expect developing countries to have anticipated that other FDI-inflow competitors would also conclude IIAs in the future (and if not, then developed countries would have pointed it out so as to get the best possible conditions for their foreign investors) and therefore that these countries would conclude as investor-friendly IIAs as they are willing to conclude from the beginning.

thought experiment, the positive statistical association would be driven by foreign firms and therefore by a foreign investment protection motivation (rather than by a competition for capital motivation). In short, although the positive statistical association arises because of the existence of a competition for capital amongst them, it does not necessarily imply that DCs concluded IIAs to 'compete for capital'.

Actually, this abstract thought experiment is not that far-fetched and might capture the conclusion of IIAs by DCs before 1990. Indeed, we have seen that a case can be made that before 1990 both the masses and domestic firms in DCs opposed IIAs,[95] so that only foreign firms supported IIAs. If foreign firms were the only supporters of IIAs, then the positive statistical association strongly suggests that DCs concluded IIAs out of a foreign investment protection motivation.

The fact that the positive association substantially decreased (possibly even disappeared) during the 1990s actually supports the aforementioned interpretation. Indeed, it was noted above that a case can be made that the masses in DCs are likely to have become supportive of IIAs after 1990.[96] This shift in the masses' preferences may yield such a reduction in the positive statistical association between developing States: if the masses want to increase FDI inflows,[97] rather than just prevent a decrease in FDI inflows due to diversions to other States, then the masses would want to conclude IIAs as quickly as possible (that is, irrespective of the IIA signings of its FDI-inflow competitors).

Insofar as this argumentation is sound, we can hold that the observed positive statistical association suggests that a foreign investment protection motivation drove, amongst others, DCs towards the conclusion of IIAs before 1990; and that a development motivation (taking the form of an increased FDI-inflow motivation) and a foreign investment protection motivation led, amongst others, DCs to conclude IIAs during the 1990s.

V. CONCLUSION

This Chapter has argued that within international investment law, a non-unitary State perspective is preferable to a unitary State perspective. By proposing a 'selectorate theory' of State decision-making in the

95 See above Section III.1.

96 See above Section III.1.

97 The dire economic prospects that developing States were facing and the perceived economic benefits promised by IIAs (see above Section III.1) strongly suggest that the masses wanted to increase FDI inflows after 1990.

context of the conclusion of IIAs, this Chapter showed that a non-unitary State perspective: (i) can be tractable despite being less parsimonious, and therefore remain fairly easy to understand and to use by a wide audience; (ii) makes predictions about the overall evolution of DCs' IIAs that are empirically consistent; (iii) allows explanation of certain State decision-making in the context of the conclusion of IIAs which a unitary State theory has a difficult time fully explaining (see the case studies of Brazil and South Africa); and (iv) makes it clear that the widespread competition for capital interpretation does not readily follow from the empirical finding that there exists a positive statistical association (that is, statistically significant correlation) between the probability of a DC signing (and arguably concluding) a BIT and the conclusion of BITs by its FDI-inflow competitors. Finally, this Chapter also showed that DCs, even though they amounted to capital-importing institutions during the twentieth century (since they had virtually no existing foreign investments and little prospects of having such investments in the near future), need not have concluded IIAs to attract FDI inflows (and therewith further development), but may have done so solely to protect foreign investments.

15. Political Economy and International Water Law: Political Economy Induced Changes to the Uptake of Benefit Sharing in International Water Law

Laurence Boisson de Chazournes and Christina Leb*

I. INTRODUCTION: THE BENEFIT SHARING NOTION AND TRANSBOUNDARY WATER COOPERATION

Over recent decades, the sharing of benefits derived from the use of natural resources has emerged as a governing principle in some Multilateral Environmental Agreements (MEAs), most notably the 1992 Convention on Biological Diversity (CBD)[1] and its 2010 Protocol on Access to Genetic Resources and the Fair and Equitable Sharing of Benefits Arising from their Utilization (Nagoya Protocol) explicitly refer to and operationalize it.[2] Interestingly, neither document defines the concept of 'fair and equitable'. As pointed out in the 2002 Bonn Guidelines, which were adopted to assist the Parties and other stakeholders in developing

* The authors would like to thank Jason Rudall for his help with the editing of the present contribution. The findings, interpretations and conclusions expressed in this Chapter are entirely those of the authors and do not represent the views of the World Bank, its Executive Directors, or the countries they represent.

[1] Convention on Biological Diversity (adopted 5 June 1992, entered into force 29 December 1993) 1760 UNTS 79 (CBD).

[2] Protocol on Access to Genetic Resources and the Fair and Equitable Sharing of Benefits Arising from their Utilization (adopted 29 October 2010, entered into force 12 October 2014) (Nagoya Protocol) <http://www.cbd.int/abs/> accessed 9 October 2014.

benefit sharing strategies, it was considered that what is regarded as fair and equitable will vary 'in light of the circumstances'.[3]

This very same argument is also reflected in the principle of equitable and reasonable utilization of transboundary water resources. Similar to the Bonn Guidelines and the Nagoya Protocol, which adopted an approach that reflects the various proportionate contributions in the distribution of benefits,[4] International Water Law (IWL) provides criteria to determine equitable and reasonable utilization. In the context of benefit sharing on genetic resources, the contributions to access, knowledge, innovation and value addition are taken into account; whereas in the context of transboundary water resources, factors such as geographic, hydrologic and climatic conditions, as well as dependence on the resource, and existing and future uses, are considered.

The differences in the factors taken into account to assess equity and their implications for benefit sharing arrangements ultimately being adopted are due to the economic, social and resource specific factors that intervene in these two areas of environmental regulation. An in-depth analysis of the International Political Economy (IPE), given the interaction between national politics and – in the context of transboundary waters more importantly – the behavior of States on the international plane, can explain the provenance of such rules and shed light on potential future trends.

In an effort to expand the discipline of IPE analysis, which has so far largely been confined to the discipline of international economic relations,[5] this Chapter analyzes the anchoring of benefit sharing arrangements between States sharing hydrologic systems in IWL. IPE analysis is mostly premised on the interaction between economic and political considerations in the context of inter-State relations,[6] and as such it represents a useful tool to analyze in a comprehensive way the considerations at stake in benefit sharing arrangements. While economic considerations are a key factor in benefit sharing arrangements, such as in the

---

[3] Bonn Guidelines on Access to Genetic Resources and Fair and Equitable Sharing of the Benefits Arising out of their Utilization (the Bonn Guidelines) para 45 <https://www.cbd.int/doc/publications/cbd-bonn-gdls-en.pdf> accessed 9 October 2014.

[4] Thomas Greiber et al., *An Explanatory Guide to the Nagoya Protocol on Access and Benefit-Sharing* (IUCN Environmental Law Paper No. 83, 2012) 58.

[5] See Anne van Aaken and Joel P Trachtman, 'Political Economy of International Law: Towards a Holistic Model of State Behaviour', above in this Volume.

[6] Ibid 10.

context of the CBD, in the case of internationally shared waters, hydrologic factors are an additional endogenous determinant to State relations. Similar to economic (for example, trade) relations between States, transboundary water systems establish interdependence, which obliges countries to engage in international relations and enter into agreements with their neighbors and countries sharing the same hydrologic system.

This Chapter responds to the questions as to why IWL emerged and on the increasing influence of local and national political processes as determinants for the international principles and norms of water law. IPE analysis is used to explain the determinants of IWL creation – law as *explanandum*. Given the strategic importance that governments attribute to their water resources, the State is the primary unit of analysis. Though, as this Chapter shows, the increasingly accented impact of the transboundary management of waters on national and local water availability (both in terms of quantity and quality) give national and local stakeholders and interest groups an increasingly deterministic role in shaping the content of IWL.

IPE analysis in this context can help highlight that the consequences of benefit sharing can be in the interests of a given State (a function of law as *explanans*). It can also add to the calculus of considerations (for example in theorizing negotiations) that were previously – advertently or otherwise – not taken into account (such as the concerns of local populations and the protection of the environment). Further still, it can be used to show that States should be discouraged from 'defecting' on their benefit sharing obligations or from exclusively pursuing narrow, short-term interests.

II. THE NOTION OF BENEFIT SHARING: ENVIRONMENTAL, SOCIAL, ECONOMIC AND LEGAL FACETS

Benefit sharing is the outcome of a process of realization that in a complex and interdependent world (i) there are fewer benefits that can be achieved by unilateral action than through cooperation with stakeholders in the same challenge; and (ii) that formulas to share the benefits of cooperative behavior need to be agreed upon to achieve equity that will spur continued cooperation.

In behavioral science and game theory this has been demonstrated through the concept of the prisoner's dilemma.[7] This is a symmetric two-person game in which non-cooperation pays for both players individually no matter what the other does. Yet, together, they are both better off if they cooperate. Through iterations of interaction, they learn over time that cooperative behavior pays off and yields higher benefits, even if there are short-term incentives for defection.[8] The situation of the iterated prisoner's dilemma is similar to the one faced in the management of transboundary water systems as States sharing these systems cannot escape their hydrologic interdependence.

II.1. The Benefit Sharing Notion and Its Origins

The physical availability of water is one of the many benefits transboundary water systems provide to riparian countries. Accessibility is a direct benefit of hydrologic systems running through or straddling a State's territory. In addition, these systems provide a wide range of other benefits that can be derived from the water flowing within. These include the food that can be produced using the resource for irrigation or animal husbandry, as well as benefits derived from non-consumptive uses such as navigation, recreation, biodiversity, fisheries and hydropower. The amount of benefits that can ultimately be derived from a hydrologic system depends to a large extent on the quality of its management. The quantity of available water for instance can be influenced through good watershed management that minimizes erosion, maximizes infiltration into the ground and thus slowing run-off, as well as through storage reservoirs of a size that can store and 'transfer' the resource from water abundant to water deficient years.[9]

In a transboundary water system, potential benefits available from the entire system cannot always be maximized by one riparian alone. In most transboundary situations, optimizing benefits requires some sort of coordination among riparian States sharing the water resources. Water creates interdependency between them; a downstream riparian, for example, may not be in a position to reduce sediment transport in the river without positive watershed management intervention upstream. At the same time, uses by one State are likely to affect one or more of its

---

[7] See Meredith Kolsky Lewis, 'International Political Economy and the Prisoner's Dilemma: Compliance with International Law', above in this Volume.

[8] This game yields the same results for two-player and multi-player settings.

[9] Claudia Sadoff, Thomas Greiber, Mark Smith and Ger Bergkamp, *SHARE – Managing Water Across Boundaries* (IUCN 2008) 21.

co-riparian States either immediately – for instance in case of serious pollution – or over time through, for example, significant abstraction that establishes existing uses and may foreclose future uses of others.

The prospective additional benefits that can be gained through coordinated activities with a co-riparian country become the driver for cooperation on transboundary water resources management and development. Cooperation is the process by which States work together to achieve a common purpose that produces additional mutual benefits that would be unavailable with unilateral action.[10] Countries cooperate where they can see that the benefits of collaboration outweigh the costs; these costs include the benefits of unilateral water uses a country has to forgo to reduce the negative impact of its uses to the country it would like to cooperate with in order to realize net gains overall. These net benefits are then being shared across boundaries and among the cooperating States.

These ideas have been analyzed in economic and political science literature and have led to the crystallization of the so called 'benefit sharing concept' in the context of transboundary water cooperation.[11] The underlying idea of the benefit sharing concept is that, to say it in a simplified way, cooperation creates win-win situations. Cooperation – rather than conflict or competition among actors – leads to an increase of overall benefits which can subsequently be shared among all actors. A useful and current illustration of the application of the benefit sharing concept to transboundary rivers has been developed by Sadoff and Grey. The two authors distinguish between four types of benefits that can be derived from cooperative management of transboundary watercourses: (1) benefits *to* the river, (2) benefits *from* the river, (3) reduction of costs *because of* the river, and (4) benefits *beyond* the river.[12] The first type of benefits focuses on the ecological benefits that occur if riparian States join together to maintain a healthy aquatic environment in the river basin.

---

[10] I William Zartman, 'Concept: Cooperation' (2008) 30 PIN Points 5–7.

[11] Conceptualizations of benefit sharing in the context of transboundary watercourses have been presented by: Claudia W Sadoff and David Grey, 'Beyond the River: The Benefits of Cooperation on International Rivers' (2002) 4 WP 389–403; David Phillips et al., *Transboundary Water Co-operation as a Tool for Conflict Prevention and Broader Benefit Sharing* (Global Development Studies No. 4, Ministry of Foreign Affairs, Sweden, 2006); David Phillips, Shaddad Attili, Stephen C McCaffrey and John Murray, 'The Jordan River Basin: 2. Potential Future Allocation to the Co-riparians' (2007) 32 WI 39–62; David Phillips et al., *The TWO Analysis: Introducing a Methodology for the Transboundary Waters Opportunity Analysis* (Report No. 23, SIWI, Stockholm, 2008); Sadoff et al. (n 9).

[12] Sadoff and Grey (n 11) 389–403; Sadoff et al. (n 9) 23–5.

To a certain extent, the authors argue, these benefits *to* the river are a pre-requisite to derive the second type of benefits, benefits *from* the river.[13] This second type is linked to the economic benefits that can be reaped from the river; again the argument goes that cooperative action will increase the benefits that can be generated. The third type of benefits comes closest to explaining how benefit sharing in itself can contribute to increasing the 'basket of benefits',[14] which is the range of different benefits that become available. Here the benefit is the reduction of costs that arise *because of the river*, alluding to the costs of political conflict over the river. Cooperation and benefit sharing can reduce these tensions. Benefits *beyond* the river are those that occur as a follow-on effect of benefits derived *from* and reduction of costs *because of the* river; they concern forward linkages in the economy into sectors that are indirectly related to the management of transboundary water resources. These forward linkages are the result of improved relationships among riparian States. They occur, for example, where riparian States experience improvements in their political relationships due to profitable or successful cooperation with respect to their shared waters and subsequently seek additional cooperative relationships in other sectors of their economy, including trade, scientific cooperation and technology exchange. Benefits that occur because of these new relationships are benefits of the fourth type.[15]

The Sadoff-Grey model[16] illustrates the various types of benefits that can be created along transboundary rivers; yet, the concept can also be applied to transboundary aquifers and lakes. The model describes benefit sharing in the context of promoting cooperation on transboundary river basins: when countries acknowledge the additional benefits that can be derived from cooperation on transboundary water systems, they are more

---

13 Sadoff and Grey (n 11) 395.

14 The term 'basket of benefits' was coined in Phillips et al., (n 11).

15 It goes without saying that successful cooperation in non-water-related sectors can be the source of cooperation on transboundary waters. Often forward linkages travel both ways.

16 Other models include Transboundary Waters Opportunity Analysis (TWO Analysis), a framework which identifies all potential benefits that can be derived from the basin and can be shared equitably among basin States (see Phillips et al., (n 11)); and the ECO^2 Model, which focuses on finding a balance between development and protection of the resource in the framework of sustainable development (see Marius Claassen, *Focus on CSIR Research in Water Resources: ECO2 – Sharing Benefits from Water Resources* (CSIR, Conference Paper presented at the Stockholm World Water Week, 13–17 August 2007) <http://researchspace.csir.co.za/dspace/handle/10204/1127> accessed 13 October 2014.

likely to cooperate in the pursuit of generating and sharing these additional benefits. The actors in this conceptualization are countries. The benefit sharing concept, however, equally applies to actors at the local, community and individual level. These are often the major stakeholders of benefit sharing arrangements between countries. Benefits that accrue between countries trickle down to government authorities, local communities, individual water users and other affected people. Other descriptions of the benefit sharing concept, such as in the literature on benefit sharing around forest development and in the context of hydropower development and its impact on local communities,[17] focus more on sharing among all those who are affected by a new project or legislation. Rather than just analyzing the benefits a project or policy brings for a country as a whole, the distribution of benefits among different communities – at the local level – is analyzed.

This Chapter investigates the question of how the concept of benefit sharing is reflected in International Law (IL) and which beneficiary parties are considered. For the purpose of this analysis, which considers the uptake of the concept in IWL, the focus will be on benefit sharing between States as the primary subjects of IL.

II.2. The Legal Framing of Benefit Sharing in International Water Law

The benefit sharing approach has been hailed by some as a new and innovative way to operationalize the principle of equitable and reasonable utilization, one of the cornerstone principles of IWL.[18] The document associated with firmly establishing the principle of equitable and reasonable utilization as one of the key principles of IWL is the 1966 Helsinki Rules on the Use of the Waters of International Rivers.[19] These rules were drawn up based on existing water treaties and State practice on the use of transboundary waters to that date. Article IV of the Helsinki Rules

---

[17] Pham Thu Thuy et al., *Approaches to Benefit-Sharing: A Preliminary Comparative Analysis of 13 REDD+ Countries* (Working Paper No. 108, CIFOR, Bogor, Indonesia, 2013); Chaogang Wang, 'A Guide for Local Benefit Sharing in Hydropower Projects' (World Bank Social Development Papers, Paper No. 128, June 2012) 1.

[18] Richard Paisley, 'Adversaries into Partners: International Water Law and the Equitable Sharing of Downstream Benefits' (2002) 3 Melb J Int L 280–300.

[19] International Law Association (ILA), *Report of the Fifty-Second Conference held at Helsinki, August 14th to August 20th, 1966* (ILA, London, 1967) 478–532.

entitles each basin State, 'within its territory, to a reasonable and equitable share in the beneficial uses of the waters of an international drainage basin'. At the heart of this principle lies the obligation to utilize transboundary watercourses in an equitable manner. This obligation is accompanied by a correlative right of each basin State to an equitable share of the uses and benefits therefrom.[20]

The first sentence of Article 5 (1) of the 1997 Convention on the Law of the Non-Navigational Uses of International Watercourses (1997 UN Watercourses Convention) expresses the obligation. It states that: 'Watercourse States shall in their respective territories utilize an international watercourse in an equitable and reasonable manner.' The second sentence of Article 5 (1) obliges watercourse States to use and develop an international watercourse 'with a view to attaining optimal and sustainable utilization thereof and benefits therefrom [...]'. According to the International Law Commission (ILC), the objective to be sought therefore is the attainment of 'maximum possible benefits for all watercourse States'.[21] As much as this paragraph refers to both actions by individual States as well as to cooperative measures, this formula anchors the benefit sharing approach in the principle of equitable and reasonable utilization.[22] States enter into agreements on benefit sharing when they expect that cooperative management and development of a hydrologic system allows them to increase the benefits available from the common resource and share them equitably.

What equity means in each specific basin context has to be first and foremost decided by the watercourse States concerned. In the case of unilateral development and the absence of cooperative development for optimal utilization, the various formulations of the principle of equitable and reasonable use in the 1997 UN Watercourses Convention and other documents provide guidance through non-exhaustive lists of criteria to consider. In line with the principle of the equality of rights, each State has an equal right to an equitable share of the water resources and benefits that can be derived therefrom.[23] State entitlements follow equity considerations that are to be based on the specific circumstances of each transboundary watercourse or aquifer system.

---

[20] International Law Commission (ILC), 'The Law of Non-Navigational Uses of International Watercourses. Draft Articles and Commentaries thereto adopted by the Drafting Committee on second reading: Articles 1–33' (1994) II(2) ILC Yb 98, para 222.

[21] Ibid 97.

[22] Ibid.

[23] Ibid 98; ILA (n 19) 487; ILC (n 20) 98.

Before discussing how equity is assessed, the following paragraphs will present an analysis of the characteristics of and the Political Economy (PE) influences on the interpretation and formulation of the principle of equitable and reasonable use.

Political economy influences on early conceptualization of benefit sharing in International Water Law

While the principle of equitable and reasonable utilization is today one of the core principles of IWL, its origins are found at the national level. Early formulations of the principle occurred in particular in the jurisdiction of the United States Supreme Court concerning disputes between federal States with respect to consumptive use of shared watercourses. In the decisions addressing interstate disputes about water apportionment,[24] the US Supreme Court referred to the 'doctrine of equitable apportionment'.[25] For example, the case *State of Kansas v State of Colorado*[26] – decided by the US Supreme Court in 1907 – concerned irrigation benefits. Kansas demanded an interdiction of diversions by Colorado of the water of the Arkansas River. Kansas claimed that the increase in the area of irrigated fields in Colorado harmed irrigation in its western counties due to a decrease in flow volume. The decision of the Court is remarkable: while acknowledging that the 'irrigation of Colorado has worked some detriment to the southwestern part of Kansas', at the same time it also noted that the material damages in Kansas did not outweigh the benefits derived from irrigation in Colorado.[27] The Supreme Court held that 'when we compare the amount of this detriment with the great benefit which has obviously resulted to the counties in Colorado, it would seem that equality of right and equity between the two States forbids any interference with the present withdrawal of water in Colorado for purposes of irrigation'.[28] The Court based its decision on the

---

[24] Stephen C McCaffrey, *The Law of International Watercourses – Non-navigational Uses* (2nd edn, OUP 2007) 384; Lucius Caflish, 'Règles générales du droit des cours d'eau internationaux' (1989) 219 Recueil des Cours 141 ff.; Report of the Special Rapporteur Stephen C McCaffrey, 'Second Report on the Law of the Non-Navigational Uses of International Watercourses' (1986) II(1) ILC Yb 129 FN 316; Report of the Special Rapporteur Stephen M Schwebel, 'Third Report on the Law of the Non-Navigational Uses of International Watercourses' (1982) II(1) ILC Yb 75 ff.

[25] McCaffrey (n 24) 385.

[26] *State of Kansas v Colorado* 206 US 46–119 (1907); case cited in Report of the Special Rapporteur McCaffrey (n 24) 129.

[27] *State of Kansas v Colorado* 206 (n 26) 113f.

[28] Ibid 114.

equitable distribution of economic benefits that were derived from the river,[29] which at that time brought economic benefits to Colorado that went far beyond the benefits that could have been and had been achieved by Kansas so far. At the same time, the Court made it clear that this decision was without prejudice to the right of Kansas to file a claim in the future in case their benefits (and harm) were no longer equitably distributed.[30]

This decision highlights that the doctrine of equitable apportionment looks at a much wider understanding of benefits derived from water than just access and right to a certain water volume. The Court looked at the gains that can be derived from the availability of water in general. In the case of irrigation, benefits include crops, food security, socioeconomic development as well as the benefit of flow regulation that ensures regular water supply to fertile grounds or otherwise non-arable land and makes agriculture resistant to unexpected rainfall variations. At the same time, the Court acknowledged that underlying circumstances may change and did not preclude future claims by Kansas.

As can be seen, the principle of equitable utilization of transboundary waters is not limited to an understanding that merely focuses on the attribution of water quantity. This would overlook the multiplicity of possibilities to generate additional benefits with efficient water management. The principle applies in a much wider scope and looks at all forms of utilization, as well as the equitable allocation of the benefits therefrom.

This and other cases, as well as treaty practice, constitute the basis for the formulation of the equitable and reasonable use principle in the International Law Association's (ILA) Helsinki Rules, and subsequently in the 1997 UN Watercourses Convention. The ILA interpreted the notion of 'beneficial use' in a broad sense; as not limited to efficiency and economic optimization considerations. The commentary of the Association notes that 'beneficial use', according to the principle of equitable utilization, 'need not be *the* most productive use [...] nor need it utilize the most efficient methods known in order to ... insure maximum utilization'.[31] Reflecting the spirit of the time when the Helsinki Rules were formulated, this interpretation in 1966 was to a large part based on

---

29 James E Sherow, 'The Contest for the "Nile of America": Kansas v. Colorado (1907)' (1990) 10 Great Plains Quarterly 57.

30 *State of Kansas v Colorado* (n 26) at 117: '[...] there will come a time when Kansas may justly say that there is no longer an equitable division of benefits and may rightfully call for relief against the action of Colorado [...]'.

31 ILA (n 19) 487.

the intention not to impose an undue burden on financially weak and technologically less advanced countries. In recognition of the economic divergence between States, in particular with respect to the new States that emerged from decolonization, the idea in the formulation of the principle was to put States under a duty of efficiency, yet one that would be 'commensurate with their financial resources'.[32]

Reframing due to changes in the Political Economy

The principle of equitable and reasonable utilization does not establish an obligation to develop and manage transboundary waters merely based on economic optimization and efficiency criteria. The absence of such a duty has not changed over time; however, the motivation behind it has changed. The objective of integrated water resources management has moved into the fore. The ILC argued in 1994 that attaining 'optimal utilization and benefits' is not about achieving maximum and most efficient use, nor about achieving the monetarily most valuable outcomes.[33] Optimal utilization is utilization that balances and integrates monetarily valuable uses with environmentally and socially beneficial uses. Thus, the motivation and interpretation of the principle has slightly shifted over time: equity with respect to economically less developed States formed an important priority in the interpretation of the principle in the mid-1960s at the height of decolonization. In the early 1990s, after the 1972 Stockholm Conference on the Human Environment and the 1992 Rio Conference on Environment and Development had taken place, the aspects of integrated management, sustainability and environmental considerations moved into the foreground.

In this evolving interpretation, the principle of equitable and reasonable utilization adopted a wider notion of what constitutes a benefit that can be derived from the utilization of transboundary water resources. The definition of 'beneficial use' has evolved and expanded over time with an increasing realization that human society and its economic activities negatively affect ecosystems and the environment. The legal definition has equally evolved. Article 5 (1) of the 1997 UN Watercourses Convention reads:

> Watercourse States shall in their respective territories utilize an international watercourse in an equitable and reasonable manner. In particular, an international watercourse shall be used and developed by watercourse States with a view to attaining optimal and sustainable utilization thereof and benefits

---

32 Ibid.

33 ILC (n 20) 97.

therefrom, taking into account the interests of the watercourse States concerned, consistent with adequate protection of the watercourse.[34]

The last clause of this paragraph shows evidence of the evolution of the notion of 'beneficial use'. Economic and social gains need to be balanced against ecosystem needs. In its commentary, the ILC puts emphasis on the concept of sustainability as one of the guiding principles for the realization of equitable and reasonable use. The spirit of aiming at sustainability is also reflected in Article 1 of the 1997 UN Watercourses Convention, which highlights the objective of achieving a balance between water uses and the protection and preservation of the watercourse itself.[35]

Criteria for equity

Legal instruments that spell out the principle of equitable utilization (as well as commentaries thereto) do not usually make a clear distinction between uses and benefits. The principle of equitable utilization aims at an equitable attribution of both uses and benefits among basin States.[36]

Equity is assessed through the consideration of a series of factors that will be particular to each individual basin and to the needs of individual basin States. For this reason, the formulation of these criteria in the 1966 Helsinki Rules and the 1997 UN Watercourses Convention remains general. Article 6 of the 1997 UN Watercourses Convention provides a non-exhaustive list of criteria to be considered. The provision opens with an affirmation that the '[u]tilization of an international watercourse in an equitable and reasonable manner [...] requires taking into account all relevant factors and circumstances.' The indicative list includes criteria of a geographic, hydrographic, climatic, and ecologic character; the economic and social needs of basin States; the dependent basin population; current and potential uses; the conservation, protection, development and

---

34 Adopted by the UN General Assembly in UNGA Res 51/229 (21 May 1997), UN Doc A/RES/51/229.

35 Art 1 (1): 'The present Convention applies to uses of international watercourses and of their waters for purposes other than navigation and to measures of protection, preservation and management related to the uses of those watercourses and their waters.'

36 The following description on the implementation of the principle draws on Laurence Boisson de Chazournes and Mara Tignino, 'Droit international et eau douce' (2013) 2900 Jurisclasseur, Environnement 1–40.

economy of water use; as well as the availability of comparable alternatives to existing or potential uses.[37]

The process of assessing benefit sharing opportunities in transboundary river basins bears a lot of similarity with the process aimed at operationalizing the principle of equitable and reasonable utilization.[38] States which apply the benefit sharing concept look at the same set of criteria that are to be taken into account when determining equitable and reasonable utilization in order to determine their proper *formulae* on how to share the benefits. For instance in the scalable three-step approach to joint identification of potential benefits in a basin developed by Granit and Claassen, the TWO Analysis is used for the assessment of joint investment opportunities.[39] According to the basic framework of the TWO Analysis, countries assess various key categories of development opportunities and related benefits – power production and trading, primary production, urban and industrial development, environmental and ecosystem services – and other basin specific opportunities and uses.[40] The framework is thus adjustable to the specific basin context as each river basin is different. In this three-step approach, the opportunity analysis is followed by two more steps, which analyze the impacts of identified investments and possible barriers to implementation.[41]

The criteria and basin conditions to consider according to the principle of equitable and reasonable allocation are those that are analyzed by countries to assess benefit sharing opportunities, as exemplified by the application of the Transboundary Waters Opportunity (TWO) Analysis in the Nile and Jordan basin contexts.[42] The legal principle establishes

---

37 Similar wording is included in the SADC Revised Protocol on Shared Watercourses (adopted 7 August 2000, entered into force 22 September 2003) (2001) 40 ILM 321, Art 3.8 and the Agreement on the Cooperation for the Sustainable Development of the Mekong River Basin (entered into force 5 April 1995) (1995) 34 ILM 864, Arts 5, 26.

38 Melvin Woodhouse, *Nile Basin Transboundary Benefit Sharing Framework* (Nile Basin Initiative, Entebbe, 2009) (on file with the authors).

39 Jakob Granit and Marius Claassen, 'A Scalable Approach Towards Realizing Tangible Benefits in Transboundary River Basins and Regions', in Laurence Boisson de Chazournes, Christina Leb and Mara Tignino (eds), *Freshwater and International Law* (Edward Elgar 2012) 140–154.

40 Phillips et al. (n 11) 7.

41 Granit and Claassen (n 39) 147.

42 SADC, *SADC Concept Paper on Benefit Sharing and Transboundary Water Management and Development*, <http://www.cdri.org.kh/shdmekong/13.SADC%20concept%20paper%20benefit%20sharing_SADC.pdf> accessed 13 October 2014, 9.

rights and obligations to equitable sharing of the uses of a transboundary basin and the benefits therefrom, whereas benefit sharing is the coming together of riparian States to agree to develop and/or increase the benefits to be had from a river and to share them. This State practice on benefit sharing has contributed and continues to contribute to the evolution of the legal principle of equitable and reasonable utilization over time.

III. BENEFIT SHARING IN LEGAL PRACTICE: AN EXAMINATION OF INTERNATIONAL WATER TREATIES

The uptake of benefit sharing can also be traced in treaty practice. Among international water treaties, one can generally distinguish between legal instruments that focus on the allocation of water itself, on the one hand, and those which provide for the sharing of benefits that can be derived from water resources. For example, the treaties between India and Bangladesh regarding the release of flow at Farakka barrage on the Ganges River[43] can be considered as a water allocation treaty falling under the first category. In contrast, the 1961 Treaty relating to the Cooperative Development of the Water Resources of the Columbia River Basin,[44] which regulates the sharing of hydropower and flood regulation benefits among the two riparian countries, belongs to the second group. Hydroelectricity production and its trade generate benefits from and beyond the river, whereas flood control reduces the costs because of the river. Here, the focus is on this second group of treaties, which regulate the generation and sharing of the additional benefits derived from cooperative water resources management and development.

Benefit sharing treaties consider the broadening of the basket of benefits beyond what is achievable by unilateral resource development and sharing of these benefits. These elements are common in agreements regulating navigation and joint infrastructure. However, they are not the

---

[43] Treaty between India and Bangladesh on Sharing of the Ganga/Ganges Waters at Farakka (signed 12 December 1996) (1996) 36 ILM 519; Indo-Bangladesh Memorandum of Understanding (7 October 1982); Agreement between India and Bangladesh on Sharing of the Ganges Waters at Farakka and on Augmenting its Flows (signed 5 November 1977) <http://ocid.nacse.org/tfdd/tfdddocs/394ENG.pdf> accessed 1 March 2015.

[44] Signed by the United States and Canada in Washington, DC on 17 January 1961.

only treaties to regulate benefit sharing; there are a number of instruments regulating other uses, or regulating overall basin development more generally that also establish principles on how benefits are shared in these individual basins.

III.1. Early Examples – Navigation

One of the oldest examples of a treaty establishing general principles on how benefits – and costs – are to be shared is the 1921 Convention and Statute on the Regime of Navigable Waterways of International Concern.[45] Navigation was one of the first uses to be recognized in treaties as having an international economic value. Article 10 of the Statute on the Regime of Navigable Waterways regulates the upstream/downstream benefit of maintaining navigability of waterways; it stipulates that a riparian which is under the obligation to undertake works in order to guarantee continued navigability of the river has the right to demand from others a reasonable contribution to the costs involved.[46] The State that creates or maintains a benefit to others, the benefit of continued navigability of the waterway, has the right to demand a contribution for the realization of this benefit and thus share in the benefits derived by others of its actions.

III.2. Benefits from Infrastructure Development

The majority of bilateral treaties developing benefit sharing rules are those establishing joint infrastructure. The infrastructure is put in place by co-riparian States in order to benefit from the joint or coordinated management and use of the transboundary water resources. In general, they include a specific formula on how benefits are shared; in particular where joint infrastructure generates benefits on contiguous river stretches these will be shared in equal parts. This is for instance the case for the Yacyretá, Itaipú and Iron Gates projects. The treaties which form the legal base for the projects[47] distribute hydropower benefits at equal parts to the respective contracting parties.

---

[45] Opened for signature 20 April 1921, entry into force 31 October 1922 (1921) 7 LNTS 35.

[46] Statute on the Regime of Navigable Waterways of International Concern (signed 20 April 1921) 7 LNTS 35.

[47] Equal sharing of power benefits according to the Treaty of Yacyreta (signed 3 December 1973) 1380 UNTS 80, Art XIII; Treaty between the Federative Republic of Brazil and the Republic of Paraguay concerning the

The case of the 1961 Columbia River Treaty[48] in which Canada and the United States agreed to a series of dam and reservoir constructions in the upper reaches for flood control and improvement of hydroelectric power generation shares similar traits. It entitles Canada to one half of the downstream power benefits that can be generated due to flow regulation on its territory and attributes one-half of the estimated value of the flood damage reduction that the Canadian reservoirs provide to this country. However, due to the impossibility of quantifying future benefits of flood control with certainty, the amounts paid by the United States to Canada remain an approximation of equal shares. Reimbursements for flood control benefits are accomplished according to a schedule of one-time payments to be effected once the agreed infrastructure is operational. Payments are reduced if the operation of storage infrastructure is delayed.[49]

The benefit sharing arrangements of the Columbia River Treaty were agreed to last for a period of at least 60 years; thereafter either party may terminate the treaty, with a minimum of ten years' advance notice. Given that 16 September 2024 is the earliest date the treaty can be terminated, both parties have actively assessed the adequacy of the benefit and cost sharing arrangements to determine whether either of them may want to make use of their right of notification of treaty termination at the earliest possible date in the fall of 2014.[50] At the time of treaty negotiation, the benefits of flood protection and energy production were of uppermost consideration; social, economic and environmental impact, in particular on local populations, received relatively less attention in the benefit sharing agreement between the US and Canada. Over the period of treaty implementation, these topics have however moved up on the priority list of political agendas in both countries and, more generally, on the international policy agenda. Today, the benefits and costs for local

---

Hydroelectric Utilization of the Water Resources of the Paraná River owned in Condominium by the two Countries, from and including the Salto Grande de Sete Quedas or Salto del Guairá, to the Mouth of the Iguassu River (signed 26 April 1973) 923 UNTS 92 (Treaty of Itaipú), Art XIII; The 1963 Agreement for the Iron Gates Project (signed 30 November 1963) 512 UNTS 10, Arts 5, 6, 8, provides for equal sharing of power and navigation potential.

48 Treaty Relating to Cooperative Development of the Water Resources of the Columbia River Basin (opened for signature 17 January 1961, entry into force 16 September 1964) 542 UNTS 244 (Columbia River Treaty).

49 Columbia River Treaty, Art VI.

50 At the time of writing (March 2016), neither party has invoked the right to terminate the treaty.

stakeholders and the environment have a different political weight than in the 1950s and 1960s when the treaty was negotiated.

The Lesotho Highlands project between South Africa and the Kingdom of Lesotho is another example where the idea of benefit sharing was pursued. The Highlands project is a river diversion project which delivers water from the Senqu/Orange River in Lesotho into the Vaal River and Gauteng province of South Africa and generates hydropower in Lesotho.[51] Ancillary benefits made possible by the investment, such as irrigation, tourism, and fisheries accrue to the country on the territory of which they occur. In the 1986 Treaty, which forms the basis for the project, two riparians of one river basin, the Senqu/Orange River Basin, agree that equitable utilization of the rivers' resources consists in diverting waters from one tributary to another. South Africa would have been able to divert this water entirely within its own territory, but this would have come at higher costs requiring a more complex system of civil works. The Lesotho Highlands project therefore represents what is called a *win-win* project for the two riparians.[52]

The agreements that have been described have the benefits *from* the river and *to* States in mind. Over time, the benefits *to* the river and to directly dependent local communities were increasingly considered by States, which can be partly attributed to a more vocal and more empowered civil society in many countries since the 1990s.

III.3. Considering Ecosystems and Local Communities

In the case of the Senegal River, initially the three downstream riparians have developed a complex treaty system which serves as a basis for equitable utilization and benefit sharing by means of specific infrastructure projects and navigation regulation, before a basin-wide framework agreement was established with the 2002 Senegal Water Charter.[53] The legal framework for joint management established by Mali, Mauretania

---

[51] Treaty on Lesotho Highlands Water Project between the Government of the Kingdom of Lesotho and the Government of the Republic of South Africa (signed 24 October 1986) (1997) FAO Legislative Study – 61 <http://www.fao.org/docrep/w7414b/w7414b00.HTM> accessed 13 October 2014, Art 4.

[52] Winston H Yu, *Benefit Sharing in International Rivers: Findings from the Senegal River Basin, the Columbia River Basin, and the Lesotho Highlands Water Project* (Africa Region Water Resources Unit Working Paper 1, World Bank, 2008) 53 ff.

[53] 'Charte des eaux du fleuve Sénégal', in Laurence Boisson de Chazournes, Richard Desgagné, Makane Mbengue and Cesare Romano, *Protection internationale de l'environnement* (2nd edn, Pedone 2005) 301–314.

and Senegal since 1972 is regularly cited as one of the prime examples of benefit sharing regimes through infrastructure development.[54] The initial motivation of the three States was to increase flood protection, hydropower, irrigation, and navigation benefits through joint management of the flow regime.[55] For this purpose a tri-partite management mechanism was set up: the *Organisation pour la Mise en Valeur du fleuve Sénégal* (OMVS).[56] Two jointly owned[57] multi-purpose reservoirs, at Diama and at Manantali, were constructed in the late 1980s, after the Council of Ministers had adopted a formula, known as the 'key',[58] for the sharing of benefits and costs associated with the two reservoirs. When the Senegal Water Charter was adopted in 2002 in order to update and consolidate the legal framework applicable to the basin, it also opened the door for participation of the fourth riparian, Guinea. Of importance for the present analysis, the Charter has placed emphasis on the Parties' objective to develop the River's resources in a sustainable way, taking into consideration, in particular, environmental and ecosystem needs and giving priority to the satisfaction of vital human needs in recognition of a human right to water. In the Charter, the Parties explicitly agree to the principle of equitable and reasonable utilization as a principle for the allocation of waters for different uses.[59] The range of uses that the Senegal Water Charter refers to is also larger than the uses enumerated in the 1972 Convention on the Statute of the River Senegal honoring the concept of Integrated Water Resources Management (IWRM) and thus adding, among others, flood risk reduction, the consideration of human uses and the protection of the environment.[60]

The principle of equitable and reasonable utilization governs the rights and duties of riparian States with respect to each other. In consequence, the majority of treaties which establish principles on how to share benefits designate only States as subjects and beneficiaries. With the

---

[54] See Yu (n 52); Paisley (n 18).

[55] *Convention relative au statut du fleuve Sénégal* (signed 11 March 1972) LEX-FAOC016004 <http://faolex.fao.org> accessed 13 October 2014.

[56] *Convention portant création de l'Organisation pour la mise en valeur du fleuve Sénégal* (signed 11 March 1972) LEX-FAOC016003 <http://faolex.fao.org> accessed 13 October 2014.

[57] *Convention conclue entre le Mali, la Mauritanie et le Sénégal relative au statut juridique des ouvrages communs* (signed 21 December 1978) <http://www.fao.org/docrep/w7414b/w7414b0d.htm> accessed 13 October 2014.

[58] For a summary presentation of the 'key' see Yu (n 52) 17–20.

[59] Charter of Water of the Senegal River (28 May 2002) <http://www.tematea.org/?q=node/6580> accessed 13 October 2014, Art 4.

[60] Ibid Art 5.

trend of increased civil society engagement on issues of international concern, there has also been an increase in the number of treaties considering benefits to local communities and their participation in the decision making process. One such example is the Convention on the Sustainable Management of Lake Tanganyika. This Convention includes '[t]he principle of fair and equitable benefit sharing by virtue of which local communities are entitled to share in the benefits derived from local resources' as one of the general principles for the sustainable development of the lake.[61] This is in particular of relevance with regard to the fisheries resources of this shared lake. Furthermore, the Convention provides for public participation in the decision making processes that affect the lake basin or the livelihoods of local populations and mandates each contracting Party to ensure that appeal or review procedures exist for decisions on activities that are likely to cause harm.[62] Another basin where the environment and public participation rights have increasingly found their way into the legal framework governing management and development is the Great Lakes Basin in North America shared by the United States and Canada. The last amendment, which became effective in 2012,[63] was drafted based on extensive consultations with local communities and other stakeholders and includes new regulations on ecosystem protection and the effects of climate change, and increases opportunities for public participation.

The increased voice of civil society in many countries and the tendency towards greater inclusion of affected stakeholder groups in the decision making process on transboundary water management has led to a new focus of international water treaties. As a result, treaties increasingly include rules that ensure benefits *to* the river and other hydrologic systems and provide for public participation and consultation in decision making, promoting a trickling down of benefits to local communities and stakeholders.

---

[61] Convention on the Sustainable Management of Lake Tanganyika (signed 12 June 2003) <http://www.ecolex.org/server2.php/libcat/docs/TRE/Multilateral/En/TRE001482.pdf> accessed 13 October 2014, Art 5.

[62] Ibid Arts 5, 17.

[63] Protocol Amending the Agreement between the United States of America and Canada on Great Lakes Water Quality 1978, as amended on 16 October 1983 and 18 November 1987 (7 September 2012) <http://www.ec.gc.ca/Publications/> accessed 13 October 2014.

IV. REASONS WHY BENEFIT SHARING IS NOT MORE WIDELY RECOGNIZED IN LEGAL PRACTICE

The practice remains limited to a small number of examples where concise benefit sharing formulae have been developed by States at the basin level, such as the 'key' in the case of the Senegal River Basin and the agreements between Canada and the United States on the Columbia River. The overwhelming majority of treaties which include benefit sharing arrangements are project related, whereas a smaller number of treaties concern categories of uses, and only in very rare instances do treaties refer to a 'principle of benefit sharing'. Benefit sharing more often seems to have arisen out of exigency or the interest in generating additional mutual benefits rather than out of a sense of duty. In some cases, it is employed as a way to raise finance for projects that one State would not be able to finance on its own; in other cases, projects – in particular those projects on contiguous stretches of rivers (for example, Itaipú and Yacyreta) – could not have been implemented by one State alone because the territory of another State is affected.

IV.1. Complexity of Negotiations Involving Issues Other Than Water

The resort to framework agreements for basin management and regional integration

Achieving agreement on defined benefit sharing rules at the basin level, rather than in the context of a specific project, is a challenging task given the multitude of benefits that are possible *to, from, because of,* and *beyond* the river. In basins that are shared by more than two countries this becomes an even more complex matter. The presence of multiple parties at the negotiation table increases the possible combinations of benefits shared exponentially and makes it more difficult to achieve an agreement that is accepted as equitable by all participating parties. Hence, the most prevalent way by which multilateral water treaties give consideration to benefits and their distribution among riparian States is by a general recognition of the contribution of cooperation and joint activities in increasing benefits and improving living standards.[64] The recognition of a

[64] Treaty for Amazonian Cooperation (signed July 1978) 1202 UNTS 71, Preamble; Agreement on the Cooperation for the Sustainable Development of the Mekong River Basin (signed 5 April 1995) 2069 UNTS 3, Arts 1, 2; Framework Agreement of the Sava River Basin (signed 3 December 2002, entered into force 29 December 2004) 2366 UNTS 479, Preamble.

common aim to share and equitably distribute benefits is expressed in a large number of treaties in their preambles or first articles. At the same time, however, the ensuing treaty text regularly does not establish any detailed rules or guidance according to which future benefits will be shared among riparian States. This is due to the fact that the majority of multilateral water treaties serve as framework agreements for basin management. They leave the regulation of specific uses or investments to subsequent bilateral or plurilateral agreements concluded by the Parties.[65] In the absence of more specific rules in framework treaties, the principle of equitable and reasonable utilization, as codified by the 1997 UN Watercourses Convention, applies, but nevertheless has its limits. It provides guidance on criteria to consider in assessing equity in the use and distribution of benefits, but it does not provide clear guidance on how to distribute the shares.[66]

One of the difficulties is the quantification of benefits in terms of their economic or financial value due to, for instance, constantly fluctuating market prices for electricity, crops and other goods, and the difficulty of quantifying costs that arise in cases of flood damage, in particular in respect of the loss of human life. Once a benefit sharing arrangement is agreed, time also presents a challenge. Circumstances – not only market prices – change over time; with a change in the structure of the economy or changes in population size or migration, water needs within countries change over time and a once agreed upon benefit sharing arrangement may, after some time, no longer be considered equitable. It is for these reasons that, for example, the 'key' which defines the sharing of hydropower, navigation and irrigation benefits in the Senegal Basin is regularly adjusted and renegotiated. Similarly, parts of the benefit sharing arrangements in the Columbia River Basin are renegotiated regularly.

Treaties which provide the flexibility of renegotiating benefit sharing arrangements are, however, rare. In most cases, States enter into legal agreements to achieve stability and predictability[67] in their relationship and therefore avoid rules that open up legal arrangements to flexibility.

---

65 Treaty of the River Plate Basin (signed 23 April 1969) 875 UNTS 11.

66 Bruce Lankford, 'Does Article 6 (Factors Relevant to Equitable and Reasonable Utilization) in the UN Watercourses Convention misdirect riparian countries?' (2013) 38 WI 130–145.

67 Laurence Boisson de Chazournes, *Fresh Water in International Law* (OUP 2013) 8.

Benefit sharing through issue linkage

A small number of agreements provide for issue linkages to benefits *beyond* the river or hydrologic system in order to increase the 'basket of benefits' under consideration for the sharing arrangements. The 1998 Agreement on the Use of Water and Energy Resources of the Syr Darya Basin[68] provides a framework based on which the Parties agree on annual energy and water sharing rules. Water management on the Syr Darya River, a tributary to the disappearing Aral Sea, is significantly challenged by conflicting water demands; on the one hand, there is increased demand for water releases during freezing Central Asian winters to produce electricity and, on the other hand, there is a need for considerable upstream water storage for irrigation and water supply downstream during the long hot and dry summer seasons. In the 1998 Agreement, the Parties express their common desire to find the most equitable solution to use the basin's water and energy resources and benefits derived from the joint management of the Naryn-Syr Darya Cascade and future hydropower facilities. Annual agreements are supposed to specify the particular water and energy sharing rules for the respective calendar year and in this way determine the distribution of benefits to the countries.[69] An interesting feature of these annual operating regimes is that the benefit transfer streams negotiated in these agreements are not limited to benefits derived from water resources utilization but include the transfer of electricity generated from natural gas and coal.[70] In order to arrive at a formula of equitable utilization acceptable for all riparian States, the 'basket of benefits' on the negotiation table was enlarged by including other natural resources so as to allow for additional trade-offs in reaching agreement.

As this case study exemplifies, the fact that agreements with issue linkages are dependent on variables that are exogenous to water resources management means they are at the same time challenging to implement.

---

[68] Finalized by Kazakhstan, the Kyrgyz Republic and Uzbekistan in Bishkek on 17 March 1998, and amended by a Protocol which adds Tajikistan as a Party to the Agreement on 7 May 1999 <http://ocid.nacse.org/tfdd/treaties.php> accessed 13 October 2014.

[69] See, for example, the Agreement Between the Government of the Republic of Kazakhstan, the Government of the Kyrgyz Republic and the Government of the Republic of Uzbekistan on Joint, and Complex Use of Water and Energy Resources of the Naryn Syr Darya Cascade Reservoirs (adopted 17 March 1998) <http://ocid.nacse.org/tfdd/treaties.php> accessed 13 October 2014.

[70] See Laurence Boisson de Chazournes, 'The Aral Sea Basin: Legal and Institutional Aspects of Governance', in Matthias Finger, Ludivine Tamiotti and Jeremy Allouche (eds), *The Multi-Governance of Water* (SUNY Press 2006) 147–171.

The water for energy trading scheme among the riparian countries of the Syr Darya collapsed in the face of fluctuating hydro-energy and fossil fuel energy market prices and diverging price expectations among the countries. While the treaty is still in force, the Parties withdrew from annual negotiations and opted for unilateral strategies to make them less dependent on the basin-level water-for-energy exchange.[71]

Role of institutions

Benefit sharing arrangements are not common in international treaties since there is often a lack of trust as to how the resulting benefits may in practice be shared. It has been observed that scenarios of this type are analogous to Stag Hunt situations.[72] That is, in a collective arrangement that will increase water availability to all concerned riparian States, all concerned Parties sharing a given water resource will have to risk, sacrifice or contribute something, whether that is the upstream State ensuring an uninhibited flow, the midstream State giving up land to facilitate the construction of a dam, or the downstream State losing control over the flow of water.[73] In a Stag Hunt situation, a Pareto-optimal outcome relies on all players cooperating to distribute the benefits after a stag is captured by one of the players. However, stag hunters have a tendency for defection after the stag has been captured, and this assumption results in a lack of trust. To mitigate this lack of trust, institutions and effective enforcement mechanisms can play a role in ensuring obligations are discharged. At the very least, institutions can be important channels of communication and dialogue, which can be vital to overcoming a lack of trust. Moreover, the coordination of water-related activities through institutions can also result in efficiency savings to the extent that duplication is avoided.

Generally speaking, basin organizations and commissions are symptomatic of the need for cooperation and can allow the participation of other actors. They offer a defined framework within which cooperation can take place and be strengthened.[74] Beyond communication and dialogue, institutions can facilitate tangible cooperation to ensure the benefits that

---

71 Alfred Diebold, 'Study on Cooperation on the Syr Darya Basin' (2012) Indecon Consulting.

72 Eyal Benvenisti, 'Collective Action in the Utilization of Shared Freshwater: The Challenges of International Water Resources Law' (1996) 90 AJIL 384, 390.

73 Ibid.

74 See Boisson de Chazournes (n 67) 176.

can be obtained from a resource are focused upon and optimized, and can help to avoid 'defection' as in the Stag Hunt scenario.

Over time, the need for a broader scope of cooperation became evident as a wider variety of uses were made of international waterways. This has meant extending representation on commissions and bodies to include non-riparian States, as well as a broadening of the issues (and potential benefits) over which such institutions have competence. In recent times, their mandates have extended to environment or energy related issues, as well as monitoring, the propagation of policy objectives, the regulation of standards or the facilitation of negotiation.[75]

IV.2. Recognition of Interests of Other (Water) Actors Not Present at the Negotiation Table

Legal developments are increasingly making space for other actors that are not directly involved in, yet are nevertheless affected by, arrangements between countries agreeing on benefit sharing arrangements. Compared to the 1966 Helsinki Rules, the 1997 UN Watercourses Convention provides a wider consideration of the interests of other watercourse States by introducing and reinforcing strong procedural requirements for the implementation of the obligation to notify planned measures with potentially significant adverse effects.[76] At the same time, Article 5 of the 1997 UN Watercourses Convention provides a 'voice' to the environment as another 'actor' interested in benefit sharing, stipulating the optimal and sustainable utilization shall be consistent with the protection of the environment. Ultimately, the Convention introduces a 'voice' to individuals through its Article 32 on the obligation not to discriminate in the access to justice for individuals who suffered transboundary harm.[77] However, in general, these other actors – the environment and individuals – are not given an equal voice as they are not party, but rather subject, to the agreement. States remain the primary authors of IL and treaties, yet an indirect voice can be given to actors not present at the negotiation table, either through their influence within the intra-State

---

[75] UN Water, 'Transboundary Waters: Sharing Benefits, Sharing Responsibilities' (2008), <http://www.unwater.org/downloads/UNW_TRANSBOUNDARY.pdf> accessed 5 October 2014.

[76] 1997 UN Watercourses Convention, Art 12.

[77] Laurence Boisson de Chazournes, 'Chapter 1', in Laurence Boisson de Chazournes and Salman A Salman (eds), *Les ressources en eau et le droit international/Water Resources and International Law* (Hague Academy of International Law 2005).

process of decision making or their 'voice' can be expressed by others, including through dispute settlement bodies.

Other basin countries

Bilateral treaties concerning one or a limited number of uses by and large distribute benefits equitably and, more often than not, equally between the two signatory States. In general, these agreements do not cause problems in basins which are shared by two States only. However, if such a bilateral agreement takes place within the context of a multi-riparian system, such as in the case of the Lesotho Highlands Project, it should be assessed *a priori* whether the specific agreement supports equitable sharing also with respect to the entire basin and all its riparians. It is possible that a bilateral benefit sharing treaty in a multi-riparian basin precludes equitable and reasonable utilization of the basin's water resources by other riparians. One way to give not directly affected States a voice and opportunity to join in the benefit sharing arrangements is by notifying planned measures to them.

The World Bank Operational Policy 7.50 on International Waterways which requires notification of all riparian States of projects that use water independent of a threshold of impact on their territories is the most progressive rule in this regard.[78] It was applied to Phase 1 of the Lesotho Highlands Water Project since the World Bank participated as financier. A large part of the water is diverted outside of the Orange/Senqu watershed and eventually evacuates into the Indian Ocean and not, as the normal flow of the river, into the Atlantic. At the time the project was conceived in the mid-1980s, the territory of Namibia was under the administration of the United Nations Council for South West Africa. Both the UN Council and the South West Africa People's Organization (SWAPO) were notified of the project; neither of them voiced an objection to the project.[79] In this case, it is an international financial institution that ensured that each basin State and interested party was heard in the process.

---

78 World Bank Operational Policy 7.50 – Projects on International Waterways <http://web.worldbank.org/WBSITE/EXTERNAL/PROJECTS/EXTPOLICIES/EXTOPMANUAL/0,,contentMDK:20064667~menuPK:64701637~pagePK:64709096~piPK:64709108~theSitePK:502184,00.html> accessed 13 October 2014.

79 Salman A Salman, *The World Bank Policy for Projects on International Waterways – An Historical and Legal Analysis* (The World Bank, Washington, DC, 2009) 126f.

Where two riparian States of a pluri-country basin intend to enter into a bilateral agreement on sharing benefits of specific uses, according to Article 5 of the 1997 UN Watercourses Convention, they should consider the interests of other watercourse States and thus the impact of their agreement on the equitable distribution of overall benefits and uses. Assessing the interests of other watercourse States requires a large amount of data and not all of this information may easily be available, in particular information which concerns future uses. The promotion of sub-basin or basin scale assessments through international organizations is therefore another useful tool to ensure that impacts on and interests of other basin countries are taken into account. The Global Environmental Fund (GEF) encourages the preparation of transboundary diagnostic assessments or strategic action plans, in part as a tool to facilitate investments addressing issues of transboundary concern.[80] These diagnostic assessments consider the panoply of possible benefit sharing trade-offs between all riparian States.

The environment

Another 'beneficiary' that receives assistance at times from third parties is the environment. In the decision on the *Gabčíkovo-Nagymaros Project*,[81] the ICJ confirmed that the environment forms part of the protection provided by the principle of equitable use. The Court pronounced itself on the question whether a water diversion carried out by Czechoslovakia,[82] was proportional in accordance with the principle of equitable and reasonable use. In deciding that the diversion was contrary to the principle, the Court noted that not only had Czechoslovakia (then still one State) diverted a disproportionate share of water away from Hungarian territory, but also that this diversion negatively impacted on the ecology of the Szigetköz.[83] The fauna and flora of the alluvial plains in that area would have been at risk of extinction.[84] The Court declared that Hungary was thereby deprived 'of its right to an equitable and reasonable

[80] GEF, *International Waters – Delivering Results* (2012) <http://www.thegef.org/gef/sites/thegef.org/files/publication/IW_DeliveringResults-2012.pdf> accessed 13 October 2014, 4.

[81] *Gabčíkovo-Nagymaros Project (Hungary/Slovakia)* [1997] ICJ Rep 7.

[82] Czechoslovakia is the predecessor State of Slovakia, one of the two parties to the dispute concerning a joint hydropower infrastructure project on the Danubian border with Hungary.

[83] *Gabčíkovo-Nagymaros Project* (n 81) para 85.

[84] Ibid para 40 on the environmental risks and impacts of the diversion.

share of the natural resources of the Danube'.[85] With this the Court confirmed that environmental concerns are an important factor to take into account in determining beneficial use. It is one of the instances[86] where an international dispute settlement mechanism ensured consideration of benefits *to* the river and its ecosystems that had not been included in the original treaty-based benefit sharing arrangements.

Affected population

Benefit sharing on international waters is most often regulated by international treaties. Affected individuals and communities are traditionally not present at the negotiation table. As discussed further above, in the last two decades the trend has been toward increasing inclusion of affected stakeholders, either through influence on their national governments during negotiations or through their inclusion in the decision making process based on treaty provisions.

At the same time, the interests of affected populations have also been promoted by third parties. International organizations have intervened in some cases to ensure benefits to project-affected populations in international benefit sharing schemes. One such case occurred in the implementation of the Lesotho Water Highlands project. The World Bank required the Kingdom of Lesotho to establish a community development fund as a prerequisite for its funding assistance. Parts of the project revenues were channeled to this fund in order to ensure employment generation, poverty reduction and improvement of the livelihoods of people living in the project-affected area.[87]

V. CONCLUSION: TOWARDS ENLARGING THE BASKET OF BENEFITS

The benefit sharing concept goes beyond the principle of equitable and reasonable utilization; though this IWL principle provides useful guidance for benefit sharing between States. Codified in the 1997 UN Watercourses Convention, this principle contains important elements that can be applied by States in setting up benefit sharing rules. The list of

---

85 Ibid para 85.

86 Others being the arbitration awards on the *Iron Rhine* (Award) (24 May 2005) and the *Indus Waters Kishenganga Arbitration* (Partial Award) (19 February 2013) and (Final Award) (20 December 2013), all available at <http://www.pca-cpa.org/> accessed 13 October 2014.

87 Yu (n 52) 61.

criteria that are to be taken into account in the assessment of equitable and reasonable use provides, at the same time, a useful list of elements to be considered in the design of benefit sharing frameworks. The fact that Article 5 does not only refer to utilizations but also to benefits encourages countries to focus their cooperation not only on the allocation of water for specific uses, but also on the increase of benefits that can be derived from alternative water uses, thereby increasing the 'basket of benefits' available to them. Alternative methods of increasing the benefits that can be derived from transboundary rivers through reservoir management, not only for flood protection but also for the optimization of energy production, become more frequent in practice. Countries develop benefit sharing mechanisms and institutions to increase the scale of benefits available to them, and also to prevent and settle disputes concerning competing demands on transboundary water resources.

The practice on benefit sharing has led to an evolved interpretation of the content of the equitable and reasonable use principle. Over time, the principle has been reframed due to changes in the PE, including in-country priorities concerning the use and management of transboundary water resources. Utilization for economic means and ends of States has been complemented over time by management principles that increasingly take the interests of local stakeholders and individuals, as well as the environment, into account. International organizations, dispute settlement bodies and national actors in one country can have an indirect spill-over effect into law making and the implementation of benefit sharing arrangements at the national level in other countries. International treaties can be the conduit through which benefit sharing with local stakeholders and for the benefit of the environment becomes harmonized across countries, including in countries where the national policy making process would otherwise not prioritize the inclusion of local stakeholders and the environment.

The IWL principle of equitable and reasonable utilization, conceived as a principle that primarily concerns the optimization of the use of shared waters and benefits derived therefrom for States, has evolved to consider the impact on the protection of the resource. The practice of States and dispute settlement bodies is opening up this principle to the integration of more holistic benefits for connected ecosystems – and the environment more generally – as well as individual stakeholders.

16. Political Economy and the Protection of Human Rights: Political Economy and Compliance with Human Rights Treaties

Ulyana Kohut

I. INTRODUCTION

The interplay between International Law (IL), politics and economics in the continuously globalizing world is no longer a mere interest of scholars in each respective field.[1] Rather it forms a top question of contemporary academic agendas, leading to the collision of theories and methodologies into a unified comprehensive 'inter-discipline'.[2]

Traditionally, International Relations (IR) scholars assume most cases of compliance with IL to be correlated with substantive benefits for signatory States (symmetric or asymmetric). However, it is generally accepted that Human Rights (HR) regimes differ from most other forms of international cooperation in both 'their ends and their means'.[3] HR treaties essentially deal with the rule- or standard-setting on the treatment of the peoples under States' direct authority; hence they lack the majority of compliance-triggering mechanisms inherent to other types of international agreements.[4] It is only logical, then, that the most frequent

[1] Anne-Marie Slaughter, 'International Law in a World of Liberal States' (1995) 6 EJIL 503 (observing that today it is nearly taken for granted that any study of the contemporary 'international system' necessarily comprises the analysis of both IL and international politics).

[2] Term used by Professor Michael R Krätke to describe Political Economy.

[3] Andrew Moravcsik, 'The Origin of Human Rights Regimes: Democratic Delegation in Postwar Europe' (2000) 54 Int Org 217.

[4] Oona A Hathaway, 'Do Human Rights Treaties Make a Difference?' (2002) 111 Yale L J 1938; Louis Henkin, *How Nations Behave: Law and Foreign Policy* (2nd edn, Columbia University Press 1979) 235.

question put by IL and IR scholars is what drives States towards compliance with HR treaties?

The interdisciplinary research on compliance emphasizes the importance of actors' interests, historical, social, political legacies and structures in determining the motivations of particular behaviour with regard to IL norms (the *why* question), but less attention is given to a systematic consideration of the compliance requirements and avenues of producing the compliant behaviour.[5] The concept of compliance is not static or immutable; rather it depends on the theory or conception of law[6] one adopts and on the nature of particular legal obligations. Hence, the appropriateness of applying the interdisciplinary methodology to a study of *compliance* with IL, or at least with some of its branches, may be legitimately questioned.[7]

The focus of this Chapter is only on *compliance* with States' obligations under HR treaties. Having said that, compliance may often be interconnected with the establishment of HR regimes and adherence to HR treaties, although there may be no direct causal relationship between them. This Chapter considers the assumptions advanced under both International Political Economy (IPE) and Political Economy (PE) approaches with the closer focus on the latter, however. It tends to make an argument in favour of the leading role and binding force of IL in the context of State action and the formation of State policies (IL as *explanans*), although it does not discard a possibility of some IL norms being determined by other factors, for example, particular interests (IL as *explanandum*).

Following the introductory Section I, Section II of this Chapter overviews some principal theories of compliance with IL[8] and then

---

5 Amarjit Singh, *A Strategy and Framework for Identifying Compliance Requirements under International Law (with an illustration relating to international human rights norms)* (2011) Ph.D. Thesis, LSE 11, 13, available at <http://etheses.lse.ac.uk/922/1/Singh_Strategy_Framework_Identifying_Compliance.pdf> (accessed 28 July 2015).

6 Benedict Kingsbury, 'The Concept of Compliance as the Function of Competing Conceptions of International Law' (1998) 19 Mich J Int L 368 (arguing that 'the concept of "compliance" with international law cannot be taken as shared, but must be given meaning by reference to a theory (or a set of interlocking theories) of international law').

7 See also Barbara Delcourt, 'Political Economy of International Law: A Convenient Alliance for the Study of Compliance?', above in this Volume.

8 For the application of game theories (specifically prisoner's dilemma) in different contexts of IL see Meredith Kolsky Lewis, 'International Political

considers the potential of the PE approach. Section III draws attention to the two fundamental sources of difficulties for any modelled, quantitative or comparative study of *compliance with HR treaties*: the complexity of the HR treaties and the concept of compliance themselves. Section IV concludes with pointing to the limits of the interdisciplinary studies on this particular subject matter.[9]

II. THEORIES OF COMPLIANCE WITH HUMAN RIGHTS TREATIES

II.1. Theories of Compliance

Most social science studies investigate *why* relevant actors behave in a particular way, while few of them inquire *how* they do (or should) comply. Both IL and IR literature derive different models of compliance through the engines that drive State behaviour with respect to IL generally or to HR in particular. The same or similar engines may be present in different models.[10] What differs is the weight given to a particular one. Traditionally, two broad approaches to compliance could be identified: 'rational actor models' and 'normative theory'.[11] However, a considerable number of studies based on constructivist assumptions allows isolating this approach as a third separate perspective.

Economy and the Prisoner's Dilemma: Compliance with International Law', above in this Volume.

[9] Further implications of the PE methodology to a study of international agreements in general, or to customary international norms on HR, are beyond the scope of this Chapter. It considers HR treaty-based norms exclusively, unless specifically indicated otherwise.

[10] Jana von Stein, 'The Engines of Compliance', in Jeffrey L Dunoff and Mark A Pollak (eds), *Interdisciplinary Perspectives on International Law and International Relations: The State of the Art* (CUP 2013) 478 (observing that these mechanisms are often interconnected and not necessarily mutually exclusive).

[11] Hathaway (n 4) 1944. This classification mirrors that of Robert O Keohane, 'International Relations and International Law: Two Optics' (1997) 38 Harv Int L J 487 ff. See also, Oona A Hathaway, 'Between Power and Principle: An Integrated Theory of International Law' (2005) 72 U Chi L Rev 477–486 (referring to these models as '*interest-based models*' and '*norm-based models*', and advancing an argument for their convergence). Similarly, see Barbara Delcourt, 'Compliance, Theory of', in Rüdiger Wolfrum (ed), *Max Planck Encyclopaedia of Public International Law*, available at <www.mpepil.com>.

Rational actor or interest-based models

This approach to compliance with IL is characterized by an accent on the interests as the primary motivation for State action and an overall reluctance to recognize the impact of legal norms on State behaviour. *Realism* focuses on the central role of power in IR and depicts States as unitary actors, who act rationally in pursuit of their interests '[given] their capacities and the constraints imposed by the power and interests of others'.[12] Even if a possibility that States may have a genuine interest in HR protection causing a certain course of action is accepted (like the economic and other interests),[13] these scholars argue compliance with the requirements of HR treaties occurs not because of the binding force of the norm, but from the coincidence of State interests and the costs and benefits calculus.[14]

Like realism, *institutionalism* views States as unitary actors pursuing their self-interests, but refuses the realist assumption that, in the absence of a central authority, the only motivation for cooperation is power-redistribution and self-interest, concentrating instead on 'regimes' (these being as a 'utility maximizing instrument' States may use in pursuit of their self-interests). This scholarship traces compliance with international treaties to the dynamics created by the domestic institutions and politics, indicating the importance of considering the 'propensity to comply' as a characteristic that varies in different States.[15] Additionally, the *reputational model*, whereby compliance is embedded in '3 Rs' (Reputation, Retaliation, and Reciprocity), argues that States comply with IL norms because they fear the sanctions and care about the reputational costs.[16]

---

[12] Kingsbury (n 6) 350. This approach implies no causal correlation between the normative value and persuasive power of legal norm *per se* and State behaviour. States comply with their requirements only where there is some self-interest or rational motivation for such action; hence compliance occurs when the costs of non-compliance are higher than the benefits from compliance. See Anne-Marie Slaughter, 'International Relations, Principal Theories', in Rüdiger Wolfrum (ed), *Max Planck Encyclopaedia of Public International Law*, available at <www.mpepil.com>.

[13] Kenneth N Waltz, *Theory of International Politics* (Addison-Wesley 1979) 200; Jack Donnelly, 'International Human Rights: A Regime Analysis' (1986) 40 Int Org 616.

[14] Richard H Steinberg, 'Wanted – Dead or Alive: Realism in International Law', in Dunoff and Pollak (eds) (n 10) 166.

[15] Barbara Koremenos, 'Institutionalism and International Law', in Dunoff and Pollak (eds) (n 10) 74.

[16] This theory is developed in various works of the author, inter alia Andrew T Guzman, *How International Law Works: A Rational Choice Theory* (OUP

Somewhat differently, *liberal theory* refuses the assumption that States act as unitary actors in determining their preferences, arguing instead that the latter are based on the 'demands of individuals and social groups, and their relative power in society'.[17] Andrew Moravcsik's recently developed liberal theory, based on the central role of non-State actors and whereby States represent the interests of some (most powerful or dominant) segments of domestic society, argues that the shape, interplay and convergence of these preferences form foreign policy prerogatives and determine State action at the international level.[18] International norms rely on the 'vertical' enforcement system, whereby they undergo the 'internalization' and integration with domestic institutions and politics.[19] The motivation for the establishment of HR regimes comes from a rational choice to delegate certain powers to an independent international institution, which in turn is an outcome of the weighting of the restrictions on government discretion (purporting some sovereignty cost) and of the reduction of domestic political uncertainty (by securing preferred domestic policy through the means of 'two-level' commitment and reducing the possibility of unfavourable policies by the future governments). However, Moravcsik correctly argues that whilst the theory accurately explains the establishment of HR regimes, it provides a marginal input on the compliance issue.[20]

2008). Criticizing this view, Brewster argues that 'compliance with international rules is a function of domestic support for the goal of the treaty regimes as well as respect for international legal obligations'. See Rachel Brewster, 'The Limits of Reputation on Compliance' (2009) 1 Int Theo 329.

[17] Andrew Moravcsik, 'Liberal Theories of International Law', in Dunoff and Pollak (eds) (n 10) 83.

[18] Andrew Moravcsik, 'Taking Preferences Seriously: A Liberal Theory of International Politics' (1997) 51 Int Org 513 ff.

[19] Moravcsik (n 17) 92–100. Similarly, Beth A Simmons, *Mobilizing for Human Rights: International Law and Domestic Politics* (CUP 2009); Xinyuan Dai, 'Why Comply? The Domestic Constituency Mechanism' (2005) 59 Int Org 363 ff.

[20] Although the author suggests that compliance with international HR commitments can be determined by three conditions: fear of domestic political uncertainty, foreign governments' support of the position of national government and international cooperation, which would help to induce domestic actors to support the maintenance of current policies. See Moravcsik (n 3) 246–247.

Normative or norm-based models

The *managerial model* assumes that States tend to comply with IL because of considerations of efficiency, interests and norms,[21] whereby persuasion represents a fundamental instrument of treaty compliance. States are generally inclined to comply with their international treaty obligations, except when the sources of non-compliance[22] come into play. Since treaties indeed generate legal norms, which include an obligation to obey the legal norms, the 'management of compliance' resolves non-compliance.[23]

Sharing some managerialist assumptions, most importantly States' propensity to comply, the *fairness model* assumes that support for international regimes (this being considered the key element of compliance) lies in and depends on the legitimacy of their constitutive norms.[24] Thomas Franck argues that the central element of treaty adherence and subsequent compliance is the perceived fairness of substantive and procedural treaty norms (being part of a wider requirement of IL fairness).[25] HR treaties are mostly fair because they result from a 'right process';[26] hence, they tend to obtain high compliance rates.

Recognizing the merits of the managerial and fairness models, Harold Hongju Koh stresses the importance of the Transnational Legal Process

---

[21] Abram Chayes and Antonia Handler Chayes, *The New Sovereignty: Compliance with International Regulatory Agreements* (Harvard University Press 1995) 3.

[22] The authors ground the sources of non-compliance in insufficient information, ambiguity and indeterminacy of treaties, and in lack of capacity or time to act, rather than in the calculus of costs and benefits or waging the State's interests. See Chayes and Chayes (n 21) 9–17; also Abram Chayes and Antonia Handler Chayes, 'On Compliance' (1993) 47 Int Org 188–197.

[23] The process of 'managing compliance' consists of aiming at transparency and clarity of the treaty requirements, effective dispute settlement bodies, and capacity building for achieving higher rates of compliance. The central instrument of treaty compliance is, however, the persuasion of non-complying States to obey their treaty obligations.

[24] Phillip R Trimble, 'International Law, World Order, and Critical Legal Studies' (1990) 42 Stanford L Rev 811 ff.; Thomas M Franck, 'Legitimacy in the International System' (1988) 82 AJIL 705 ff.

[25] Thomas M Franck, *Fairness in International Law and Institutions* (Clarendon Press 1995) 7.

[26] Delcourt (n 11); Franck (n 25) 124 (Franck argues that for their central role in international legal and political life, a violation of any HR norm is viewed as an action against the public policy of the international community).

(TLP).[27] His *transnational model* distinguishes four relationships between international norms and State conduct: coincidence, conformity, compliance and obedience.[28] Positive transformational effect (leading to compliant behaviour or obedience) of repeated interactions in TLP is determined by countless constantly repeating transactions within the process, whereby a variety of actors interact and interpret legal norms, and subsequently seek to internalize them into their domestic legal orders.[29] For States which are reluctant to denounce HR violations of other States for political, economic or other reasons, 'horizontal problem-solving managerial' or 'philosophical value-based' compliance strategies seem to be insufficient, while a vertical strategy of interaction between a variety of actors, including the so-called 'epistemic community'[30] interpretation, and internalization are argued to be more effective.[31]

Constructivism

Theories grounded in 'sophisticated constructivism'[32] explain State practice by the combined impact of power, incentives, material benefits or sanctions on the one side, and of repeated interactions, international socialization, and gradual social change brought about by the international norms on the other side. Constructivism argues that a key to understanding State identity and behaviour lies in a combination of factors: historical path, tradition, institutions, discourse, ideals and social

---

[27] TLP is 'the complex process of private and public, domestic and international institutional interaction of various actors – nation-States, international organizations, multilateral enterprises, non-governmental organizations, and private individuals – whereby global norms are not just debated, made, interpreted or enforced, but ultimately internalized by domestic legal system'. See Harold Hongju Koh, 'Transnational Legal Process' (1996) 75 Neb L Rev 183–184.

[28] Harold Hongju Koh, 'Why Do Nations Obey International Law?' (1997) 106 Yale L J 2600 (fn 3).

[29] Ibid at 2651. For Koh 'internalized compliance' is obedience. Ibid 2646.

[30] Harold Hongju Koh, 'How is International Human Rights Law Enforced?' (1999) 74 Indiana L J 1407–1408 (observing that involvement of the 'epistemic community' and other types of pro-HR activist in the process is feasible to combat a general tendency of States not to enforce HR norms against a violator State, and also they are capable of facilitating the legal internalization through means of incorporation, judicial interpretation, acceptance of a norm by political elites).

[31] Koh (n 28) 2656. They further generate norms, which enter into domestic legal orders through a process of social, political and legal internalization. Ibid 2656–2657.

[32] Elizabeth Stubbins Bates, 'Sophisticated Constructivism in Human Rights Compliance Theory' (2014) 25 EJIL 1169 ff.

norms.[33] Focus on actors' belief and identity leads this scholarship to concentrate on social norms and on non-State actors, emphasizing that these may play a decisive role in shaping State beliefs (non-State actors as 'norm-entrepreneurs') or induce international institutions to seek the maximization of their own interests.[34] Compliance cannot be separated from other IL processes (like making and maintenance of, change in, law etc.) and the role of IL and legal argumentation in general is viewed as fundamental for compliance. In recent years, these scholars have developed a set of models, which combine the rational actors' 'logic of consequences', where applicable, with the constructivist 'logic of appropriateness'.[35]

II.2. Potential of the Political Economy Model Developed by Anne van Aaken and Joel P Trachtman above in this Volume

The model developed in Chapter 1 of this Volume (the Model) also draws upon the elements of different theories, principally on some liberal and constructivist assumptions. Its theoretical framework points to the fact that, as in many other spheres of IL, a decision to comply with HR norms is (almost) never purely international. However, it also recognizes a possibility of domestic politics and processes to be influenced by systemic and transnational factors.[36] It follows that the role of non-State

---

[33] Slaughter (n 12); Jutta Brunnée and Stephen J Toope, 'Constructivism and International Law', in Dunoff and Pollak (eds) (n 10) 121.

[34] Slaughter (n 12); Michael Barnett and Martha Finnemore, *Rules for the World: International Organizations in Global Politics* (Cornell University Press 2004); Andrew T Guzman, 'International Organizations and the Frankenstein Problem' (2013) 24 EJIL 999 ff.

[35] Thomas Risse and Stephen C Ropp, 'Introduction and Overview', in Thomas Risse, Stephen C Ropp and Kathryn Sikkink (eds), *The Persistent Power of Human Rights: From Commitment to Compliance* (CUP 2013) 12. This volume is a development of the previously elaborated 'spiral model' of HR change, demonstrating the path from the 'repression' (massive HR violations) to 'rule-consistent behaviour' (compliance). The original 1999 model applied only the constructivist assumptions of State behaviour; however, the 2013 improved model combines rational choice with constructivist assumptions. The original 1999 model appears in Thomas Risse, Stephen C Ropp and Kathryn Sikkink (eds), *The Power of Human Rights: International Norms and Domestic Change* (CUP 1999).

[36] Peter M Haas, 'Choosing to Comply: Theorizing from International Relations and Comparative Politics', in Dinah Shelton (ed), *Commitment and Compliance: The Role of Non-binding Norms in the International Legal System* (OUP 2000) 43.

actors often becomes crucial in shaping the State decision to comply through the power of interested States or through their influence on public opinion and domestic preferences.

The Model also illustrates that reputation and pressure from HR treaty bodies may provide more incentives to comply.[37] This points to the need to strengthen the HR treaty bodies and to give them the tools to reach the goals of their respective treaties.[38] Moreover, it points out the need to overcome the lack of coherence between different HR treaty bodies, especially those of universal nature. This problem is already recognized in legal scholarship emphasizing the need for a comprehensive reform, which would help to bypass Guzman's 'Frankenstein problem' of IOs[39] and would truly strengthen universal HR treaty bodies. Strong HR institutions, with the power to adjudicate and prescribe sanctions, or ideally the utopian 'World Court for Human Rights'[40] as the final

---

[37] In a study examining the extent to which member States of the Council of Europe (CoE) comply with their HR obligations, and whether a dialogue between the organization and a particular country results in a learning process, Pamela Jordan demonstrates that the CoE has acted as an 'effective mechanism of compliance' relying on soft power of 'pressure, shaming, and the threat of expulsion' and supplied by the internalization of respective HR into domestic legal systems. See Pamela A Jordan, 'Does Membership Have Its Privileges?: Entrance into the Council of Europe and Compliance with Human Rights Norms' (2003) 25 HR Q 667, 686. Similarly, on the 'naming and shaming' strategy in criticizing HR performance employed by the UN Human Rights Commission (now UN Human Rights Council) see Ann Marie Clark, 'The Normative Context of Human Rights Criticism: Treaty Ratification and UN Mechanisms', in Risse, Ropp and Sikkink (eds), *The Persistent Power* (n 35) 125–144.

[38] For a remarkable account of the evolutionary status of regional HR courts and organizations and their influence on State action in the field of HR, presenting a comprehensive amount of empirical evidence, see Alexandra Huneeus, 'International Criminal Law by Other Means: The Quasi-Criminal Jurisdiction of the Human Rights Courts' (2013) 107 AJIL 1 ff. Also Courtney Hillebrecht, *Domestic Politics and International Human Rights Tribunals: The Problem of Compliance* (CUP 2014).

[39] Guzman (n 34) 999, 1002. The author compares the problem of IOs to Mary Shelley's story about Dr Victor Frankenstein. Guzman argues that when States create an IO, they give that entity 'a life of its own and [it] cannot be fully controlled by individual States'. The Frankenstein problem essentially means 'the need for each State to balance the potential benefits of an IO against the risk that the IO will behave contrary to the interests of the State'.

[40] Andrew Clapham, 'Overseeing Human Rights Compliance', in Antonio Cassese (ed), *Realizing Utopia: The Future of International Law* (OUP 2012) 318 (arguing that 'to consider an international court [for HR] as the final

guardian in the protection of the international HR, are expected to be more effective in inducing compliance with HR treaty obligations.

II.3. Human Rights as State Interests

Interdisciplinary theories of compliance described above comprise a wide range of mechanisms that may ensure State compliance with HR obligations. They recognize that international HR law is a cornerstone of modern inter-State relations, but observe that the very concept of HR is deeply integrated with the limitations of State sovereignty. Although this 'limitation-power' is somewhat blurred in the field of treaties (for they are a consent-based type of IL), they nevertheless purport some sovereignty costs. Hence, PE suggests that States accept only limitations they have agreed upon, but they still seek to protect their sovereignty and to reduce the connected costs by establishing HR treaty bodies with weak monitoring and supervisory power.[41]

This may explain why more democratic States tend to be willing to accept less rigorous HR obligations, whereas they remain reluctant to undertake formal binding ones with strong enforcement or monitoring mechanisms.[42] But it cannot fully account for the gradual deepening of HR regimes, whereby States who opposed any strong international HR

---

guarantor may seem naïve, but this destination is simply the logical development of the project to protect human rights through international law').

[41] See Andreas von Staden, 'The Political Economy of the (Non-) Enforcement of International Human Rights Pronouncements by States', above in this Volume (arguing that 'States seek to limit (especially unanticipated) sovereignty costs, including those linked to their expectation as to the probability of future enforcement').

[42] See Moravcsik (n 3) 217 ff. and n 43 below on the European countries. Similar observation may be made with regard to the US and Canada. Both possess strong domestic mechanisms for the protection of civil, political and other fundamental HR; their representatives were the supporters and promoters of the UDHR (suffice to think of Eleanor Roosevelt (US) or John Peters Humphrey (Canada)). However, with the emergence of the stronger Inter-American HR regime, both the US and Canada refused to accept the 'jurisdictional arm' of the system. For a recent overview of the US approach see Francisco J Rivera Juaristi, 'U.S. Exceptionalism and the Strengthening Process of the Inter-American Human Rights System' (2013) 20 Human Rights Brief 19 ff. (observing that the lack of the ratifications of the HR treaties 'raises serious questions about the effectiveness and legitimacy of the System' and urging 'the United States *to pay its true debt* to the Inter-American Human Rights System by fully engaging the System and by finally ratifying the American Convention on Human Rights' (emphasis added)).

commitment, supporting only the declaratory nature of HR treaties, gradually bind themselves with international adjudication and develop a culture of compliance.[43]

The nature of HR and their fundamental role in the international community suggest that States may be genuinely committed to promote and protect them everywhere. Change in social values over the last few decades has had an impact on States; hence, they are more and more likely to act as the 'agents of humanity'. The establishment of the international and mixed criminal tribunals and of the International Criminal Court (ICC) evidences that States are willing to act collectively in order to protect the fundamental values of the international community (enshrined, inter alia, in the international HR norms) and to hold their violators accountable.[44]

In fact, many HR treaty norms are not a reflection of reality, but rather they seek to guide the reality in a certain direction. States may commit to them in an effort to 'lock in' a certain course of policy domestically and as well for the community of nations. These fundamental values (or international norms recognizing and protecting them) may constitute an independent and powerful interest. Hence, State action in the field of HR protection can be motivated by cross-consideration of two types of interests: (*i*) their respective national interests (determined by domestic political processes), and (*ii*) collective interests of humanity. Only the action in the collective interests of humanity may preserve a certain benefit for national interests (reputation, membership, socialization) *and* contribute to the process of developing long-term peace, security, well-being of the world and the maintenance of the law-centred international system.

---

[43] For example, the UK firmly opposed any 'strong' legally binding obligations during the CoE negotiations of the European Convention for the Protection of Human Rights and Fundamental Freedoms (ECHR) (Moravcsik (n 3)). Nevertheless, it came to accept the binding nature of the European Court of Human Rights (ECtHR) judgments and even modified its domestic legal provisions in conformity with the Court's jurisprudence.

[44] Geoff Dancy and Kathryn Sikkink, 'Ratification and Human Rights Prosecutions: Toward a Transnational Theory of Treaty Compliance' (2012) 44 International Law and Politics 751 ff. See also Risse and Ropp (n 35) 3, citing Nicole Deitelhoff, 'The Discursive Process of Legalization: Charting Islands of Persuasion in the ICC Case' (2009) 63 Int Org 33 ff.; Kathryn Sikkink, *The Justice Cascade: Human Rights Prosecutions and World Politics* (Norton 2011).

III. COMPLIANCE WITH HUMAN RIGHTS TREATIES: A CASE AGAINST POLITICAL ECONOMY APPROACH?

III.1. Complexity of Human Rights Treaties

HR treaties are not new to the international community. Rather the framework of protecting the rights of *all* human beings[45] and 'the effort to institutionalize HR regimes in a series of multilateral treaties' is new.[46] The pursuit of this effort has led to the spread of more specific and normative HR treaties with independent supervisory and monitoring bodies.[47] Today the establishment and evolution of modern HR regimes is considered one of the biggest achievements in the promotion and protection of HR internationally, for they accelerate the translation of an aspirational idea of universal HR into legally enforceable rights.

Formally speaking, HR treaties are subject to the regulation of the Vienna Convention on the Law of Treaties (VCLT). But the humanizing potential and specific normative character of HR treaties is widely recognized.[48] They express a commitment to norms and values, but do not represent a traditional exchange of policies or benefits.[49] The

---

[45] HR treaties refer to rights, which derive 'from the inherent dignity of the human person' (International Covenant on Civil and Political Rights (ICCPR) Preamble).

[46] Jack L Goldsmith and Eric A Posner, *The Limits of International Law* (OUP 2005) 107.

[47] See also the 'Introduction' to Andreas von Staden, 'The Political Economy of the (Non-)Enforcement of International Human Rights Pronouncements by States', above in this Volume.

[48] As recognized, inter alia, by the ECtHR in a number of cases (for example, the *Wemhoff v. Germany*, App No. 2122/64, Judgment (of 27 June 1968) para. 8; *Ireland v. United Kingdom*, App No. 5310/71, Judgment (of 18 January 1978) para. 42; *Loizidou v. Turkey*, App No. 15318/89, Judgment (of 23 March 1995) para. 25). In the latter case cited, the Court even refers to the ECHR as a 'constitutional instrument of European public order'.

[49] Matthew Craven observes, referring to the Genocide Convention, that the treaty does not '[represent] an exchange of interests or benefits between contracting States', but rather embodies a 'commitment of the participating States to certain norms and values recognized by the international community'. See Matthew Craven, 'Legal Differentiation and the Concept of the Human Rights Treaty in International Law' (2000) 11 EJIL 491 (the author refers to the position expressed in the Separate Opinion of Judge Weeramanty in the Case concerning the *Application of the Convention on the Prevention and Punishment*

asymmetry of interests and actors involved sets a limit to the traditional reciprocal structure of inter-State relations. The complexity of HR treaties, hence, is the first source of difficulties for any quantitative comparative or unified modelled general study. The issue of complexity is stressed here in the following general considerations, all of which point to (*i*) the difficulty to isolate the impact of a particular norm or a single institution on behaviour; and/or (*ii*) even greater difficulty to perform a unified and systematic quantitative comparative analysis.

Specificity and typology of treaties, rights and obligations

PE models largely draw on the reciprocal relations between States. However, strict reciprocity – meaning an equivalent reaction of State A to the action of State B – is missing in the field of HR law for it is by definition a 'non reciprocal law'[50] and the rights recognized and protected by this body of law are non-reciprocal rights.[51] This implies that the co-operation in this field does not represent an exchange of interests or benefits between the contracting States. Hence the role of inter-State 'contractual bargaining' is not present or is very weak.[52]

Moreover, the corpus of 'HR treaties' includes international agreements, which are distinct in their form, content and institutional design. James Crawford, for instance, divides them into four general categories:[53]

---

of Genocide (Bosnia-Herzegovina v. Federal Republic of Yugoslavia, ICJ Rep (1996) 645).

50 Henkin (n 4) 235 (arguing that the law of HR is 'not reciprocal between States; there is no other State that is the victim or otherwise offended when a State violates its human rights undertakings').

51 Here the present author assumes that legal rights under HR treaties do not purport the reciprocity in rights or duties between States and individual beneficiaries of the rights, neither they purport traditional reciprocal relations between States. Human Rights Committee's General Comment No. 24, for example, points to the specific character of the HR treaties, where 'inter-State-reciprocity' has no place, except 'in the limited context of reservations to declarations on the Committee's competence'. It further states that HR treaties 'are not a web of inter-State exchanges of mutual obligations', but rather 'they concern the endowment of individuals with rights'.

52 Louis Henkin, 'International Law: Politics, Values, and Functions' (1989) 216 Recueil des Cours 253. A more complex approach to reciprocity may include cross-retaliation in other sectors of cooperation. For example, interested actors may use cooperation in other sectors as leverage in order to induce compliance with HR obligations. This, however, may be a motivation for occasional conforming action, but not for long-term culture of compliance.

53 James Crawford, *Brownlie's Principles of Public International Law* (8th edn, OUP 2012) 638.

(1) comprehensive international treaties with the universalist aspiration;[54] (2) regional conventions;[55] (3) conventions dealing with specific wrongs;[56] and (4) conventions dealing with the protection of specific categories of people[57]

All the above-mentioned treaties include an array of rights of a different nature, entailing varying State obligations and available means of protection (from the most obvious issue-specific rights, to the division on 'substantive or procedural'; 'individual or collective' etc. purporting the State 'obligations of conduct or obligations of result', 'positive or negative' obligations etc.). This diversity (often even within the same treaty) means that not all rights or treaties may be measured or compared using the same models[58] and some may not be measured at all.

Diversity of human rights institutions

Some HR treaties provide for inter-State[59] and/or individual (or group) communications,[60] while others also envisage, in one form or another, specific mechanisms enabling a treaty body to investigate the violations of treaty obligations or a mandate to carry out State visits to monitor

---

[54] ICCPR; International Covenant on Economic, Social and Cultural Rights (ICESCR).

[55] ECHR; American Convention on Human Right (ACHR); 1981 African Charter on Human and Peoples' Rights (AfrChHPR).

[56] Convention on the Prevention and Punishment of the Crime of Genocide (the Genocide Convention); Convention on the Elimination of all Forms of Racial Discrimination (CERD); Convention against Torture and Other Cruel, Inhuman or Degrading Treatment or Punishment (CAT); International Convention for the Protection of All Persons from Forced Disappearance (CED).

[57] Convention on the Elimination of all forms of Discrimination Against Women (CEDAW); Convention on the Rights of the Child (CRC); International Convention on the Protection of the Rights of All Migrant Workers and Members of Their Families (ICMW); Convention on the Rights of Persons with Disabilities (CRPD).

[58] Dai observes that 'to date, no comprehensive dataset exists to capture States' compliance with all human rights treaties or all rights covered in any particular treaty'. See Xinyuan Dai, 'The "Compliance Gap" and the Efficacy of International Human Rights Institutions', in Risse, Ropp and Sikkink (eds), *The Persistent Power* (n 35) 90.

[59] ICCPR, Art. 41; 2008 Optional Protocol to the ICESCR, Art. 10(1); CAT, Art. 21(1).

[60] The 1966 Optional Protocol to the ICCPR, Art. 1; 2008 Optional Protocol to the ICESCR, Art. 2; 1999 Optional Protocol to the CEDAW, Art. 2; CAT, Art. 21(1).

compliance with the treaty obligations.[61] All of the HR treaties mentioned above establish a treaty body with the task of supervising and monitoring the implementation of treaty obligations; hence, they produce at least some impact on State decisions. But differences in their composition and mandate, financing (which influences their capacity) and the proliferation of universal, sub-national and national HR institutions[62] operating under the same HR treaties make it nearly impossible to conduct a systematic analysis, which would allow identification of their individual input on compliance.

Domestic factors

The treaty norms fundamentally set the corresponding legal obligations on contracting Parties to 'respect and ensure' the rights recognized therein to all the individuals within their territory and subject to their

[61] For example, the 2002 Optional Protocol to the CAT (in force 22 June 2006) tends to establish, on the one hand, a system of 'regular visits undertaken by international and national bodies to places where peoples are deprived of their liberty' in order to prevent the acts prohibited by the CAT (Arts. 1, 13) and, on the other hand, 'national prevention mechanisms' (Art. 17). The CAT Subcommittee on Prevention is mandated to perform State visits and make recommendations (Art. 11(1)(a)). In addition, the Convention also provides for a confidential inquiry procedure, where the Committee receives reliable information on the systematic practice of torture in a State (CAT, Art. 20). The 1999 Optional Protocol to the CEDAW (in force 22 December 2000), the Optional Protocol to the CRC, the Optional Protocol CRPD, and the CED also envisage only similar inquiry procedures.

[62] Andrew Wolman, 'Sub-National Human Rights Institutions and the Domestication of International Human Rights Norms' (2015) 33 NQHR 225–226 (italic in the original text) (arguing that National HR institutions (NHRIs) include national HR commissions, HR ombudsmen and alike, and sub-national HR institutions comprise 'those sub-national equivalents of NHRIs that are defined here as *independent non-judicial governmental institutions that possess a sub-national mandate, and whose mission includes the implementation of human rights norms*'). See also Richard Carver, 'A New Answer to an Old Question: National Human Rights institutions and the Domestication of International Law' (2010) 10 HR L Rev 6–7 (indicating that 45 per cent of analysed NHRIs include international HR treaties as the applicable law under their mandates, and the same percentage does not specify the applicable norms); Wolman affirms a similar pattern in the case of supra-national HR institutions, whereby a significant number of them are authorized to use international HR norms under their mandates, although many are confined to operate with and implement domestic HR norms, hence dealing with international HR law only indirectly through the overlapping normative content of some domestic and international HR norms. See Wolman, in this fn, at 231.

jurisdiction.[63] States Parties accept 'to take the necessary steps [...] to adopt such legislation or other measures as may be necessary to give effect to the rights recognized'[64] and to submit periodic reports 'on the measures they have adopted which give effect to the rights recognized therein and on the progress made in the enjoyment of those rights'.[65]

It follows that the rights become primarily available to an individual or a group of individuals through the domestic legal system. States must provide specific domestic mechanisms, including juridical, for recognition and protection of individual and collective rights. Therefore the standards of the HR treaty norms enter into domestic law, often at the constitutional level, but there will necessarily be a number of national, regional and provincial level institutions involved in giving effect to the norms. This implies the need to consider also their combined capacity to comply. The differences in domestic legal structures and processes further hamper a unified analysis of the HR performances of differently structured States.

Changing interpretation

HR treaties are living instruments. The content and meaning of the rights recognized in most universal and regional HR treaties may change in response to societal changes. International HR tribunals and domestic courts develop the interpretation of HR treaties, which often departs from the original will of the drafters.[66]

In the same manner, the interplay between the rights recognized in different treaties and soft law acts, but which contribute to the protection of the same value,[67] leads to a situation where some rights and the

---

[63] ICCPR, Art. 2(1).

[64] ICCPR, Art. 2(2); similarly ICESCR, Art. 2(1).

[65] ICCPR, Art. 40(1).

[66] Cesare Pitea, 'Interpreting the ECHR in the Light of "Other" International Instruments: Systemic Integration or Fragmentation of Rules on Treaty Interpretation?', in Nerina Boschiero, Tullio Scovazzi, Cesare Pitea and Chiara Ragni (eds), *International Courts and the Development of International Law* (Asser Press 2013) 545–559.

[67] Consider, for example, the rights of the child. They originate from the 1948 UDHR and the 1959 Declaration of the Rights of the Child. Some rights are recognized in legally binding international agreements (for example, the ICCPR (Art. 24) and the ICESPR (Arts. 10 and 40)) and upheld indirectly in other subject-matter instruments (for example, Agreement No. 182 of the ILO on the worst means of infantile work and its immediate action for its elimination from 17 June 1999). Further, they are recognized in a specific convention, the 1989 CRC, and the two Optional Protocols on the Involvement of Children in

respective State obligations are interpreted in the light of different instruments.[68] Moreover, HR treaties uphold the values that are sometimes protected also by other areas of IL (e.g., *jus cogens*) and the whole idea of HR protection and promotion is enshrined in the UN Charter.[69] What is more, the overall complexity of HR law[70] is aggravated by its strong dependence on the soft law, especially in interpretation and determination of the content of various rights recognized in the HR treaties. The magnitude and legal relevance of HR soft law acts may vary,[71] but their interactions with HR 'hard' law 'shape the content of the international [HR] obligations'.[72] Together general IL and HR (soft and 'hard') law norms create Kingsbury's 'operative normative environment' and have a combined effect on the process of State compliance with HR

Armed Conflict and on the Rights of the Child on the Sale of Children, Child Prostitution and the Use of Child Pornography. Similar repetition of the rights in different instruments with varying legal force may be observed at the regional level. It is often not evident which action is taken in giving effect to or in compliance with precisely which international norm. States may take a particular action in compliance with two or more international norms if they aim at the protection of the same value. See Fabián Novak, 'The Inter-American Court of Human Rights and Its Contribution to the Protection of Children's Rights', in Nerina Boschiero, Tullio Scovazzi, Cesare Pitea and Chiara Ragni (eds), *International Courts and the Development of International Law* (Asser Press 2013) 513–515.

[68] In a recent case the ECtHR interpreted Art. 11 of the ECHR in the light of other international instruments, relying, inter alia, on the interpretation of Arts. 5 and 6 of the 1996 European Social Charter by the European Committee on Social Rights. See *Demir and Baykara v. Turkey*, App No. 34503/97, Judgment (21 November 2006).

[69] Charter of the United Nations (UN Charter), Preamble, Arts. 1(3), 55, 56.

[70] Dinah Shelton, 'Commentary and Conclusions', in Shelton (ed) (n 36) 449: 'the very complexity and proliferation of human rights norms could be a disincentive to compliance'.

[71] HR texts classified as soft law include: (1) *'primary' soft law*, which may (a) set forth new standards, or (b) reaffirm previously accepted standards, or (c) further elaborate previously accepted vague or general standards; and (2) *'secondary' soft law*, including the pronouncements of HR treaty bodies, jurisprudence of regional HR courts and commissions, and resolutions of political organs applying primary norms, which may (a) make general comments or interpretative declarations, or (b) issue specific recommendations to particular States. See Dinah Shelton, 'Compliance with International Human Rights Soft Law', in Edith Brown Weiss (ed), *International Compliance with Nonbinding Accords*, Studies in Transnational Legal Policy No. 29 (ASIL 1997) 120–127.

[72] Ibid at 141.

treaties. International HR treaties, hence, operate and should be interpreted as part of the international legal system.[73] It is difficult to isolate the extent to which each particular norm has contributed to a specific State behaviour.

Asymmetry

Bassiouni has argued that the last phase in a rights-development regime is the criminalization stage, where the values contained in the violated right are protected and enhanced by the penal proscription.[74] This traditionally takes place at the domestic level, but the establishment of the individual criminal responsibility under IL serves as an additional deterrent factor, capable of triggering compliance. This mode of international accountability supplements the traditional State responsibility paradigm, which, in the context of inter-State relations, applies rarely in this field, in case of abusive violations. The former introduces an additional mode of protection for a limited group of rights (especially 'physical integrity rights'), causing the asymmetry in the legal means of protection envisaged in different treaty regimes and the consequent asymmetry in the compliance requirements.

III.2. The Concept of Compliance

Perhaps the majority of literature on compliance with IL quotes Louis Henkin, who famously observed that 'almost all nations observe almost all principles of international law and almost all of their obligations

---

[73] *Fragmentation of International Law: Difficulties Arising from the Diversification and Expansion of International Law*, Report of the Study Group of the International Law Commission finalized by Martti Koskenniemi, UN Doc. A/CN.4/L.682 (13 April 2006) para. 413 (indicating that international treaties are the creation and a part of the system of IL and shall operate as such, hence the 'international obligations are interpreted by reference to their normative environment'). Similarly, the ECtHR held that 'when it [the ECtHR] considers the object and purpose of the Convention provisions, it also takes into account the international law background to the legal question before it'. See *Demir and Baykara v. Turkey* [GC], App No. 34503/97, Judgment (12 November 2008), para. 76. See also Ragnar Nordeide, 'Demir & Baykara v. Turkey, App. No. 34503/97' (2009) 103 AJIL 573 (observing that 'the Court [ECtHR] supports the idea of a structural relationship between the Convention [ECHR] and other international law. The Court's approach reflects its understanding of the Convention within a broader context').

[74] Cherif M Bassiouni, 'International Criminal Law and Human Rights' (1982) Yale Journal of World Public Order 193.

almost all of the time'.[75] The fundamental reason for the 'almost' is the lack of clarity with the identification of the precise compliance requirements of many international norms and the varying meaning of the concept of compliance. Any reference to 'compliance' with treaty norms may comprise three dimensions: (*i*) compliance with procedural obligations, (*ii*) compliance with substantive obligations, and (*iii*) compliance with the spirit of the treaty,[76] but, as Lisa Martin observes, most interdisciplinary studies on compliance indeed 'lack the conceptual clarity about the difference between compliance, cooperation and effectiveness'.[77] It becomes evident that the concept of compliance itself represents a second major source of difficulties in a study of HR treaties.

The definitions of compliance in legal studies often differ, but they all purport a common denominator – a certain degree of conformity between the conduct and requirements of the legal rule.[78] What is often omitted is that compliance may mean both: the state of factual conformity to the rule and the process of reaching full conformity.[79]

---

[75] Louis Henkin (n 4) 47 (italics in the original text).

[76] Edith Brown Weiss and Harold K Jacobson, 'A Framework for Analysis', in Edith Brown Weiss and Harold K Jacobson (eds), *Engaging Countries: Strengthening Compliance with International Environmental Accords* (MIT Press 1998) 4.

[77] Lisa L Martin, 'Against Compliance', in Dunoff and Pollak (eds) (n 10) 605 (arguing also that perhaps compliance as a measurement of interests is not the best way to study the effects of legal norms. Ibid 607).

[78] For example, *compliance* has been defined as 'sustained behaviour and domestic practices that conform to the international [HR] norms' (Risse and Ropp (n 35) 10), or as a concept that 'includes implementation, but is broader, concerned with factual matching of State behaviour and international norms' (Dinah Shelton, 'Introduction. Law, Non-Law and the Problem of "Soft Law"', in Shelton (ed) (n 36) 5); or as 'conformity between the conduct required of the State by [an international] obligation and the conduct actually adopted by the State – that is, between the requirements of international law and the facts of the matter' (James Crawford, *International Law Commission's Articles on State Responsibility: Introduction, Text, and Commentaries* (CUP 2002) 125); or simply as 'a state of conformity or identity between an actor's behaviour and a specific rule' (Kal Raustiala and Anne-Marie Slaughter, 'International Law, International Relations and Compliance', in Walter Carlnaes, Thomas Risse-Kappen and Beth A Simmons (eds), *Handbook of International Relations* (Sage Publications 2002) 539).

[79] An example may be the Montreal Protocol on Substances that Deplete the Ozone Layer. Its Article 8 establishes the procedures and institutional mechanism 'for determining non-compliance with the provisions of this Protocol and for treatment of Parties found to be in non-compliance'. Kingsbury observes that 'in

There may be a state of factual compliance with certain requirements of a norm or a group of norms and, at the same time, non-compliance with other requirements of the same norm (or a correlated norm, or a set of norms expressed in a treaty etc.), because compliance is often intended as a process of reaching (and often also the process of developing the capacity of reaching) a fully compliant behaviour. This implies that there are accepted levels of non-compliance and that there are cases where non-compliant behaviour is not a voluntary act, but depends on the actor's capacity to comply.[80] The failure to view compliance with legal norms as a continuous process may lead to confusion of this concept with effectiveness of a particular norm, treaty or the correspondent international regime.[81] Here compliance is indeed logically interconnected with the notion of effectiveness, making it difficult to separate the two concepts in a given study.

In addition and as observed above, a particular norm alone, extracted from the wider normative environment in which it exists, may produce little independent effect on behaviour. As Benedict Kingsbury argues, '[any] social system includes a wide variety of legal and non-legal norms that may act simultaneously to affect behaviour'.[82] Similarly, the same rights may be regulated by different HR or other treaties, hence, they

---

the Montreal Protocol case, "compliance" may be conceptualized as conformity with rules, but in practice even the narrow "legal" concepts of 'compliance and "non-compliance" are more completely described in terms of a *process* involving relevant international institutions, the regulated States, and other States' (emphasis added). See Kingsbury (n 6) 367.

80 Chayes and Chayes (n 22) 176; Chayes and Chayes (n 21) 9–17. One recent study recognizes that actors' capacity to comply is crucial to the 'rule-consistent behaviour', stressing the attention on the weak or limited statehood as a 'major obstacle with regard to domestic implementation and compliance'. See Tanja A Börzel and Thomas Risse, 'Human Rights in Areas of Limited Statehood: The New Agenda', in Thomas Risse, Stephen C Ropp and Kathryn Sikkink (eds), *The Persistent Power* (n 35) 63–84.

81 Often compliance with the requirements of the norm is a first step to its effectiveness, which may sometimes be measured by the levels of compliance. But the two are distinct concepts. Oversimplification of this observation is that norms set certain rules of behaviour; *compliance* with such norms would mean a conduct or abstention therefrom in accordance with the rules, whereas the *effectiveness* of the norm would be evaluated in terms of the conditional impact of that norm on the behaviour of particular actors combined with its ability to solve the problem at hand ('effectiveness is the question whether the goals of the norm are achieved'. See Shelton (n 78) 5).

82 Kingsbury (n 6) 363. For example, the ICCPR states in its preamble that the articles of the treaty are recognized taking into account 'the obligations of

benefit from the impact of two or more treaty regimes,[83] and it is difficult to identify what particular norm has contributed to a given State behaviour.

III.3. Summarizing the Methodological and Substantive Limits of Interdisciplinary Research

All the interdisciplinary studies reveal the subjective evaluation and measurement problems, although to a different extent and at different stages of analysis. The 'standard-setting' nature of most HR treaties demonstrates the importance of the complex consideration of the two facets of 'compliance' – compliance as a factual state and compliance as a process. Different levels of required behaviour point to the need to 'rank' the severity of the violation, whereby only an abusive behaviour or excess of non-compliant action causes a strong reaction. The measurements of compliance may also involve the evaluation of minor non-compliant activities by way of standard-based evaluation of the norms, but such approach 'involves setting levels of performance that are *deemed* to indicate compliance'.[84]

What follows is the centrality of conceptualization, judgment[85] and subjective evaluation of the perceived facts or events, which presents a double-layer problem. On the one hand, any quantitative or qualitative

States under the Charter of the United Nations to promote universal respect for, and observance of, human rights and freedoms' (para. 3).

[83] For example, Article 7 of the ICCPR recognizes that 'no one shall be subject to torture or to cruel, inhuman or degrading treatment or punishment'. Further, making a clear reference to the UN Charter, UDHR, and to the above-mentioned Article 7 of the ICCPR, the specific 1984 CAT was adopted in order to strengthen the international effort to fight these phenomena.

[84] Shelton (n 71) 133 (emphasis added). But, as the author argues, the employment of this type of measurement also differs in the practice of different organizations performing the measurement and evaluation of compliance. Similarly, Dai observes that the same data sets (PTS and CIRI) use annual country reports by the US State Department and Amnesty International on the respect for personal integrity rights, however, categorizing them into different levels; as a result, 'the data in both datasets seem to suggest that the global average of States' respect for personal integrity rights improves slightly by Amnesty International coding and worsens slightly by the State Department coding'. See Dai (n 58) 89.

[85] George A Lopez and Michael Stohl, 'Problems of Concept and Measurement in the Study of Human Rights', in Thomas B Jabine and Richard P Claude (eds), *Human Rights and Statistics: Getting the Record Straight* (University of Pennsylvania Press 1992) 218.

analysis of HR norms involves the determination of what is perceived as a HR violation. Is it only a strict violation of a treaty norm or is it also a disdain for 'human dignity' that is perceived as infringing the correlated HR? HR treaties sometimes leave many subjective categories and concepts undefined.[86] As a consequence, they do not generally specify what constitutes a violation (or at least, do not indicate *all* the instances that would constitute a violation). On the other hand, such an analysis involves collection and examination of information, which often is not sufficiently accurate, reliable or nuanced (especially on the HR violations).[87] Quantitative or qualitative studies on HR treaty norms include the evaluation of the information on the substantial and procedural requirements of HR treaties and on the diverse domestic actors and national legal systems – differences that are difficult to comprise in a single model or measurement protocol.[88]

Further, international legal order is an extremely complex system and social science samplers fail to take into account a set of small but important details.[89] Continuously evolving and socializing international community and globalization have their part in the change of both domestic and international decision-making processes.[90] On the one

---

86 For instance, the ICCPR, Art. 10(1) provides that 'All persons deprived of their liberty shall be treated with humanity and with respect for the inherent dignity of the human person', but while specifying some requirements of the norm in the subsequent paragraphs, it does not define what exactly constitutes 'inherent dignity of the human person'.

87 Lopez and Stohl (n 85) 217: 'quality and quantity of this information often inconsistent across nations, over time, and vis-à-vis different rights'.

88 Even if other methodologies are applied to determine compliance, the *causal* dimension of compliance (especially the path from recording a violation to tracing its cause) remains difficult to demonstrate. See Shelton (n 71) 139. See also n 60 above in this Chapter.

89 Dinah Shelton asserts that any effort to assess the 'overall compliance of States with human rights norms can produce vastly different results, stemming from the disagreement over the contents of the human rights catalogue and the scope of permissible limitations, as well as what amounts to a violation' and points out that 'one early effort to measure compliance by producing a single scale of human rights compliance evaluated fifty criteria of respect for human rights, in the process *equating freedom to purchase alcohol with freedom from torture*'. See Shelton (n 71) 135 (emphasis added).

90 Globalization 'represents [...] a *qualitative* transformation of the international system with lasting implications for the public and private sectors alike, including changes in the nature of the legal processes and structures that shape the relationships and interactions among States' and not only 'a *quantitative* change in the volume of cross-border activity'. See Wolfgang H Reinicke and Jan

hand, globalization influences both individual and collective choices. Being primarily driven by private actors,[91] it allows their activities to affect developments in the international public sphere. Hence, it contributes to the building of capacity to comply and represents a powerful engine to induce compliance with international HR treaty norms.[92] Theorizing HR from the PE perspective, however, fails to account for the impact of many such actors on compliance treaty norms. Most importantly it misses national and sub-national HR institutions, which influence other actors, domestic or international, through the process of 'domestication of international human rights law'.[93] On the other hand, it fails to comprise the international socialization, whereby repeated interactions between actors, through 'acculturation',[94] may lead to the development of the culture of compliance. Acculturation induces desired behaviour through the 'pressure to assimilate', purporting a change of 'incentive structure or mind' of a targeted actor and changing his social environment.[95]

However sophisticated and comprehensive models may the interdisciplinary approach – such as PE – provide, they seem to fail to account for the whole complexity of HR treaties and to underestimate the value of a legal norm itself. HR treaties and the decision to comply with their norms should be studied as a part of the complex system of international norms, and not as an autonomous, self-sufficient and self-executing set of rules. Empirical testing of the PE models faces the

---

Martin Witte, 'Interdependence, Globalization, and Sovereignty: The Role of Non-binding International Legal Accords', in Shelton (ed) (n 36) 75.

[91] Ibid at 78 (stating that 'in contrast to economic interdependence, globalization is a process mostly structured by private actors' that 'have begun to recognize themselves on a transnational scale').

[92] '[Regulatory] treaties are formally between States, and the obligations are cast as State obligations [...]. The real object of the treaty, however, is not to affect State behaviour, but to regulate the activities of individuals and private entities'. See Chayes and Chayes (n 21) 14.

[93] Carver (n 62) 6–7; Wolman (n 62) 224, 231.

[94] 'Acculturation' here means 'the general process of adopting the beliefs and behavioural patterns of the surrounding culture' and may be viewed as the third mechanism (along with coercion and persuasion) through which IL may change State behaviour. See Ryan Goodman and Derek Jinks, 'How to Influence States: Socialization and International Human Rights Law' (2004) 54 Duke L J 638.

[95] Ibid. The research in this field demonstrates that there is a significant amount of theoretical and empirical evidence to suggest that cultural and associational aspects of IR produce a positive correlation between acculturation and State policy. Ibid at 646; Ryan Goodman and Derek Jinks, *Socializing States: Promoting Human Rights Through International Law* (OUP 2013).

same old problem – 'measuring may not be able to identify what practices result from implementation of international norms'.[96]

IV. CONCLUSION

Legal scholars should identify legal problems and seek to find the solutions by the 'invocation of law',[97] through legal argumentation and reasoning. While, even for an idealist, it would be naïve to argue that States comply with HR treaties only from the sense of legal obligation, it seems likewise not very realistic to imply that States do so only from the costs-benefits calculus, while guided primarily or exclusively by their 'egoistic' interests or domestic preferences. Whether States comply or not with a HR treaty norm, they avoid expressly admitting the fact of acting in direct 'violation of IL', and especially so in the field of HR. Rather, States use other norms available in the IL's 'normative arsenal' to justify or excuse their action (e.g., national or international security concerns). But once they have undertaken to conform to HR treaty norms and have accepted their legitimacy – such justificatory discourse becomes more difficult.

HR law is not a traditional 'inter-State' law. It is a particularly sensitive social construct, which presents a challenging case for the PE methodology. The diversity and complexity hamper the construction of a comprehensive model, which would account for all the dynamics of that law. The non-static concept of compliance itself presents another challenge. As a result, it is difficult to draw any concrete normative framework for the improvements of the HR treaty mechanisms from these studies alone.

Many international lawyers criticize the mix of legal studies with IR theories, arguing that the 'goal of law is to shape and judge behaviour, and not to explain or predict it'.[98] What IL is (or should be) concerned about is what the law is, how to apply it and how to improve it. Questions of why the law is the way it is, or why the norm is applicable to one but not to the other, are concerns of philosophy, history or politics. To this end, the PE approach seems to be a great intellectual exercise,

---

[96] Shelton (n 71) 134. The development of the HR data, based mostly on monitoring the violations of HR, itself presents a problem, be it an '*event-based data*' (data on individual violations) or a '*standard-based data*' (measures HR performance at the national level).

[97] Steven R Ratner, 'Persuading to Comply: On the Deployment and Avoidance of Legal Argumentation', in Dunoff and Pollak (eds) (n 10) 585.

[98] Brunnée and Toope (n 33) 119.

which is able to identify certain problems of law and to try to explain underlying processes, interests, motivations leading to particular behaviour of various actors. Nevertheless, such an approach should seek to answer also the *how* question, not only the *why* one, in order to generate a valid normative input.

17. Political Economy and International Migration Law

Daniela Vitiello* **and Marion Panizzon****

I. THE INTERPLAY BETWEEN IL AND PE IN THE FIELD OF MIGRATION

In a world where roughly 232 million people live outside their country of origin,[1] international migration has been rightly acknowledged as one of the major global issues of our time.[2] However, its direct and indirect impact on development is yet to be fully understood.[3]

To disentangle the complexity of this phenomenon and its repercussions, it is best to bear in mind that human migration is not a distinctive feature of contemporary history. Although a man is, according to Adam Smith, 'of all sorts of luggage the most difficult to be transported',[4] men and women have always migrated, both voluntarily and forcibly. Forced migration is the only way to escape a situation of risk or violation of fundamental human rights, by reason of ill treatment, torture or persecution. Voluntary migration is instead the result of a choice leading migrants to leave their homeland, their family and their certainties in pursuit of a better life abroad.

From an economic perspective, the decision to migrate is the result of a careful cost-benefit analysis, in which the economic and non-economic

---

* Author of Sections I, V, VI.

** Author of Sections II, III, IV.

1 IOM, *Global Migration Trends: An Overview* (2014) 1.

2 IOM, Statement at the Council by Nassir Abdulaziz Al-Nasser, UNGA President (66th session), 6 December 2011.

3 OECD, *Boosting Productivity to Meet the Middle-Income Challenge* (Perspectives on Global Development 2014).

4 Adam Smith, *An Inquiry into the Nature and Causes of the Wealth of Nations* (William Clowes and Sons 1835) 189.

costs of the departure are balanced with the potential benefits in terms of wellbeing, security and integration in destination countries.[5]

In forced migration, the result of this balancing exercise is predictable, since one of the two options (in other words, the stay) is practically unavailable. The peculiar vulnerabilities in which involuntary migrants find themselves as a result of the lack of alternatives have eventuated in the 'internationalization' of their plight. From a legal perspective, it has lead to the recognition of different protection statuses at the international, regional and local level.[6]

In cases of economically driven transnational movements, migrants are assumed to have alternatives. Their migration path is much less safeguarded by International Law (IL), due to a normative tension existing between the individual's right to move across international borders and the discretionary power of States to refuse entry of aliens.[7] This asymmetry mirrors the view, strongly entrenched in IL and practice, that migrants' legitimate expectation of a better life should be counterbalanced with the States' sovereign prerogative to determine conditions (*an*) and modalities (*quomodo*) of aliens' entry and stay in their territory, which represents the quintessence of statehood.[8]

Such a prerogative has inhibited the formation of a comprehensive and integrated system of law dealing with international migration[9] – apart from a *noyau dur* of customary rules limiting States' power in the phases

---

[5] Oliver Falck et al., 'Cultural Biases in Migration: Estimating Non-Monetary Migration Costs' (Institute for the Study of Labor – IZA DP No 8922, 2015) 2.

[6] Refer respectively and chiefly to: the refugee status, as set forth in the Convention Relating to the Status of Refugees (CRSR), the subsidiary protection status, developed in the EU, together with the temporary protection, and the right to asylum and the humanitarian protection, set forth in many domestic legislations.

[7] Vincent Chetail, 'Droit international des migrations: fondements et limites du multilatéralisme', in Habib Gherari and Rostane Mehdi (eds), *La société internationale face aux défis migratoires* (Pédone 2012); Thomas A Aleinikoff and Vincent Chetail (eds), *Migration and International Legal Norms* (Asser Press 2003).

[8] See, for example, US Supreme Court, *Nishimura Ekiu v. US et al.* [1892] 142 US 651, 659 (Gray LJ); Inter-American Convention on Rights and Duties of States (IACRDS) [1933] OAS TS 881, art 3.

[9] Richard B Lillich, *The Human Rights of Aliens in Contemporary International Law* (Manchester University Press 1984) 122; Thomas A Aleinikoff, 'International Legal Norms on Migration: Substance without Architecture', in Ryszard Cholewinski et al. (eds), *International Migration Law. Developing Paradigms and Key Challenges* (Asser Press 2007).

of the entry and exit of aliens (in other words, the right to leave any country,[10] the general prohibition on *refoulement*,[11] and some procedural guarantees surrounding the expulsion procedure).[12]

The solidity of the sovereign prerogative on the design of migrants' rights across and within the borders is pronounced by both the preference for soft law instruments[13] and the fragmentation of international obligations that have arisen in this field, building up a multilayered but patchy body of hard law. The oldest part of this *corpus juris* is composed by Customary International Law (CIL) on the treatment of foreign nationals, which qualifies as a right of the States, granted on a reciprocal basis, of which the individual is the beneficiary.[14]

Conflated in this body of law are also human rights, which presuppose a strengthened protection of vulnerable persons and contain an absolute prohibition of certain conducts (for example, torture, ill treatment and race discrimination).[15] In this area, the central rule with reference to aliens is the non-discrimination principle, which has been widely acknowledged as a key legal foundation of the claim for migrants' access to rights – regardless of their legal status.[16] However, this is merely a legal trend, as yet untranslated into positive law. Indeed, in contemporary Public International Law (PIL), the non-discrimination principle does not

---

[10] It limits States' power to forbid the exit of aliens from their territory. See Universal Declaration of Human Rights (UDHR), art 13 (2), International Covenant on Civil and Political Rights (ICCPR), art 12 (2).

[11] It restrains States' discretion in case of removal of aliens (thus not just refugees and putative refugees) towards territories where they risk seeing their fundamental rights jeopardized. See International Law Commission (ILC), Draft Articles on Protection of the Human Rights of Persons Who Have Been or Are Being Expelled (APHRPE) [2014] UN Doc A/CN.4/L.832, arts 23–24.

[12] Ibid, art 13 and art 21, para 3.

[13] See, for example, Declaration on the Human Rights of Individuals Who Are Not Nationals of the Country in Which They Live [1985] UN Doc A/RES/20/144; Multilateral Framework on Labor Migration (International Labour Organization – ILO 2006).

[14] See, for example, *Mavrommatis Palestine Concession Case* [1924] PCIJ Rep Ser A 2, 12.

[15] Anne F Bayefsky (ed), *Human Rights and Refugees, Internally Displaced Persons and Migrant Workers. Essays in Memory of Joan Fitzpatrick and Arthur Helton* (Nijhoff 2006) 551.

[16] Daniela Vitiello, 'The Right to Health Care for Undocumented Migrants in Times of Economic Crisis. The EU Experience', in Giovanni Carlo Bruno et al. (eds), *Human Mobility. Migration from a European and African Viewpoint* (Rubbettino 2013).

spell out the parity of treatment between citizens and denizens,[17] since the notion of 'national origin' as a ground for equal treatment is mostly intended in a meta-juridical sense.[18] Therefore, it does not oblige States to equate aliens' treatment to that stemming from citizenship or naturalization.[19] Rather, provided that limitations to aliens' rights are legitimate (that is, necessary and proportionate), these limitations can apply under the principle of non-discrimination. In fact, human rights conventions legitimate a balancing exercise between individual rights and 'democratic society's interests' (for example, arts 14, 21, 22 ICCPR and art 15 ECHR) or even States' interest in 'promoting the general welfare' (art 4 ICESCR), with the only exception, a core of intangible and absolute rights.

The third set of international norms concerning migrants' treatment refers to the protection of migrant workers. Conventions adopted under the auspices of ILO,[20] but also the International Convention on the Protection of the Rights of All Migrant Workers and Members of their Families (ICMW),[21] set forth standards of migrants' treatment, partially independent from the regularity of their residence status. The ICMW, in particular, has represented an attempt to mitigate the traditional econocentric view of migrants as mere workforce. However, receiving States have largely boycotted its implementation through low ratification record, rendering this convention – the UN's 'best-kept secret' – ineffectual.[22]

Lastly, there is the multilateral trade regime designed by the General Agreement on Trade in Services (GATS) and its Mode 4 on the movement of natural persons. As currently maintained, it fails to address the major concerns of developing and labour-sending countries. At the same time, it leaves developed and labour-receiving countries a wide margin of discretion as to the sectors to subject to Mode 4 constraints and excludes from its scope permanent migrants and foreigners 'seeking

---

17 On the notion of denizen, see Tomas Hammer (ed), *Democracy and the Nation State: Aliens, Denizens and Citizens in a World of International Migration* (Aldershot 1990).

18 Council of Europe (CoE), *The Position of Aliens in Relation to the European Convention of Human Rights* (HR Files No 8, 2001).

19 See, for example, European Court of Human Rights (ECtHR), *Biao v Denmark* App no 38590/10 (25 March 2014), para 79.

20 ILO Migration for Employment Convention (Revised), 1949 (No. 97); ILO Migrant Workers (Supplementary Provisions) Convention, 1975 (No. 143).

21 ICMW [1990] UN Doc A/RES/45/158.

22 Raffaele Cadin, 'Protection "of" or "from" Migrants? The Failure of Western Countries to Ratify the UN Convention on Migrant Workers' Rights' (2014) 4 KoreEuropa 14.

access to the labour market'.[23] This legal formulation disconnects issues of entry, stay and treatment from questions of market access, discriminating among workers on the ground of their economic role in the country of destination (temporary v. permanent migration) and prioritizing destination market needs asymmetrically.[24]

The impact of such an international framework, which ends up regulating migration on a global scale, should be carefully considered. PE can provide clarification of the causes of fragmentation, revealing the logical nexus between economic concern and law formation. This result can be accomplished through an analysis of the motivations/constraints of participating constituencies and the assessment of their impact on the international normative output.[25]

However, understanding the interplay between PE and international migration law will be complicated due to the distinctive nature of migrant workforce among the other production factors, epitomized in the famous aphorism by Max Frisch.[26]

At the micro level, the *punctum crucis* is the identification of sources of migratory costs and benefits and the quantification of their reciprocal impact on the decision to migrate. Identifying these costs/benefits can help countries leverage their competitive advantages in attracting those migrants more likely to contribute to economic growth. Thus, identification of such costs is essential in the crafting of domestic migratory policy aiming to adjust the dimension and typology of influx to domestic market needs and welfare constraints. However, apart from some identifiable factors (in other words, the access to political freedoms and the existence of migrant social networks), the outcome of the individual cost-benefit analysis cannot be predicted with any certainty, especially due to the inherent difficulty in assessing the weight of non-market-induced determinants of migration.

No less a challenge is the evaluation of relevant stakeholders' competing interests at the meso level, since it is affected by public (real and

---

[23] Joel P Trachtman, *The International Law of Economic Migration. Toward the Fourth Freedom* (WE Upjohn Institute 2009) 241.

[24] Tomer Broude, 'Explaining the Normative Duality of Trade and Migration Agreements' (2011) 105 ASIL Proc 407, 421.

[25] Eyal Benvenisti and George W Downs, 'The Empire's New Clothes: Political Economy and the Fragmentation of International Law' (2007) 60 Stanford L Rev 595.

[26] 'Man hat Arbeitskräfte gerufen, und es kommen Menschen'. See also the ILO Declaration of Philadelphia [1944], emphasizing: 'labor is not a commodity'.

perceived) benefits, market needs, political welfare, group agency and migrants' own interests. Clearly, the crafting of migratory policies – in a way consistent with the final goal to enhance public welfare – is an extremely delicate undertaking.

It is then essential to understand that migration 'does not display the same pattern of domestic interests as trade' in the crafting of policy.[27] On one hand, it is widely accepted that the liberalization of labour mobility across borders is potentially Pareto efficient by virtue of a better allocation of workforce, the cross-fertilization of ideas and knowledge spill over[28] (models based on empirical evidences have convincingly projected that in the long run it would result in almost doubling of world GDP).[29] On the other hand, *ceteris paribus*,[30] free migration produces distributive differentials in risks and gains, not only among the relevant stakeholders operating in the domestic context (micro-meso level), but also between countries of origin and destination at the macro level. If not tackled, such imbalance can impair or at least unfavourably nuance the positive correlation between free migration and welfare gains, causing substantial losses.

Due to the transnational nature of the challenge, it is unquestionable that its tackling entails a wholehearted cooperative response. To this end, Trachtman interestingly proposes the adoption of an international framework agreement allowing for negotiation of compensatory adjustment mechanisms for welfare losses while minimizing transaction costs.[31] Unfortunately, this solution has not yet encountered strong international support by States and, apart from minor regional achievements, liberalization of migration is yet to come. It appears, rather, as a more distant goal as a consequence of the changing landscape of international migration.

---

[27] Joel P Trachtman, 'The Political Economy of International Migration Law', in David A Deese (ed), *Handbook of the International Political Economy of Trade* (Edward Elgar 2014) 502.

[28] Gilles Duranton, 'California Dreamin': The Feeble Case for Cluster Policies' (2011) 3 Rev Econ Anal 3; Michael A Clemens, 'Economics and Emigration: Trillion-Dollar Bills on the Sidewalk?' (2011) 25 JEP 83.

[29] Nathan Smith, 'Open Borders and the Hive Mind Hypothesis' (2015) available at <http://openborders.info/blog/open-borders-hive-mind-hypothesis/> (accessed 30 October 2015).

[30] History, demagogy, racism, economic downturns and income inequality are some of the relevant variables impacting on the determination of migratory policies, which the *ceteris paribus* assumption is intended to exclude from the analysis.

[31] Trachtman (n 27) 524.

Taking into account the special nature of migrant workforce among other production factors, this Chapter aims to advance the debate over international migration, the true significance of which has been framed as 'the missing link between globalization and development'.[32] To this end, in the first part of the analysis, key PE theories are reviewed in order to provide insight on the proper combination of these theories that could assure a better understanding of migration dynamics. In the second part, the suitability of current instruments of transaction over migration is discussed in light of new migratory trends and challenges.

II. WHICH PE FOR THE BETTER UNDERSTANDING OF MIGRATION DYNAMICS? THE CLASSIC PE THEORY AND THE GLOBAL PUBLIC GOODS THEORY

There is not one PE of migration, but rather several theories attempting to understand the motivators of migration[33] – an insight that reflects the circumstance that there is not a single migration dynamic but rather a multiplicity of vulnerabilities and agencies impacting on a migration decision and shaping its context.[34]

Until the 21st century, migration theories have been mostly 'individualistic': migration was approached as individuals' relocation between countries and the reasons underlying this choice analysed. More recently, migration theories have become more 'structuralist', their focus being on social factors influencing the migratory movement, considered as one type of cross-border mobility within other transboundary flows, including goods, services, capital.[35]

Classic PE of migration studies how States have adapted their response to markets through law and policy. It explains migration in terms of income differentials and labour market demand, shedding light on why – despite global welfare gains from migration exceeding those of trade

---

32 IOM, Statement by the UNCTAD Secretary General, Rubens Ricupero, at the IOM Forum 2001.

33 Douglas S Massey et al., *Worlds in Motion: Understanding International Migration at the End of the Millennium* (Clarendon 2009) 3.

34 Douglas S Massey and Edward J Taylor, *International Migration: Prospects and Policies in a Global Market* (OUP 2004) 383.

35 Aristide R Zolberg, 'The Next Waves: Migration Theory for a Changing World' (1989) 23 Int Migr Rev 403.

liberalization – destination States restrict immigration.[36] Among studies analysing the role of the State in the migration process, two perspectives are distinguishable: some studies consider the material and formal sources determining the emergence of migration regulation,[37] others investigate how the design of migration regulation influences the would-be migrant's decision-making.

In the latter perspective, one may collocate the rational choice theory (De Jonge), putting the migrant cost-benefit decision-making at the centre of the migratory process and lessening the power ascribed to wage differentials as a chief factor triggering migration. New Economics of Labour Migration (NELM), coined by Stark, also considers migration in a rational choice perspective. However, it situates the cost-benefit analysis at a family rather than individual level, showcasing parallels to system theories, where the migrant's decision is considered as a part of a greater transnational network.[38]

In the first perspective, one may collocate the typical PE dilemma about trade liberalization and its effect on migration. Trade liberalization has the effect of substitution on labour migration until enterprises are able to compete with foreign multinationals and products.[39] Thus, in the short run, trade liberalization's adjustment costs trigger more migration.[40] Only in the long run, international trade creates jobs in developing countries, and shortens the social and financial distance between receiving and host societies,[41] reducing migration pressure while favouring cross-border movement of persons – a phenomenon described by Martin

---

[36] Trachtman (n 23) 115.

[37] Stephan Castles, 'The Factors that Make and Unmake Migration Policies', in Alejandro Portes and Josh DeWind (eds), *Rethinking Migration* (Berghahn 2007).

[38] Jan De Jonge, *Rethinking Rational Choice Theory. A Companion on Rational and Moral Action* (Basingstoke 2012); Oded Stark and David E Bloom, 'The New Economics of Labor Migration'(1985) 75 Am Econ Rev 173. See below, Section III.

[39] On the contrary, for the Stolper-Samuelson human capital theory, labour flows accompany capital so that developing countries are not only migrant sending but also migrant recipient countries.

[40] William Gois, 'Opinion Piece: Exploring migration and Development Linkages and Reclaiming What is Human and Right in the Discourse' (2009) 28 Refugee Surv Q 201.

[41] Caroline Brettell and James F Hollifield (eds), *Migration Theory: Talking Across Disciplines* (Routledge 2007).

and Taylor as the 'migration hump'.[42] This being the theory, in practice certain aspects of trade protection in the North may exacerbate the migration pressure since they prevent developing countries from gaining access to the most important markets. Lucas criticizes not only trade protectionism but also the inconsistency of trade and migration policies, explained through the failure to coordinate by domestic political constituencies in developed countries[43] and their reluctance to open labour and services markets. As a result, migration is left off the negotiations over free movement of goods and capital across nations,[44] making it the 'missing global flow'.[45]

Hatton, Williamson[46] and Mayda[47] have been the first to label the dichotomy between trade liberalization and free migration as the 'dual policy paradox', illustrated by the evidence that industrialized countries obstacle the latter, despite the fact that its welfare gains are predicted to significantly exceed those from the former. The explanation of this paradox is in the evidence that trade is a two-way street, based on reciprocity, whereas in the field of migration not all countries have, for example, an import interest for low-skilled workers.[48]

Within the PE of migration the second explanation for a missing international regime is provided by the Global Public Goods (GPGs) theory. This theory is advanced notably by Betts who finds that migration splits into club and private goods, but that there is no GPG that would

---

[42] Philip Martin and Edward J Taylor, 'The Anatomy of a Migration Hump', in Edward J Taylor (ed), *Development Strategy, Employment and Migration: Insights from Models* (OECD 1996) 43.

[43] Robert E B Lucas, 'International Labor Migration in a Globalizing Economy' (Carnegie Papers No 92, 2008) 15.

[44] L A Winters et al., 'Liberalising Temporary Movement of Natural Persons: An Agenda for the Development Round' (2003) 26 World Econ 1137.

[45] Gustav Ranis, 'Migration, Trade, Capital and Development: Substitutes, Complements and Policies' (Yale University EGC DP No 950, 2007) 285.

[46] Timothy J Hatton and Jeffrey G Williamson, 'A Dual Policy Paradox: Why Have Trade and Immigration Policies Always Differed in Labor-Scarce Economies' (IZA DP No 2146, 2006).

[47] Anna M Mayda, 'Why Are People More Pro-Trade than Pro-Migration?' (IZA DP No 2855, 2007).

[48] Timothy J Hatton, 'Should we Have a WTO for International Migration?' (2007) 22 Econ Pol 339; Sherry Stephenson and Gary Hufbauer, 'Increasing Labor Mobility: Options for Developing Countries', in Olivier Cattaneo et al. (eds) *International Trade in Services, New Trends and Opportunities for Developing Countries* (WB 2010) 29.

justify the case for migration governance.[49] As a result, the only existing multilateral trade agreement concerning labour migration is framed to give prevalence to club goals. In fact, in the field of migration, States cannot organize to act collectively so that the GPG is no longer undersupplied and its benefits accrue evenly and universally to all States because not all benefits are non-excludable. Only refugee protection and the fight against human smuggling and trafficking are GPGs, since there is no possibility to keep their gains private. To Betts, one has to distinguish the gains of free migration (for example, remittances, diaspora networks, supply of highly skilled) from the gains of managed migration, seeking to minimize the risks of free migration (for example, brain drain, visa overstays, migrant worker exploitation). Both are excludable, thus not GPGs. As to the consumption, protecting refugees is non-rivalrous because if one State admits a refugee, the others can free ride on this benefit. Whereas the same is true for low-skilled migrants (they are abundant and the consumption by one State does not diminish the supply to other States), it is not true for highly skilled migrants. Thus, for Betts high-skilled migration amounts to a private good, whose benefits are excludable and the supply of which is of limited volume, whereas low-skilled migration amounts to a club good, which is infinite in supply but the regulation of which is excludable.

A different view is brought foreword by Trachtman, who sees both highly and low-skilled migrants as GPGs producing non-excludable benefits: the former, through skills and education, the latter because other destination countries may free ride on the fact that there is less migratory pressure emanating from a given source country. Thus, each destination country should take on both skilled and unskilled migrant workers, while source countries should be compensated for their human capital losses. In Trachtman's view, highly skilled migration is an unlimited resource and the risk or externality cost is the lack of investment in education by source countries, not the refusal of host countries to liberalize access to their markets for migrants (as for Betts). Therefore, for Trachtman it is easier to make a case for the top-down multilateral regulation of migration, while Bett's theory explains better the 'agreement dualism', described by system theories.

---

[49] Alexander Betts (ed), *Global Migration Governance* (OUP 2011).

III. SYSTEM THEORIES: THE WORLD SYSTEM THEORY, THE MIGRANT TRANSNATIONALISM AND THE ECONOMIC DUALISM

In migration studies, we distinguish World System Theory (WS) from Migrant Transnationalism (MT) as the two main sets of system theories.

WS (also known as migration system theory) focuses on the inter-linkages between the flow of persons and other flows including information, goods, services and ideas. It clarifies the distinction between 'relational' networks (family and migrant agency activity) and 'regulatory' relations (State-to-State linkages).[50] In addition, it is one of the few theories analysing how migration has been transformed by the globalization and internationalization of labour markets throughout the spread of multinational companies, the proliferation of treaties enacted to create supranational jobs (for example, NAFTA, ASEAN, MERCOSUR) and the development of migrant networks.[51]

WS shares with MT the conviction that migration is just another type of flow alongside information, capital, services and ideas. Migration occurs because the capitalist mode of production incorporates new regions in its path towards unifying the world economy. This penetration, 'in combination with processes of modernization and commercialization of agriculture leads to dislocations and disruptions',[52] and consequently to displacement of a large volume of population. The upside of WS is that it fails to clarify migratory flows between less connected countries, as well as the determinants of migration and why migration of highly skilled follows different patterns than the migration of lower skilled. On the contrary, MT emphasizes a more pro-active engagement of migrants in shaping their destiny.[53] MT (including the migrant network theory, the theory of cumulative causation, the theory of social capital) explains both the determinants of migration and the perpetuation of migration. It builds upon the assumption that interpersonal relations linking migrants to their networks reduce migratory costs and uncertainty, triggering a multiplier effect that leads to chain migration. Its merit is to provide a theory that situates itself in between the macro-level structural theories and the

---

[50] James T Fawcett, 'Networks, Linkages, and Migration Systems' (1989) 23 Int Migr Rev 673.

[51] Massey et al. (n 33) 61.

[52] Joaquin Arango, 'Explaining Migration: A Critical View' (2000) 52 ISSJ 290.

[53] James F Petras et al., *Class, State and Power in the Third World, With Case Studies on Class Conflict in Latin America* (Osmun 1981).

micro-level of rational choice. However, it does not clarify the consequences of the saturation in the dynamics of networks and why high-skilled migration follows different paths and types of regulation. In addition, as the WS, it has not been empirically tested, remaining in the realm of conceptual frameworks.

The new structural theories, focusing on the demand side of migration, are: the Immigration Market Theory (IM) and the Labour Market Segmentation Theory (LMS), both based on the theory of Economic Dualism (ED), as described notably by Piore.[54] He could demonstrate that supply of migrant workers is highly elastic and, in Europe and the US, it was functional to capitalism and eventually permitted a segmented labour market.[55] Thus, in these theories migration is explained by macro-level factors (structural demand), rather than by micro-level rational choice. Contrary to human capital theory, they conclude that labour market segmentation is a by-product of the flexibility of the economy due to globalization,[56] applying as a 'critique of neoclassical economic theory's assumption of a single homogeneous competitive labour market'.[57] These theories find that push-factors (including unemployment and poverty) are less relevant in determining migration than the structural demand for migrant labour in industrialized countries (pull-factors).[58] This is because native workers over time move up the skill ladder and populate the higher capital-intensive segment of the labour market, leaving the lower segment to migrant workers. Their merit is to explain both why structural unemployment coexists with demand for foreign labour (think to the '3D jobs': dirty, dangerous and demeaning) and why immigrants do not necessarily compete with native workers – as has been otherwise suggested by human capital theory or implied by rational choice and system theory. In fact, LMS demonstrates that it is difficult to switch from the secondary to the primary labour market and social mechanisms keep wages down in the latter, even when the supply

---

54 Michael J Piore, 'Dualism in the Labor Market: A Response to Uncertainty and Flux. The Case of France' (1978) 29 Revue Economique 26.

55 Michael J Piore, *Birds of Passage: Migrant Labor and Industrial Societies* (CUP 1979) 187.

56 Philip G Cerny, 'Globalization, Governance and Complexity', in Aseem Prakash and Jeffrey A Hart (eds), *Globalization and Governance* (Routledge 2000) at 204.

57 Randy Hodson and Robert L Kaufman, 'Economic Dualism: A Critical Review' (1982) 47 Am Soc Rev 737.

58 Alexandre Abreu, 'The New Economics of Labor Migration: Beware of Neoclassicals Bearing Gifts' (2012) 16 Forum Soc Econ 46.

of low-skilled migrant labour decreases.[59] This is not true for highly skilled migrants, who are a scarce resource, joining the natives on the primary market as a consequence of employers' competition for skills. Interestingly, it leads to a divided labour market not only between natives and migrants, but also among migrants.[60]

Some criticisms have been voiced against these theories: first, they fail to explain the inflows of highly skilled migrant workers. One of the few attempts to explain the link between economic restructuring and highly skilled migration is provided by Borjas's IM.[61] He shares the view that not only wage differentials create demand for migrant workers, but also active recruitment by employers. In a globalizing economy, States, as well as transnational corporations and recruitment agencies, are in competition for international skills. The role of the State is increasingly important not only in migration control but also in the global competition for talent;[62] a trend that – according to Koser and Salt – 'may be reinforced if it is accompanied by politically initiated regionalization of the international labour market'.[63]

The second downside of these theories is that they underestimate migrants' resources and vulnerabilities. As Zolberg points out, migrant workers are able to overcome restrictions on rights and bargain for labour conditions closer to those of native workers; in addition, often they create jobs that would not exist without them, rather than filling in for pre-existing jobs that natives have shunned (hypothesis not contemplated in LMS).[64] This is truer nowadays, since processes of social transformation and transnationalization deeply influence labour market structures.

Third, these theories are difficult to prove empirically and segmentation into primary and secondary markets may be arbitrary. On this point, Dustmann and Frattini find empirical evidence for economic dualism in Europe in relation to how occupational and earnings distribution differ between EU immigrants, non-EU immigrants and natives.[65] In addition,

---

59 Tobias Müller, 'Migration Policy in a Small Open Economy with a Dual Labour Market' (2003) 11 Rev Int Econ 130.

60 See below, Section IV.

61 George Borjas, *Friends or Strangers* (Basic Books 1990).

62 Allan Findlay, 'A Migration Channels Approach to the Study of High Level Manpower Movements: A Theoretical Perspective' (1990) 28 Int Migr 15.

63 Khalid Koser and John Salt, 'The Geography of Highly Skilled International Migration' (1997) 3 Int J Popul Geogr 291, 293.

64 Zolberg (n 35) 408.

65 Marion Panizzon, 'Migration and Trade: Prospects for Bilateralism in the Face of Skill-Selective Mobility Laws' (2011) 12 Melb J Int L 95.

they could show a variance within employment probability, occupational and earnings distribution, which is important for the hypothesis that the new labour market segments along skills rather than nationality. However, their model has been criticized for ignoring resources, vulnerabilities and social relations,[66] which could be best factored by adopting a livelihood approach and a relational PE analysis,[67] offering a more context-specific viewpoint of migration outcomes and allowing an interactional, behavioural assessment.

More generally, these theories can clarify why there is more migration today than before but fail to explain how to govern such migration internationally. On this point, the evidence is that international cooperation over labour migration draws upon two categories of tools: Regional Trade Agreements (RTAs), used to facilitate the mobility of the highly skilled, and bilateral agreements, used to contain the mobility of the low-skilled. This bifurcation mirrors the labour market segmentation, where lower skilled migrants are subject to highly restrictive mobility schemes for the sole reason that their movement is associated with irregular migration, while highly skilled are the object of the global hunt for talent and thus provided with preferential channels. Taking up Rosenau's idea of 'fragmegration', and extrapolating for the field of migration, we find that there is a fragmentation between highly skilled migrants, whose admission and stay is made more attractive, and lower skilled, whose return is promoted.[68] In addition, Rosenau's idea of 'distant proximities' plays into the emerging transnationalization of migration, whereby most migratory movements no longer occur among geographically proximate areas but instead between spaces linked to each other through transnational networks, which have emerged in the face of globalization. Castles validates these findings implying the emergence of a 'skill divide', with its proper translation into different migratory legal statuses.[69]

---

[66] Randy Hodson and Robert L Kaufman, 'Economic Dualism: A Critical Review' (1982) 47 Am Soc Rev 737.

[67] Sarah Collinson, 'The Political Economy of Migration Processes: An Agenda for Migration Research and Analysis' (IMI WP No 12, 2009).

[68] James N Rosenau, 'Emergent Spaces, New Places, and Old Faces: Proliferating Identities in a Globalizing World', in Jonathan Friedman and Shalina Randeria (eds), *Worlds on the Move, Globalization, Migration, and Cultural Security* (Tauris 2004).

[69] Stephen Castles, 'International Migration at the Beginning of the Twenty-first Century: Global Trends and Issues' (2002) 52 ISSJ 271.

IV. THE SOURCE OF THE SKILL DIVIDE: MARKET OR REGULATOR?

Whereas we manage to adapt theories of LMS and ED to the high vs. low-skilled dichotomy and we draw on these theories to identify the phenomenon dividing up the market into two segments, the explanation we gather on the skill divide appears still incomplete. One specific unanswered query – emerging as a chicken and egg dilemma – is whether the regulator simply implements a separation between high and low-skilled migrants (which already plays out on the labour market); or anti-immigrant sentiments lead politics to pressure law to differentiate the legal regimes governing high and low-skilled migration (with the labour market playing no role in this segmentation).

The second hypothesis has been maintained by Hainmueller and Hiscox, who find empirical evidence for Europe that natives prefer highly skilled migrants and that this preference does not decrease depending on the natives' skill level.[70] Whereas poor natives fear constraints on welfare benefits, rich natives' economic self-interest in relation to low-skilled immigration is the fear of increased taxes. Therefore, governments design immigration law channels that distinguish between high and low-skilled migrants. However, they also have to cater to employers' demands for lower skilled workers and consider source countries' willingness to cooperate on readmission. For these reasons, governments need 'escape clauses' to circumvent voter sentiment biased against low-skilled workers (for example, bilateral agreements granting access to lower-skilled professions in shortage in the destination country, in return for source country cooperation on readmission).[71] In short, migration is conceived as an instrument adjusting skills, age and sectorial composition of national and regional labour markets.[72] It is thus the cheap alternative to

---

[70] Jens Hainmueller and Michael J Hiscox, 'Attitudes Toward Highly Skilled and Low-Skilled Immigration: Evidence from a Survey Experiment' (2010) 104 Am Pol Sci Rev 61.

[71] Marion Panizzon, 'Franco–African AJMs on Migration: Bilateralism Revisited in Multilayered Migration Governance', in Rahel Kunz et al. (eds), *Multilayered Migration Governance: The Promise of Partnership* (Routledge 2011) 209.

[72] Lant Pritchett, 'Let their People Come: Breaking the Gridlock on International Labor Mobility' (Center for Global Development – CGD 2006) 111; María L Palma Martos and José L M Navarro, 'Globalization and Migration Flows. Some Effects of Immigration on the Spanish Labour Market in the Last

trade liberalization and the structural adjustment of markets to the forces of globalization.[73]

Dauvergne argues that the States design immigration law with the purpose of shaping the economy and controlling globalization forces. Following this line of argument, the economy should be pushed towards recruiting only the best and the brightest, while eliminating industries which use low-skilled migrants as a substitute for product innovation and technological adjustment.[74] However, she admits that there is an inroad to the State's skill-selectiveness, which is made by human rights standards and the rule of law.

Castles does not deny that also the State is responsible for the skill divide, however he argues that the 'global migration market' – linked to the 'informal social networks, which develop within the migratory process' – may become more 'powerful in shaping population flows than the policies of States'.[75] This line of reasoning could uphold the idea of a primacy of market forces, tempered with the human rights perspective. To this end, it could be useful to draw a parallel with Rosenau's idea of 'bifurcation of global structures', whereby State centrism is softened at the cost of the rise of subnational and transnational entities.

This has been surely the case for highly skilled migrants, in the sense that migration law has been adapted to the primary market needs of a skilled migrant workforce.[76] For low-skilled migration, instead, States tend to ignore market demand and cater to anti-immigrant sentiment by installing restrictive entry schemes. This is particularly true in a post-9/11 world, where the market-driven demand for unskilled migrant labour, neglected by skill-selective schemes, is met by other means, notably 'increases in people smuggling, trafficking and undocumented migration,

---

Decade' available at <http://anale.feaa.uaic.ro/anale/resurse/mec2martosn.pdf> (accessed 30 October 2015).

[73] James F Hollifield, 'Migration and the "New" International Order: The Missing Regime', in Bimal Ghosh (ed), *Managing Migration: Time for a New International Regime* (OUP 2003) 87.

[74] Catherine Dauvergne, 'Sovereignty, Migration and the Rule of Law in Global Times' (2004) 67 Mod L Rev 604.

[75] Stephen Castles, 'Globalization and Migration: Some Pressing Contradictions' (UNESCO 1998) 179, 181.

[76] Adrian Favell and Randall Hansen, 'Markets Against Politics: Migration, EU Enlargement and the Idea of Europe' (2002) 28 J Ethn Migr Stud 581.

at […] significant and rising human costs [which are] unintended and undesired outcomes'.[77]

In conclusion, a combination of the State's response to anti-immigrant sentiments and the segmentation of labour markets explains the skill divide, which reverberates in the discriminatory legal treatment between these two migrant categories. The divide is triggered by a global competition for the 'best and the brightest'[78] but also by the desire of States to improve control over migration, both leading to a perpetuation of the 'the North-South development divide'.[79]

V. RE-SETTING THE STAGE: THE DECLINING CENTRALITY OF TRADITIONAL DIVIDES IN THE DECISION-MAKING PROCESS REGARDING MIGRATION AND THE UPCOMING CHALLENGES FOR IL

Previous paragraphs highlight how PE theories can be used to explain the bifurcation of migration steering tools. Their key focus is the international legal movement of workforce, which poses complex challenges upon national welfare, making it vital for States to undertake forms of cooperation for mobility distinguishing the 'wanted' from the 'unwanted' migrants.[80]

---

[77] Hein de Haas and Simona Vezzoli, 'Leaving Matters: The Nature, Evolution and Effects of Emigration Policies' (IMI WP No 34, 2011) 5; Frank Düvell, *Illegal Immigration in Europe. Beyond Control* (Palgrave Macmillan 2005).

[78] Devesh Kapur and John McHale, *Give us Your Best and Your Brightest, The Global Hunt for Talent and Its Impact on the Developing World* (CGD 2005).

[79] David Ellerman, 'The Dynamics of Migration of the Highly Skilled: A Survey of the Literature', in Yevgeny Kuznetsov (ed), *Diaspora Networks and the International Migration of Skills: How Countries Can Draw on Their Talent Abroad* (WB 2006) 21, 31.

[80] Instances of regional cooperation for labour mobility are provided by EU Directives on highly skilled workers, Blue Card holders, researchers and students, family reunification and long-term residence. It is also feasible to incorporate free mobility clauses in FTAs, as in the case of the provisions facilitating mobility of qualified professionals among NAFTA countries. There is also a wide record of bilateral agreements, mostly dealing with temporary migration (seasonal, guest and holiday workers) and low-skilled labour workforce. See *International Migration Outlook* (OECD 2014, ch 3) 192–193.

In these analyses, forced migration remains mostly excluded, due to the non-discretionary control that States exercise upon it, and the subject of irregular labour migration is minimized, by reason of its low impact on governments' maximization of political support. However, as globalization modifies and shapes migratory processes, migration theories need to be readapted and updated. This is particularly the case in the present global context of structural change in migration dynamics, where one may question the suitability of traditional divisions in both shaping domestic policies and framing or orienting international transactions regarding migration.[81]

Looking at the data provided by the OECD in 2014, the first divide affected by the current situation is that between 'discretionary' and 'non-discretionary' migrants. Indeed, the quantitative dimension of forced migration, accounting for an unprecedented portion of the total, raises (*inter alia*) the question of how to maximize the contribution from non-labour migration[82] while receiving countries often seek to exploit the margin of appreciation left by international rules to somewhat curtail refugee rights. At the same time, the situation is complicated by a number of international obligations to admit foreigners, which have arisen in the field of labour migration, limiting States' traditional discretion in this area.[83]

The second divide affected by the intensification of globalization processes is the skill dichotomy. As the trend toward specialization moves further, skills typologies and their association to traditional markers are shifting, so that the match between the market's needs and migrants' skills becomes problematic.[84] This may result in both thwarting the global competition for talent and rendering less foreseeable the outputs of selective migration policies based on qualifications. This deconstruction of skill dichotomies represents a major challenge also because the existing web of international trade instruments concerning labour migration is built upon the traditional market-driven dualism that exists between highly and low-skilled migrants, which also conditions the

---

[81] Catherine Dauvergne, *Making People Illegal, What Globalization Means for Migration and Law* (CUP 2009) 5.

[82] Claudio Matera and Amanda Taylor (eds), *The Common European Asylum System and Human Rights: Enhancing Protection in Times of Emergencies* (Centre for the Law of EU External Relations – CLEER WP No 7, 2014).

[83] Examples can be found in OECD (n 80) 146–147.

[84] Thomas Liebig et al., 'How can migrants' skills be put to use?' (2014) available at <http://www.oecd.org/els/mig/migration-policy-debates-3.pdf> (accessed 30 October 2015).

modality of transaction – that is, the option for multilateralism or bilateralism.[85]

The third divide influenced by current migration dynamics is that between temporary and permanent migrants. Due to the proliferation of different residence and protection statuses, the temporariness of residence and work permits can be more easily circumvented by migrants[86] and does not impact substantially on their decision to stay or leave. As a result, policies modelling migratory pathways throughout the duration of stay are proving to be less effective and no longer function as a steering tool for unemployment mitigation.[87] Apart from this, the underlining problem of the distinction between permanent and temporary statuses is that migrant workers do not leave a host country simply due to job loss (in economic terms, this signifies that labour is less flexible than other production factors).

Lastly, the proliferation of irregular pathways[88] is making it more difficult to match migration goals and steering tools. This is often the paradoxical result of political attempts to reconcile the trade-off between free migration and the welfare state in receiving countries. In fact, since irregular migration does not qualify for welfare and lacks organization and agency, its claim for rights is rarely incorporated in process outputs and its failure to influence domestic decision-making processes does not produce any political cost.

As Milton Friedman sharply pointed out, in Americans' eyes migration 'is only good so long as it is illegal',[89] since illegal migration greases the economic wheels while limiting the costs that migrants' reception imposes on taxpayers and the risk of rent seeking. Not surprisingly, in many receiving countries, the opposing socio-economic interests of domestic communities – claiming a reduction of immigrants' welfare uptake – employers – demanding flexible low-cost labour force – and

---

85 Jürgen Bast, 'Bilateralism and Multilateralism in International Migration Law' (2011) 105 ASIL Proc 407, 412.

86 See, for example, the issuance of a permanent permit after five years' residence established in the EU Council Directive 2003/109/EC, OJ L 16/44, whose scope has been extended to third countries nationals eligible for international protection by Directive 2011/51/EU, OJ L 132/1.

87 Even in regional systems, based on common rules, one often finds such a mottled application of the common legal setting to prejudice the result of a uniform impact on migrants' choices. See OECD (n 80) 149.

88 See World Migration Rep (IOM 2010, ch 4) 29; OECD (n 80) 134.

89 See 'Friedman on Immigration and the Welfare State' (2006) available at <http://openborders.info/friedman-immigration-welfare-state/> (accessed 30 October 2015).

migrants – seeking the recognition of right to free movement – have been reconciled by government toleration of a certain amount of undocumented migration.[90] Meanwhile, at the international level, cooperation against irregular migration has become a priority since the political debate has spotlighted a nonmarket-driven goal – that is, security – on other objectives associated with economic migrations, especially in bilateral agreements.[91] This trend has been exasperated by the current economic downturn, which has nurtured a widespread aversion to free migration by public opinion. In spite of the fact that free labour mobility has been proven to enhance the adjustment capacity of integrated labour markets to cope with asymmetric shocks,[92] the number of aliens – whether holding a regular or irregular status – has become an issue in many receiving countries.[93]

Policy makers have struggled to factor the impact of claims for a restrictive approach into negotiations. At the domestic level, this has resulted in a mixture of deterring policies, whose main features are: the increasing recourse to restrictions on family reunification; the implementation of civic integration tests as a condition for entry and stay; the limitation on the access to rights; the criminalization of irregular immigration; the imposition of a wide variety of controls on egress (not always compatible with international obligations); and the strengthening of traditional tools, such as numerical limits and quotas, detailed selection, ranking criteria, labour market tests and shortage lists.[94] The need for a response to new challenges has led to a sophistication of means composing States' toolbox on migration management and to the adoption of hyper-selective policies, such as those based on the 'expression of

---

[90] Mats Tjernberg, 'The Economy of Undocumented Migration: Taxation and Access to Welfare' (2010) 12 EJML 149; Daniela Vitiello, 'The European Doorway to Social Rights for Undocumented Migrants' (2010) 48 AWR Bull 110.

[91] Alexander Betts and James Milner, *The Externalisation of EU Asylum Policy: The Position of African States* (COMPAS WP No 36, 2006); Aderanti Adepoju et al., 'Europe's Migration Agreements with Migrant-Sending Countries in the Global South: A Critical Review' (2010) 48 Int Migr 42, 61.

[92] Julia Jauer et al., *Migration as an Adjustment Mechanism in the Crisis? A Comparison of Europe and the United States* (OECD, SEM WP No 155, 2014).

[93] US German Marshall Fund, *Transatlantic Trends* (2014) available at <http://trends.gmfus.org/transatlantic-trends/> (accessed 30 October 2015).

[94] This is the case in the EU, but also in Australia, where labour market tests for immigrants have been strengthened, and in Canada, where the option for shortage lists has served to increase public consensus. See OECD (n 80) 178.

interest' (that is, an evolution of the point-based system),[95] coupled with incentives designed to retain the 'wanted' migrants (for example, the so-called 'red carpet treatment'),[96] and expanding upon the concept of citizenship for the purposes of cross-border attraction of human capital.[97]

At the bilateral and regional level, the emphasis placed on the security discourse has further prioritized the negotiation of readmission agreements, 'non-arrival' strategies and diversion policies, whose bargaining object is an enhanced cooperation in the restriction of movement of people in return for economic aid to sending countries.[98] The net result of the pursuit of containment goals has been the shift of responsibility back onto sending and transit States, least able to cope with international migration and already bearing the lion's share of it, as well as the proliferation of illegal ways for migrants to leave their countries, with serious humanitarian backlashes. Lastly, the international negotiations on migration have spotlighted the criminal issue, rounding out new proposals of strategic cooperation in the fight against irregular immigration and transnational crimes involving the movement of natural persons,[99] with particular reference to migrant smuggling and trafficking in human beings.[100]

In light of these developments, the traditional 'skill divide' – triggered by market-driven concerns – seems to be coupled with a new 'security

---

95 Ibid, 168.

96 Ibid, 188–190.

97 Aylet Schachar, 'Highly Skilled Immigration: The New Frontier of International Labor Migration' (2011) 105 ASIL Proc 407, 416.

98 This is especially the case in the EU, where 'preventive' strategies substantiate mainly in enhanced operative cooperation between the Union (and its Member States) and third countries by means of joint sea patrols, deployment of liaison officers and carrier sanctions, while 'diversion' policies concern the readmission of irregular migrants and asylum seekers through the 'safe third country' clause and the 'protection in region' mechanism. In a similar vein, the Australian 'Pacific Solution II' envisages 'tow-backs' to the country of departure of migrants headed to Australian shores, their transferring to 'offshore' processing centres located in Australian overseas territories and the Australia-Malaysia People Swap' Arrangement, aimed at deterring 'boat people' from landing on Australian shores by threatening them with deportation to Malaysia. See Daniela Vitiello, 'La cooperazione operativa tra Frontex e i paesi terzi nel contrasto all'immigrazione irregolare', in Francesco Cherubini (ed), *Le migrazioni in Europa – UE, Stati terzi e migration outsourcing* (Bordeaux 2015) 163, 254.

99 See, for example, EU, *A European Agenda on Migration*, COM(2015)240 final.

100 Convention against Transnational Organized Crime (CATOC) [2000] UN Doc A/55/383, and its two Protocols on smuggling and trafficking.

divide' – prompted by a revival of the logic of State control over migration and resulting in discriminatory practices. This new divide is apparent even from the lexicon used to distinguish the 'expats' (white, coming from developed countries and sharing the same culture and values – thus presumed not dangerous for local communities) from mere 'immigrants' (black or yellow, coming from developing countries and holding a different culture and values – thus presumed to carry threats).[101]

The 'delocalisation' of European border controls[102] and the ongoing dismantling of the Schengen cooperation in Europe provides a convincing example. As migrants' surge by sea started to be connoted as an extraordinary 'emergency',[103] in the aftermath of the Arab Springs,[104] European States re-emphasized 'the importance of the elusive national borders for the most vulnerable group of the population – the migrants and residents without EU citizenship'.[105] This led first to the recast of the Schengen Borders Code in order to introduce a security net.[106] Then, very recently, the dispute between EU States on migration management peaked,[107] seriously narrowing the room for mediation among different stances and risking impairing one of the most qualifying results of European integration – the 'fourth freedom'.[108]

Building public confidence in migration issues should be the first step in reversing this trend. In addition, policy reforms aiming at reconciling

---

[101] Mawuna Remarque Koutonin, 'Why are White People Expats When the Rest of Us Are Immigrants?' (The Guardian, 13 March 2015).

[102] See, for example, the priorities of the EU Global Approach on Migration and Mobility (COM/2011/743 final) in relation to third countries of origin and transit.

[103] On the diffusion of the narrative of migration 'emergency' see Tamás Molnár, '(Ab)normality of International Migration Law: Normative and Structural Asymmetries and Contradictions' (2015) available at <https://migreflaw.wordpress.com/2015/05/11/> (accessed 30 October 2015).

[104] Daniela Vitiello, 'The "Lampedusa Case" from a Domestic and European Standpoint' (2011) 49 AWR Bull 282.

[105] Dimitry Kochenov and Martijn van den Brink, *Pretending There Is No Union: Non-Derivative Quasi-Citizenship Rights of Third-Country Nationals in the EU* (EUI WP Law No 7, 2015) 23.

[106] See art 26 of the Regulation (EU) No 1051/2013 amending Regulation (EC) No 562/2006, OJ L 295/1, providing for common rules on the temporary reintroduction of border controls at internal borders in exceptional circumstances.

[107] Philippe Euzen, 'A la frontière franco-italienne, l'incessant va-et-vient des migrants refoulés' (Le Monde, 19 June 2015).

[108] Trachtman defines it as the 'legally authorized free movement of labor'. See Trachtman (n 23) 4.

short and long-term objectives and enhancing migrants' contribution to domestic economies should look at viable strategies to adjust universal measures to targeted strategies, untap immigrants' potential through integration, and balance the share of responsibility among all relevant stakeholders. Of course, a general model of migration management applicable with success in every national context is not feasible because the appropriateness of the various tools derives from a number of local conditions. However, analysing different policies implemented in the OECD countries from 2002 to 2012,[109] one discovers that the more effective approaches are those capable of reacting to change. Their common benchmark is represented by the flexibility – in other words, the capacity to match goals with appropriate tools and to respond to inherent trade-offs among multiple stakeholders assuring the fulfillment of competing goals.[110]

VI. CONCLUSION

International, regional and local decision-making processes over migration have long shaped migratory flows, so that only the 'wanted' embarked on the journey. States have kept their hands on the tiller of migration policies by disconnecting the question of territorial admission, sojourn, and (even) treatment of foreigners from that of labour market access. In addition, the option for an econo-centric approach has led to discrimination among migrants on the ground of the 'scarcity' of their skills (this approach being also entrenched in the only multilateral hard law framework dealing with the access of migrants to contracting parties' labour markets – the GATS Mode 4). Therefore, the dichotomy between migrant rights' protection and free movement has been recomposed only with regard to highly skilled migrants.

Although not completely satisfactory, this market-oriented framework and its 'embedded governance' of international migration[111] have long

---

[109] *Free Movement of Workers and Labor Market Adjustment: Recent Experiences from OECD Countries and the European Union* (OECD 2012).

[110] For proposals regarding the EU context see Peter Bosch, 'Towards a Pro-Active European Labor Migration Policy. Concrete Measures for a Comprehensive Package' (EUI, MPC Paper No 3, 2015).

[111] Sabine Corneloup, 'Can Private International Law Contribute to Global Migration Governance?', in Horatia Muir Watt and Diego P Fernández Arroyo (eds), *Private International Law and Global Governance* (OUP 2014) 301, 304.

counterbalanced a restrictive unilateralism, creating room for international cooperation on migration.

Yet, together with the maturation of globalization processes, the evolution of dynamics in human mobility has rendered inadequate the steering tools at the disposal of the international community. In the search for smart policies to support economic growth, policy makers must now take into account emerging tendencies related to structural changes (in other words, the modality of migration, the evolution of protection statuses, the modification of labour markets, the shrinking capacity of the national welfare state). Understanding the impact of these trends on the current global order implies a multidimensional analysis that places in the right perspective all relevant variables, including the public perception of genuine and forced migration, not to mention the concern for demographics.

To this fairly daunting array of challenges one must add the current economic downturn. In receiving countries, it has exasperated the trade-off between market demand for a flexible workforce to relaunch the economic cycle and regulators' attempts to reduce immigrants' numbers and their welfare uptake (both influenced by public aversion to migration and exploiting it to make migration an easy scapegoat issue for political advantage).[112]

In sending countries, the downturn has exacerbated the pressure to migrate from both highly and low-skilled workers: the former have managed to leave through preferential channels; the latter have seen their ambitions often frustrated, due to bilateral commitments to control departures. This state of affairs has accelerated brain drain while reducing remittances and return migration – further impairing the migration-development nexus.

The economic crisis has succeeded in straining cooperation among States, making more than ever restrictive unilateralism 'the elephant in the room'.[113] In addition, it has prioritized the containment objective, raising appeals to address issues relating to transnational crime and limiting migrants' rights in favour of States' security.

From a PE perspective, the shift from the narrative of 'quasi-open borders' to that of 'migration control' can be described as a market failure, affecting all levels of governance on migratory issues: at the local level, it curtails human and social welfare while impeding free mobility

[112] Pascal Lamy, *Key Note Speech at the OEDC High Level Policy Forum on Migration*, 17 December 2014.

[113] Bast (n 85) 415.

of labour to act as an 'adjustment mechanism' in times of economic downturn; at the bilateral and regional level, it prevents States from achieving welfare-enhancing agreements; at the multilateral level, it tarnishes the interlinkages between migration and development.[114]

The trend towards the prioritization of non-economic concerns in migration transactions represents the last bulwark of sovereignty in the face of globalization. The impact of this trend has to be carefully factored when proposing feasible migration strategies, aimed at the redistribution of power and welfare in favour of displaced peoples, not only because it renders migration management somewhat economically inefficient, but also because it erodes the legal position of the migrant under IL and undermines the progressive development of a *jus migrandi*.

Clearly, the recipe for efficient and coherent international migration management could not be more challenging and the recasting of existing instruments is difficult to foresee as these depend on the States' interests.[115]

However, insights to address the upcoming challenges can be extrapolated from the existing imperfect framework of rules on migrants' rights and trade law and, more precisely, from the conceptual primacy it assigns to individual liberalism, *de facto* limiting States' sovereignty.[116] Although developed in a 'piecemeal fashion',[117] this legal system shows some convergence in recognizing the distinctive nature of migrant labour in economic negotiation and is equipped with a number of tools to cope with normative antinomies.[118]

---

[114] In fact, although developed countries increasingly depend upon a migrant workforce – also low-skilled – and sending countries' development is bound to the revenue it creates – the flows of migrants' remittances almost outclassing development aid in scope and relevance – the former prefer to renounce the benefits of labour mobility in the name of domestic consensus over the containment of migrants' mobility, the latter do not hold sufficient bargaining power to reverse this trend. See Daniel Bethlehem, 'The End of Geography: The Changing Nature of the International System and the Challenge to International Law' (2014) 25 EJIL 9, 16.

[115] The possibility of further liberalization has been at stake in the Doha round of trade negotiations without significant evolution. See Brian Opeskin, *The Influence of International Law on the International Movement of Persons* (UNDP RP No 18, 2009) 21.

[116] Jagdish Bhagwati, *In Defense of Globalization* (OUP 2004).

[117] UNDP (n 115) 27.

[118] Chantal Thomas, 'Convergences and Divergences in International Legal Norms on Migrant Labor' (2011) 32 Comp Lab L Pol J 405, 434.

In addition, the impact of the empowerment of civil society and IOs on international transactions over migration should not be underestimated, 'as the salience of international legal rules as norms can precede or exceed their effectiveness as rules of positive law'.[119] While States are the final arbiters in the recasting of the international migration regime, IOs and NGOs play an increasingly crucial role in restraining and routing State authority over the transborders movement of persons, especially when entrusted with effective monitoring powers.

The classic example is the evolutive interpretation of human rights by monitoring treaty bodies, which take upon themselves the assessment of what is legitimate in areas where States enjoy a margin of appreciation.[120] No less important is the advocacy role of IOs and NGOs. They promote States' compliance through 'naming and shaming' and deliver priorities in international agendas on migration, including through the formulation of codes of conduct on ethical recruitment (IOM, ILO, WHO).[121]

Ultimately, this trend has the potential to contribute to a 'qualitative jump' in the (re)formation of a *jus migrandi* in IL, enabling significant changes in the traditional balance between State sovereignty on migratory issues and migrants' rights, particularly with respect to the call on liberalizing constraints on low-skilled migration.[122]

It is worth stressing that the development of a *jus migrandi* in IL is not a necessary outcome of a human rights approach, unlinked or in contrast with economic concerns. The non-economic nature of some challenges should not contribute to clouding the PE lens in the search for optimal solutions. Indeed, as shown by the CJEU's jurisprudence, it is possible to recompose the fracture between economic and human rights concerns in light of the economic finality of agreements on free movement of labour. The need to assure the *effet utile* of these agreements can justify the reconnection of the migrants' right to employment to their right to sojourn, implying the latter to be embedded in the former.[123]

---

119 Ibid, 407.

120 On the jurisprudence of the ECJ see Catherine Barnard and Steve Peers (eds), *European Union Law* (OUP 2014) 356, 777.

121 Jutta Brunnée, 'International Legal Accountability Through the Lens of the Law of State Responsibility' (2005) 36 NYIL 3.

122 UNDP, 'Making Global Trade Work For People' (Earthscan 2003).

123 See, inter alia, *Sevince* Case C-192/89 (20 September 1990), para 29; *Dogan* Case C-383/03 (7 July 2005), para 14; *Gülbahce* Case C-268/11 (8 November 2012), para 38.

However, one may wonder whether the traditional econo-centric approach is still sufficient to unlock welfare gains. Regarding this, Broude argues that the unfettered liberalization of migration should not be considered a win-win solution uncritically and that, aside from compensation of the losers in international negotiation on migration, it may be desirable to introduce into the transaction safeguarding clauses that aim to preserve core non-economic values, including 'elements of global distributive justice [and] human rights protection'.[124] This could lead to a different reading of the various modalities of cooperation, whose appropriateness would be more dependent on the symmetry of commitments undertaken by the parties involved than on their multilateral or bilateral nature.[125]

Venturing into the realm of the progressive development of IL, the option for a more inclusive approach to migration is not likely to uphold a perfect individual right 'to seek and be granted a better life'.[126] However, the increasing relevance of non-State voices in the international institutional setting may help fill in some of the gaps towards the maximization of individual, national and global welfare, which can but pass through more equitable burden/reward sharing mechanisms and the incorporation in a cooperative framework of peoples' claims for freedom of movement, human security and human capital development.

---

[124] Tomer Broude, 'The WTO/GATS Mode 4, International Labour Migration Regimes and Global Justice', in Roland Pierik and Wouter Werner (eds), *Cosmopolitanism in Context. Perspectives from International Law and Political Theory* (CUP 2010), 104; Tomer Broude, 'A Minimal Liberal Defense of (Some) Discrimination in Migration Regulation' (2013) 36 Fordham Int L J 575.

[125] See Bast (n 85).

[126] The wording ironically recalls art 14, para 1 of the UDHR, on the right to seek and be granted asylum from persecutions. *Contra*, see Colin Grey, 'The Right of Migration' (2014) 20 Legal Theory 25.

PART V

Conclusions

18. Political Economy and International Law: Paradoxes and Potential

Eyal Benvenisti and Jan Wouters

I. INTRODUCTION

This Book breaks new ground in that its chapters look consistently through the lenses of Political Economy (PE) at a wide set of International Law (IL) issues: from sources to enforcement and various substantive areas, such as trade agreements, investment law, water law, human rights and migration law issues. The chapters unravel the dimensions of PE behind the most diverse issues, like benefit sharing in water law, the strategies used by judges when identifying customary norms, the non-written waiver which facilitates regional trade agreements, and the problem of many hands in the law of international responsibility.

Instead of a one-size-fits-all approach, the authors have followed their own methodologies in considering PE as their object of study. Some of them are enthusiastic about the insights which PE offers to the study of IL; others are downright skeptical. The 'holistic model of State behavior' advanced by Anne van Aaken and Joel Trachtman has inspired some authors, while other contributors do not hide their criticism. A veritably pluralistic volume! The unifying strength of this colorful bouquet of essays is that they have all been written by the most seasoned and highly regarded scholars – we would almost be tempted to say: 'the most highly qualified publicists' within the meaning of Article 38(1)(d) of the Statute of the International Court of Justice – in their areas of expertise.

In this short conclusion we develop some reflections on the relationship between the disciplines of IL and PE: what can each learn from the other? It turns out to be a story of paradoxes, but also one which carries great potential. In the end, we will make the case for more interdisciplinary legal education and research.

II. SOME PARADOXES

The discovery of a PE approach by international legal scholarship carries its own surprises.

A first paradox: it has been rightly stressed in the past and today that a good mastery and scholarship of IL is inconceivable without at least a dose of economics, history, politics and sociology. Everyone knows that IL is deeply affected and shaped by historical and political realities and that the rule formation processes themselves depend highly on the social behavior and interactions of their main subjects, States. In other words, when as international lawyers we apply a PE approach to IL, we may find ourselves in the situation of Mr. Jourdain in *Le Bourgeois Gentilhomme* of Molière. Mr. Jourdain found out to his own surprise that he had been speaking prose all of his life, and did not even know it. Have we always been practicing an implicit PE approach to IL without knowing it? The very methodology of IL presupposes a recourse to empirical research tools: otherwise, how could one even start to demonstrate the existence of a sufficiently critical and uniform body of State practice when identifying certain rules of Customary International Law (CIL)? However, therein lies the rub: the fact that IL actors (from the International Court of Justice and national courts to legal scholarship) have never developed a full methodology for this empirical part of ascertaining CIL is an important failure. It is to be hoped that the current work of Sir Michael Wood within the International Law Commission (ILC) will bring more clarity and rigor in this respect. Interestingly, for Sir Michael Wood and the ILC the 'identification of customary international law' project is not born out of academic curiosity, but out of a sincere and correct conviction that a better methodology to establish CIL is desperately needed at the practical level.

This leads spontaneously to a second paradox. One can illustrate it by looking into early critical book reviews of the magisterial treatise *Théories et réalités en droit international* (*Theories and Realities in International Law*) by Charles de Visscher, first published in 1953 immediately after his unprecedented combined term of 15 years at the PCIJ and ICJ. De Visscher wrote his book in order to bridge the gap between legal and political approaches to IL. As Marcel Merle observed in his book review in the *Revue française de science politique* in 1955, Charles de Visscher tried to demonstrate that the two disciplines of IL and international relations had to '*marcher de pair sans pour autant se confondre*.' But the same reviewer was harsh in his criticism of the book: '*M. de Visscher a fait la part si belle au phénomène politique qu'on en vient à se demander si l'autonomie de la science juridique dans les rapports internationaux n'est pas une simple illusion.*'

That is indeed a fundamental question which a book such as the present one cannot avoid, and a second paradox brought to the fore by the discovery of PE approaches by IL scholars: what is the 'autonomy' or 'proper place' of international legal scholarship vis-à-vis other disciplines?

It is good to dwell on this question for a brief moment. What is the proper contribution of international legal scholarship to our knowledge? If PE offers answers to the 'why' question, and if it can help to explain 'who wins, who loses', then what addition to genuine knowledge development does the legal approach have? Charles de Visscher, in his aforementioned book, submitted that the essential role of the law is 'teleological' ('*l'étude du droit, comme de toute science normative, est dominée par une attitude essentiellement téléologique*'). That very premise may help us to understand the development in IL of legal categories which, admittedly, often fail to live up to empirical realities: from *jus cogens* and the common heritage of mankind to sustainable development, the principle of solidarity, common but differentiated responsibility, etc.

There may be more than teleology, though. In his aforementioned book review, Merle wondered whether 'systematization' ('*la systématisation*') too is not an essential part of the proper contribution of legal science. He takes the example of the 'international community', a notion which can be derided for its lack of empirical reality, but of which one can wonder what IL and practice could do in its absence. However this may be, it is one of the challenging side effects of a book like the present one that it triggers legal scholars into an exercise of introspection, in other words, an examination of their legal scientific conscience. In the aforementioned systematization perspective one can see the merits of such ventures as the elaboration of a 'rules-based system'/'international order based on the rule of law', codification, generation of legal certainty and predictability, increasing consistency, tackling fragmentation, etc.

An introspective self-examination of legal scholarship pushes lawyers not only to look into the nature of our legal discipline as a science, but also as an *art*. We have been foretold by our teachers for many centuries that *ius est ars boni et aequi* – law is the art of the good and the equitable. The conference which gave rise to the present Volume was held at the premises of *La Sapienza* University in Rome. In that sense it is good to remind oneself that the aforementioned definition comes from one of the most distinguished jurists of Roman antiquity, Publius Iuventius Celsus. The present Volume is naturally littered with a great number of economic notions, from externalities to moral hazard, Pareto efficiency and prisoner's dilemmas. However, apart from a few contributions, there is precious little attention granted to justice and equity. It is heartening that the authors who have contributed human rights-related chapters to this Book come to the finding that sub-fields of IL where values and the search of justice are more strongly at the core, like human rights law, international humanitarian law and international criminal law, may be less prone to be inspired by a PE approach (but see below). It is indeed not obvious to apply concepts of contractualism and reciprocity to these areas. Reciprocity, as we know, has even been explicitly banned from international humanitarian law with the demise of the *si omnes* clause in the course of the twentieth century. As Joel Trachtman rightly observed, PE is most useful in a *lex ferenda* perspective. But even there it cannot be the sole frame of reference, as it does not provide much normative guidance: it does not explain compassion and honor. Even with regard to the 'why' function, further work is needed on the PE side to fully explain the dynamics of international rule-making, especially in a multilateral context that is different from 'multilateralized bilateral contractual arrangements' like the World Trade Organization. To problematize this further: what about a PE approach to 'multi-level rulemaking', a phenomenon with which one is constantly confronted in the European Union and where the lines of authority (and accountability) are very often diffuse? In IL proper, what about areas such as peace and security, disarmament and human rights? Niels Peterson points to the 'deliberative trap' thesis of Thomas Risse, but he also concludes that it is the human rights example that should make us very cautious in using PE as a universal analytical toolbox, as we would then miss important aspects in the analysis of the international legal order.

III. THE DIFFERENCE BETWEEN INTERNATIONAL LAWYERS AND POLITICAL ECONOMISTS

Political economists examine how economic forces and competing interests shape policies, laws and institutions. Their analytical tools and insights offer tantalizing explanations for the evolution of international norms and institutions and the dynamic interaction between IL and domestic law. They shed new light on many areas of IL, as the present Volume shows, and even beyond. Even the laws of war can benefit from the inquiries of political economists: they can, for instance, tell us about the prospects of soldiers as 'agents' on the loose or of war that erupts because of asymmetric information problems. These explanations inform us that in order to engage with, and benefit from, the insights of PE, international lawyers must make a brave decision: to temporarily put aside some of the basic assumptions of our discipline and instead entertain other assumptions even though for many of us those assumptions could sound almost sacrilegious.

The fundamental difference between lawyers and political economists is that lawyers are brought up to put faith in the script. Our expertise in interpreting texts leads us to believe that words matter and that the written norm makes a difference in the real world. Therefore, if the law stipulates that judges are independent, then independent they are; when the Constitution states that the legislature is supreme, then the legislature can bind the executive; and if IL regards States as the building blocks of the system, then international lawyers should focus on what 'States' do and what they consent to. But political economists treat the script as 'cheap talk': they invest little – probably too little – effort to understand what the law says. They focus on action. For them the law is just another resource that is the object of competition: lawmakers 'sell' their product – law – to the highest bidders (the voters or special interests), because they wish to stay in power; judges are not devoid of personal and institutional desires and will tailor their judgments to enhance the institutional role of the court and even to please those who can renew their term in office. Thus, the judge will be independent only if she or he is promised complete insulation from any pressure, and the legislator will be independent of the executive only if re-election to parliament is not in the hands of the party leaders who head the executive branch and can therefore 'punish' legislators from their own party who have given the executive a hard time. Political economists identify potent actors that have no name in the realm of formal law. They see 'capture' almost everywhere by 'special interests' that drives not only law-making but also the making – and unmaking – of IL.

What seems, certainly for lawyers, as a bleak and cynical worldview, is regarded by political economists as a crucial exercise for identifying and mending the flaws of the system of public decision-making. One must understand the hidden or not so hidden agendas of the various actors and the myriad ways that are available for them to promote their own interests in order to be able to design mechanisms to limit those options and thereby to ensure that the public interest is served.

IV. THE POTENTIAL FOR SYNERGIES AND COMPLEMENTARITY

It is here that lawyers can join forces with political economists by assuming a remedial function. The legal discipline does not only teach us how to interpret a text. It also hones our sensitivities to the importance of judicial review and of other checks and balances as means to promote the rule of law. Moreover, as lawyers we gain experience about what makes such review mechanisms effective or not. This is the type of discipline that complements the work of political economists. Not the law of words, but the law of institutions – institutions that provide checks against capture and insulate certain reliable actors (judges, heads of central banks, etc.) from illegitimate influence. The political economists look for allies in lawyers who will act more as engineers that construct elaborate institutions than as linguists who see the script as the key to salvation.

As engineers of effective review mechanisms, we lawyers can make good use of the insights of political economists that help us to identify problems and design the solutions. For example, political economists identify asymmetric information as a key challenge for democratic decision-making. Those with better access to information will gain the upper hand in standard-setting: if only farmers knew the relative risks of pesticides they would pressure regulators to allow the use of those pesticides that were more harmful to consumers but less harmful to the farmers. Lawyers excel in constructing procedures that overcome asymmetric information problems by ensuring more diverse representation and public participation in decision-making, etc.

One of the main insights that PE has to offer international lawyers is that 'States' are not the only, not even the most important, actors in the international realm. The 'State' is composed of individuals who vie for power and use the various State institutions as a tool to promote their self-interest. As a result of their influence, State practice and even treaties may reflect the interests of certain economic élites rather than the interests of the general population in the respective countries. Here too, lawyers as 'legal engineers' can contribute by understanding the ways by which IL and international institutions can be used as tools to overcome asymmetric information and reduce capture of narrow interests.

In some sense, international lawyers are closer to the PE worldview than many domestic lawyers. As students of a fragmented system of law that has no central legislature, courts or police, they develop intuitions about the role of power, of reputation, of economic and social forces. The promise of this Book is that it paves the way for acknowledging the fact that these intuitions deserve systematic treatment, because such treatment will make for more effective international lawyers. The bleak world view of political scientists can be enlisted to improve the ways in which to ensure that IL promotes the interests of all.

V. THE NEED FOR MORE INTERDISCIPLINARY LEGAL EDUCATION AND RESEARCH

If this Book yields one major insight for academics, it is that we need to change our legal teaching curriculum. Especially in Europe, law students are still overwhelmingly rendered intellectually myopic by a strongly embedded tradition of 'black letter' approaches to the study of law. PE approaches should be part and parcel of legal curricula, in an integrated manner – and not just in the form of some introductory courses in economics, sociology and philosophy.

There is much more to be done. One could think in particular of doctoral research programs. Especially in Europe, such programs often perpetuate the monodisciplinarity and doctrinal approaches of the previous steps in legal education. Researchers in IL often do not receive sufficient methodological training in disciplines other than the legal one. There are interesting tendencies in doctoral training programs across a number of academic institutions, and we should arguably exchange more good practice in this respect to see in which ways we can optimize the doctoral training and open up our doctoral researchers' eyes to non-legal approaches. This being said, in order to conduct sound multidisciplinary or interdisciplinary research, one has to be in the first place very strong in one's own discipline. This implies, interestingly enough, that parallel to opening its eyes to non-legal approaches, including PE, legal scholarship must further develop and deepen a sound *legal* methodology. In IL, this requires at the very least a less doctrinal approach and a stronger openness for empirical realities and ways of measuring and evaluating them, including non-traditional normative processes, non-State actors and, importantly, the dynamic interactions between public and private legal processes. In many respects this means going right back to our academic roots, and to the times when disciplines were less carved up than they are today. In that sense, (re-)discovering PE constitutes for international lawyers both a fascinating journey to the future and a revisiting of our own intellectual heritage.

Index

acculturation
human rights, and 406–7
State interests, and 59–60
ad hoc tribunals
judicial appointments 209–10
State attitudes towards 209
adherence *see also* compliance
public international law lobbying, and 34–5
model for 35–43
reciprocity, and 31–3
regional trade agreements 316, 319, 326
welfare influences 31
Al-Khawaja and Tahery v. UK (2009, ECtHR) 221–2
Albert, Hans 12
Alvarez, Jose 169, 173
Anti-Ballistic Missile Treaty 1972 186, 192
anti-formalism 167
arms races 185–6
Attorney General v. Burgoa (1980, EU) 121
Australia – Apples dispute (2010, WTO) 191

behavioural economics 13–14, 101
Behrami v. France (2007, ECtHR) 294
Belgium v. Senegal (2012, ICJ) 218–19
Betts, Alexander 417–18
bilateralism *vs.* multilateralism 41
Bonn Guidelines 2002 356–7
Borjas, George 421
Bosnian Genocide case (2007, ICJ) 298–9
Brazil
international investment agreements 348–50
Broude, Tomer 435
Brunnée, Jutta 176

Canada
water treaties, benefit sharing 371–2
Castles, Stephen 422, 424
Cheyes, Adam 193
China
jus cogens, and 92–3
climate change remediation 184–5
State responsibility and cooperation 302–3
Cohen, Benjamin 18–20
Cole, Daniel 302
comparative law
constitutional texts 269
role of 268–70
compliance
causal effects, and 176–7
constructivism, and 390–91
customary law norms, with 55–61, 402–4
constructivism, and 58–60
human rights obligations 60
precedent-setting 56–7
rational choice 55–9, 61
reputation, and 57–8
definitions 159–61, 402
dimensions of 402
enforcement mechanisms 161, 171–2
focus trends 176–7
human rights
challenges 407–8
constructivism, and 390–91
domestic influences 398–9
enforcement 231–2, 242
good faith principle of 240
interconnectedness 385
measurement of 404–5

mechanisms for 384
motives for 384–91, 407–8
non-State influences on 391–3
obligations 398–9
political economy approach 395–407
rational choice, and 387–8
reputation, and 387
supervisory body powers, and 231–2, 239–40
theories of 385–91
trends 231–2
identification conflicts 166–8, 173–5
institutional effects on 170–71, 387
interdisciplinarity, and 176–7
judicalization and internalization 165–6
legalization 165–7
motives 55, 63–4
non-compliance
accepted levels of 403
efficient breach 71–2
implications 56–7
influences on 64, 161–4, 170–71
punishment mechanisms 56–7
political economy, and 170
prisoner's dilemma, and 183–4
analysis challenges 189–92
application challenges 188–9
enforcement mechanisms, with 194–6
enforcement mechanisms, without 192–4
failure of 196–9
reasons for 192–3, 196–201
reciprocity, and 32, 49–50, 66–7, 194–6
shock or crisis, and 199–200
public international law lobbying, and 34–5
model 35–43
purpose 160–61, 170, 403
realism, and 387
reasons for 64, 161–4, 170–71
reciprocity, and 31–3, 55–8, 61
regulatory tool, as 55–6
reputation, and 57–8, 304
retaliation, and 57–8
self-interest 164
social science influences on 176–7
studies of 161–3, 167–8, 176–7
design 171–3
limitations 172–3
understanding, and 168–71, 173–4
theories of 385–91
fairness model 389–90
legitimacy model 163–4, 167
liberal theory 165–6, 173, 388
managerial model 163
norm-based model 388–9
pluralist model 167–8
rational choice theory 35–43, 164, 385–8
transnational model 164–5, 389–90
vs. cooperation 161
vs. responsibility 176
welfare influences 30–31
WTO dispute settlement rules 161
constructivism 20, 22
compliance, and 58–60, 390–91
transnational model 164–5
contemporaneity, principle of 105–6
Convention on Biological Diversity 1992 356
Corfu Channel case (1949, ICJ) 289
custom *see* customary international law
customary international law *see also jus cogens*
breach of
predictability and assessment 71–2
compliance with 55
rational choice 55–8
reciprocity, and 56–8, 61
self-interest, and 63–4
concept development 47, 62
evolutive interpretation 108–11
Soviet influences on 77–9
cooperation, limitations on 49
creation 64–6
bilateral *vs.* multilateral parameters 65–6, 69–70
ergo omnes concept 69
identification, and 67–8
justification for conduct 67
opinio iuris principle 68, 70

prisoner's dilemma, as 65–7, 178–9, 184, 186–8, 195
rule codification 70
State role in 72–3
fundamental human rights 53, 60
game theory, and 48–9, 65–7
identification 67–8
judicial, constraints on 51–5
interpretation 70–72
priority variations 71–2
rationality, and 71
legal certainty, and 51–3
opting-out mechanisms 53
political economy
identification role 65–9, 73–4
interpretation role 70–72
principles 48–9, 62
social science, and 48
State responsibility and obligations 67–9, 72–3
vs. social conduct 67–8
customary law *see* customary international law

Dauvergne, Catherine 424
de Visscher, Charles 440–41
decision-making, selectorate theory of 334–5
causal influences on 338–9
FDI policy influences 339–40
interest groups, and 336–7
political contributions 338–9
political influences on 335–7
dependency theory 19
developing countries
international investment agreements
adherence 329–30
Brazil, in 348–50
corporate role, domestic *vs.* foreign 343–4, 351–2
economic benefits 342–3
FDI inflows, and 341–3, 352–4
imitation of peers, and 345–6
influences on 340–43, 346–7
labour unions, and 343
motives 330–32
neo-colonialism, and 341–2
non-ratification, reasons for 348–50
non-unitary State perspective 353–5
predictions 347–8
public opinion 341–2
rational choice, and 344–5
South Africa, in 350–52
national court cooperation 267
prisoner's dilemma
Least-Developed Country BITs 186–7
Least-Developed Country FTAs 187–8
dispute settlement
diffusion of State responsibility, and 295
human rights 233, 236
international investment agreements 329
international mandates 207
WTO mechanism 175, 196–8
Dunoff, Jeffrey 172, 176

EC – Hormones dispute (1998, WTO) 191, 200
economics
international political economy, and 17–21
social science, as 17–18
efficient breach hypothesis 118
emerging technology
informal law approach 137–8
nanotechnology regulation 139–42
state actor perceptions of 142–54
enforcement *see also* compliance; human rights
definition 241–2
purpose 242
ergo omnes concept 69
European Court of Human Rights
enforcement powers 245
European Union
migration restrictions 430
Russia South Stream dispute 115–16
TEFU, compatibility with other treaties 120–24

fair and equitable, interpretation 356–7
fairness model of compliance 389–90
Finnemore, Martha 172
Fitzmaurice, Gerald 105–6
folk theorem 118
Franck, Thomas 163–4, 389
free-riding 50–51, 418
Friedman, Milton 427
Frisch, Max 413

Gabcíkovo-Nagymaros Project (1997, ICJ) 381–2
game theory 25–6, 118–19
  blame games strategies 300–301
  customary international law 48–50
  limitations 48
  multiple equilibria, influences of 49–50
  public-good games 50–51
General Agreement on Tariffs and Trade Article XXIV 321–8
Germany v. Italy (2012, ICJ) 86–91
global public goods theory 417–18
globalization
  human rights, and 405–6
  international law interpretation, and 2, 259–60
  migration, and 419, 421, 424–7, 432–3
  national court role 276–7
Goldsmith, Jack 48–50, 67
Goodman, Ryan 59
Gourevitch, Peter 25
greenhouse gas emissions 185
Grey, David 360–62
Grossman-Helpman political support model 26–31
Guzman, Andrew 164, 167

Habré v Senegal (2010, ECW) 218
Hatton, Timothy 417
hearsay 220–22, 228
hegemonic stability theory 19
Helsinki Rules on the Use of Waters of International Rivers 1966 362–3, 365–7
Henkin, Louis 232, 401–2
human rights
  attitudes to, changing 399–401, 405–6
  community norms, as 243
  compliance
    challenges 407–8
    constructivism, and 390–91
    domestic influences 398–9
    enforcement 231–2, 242
    good faith principle of 240
    interconnectedness 385
    measurement 404–5
    mechanisms 384
    motives for 384–91, 407–8
    non-State influences 391–3
    obligations 398–9
    political economy approach 395–407
    rational choice, and 387–8
    reputation, and 387
    supervisory body powers, and 231–2, 239–40
    theories of 385–91
    trends 231–2
  criminal responsibility, and 401
  customary international law, and 53, 60
  discrimination 237
  dispute settlement 233, 236
  enforced disappearance 238–9
  enforcement
    compliance with 231–2
    costs 242, 247–52
    countermeasures 244
    definition 241–2
    domain characteristics, and 250–52
    humanitarian justifications 251–2
    issue specificity, and 252–4
    legal status influences on 241–6, 255–6
    methods 242–6
    powers 244–5
    pronouncements 246–56
    purpose 242
    rational choice, and 247–50
    reciprocity, and 250–51, 387, 396–7, 442

responsibilities and obligations 241–4
soft law 255–6
trends 246–7, 252
globalization, and 405–6
hearsay, and 220–22, 228
Helsinki Declaration 79–80
institutions, diversity of 397–8
interest groups, role of 110–11
international protection regime 230–31
jus cogens, and 79–81, 86–92, 400
migration law, and 411–12, 418, 434–5
monitoring bodies 434
prisoner's dilemma, and 192–3
prisoners' right to vote 253–4
pronouncements
binding *vs.* non-binding 242–3, 255–6
concluding observations 236–7
dispute settlement rulings 233, 236
enforcement 246–56
general comments 238
inquiries and urgent actions 238–9
interim measures 236, 240–41
legal status 239–41
rape 237
right to fair trial 253–4
soft law, and 400–401
sovereign immunity, and 90–91, 214–15
State controls over 86–92, 256–7, 393–4
State interests, as 393–4
State obligations 236–41, 243–4, 398–9
supervisory bodies 230–31
legal status 239–41, 255–6
output trends 234–5
powers 231–2, 245–6
pronouncements 233–9
torture 237–8
treaties
complexity of 395–6, 406–7
regulation of 395–6
research limitations 404–7
types of 396–7
Hussein v. Albania (2006, ECtHR) 294, 296

immigration *see* migration; migration law
individualism 23–4, 27–8
institutionalism
human rights compliance, and 387–8
interest groups
decision-making, role in 336–7
evolutive interpretation, role in 110–11
international constitutionalism 16
international cooperation
conditional cooperation 56–7
forms of 118
limitations 49–50
national courts, inter-judicial cooperation 264–77
organizational structures for 22–3
political economy, and 117
prisoner's dilemma, and 266–7
public-good games 50–51
public international law lobbying model 35–43
reciprocity *vs.* retaliation 31–3, 49–50, 56–7, 61
soft law, and 118
transboundary water systems 360–61
trends 137
International Court of Justice
consular notifications and post-conviction remedies 219–20, 227–8
customary international law, identification 51, 54–5, 68, 214
international crimes, retroactivity 218–19
jurisdiction 205–6
jus cogens 86–91
limitations on 228
sovereign immunity interpretation 86–91, 214–15, 224–5
treaty interpretation 99–100, 102–4
international courts and tribunals
ad hoc tribunals 209–10

consular notifications and post-conviction remedies 219–20, 227–8
human rights, and 220–22, 228
international criminal law
hearsay, and 220–22, 228
imputed responsibility for crimes 222–3, 228–9
retroactivity, and 217–19
investment tribunals 215–17
judiciary
appointment 208–10
retention 210–11
jurisdiction 205–8
dispute settlement mandates 207
influences on 213
limitations 205–7
standing rules 206
withdrawal from 206–7, 225
purpose 204, 213–14
regional tribunals 213
sovereign immunity rulings 214–15
special purpose tribunals 213–14
State interests, responsiveness to 212–13
State relationships with 204–11
taxation as appropriation 215–17, 225–6
international criminal law 217–19
extraterritoriality, and 217–18
human rights, and 401
hearsay 218, 220–22
imputed responsibility for crimes 222–3, 228–9
principle of legality 217
retroactivity, and 217–19, 227
International Criminal Tribunal for the Former Yugoslavia 222–3, 228–9
International labor Organization Treaty 193–4
international law *see also* customary international law; public international law
adherence, welfare influences on 31
comparative analysis, and 268–70
compliance
influences on 30–31, 63–4
motives 67
welfare, and 30–31
domestic causes of 24–6
evolution of 91–3
identification of 64–5
informal mechanisms 128–31
negative reasons for 131–5
positive reasons for 135–8
interest groups, influence of 110–11
legal scholarship, role of 440–41
normative conflict 111–19
AB/AC conflict model 113–19
judicial mechanisms 112–13
presumption against conflict 112–13
political economy, and 82–3
political support model 26–31
prisoner's dilemma, and
arms races 185–6
climate change remediation 184–5
compliance with customary law 183–4
creation by 65–7, 178–9, 184, 186–8, 195
economic protectionism, and 181–4
purpose 67–8
sanctions role in 67–8
soft law role in 132–7, 154–5
State roles 72–3
systematization 441
trade protectionism, and 181–4
two-level game, as a 20–26, 111, 205, 260–61
international organizations
characteristics 127–8
diffusion of State responsibility, and 286–8, 291, 299
governance/ law-making role 127–8
advantages 145, 150–54
decision-making process 142–4, 146–8
emerging technology 137–8
expertise 144–5, 148–50
political economy approaches 130–31
studies, generally 128–9
migration law policy design role 434
international political economy

analysis, limitations 20–21, 95–6
diversity of approaches, influences on 18–20
economic approach 17–18
evolutive interpretation of law 108–11
interest groups, role of 110–11
political decision-making theory 20–21
role of 13, 95–6
study trends 95–6
variations in 17–21
international relations
acculturation influences on 59–60
compliance role in 160
game theory, and 25
individualism 23–4
judicial welfare function 102–4
liberal theory 23–4
public international law lobbying model 35–43
social psychology, and 59–60
social science approach 10
study trends 96–7
investment agreements
definition 329
developing countries, by
adherence 329–30
Brazil, in 348–50
corporate role, domestic *vs.* foreign 343–4, 351–2
economic benefits 342–3
FDI inflows, and 341–3, 352–4
imitation of peers 345–6
influences on 340–43, 346–7
labour unions, and 343
motives 330–32
neo-colonialism, and 341–2
non-ratification, reasons for 348–50
non-unitary State perspective 353–5
predictions 347–8
public opinion 341–2
rational choice, and 344–5
South Africa, in 350–52
dispute settlement 329
features of 329
motives 329–31
selectorate theory of decision-making 331–2, 334–5
causal mechanisms 338–9
FDI policy influences 339–40
interest groups, and 336–7
political contributions 338–9
political influences on 335–7
Iraqi State v. Corporation Dumez GTM (2006, France) 272
ISO Technical Committee on Nanotechnology 139–42
Italy
right to fair trial 253–4

Jenks, Wilfred 112
Jinks, Derek 59
Jongryn Mo 26
judicial law-making 202
globalization, and 2, 259–60
international courts and tribunals, by
consular notifications and post-conviction remedies 219–20, 227–8
human rights, and hearsay 220–22, 228
international crimes, imputed responsibility for 222–3, 228–9
international crimes, retroactivity 217–19, 227
model for 203, 229
sovereign immunity 90–91, 214–15, 224–5
taxation as appropriation 215–17, 225–6
national courts, by
benefits of 270–77
comparative law role 268–70
domestic democratic processes, and 262–4
higher courts, role of 266–7
inter-judicial cooperation 264–77
international law implications 262–4
international law obligations 258
limitations 260, 263
motives 259–67

trends 259
judiciary
evolutive interpretation 109–10
international courts and tribunals, in
appointment 209–10
retention 210–11
judicial welfare function 102–4, 109–10
political economy studies of 109–10
role of, legal model interpretations 101–2
treaty interpretation 102–3
jus cogens
functions 77–8, 81, 92–4
historical development 76–82
human rights law 79–81
Soviet theory 77–9
treaty law 78–9
US influences on 80
international law, and
continuing evolution 90–94
ICJ interpretation 86–91
litigation, role in 84–5
place in 77, 81, 84
public choice theory, and 84–6
stakeholder interactions 84–5
State sovereignty, and 78–81, 86–94
peaceful coexistence theory 78–9, 85–6
political economy, and 75–6, 92–4
principles of 75, 77, 81, 84

Kadi case (2008, EU) 121, 271–4
Kansas v. Colorado (1907, US) 364–5
Kantorowicz, Hermann 11–14, 21
Kelsen, Hans 111
Kennedy, David 174–5
Keohane, Robert 31
Kingsbury, Benedict 160–61, 400–401, 403–4
Koh, Harold 164–5, 389–90
kompetenz-kompetenz principle 205
Koser, Khalid 421
Koskenniemi, Martti 175–6
Kyoto Protocol 185

Lance Armstrong v. Tygart (2012, US) 275–6
law, generally *see also* judicial law-making; soft law
concept interpretations 167
evolutionary nature 108–9
intention, and 100–102
law-making methods 133–5
law *vs.* non-law 132–3
vs. economics 174
wealth maximization, and 175
legal norms
comparative analysis 268–70
compliance, and 402–4
conflict 111–19
AB/AC conflict model 113–19
judicial anti-conflict mechanisms 112–13
lex prior vs. lex posterior derogat priori 113–14
presumption against 112–13
executive authority, and 134–5
moralization, and 284–6
pyramid of 111
soft law, and 132–7
legal positivism 15–16
legalization, concept of 132–3
liberal theory of international relations 23–4
compliance, and 389
lobbying
political support models 27–31
public international law lobbying 33–5

Malloy, Robin 173–4
managerial model of compliance 389–90
many hands problem 279–81, 289–94
Marovcsik, Andrew 23
Martin, Lisa 170–71, 176–7, 402
Mayda, Anna 417
Merle, Marcel 440–41
Meron, Theodore 53
migration
anti-immigrant sentiment 424–5
burden shifts 429, 431
illegal migration 424–5, 427–9

reasons for 409–10, 413–16
system theories 419–22
temporary *vs.* permanent 427
trends 409, 424–7
voluntary *vs.* forced 409–10, 418, 426–7
migration law
asymmetry in 410
costs and benefits identification 413–14
free riding, and 418
globalization impacts 419, 421, 424–7, 432–3
human rights, and 411–12, 418, 434–5
illegal migration
policy approaches 427–8
trends 424–5, 429
migrant workers
agreement dualism 418
protections 412–13
regulation, influences on 423–5
skilled *vs.* unskilled workers 418, 421–7, 430–31
temporary *vs.* permanent migration 427
trade liberalization, and 416–17, 424
non-discrimination principle 411–12
policy design
economic crisis, and 431–2
influences on 423–5, 428–9, 431–5
international organizations role 434
non-arrival strategies 429–30
non-economic influences 433–5
political economy approaches 413–17, 425–6, 432–3
trends 428–34
public welfare, and 414
conflicts 427, 432–3
refoulement prohibition 410–11
refugee protections 418, 426
soft law role 411
stakeholder interests 413–14
State prerogatives 410–11
State self-interest, and 423–5
theories
economic dualism 420–22
global public goods 417–18
immigration market theory 420–21
individualism 415
labour market segmentation theory 420–22
limitations 421–2
migrant transnationalism theory 419
rational choice 416, 419–20
structural theories 415, 419–21
world system theory 419–20
trade agreement influences on 422
trade in services agreement 412–13
voluntary migration protections 410, 418
Milner, Helen 19
Minors Oposa case (1994, Philippines) 268
Mitrany, David 22–3
Moavcsik, Andrew 388
moral behaviour
common and shared responsibilities 288–9
judicial welfare function, and 109–10
moralization trends 284–6
political economy, and 82–3
Morelli, Gaetano 67
multilateral environmental agreements
benefit sharing 356–8
multilateralism
cooperation limitations 49–50
creation of customary international law, and 65–6, 69–70
vs. bilateralism 41

nanotechnologies
informal law
approach 137–8
state actor perceptions 142–56
ISO Technical Committee on 139–42
national courts, generally *see also* judicial law-making
international law, and
comparative law role 268–70
constraint variations 211–12
developing countries, and 267

domestic democratic process relationships 260–64
evolution, influences on 262–3
global private regulation, and 276–7
higher courts role 266–7
inter-judicial cooperation 264–77
judicial law-making, benefits of 270–77
two-level game, as a 20, 260–61
purpose 204
NATO Treaty 78
Navigable Watewrways Convention 1921 370
neo-institutionalism
treaties, interpretation 101–2
neo-liberalism
wealth maximization 175
Nicaragua v. US (1986, ICJ) 55, 67, 207–8, 222
non-compliance *see* compliance
non-government organizations *see* international organizations
Norman, George 32, 49–50
nuclear weapons
prisoner's dilemma 185–6, 192

Ohlin, Jens 193
Open Economy Politics 19–20
Open Skies cases 122–3
opinio iuris principle 52–3, 55, 68, 70

Piore, Michael 420–21
pluralism 167–8
political economy, generally *see also* international political economy
benefits of 1–2, 154
definition 1, 82
economic approach 17–18
historical background 17
interest groups, role of 110–11
international law, and
creation and identification 65–9, 73–4
differences in approach 442–3
evolutive interpretation 108–11
integration into 11–16
interdisciplinary research needs 445
interpretation 70–72, 440
paradoxes 440–42
rational conduct 67–9
rule codification 70
synergies and complementarity 444–5
interstate cooperation theories, and 117
limitations 82, 174
methods 74, 96–7
role of 10, 13, 16, 63–4, 70, 82–3, 95–6
political support model 26–31
political welfare 22, 30–31
Pollack, Mark 172, 176
positivism 167
Posner, Eric 48–50, 67, 101, 175, 195, 198, 209
prisoner's dilemma 32, 65
arms races 185–6, 192
climate change remediation 184–5
compliance with customary and international law 183–4
analysis challenges 189–92
application challenges 188–9
enforcement mechanisms, with 194–6
enforcement mechanisms, without 192–4
failure of 196–9
non-compliance 196–9
reasons for 192–3, 196–201
reciprocity, and 32, 49–50, 66–7, 194–6
shock or crisis, and 199–200
coordination and cooperation 266–7
creation of customary and international law 65–7, 178–9, 184, 186–8, 195
difficulties with 66–7
economic protectionism, and 181–4
human rights, and 192–3
Least-Developed Country BITs 186–7
Least-Developed Country FTAs 187–8

limitations 189
political economy, and 200–201
principles 179–80, 359
public-good games 50–51
rational choice, and 200
reciprocity, and 32, 49–50, 66–7, 194–6
regional trade agreements, as 320
repeated games 189–90, 200
State interests, and 32, 49–50, 65
WTO, and 186–7, 190–91, 194, 196–9
Prosecutor v. Tadic (2000, ICTY) 298
Protection of the Rights of Migrant Workers Convention 1990 412
protectionism
political support model 27–9
prisoner's dilemma, and 181–4
public choice theory 21–2, 83
international law application 83
jus cogens, and 84–6
non-market decision-making, and 175
public international law lobbying 34–5
public goods
compliance with customary norms 59–60
migration, and 417–18
State responsibility, and 305
public international law
causes and effects 13–14, 21–3
compliance role in 160
doctrinal perspective 12–14
interpretation variations 15–16
law application perspective 14–16
lobbying 33–5
normative perspective 12–13
object and purpose 14–16
political economy integration into 11–16
positive perspective 12–13
sociological perspective 12–13, 15–16
State interests, and 21–3
trends 9
public international law lobbying 33
compliance and adherence, and 35–6
model 35–43
purpose 34–5
public welfare 22, 30–31
migration law, and 414, 427, 432–3
public-good games 50–51
Pulkowski, Dirk 160, 169, 171
Putnam, Robert 25–6

R v. Secretary of State for Defence (2007, UK) 272
rational choice *see also* prisoner's dilemma
customary international law
compliance, and 55–9, 61
interpretation 71
limitations 42–3
models of compliance and adherence 35–43
human rights enforcement, and 247–50
international investment agreements
developing countries, by 344–5
theory 13, 19–20, 169
compliance, and 387–8
limitations 175
migration, and 416, 419–20
treaty interpretation, and 100–101, 103
Ravenhill, John 318–19
realism
human rights compliance, and 387
reciprocity 31–3, 63
customary International law
compliance, and 56–8, 61
prisoner's dilemma 32, 49–50, 66–7, 194–6
human rights enforcement, and 250–51, 387, 396–7, 442
limitations 32, 49–50
public international law
lobbying model 35–43
specific *vs.* diffuse 56
Regina v. Horncastle (2009, UK) 221
regional trade agreements
adherence 316, 319, 326–8
definition 312–13
economic benefits 317
features 313–14, 327

hubs and spokes 314–15
international law
conflicts between 324–5
coordination mechanism 321–8
customary regional exception 325–6
margin of appreciation 325–6, 328
place in 321, 326–7
transparency mechanisms 323
labour migration, and 422
motives 316–20
political economy, and
conflicts between 311, 324
interpretation 312–13
purpose of RTAs 316–20, 324
prisoner's dilemma, as 320
trade creation *vs.* trade diversion 317
trade liberalization, and 315–16
trends 311–14
WTO trade agreement regime, and 321–8
reputation 57–8, 304, 387–8
retaliation *vs.* reciprocity 32–3, 61
Risse, Thomas 60
Rosenau, James 422
Russia
EU South Stream dispute 115–16
Soviet *jus cogens* theory 77–9

Sadoff, Claudia 360–62
Salt, John 421
Sari v. Turkey and Denmark (2001, ECtHR) 292
self-interest, influences of 63–4, 164, 242
Sengal Water Charter 2002 372–3
Serbia and Montenegro v. Belgium (2004, ECJ) 296
Sikkink, Kathryn 172
Smith, Adam 409
social psychology
compliance with customary noms 59–60
social sciences
customary international law, and 48
international constitutionalism, and 16
international law design, and 16
international relations, in 10
perspectives of law 12–16
treaty interpretation, and 14–15
soft law
distributive approach 136
emerging technology 137–8
human rights, and 255–6, 400–401
international law-making, and 128–31, 135
interpretation 15–16, 123–34
interstate cooperation, forms of 118
legalization 132, 136–7
migration law, in 411
nanotechnology regulation 139–42
reasons for
negative 131–5
positive 135–8
state actor perceptions 142–54
trends 154–5
South Africa
international investment agreements 350–52
Lesotho Highlands Project 372, 380
sovereign immunity
human rights, and 90–91, 214–15
jus cogens, and 90–91
Stark, Oded 416
State interests
acculturation, and 59–60
conduct, influences on 59–60
cooperation, and
attitudes towards 31–3
free-riding 50–51
organizational structures for 22–3
customary international law
change of attitudes or conduct 72–3
conflicts with 67
dualism, and 72–3
human rights as 393–4
international relations, and
adherence 31–3
causal influences 24–6
compliance 30–33
domestic bargaining 26
game theory 25–6
liberal theory 23–4
political support models 26–31

public international law lobbying 33–43
reciprocity *vs.* retaliation 31–3, 61, 63
jus cogens, and 86–93
non-compliance, and 64
prisoner's dilemma, and 32, 49–50, 65
public *vs.* political welfare models 21–2
self-interest influences 63–4
State responsibility, and 298
State responsibility
diffusion 307
benefits 302–3
blame game strategies 300–301
bystander effect, and 292–3
common and shared responsibilities 280–81, 287–9
concerted action, and 279–80, 299
cooperation obligations, and 282–4
cooperation, willingness 303–4
costs 303–7
definition 278–9, 301–2
delegation 300
dual attribution 293–4
examples 280–81
identifying responsibility 290–94, 296–7
incentives 304–5
independent responsibility principle 290, 292–4
influences on 282–7, 296–7
informational influences 296–7
institutional limitations 294–6
interdependence, and 282–4
international organizations, and 286–8, 291, 299
justice for victims, and 306–7
many hands problem 279–81, 289–94
moral dimensions 284–6, 288
multiplicity of actors, and 286–7, 299
normative challenges 289–94
obligations, assignment of 291–2, 305
orchestration 300
performance obligations, and 304–5
political influences on 297–9
private actors, and 286–7
private costs 306–7
public goods, and 305
reparation and restitution 304–5
reputation of international law, and 304
responsibility gaps 289–97, 302–7
soft powers 298–9
State interests, and 298
strategies 299–301
international law principles 67–9
Stockholm Declaration 1972 288
Swaine, Edward 49
Sykes, Alan 195, 198

tariffs, and protectionism 181–4
Thompson, Dennis 279–80, 289–94
TMPH (many hands problem) 279–81, 289–94
Toope, Stephen 176
trade agreements *see also* international investment agreements; regional trade agreements; World Trade Organization
lobbying 27–31, 34–5
prisoner's dilemma 186–7, 320
trade creation *vs.* trade diversion 317
welfare effects 28–9
WTO trade agreement coordination regime 321–4
trade liberalization
dual policy paradox 417
migrant workers, and 416–17, 424
reciprocity, and 33
regional trade agreements, and 315–16
transnational model of compliance 164–5, 389–90
treaties
boundary treaties 103
definition 98–9
interpretation 14–15, 62, 99–100, 102–3
approaches 107–8

    conflicts 113–18
    context-dependence 103–4
    evolutive interpretation 105–11
    existence of, disputes over 99–100, 102–4
    generic terms 108
    intention, and 100–102, 105–7
    lex prior vs. lex posterior derogat priori 113–14
    non-State determination 102–3
    political economy role in 104–5, 108–11, 125–6
    principle of contemporaneity 105–6
    rights and obligations 121
    TEFU compatibility with other treaties 120–24
  jus cogens, and 78–9
  nature 96, 106
  object and purpose 14, 65, 107
  political economy, and
    interpretation role 104–5, 108–11, 125–6
    study trends 96, 98–9
    termination of treaties 119, 124
  public international law, and 95
  rational choice theory, and 100–101, 103
  termination
    compatibility of treaties 120–24
    political economy, and 119
Turkey
  human rights obligations 254

unitary State perspective 2
United Kingdom
  prisoners' right to vote 253–4
United States
  Columbia River Treaty 1961 371–2
  International labor Organization Treaty 193–4
  political campaign contributions 338
  water treaties, benefit sharing 371–2
  WTO agreement compliance 190
US – Byrd Amendment dispute (2004, WTO) 197–8
US – Cotton Subsidies dispute (2009, WTO) 197–8
US – FSC / US – 1916 Act disputes (2002, WTO) 197–8
US – Gambling dispute (2007, WTO) 198
US v. Iran (1980, ICJ) 207–8

van Gend en Loos case (1963, ECJ) 275–6
Viner, Jacob 317
Voeten, Eric 212–13
von Stein, Jana 172
von Verdross, Alfred 77–8

Waite and Kennedy v. Germany (1999, ECtHR) 274–5
water law
  benefit sharing
    basin management agreements 375–6
    basket of benefits concept 361, 369–70, 377, 382–3
    beneficial use, interpretation 366–7
    benefits, interpretation 376
    benefits model 360–62
    concept development 356–8, 364–5
    ecosystem and community protection agreements 372–4
    environmental impacts 381–2
    equitable and reasonable use principle 357–8, 362–7, 373–4, 376, 382–3
    equitable apportionment 364–5
    equity criteria 367–9
    flexibility, and 376
    infrastructure agreements 369–72
    institutional roles 378–9
    international law, place in 362–9
    issue linkages, and 377–8
    limitations 375–82
    navigation agreements 369–70
    non-party State entitlements 380–81
    non-State actor interests, and 379–80, 382
    opportunities, assessment of 368–9
    political economy, and 357–8, 366–7, 383

population impacts 382
principles 358
regional agreements 375–6
time challenges 376
water allocation agreements 369
water treaty approaches 369
Columbia River Treaty 1961 371–2
Helsinki Rules 1966 362–3, 365–7
Lake Tanganyika Water Management Convention 2003 374
Lesotho Highlands Project 372, 380
Navigable Waterways Convention 1921 370
Sengal Water Charter 2002 372–3
transboundary water systems
benefits 359–62
coordination and cooperation 360–61
interdependence 358–60
State obligations 362–3, 366
TWO analysis 368–9
Watercourses Convention 1997 363, 365–7, 376, 379, 382–3
Watercourses Convention 1997 363, 365–7, 376, 379, 382–3
wealth maximization 175
Weber, Max 12
welfare 21–2
adherence, and 31
compliance, and 30–31
judicial welfare function 102–4, 109–10
lobbying, and 26–7
maximisation 181–4
public-good games 50–51
public welfare
migration law, and 414, 427, 432–3
vs. political welfare 22
regional trade agreements, and 317
total welfare 27–8
welfarism 17
Williamson, Jeffrey 417
Wolfe, Robert 168, 175
World Trade Organization
compliance challenges 190–91
dispute settlement mechanism 175, 196–8
GATS and movement of persons 412–13
GATT Article XXIV 321–8
prisoner's dilemma
compliance with customary and international law 190–91, 194, 196–9
creation of customary and international law 186–7
regional trade agreements, relationship with 321–8

Yoo, John 209
Yukos v. Russian Federation (214, PCA) 215–17

Zolberg, Aristide 421